GLASS NOTES

A Reference For The Glass Artist

Henry Halem

Version 4.0

Glass Notes: A reference for the glass artist

© 2006 Franklin Mills Press
Published by Franklin Mills Press
P.O. Box 906
Kent, OH 44240-2303, USA
Web: http://www.glassnotes.com
E-mail: hhalem@glassnotes.com
Tel: 330/673-8632

All rights reserved. No part of this book may be reproduced in any form or by electronic or mechanical means, including information storage and retrieval systems, without permission in writing from the publisher, except by a reviewer, who may quote passages in a review. Accuracy of any and all information contained in this book is assumed but not guaranteed.

Editor: Chad Wickman
Front and back cover design: Marty Timmerman
All photos by the author unless noted

Articles not written by the author are attributed to the author of origin and reprinted with their expressed permission.

First edition: 1993
Second edition: 1994
Third edition: 1996
Fourth edition: 2006

Cover photos from top left to right: Dick Ritter, Murrine's, 1974; Jaroslava Brychtova and Stanislav Libensky, Pilchuck, 1987; plaster mold blow, Pilchuck, 1987; Dick Ritter gathering, Penland, circa 1974; Libensky, casting glass color easel; Everett "Shorty" Finley at Blenko Glass, 1976; emptying a factory furnace; Dick Marquis working at Kent State University, 1981; polishing at Steuben; Harvey Littleton, Berkeley, 1968; Jim Mongrain working at Kent State, 2005.

Back cover photos are works by Henry Halem and are representative of pieces created from 1972 through 2005.

Contact the Author:

Henry Halem provides consulting services as well as workshops and lectures. Inquiries about his availability should be directed to his E-mail above. Readers of this book are also encouraged to contact the author with comments and ideas for future editions.

Attention Colleges, Universities, and Glass Schools: Student discounts are available for quantities shipped to one address. Special booklets or book excerpts can be created by Franklin Mills Press to fit your specific needs. For information contact Franklin Mills Press.

ISBN 1-885663-06-4
ISBN 978-1-885663-06-1

In loving memory of my big brother Bob. He is missed.

Like glass, life is fragile.

Table of Contents

Introduction to Batching 9
       Compatibility, Colorants, LEC

Annealing 39
       Determining the A.T., Controllers, Annealing Castings, Stress & Compatibility

Casting 61
       All Kinds of Molds, Sand Casting, Kiln Casting

Refractories 135
       Bricks, Insulation, Furnaces, Recuperation

Glory Holes 189
       Fiber, IFB, Square Hole, A Garage

Burners 223
       Flame Safety

Annealers 241
       IFB, Skamol, Roll-Out, Electrical Information

General Information 283
       Adhesives, Enameling, Scavo, Mold Separator, Fuming (Iridizing), Color Bar Breaker,
       Pipe Cooler, Benches, Make-up Air, CFM, Diamond Drill Speeds

Suppliers 321

Conversions 341

Letters to Dr. Glass 345

Index 348

The page numbers in this table of contents will take you to the section heading page where you will find a specific content table. For specific subjects, use the index.

Acknowledgments

This, the 4th edition of *Glass Notes,* would not have been possible without the collective knowledge of others working in the field. *Glass Notes* is not all my book, but as you will see, is a compendium of information on and about glass gathered from many sources. It is important that I give credit and thanks to those who so willingly contributed their knowledge and insights to me for publication. First, I wish to thank all those gurus of glass that shared information with me in the previous edition: Fritz Dreisbach, Stanislav Libensky and Jaraslova Brychtova, Bob Carlson, Nick Labino, Mark Peiser, Dan Schwoerer, Tom Ash, Rick Mills, Klaus Moje, José Chardiet, Rik Allen, Dudley Giberson, Ed Francis, Jaroslav Zahradnik, Rudy Gritsch, Tom Armbruster, and John Chiles. For this edition, others have shared their knowledge as well as encouragement, and they include, along with those names above: Dr. Frank Woolley, Pete VanderLaan, Hugh Jenkins, Charlie Correll, Sean Mercer, Alicia Lomné, Jeremy Lepisto, The Bullseye Glass Co., The Corning Museum of Glass, Steve Abell, Art Allison, and Peet Robison.

I would also like to thank my editor, Chad Wickman, whose eagle eye dotted all the i's, crossed all the T's, inserted all the commas, and helped clarify the obscure. The great lunches and dinners with Marty Timmerman where we talked about life, love, and his great graphic front and back covers. No acknowledgement would be complete without my thanking those teachers who filled my head with ideas and pointed me in my life's direction, especially my high school art teacher Sylvia Weil who believed in my ability to make art. The circle would not be complete if I didn't thank all my former students who continue to build our rich history.

Last but of course never least, my biggest fans, my wife, playwright Sandra Perlman and my daughter Jessica.

Henry Halem,
Kent, Ohio
September 2006

Preface

This, the fourth edition of *Glass Notes*, has taken a great deal of effort. It attempts to bring up to date and clarify a good deal of the information found in the 3rd edition as well as add a good deal of new information pertinent to the art glass studio. In the last 10 years, there has been a sea change in studio equipment and glass techniques. With the costs of energy rising precipitously, studios are finding it imperative to include recuperators on their furnaces in order to be able to meet their monthly costs of operation. Hand tools are now crafted to meet the demands of the off hand blower, formulas and techniques for constructing high strength casting molds have been developed to accommodate complex castings, and the list keeps on growing. Artists now have access to the internet and discussion boards where they can find answers to technical as well as technique questions. If you've never accessed one of these boards, I recommend you do; the discussions are lively and sometimes insightful. Every manufacturer of products applicable to the glass studio has a site where one can order products. *Glass Notes* is by no means a definitive text but should be used as a resource to give you an idea of what is entailed in building studio glass equipment as well as some of the techniques available to you, the artist. I am proud of the result of my labor and the labor of others who agreed to let me include the information they developed over the years. I hope you find within these covers the information you seek.

On the following pages, you will find information concerning the technical aspects of the glass studio as well as descriptions of some glass processes. The equipment described in words and illustrations is not meant to be the definitive vision but is only an insight into one method of construction. If you intend to build a furnace or annealer, I recommend you visit studios that have equipment similar to what you intend to build as some of this information can be quite complex. Many who have purchased this book have telephoned or E-mailed me seeking further clarification, but remember, if you do contact me I'm on EST. Although it's exciting to build a furnace, light it up, and melt batch, don't feel that you have to as there are many excellent glass artists who know nothing about batching or building furnaces and run very profitable glass studios.

The primary concern of the artist is aesthetics. It's the object that matters and not its degree of difficulty. I've seen some bad glass come from great furnaces and vice versa. A knowledge of technique combined with a keen aesthetic makes art, or, $T \times A = A^2$. Einstein I'm not, but I do know the making of art is hard work. Building a furnace is easy, at least relative to the making of art that is. Knowledge of how the glass studio works and is built can be very rewarding, but it is only a tool for making art. There is nothing wrong with purchasing a well-built furnace and annealer, and some really good companies are building furnaces and annealers. Contact information for those companies can be found in the back of the book.

My point is this: first things first. Find out why you came to the swamp. Don't get up to your ass in alligators when all you wish to do is make art. You will learn how to build safe and efficient equipment when it becomes important. Knowing how things work and how they are made is only part of "the big picture," and there's more to glass than fancy batch and a fancy furnace. If you're ready, I hope that some of that technical information you've been searching for can be found between these covers.

Henry Halem

Kent, Ohio
September, 2006

Authors Bio

Henry Halem has been actively involved in the glass movement since 1968. His undergraduate degree comes from the Rhode Island School of Design where he received his BFA in ceramics in 1960. After serving as the first Resident Craftsman for the Virginia Museum of Fine Arts in Richmond, Halem returned for his MFA work in ceramics at the George Washington University where he received his MFA in 1968. During this time, he was an Instructor of Ceramics at Mary Washington College of the University of Virginia and a working artist, all while exhibiting his work extensively throughout the US.

Halem saw the energy and excitement generated by artists using glass, particularly as they emerged in the studio movement of the late 1960's. He returned to post graduate studies in glass as Harvey Littleton's assistant at the University of Wisconsin for one year. In 1969, Halem assumed a teaching post at Kent State University with the mandate to create a Glass program within the Crafts Division of the School of Art.

In 1998, after 29 years of teaching at Kent State, Halem left the university. During his tenure, Halem built the Kent State University glass program into one of international reputation. Many of his former students have become major names in the glass art field and maintain studios throughout the United States.

Halem has taught on numerous occasions at the historic Penland School of Crafts in North Carolina, the internationally known Pilchuck Glass School, The Nijjima Glass School in Japan, and at the Studio at the Corning Museum of Glass. He has presented workshops at major glass institutions in the US., Europe, Japan, and Australia. Previously, Halem has been invited as a representative of the U.S. to participate in prestigious international symposiums in The Czech Republic and the former Soviet Union.

Halem with Fritz Dreisbach, Mark Peiser, Joel Myers, and Marvin Lipofsky, founded the Glass Art Society and was elected its first president. The Glass Art Society at its Toledo meeting in 1993 presented him its honorary life membership. The following year (1994), Halem was installed as a Fellow of the American Crafts Council--their highest honor--and that same year he received the Governor's Award in Ohio for his contributions as an artist and educator. In 1998 he was presented with the President's medal from Kent State University.

Since the late 60's, when he moved from being a potter and began his love affair with glass, Halem's work has grown from purely blown vessels, through kiln casting, sculptural wall pieces, and into multi-media glass constructions. "I try to define my art by content and not by material. Art is about ideas; ideas that spring from observation, the persistence of memory and experience. In some cases the ideas spring from the material itself. Glass as a fragile material, glass as container, glass translucent, precious and ceremonial. Glass lifted from the commonplace and made holy. The shards of the past preserved. Glass holds dear the light within."

Halem's art has been chosen for exhibition in numerous group shows and also has an independent exhibition record. He was one of four national artists featured in the 1982 *LIFE* magazine article about the rise of contemporary glass.

Halem's work is found in many major private and museum collections including the Cleveland Museum of Art, The Philadelphia Museum of Fine Art, The Czech Museum of Art in Prague, the Hokkaido Museum in Sapporo, Japan, the High Museum of Art in Atlanta, and the Toledo Museum of Art.

His years of experience with glass make him eminently qualified to write and edit this book, *Glass Notes*.

In the Beginning

The two gentleman pictured below are the progenitors of contemporary studio glass. On the left is Harvey Littleton (1968) whose vision, in the early 60's, that we could build furnaces, melt glass, and make art, captured our imagination, energy, and "can-do" spirit. His vision gave rise to the thousands of artists working in glass throughout the world as well as to the hundreds of schools teaching this ancient art.

All the above probably wouldn't have been possible if not for the engineering abilities of the late Dominic Labino. It was Nick who demonstrated to Harvey how to build a practical glass furnace that would serve the needs of the small studio as well as the universities teaching glass. Nick also introduced us to the JM 475 glass marble that became the first glass melted in our furnaces. In later years, he would develop for Harvey the now famous SP 87 Batch.

Harvey Littleton, 1968

Nick Labino, circa 1976

The Glass Studio at the University of Wisconsin, 1963

Introduction to Batching

Chapter Contents

The Properties of Glass	10
Introduction to Glass	12
A Very Brief History	12
Explanation of Raw Materials Table	15
Opacifying Agents	19
Dr. Frank E. Woolley	20
Colored (Coloured) Glasses	21
Colorants for Batch	23
Colorants for Cullet	24
Glass Batching	25
Introduction to Batching	26
Assorted Notes for Batching	31
Some Batches	32
Compatibility	34
The Search for Compatibility	35
Factors for Calculating Linear Expansion	37

The Properties of Glass

The Corning Museum of Glass

Properties Of Glass: Chemical

The properties of glass can be varied and regulated over an extensive range by modifying the composition, production techniques, or both. In any glass, the mechanical, chemical, optical, and thermal properties cannot occur separately. Instead, any glass represents a combination of properties. And in selecting an individual glass for a product, it is this combination that is important. Usually, one property cannot be changed without causing a change in the other properties. It is the art of the glass scientist to produce the most favorable combination possible.

Chemistry Of Glass / Chemical Cousins

Thousands of different chemical compositions can be made into glass. Different formulas affect the mechanical, electrical, chemical, optical, and thermal properties of the glasses that are produced. There is no single chemical composition which characterizes all glass.

Typical glass contains formers, fluxes, and stabilizers.

Formers make up the largest percentage of the mixture to be melted. In typical soda-lime-silica glass, the former is silica (Silicon dioxide) in the form of sand.

Flux lowers the temperature at which the former will melt. Soda (Sodium carbonate) and Potash (Potassium carbonate), both alkalis, are common fluxes.

Stabilizers make the glass strong and water resistant. Calcium carbonate, often called calcined limestone, is a stabilizer. Without a stabilizer, water and humidity attack and dissolve glass. Glass lacking lime is often called "waterglass."

The Glassy State (Glass is a state of matter)

Glasses combine some properties of crystals and some of liquids but are distinctly different from both.

Glasses have the mechanical rigidity of crystals, but the random, disordered arrangement of molecules that characterize liquids.

Glasses are usually formed by melting crystalline materials at very high temperatures. When the melt cools, the atoms are locked into a random (disordered) state before they can form into a perfect crystal arrangement.

Composition

Glass products include three types of materials:

- FORMERS are the basic ingredients. Any chemical compound that can be melted and cooled into a glass is a FORMER. (With enough heat, 100% of the earth's crust could be made into glass. *If we're not careful we just might get there.*)

- FLUXES help FORMERS to melt at lower, more practical temperatures.

- STABILIZERS combine with FORMERS and FLUXES to keep the finished glass from dissolving, crumbling, or falling apart. We call this durability.
- Chemical composition determines what a glass can do.

Formers

Most commercial glass is made with sand that contains Silica, the most common former.

Melting sand by itself is too expensive because of the high temperatures required (about 1850° C, or 3360° F). THEREFORE...

Fluxes

are added which let the FORMER melt more readily and at lower temperatures (2370° F, 1300° C). These include:
- Soda Ash
- Potash
- Lithium Carbonate

Fluxes also make the glass chemically unstable, liable to dissolve in water or form unwanted crystals. THEREFORE ...

Stabilizers

are added to make the glass uniform and keep its special structure intact. These include:

- Limestone
- Litharge
- Alumina
- Magnesia
- Barium Carbonate
- Strontium Carbonate
- Zinc Oxide
- Zirconia

Hopefully these two pages and subsequent pages define for you what glass is in technical terms. What you will find in some of the pages beyond this introductory chapter is how this ubiquitous material, glass, can be and is used for the making of great art and craft. It is for you to define what the art is and what the craft is. As I have stated in previous editions of this book, always remember why you came to the well. If it is to make art, then make that your goal. If understanding the technical aspects of this material is helpful in that quest, then by all means learn those aspects, but never lose sight of your ultimate goal, to make beautiful glass.

Glass: an inorganic product of fusion that has cooled to a rigid condition without crystallizing.

Introduction to Glass
A Very Brief History

Glass is a liquid; at high temperatures it flows, and at low temperatures it doesn't. These simple statements embody a broad technology, most of which is empirically based.

During the early days (1962 – 1971) of the glass movement, as it came to be known, the studio artists and students blew a cullet known as JM 475 from fairly crude furnaces. This glass cullet came to us in the form of a greenish, hard, boron based glass marble. This glass marble, developed by Nick Labino for the Johns Manville Corp., was actually developed for the spinning of insulating glass fiber. In order to find out how we came to use the JM 475 marble required a bit of detective work on my part, and I feel the story is interesting enough to be retold.

To begin, my investigation I called my friend Fritz Dreisbach who I knew was there in Toledo when Harvey Littleton's workshops were presented. Fritz related to me that the first furnace Harvey developed in March of 1962 was a crude type of crucible pot furnace that was fired with a weed burner. Harvey's intention was to melt a batch formula he had developed, but as fate would have it, he either couldn't get enough heat, or the batch was of poor quality and wouldn't melt properly. At that time, Nick Labino was in attendance and had observed Harvey's attempts at melting glass. Nick saw the problems Harvey was having melting the batch and took two of the participants, Tom McGlauchlin and Clayton Bailey, back with him to his farm outside of Toledo and gave them a box of the JM 475 glass marbles. Nick told them to get rid of the batch and charge those marbles instead. Tom and Clayton went back to Toledo and gave Harvey the box of marbles to melt. The melt worked better, but the furnace still required some tweaking. Since no one really could blow glass, a few trinkets were fabricated, but unfortunately none have survived. Regardless of all the problems encountered at that first workshop it was considered a success by all in attendance; all agreed to get together again in June of 1962. And so it came to pass that the second Toledo workshop was held with the JM 475 marbles being the glass of choice. Harvey was still using the crude pot furnace from the first workshop, but I believe it had been improved upon and was capable of greater temperatures. Nick eventually steered Harvey away from his crude crucible furnace and introduced him to the small day tank melting unit which eventually populated all our studios. It is believed that the Labino day tank style furnace was introduced at the Crafts Conference held at Columbia University in NY the following year. The reader should note that the day tanks that are still in use in many studios and universities are very similar and directly related to the one that Nick developed in the early 60's. Since no one in those early days had any idea about melting batch glasses, and the fact that the JM 475 marble was cheap and easy to obtain, it became the glass we used at the University of Wisconsin in Madison and eventually in all the schools that were teaching glass until about 1971.

> **The usual requirements for a glass are:**
> a. it not crystallize upon cooling,
> b. it not dissolve in water, and
> c. it be stable in the molten state.

The 475 marble was a stiff green glass that, when blown, required one to move very quickly or it would set and become almost impossible to work. With all its inherent drawbacks, we managed to produce some, how shall I say, interesting objects. One should also keep in mind that our early furnaces had very crude burner systems that were incapable of achieving an adequate temperature. This only added to the stiffness of the 475 marbles. Another problem was the fact that most of us did not have glory holes, and we used the furnace gathering port to reheat. It all seems quite quaint now, but I must say it all was very exciting-- we were glass blowers with a mission and little stood in our way. We fanned out all across the country, spreading the word and teaching all who showed an interest in learning how to blow glass.

A few years ago, Steve Feren at the U. of Wisconsin arranged a small glass blowing reunion for a few of us hardy souls, and for old time sake, they charged the furnaces with the 475 marbles. Like I said, the glass was still stiff as hell.

As time progressed and universities began to include glass in their art school offerings, those who taught within those programs wanted glasses that were more applicable to the growing sophistication of our skills. After some research, we discovered a couple of companies as well as glass factories that either sold cullet in bulk or offered us their scrap glass for the taking. There had to be a glass that was softer and easier to blow than the 475 marbles. Suffice it to say, the quality of some factory cullets was a vast improvement over the marbles. We even found that the Fenton factory offered a clear cullet with a few compatible colors. Wow, compatible colors! The only catch was that we had to purchase the Fenton cullet through the Gabbert Cullet Co. located in Williamstown, WV, and run by one of the great characters that entered our lives, O.J. "Jiggs" Gabbert. Gabbert in my estimation was instrumental for the expansion of the studio glass movement (as it came to be known) because he sold good, clean crystal in an endless supply and at a reasonable price. Because of Jigg's contributions to the studio glass movement, I nominated him and he received an Honorary Lifetime Achievement award from the Glass Art Society in 1985. Jiggs has since passed away, but his company is still selling cullet to many schools around the country.

As an aside, we figured out early on in the 60's at Madison how to colorize the 475 marbles. The simple addition of a metallic oxide was all it took. I think it was Robert Barber who showed us how it was done. It's hard to believe how awed we were when Bob added a bit of Cobalt to a bunch of marbles and out came the most beautiful blue glass one could imagine. I think we all believed that Bob had invented the wheel.

During these early days, there were a few hardy souls that began to get a grasp on the chemistry of glass by reading Sam Scholes' *Modern Glass Practice*. From this text, one could configure a batch recipe, although it was not known if the resulting glass would fit our base crystal or any crystal for that matter since LEC was not part of our vocabulary. To my knowledge, it was Mark Peiser who started the ball rolling. Mark's first attempt was to develop an opal that would work with the 475 marbles. I believed he first tried using the Selenium red base glass that was published in the Scholes book. Even stranger was that with some tweaking he actually did develop that opal, but it didn't fit anything in our known world. On the heels of or concurrently with Mark's work, Dudley Giberson was working in New Hampshire and developing his batch recipes. In the spring of 1970, ten of us got together at the first GAS meeting in Penland. At this meeting as well as the subsequent year, we compared notes on what we were all doing in our respective studios and schools. Mark and Dudley showed and described to us what they had done with batching. It was all very exciting. I remember a group of us standing in front of Mark's furnace being totally awestruck by the fact that we could actually see the bottom of the furnace through 4 inches of crystal which was never possible with the marbles. Apparently, Mark also had figured out how to make an excellent crystal that really did fit his opals. Ah, those were heady days.

As Pete VanderLaan recalls: "In 1978 a conference was proposed in Boulder Colorado as an information-sharing project which published it's proceedings. It was known as "The Hot Glass Information Exchange". It was spearheaded by John Bingham, John Nickerson, Peter VanderLaan, and Henry Summa. All the participants were owners of private studios making glass with the notable exception of Andy Billici who was teaching at Alfred University at that time.

Pete continues: "The cost of admission was a technical article on some aspect of running a studio. The responses were wide and varied, anywhere from batch making issues to grinding facilities and how to build them. Shorty Finley came out from Blenko, and we all played with glass with Shorty whose facility with the material was a joy to watch. Participants included Bill Worchester, Josh Simpson, John Lewis, Steve Smyers, Jaffa Sikorsky, and a host of others. The proceedings were put in book form, and three editions were printed and sold. None of the participants wanted the profits outside of a flue gas analyzer which made the rounds from studio to studio. It's still possible to purchase copies of the book from Whitehouse-books.com. Be advised, though, they are Xerox copies but worth the read."

Well, it's now 2006 and we've come a long way. We did re-invent the wheel--at least in the blowing and casting areas and have passed all that knowledge on to all who would listen or take our classes. Yet, the one area that has not grown much within glass schools has been the teaching of glass chemistry. Yes, there were and are a few hardy souls that toil endlessly, mastering the art of glass batching; but, in my opinion, because of the fact that decent cullet was and is available along with compatible color bars and now premixed batch, not many care to take on the task of mixing their own colors. I fully understand why most studios do not get involved in batching: it is not for the faint of heart, equipment and material can be expensive as well as take up precious space, and material storage can and is problematic. But just think of the extraordinary reward you're missing when you batch that fantastic warm green, red, or opal yellow and it all fits your bright, soft crystal.

So much for the history lesson; it's time to move on and get to the business at hand which is to try and get you, the reader, involved and excited about developing your own glass colors. Before moving on, however, I have two people to thank for the information that follows.

A Big Thank You!

The two people who have agreed to share their vast knowledge of glass chemistry and their practical application of the same are Pete VanderLaan and Dr. Frank E. Woolley. I am indeed in their debt for allowing me to print the information they have so graciously provided. The reader should note that my thank you below is not in the order of importance as since they both are equals.

Pete VanderLaan to my knowledge is the one person in the U.S. who has taken on the task of developing the art of batching color and does not hesitate to share what he knows with all who will listen. Pete has been seriously involved in glass chemistry and has been making his own colors for 35 years. A few years ago, Pete removed the veil of secrecy that surrounds this all too secret medieval art and has "gone public" with his vast knowledge of glass chemistry. Pete is also the moderator of the CraftWeb board on the Internet (http://talk.craftweb.com/). This board is a clearinghouse for all questions as they pertain to hot glass and other glass techniques. Many gather at this board on a daily basis asking and answering questions from all over the world. By far the most questions asked concern glass batching and Pete really shines when those questions appear. I am indeed fortunate that Pete has agreed to share some of that knowledge with my readers. I know he is doing this because he feels anyone who is serious about being an artist with glass and uses color should develop color batches that suit their needs instead of buying those "on again, off again," color bars.

The other person I would like to thank is Dr. Frank E. Woolley for his contributions to this and other chapters in this book. Prior to his retirement Dr. Woolley was manager of melting research in the Science and Technology Division of the Corning Glass Works. Dr. Woolley produced a collection of lecture notes in a manual titled *Glass Technology for the Studio (1998)*. This manual was presented to all those students that attended his lectures. Dr. Woolley has graciously agreed to let me include information found in the pages of that manual. I have, with his permission, taken some of that information as it applies to this particular section and put that information in a narrative form. A brief bio on these two gentleman appears at the heading of their particular sections. Pete, Frank, and I hope the information that follows will stimulate all who are interested in carving out a section of their studios and devote it to the formulating of glass color.

Because they codify my thoughts on art and technology, I think I should end this introduction with Dr. Woolley's own words found in the preface of his manual: "The goal of these notes is to present in more understandable terms some of the modern understandings of glass science and technology, so that glass artists can be freed from technical constraints, and can find new ways to express themselves in a broader range of materials, processes and forms."

JM 475 Marbles

14 Glass Notes

Explanation of Raw Materials Table

Information: Ceramic Industry Materials Handbook

The following information gives the composition of the principal raw materials used in glass making in terms of the oxides remaining in the glass after the melting processes. Although these materials are seldom chemically pure enough to represent accurately by chemical formulas and by percentage compositions corresponding to these formulas, it is best for our present purpose to assume that this is the case. Some exceptions are made for those minerals which are so seldom perfectly pure or truly represented by chemical formulas that it is better to choose typical compositions of the minerals as supplied. It must be understood that the fractions and factors given for heavy chemicals apply to chemicals of 100% purity, whereas the usual degree of purity is more apt to be about 99%. Practically, it is necessary to rely upon recent analyses of the actual stocks of materials on hand if very accurate calculations are desired.

Effect on the chemical and physical properties of the different oxide constituents generally employed in glass

Silica (SiO_2, Glass sand) Uniform grain size is perhaps of more importance in a glass sand than the actual size of the grains themselves. If the sand grains are too fine, the first reaction will take place so rapidly that the large volumes of carbon dioxide liberated will cause the batch to foam badly. Too fine a sand also may be responsible for the formation of a fine, persistent seed in the glass. In glass compositions, silica confers high viscosity, good chemical resistance, and a low coefficient of thermal expansion.

Boric Oxide (B_2O_3, Borax) facilitates the melting operation, improves chemical resistance, produces glass of low thermal expansion giving good resistance to thermal shock, and inhibits devitrification. Mechanical strength and scratch hardness are also increased. Borax decreases the viscosity of glass but decreases working time. It may produce seeds and is rough on refractories.

Soda (Na_2O) Is used as the primary flux in glasses. Gives easy melting and rapidly lowers the viscosity of glasses, reduces resistance to chemical attack, lowers the mechanical strength, and increases thermal expansion.

Potash (K_2O) Is similar to soda in its general effects, but viscosity and thermal expansion changes are not so marked. It improves appearance or brilliance. The mixed alkali glasses are invariably more durable than those containing only Na_2O. K_2O improves color development in many glasses. It should be noted that the use of potash alone when batching Cad/Sel glass will lead to a decrease in the amount of selenium needed.

Lead Oxide (PbO) The usual form for glass is Lead Monosilicate. Lead Monosilicate is easier to handle, dustless, and safer than pure PbO. when used in proportions of about 30% by weight, it gives easy melting glasses as in lead crystal glasses. It imparts considerable density to the glass and has a high refractive index. It improves melting characteristics of glass when used in percentages of 4% or greater.

Lime (CaO, Calcium Carbonate) For glass, lime is introduced as limestone, burned lime (calcined limestone), and dolomite. The commercial limestones are classified according to their relative content of CaO and MgO. The term lime, when used with reference to glass, may mean either a high calcium limestone or a dolomitic limestone or the oxide as burned lime made from either of these types of stone. Lime is one of the most important of the common batch ingredients. When added in proper quantities Lime gives to glass, durability, hardness, viscosity and tenacity, and facilitates melting and refining. When present in high proportions, it gives glasses of great fluidity when molten and makes them set rapidly as they cool down. High lime glasses are prone to devitrification. It should be noted that limestone is also a source of batch impurities. The form most used is the dolomitic variety of limestone because of its low iron content as well as a powerful fluxing action. It is thought that glasses containing dolomitic limestone will fine faster than those with other forms of lime.

Lithia (LiO_2) Glasses containing lithia are much more fluid in the molten state than those containing proportional amounts of sodium or potassium. Much smaller amounts of lithia are required to produce a glass of the necessary fluidity for working without sacrificing the desired physical and chemical properties.

Magnesia (MgO) performs a similar function to lime; however, it shows less tendency to devitrification while decreasing the setting rates. Improvement is noticeable in resistance to weathering. It is usually found in conjunction with lime. Magnesia can also improve working properties.

Barium Oxide (BaO) is used as Barium Carbonate. The properties imparted, in most cases, are similar to those given to glass by calcia or magnesia. Glasses high in Barium are less durable than a corresponding lime glass. The addition of Barium to lime glasses will increase brilliance.

Calcium Phosphate ($Ca_3(PO_4)_2$) is chiefly employed in the production of opal glasses similar to those produced by the use of fluorine compounds. The addition of barium aids in the action of the phosphate. For example, pharmaceutical containers are frequently phosphate opals.

Alumina (Al_2O_3) produces glasses of high viscosity and high durability. Alumina is usually supplied through feldspar, commonly nepheline seyenite. Alumina in opal glass makes for greater fluorine retention, not necessarily greater opacity.

Zinc Oxide (ZnO) Zinc imparts brilliance and good stability. It is also a substitute for the more soluble alkali constituents; it also lowers viscosity. A 1% addition improves durability and maintains good workability. It is a main constituent of fluoride opal glasses. The addition of 10% zinc oxide assists in the development of the color of cad/sel ruby glasses.

Author's note: The information provided was gleaned from the January issue of Ceramic Industry *(www.ceramicindustry.com). The January issue of this publication lists every chemical used in the ceramic, glass, and enameling industry. The text that accompanies the chemical listing delineates in great detail its effects upon the glass melt. I highly recommend getting a copy.*

Reasons for employing certain raw materials to the glass

- Calcined alumina, hydrated alumina, allows alumina to be introduced into the glass without adding alkali at the same time. This is essential in the alkali-free glasses.

- Feldspars, nepheline syenite, allows alumina to be introduced more easily into the composition while adding alkali simultaneously.

- Antimony oxide is a reducing agent with some refining action. It is generally employed for this purpose in pot melted glasses, and its effects take place at a slightly lower temperature than when using arsenic. (Toxic)

- Arsenic has an oxidizing action on ferrous iron and a refining action at somewhat higher temperatures than with antimony. It is used widely as a stabilizer when decolorizing with selenium. (Highly poisonous)

- Manganese oxide is an old-fashioned decolorizer employed in pot melting. It also is used for the production of purple glasses.

- Selenium, as noted, is the universal decolorizer employed in tank melting practice. It is used in conjunction with cadmium sulphide for the production of ruby glasses ranging in color from amber to deep red.

- Sodium and potassium nitrates are oxidizing agents nearly always used in pot melting practice; excess causes rapid attack on the refractories.

- Saltcake prevents the formation of silica scum. It is principally used in sheet and plate glass manufacture where large surface areas of molten glass encourage this scum formation. It is also an oxidizing agent.

- Calcium carbonate, chemically prepared, is free from any trace of iron oxide and is often used in the preparation of optical glasses where the much cheaper limestones cannot be used because of the impurities they contain.

Conversion from Oxide Weight (%) to Batch Recipe (Pounds)

Oxide	%	Material	Reciprocal	x's	% in Glass	=	Weight of Material in Pounds
SiO_2	72.0	*Silica	1.000	x	72	=	72.0
Al_2O_3	2.0	Calcined Al	1.000	x	2	=	2
MgO	3.5	**Dolomite	4.580	x	3.5	=	16
CaO	6.5	Minus 4.8 included in dolomite (taken as calcium carbonate)					
CaO	1.7	Limestone	1.786	x	1.7	=	3.0
Na_2O	16	Soda Ash	1.710	x	16	=	27.3
Totals	100%				Total Weight		120.3

*Silica Sand conversion factor is understood to be 1.000 and is usually not listed in tables.

**Dolomite is a compound material which yields MgO, CaO, and CO_2. It is usually used to fill the MgO requirement and helps by partially filling the CaO. Using the reciprocal fraction from the Composition of Raw Materials chart on pg. 18 we find:

Dolomite yields .304 CaO
.216 MgO
.480 CO_2 which is expelled as a gas

Solving first for the MgO: 3.5 x 4.574 = 16.0 lbs. Of this 16.0 lbs., .304% is CaO; therefore, 16.0 x .304 = 4.8% CaO included in the dolomite must be subtracted from the total CaO requirement. 1.7% CaO remains to be satisfied to complete the CaO requirement (usually taken as calcium carbonate refered to as limestone; see above).

Final Batch in pounds
(Not a real batch, sample only)

Sand ---------------------- 72.0
Alumina -------------------- 2.0
Dolomite ----------------- 16.0
Limestone ----------------- 3.0
Soda Ash ---------------- 27.3

Factory batch barrows ready to charge.

Composition of Raw Materials

Materials	Alternate Name	Theoretical Formula	Oxide Supplied	Fraction	Reciprocal*
Alumina	Calcined Alumina	Al_2O_3	Al_2O_3	1.000	1.000
Alumina Hydrate	Hydrated Alumina	$Al_2O_3 \cdot 3H_2O$	Al_2O_3	.654	1.531
Feldspar	Microcline (typical)	$K_2O \cdot Al_2O_3 \cdot 6SiO_2$	Al_2O_3	.180	5.556
			$K_2(Na_2)O$	.130	
			SiO_2	.680	
Nepheline Syenite	Nephy, Neph Sy (Typical Composition)		Al_2O_3	.250	4.000
			$Na_2(K_2)O$	.150	
			SiO_2	.600	
Kyanite		$Al_2O_3 \cdot SiO_2$	Al_2O_3	.567	1.763
			SiO_2	.433	
Kaolin	China Clay	$Al_2O_3 \cdot 2SiO_2 \cdot 2H_2O$	Al_2O_3	.395	2.57
			SiO_2	.465	
Cryolite	Kryolith	Na_2AlF_6	Na_2O	.443	2.258
			Al_2O_3	.243	4.118
			F_2 loss on Volatilization		
Antimony Oxide		Sb_2O_3	Sb_2O_3	1.000	1.000
Arsenious Oxide	Arsenic	As_2O_3	As_2O_5	1.160	.860
Barium Carbonate		$BaCO_3$	BaO	.777	1.288
Barium Oxide	Baryta	BaO	BaO	1.000	1.000
Barium Sulfate	Barytes	$BaSO_4$	BaO	.657	1.523
Boric Oxide	Boracic Acid	$B_2O_3 \cdot 3H_2O$	B_2O_3	.563	1.776
Borax	Borax (10 Mol)	$Na_2O \cdot 2B_2O_3$	B_2O_3	.365	2.738
			Na_2O	.163	6.135
Anhydrous Borax	"Pyrobar"	$Na_2O \cdot 2B_2O_3$	B_2O_3	.692	1.445
Lime, Burnt	Burnt Lime	CaO	CaO	1.000	1.000
Lime, Hydrated	Calcium Hydrate	$CaO \cdot H_2O$	CaO	.757	1.322
Limestone	Calcium Carbonate	$CaCO_3$	CaO	.560	1.786
Calcium Carbonate	Whiting	$CaCO_3$	CaO	.560	1.786
Lime, Dolomitic	Burnt Dolomite	$CaO \cdot MgO$	CaO	.582	1.720
			MgO	.418	2.390
Dolomite	Raw Limestone, Dolo.	$CaO \cdot MgO \cdot 2CO_3$	CaO	.304	3.290
			MgO	.216	4.580
Lime, Hydrated, Dol.	Finishing Lime	$CaO \cdot MgO \cdot 2H_2O$	CaO	.423	2.363
			MgO	.304	3.290
Litharge	Lead Oxide, Yellow	PbO	PbO	1.000	1.000
Red Lead	Minium	Pb_3O_4	PbO	.977	1.024
Lithium Carbonate	Lithium	Li_2CO_3	Li_2O	.404	2.473
Fluorspar	Calcium Floride	CaF_2	CaF_2	1.000	1.000

Material	Alternate Name	Theoretical Formula	Oxide Supplied	Fraction	Reciprocal*
Bone Ash	Calcium Phosphate	$3CaO \cdot 2P_2O_3$	CaO	.372	2.700
			P_2O_5	.628	1.592
Sodium Fluosilicate	Sodium Silicafluoride	Na_2SiF_6			
Iron Oxide (Red)	Iron Oxide	Fe_2O_3	Fe_2O_3	1.000	1.000
Potassium Hydrate	Caustic Potash	KOH	K_2O	.838	1.194
Potassium Nitrate	Saltpeter	KNO_3	K_2O	.465	2.151
Potassium Carbonate	Calcined Potash	K_2CO_3	K_2O	.681	1.469
Glassmaker's Potash	Potassium Carbonate (Hydrated)	$K_2CO_2 \cdot 1.5H_2O$	K_2O	.570	1.754
Sand	Glass Sand, Quartz	SiO_2	SiO_2	1.000	1.000
Soda Ash	Sodium Carbonate	Na_2CO_3	Na_2O	.585	1.709
Sodium Nitrate	Saltpeter	$NaNO_3$	Na_2O	.365	2.741
Salt Cake	Sodium Sulfate	Na_2SO_4	Na_2O	.437	2.290
Strontium Carbonate		$SrCO_3$	SrO	.702	1.425
Silver Nitrate		$AgNO_3$	Ag_2O	.682	1.466
Gold Chloride		$AuCl_3$	Au	.649	1.540
Black Uranium		U_2O_8	UO_3	1.019	.981
Zinc Oxide	Zinc Oxide	ZnO	ZnO	1.000	1.000

Opacifying Agents

Material	Alternate Name	Theoretical Formula	Oxide Supplied	Fraction	Reciprocal*
Calcium Fluoride	----------	CaF_2	CaO	.718	1.392
			F_2 Loss on Volatilization		
Cryolite	----------	Na_3AlF_6	Na_2O	.443	2.258
			Al_2O_3	2.43	4.118
			F_2 Loss on Volatilization		
Calcium Phosphate	Bone Ash	$Ca_3(PO_4)_2$	CaO	.542	1.844
			P_2O_5	.458	2.185
Tin Oxide	Tin Oxide	SnO_2	SnO_2	1.000	1.000
Zirconium Oxide	----------	ZrO_2	ZrO_2	1.000	1.000
Salt	----------	NaCl	Na_2O	.530	1.866
			Cl_2	.607	1.648
Potassium Chloride	----------	KCl	K_2O	.632	1.583
			Cl_2	.476	2.103
Sodium Phosphate	----------	$NaPO_3$	Na_2O	.304	3.390
			P_2O_5	.696	1.437

* This column gives pounds of material required to supply one pound of oxide.

Dr. Frank E. Woolley

A few years ago, I was shown a technical booklet titled *Glass Technology for the Studio* written by Dr. Frank E. Woolley. Dr. Woolley had written this text for a course he was teaching at the Corning Museum School. His book is a treasure of technical information written in a language that most studio artists can understand. I am extremely grateful that Dr. Woolley has given me permission to reproduce in *Glass Notes* what I find applicable for my readers. The information included from his book is so noted with his name. I have in some instances added information in order to clarify some of the facts as stated by Dr. Woolley. I have also changed some of his formats to a more narrative style. For those that are not familiar with Dr. Woolley's background in the field, I have included a short bio below.

Brief Bio

Dr. Woolley is a technical consultant who specializes in glass melting. He is retired from Corning Inc. where he was Manager of Melting Research in the Science and Technology Division. His group investigated the fundamental processes of glass melting and developed new industrial melting processes for Corning's domestic and international glass melting. He received B.S. and M.S. degrees in Chemical and Metallurgical Engineering from the University of Michigan, and a Sc.D. in Chemical Metallurgy from MIT in 1966. He also received a M.B.A. degree from Syracuse University in 1980. Dr. Woolley was with Corning from 1966 to 1998, except for service as a Powder Metallurgist with the U.S. Army from 1967 to 1969. He managed various groups in RD&E at Corning, NY and Fontainebleau, France, engaged in testing and selection of refractories and raw materials, laboratory- and pilot-scale glass melting and forming, development of glass compositions, ceramic processing, and vapor deposition of glasses for optical fibers. Dr. Woolley has taught glass technology at Alfred University and at the Center for Professional Advancement. He has also taught glass technology to glass artists at The Studio of the Corning Museum of Glass in Corning, NY. Dr. Woolley was elected a Fellow of the American Ceramic Society in 1997. He is past chairman of Technical Committee 14 on Gases in Glass of the International Commission on Glass. He is a past member of ASTM Committee C-8 on Refractories, the Society of Glass Technology, and the American Institute of Chemical Engineers. He currently consults for the US Department of Energy and its contractors on vitrification of radioactive wastes. Dr. Woolley now makes his home in the great state of Massachusetts.

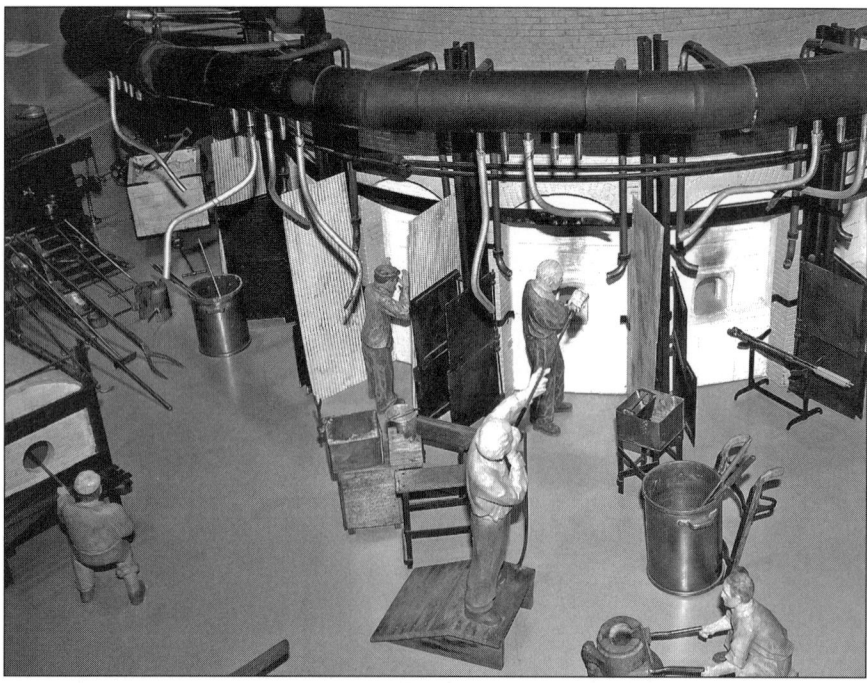

Model of Glass Factory
Corning Museum of Glass

Colored (Coloured) Glasses

Dr. Frank E. Woolley

The Nature of Coloration in Glasses

The two principal methods of creating color in glasses are to dissolve elements that absorb light of specific wavelengths, or to create dispersions of extremely fine particles, called colloids, that also absorb light of specific wavelengths.

The amount of light absorbed by either method depends only on the wavelength and the amount of the colorant that is in its path.

This means that the intensity of the color depends on the product of the thickness of the glass and the concentration of colorant in the glass; thick colored glass looks darker or more colored than thin glass of exactly the same composition, in direct proportion to the glass thickness.

Some glasses are opaque as well as colored; these are opal (white) glasses to which the same colorants that produce transparent colors have been added.

Components That Color Glasses

Solution colorants

The most common dissolved colorants are elements of the transition metal family; the nonmetals sulfur and selenium, and metals of the rare earth family are also used as glass colorants. *Author's note: See chart on page 23 for the colorants and the resulting colors when employed in a batch.*

The color is created by a process within the atom. This means that a color recipe for one glass will usually work for other glass compositions (if they both have the same oxidation state).

In general, potassium silicate glasses (K_2O) give "clearer" colors (narrower absorption bands) than sodium silicate glasses (Na_2O).

Transition metals dissolve in glass as "ions," which are atoms with one or more of their electrons removed.

The number of electrons removed depends on the "oxidation state" of the glass or how much oxygen is chemically available to react with the transition metal element; this is controlled by adding oxidizing and reducing agents in the batch, and by contact with the furnace atmosphere.

Very pure reds, oranges, and yellows can be obtained by precipitating colloids of cadmium with sulfur (yellow) and selenium (red).
Because of the extreme toxicity of cadmium and selenium, these glasses require careful batch handling and very effective dust and exhaust removal.

Since both components are lost from the melt by volatilization, the color changes with time in the furnace or the flame as does the LEC.

Adding Colorants to Pre-Mixed Batches

Colorants added to premixed batch need to be fairly well dispersed in the batch; since most of them have higher densities than the clear glass, they tend to drop to the bottom of the melter if they are poorly mixed.

If there is good convection in the melter, the colorants do not need to be mixed throughout the entire charge; they can be dispersed in a portion of the fill. It should be noted though that small tanks and crucibles have very low convection currents.

Interactions between colorants and fining agents

Since oxidation state is important for many of the colorants, and is critical for the colloidal (cadmium and selenium) colorants, there is a natural conflict between the colorants and the fining agents. Fining agents are oxidizers and remove sulfur and selenium during melting.

It should be noted that Spruce Pine and many other batches contain antimony, which creates an oxidizing condition at the fining temperature. Antimony becomes a reducing agent as the glass is cooled; this helps the precipitation of metallic colloids but decreases the intensity of manganese and copper colors.

Adding Colorants to Cullet

It is not that difficult to add common mettalic colorants to cullet. The color will disperse more easily if the cullet is in small pieces and not large lumps. *See pg. 24 for a list of colorants that work well with cullet.* Because you don't know the specific formulation of the cullet, it is difficult to predict the exact color one gets when adding the mettalic oxides, but I can guarantee you that you will get blue when adding cobalt. **Please note: You cannot add Cadmium or Selenium to cullet.**

Further reading

Section 18 on Optical Properties in Fay Tooley's *Handbook of Glass Manufacture* 3rd ed. (Ashlee Publishing Co., 1984) has an excellent discussion of colored glasses and the behavior of many colorants. This book is no longer in print, but you may be able to obtain a copy from Whitehouse Books.com (www.whitehouse-books.com).

The classic text is Woldemar A. Weyl, *Coloured Glasses* (Pub. by, Society of Glass Technology, Sheffield, England, 1951). Although over 50 years old, there is no more complete source of information on the effects of each colorant in a wide range of base glasses. This book is available from Whitehouse-Books.com. This book can be difficult for the novice but is worth having if you get serious about batching your own glass.

Color in Glass and the Effect of Atmosphere

Making colored glass is a complex process, due to the composition of the glass itself, the furnace conditions, and because the same metal oxide can produce a range of colors depending on quantity added. The state of the furnace is of particular importance since the amount of oxygen being consumed by the fuel will affect the reaction between the added metal oxide and the glass batch. A reducing environment is produced when the fuel is oxygen hungry. As the fuel burns oxygen, it is drawn out of the furnace atmosphere and out of the glass batch as well thus altering the number of oxygen ions in the molten glass. The reduced metal oxide does not melt, but instead is distributed evenly in tiny particles, creating a suspension (colloid) which reflects light and produces the appearance of color.

An oxidizing environment, on the other hand, is produced when the fuel has been more fully burned, and requires less oxygen to maintain itself. In this case, the metal oxide added to the glass batch fuses with the silica to produce a colored silicate, and the higher levels of oxygen ions in the glass produce a different range of colors.

Author's Note: All chemicals if handled improperly can be dangerous to your health. Some chemicals that are more dangerous than others and should be avoided by the inexperienced. Those chemicals are: Barium, Lead, Zinc, Cadmium Sulphide, and Selenium. When handling any batch chemicals one should wear an adequate dust mask and have adequate ventilation. A Tyvek suit would not be out of the question either.

Always melt glass under a good exhaust hood. The products of combustion can and often do contain heavy metals, caustic materials, and carcinogens.

Colorants for Batch

Chart Supplied by Pete VanderLaan

Color	Condition	Colorant	Influential Flux	Degree of Difficulty
Dark Blue	Oxidizing	Cobalt Oxide or Carbonate	No Special	Easy
Turquoise Blue	Oxidizing	Copper Oxide or Carbonate	Barium Brightens Substantially	Easy
Pale Blue	Oxidizing	Iron Oxide	Soda or Potash	Easy
Brown	Oxidizing	Selenium and Iron	Sodium	Easy but Toxic
Black	Oxidizing	Cobalt and Copper	Soda or Potash	Easy
Brown	Oxidizing	Nickel	Sodium	Nickel is somewhat refractory
Gray	Oxidizing	Manganese and Iron	Sodium	Fine Balance
Purple	Oxidizing	Manganese	Potash	Easy
Purple	Neutral	Gold and Cobalt	Lead	Advanced Skill
Violet	Neutral	Neodymium	Soda or Potash	Easy
Deep Green	Neutral	Copper and Iron Oxide	Lead	Easy and Toxic
Medium Green	Reducing	Copper and Iron Oxide	Soda or Potash	Fine Balance
Yellow Green	Neutral	Potassium Dichromate	Soda or Potash	Hard to Melt Cleanly
Emerald Green	Reduced	Potassium Dichromate	Soda or Potash	Hard to Melt Cleanly
Blue Green	Neutral	Potassium Dichromate and Copper Oxide	Soda or Potash	Hard to Melt Cleanly
Deep Red	Neutral	Copper Oxide, Stannous Oxide, Zinc Oxide	Soda and Potash	Hard to find Chemicals
Wine Red	Neutral	Gold Chloride and Selenium	Lead and Potash	Fine Balance and Expensive
Lipstick Red	Neutral to Reducing	Cadmium Sulphide and Selenium	Zinc and Potash	Toxic Melt Requiring Fine Balance
White	Oxidizing	Cryolite	Soda Potash and Barium	Hard to Calculate Expansion
Opal Swirl	Neutral	Stannous Oxide, Silver Nitrate, Zinc Oxide, Iron Oxide	Soda and Potash	Wildly Unpredictable
Pink	Neutral	Selenium	High Potash	Toxic
Amber	Neutral	Sulphur	Black Tin and Sulphur	Really Stinks Forever

Colorants for Cullet

It is assumed that these colorants are being used with a basic clear soda/lime factory cullet. I have used these colorants on and off over the years and know some will go into solution easily while others need a bit of "coaxing." Some of these colorants, used in different ratios with each other, can produce changes in the resultant color. It can be fun but rather expensive to experiment with the ratios. If you wish to reproduce your results, it is imperative to weigh the ratio of colorant to cullet. The colorants are always added as a percentage of the weight of the cullet. You will need a fairly good triple beam balance to weigh your colorants as well as a conversion chart to convert from our archaic ounces and pounds to grams (metric). Radio Shack sells, or did sell, a very inexpensive metric conversion calculator. I would be lost without mine. If you use a computer, there are a few excellent sites that can do the calculations for you. One that I use is **http://www.convert-me.com/en/**. If you make colorant additions over 1%, you may change the coefficient of expansion of your glass, making it incompatible with your crystal. I have not found many problems when I used more than 1%. I only mention it as a precaution and as a way for you to trace the cause of checking, if that becomes a problem. One way to get a good dispersion of the colorant in the glass is to wet the cullet and then sift colorant onto the wet cullet. The colorant will readily stick to the glass.

- **Manganese** Blue violet. In the carbonate form, manganese will "boil" quite violently but will eventually settle down. It is difficult to state how much one should add to the cullet to create the desired color. Manganese tends to be a "fugitive" colorant. That is, it tends to vaporize quite easily from the melted glass with a resulting color that is rather washed out. It also has a tendency to settle to the bottom of the tank. A nice trick is to gather the boiling manganese glass. The resulting glass surface is pitted purple, which can be quite effective under certain circumstances.

- **Copper** Greenish blue. Copper is very reliable and easy to use. When used in combination with iron oxide, it is possible to produce green. Start with equal quantities of copper and iron. Back in the 60's when we were blowing 475 marbles (see my introduction to this section) Bob Barber made small additions of copper to the cullet, subjected it to a reducing flame for 3 days, and made sort of copper ruby. At least that's how I remember it.

- **Iron** Greenish, brownish, bluish. The colors produced by iron are dependent on the quantity used as well as the ph of the base glass and the atmosphere of the furnace.

- **Cobalt** Blue, and I mean blue. Although cobalt is very expensive, it should be used in minute quantities to create a strong blue. It is best to mix cobalt with some fritted cullet in order to disperse it before charging.

- **Nickel** Brown or purple. The depth of color produced by nickel depends on the character of the alkali in your cullet. High potash (potassium) glass tends toward violet; on the other hand, soda (sodium) glass tends toward a brownish color. Nickel oxide is very refractory and doesn't want to go into solution readily. You will need to melt your cullet at a higher temperature if it doesn't go into solution.

- **Potassium Dichromate** Green. If you're not careful, the dichromate will produce corundum (black) specks in your glass. A high saturation of this material can produce an aventurine glass. Peet Robison and I made a green aventurine with this material but as I remember it we always got some black corundum specks.

- **Silver Nitrate** Yellowish. When fresh, turns opaque bluish; yellowish when allowed to sit in the pot. We used it to create Schmaltz Glass back in Madison in the 60's. Never touch silver nitrate with your hands or let it touch any part of your body. It will create "burns" on your skin. Silver Nitrate is also very expensive.

Some of these oxides can be purchased as carbonates and or dioxides as well as in the pure oxide form. The pure oxide will always require a smaller percent addition than the carbonate or the dioxide for a particular color.

Glass Batching

The information found on the preceding pages included some of the technical information needed prior to your setting up a batch room. The information that now follows includes the practical aspects of actually making that batch.

In recent years, a great number of studio artists have become interested in mixing their own batch colors but have shied away from doing so because of imagined difficulties. Pete VanderLaan has been batching glass for many years and has agreed to share with you and his many fans how to get started in this very rewarding aspect of glass. Some of you might think that the commercially available color rods and glass batches preclude the need to know anything about glass batching. For some that might be true, but you know I'm rather bored with seeing the same colors day after day and year after year. Wouldn't it be nice if you could make your own colors, colors with subtlety, colors that really fit, colors that are yours and no on else's. Well, it is not only possible but is easier than you might think. Yes, it will take work and an investment of your hard earned cash to get started, but ask yourself how much you've spent over the years buying color rods, cullet, or batch and how much you will be spending in the future for all those materials. In the long run it is the do-it-yourselfer that spends the least. Do you remember when you blew your first glass and drank from it well it's that same feeling of satisfaction when you melt your first batch. I won't fool you though; there are going to be problems to solve and headaches when you batch, but as they say, "no guts no glory."

Pete VanderLaan began working in glass in the late 60's in a private studio in Santa Fe, New Mexico. At that time, if one wanted colored glass, one made it themselves. Kügler color would not be imported for another five years. VanderLaan began to color cullet but quickly realized that it was totally limiting. With the encouragement of pioneers like Dudley Giberson and Mark Peiser, began mixing his own formulas for colored and clear glasses. Over the decades, this has been refined more and more. Pete often talks about the transition from being the student to being the teacher. "I don't know quite when it happens but eventually you realize that you are being asked way more questions than you are asking, and that the group you can ask is getting smaller and smaller." As John Croucher from Gaffer has said, "there aren't a lot of people you can sit down with and shoot the breeze about making color rods. I think a big difference for me is that I think it is important to pass that knowledge along while many people want to sit on it. In the long run, we are only going to be as good as the people whose shoulders we were allowed to stand on."

Pete now lives and works with his wife MaryBeth Bliss in Chocorua, New Hampshire. He is also the distributor for Engineered Ceramics crucibles.

Pete VanderLaan

One great advantage to batching your own color is that you will not have to buy these anymore.

Introduction to Batching

by Pete VanderLaan

I am highly suspicious of the commercially available high-lead color rods in the off-hand glass studio that are used by most of the glass studios around the world. The notion of combining two or more radically different glasses in one piece of work and expecting that everything will be okay throughout the ages is something that my experience tells me is not going to work all that well. It is because of the problems inherent in using commercially available color rods that I decided to become involved in the batching of my own colors. Over the past 45 years, I have become quite adept at developing many types of glasses and find great satisfaction in the intricacies of glass chemistry. Although the history of glass chemistry within the glass factory and studio has and is highly secretive, I believe it important to share what I know with those who have the desire and wherewithal to become involved in the "alchemy" of glass batching. It is helpful to have some knowledge of chemistry in order to understand the differences between each of the materials that constitute a glass batch. If you do not and even if you do have a knowledge of chemistry, I recommend you read *Modern Glass Practice* by Sam Scholes. This text is an excellent primer on all the raw materials that go into the glass batch. Once you have a thorough understanding of batch materials, you should be ready to tackle the ins and outs of producing your very own glass.

One thing that I stress throughout this primer on glass batching is safety. There are any number of materials found in the batch room that can kill quickly or over time. Yes, you have read that correctly, kill you. It is imperative that you protect yourself as well as those around you by outfitting the batch room with the necessary ventilation and yourself with the correct filter masks and clothing. If you do not, I and the author of this book cannot take responsibility for your health and welfare. Consider yourself warned.

Getting Started

The Batch Room

The batch facility should be a room large enough to store all your materials and also as your batch mixer. Ideally it should be heated and have a smooth cement floor as well as good exhaust system. Some of the materials used in batching are quite caustic, and some dangerous. All the batch chemicals must be stored safely, especially if there are children and pets in the area.

The Tools

Before getting started, The following is a list of tools that you will need to successfully set up a batch mixing area. Some are absolutely critical and are marked with an asterisk (*).

A clean mixer, preferably new, but if not, then very clean. Cement mixers work fine. Mortar mixers don't. It should be capable of holding at least one hundred pounds without spilling anything. You are going to make a gasketed lid for this mixer.

1. A good gram scale. These are getting much more interesting to buy than you might think. Get weights for it that let you go up to 2500 grams.
2. A very good platform scale. This should be capable of weighing batch materials of at least 100 pounds (45.3 kg.) and <u>should be really accurate</u>. Accuracy is the key to success! It should be in increments of 1/16 lb. which is one ounce or 28 grams. If you can afford it I would recommend purchasing a good, heavy duty digital platform scale. Digital scales are extremely accurate. You can sometimes find good used scales at factory auctions. (If you use a platform scale like I do, I might recommend you have two scales. The second scale is for double checking the accuracy of the last scale. You won't regret this if you get serious. I use a stainless steel platform scale that is digital and reads in 100th's of a pound up to 100 pounds. I always weigh on the first scale and double check sliding to the next one. Use only one scale at your own risk.)
3. A wooden frame with window screen in it for screening materials. It should fit over a 35 gallon can.
4. Various size screen materials are available at any good hardware store. Several different ones are nice.
5. A calculator that won't ever leave the room. Radio Shack sells a great little calculator that converts pounds to grams and back.
6. As good a respirator as you can afford. This is not the area you should get cheap in. Your respirator is your friend. It should be approved by the bureau of mines (read the label) to filter silica dust. I use an organic vapor and dust dual cartridge unit. Always keep replacement cartridges on hand. If you use one that also filters organic vapors, then it is important that you store it in a zip lock bag. Why you ask? Because storing it that way will extend the life of the charcoal filter.

The Small Stuff

- Latex or plastic throw away gloves.
- A couple of big funnels
- A few 1 gallon plastic jars
- 20 five gallon buckets, new with lids
- 500 paper "beer bags"
- A magic marker
- Yellow pads and pens.
- A roll of unprinted newspaper
- Waybill envelopes from USPS or Fed Ex (those clear plastic sticky back thingies found at Kinko's-and they're free)
- Hair nets (they're chic, so use 'em)
- Tyvek disposable suits (wear 'em)

Chemicals to Get Started

Many batch materials get substantially cheaper as you buy in larger quantities. The trouble with buying large quantities is that it is just the same as putting money on a shelf. Don't buy more than you will use in six months when considering the bulk materials used in glassmaking. They don't store well. It's okay to store the metallic oxides used to color glass as they are usually purchased in small quantities and are not affected by humidity or temperature.

The Bulk Chemicals (Chemical grade and vendor found at the end of this section)

- 1000 lbs. of Silica- 140 to 200 mesh. (Optical glass grade.) 250 lbs. of Soda Ash, light or dense (Sodium Carbonate)
- 200 lbs. of Potash (Potassium Carbonate)
- 200 lbs. of Hydrated Lime Type "N" hydrate (Don't confuse this with type "S")
- 200 lbs. Borax 5 mole (the most common)
- 200 lbs. Whiting, (Calcium Carbonate or Limestone)
- 200 lbs. zinc oxide (palletized)
- 200 lbs. feldspar (I prefer Potash Spars, but they are all dependent on availability)
- Spars have what would be called "typical analysis. A "soda" spar would probably be 17-18% Sodium, and the rest Silica and Alumina. It will also invariably have what we call "tramp iron" in it which discolors the glass. Spars vary from region to region since many are mined locally. A potash Spar would have 17-18 % Potassium instead of sodium.
- 100 lbs. Cryolite (synthetic)
- 50 lbs. Potassium Nitrate
- 50 lbs. Sodium Nitrate
- 50 lbs. Lithium Carbonate
- 50 lbs. Barium Carbonate (Toxic)
- 50 lbs. fluorspar (Calcium Fluoride)
- 50 lbs. Boric Acid

The Colorants

- 5 lbs. Cuprous oxide (red copper)
- 3 lbs. Cobalt oxide or Carbonate
- 10 lbs. Manganese Dioxide
- 3 lbs. Ferrous oxide (Red iron)
- 3 lbs. Nickle oxide black
- 3 lbs. Potassium Dichromate (Poisonous)
- 3 lbs.. Neodymium Oxide
- 3 lbs. Selenium Powder (Poisonous)
- 3 lbs. Cadmium Sulphide (As toxic as it gets)
- 1 lb Cadmium Oxide (As toxic as it gets)
- 1 lb Silver Nitrate
- 1 oz. Gold (not for the faint of heart!)
- 1 lb Titanium Dioxide
- 1 lb Cerium oxide
- 3 lbs. Black Tin (Stannous Oxide, NOT Stannic Oxide which is white)
- 3 lbs. Antimony Oxide (Poisonous)

Other Chemicals You May Need

(Advanced Technique)

- 1 lb. Sodium Bromide (Making Silver Bromide)
- 1 Liter Nitric Acid (for gold sand preparation and making silver Nitrate).
- 1 Liter Hydrochloric acid (For gold sand preparation)
- Lead Monosilicate (For Advanced glassmakers with excellent ventilation and a healthy respect for Lead.) (Poisonous)

There are more chemicals, but these will get you started. I do want to issue a very strong warning here: **Lead and Cadmium will kill you if handled improperly**. If you can't ventilate the furnace perfectly, don't even consider melting these compounds!

This is enough to get you started. There are other forms of metallic oxides that are commonly in use that I have not listed here. The carbonates in general are a "softer" way of coloring glass, but buying everything is expensive. I think it best to wait and see if you get hooked on making your own glass or whether you would really rather simply buy color rods.

The Batch Room Layout

I have seen a lot of different rooms for mixing glass, ranging from 100 square feet to about four hundred square feet. The biggest I have seen actually involved a front end loader going into individual rooms and picking up raw materials in the bucket to go to the batch mixer! I use a room that is about 200 square feet. It has lots of shelves.

I try to keep my bagged raw products on racks that are all above waist level. I don't like leaning over to pick up anything. I store enough materials inside the batch room to make at least two weeks worth of glass. The rest is out on the covered porch under tarps. My neighbors just love this.

I fill 35 gallon garbage cans with my basic raw materials. These include Soda Ash, Potash, Borax, Lime, Cryolite, Zinc and Whiting. Occupying five gallon buckets are Feldspar, Barium Carbonate, Lithium Carbonate, Lead monosilicate, and finally, Potassium and Sodium Nitrates. In one gallon jar land I keep my metallic oxides: red and black copper, Nickle oxide, Manganese di-oxide, copper carbonate, Neodymium oxide, Black tin, White tin, Cobalt oxide and carbonate, Selenium metal powder, Cadmium Sulphide. Cadmium oxide, Potassium Di-Chromate, Red and Black Iron, Antimony, Arsenic, Zinc Sulphide, Cerium and Titanium.

Counters

Make sure you have at least a 2' x 5' counter space at normal table height. Set your scales so that the tops of your buckets are at normal counter height. Try to leave space around the scales so that spillage can be cleaned up easily. On my counter, I have a newsprint roll dispenser at one end. I pull out fresh paper whenever the table begins to look messy. I believe that a messy batchroom leads to errors. (This does not mean that I keep a clean batch room, but it keeps Henry happy, and he's in charge.)

Mixers

Some people get all worked up about mixers. I don't I judge the success of the mixers by the quality of the glass that is melted. I melt clean, cord-free glass. The old adage of "Well mixed is half melted" is very true. I find that cement mixers work just fine.

I have three cement mixers in my batch room. For individual use, you really only need one. There is only one cardinal rule with a cement mixer: it has to be perfectly clean. If you use an old mixer, that's fine, but sandblast the inside of the drum. I have been told that a pint of kerosene thrown in the drum and lit will make the drum hot enough to pop any cement off the metal surface. I have never tried it, and it sounded kind of dangerous, but I do throw it out there as yet another way to avoid spending money on tools.

The mixer needs to have a few things done to it. The first is to close off the central shaft from batch materials. I do this with a big plastic cup duct-taped to the drum itself. This sometimes comes apart but after a few attempts, and an appreciation for how much tape to actually use, the thing settles down and behaves itself. If you don't put protection over the center shaft, batch materials will get down in the bearings and make a noise that will wake the dead. There are new mixers made which have closed bearings and easily removable drums. I have one of these and it is an I-MAX. It was cheap at $350.00, and the drum is easily removable, which is more than I can say about my old Montgomery Wards mixers. I did, however, have to add additional blades to the I-MAX. Don't buy a mortar mixer. They are too small and don't mix well.. If you can get a commercial sized bread mixer; they work great. If you are a true do it yourselfer, the old book *Handbook of Glass Manufacture* by Hodkin and Cousins has some good drawings of mixers. Henry Summa built a nice chain drive mixer with a salvaged drum that has been going strong for twenty five years. Peet Robison has one that is made from a 30 gallon garbage can.

So, motorize your mixer. Gear motors work best. Chain drives will never let you down. My take is that cement mixers work fine and you are up and running pretty quickly.

You will need a lid for the mixer. I drilled three holes in mine, near the opening and put bolts through the holes. Using the bolts as anchors, I cut a piece of plywood that fit perfectly into the opening of the mixer. I took this circle and screwed it to a larger piece of plywood and stuck it in the mixer opening. Then I drilled three holes in the plywood and ran bolts down from the upper set of holes to the lower set. I made the bolts "J" shaped so they would hook around the fixed bolts in the mixer.

The lid then needs some gasket material for a tight seal. I used foam door and window insulating material.

Scales

You are going to need three scales. You may be able to afford only two. Correct this as soon as is financially possible. Your scales need to be either beam balance or digital. I would never consider a spring loaded bathroom or postal type scale to be workable in a batch room. If you use a beam scale, it should have a big platform, 16 inch by 24 inch. The old Wells Fargo type scales are great! It should read in increments of $\frac{1}{16}$ of a pound up to 50 pounds and should have provisions for extra weights. Check it for accuracy, carefully using known value weights to do your checking. I have my scales certified once every few years by a professional service.

Your digital scale should read from zero to one

hundred pounds in increments of one hundreth of a pound. It should be capable of being "zeroed". It is nice if it can read in pounds, Kilograms, or ounces. It is best made of stainless steel. These are expensive but worth the price. It also should have as large a platform as possible.

You also need a gram scale. These are getting a bit more awkward to buy given the drug trade, but they are available to legitimate users of sensitive scales. Jewelry suppliers handle them as well as Laboratory supply houses. You need a beam balance that preferably reads up to 500 grams in as little as $^1/_{10}$ gram increments. It should be capable of handling 2000 grams of extra weight. Keep this scale clean. It doesn't take much junk in the beam to render it inaccurate.

Digital scales are a Godsend but can be finicky. I have sent them back to the shop for repairs simply by blowing on them with a compressed air gun. They can also break if they are overloaded. Digital scales can be finicky. I have always thought it was dumb to have a scale that had a 100 lb maximum and that if you put on more it was toast. If I knew what the item weighed, I wouldn't have needed a scale. So I admit to a love/hate relationship with my digital balance.

Garbage Cans

About the only really substantive thing you can talk about here is durability. Rubbermaid garbage cans are the Cadillac of cans but they are pricey. I do prefer plastic cans over galvanized steel in areas with a lot of humidity, but while they don't corrode, they do crack easily. In Santa Fe, there is no humidity at all, and I am still using metal cans I bought in 1974. I doubt they would last three years in Missouri. So buy the best you can afford, especially if you plan to drag them around at all.

Five Gallon Buckets

Get them with lids. Big discount houses sell them for about $3.50 each. If you get serious about batch mixing you will be surprised at how many you will need. I have about 150. I stick the UPS waybill envelopes to the buckets and then slip a label indicating what the bucket holds inside of the waybill pouch. You have to keep any buckets for Cadmium or Selenium glasses totally clean and to themselves. Copper, cobalt, or chrome in even minute amounts will destroy the color of a Cad/Sel yellow or red.

One Gallon Cans

I buy mine from the House of Cans. They are cheap, but you have to buy about 100 of them at a time, so I'd advise looking somewhere else for plastic cans. Get-screw on lids.

Dark Jars

Keep Silver nitrate in dark brown bottles.

Vacuum

They aren't as good as they used to be but, Sears Shop Vacs are still very handy in the Batch room. Remember when you vacuum to wear a respirator since the finest dusts will still pass through a vacuum filter unless it is a HEPA vacuum (big bucks).

Floor Compound

You really need this stuff. It is an oiled sawdust. Graingers sells it in 50 lb boxes. Sprinkle it on the floor liberally and sweep us your messes. It really handles fine dusts well. I can't say enough good things about floor compound.

Beer Bags

Thats what they call them at Sam's Club. They come in bundles of five hundred. I usually put six or seven pounds of batch in one of the labeled bags. It makes it easy to move them around the studio. I put them in a shovel and drop them directly into the pot. It really beats ladling dusty batch and spilling it all over creation. Mark your bags with what's in them; you won't regret it. I have lots of bags in my batch room that are unmarked. The only way to find out what's in them is to throw them in the furnace.

Hair Nets & Tyvek Suits

Wear them both and keep all of those dusts off of your skin and clothes. With the orange Playtex gloves you will make a smashing fashion statement. Cadmium in your household laundry won't endear you to anyone. Keep these chemicals in the batch room!

Respirator

They are not created equal. Find one that fits your face. It needs to be dual cartridge. I use organic vapor cartridges with nuisance dust covers. You should replace your respirator about every eight months if you are doing this seriously. The rubber fatigues and does not fit well after time. After all, it's the only set of lungs you've got. Don't hang your respirator up by the flexible band. It will stretch and be worthless immediately.

Timer

I use a big timer from a darkroom. It has movable hands and a big noisy buzzer. It helps to remind you when to turn of the mixer. I have my timer wired into the motor on the mixer.

Ventilation

I have three 24" fans in the walls behind each mixer pulling about 9,000 cubic feet of air per minute through the room. It gets cold in the winter. If you can't ventilate your batch room and furnace room, you have no business melting raw glasses. It will kill you.

Miscellaneous

A crescent wrench, a grease gun, small stainless steel mixing bowls (scoops), 409 cleaner, paper towels, a calculator, file cards, yellow pads, pens, garbage bags, bins to go under mixers...you know the drill. If you feel you're now your ready to mix that batch proceed to the next section.

The Basics

Okay, you have all these tools and all these chemicals, so now what?

Now is the time to look at the different elements that go into making glasses and what they do. The primary ingredient in glass is Silica. It will be present in glass commonly between 62-70%. Silica, by itself, will melt at temperatures over 3,000° F (1648° C). For our needs it has to melt at a lower temperature to be useful.

Alkaline fluxes fill this gap nicely. Sodium or Potassium Carbonates will lower the temperature of the silica significantly. Depending on the volume of flux used, the melt temperature can fall as low as 1400° F (760° C). The mix unfortunately needs something to stabilize it and that is commonly done with calcium and occasionally with zinc. This trinary structure is the most common in modern glasses.

Each of these chemicals determines the viscosity of the glass, the temperature at which it will anneal, and the amount that the glass will expand upon being heated. The expansion of the glass will be of great concern to you as a batch maker. In order to hopefully fit, two differing glass must be within one and one half ten thousandths of an inch of each other in expansion based on the following test. Each glass has a 4" cane cut of it 4 mm in diameter. The cane is heated in a quartz tube from 19° C to 300° C. The expansion, which will be linear, can be measured. It is necessary that for two samples to "fit" that they expand within a range of 1.5×10^{-6}. There are other factors that can prevent fit, namely viscosity and annealing range. The expansion issue would appear to be the one of greatest concern in blown glasses. In cast glasses, all three are of paramount importance. Most commercial glasses have expansions between 90-96 ten thousandths and most color is manufactured in this range. There are notable exceptions, and it is always wise to test your glasses. This test commonly known as "Dilatometry," only tells you the differences in expansions while at 300° C. Not all glasses expand on a linear basis. Ideally, the glass maker's concerns should lie with the difference between the glasses in question when checked at room temperature. This is best done with a polarimeter, making what is commonly known as a " Hagy" or "Trident" seal (see pg. 59). The seal is examined in the polarimeter for strain. The great problem with the Polarimetry test is that the tool is really expensive and beyond the practical means of the average studio. It is also true that if the glasses to be tested are not pretty close already that the seals will break on being made. Then you have no information at all. I do use both testing methods and they perform different functions.

Please read the following before proceeding

All chemicals if handled improperly can be dangerous to your health. Some chemicals are more dangerous than others and should be avoided by the inexperienced. Those chemicals include: Barium, Lead, Zinc, Cadmium Sulphide, and Selenium. When handling any batch chemicals, one should wear an adequate dust mask and have adequate ventilation. A Tyvek suit would not be out of the question, either.

Always melt glass under a good exhaust hood. The products of combustion can and often do contain heavy metals, caustic materials, and possible carcinogens.

Assorted Notes for Batching

The assorted notes below were taken from telephone conversations I had with Mark Peiser back in the 70's. The notes were scribbled on a yellow pad and were answers Mark had for the questions I threw at him. His answers to those long forgotten questions were very helpful in solving many of my batching problems. All I knew at the time was what I figured out from Scholes' *Modern Glass Practice*. Mark had the practical know-how and that was what I needed; indeed it is what we all need, someone that has been there and done it. I have left the notes in the book in their original form as Mark's information then is still applicable in many instances today. It is obvious that some of the statements are rather enigmatic and ambiguous as one does not know what the question is. It's sort of a Jeopardy game for glass artists, but maybe you'll have that question and find the answer here.

Notes on Phosphate Opals

1. For good phosphate opals, remove tri-calcium phosphate and replace with tri-Sodium phosphate. Do not recalculate. Use anhydrous TSP.
2. Borea promotes phase separation of phosphate and silica; this is good. Some borax should be used in making a phosphate opal.
3. Mono-calcium phosphate or tri-sodium phosphate will give an alumina phosphate which retards opacity. Alumina goes into secondary phase.
4. Strontium nitrate or strontium carbonate will go into phosphate phase and help prevent devitrification without damaging opacity. It will take glass toward red transmission and away from blue transmission.
5. Barium in phosphate opal increases opacity and reduces devitrification.
6. Mono-calcium phosphate above 12% is no good.
7. B_2O_3 increases opacity, decreases scumming, decreases viscosity, and decreases expansion, but increasing B_2O_3 beyond a certain point will screw up phosphate opals. This is true.
8. An increase of strontium to high percentages shows no visible effect on glass, and it may help in striking.
9. Zinc creates no apparent change but helps workability.
10. Dolomitic limestone may retard striking.
11. Lithium eliminates scum and helps in the melt. Keep lithium under 1%.
12. Strontium seems to help color formation. Start at 4% and increase by 2s.

Assorted Information

Potash, Soda ratio--substitute soda for potash to decrease surface tension. Some Lithium will help. 1 ½ % will make a glass with a low viscosity. Low viscosity glasses attack refractories. Increase the fluoride content when adding lithium to retain opacity.

Sodium nitrate starts the melting process at a lower temperature. It is also an oxidizing agent. It helps make copper blue. If you are making red glass do **NOT** use sodium nitrate.

Fining

Sodium sulfate helps in fining; use ½%.
Use Arsenic for fining ¼ % is adequate **(ARSENIC IS VERY DEADLY)**; don't use if you can avoid it.
Antimony, ¼ to ½ %. Should use some niter when using antimony **(ANTIMONY IS VERY DANGEROUS)**. Antimony is a multivalent element, being monovalent at high temperatures and pentavalent below 2100° F. This allows the material to absorb gasses back into solution once the melt is completed and cooled. A little fluorspar opens the network while helping durability and workability.

Some Batches

Red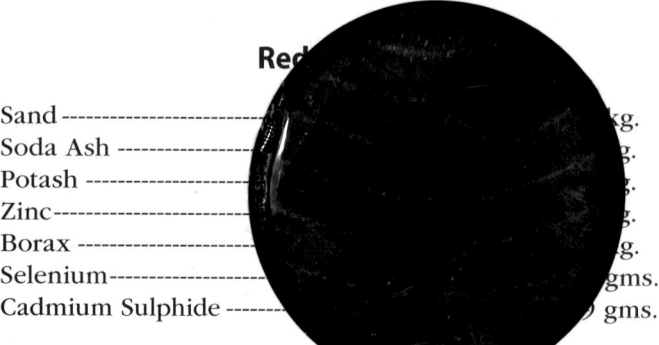

Sand	kg.
Soda Ash	
Potash	
Zinc	
Borax	kg.
Selenium	gms.
Cadmium Sulphide	gms.

Author's Note: This glass formula has been attributed to Scholes from the first edition of his book, Modern Glass Practice, *but if you look closely at this entry, there is a footnote. Scholes gives attribution to, drum roll please, Kirkpatrick & Roberts,* Journal of the American Ceramic Society, *1919, p. 896.*

Sample Phosphate Opal Batch

From Mark Peiser

Sand	100.00 lbs.	45.36 kg.
Soda	43.86 lbs.	19.89 kg.
Lime	18.00 lbs.	8.16 kg.
Nephy	10.00 lbs.	4.53 kg.
Borax (10 mol.)	4.00 lbs	1.81 kg.
Florspar	2.00 lbs.	.90 kg.
Tri-Calcium Phosphate	10.38 lbs.	4.70 kg.

Remember, a phosphate opal is a striking opal; that is, when working it you must cool it down and then upon reheat it will strike.

A Red That Might Fit Your Crystal

From Pete VanderLaan

Sand	50.00 lbs.	22.68 kg.
Soda Ash	11.90 lbs.	5.39 kg.
Potash	8.50 lbs.	3.85 kg.
Lime Hydrate	5.25 lbs.	2.38 kg.
Zinc Oxide	4.25 lbs.	1.92 kg.
Cadmium Sulphide	600.00 grams	
Selenium	220.00 grams	

Melt at 2200° F (1204° C) in a neutral atmosphere and raise the temperature to 2300° F (1260° C) when the last charge has gone flat. Squeeze at 1900° F (1038° C). This is a drop dead red that fits Spruce Pine 87 like a glove. C.O.E. 96.

Sample Fluorine Opal White

From Pete VanderLaan

Sand	54.50 lbs.
Soda	11.50 lbs.
Potash	4.00 lbs.
Whiting	4.30 lbs.
Zinc	5.00 lbs.
Cryolite	9.13 lbs.

General Limits for Batch Formulation

SiO_2 ---------------------------------- 63% - 73%
Al_2O_3 ------------------------------- .5 - 2%
LiO_2 ---------------------------------- .25 - 1%
Na_2O, K_2O ----------------------- 17.5% or less
MgO, CaO, BaO, ZnO --------- 8% total of all

You may well be asking the question: What are limits? The limits listed above give parameters in percentages for the amounts of those specific materials that should be used when formulating a soda/lime glass. Developing a glass with percentages above and possibly below the limits listed can cause problems in the final melt. What are those problems? A glass too difficult to blow or melt, or a glass that lacks durability or that is so active that it eats your refractory for lunch. It is never a bad idea to test any glass you formulate for durability. When testing for durability it is a good idea to compare your new glass against one of known durability. See pg. 60 to learn how to test your glass for durability.

Here is what we do know about some of the numbers found above. High SiO_2 (above 72%) gives good durability but cannot be blown easily. More than 1.5% Al_2O_3 can make glass too stiff. Fluxes above 17% either alone or together may create a glass that lacks durability. Lithia makes glass softer to blow, but be careful when using more than 1%. Lithia affects viscosity, and the lower the viscosity the more your glass will attack the refractory and cause it to fail prematurely.

Once you start formulating your own glass, the numbers will become familiar to you and you will know where good starting points are for glass calculations.

This photo was taken at Mark Peiser's studio in North Carolina. It shows Mark's opal tests. It is unfortunate that this photo is not in color as the beauty and subtlety of color that Mark is capable of achieving is just extraordinary.

Compatibility

Dr Frank E. Woolley

Why colored glasses are often incompatible

Colored glasses have different chemical compositions than the clear base glasses.

In some cases, colors can be obtained just by adding a very small amount of colorant to the base glass.

Some of the simplest colors, like cobalt blue or chromium green, are so dilute that the composition and glass properties are identical to the clear base.

More complicated colors, like reds and yellows, and all the opaque colors, require substantial modification of the base; their properties are usually much different than the clear base.

Each glass composition has a characteristic thermal expansion curve and viscosity curve, showing how length and viscosity vary with temperature.

Two glasses of different chemical compositions nearly always have different thermal expansions or viscosities.

How combining two glasses causes permanent stress

- If two glasses of different chemical compositions are sealed together while hot, each one will contract by a different amount as they cool down together.
- The difference in the total contractions of the two glasses, from the Setting Point of the softer of the two to room temperature, must be accommodated by elastic deformation of the glasses, leaving a permanent stress in both glasses.

The Effects of Cooling

Each glass contracts as it continues to cool, but by different amounts.

The glass that contracts the most must stretch to stay attached to the other glass, which must compress. The glass which contracts more (higher thermal expansion) will be left in tension, while the lower expansion glass will be left in compression.

Stress pattern in the piece depends on the location of the higher expansion glass:

If the higher expansion glass is on the outside, the surface will be in tension, and the piece may break when it is touched.

If the higher expansion glass is inside, the interior surface will be in tension; the piece may not break immediately, but it may break violently when touched on the inside, or when cold worked, scratched deeply, or bruised.

Definitions

- SEALS also known as prunts, handles, wraps, etc. are created whenever two different glasses are fused together, whether as a coating, an embedded layer, or as an attachment.
- MISMATCH is the difference in thermal expansion from room temperature to the **Setting Point** of the softer of the two glasses.
- COMPATIBILITY is the condition where stress in a seal is too low to cause breakage of the seal under reasonable use conditions of the article; it depends on mismatch, but also on seal geometry and use to which the piece will be put.

The Search for Compatibility

Dr. Frank E. Woolley

If one searches hard enough, charts can be found that give rough guidelines for compatibility of commercial colors with clear glasses that have known expansions, i.e., S.P. 87, Phillips, East Bay, etc. Under some circumstances, those charts can be used, but they are not reliable indicators of compatibility for the following reasons:

Each color from a single manufacturer has a different composition and thermal expansion, so these guidelines are not valid for all colors made by that manufacturer. The composition and thermal expansion of colors may vary from lot to lot. It should also be noted that the composition and thermal expansion of clear glasses changes slowly with time in the tank or pot. There is also a slow volatilization and refractory corrosion which will also lower the thermal expansion and raise the viscosity. Your best bet is not to use these charts but to call someone that uses the same base glass as yours and ask them what colors fit from which manufacturer. Even when you think you have a sure thing, you're going to find out there is no such thing as a "sure thing"

Thermal Expansion
Most glasses expand when heated and contract by the same amount when cooled

Linear Expansion Coefficient (LEC), Coefficient of Thermal Expansion (CTE), Coefficient of Expansion COE)

LEC, CTE, and COE all mean the same thing. For our explanation we will only use LEC. LEC gives the average fractional change in length for a unit change in temperature over a specified temperature range. Thermal expansion is important because stresses arise if temperature differences are created in different parts of a piece of glass when it is heated or cooled; glasses of lower LEC have better thermal shock resistance and can be annealed more rapidly.

Compatibility

When two glasses are sealed together, each glass will try to contract differently as they cool to room temperature. The difference in total thermal contraction of the two glasses as they cool from the setting point of the softer glass to room temperature determines the amount of stress produced by the requirement that they remain sealed together (that is, that they remain the same length).

Compatibility depends on having a small difference in total thermal expansions; this is the case if they have nearly the same LEC, or if one glass is very soft.

Durability

Resistance to chemical attack--by moisture in the atmosphere (weathering), by acids (as in foods), or by bases (as in alkaline detergents). Glasses with poor durability acquire a hazy or frosted surface over time as the surface is roughened or etched and corrosion products build up.

Glass Stability

The practical definition of a glass is a material which becomes rigid and non - crystalline on cooling at a moderate rate; unstable glasses require higher cooling rates. Stability means the resistance to devitrification (crystallization) – important to prevent defects from forming during gathering, slumping, sintering, sagging or annealing.

Liquidus temperature is the temperature **above** which crystals cannot form; for soda/lime glasses it is around 1750 – 1850° F (950 – 1000° C).

Crystallization rate is low near the liquidus but usually is highest 100 – 200° F (50 – 100° C). It declines at lower temperatures and is usually negligible at the softening point. *Author's Note: Temperatures have been rounded off.*

Viscosity at the liquidus limits the choice of forming processes; unstable glasses can not be drawn or hand worked but must be cast or pressed.

Other Characteristics Important in the Studio

Keep in Mind

- A source of batch or cullet is useful to the extent that it is available repeatedly with a consistent chemistry and free from contamination.
- The time required to determine the compatibility and melting and annealing cycles for a new composition make it uneconomical to use small lots of glass of unknown properties.
- Contamination in cullet can result in a variety of defects in the glass (color, stones, knots, cords, bubbles); metal in the cullet can cause accelerated attack on crucibles and liners. That means a stray bottle cap charged with that "free" cullet you got from the recycling plant down the street can drill a hole through your crucible.

Cost

- Usually the cost of batch or cullet is a small part of the total cost of finished pieces; a "bargain" source of batch or cullet may prove to be very expensive if it leads to high losses of pieces due to defects or breakage or if much time is required to learn how to work with it.
- In the immortal words of Click and Clack, "it's the stingy man that pays the most."

Composition and the Coefficient of Thermal Expansion

The various glass-forming oxides have rather definite effects upon the expansivity of glasses. Silica, as the least expansive oxide in the pure glassy condition, has a powerful effect in reducing expansion in commercial glasses. Boric oxide, in small quantities, is even more favorable than silica in this respect. This is true notwithstanding the fact that boron oxide itself, as a glass, has about thirty times the expansivity of fused silica. When boron oxide is present in amounts above 15%, it begins to have the opposite effect and cannot be substituted further for silica without increasing the coefficient of expansion of the glass.

The alkalis have the opposite tendency and increase the expansivity of glasses much more than do any other oxides. The RO bases have an intermediate effect; of these, MgO exerts the least influence to increase the expansion. Al_2O_3 in small amounts adds less to the expansion than any of the bases.

Mark Peiser's Pot Furnace

36 Glass Notes

Factors for Calculating Linear Expansion

Establishing the Linear Expansion of a given glass is a simple matter. Multiply the percent (%) of each oxide in any given glass by the factors and add the column. The resulting answer is the linear expansion of that particular glass. To formulate compatible glasses, it is important that they have similar expansions as well as similar viscosities. Similarly, two different glasses that express the same expansions on paper will not necessarily "fit" in reality. There is no substitute for doing actual melts to test for compatibility and annealing. The chart should only be used to get you "in the ball park."

It should be noted that the E & T chart found on this page and used for calculating Linear Expansion is only one of a few charts that have been developed by others over the years. We use the E & T Chart because it was the one adopted by the studio glass artists many years ago and is still in use today. The expansion factors found on color rod charts and commercially available batch formulas have been derived from this chart as well.

Once you start developing your own glasses from scratch and make them fit your base glass, you will never again buy those pesky color bars that fit one day but not the next. Good luck on your quest for that perfect color that you've had in your imagination for years, and remember, don't give up.

Example for Calculation of Linear Expansion

English & Turner E & T	
SiO_2	0.05×10^{-7}
Al_2O_3	0.14
B_2O_3	-0.65
Na_2O	4.32
K_2O	3.90
CaO	1.63
MgO	0.45
PbO	1.06
ZnO	0.70
ZrO_2	0.70
BaO	1.40
LiO_3	4.50

	%		Factors		Expansion
SiO_2	72.40	x	.0.05	=	3.62
Na_2O	14.61	x	4.32	=	63.11
B_2O_3	0.72	x	-0.65	=	-.46
Al_2O_3	1.77	x	0.14	=	0.24
CaO	6.11	x	1.63	=	9.95
MgO	4.39	x	0.45	=	1.97
	100%		Total		78.43

Simply stated, the above glass has an E&T expansion of 78.43×10^{-7}

Conclusion

Well, there you have it! It may not be everything you need to know about batching your own glass, but in my estimation, all the information you'll need to get you started. We certainly owe a debt of gratitude to Dr. Frank E. Woolley and Pete VanderLaan for sharing their vast knowledge with you, the reader. From a personal point of view, I would say it's people like Frank and Pete and all those who choose to share "their secrets" that have pushed the art of glass making to heights never before seen in the history of glass. We are all indeed fortunate.

NOTES

Annealing & Compatibility

Chapter Content

Annealing Glass 40
Annealing 42
Shape Effect on Stress 44
About Annealing Charts and Other Stuff 46
Determining Annealing Temperature, The Cane Test 48
Controllers and Relays 49
Annealing Charts 49
Annealing of Cast Glass Pieces 50
Annealing of Castings 51
Libensky Method of Annealing 52
The Libensky Method 53
Laboratory Testing for Annealing and Strain Point 54
Testing Stress and Compatibility 55
Testing for Compatibility 58
Glass Durability Testing 60

Annealing Glass

This section will hopefully unravel some of the mysteries about annealing and cooling glass. Annealing and cooling can be summed up in four simple words: "patience is a virtue."

When glass is formed it can and often does take on variations in thickness as well as intricate shapes. This complexity often leads to problems in annealing and cooling. It is the intricacies of shape that prevents the development of annealing schedules based on mathematical formulas although one can use a chart as a starting point. It is the complex form that sets up strain between differing areas of the work. Without proper annealing and cooling the inherent strain found in the work can combine and create tension sufficient to break the form.

Temperature gradients within the work are created during forming and others during cooling. The object of annealing is to remove these gradients by soaking at a constant temperature within the annealing range for a suitable length of time. The time relates directly to the glass properties and thickness. It should be noted that one can anneal for the proper length of time for a specific form but strain can be reintroduced during the cool down from the <u>annealing point to the strain point*</u> if the work is not subjected to equal cooling rates at any given time. The cooling rate is dependent on glass properties and thickness. Another way to state the above: Glass expands when hot and shrinks when cool. Since the glass being annealed has thickness it must shrink at a rate consistent with its thickness. If it does not, the outside of the glass will shrink at a rate greater than the interior and will begin to form strain until it reaches a point wherein the mechanical strength of the glass is no longer sufficient to contain the strain and the piece checks.

The optimal annealing temperature is usually, but not always, 50° F below the softening point of your glass. Glass cannot be annealed below the strain point. Although glass can theoretically anneal at any temperature in the transition range, it is most efficient to anneal at the high end annealing point.

If you are doing castings or complex blown forms, it is very important to find out what the strain point is of the glass you are using. In order to find the strain point of any glass one must send a sample to testing lab. See pg. 54.

Proper annealing is more than just following numbers on a chart, and rarely is a piece of glass relieved of all strain. It is also important that your annealer does not have any serious heat differentials sometime referred to as thermal gradation. Thermal gradation is discussed later in this section. The temperature must be even throughout the annealer. Heat differentials can create serious annealing and cooling problems.

*referred to as the transition range.

Bob Barber's controller as presented at GAS 1, Penland, NC, 1970

40 Glass Notes

Peiser Controller, circa early 1970's

Dear Dr. Glass

Dear Dr. Glass, My glass goes into the annealer in one piece but comes out checked. What am I doing wrong?

Signed, DC

Dear DC,

Ans.- The simplest answer would be that you may not be annealing your glass correctly. Remember the total piece of glass has to be brought to thermal equilibrium at the annealing temperature before you begin to cool it. The thicker the piece of glass the longer it will take.

Ans.- If you anneal far enough below the annealing point you will not relieve the glass of enough strain in the time allotted.

Ans.- You've cooled your glass to quickly through the transition range and reintroduce strain.

Ans.- You may think you are annealing at the correct temperature but your pyrometer is reading incorrectly. This is a common problem and can be corrected by doing the cane test (see pg. 48). Stop being cheap and spring for a good controller with matching thermocouple. Remember, your annealer is only as good as your controller. See pg. 246.

All these scenarios will get you into trouble. Accuracy is important. Read on, DC...

Some other explanations for checked glass are:
- You changed cullet or batch and you have not determined its proper annealing temperature.
- It is also possible that your piece checked before it went into the annealer because your glove chilled the glass when you picked it up to put it in the oven.
- Your punty was very violent.
- You hit your piece against another piece when you put it in the annealer.
- You held the door open too long when putting another piece away and your oven cooled down too much.
- Your annealer has serious temperature gradients.

There are endless reasons why glass checks. I have only mentioned some of the mechanical problems. There are other possible problems above and beyond compatibility that can cause checking. Many problem solutions can be traced to the type of check you have in the glass. Try to analyze the check when attempting to solve your problem. Before blaming compatibility check your annealing and cooling rates, know if your annealer has any heat differentials, if your annealing temperature is correct, if your thermocouple is reading correctly, and your controller is accurate.

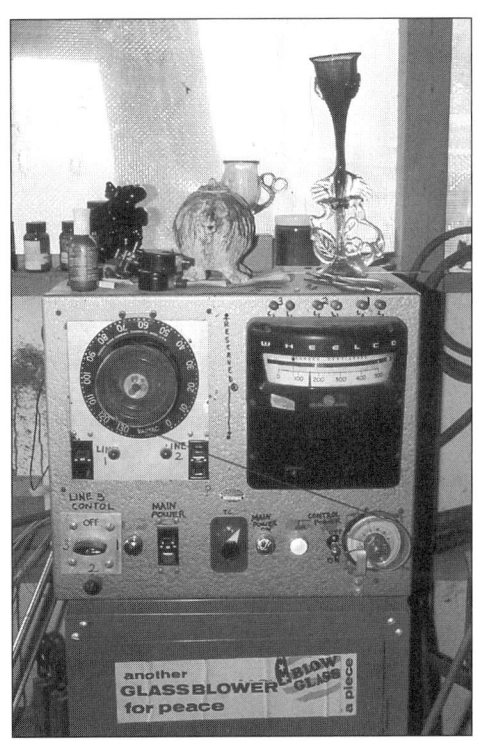

Fritz's Controller, circa early 70's

Glass Notes 41

Annealing

Dr. Frank E. Woolley

Annealing has two Goals:

1. To eliminate permanent stresses in the piece that result from rapid and uneven cooling during and after forming and:
2. Avoid creating new permanent stresses during cooling to room temperature.

This is accomplished by first holding the piece in a temperature range where internal stresses are relieved (without being so hot that the piece deforms under its own weight), then by cooling slowly enough that the permanent stresses left in the piece are acceptable for the application.

Annealing Schedules

If one attempts to develop an annealing schedule it is imperative to design the schedule for the glass composition and shape, as well as for the acceptable level of permanent stress in the piece.

A Typical Annealing Schedule Has Four Parts

1. Fast reheat to annealing temperature (only needed if pieces have been cooled without adequate annealing after forming).
2. A soak slightly above the annealing point to relieve forming stresses.
3. Slow cooling to below the strain point.
4. Faster cooling to room temperature.

- The most time-consuming part of the schedules the annealing and the slow cool through the transition range.
- The times and temperatures in the annealing schedule depend on the thickness of the piece and on LEC of the glass.
- The rate of cooling is inversely proportional to thickness squared so thicker ware must be cooled at a slower rate.
- The rate of cooling is directly proportional to the LEC, so high-expansion glasses have to be cooled more slowly.

Step	Purpose	Limitations
Fast Reheat	Return cold ware to annealing temperature	Thermal upshock breakage
Soak	Remove forming stresses	Slumping
Slow Cool	Cool from plastic to elastic range	Avoid large temperature gradients that will cause permanent stress
Fast Cool	Cool to room temperature	Thermal down-shock breakage

Shape Effect On Stress

The diagrams on the following pages describe stress and how it distributes within specific forms. Large flat plates have the simplest stress distribution; real pieces have much more complicated stress distributions.

Disks and spheres

For disks or spheres, the center is in tension, the surface in compression. Hollow disks and spheres are in tension on the inner surface.

Flat-bottomed vessels

If the bottom cools more slowly than the side (because it is setting on an insulator, or is thicker) then it will try to contract after the sides have reached the strain point; this will cause tension in the bottom of the wall.

In severe cases, the piece will "wring off" or crack just above the bottom.

If the bottom is domed (a "kick" bottom), then part of the contraction of the bottom will be accommodated by elastic flattening of the dome, reducing the stress in the walls.

Closed loops

A handle or other attachment that is thicker than the wall to which it is attached will cool slower, and will try to contract after the sides are cold and rigid; this will cause tension in the handle and in the wall where it is attached. *Swedish pitchers that have thick handles start at the base and do not touch at the top of the pitcher in order to avoid this problem.* A ribbon handle of the same thickness as the wall will cool at the same rate, so no stress will develop.

Complex shapes

For any shape, the same analysis can be applied:

Look for the region which will cool most slowly. This region will try to contract after the rest of the piece has reached room temperature. This region usually will end up in tension, surrounded by portions which are in compression. To reduce stress, design thicknesses and support during annealing to allow all parts of the piece to cool at the same rate. *Author's Note: Never compromise aesthetics for function.*

Author's Note: The drawings on the following pages have been redrawn from the original drawings provided by Dr. Woolley.

It is impossible to heat or cool glass without some temperature gradient within the piece.

Shape Effect on Stress

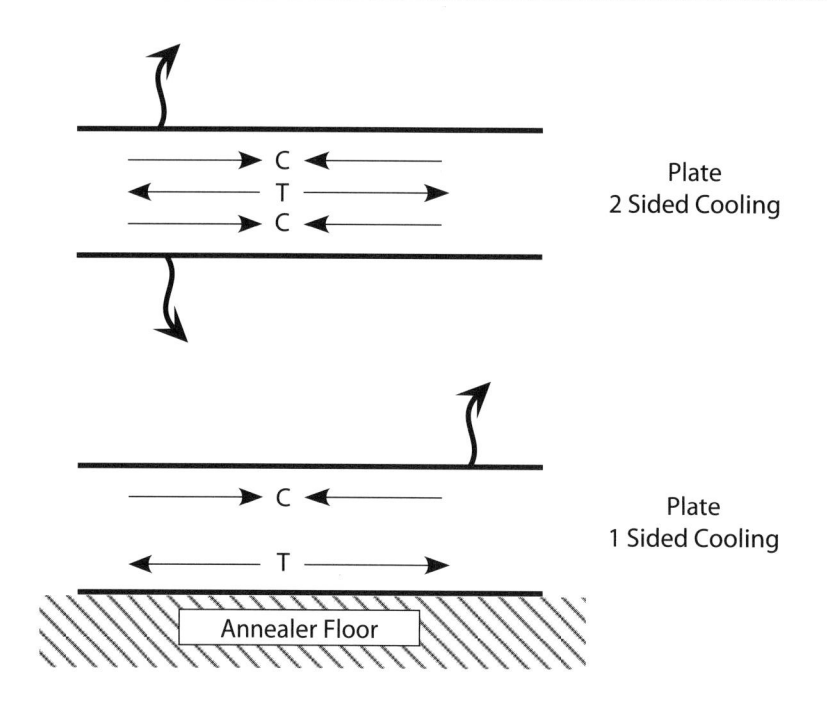

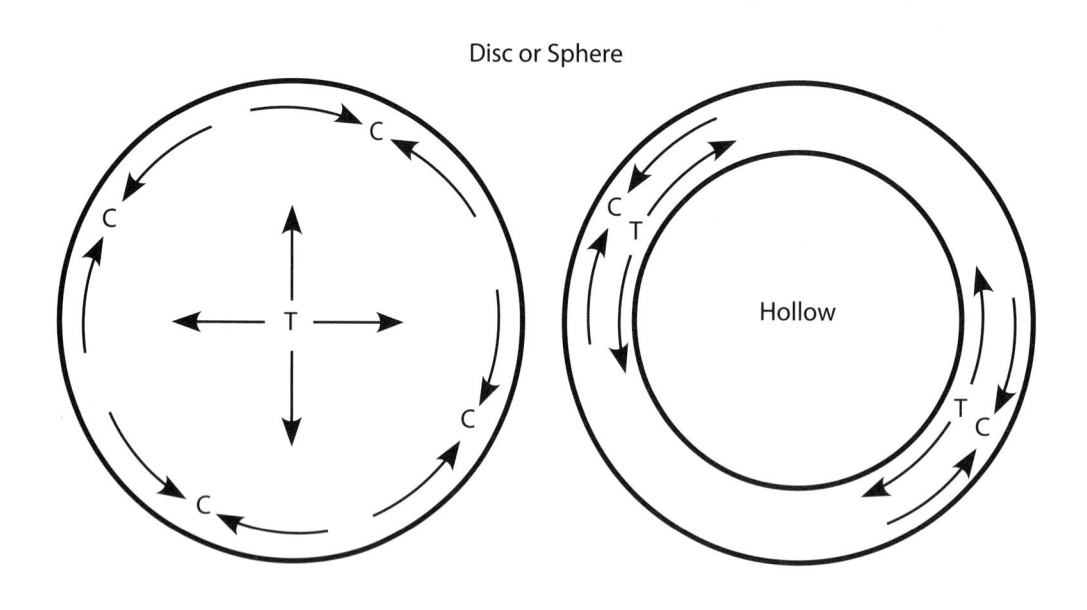

Plate
2 Sided Cooling

Plate
1 Sided Cooling

Annealer Floor

Disc or Sphere

Hollow

C = Compression
T = Tension

Note the following: A 1" plate cooling from two sides will anneal in ½ the time than if it was cooling from one side.

44 Glass Notes

Cylinder With Flat Bottom

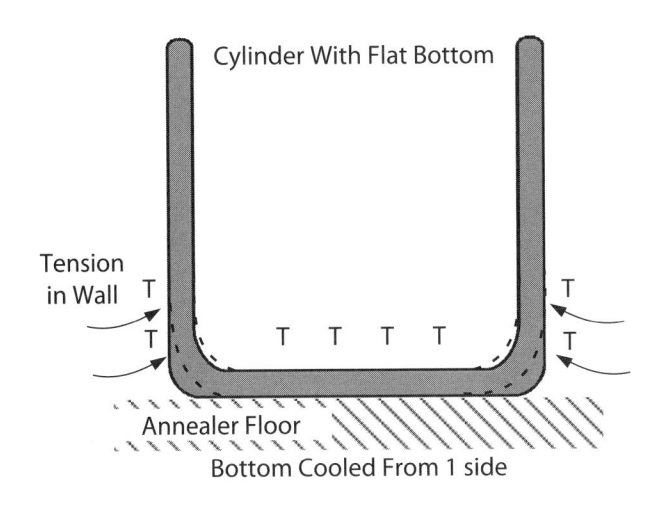

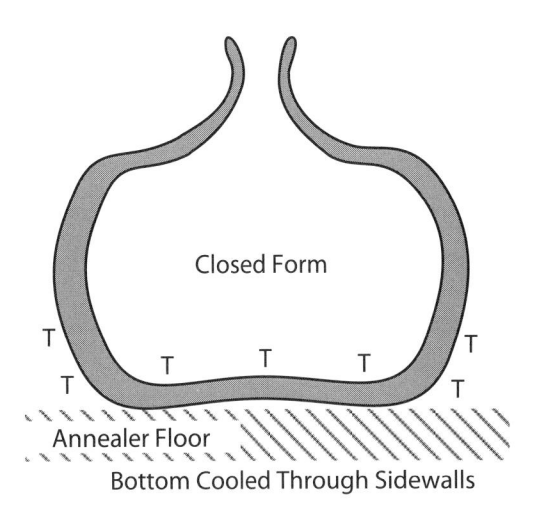

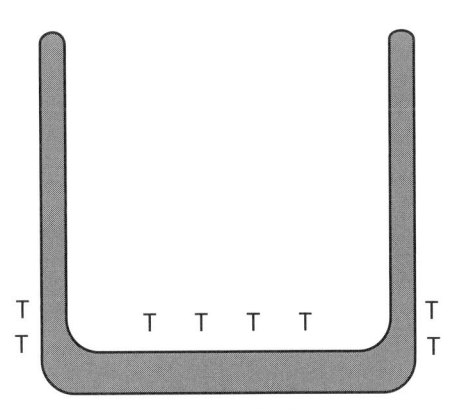

Tension in Wall

T T T T T T

Annealer Floor

Bottom Cooled From 1 side

Closed Form

T T T T T

Annealer Floor

Bottom Cooled Through Sidewalls

Bottom 2x Thicker Than Sidewalls

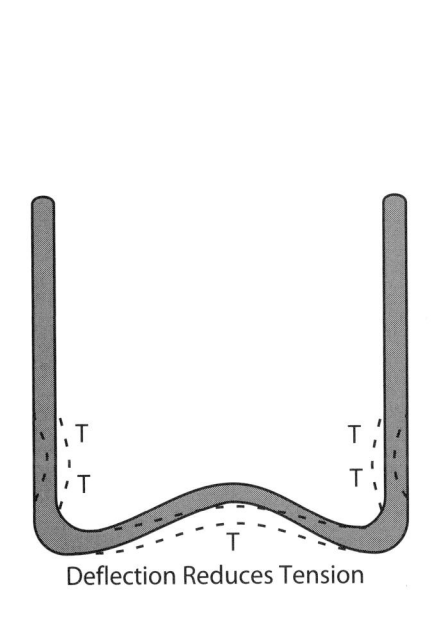

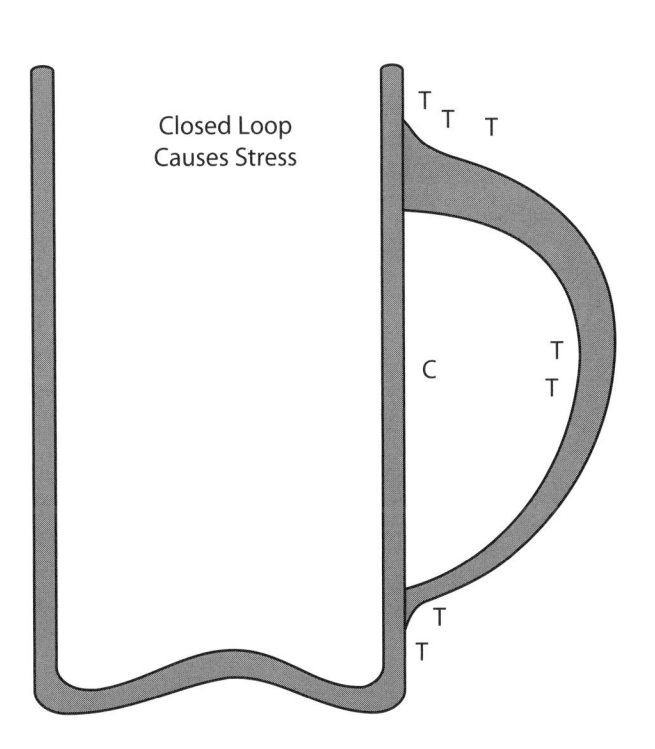

T T T T T T T

Deflection Reduces Tension

T T T T T

Closed Loop Causes Stress

T T T

C

T T

T T

Glass Notes **45**

About Annealing Charts and Other Stuff

The annealing chart on page 51 and related material was distilled from the 3rd Edition of the *Glass Engineering Handbook* by George W. McLellan and E.B. Shand. Dan Schwoerer of The Bullseye Glass Co. organized and produced the chart. This chart is a final distillation of actual annealing and cooling tests Dan and his staff undertook at Bullseye. In other words, the numbers expressed are real world numbers and not numbers derived from mathematical formulas.

- When calculating the thickness of a casting you need to consider the thickness of the mold as well as the thickness of the glass.
- Try not to wash your casting until it has sat around for a few days.
- Don't wash your casting with really hot or real cold water.

It is a known fact that annealing is accomplished within the defined transition range of the glass being annealed. Glasses of differing compositions have differing transition ranges. The transition range is the range between the high end annealing temperature and the strain point. This is the only area where glass is annealed (relieved of permanent strain) If your casting glass in rather thick sections it is very important to know the strain point of your casting glass. Although the high end annealing temperature can be determined by you the artist (pg. 48) the strain point cannot. In order to determine the strain point, you will need to send a sample to a lab that can do that type of testing. The address of a lab that does that type of testing can be found on page 54.

As stated earlier, there is no chart that is fail safe for art glass, castings, fusing's, etc.. Any and all charts that one wishes to employ will only give an approximation of actual values. Your actual values will be empirically based and will vary from object to object unless the objects are mirror images of each other.

Design Considerations

There are certain design considerations that one must take into consideration when using the chart. If you are annealing an object with a smooth flat surface, then annealing is very straight forward and the numbers in the chart are accurate. If your casting has sharp angles and or large variations in thickness, then the chart may not be adequate, but it is an excellent starting point to figure out your annealing schedule. Angles and variations in surface continuity will create concentrated stress at what is described as "the angle of re-entry." If you have angles of re-entry I would recommend you retard the cooling rates by a factor from 1.5 to 4.0 times the rates shown in the tables. Annealing times increase as the thickness increases.

Angles of re-entry are more serious when they extend to the edges of the casting. I was first made aware of this problem when I attempted to anneal 3" thick blocks with serious angles of re-entry. While in Pilchuck I had a discussion of this problem with the wonderful glass artist Ann Robinson of New Zealand. She was having the same problem with her pieces and had fortunately met with an annealing expert from The Corning Glass Works who apprised her of the problem created by angles of re-entry. I changed my annealing schedule to compensate for the angles of re-entry and found it all but solved my annealing problem.

Other Problems

There are other problems for checked castings and blown ware that have nothing to do with annealing but relate to thermal gradients within the annealer. Thermal gradients are heat differentials within the annealer. It stands to reason that if you have one temperature at the back of your oven and another in the front, your glass will not anneal correctly. The same holds true for top to bottom. It is very important to know if all the zones of your annealer maintain an even and accurate temperature. Another point to remember is that it is important to have your thermocouple(s) in the zone where the ware that is being annealed is. An interesting test is to put a thermocouple at the top of your annealer and another one at the bottom as well as back to front. You may be amazed to find a serious heat differential within each quadrant. The diagram on pg. 277 shows how to solve the problem of thermal gradation in a large annealer.

Thoughts on Annealing Charts: A re-statement

For as long as I can remember there have been innumerable annealing charts published in some form or other. My previous edition of this book published at least 3 or 4 charts and you, the artist, could take your pick of which one you thought would fit your particular annealing situation. I have received any number of phone calls from my readers concerning these charts and some tell me how great this or that annealing chart is and thank me for publishing it. On the other hand I get phone calls from other readers that use the same chart that works so well for that other guy and am told the chart is crap and doesn't work at all. Regardless of who or what is at fault I've become skeptical of annealing charts that purport to be the "Rosetta Stone" for annealing all sizes, shapes and types of glass.

The bottom line is: When it comes to annealing there are no "one size fits all" charts to calculate annealing. All the charts, except for the Bullseye chart, that I am familiar with are industrial in origin and only cover very specific glass annealing situations, and I can guarantee you they do not take into account all the weird stuff we put into and onto our hot glass masterpieces. Only use a chart to get "into the ballpark." You must develop your own chart to cover your particular cast or blown shapes as well as the type of glass you're using. If you do not understand the principles of annealing it stands to reason that you cannot fix what you don't understand. Take notes and learn from your mistakes. Remember an annealing chart is only a starting point.

Thermal Gradation

In industry one finds very large lehrs (a lehr is an annealing and cooling oven but has a moving belt to move the ware from one heat zone to another) which must maintain very accurate and even heat throughout. This is accomplished through air movement. A pusher fan is usually employed to circulate the hot air, and because of this air movement, the temperature is constant throughout each of the heat zones.

Thermal gradation problems in large annealers can be solved by providing a system to gently circulate the air. What you're actually creating is a convection oven. The drawings on pg. 277 show how to install the device.

I created a convection oven by simply running a stainless tube (½" in diameter, 1.27 cm) that had a tiny hole drilled every 1" or so (2.54 cm) along the length of the tube. The actual diameter of the tube is not really that important, but don't make the tube overly narrow. The tube was the length of the annealer. The holes were, in my case, facing the top of the annealer. I created a "T" shaped manifold with the top of the manifold extending out the top of the annealer. This was attached to an air line which extended to a compressor. There was an oil and air filter in the line. Clean air is important. During the casting, annealing and cooling cycle I ran about 2 to 5 lbs. of air pressure through the manifold. This was a sufficient amount of air circulation to mitigate any heat differentials within the annealer. There are many ways to install this system; it can be at the bottom of your annealer, along the sidewalls if you have top loader. I believe any location within the annealer that permits you to install this system and does not blow directly on the ware will work.

Digitry Controller's at the Pittsburgh Glass Center

Determining Annealing Temperature, The Cane Test

By Fritz Dreisbach

- Make a few canes of glass from the glass to be tested. The canes should be about 18" long and the thickness of a #2 pencil. Estimate what you think the annealing temperature or annealing point is. As an example, let us assume the A.T. to be 1050° F (565° C).

- Bring the oven up to the assumed 1050° (565° C) A.T. and stabilize it at this temperature for a couple of hours.

- Stand the cane in the corner of the oven at about a 45° angle and check it after one hour.

- If the cane is bent, your oven is too hot and you need to lower the temperature about 50° F (28° C) and stabilize for a couple of hours. Repeat Step 2. Always use a new cane when repeating the test. Keep lowering the temperature and repeating Step 2 if the cane continues to bend after one hour.

- If the cane is not bent after one hour but is slightly bent after 4 hours, you have hit the annealing temperature on the nose. A word of caution: if you are annealing thin ware such as long-stemmed goblets or any ware that is top heavy, it is advisable to lower the annealing temperature slightly and hold your soak longer. Keep a cane propped in the corner of your annealer, out of the way, to check your annealing

- If the cane is still not bent after 1 hour plus an additional 4 hours, the oven is too cold. Raise the temperature 20° to 30° F (11° to 17° C) and stabilize for a couple of hours. Repeat until you achieve B above. Remember to record the A.T. for the oven being tested. Doing this test requires patience. Because pyrometric temperature readings may vary for each oven, it is important to repeat the cane test for each oven.

- Each oven should be tested to determine the optimum annealing temperature. An oven that is cool by as little as 50° F (28° C) can increase the soak time necessary to remove stress by as much as ten times.

- Soaking at the A.T. is the most effective way to remove stresses induced in forming hot glass.

Author's Note: It is assumed that your thermocouple and pyrometer are in working order and reading your oven temperature accurately.

The Cane Propped in the Annealer

Controllers and Relays

The reader should note the following: If you do not have a fairly sophisticated controller and relay (Mercury Displacement Relay*, (MDR) or Solid State) you will have trouble maintaining the parameters needed to achieve annealing accuracy. Mechanical relays will work but won't give the extreme accuracy of the aforementioned relays. Problems with annealing can be quite complex. Never assume that because your work is checked after annealing it is because of a poor annealing cycle. There are a host of other problems that can create checked glass. Poorly insulated annealers as well as poorly placed heating elements are but two of a host of situations that will create annealing problems. Good luck in your search for strain relief.

See pg. 246 and 279 for information on controllers and relays. Page 339 lists the mainline controller companies.

* Mercury displacement relays MDR's) contain mercury and some local codes may preclude their use. Check your local codes before using an MDR. It should also be noted that MDR's are no longer available in Canada and Great Britain and I believe the U.S. will soon follow.

Annealing Charts

The charts on this and the following pages, if followed, will introduce you to the world of annealing and all its intricacies. The charts found in the literature are based on annealing coherent thicknesses of glass; that is, they do not account for all the anomalies found in studio art glass. Those anomalies include variable thicknesses, blobby additions, prunts, and all the other stuff we add to our glass. Because of the variables found in art glass we should only use these charts as a starting point. In reality there is no "one chart fits all" for annealing and for that reason you must keep accurate records when you anneal and note the various time additions you must make to successfully anneal your glass.

The chart below is a basic time temperature curve for blown ware cooling on two sides. The standard for blown glass with an open shape has always been to anneal one hour for every quarter inch of glass. If you are blowing closed forms, bottles, globes, etc., it may then become necessary to increase your annealing and cooling rates.

An explanation of the chart is as follows: t = thickness, A.T. = annealing temperature, A.T. -200° F (minus 111° C) = the annealing temperature minus 200° F (minus 111° C). If your glass is 1" thick and has been soaked at 950° F (510° C) for 4 hours, it will take you another 4 ½ hours to cool your glass to 750° F (398° C). A.T. -300°F (167° C) = another decrease in temperature of 100° F (56° C). The same piece of glass can be cooled the next 100° F (56° C) to 650° F (343° C) in 1 hour more and so on. This chart, like the one that follows, cools the glass slowly from the soaking temperature through the annealing range and increases in speed as it drops below this range. Don't peek. Allow the oven to cool naturally to below 200° F (93° C) before cracking the door.

Elapsed time in hours for each step of annealing for a given thickness.

t = cm	.317	.635	1.27	1.90	2.54	5.08	7.62	10.16	12.7	15.24
t = inches	⅛"	¼"	½"	¾"	1"	2"	3"	4"	5"	6"
A.T.	0.5	1	2	3	4	8	12	16	20	24
A.T. -200° F (111°C)	0.7	1.5	3.7	6.2	8.5	18	33	54	80	109
A.T. -300°F (167°C)	0.8	1.7	4.2	7	9.5	19.5	36	59	88	120
A.T. -400°F (222°C)	1	2.0	4.7	7.5	10.5	20.5	38	63	95	130
A.T. -550°F (305°C)	1.25	2.25	5.0	8.0	11.25	21	40	67	100	140

Use your annealing temperature for the A.T. in the above chart and subtract the temperatures as indicated.

Annealing of Cast Glass Pieces

By Dan Schwoerer

Cast glass pieces by their nature are usually thick, ranging from ½" to over 8". Over the years I have been getting increasing numbers of calls asking for annealing schedules for cast pieces of various thicknesses. The table on pg. 51 is what I now recommend. It is extrapolated from TABLE 4-1 in the 3rd Edition of *Glass Engineering Handbook* by George W. McLellan and E.B. Shand. As stated earlier in this section; The original chart has undergone changes based on empirically derived factors. The table was specifically adapted to Bullseye's 1101 and 1401 clear casting glasses but applies to other glasses by substituting the appropriate annealing and strain points.

How the Chart is Laid Out

- A soak at the annealing point (for Bullseye this is 960° F. For other glasses, use what the manufacturer recommends.)
- An initial cooling rate through a range from the anneal soak temperature to some lower temperature below the strain point (this lower temperature decreases with increasing thickness).
- A second cooling rate through the next 90° F (this rate is twice the initial rate).
- A final cooling rate to room temp. (this rate is 10 times the initial rate).

The other factor considered is whether the piece cooling is a hollow cast shape or a solid cast shape. The table shows cooling rates for cooling solid as well as hollow cast shapes.

Another factor that should be considered is the shape of the casting. Design induced stress shapes (i.e.: sharp angles and inside corners) concentrate stress. Pieces with large variations in thickness are also more difficult to anneal. For these situations I recommend increasing the cooling rates by factors from 1.5 to 4.0 times the rates shown in the tables. As can be seen, anneal times increase greatly as the thickness increases.

Dan at his desk

Annealing of Castings

Thickness (Inches) (mm)	Anneal Soak Time @ 960°F @ 516°C	Initial Cooling Rate (°F/Hr) (°C/Hr)	Initial Cooling Range (°F) (°C)	2nd Cooling Rate (°F/Hr) (°C/Hr)	2nd Cooling Range (°F) (°C)	Final Cooling Rate °F/hr °C/hr	Final Cooling Range (°F/Hr) (°C/Hr)	Total Minimum Time Hours
.5 in	2 hr.	100	960 - 800	180	800 - 700	600	700 - 70	6
12 mm		55	516 - 427	99	427 - 371	330	371 - 21	
.75 in	3 hr	45	960 - 800	81	800 - 700	270	700 - 70	10
19 mm		25	516 - 427	45	427 - 371	150	371 - 21	
1.0 in	4 hr	27	960 - 800	49	800 - 700	162	700 - 70	16
25 mm		15	516 - 427	27	427 - 371	90	371 - 21	
1.5 in	6 hr	12	960 - 800	22	800 - 700	72	700 - 70	33
38 mm		6.7	516 - 427	12	427 - 371	40	371 - 21	
2.0 in	8 hr	6.8	960 - 800	12	800 - 700	41	700 - 70	56
50 mm		3.8	516 - 427	6.8	427 - 371	22	371 - 21	
2.5 in	10 hr	4.3	960 - 800	8	800 - 700	26	700 - 70	84
60 mm		2.4	516 - 427	4.3	427 - 371	14.4	371 - 21	
3.0 in	12 hr	3	960 - 800	5.4	800 - 700	18	700 - 70	119
75 mm		1.7	516 - 427	3.1	427 - 371	10	371 - 21	
4.0 in	16 hr	1.7	960 - 780	3.1	780 - 680	10	680 - 70	216
100 mm		0.94	516 - 416	1.7	416 - 360	5.6	360 - 21	
6.0 in	24 hr	0.75	960 - 760	1.3	760 - 660	4.5	660 - 70	499
150 mm		0.42	516 - 404	0.76	404 - 349	2.5	349 - 21	
8.0 in	32 hr	0.42	960 - 740	0.76	740 - 640	2.5	640 - 70	916
200 mm		0.23	516 - 393	0.42	393 - 338	1.4	338 - 21	

If your controller cannot be programmed for degrees per hour it will be necessary to do the following conversion to convert from degrees per hour to hours per degree. Find the row you will be using (Thickness) and subtract the degrees in the Initial Cooling Range. Example: Your casting is solid and it is 3 inches thick: Subtract 800° from 960° (960° -800° = 160°) Divide the answer (160°) by the degrees per hour (3°) 160 ÷ 3 = 53.3 hrs. (round it up to 54 hrs). This answer is the number of hours required to lower the temperature to 800 degrees at the given rate of 3 degrees per hr. Repeat for the Second Rate and for the Final Cooling Rate.

This annealing chart is derived from Corning's method as shown in McLellan and Shand. It is based on a flat slab of uniform thickness that is set up in such a fashion that it can cool equally from top and bottom.

If the glass is not set up in such a fashion that it can cool equally from top and bottom or is anything besides a flat slab of uniform thickness, select an annealing cycle for a piece that is twice the thickness of the thickest area of the piece.

Even a very conservative annealing cycle may not work if the annealing oven is not capable of cooling evenly. If your glass checks, check your oven before you blame the chart.

This chart re-printed through the courtesy of Dan Schwoerer, The Bullseye Glass Co.

Libensky Method of Annealing

The Libensky method of annealing assumes that the glass will be relieved of strain as it cools from the high-end annealing point (G) to the strain point (H). The theory behind this method is that proper annealing can take place at any point within the annealing (transition) range if you cool down at a slow enough rate (degree based). You should know the high-end annealing temperature as well as the strain point in order to use this method although it isn't absolutely necessary to know the strain point. You can assume 700° F (370° C) as the strain point of any glass used by the glass artist although I really do recommend you find the true strain point for your casting glass. To use this method of annealing, it helps to have a fairly sophisticated controller (self tuning) with at least a mercury displacement relay. The American system anneals and then cools (time based). The annealing/cooling chart found on the next page was given directly to me by Prof. Libensky many years ago. I am quite proud to publish it for you to use. Although American glass artists

Jaroslava Brychtova and Stanislav Libensky, Pilchuck, 1987

who cast do not usually use this method, I have used his method but do a bit of cheating; I anneal from G-G1 when I have casting 2" or more in thickness. Americans usually anneal for a specific length of time (G-G1) and then cool the glass (G1-H) for the appropriate length of time. For blown ware cooling from two sides the standard, anneal 1 hour per ¼" works just fine. I have added G1 to indicate where to hold for high-end annealing. The casting temperature, E and F, depicted in this chart is a theoretical casting temperature. You need to determine the optimal temperature at which your casting glass will work. To use this chart, plug in the appropriate numbers for your casting glass: E, G, and H. A, B, C, and D are for curing the plaster/flint mold properly and are accurate regardless of the casting glass you use. If your molds are constructed properly and if you air dry your molds before firing, you will realize the least amount of mold cracking. If you must fire wet molds, dry them in the oven at about 220° F (104° C) for the length of time it takes to totally dry the mold. You will be amazed at how long it takes to dry a wet mold in an oven. It is possible to tell if the mold is dry by holding a piece of glass over the cracked door, if you see moisture form on the glass then the mold is obviously still giving off moisture. To understand the subject and learn about making molds go to pg. 62.

The Libensky Method

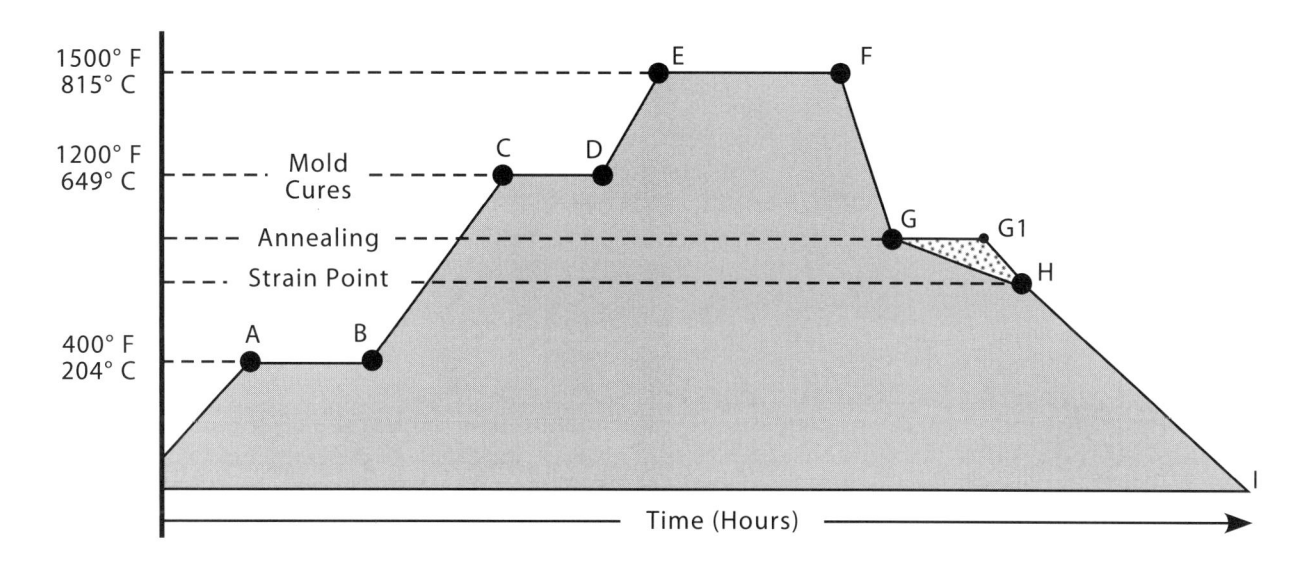

Points G & H reflect an assumed annealing temperature and strain point. I have introduced G1 for those that wish to anneal for a specified length of time (G-G1) and then cool (G1-H) You may substitute your annealing temperature and strain point without affecting the time/temperature curve. The strain point for any glass is established with a dilatometer. A sample of your glass must be sent to a lab that does this type of testing. See pg. 54 for information on strain point testing.

	A	B	C	D	E	F	G	H	I
							Anneal	Strain	
C°	200°	200°	650°	650°	800°-850°	800°-850°	510°	370°	50°-100°
F°	400°	400°	1200°	1200°	1500°	1500°	950°	700°	200°
1-1.5" 2.5-3.8 cm	3 hr.	4	4	4	1	1.5	...	12	12
2-2.5" 5-6.3 cm	4 hr.	4	4	4	1	2	...	24	24
3-4" 3-10 cm	4 hr.	4	6	6	1.5	2	8	48	48
4-6" 4-15 cm	8 hr.	8	8	8	1.5	2	10	96	96
5-8" 5-20 cm	8	12	8	8	2	3	12	190	190

Glass Notes

Laboratory Testing for Annealing & Strain Point

The actual annealing point and strain points of any given glass can be determined in a laboratory. If you are going to get serious about casting it is recommended that you have a lab determine, if not the high end annealing temperature then at least the strain point of your glass. It is generally accepted practice to use a temperature of approximately 30° F – 50° F below the high end annealing point as the temperature to hold the oven for anneal/soak. Most glass artists and schools of glass use the actual annealing temperature as established by the cane test described on page 48.

If you wish to send your glass off to a lab for testing and establishing the actual annealing temperature as well as the strain point here is that information:

ASTM C-336 ANNEALING POINT AND STRAIN POINT OF GLASS BY FIBER ELONGATION-T9502
The annealing point of a glass is defined as the temperature at which a round fiber, nominally 0.65 mm in diameter elongates under a load of 1.0 kg at a rate of 0.14 mm/min when it is cooled at a rate of 4°C/min. The strain point is determined by extrapolation of the annealing point data as the temperature at which the elongation rate is 0.0316 times that at the annealing temperature. A representative specimen of 50 gm or more of flame workable glass in pieces a minimum of 5 mm in diameter is required. Fritted or ground specimens must be remelted to obtain a piece large enough from which fibers can be drawn.
$200 per specimen to 800°C – 1472° F
$150 per specimen for glass fiber preparation

ORTON
Materials Testing & Research Center
6991 Old 3C Highway
Westerville, Ohio 43082
Phone: 614-895-2663
Fax: 614-895-5610
E-mail: homeny@ortonceramic.com
Website: www.ortonceramic.com

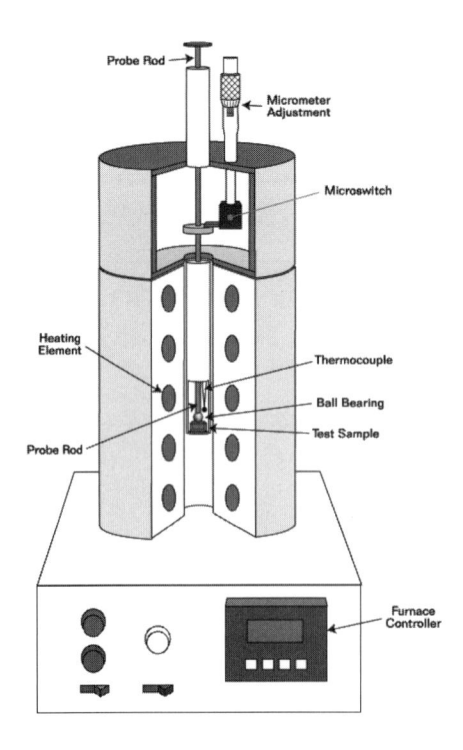

Dilitometer

Testing Stress & Compatibility

Dr. Frank E. Woolley

Now that you've batched and melted those spiffy new colors it's time to determine if they actually fit. You've determined on paper they do, but we know from experience reality does not always follow theory. There are tests you can perform in your studio that will tell you if your color will fit your base glass. The descriptions of these tests have been outlined in Dr. Frank E. Woolley's book *Glass Technology for the Studio* and presented below.

Testing for compatibility of two glasses

These are all seal tests, in which the combined effects of thermal expansion and viscosity are acting, just as they do in ware made from more than one glass

The seal tests are more reliable than separately measuring or estimating the thermal expansions and strain points of a pair of glasses

Pull test (parallel fibers)

This is the simplest and quickest test, but not always reliable for estimating the amount of mismatch and is usually used with glasses using a similar base but even then can be problematic.

- A ⅛" rod of the base glass and a ⅛" rod of the unknown glass are placed next to each other. The tips of the rods are carefully heated in a torch until they fuse together.
- With a tweezer carefully pull a thread a thin thread of equal amounts. It is important that you do not twist the thread.

Results:

On cooling, the composite fiber bends toward the glass having a higher expansion.

It is hard to interpret the results in terms of the expansion mismatch, since the deflection of the double fiber depends sensitively on the overall diameter and on the ratio of cross sections of the two fiber

Split cylinder (ring) test

This test follows the same principle as the pull test, but in a hollow cylinder rather than parallel rods. Unlike the thread test the ring test is reliable and can be depended on as a good test for compatibility.

The unknown glass is encased with the base glass and then blown as a straight cylinder approximately 3" (7.5 cm) in diameter; after annealing, a ring is cut out of the central part of the cylinder; the ring is scored and cracked along its axis to relieve any stresses in the piece. If this test is done very carefully, it can reveal a small mismatch; it cannot be used if the mismatch is large, because the piece will break when you attempt to cut rings.

Results:

If the inside is in tension, the crack will overlap.
If the outside is in tension, it will gap.
If there is no movement either way one can assume similar expansion.

The ring test is more difficult to make than the pull test but has a higher degree of accuracy. The size of the gap or overlap depends on total wall thickness, uniformity of the wall thickness, and the ratio of thicknesses of the two glasses.

Ball Test

This test differs from the previous tests in that the stress and mismatch can be estimated more accurately. It is easier to get reproducible results than with pull or ring tests.

The unknown glass 1" in diameter is encased with a 1" layer of the clear, known glass. Once made it is annealed alongside a ball of only clear glass of the same diameter, to eliminate the risk of confusing annealing stress and compatibility stress

The stress and mismatch can be estimated at four levels:
- Radial cracks in the case show the color is lower expansion; circumferential cracks in the color show the color is higher expansion
- The cracks may take hours to days to develop.
- At lower stress, the piece will not crack spontaneously, but will crack irregularly when you try to saw it with a diamond saw.
- At high stress the piece will crack spontaneously.

At even lower stress, it will saw satisfactorily, but will show stress in the polariscope; there will be a stressed region in the clear glass close to the central ball of color which is light or even colored in the polariscope.

If the stress is low enough that you can cut and polish a slice through the center, then the stress can actually be measured in the slice with a polarimeter.

A ball test which has no colors and only slight lightness in the polariscope is safe to cold work; success with higher stress levels depends entirely on the design.

Trident or Sandwich Test (two-glass seals (Sometimes referred to as the Hagy test)

These are considered by some to be the most accurate of all the tests for compatibility. This test can give numerical results useful in adjusting composition and leaves no doubt about compatibility.

This test has no advantage over the pull or ball tests if the mismatch is so large that the piece breaks. It requires a polarimeter to perform the test. According to Pete VanderLaan, "It is the absolute best test for glass compatibility. If you want to cast thick glass you want this test."

This test is made by sealing three parallel canes together at the ends, then annealing; this results in an assembly in which the canes are in simple tension and compression, and the amount of stress can be readily measured with a polarimeter or polarizing microscope

Make canes of the colored and clear glasses. The canes need to be 2-3 mm (0.080-0.120") diameter, and should be 35-40 mm (1-⅜ to 1-⅝") long. It is important that they be round and uniform in diameter. Out-of-round and taper should be less than 0.05 mm (0.002"). The two color canes should have the same average diameters within 0.2 mm (0.008"), and their average diameters should be within 0.5 mm (0.020") of that of the clear cane.

Arrange the canes as shown in the diagram on pg. 59, with three canes placed parallel, where the central cane is clear and the two outside are of the colored glass. In the attached figure, A is the colored glass and B is the clear. The ends are sealed by flame working. In the finished seal, the canes should be parallel and in the same plane.

After flame working, the assembly is annealed at a rate appropriate to the cane diameter.

Results:

Stress is measured in the clear cane using the polarimeter or polarizing microscope.

Note: The canes may also be sealed together in the hot shop by pressing a rod of hot glass across each end of the array of three canes, then annealed.

End Notes from the Author

It should be noted by all that, regardless of what test you use for compatibility, there is no substitute for real world results. The conditions under which you test for compatibility may vary from your real world melting conditions. If you test your glasses when they are fresh, the results may vary from when your base glass is 3 days old. For various reasons, glasses change expansion the longer they sit in a furnace.

If you've tested for compatibility and all seems to fit but your work is checking, it then becomes important to analyze the type of check you're getting as there are many reasons that glass checks; compatibility is only one.

If you have glasses that you've used and have demonstrated themselves to be compatible and then suddenly start to check for reasons that are definitely compatibility issues, it then becomes necessary to know if that batch glass you've been using from one of the batch companies has been altered in some way. More likely though you will find the color rod company has changed their formulation for those spiffy colors you've used for umteen years.

If your income is dependent on your daily production or your one of a kind castings, it is imperative that you develop some method of testing your glasses to insure success. It's no fun to ship a set of colorful goblets to a client or install that solid glass wall and have it all fall apart after you've spent the money. You never outgrow your need for testing. Vigilance over all aspects of your studio will save you heartache as well as a lot of money. Compatibility issues are an important aspect and a measure of your technical success.

Testing for Compatibility

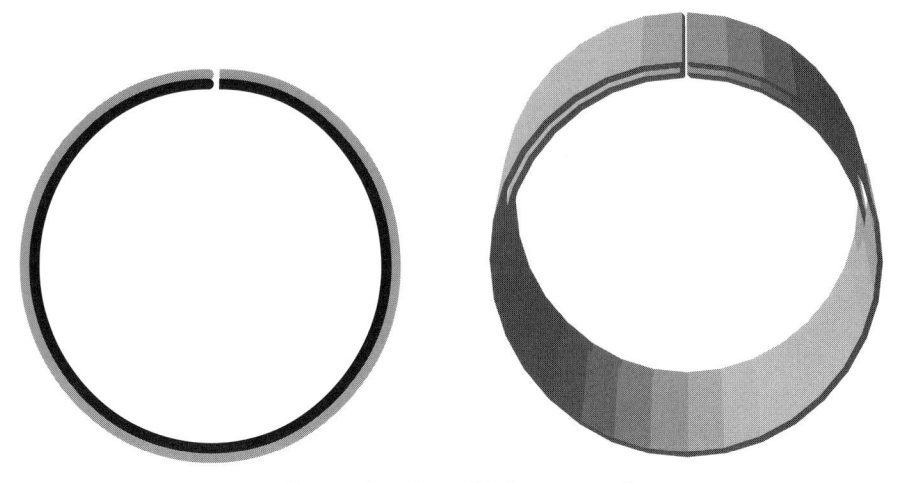

Outer glass has a higher expansion
Inner glass has a lower expansion

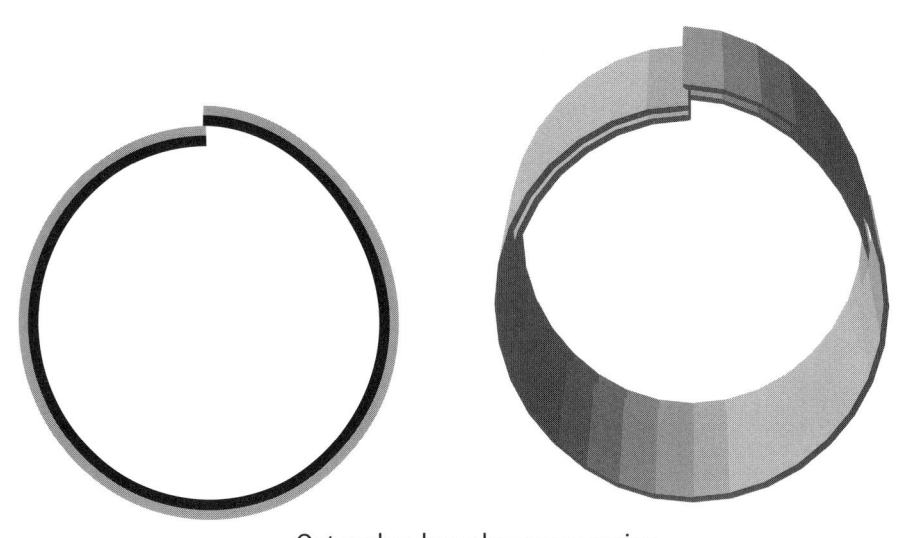

Outer glass has a lower expansion
Inner glass has a higher expansion

Ring Test

The Cane Test

Color | Clear

18+ "

Glass on the inside has higher expansion

Ball Test

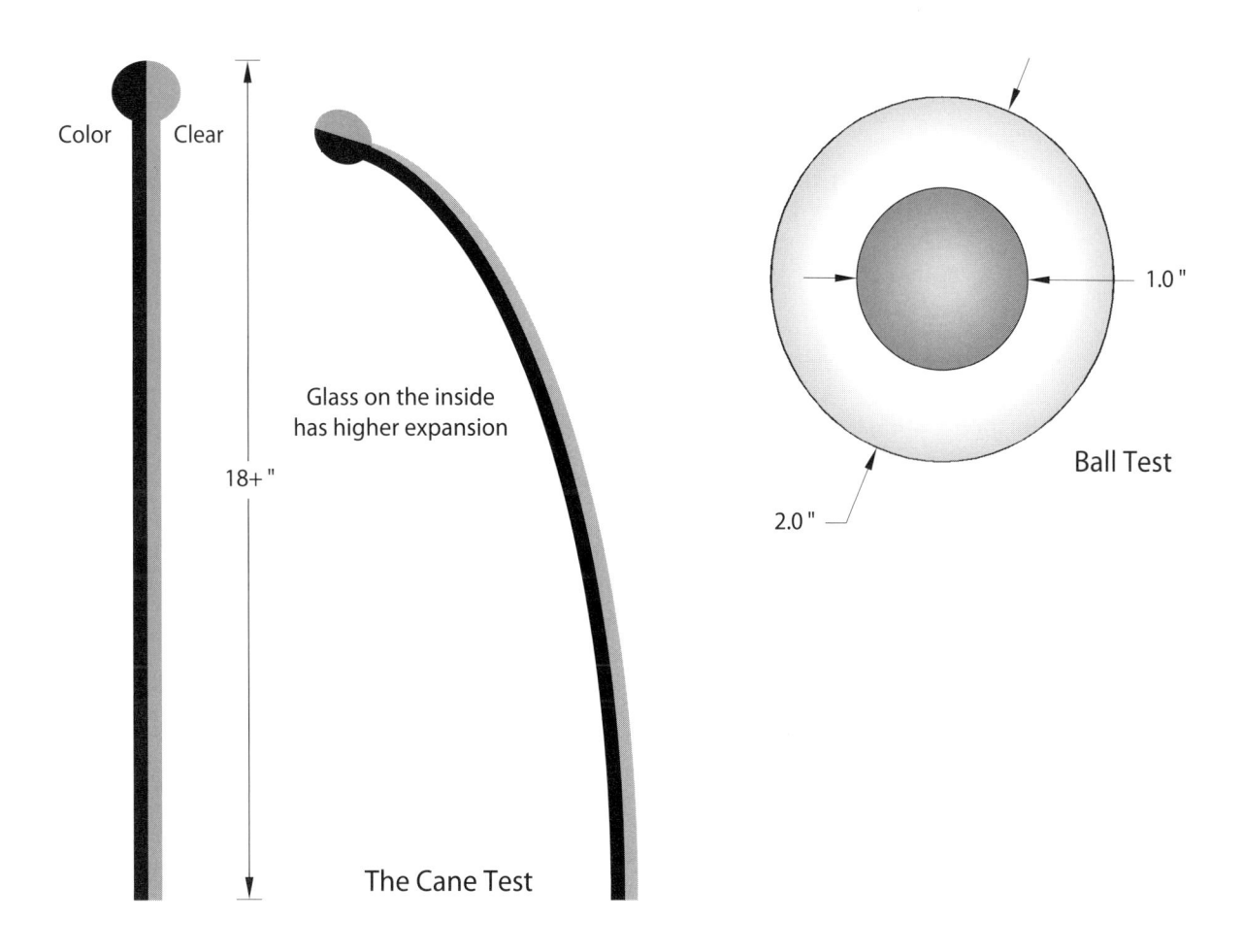

1.0 "
2.0 "

Preparation and measurement orientation of trident seal

1. Three glass rods with axes in one plane.
2. Rods flame-sealed at one end.
3. Flame sealed at both ends.

After assemblage is annealed, optical retardation in central rod is measured along a diameter with rod axes perpendicular to light path.

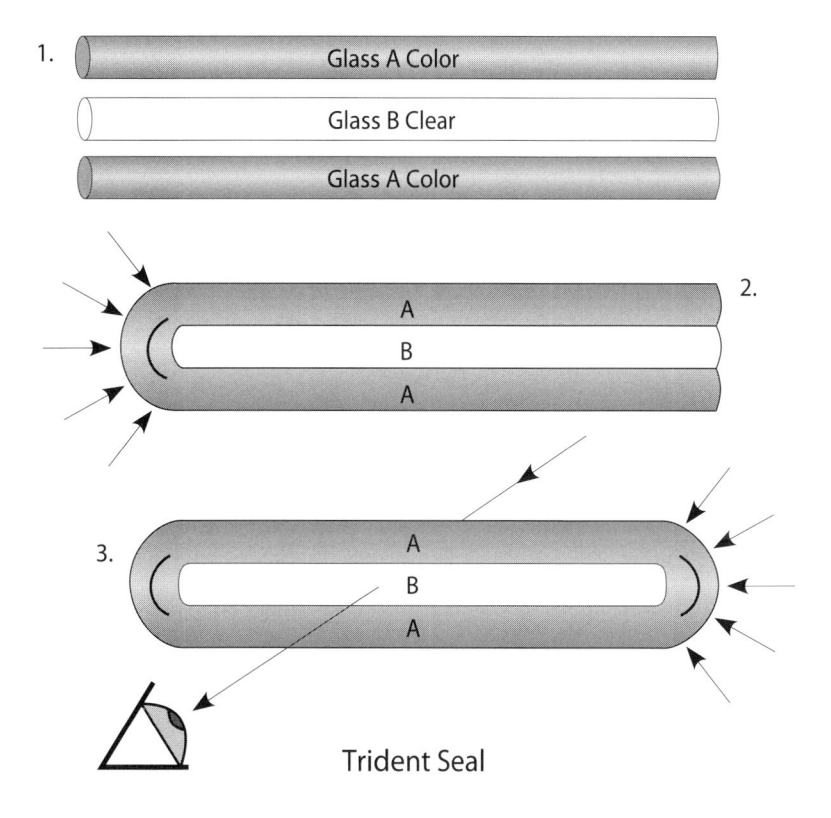

1.
Glass A Color
Glass B Clear
Glass A Color

2.
A
B
A

3.
A
B
A

Trident Seal

Glass Notes 59

Glass Durability Testing

In April of 1976 I visited with Nick Labino at his studio in Maumee, Ohio. At that time he demonstrated for me ways of testing glass for durability. There was one test that I found to be applicable to the studio artist and that was the titration method described below.

Nick was always willing to share technical information if he felt you had been "doing your homework." If he felt you were only fooling around, he wouldn't give you the time of day. I fell into both categories.

The titration test is for soda-lime glasses and is done to evaluate the resistance of glass containers to chemical attack. Nick recommended they should first be done to a known durable glass, such as window glass or bottle glass, in order to establish a known standard of durability. If your test sample does not pass the chemical durability test as it compares to the window or bottle glass control, it does not necessarily mean that the sample you are testing is not durable, although that might be the case. It only means that your glass is not durable in relation to the standard you are using. It is important to establish a parameter of durability. According to Nick, window glass was not all that durable anyway, but it was a standard. Since windows were always being cleaned, usually with an ammonia-based cleaner, any signs of surface devitrification were washed away by "the woman of the house." I guess Nick didn't do windows. If you are using factory cullet and not altering it in any way, then it's probably not necessary to test for durability. If you are batching, it is important to establish a standard of durability. It's not fun if that really sweet glass you've been blowing all week suddenly dissolves when you pour beer into it.

Testing for Durability

The equipment for this test is available from any chemistry supply house, college, or university chemistry department. If you work at a university, check out the chemistry department to see if it has a lamp worker. If so, make friends. He or she has the key to the stock room, and the stock room has all the equipment you'll need.

In a stainless steel mortar or stainless steel ball mill, grind up 20 grams or more of your sample to go through a 40 mesh screen and not a 50 mesh screen. Take the sample on the 50 mesh screen and pass a good strong magnet through it to remove any iron scale contamination. Wash the sample with acetone 3 times to dissolve the glass "dust." The sample is now ready for use. Use 10 grams of the cleaned glass sample.

Take slightly more than 100 cc of distilled water, referred to as filtrate, and boil half of it to eliminate the CO_2. Mix the water back together.

Put the 10 gram sample of glass in 100 cc of filtrate and boil the solution for 4 hours. Make sure you boil the solution in a beaker covered with a watch glass.

After boiling, cool down the filtrate to room temperature and add 5 drops of methyl red indicator, which will make the solution slightly yellow.

With a 50th normal sulfuric acid solution in a titration column, add, drop-by-drop, the acid solution to the filtrate glass solution. Keep the solution stirred while adding the acid. When the solution turns pink, it is neutralized. Let the solution stand for an hour or two to see if it remains pink. If the solution turns yellowish again, it means the alkali is still going into solution and more acid needs to be added to completely neutralize the solution.

Count the milliliters needed to neutralize the solution and compare the amount against your window or bottle glass control. You should only need about 2-3 milliliters to neutralize the solution. If you have used more acid to neutralize the solution than it took to neutralize the window or bottle glass, then your sample is not durable. If you used the same or less, you're home free.

Author's note: Nick Labino used window glass as his standard. You can use any glass that you think is durable as a standard. The reason window or bottle glass is used is that it is a known durable glass. His durability test varies a great deal from the ASTM approved test but is just fine for the studio glass artist. The ASTM test is quite rigorous and probably not really necessary for anyone making art glass, but if you're interested, here is how to obtain a copy of the ASTM test. Their web site: www.astm.org and search for C225-85. The cost of this abstract is $34.00

Mold Making & Casting Techniques

Chapter Contents

Making a Mold for Casting	62
Making a Mold	66
Libensky/Brychtova Casting Technique	67
Libensky/Brychtova Casting Technique (Pilchuck)	72
Mold Box	76
Making a Plaster Positive	79
The Casting Glass and Annealers	80
Casting Calculations and Other Useful Information	81
Ratio of Plaster/Silica to Water	83
Casting into Plaster/Silica Molds	84
Introduction to Kiln Casting	84
Flower Pot Casting	85
Determining quantity of glass needed for casting	87
Ann Robinson't Investments	88
Other Mold Materials	89
Sodium Silicate Sand Casting	90
Rigid Sand Molds for Casting	92
Making the Mold	94
Chem Bond 4905 No-Bake Resin System	96
Plaster Blow Mold	97
Sand Casting	99
Bentonite/Sand Casting	105
Cast and Blow	108
Bob Carlson Break-Away Box	110
The Klaus Moje Method of Kiln Casting	115
Strip Stacking	118
Kiln-Forming Temperature Ranges	121
Basic Fusing & Slumping Chart	122
Kiln Forming, Jeremy Lepisto	123
Pâte de Verre, Alicia Lomné	124

Making a Mold for Casting

Additional information for this section was provided by the artist Dan Clayman. Dan has an excellent handout that he uses when he teaches the glass casting process. His class is highly recommended. If you see it being offered, Henry says "take it."

This short section will explain in detail the basic principals for fabricating a mold for glass casting. The mold described will allow you to cast glass by employing any number of the following techniques: hot pads; "chunke de verre;" pâte de verre; coarse frit; cullet; and, under some conditions, molten glass. Each method of glass casting produces an aesthetic indigenous to that process. To cast glass successfully, you, the artist, must have a thorough knowledge of the casting techniques employed.

Mold Materials

Plaster: All the recipes that I am familiar with include some type of plaster. There are many different types of plaster, but only few are applicable for glass casting. Plaster is the fundamental material that holds the mold together when formed and as it heats to casting temperature. The most common plasters used for mold making are #1 Molding Plaster, Pottery Plaster, and sometimes additions of Hydrocal. The pottery plaster is exactly the same material as molding plaster but has a bit of hydrocal in it. The hydrocal adds a slight degree of toughness to the mold surface. The toughness is needed by potters that use it for slip casting.

Silica: The addition of silica to the plaster serves two purposes: it allows the plaster to maintain its integrity through the total process, it adds strength at high temperatures and reduces shrinkage. The silica grain size should be 200 – 325 mesh for fine detail.

The Mold Must

1. Not shrink, crack, warp, or deteriorate when subjected to high heat (1500° F) (815° C).
2. Retain detail throughout the length of casting.
3. Have a similar expansion to the glass being used.
4. Clean easily from the glass surface after casting.

Overview

The mold is usually composed of plaster and silica in a 1:1 ratio by weight. By weight is very important. Some casters use a 1.5 silica to 1 plaster ratio. This ratio gives a somewhat softer mold and tends to shrink a bit less. Silica is also referred to as flint and is obtainable from any good ceramic supplier. Silica is a pure sand that has been ground into a very fine (200+ mesh) powder, and plaster is "gypsum" that has been ground and subjected to high heat. The heat drives out the chemically–bonded water. When plaster is remixed with water, the process is reversed and the "gypsum" hardens. Plaster by itself will not work for casting as it does not have any ability to withstand heat and will fall apart if used without the addition of silica.

The silica is capable of withstanding elevated temperatures without deforming and gives the plaster/silica mixture the characteristics described in #1 as well as maintaining all the other aspects needed for our mold.

When making a mold, always use fresh plaster. Old plaster will not work well as it probably has taken on some water from the atmosphere and, because of that, may not set properly. The 1:1 ratio is the most common one used for fabricating casting molds. The 1:1 ratio will fulfill all the prerequisites described. It is also important to note that the mold is not affected by the expansion of the glass and can therefore be used for casting pieces with undercuts.

After making the mold, it should be handled carefully as it is rather soft and will injure easily.

If you are making castings of objects with undercuts, the model should be made from a soft material such as clay or soft rubber. This will ensure that they can be removed from your mold without injuring it.

Beginners should make their first castings a reasonable size, avoid severe undercuts, and sculpt from water–based clay or sculptures wax (micro crystalline). Plasticine (oil–based clay) is difficult to remove from the mold. Take note, however, that it is not wise to leave water based clay in the mold for any length of time after making the mold as the mold will draw the water out of the clay, and it will become very hard and difficult to remove.

Other Casting Products

Some products are available as additives for molds, and others help maintain mold integrity as follows.

Mold Additives

Alumina Hydrate allows the mold to withstand higher temperatures.

China Clay acts as a binder and helps maintain mold integrity at higher temperatures. The drawback to any clay additive is that if it is used in too high a quantity, the clay will have a tendency to stick to the surface of your casting. It can also make too hard a mold and cause the glass to crack when it cools.

Fiberglass Needles should be approximately ½" in length. They make a very strong mold when used as an addition to the plaster/silica. 1" strips of fiberglass blanket can also be dipped in the plaster/silica and horizontally wrapped around the outside of the mold to increase mold strength. This is especially helpful when making pâte de verre molds.

Grog is a very course ground up fired clay and is very good for strengthening molds when used as an additive to the last mold layer.

Fiber Blanket when shredded acts much the same way as the fiberglass needles discussed above.

High Temperature Mold Coatings

KS-4 Plus and **Mizzou** castables are sometimes used to back-up the plaster/silica mold. They are troweled onto the mold face coat as a back-up material about an inch or two in thickness. These materials give great strength to your mold and allow you to have thinner molds.

R&R 910 is a fairly hard casting material. Because of its strength it allows the caster to cut down on the mold thickness. Unlike the KS-4 and Mizzou, it can be used as the total mold, as the glass will not adhere to it at elevated temperatures. Some casters use it for the total mold and others use it as a back-up similar to how one would use the KS-4. Regardless of how you use these materials the added mold strength is ideal for large castings, and they do not break down at elevated temperatures.

To use these mold coatings, do the following: Apply either the Mizzou or KS-4 in separate batches with a trowel after you've created a thickish face coat. The final mold has a shape similar to the object being cast, and because of that, the heat penetration through the mold wall is equal throughout the annealing and cooling process, and cracking is held to a minimum. As stated above, these coatings are usually not used on smaller style molds.

Regardless of how you construct your mold, it is always a good idea to have chicken wire in the mold to reinforce it.

It is best to air dry your mold prior to casting. Air drying in a warm room for a week or two is ideal. If you're in a hurry, then you can dry your mold in the kiln at about 220° F (104° C) for the requisite length of time. Large molds take a very (and I mean <u>very</u>) long time to dry.

Fire very slowly up to 1200° F (649° C). Speed also depends on thickness. If you go quickly, you will get severe cracks as there is chemically-bonded water within the molecular structure of the plaster. This water needs time to escape, and if you go too fast, the escaping water will expand and crack the mold.

Go particularly slow from 900–1100° F (482–593° C). This is where the quartz inversion happens. The silica actually expands a bit in this range, and if you rush through this range, you run the risk of exacerbating the molds' tendency to crack.

Preparation (Illustrations at the end of this section)

Prepare the sculpture to be cast, avoiding very thin edges or thin protrusions as they will break easily when de-molding the casting. Most undercuts will cast, but if they are too complicated, they might present a problem when you try to remove the clay from the mold. It is best to start with a simple, open–faced mold.

Mold Boards should be constructed from a material that has good strength and will not suck water from the mold material when it is poured. Materials I have used that work are old formica counter tops cut into appropriate sizes, plywood that has enough thickness that it does not bend easily and has been coated with a material that makes it waterproof, aluminum strips at least ⅛" thick that have ends bent at a 90° angle. Regardless of what type of board you use, I recommend putting a thin coating of mold release on the boards to make sure the mold releases easily after it has set. This coating is especially useful when using aluminum collet boards, as the mold material has a tendency to stick to the aluminum. The separator that I recommend is the Vaseline/Kerosene mold separator. See page 295

> If your face coat is a different density from the rest of the mold, it will have a tendency to separate when fired to temperature. Use the chart on page 83 to guarantee density.

Collet Boards (mold boards) are placed around the model, leaving about 2" of space between the model and the box. It is best to construct the mold on a flat, level surface, preferably one that is totally water proof. Create a plaster dam around the bottom (outside) of your collet and up the side where the boards come together. If you use rigid collet boards you can use a clay dam. This will keep the plaster/silica mixture from running out of the box when you pour it.

For convenience it is probably a good idea to pre-mix the dry plaster/silica before using. The bags of plaster and silica come in standard weights, 50 lbs. for plaster and usually 100 lbs. for silica. If you have a large plastic or fiber drum that has a secure, tight-fitting lid, you can put equal amounts of plaster and silica in the drum and roll it around until you're sure the two materials are mixed. A drum style cement mixer works well, but it is imperative to use a lid with a gasket when mixing. Wear a good dust mask, not the hospital type, but one approved by the Bureau of

Mines for silica dust. The silica can cause silicosis.

In a clean bucket (flexible plastic), add clean cool water. Do not use warm water. If you haven't pre-mixed your plaster/silica, then sift equal amounts by weight of plaster and silica into the water; distribute the materials evenly until you've added the quantity of material called for from the chart on page 83. The general rule for the plaster/silica to water ration is 1:1.75, 1 being the water. Remember, by adding the mixture to the water, you will almost double the volume, so don't fill the bucket more than half way with water. Always add the mixture to water, never vice-versa; you get kaka if you do. Do not stir as you add the materials to the water. On pg. 82 you will find the information on how to calculate the quantity of material needed to fill your mold.

Let the plaster/silica sit (slake) for about two minutes. This is the length of time it takes for the plaster to re-hydrate. For large volumes (1 gallon or more of plaster/silica), you can use a paint mixer attached to an electric drill to stir the mixture. Use a cheap electric drill, but be careful not to let the drill come in contact with the water as you will go up in flames. If you use a drill, it is a good idea to use an extension cord with a built–in Ground Fault Interrupter (GFI). A good battery powered drill will also work. The mixer and drill will make the product ready to use in a very short time. The faster you stir, the quicker it will begin to set. For small amounts of plaster/silica, use your hand. Be careful not to stir a lot of bubbles into the plaster mixture. Pay attention as you stir. If the mixture begins to thicken while mixing, it must be poured immediately or you will end up with a mixture too thick to use.

Pour the mixture into the box containing the model. Pour off to the sides of the box to keep from injuring your model if it is soft. If you are pouring onto a rubber model, don't worry about pouring directly onto the model. Make sure you do not cause the chicken wire to come in contact with the model. After you have finished pouring the mixture, shake the table or the board to release any bubbles that may have been trapped when you poured. Don't shake too violently as you may loosen the dam around the collet and create one big mess. It is not necessary to pour more than 1 ½ to 2 inches or so above the model.

After the mixture has set for about ½ hour, you can remove the box from around the mold. Turn the mold over and carefully remove the clay. Clay will leave a residue on the surface of the mold. This residue must be cleaned off with a very soft brush and cool running water. Carefully remove all bits and pieces of clay remaining in the cracks and crevices. Dental tools, tooth picks, and some compressed air work well to remove the small pieces of clay that adhere to the mold. Be careful of any thin edges. As stated previously, before your mold is ready for casting it should be air dried. Drying the mold will give it added strength and minimize the amount of cracking that happens at elevated temperatures. Most of us are usually too impatient to wait for our molds to air dry and force dry them in the annealer. This will work but is not as good as air drying.

Author's Note: If you dry the mold in an annealer, it is important that you not raise the temperature of the annealer beyond 220° F (105° C) in order to avoid cracking. Let the mold sit at that temperature until all the moisture is gone. To test for moisture, hold a piece of glass above the slightly open annealer lid or door and see if moisture forms on it. Big molds take a long time to dry. Remember, once a mold is heated above 220° F, it might begin to crack if cooled. The higher the temperature, the more severe the cracks will be. Drying the mold at a low temperature only drives out the mechanical water, that is, the water mixed with the plaster/silica. There is still chemically bonded water in the mold and therefore the mold must be heated slowly to 1250° F (676° C). If you heat the mold too quickly, you may crack the mold.

Some Problems

Q. My Mold sets but is very soft, why?

Ans. Plaster/silica ratio is not accurate. If you do not add enough plaster to the silica, the mold set will be inadequate. To the untrained eye silica looks like plaster. Make sure you use fresh plaster.

Ans. Proper quantity of plaster/silica mixture to water is not correct. If you do not add enough plaster/silica, the mixture will be thin and leave you with a very inadequate set. It will be very "punkie" and not work. When you remove your hand from the mixture while stirring, you should not see the skin on your hand. Use the chart on pg. 83 to avoid any problems

Ans. Student did not pay attention when reading this section or during the teachers dynamic demonstration, and does not know what the hell he or she is doing. Make sure you know the difference between plaster and silica.

Q. I've done everything has been done correctly so why will the mold not set, oh learned one?

Ans. The answer to this problem is usually that the plaster used was old and has taken on water from the atmosphere thus rendering it useless. Always use fresh plaster.

Melt Out

If you have made your model from wax and attempt to do a wax burnout using the standard sculptor's method, you will create serious problems which can adversely affect the mold and possibly destroy your electric annealer. The most effective method is to steam the wax out of the mold. The advantage of steaming out the wax is that the wax will not seep into the mold, which creates a problem when you attempt to do the casting. Steaming also keeps the temperature of the mold below 200° F (93° C). Your mold should be wet when doing a steam-out. If it is dry, the wax will "wick" into the plaster and can create problems when the mold is heated for casting.

Steam-out Methods

One method is to use a pressure cooker with a plastic hose firmly attached to the steam stem on the lid (see below). Put the end of the plastic hose into your mold, and the steam generated will eventually heat the wax and permit it to run out of the mold. This method is usually used when you have a mold with deep crevices such as sculptural pieces and vessel castings. Another method is to use a wallpaper steamer.

For large, open-faced molds or a group of open-faced molds the following method works very well. Take a torch to a 55 gallon drum, cut the bottom third of the drum off or cut it lengthwise. If you cut it lengthwise, you will need to weld the half lid back on. Make sure you weld it so there are no holes, as you will be filling the drum with water. Put a good quantity of water into the drum, and place it on a sturdy steel stand over a good propane stove burner or a natural gas burner. I use a small cast iron stove sold for trailers.

Unlike sculptors that melt out wax in kilns designed for that purpose, the glass caster must melt out the wax using steam. This is because the wax must be removed at a much lower temperature than the sculpture molds designed for bronze casting. If the glass casting mold is taken to a temperature above 220° F (105° C) the mold will begin to crack. The illustrations on this page depict a pressure cooker steam-out and a large water steam-out. The objective is to get the mold as close as possible to the vigorously boiling water and to cover it completely in order to trap the steam. The hot steam will not affect the plaster/silica mold unless it takes an inordinate length of time to effect a steam-out. The hot steam will soften and melt the wax. It is important that the plaster/silica mold be wet prior to the steam out. If it is not wet the melting wax will have a tendency to soak into the porous mold, and the smoking and burning wax can adversely affect the glass casting when brought up to casting temperature. If your mold is dry prior to the steam-out, you can carefully soak it in cool water to re-wet it. If you do the steam-out correctly, the mold should look nice and clean. You may see a hint of wax residue on the mold surface, but that should not have any effect on the casting. When done, put your mold in a warm place to dry. Dry molds tend to crack less when fired.

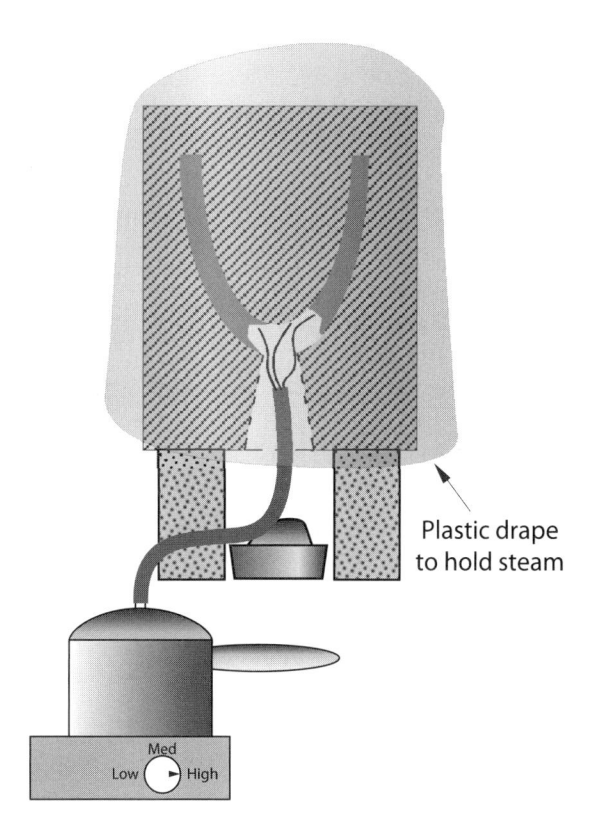

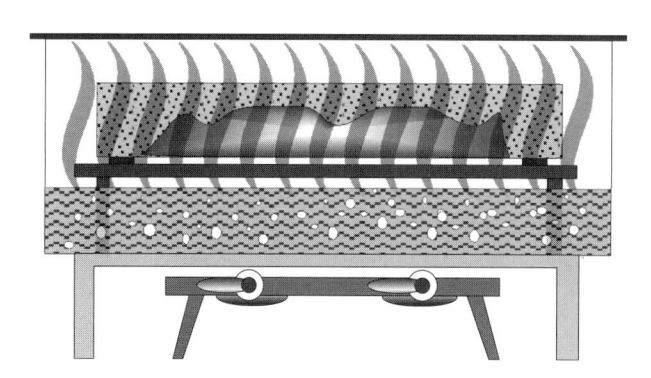

Plastic drape to hold steam

Making a Mold

These are the steps to make a simple, open-faced mold for casting. In this case, the model is made from clay.

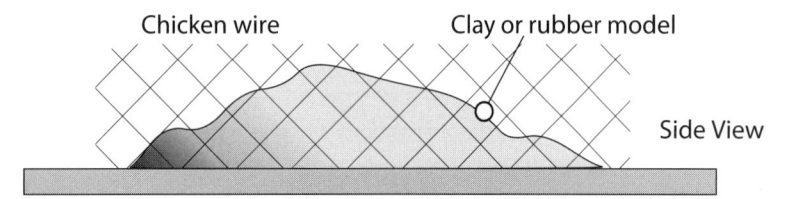

Chicken wire — Clay or rubber model

Side View

shellacked plywood, marble, glass, or Formica

Soda/lime glass does not make a very good casting glass. It usually devitrifies at casting temperature. Bullseye, Uroboros, Schott, and Gaffer are very good casting glasses.

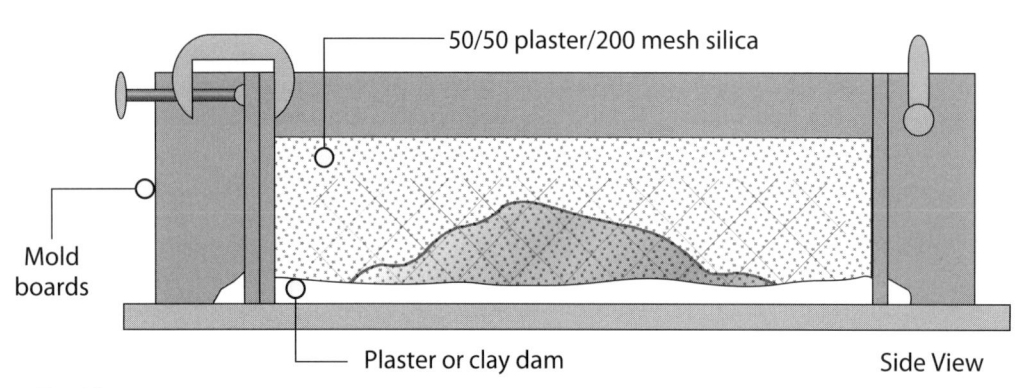

50/50 plaster/200 mesh silica

Mold boards

Plaster or clay dam

Side View

Top View

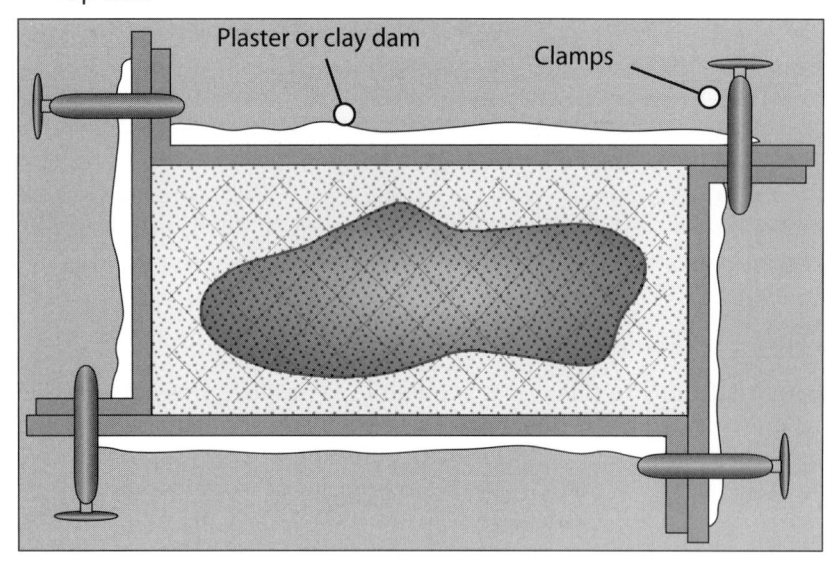

Plaster or clay dam

Clamps

Remove clay and clean clay residue from mold with a soft brush. Place mold in oven on a bed of clean sand and level. Place correct amount of casting glass in mold. *See formula for calculating glass quantity on page 82.

Don't give up if things don't work the first time. It takes many years to master the art of casting. Keep good notes and pay attention to what you're doing.

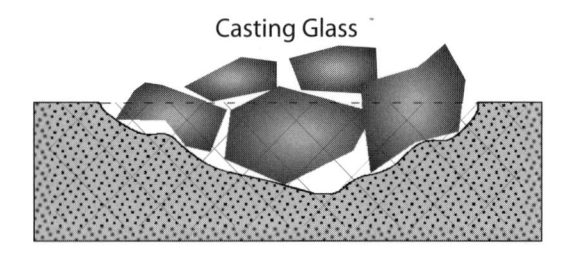

Casting Glass

Side view after casting

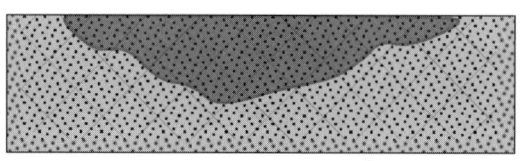

66   Glass Notes

Libensky/Brychtova Casting Technique

This section was written in 1986 and was a handout for a class that Stanislav Libensky and his wife Jaroslava Brychtova taught at Pilchuck. For the most part, I have kept it as written but have made some relevant changes noted in *italics*. It should also be noted that when this was written, quality casting glass was not available in the U.S. This is not true now as one can obtain excellent casting glass from Schott, Bullseye, Uroboros and Gaffer. The Gaffer casting glass comes closest to the quality of the Czech material. It should finally be noted that lead laws have been instituted throughout the world and what was once readily available in the Czech Republic is now very difficult to obtain. Sadly, Prof. Libensky passed away in 2002, but his contributions to the world of art live on. He is missed by all who knew and loved him.

My name is Jaroslav Zahradnik. I am living in The Czech Republic in a place called Zelezny Brod. A chemistry graduate from the Prague University, I come from a glass making family and the old glass making town of Zelezny Brod. I have developed professional interest and ability in the technical execution of the works of art of my parents, Stanislav Libensky and Jaroslava Brychtova. To be able to produce the glass casting ourselves, we constructed an architectural glass maker's studio at Zelezny Brod. The work was started in 1978, and successive extensions and additions to the studio included several glass ovens; various kinds of hot glass working equipment followed in due course. In 1983 we completed the construction of a large glass oven with inside dimensions of 6' 3" long x 3' wide x 28" high (1.9 meters long x 1 meter wide x .75 meters high). It is designed for casting large glass sculptures. The particular forming and melting techniques used to produce the glass sculptures were developed by my parents between 1955 and 1970. Designed originally for the production of architectural glass reliefs, the techniques were gradually adapted to the production of other glass objects as well. By this method, lump glass is heated up to the flow point directly in the mold of special design and, after cooling, the glass castings are worked mechanically by grinding and polishing.

Stanislav Libensky in his office at the Academy of Applied Art in Prague, circa 1991

In this way it is possible to produce glass castings of large dimensions and sophisticated shapes, the only limiting factors being the mold shape, weight, and the availability of the technical accessories needed.

Their idea is based on the principal characteristics of glass that, as a product of a melting process, will eventually solidify into a solid material without crystallization. Heating up to the flow point followed by controlled cooling makes the glass adopt the shape of the mold without changing its optical properties, and the casting obtained can be finished as may be required. The mechanical properties of the casting, however, are determined by the cooling procedure used.

The most suitable glass, because it is readily available in The Czech Republic, appears to be full lead crystal owing to the properties listed below:

The higher lead content gives the glass a high specific weight and increases both the index of refraction and the scattering of light. A chromatic decomposition of the white light takes place.

The full lead glass has a low viscosity which improves its binding power (no risk of cord formation) as well as its flow in properties in more sophisticated molds.

The low flow point is of great advantage with composition plaster molds and ovens with normal lining and electric heating elements.

The full lead glass is less prone to crystallization during the melting and cooling processes.

The full lead crystals exhibit a permanent stable surface (no fogging) and a very good resistance to atmospheric humidity.

The negative properties of full lead crystal include: lower mechanical strength, fragility, lower scratch resistance, lower modulus of elasticity, higher specific weight, and higher price. The full lead crystal used at present contains about 40% PbO.

Author's note: Not all lead crystals will suffice as a quality casting glass as their formulations might contain other materials that encourage de-vitrification within the casting range. There are two lead casting glasses I know of that are available to the studio artist: Schott Crystal and Gaffer casting glass. The Gaffer is available in many colors. It is not necessary for casting glass to be a "lead crystal" in order to cast well. Bullseye and Uroboros casting glasses work extremely well and are available in colors. Neither of these two types of casting glass contains lead. See Vendors section at the back of the book to find out where to purchase these glasses.

The preparation of the molds

The original model usually made of clay or other material is used as a positive. From this positive, a plaster negative is created. All undercuts are taken into consideration which may result in a piece mold. If it is a piece mold, then a mold separator must me used between each section. The model is removed from the final mold. The mold is then coated with two to three coats of shellac. After that dries, we coat the surface with a solution of 1 part kerosene to 1 part beeswax heated in a double boiler.

From this mold a new plaster positive is made. The surface of this positive is worked to meet the exact specifications of the final sculpture. A new "mother" mold is fabricated in a fashion similar to what has been described in the previous paragraph from this negative mold.

The master positive is then made of silicone rubber. The final negative mold for melting is made of a mixture of Dental plaster and fine 200 mesh silica, in a weight ratio of 1 part Czech dental plaster to 2 parts silica.

Author's note: American dental plaster is somewhat different than Czech dental plaster, and as a result, the weight ratios change to 1 part American dental plaster to 1.5 parts silica. This compound satisfies the requirements of expansibility, heat resistance, and mechanical strength.

The factors that limit the shape of the mold include: the melting technique, the elasticity of the rubber or gelatin positive, and the mechanical strength of the mold material. Before the start of the melting process, the mold should be allowed to dry slowly; this has an essential effect on the mold strength and surface hardness. Allowing the mold to totally air dry as opposed to forced kiln drying does increase the physical mold strength. As the bound water (chemical water) is liberated from the mold material at temperatures above 266° F (130° C), an adequate lag should be used when increasing the temperature in the casting oven. Increasing the temperature at too fast a rate will result in large cracks.

Melting and cooling the glass

For melting we use normal ovens with a refractory fire clay lining. The furnaces are heated electrically. The heating elements are placed in channels provided in the lining of the furnace walls, roof, and bottom. The furnace bottom is covered with slabs of silicon carbide. A rugged, strong furnace structure is of prime importance to allow easy and safe handling of the heavy molds inside the furnace jacket. It is important that a vent hole be provided in the furnace roof and that the vents in the lower part of the door can be opened, if necessary. As water is liberated from the plaster molds during the heating period, it is important to completely remove the water vapors from the furnace before the flow point of the glass is attained, i.e., before the glass is liquefied.

As the glass is heated up in the mold, the glass viscosity decreases at about 1475° F (800° C) and the glass becomes quite liquid, filling in the mold relief. After a slight temperature increase, the melting process is complete.

Author's note: It is not recommended that the casting temperature exceed 1550° F (843° C) as the mold will begin to deteriorate at a rapid rate thus causing large cracks.

During this final melting phase, air bubbles are liberated from the glass. In addition, cords caused by bonding of different glass lumps as well as surface unevenness of the glass lumps and the surface structure are partially removed. The final melting time is determined by the glass thickness, the mold division, and the immediate condition of the plaster mold; the latter may be affected by the glass weight, the unevenness in the mold, or the heat stress. The final melting process is performed at a temperature of 1544° F (840°C) for a period of approximately 3 hours.

When the melting process has been completed, the temperature of the molten glass should be lowered to 1112° F (600° C) to avoid possible devitrification, which usually takes place at temperatures around 1290° F (700° C). With the furnace door open, the aeration is continued for about 1 hour. At the temperature level of 1110° F (600° C), the glass viscosity is increased again so that shape changes due to mold deterioration can no longer occur. Subsequently, the temperature continues to spontaneously decrease to the upper cooling temperature level beyond which the actual cooling process begins.

Author's note: The annealing and other temperature related information stated in this section is for the high lead Czech casting glass and not any other glass.

The cooling process within the transformation temperature range of the glass is a determining factor of the mechanical properties of the glass casting. Inadequate cooling within the transformation range is responsible for the generation of permanent internal stress in the glass, eventually causing the glass casting to crack when in the furnace or during the mechanical working. The actual annealing, at which the permanent stress is removed from the glass, takes place between the upper cooling temperature, i.e. the annealing point, and the lower cooling temperature, i.e., the strain point. The respective temperatures and the annealing rate within the annealing interval are specified by the glass producer. It is easy to establish the high end annealing temperature, but in order to establish the strain point, you must send a glass sample to a testing lab. The name and address of that lab is found on page 54.

Author's note: the above information is an excellent description of what annealing and cooling is all about.

For the melt, we use the annealing point 788° F (420° C) and a strain point of 680° F (360° C). The annealing rate is determined especially by the thickness of the glass casting, its shape, and the amount of stress required in the cooled casting. For instance, with a casting 6" (15 cm) thick, I would use an annealing rate expressed in a temperature drop of 1° C/hr., whereas with a casting 2". (5 cm) thick, the rate would be in the order of 3° C/hr . Below the strain point, it is important to maintain the strain point cooling rate which is approximately 2 to 3 times higher than that used within the annealing period. This is important in order to avoid the admissible transition stress in the glass during the cooling of the casting.

Author's note: The Centigrade degree is a longer temperature interval than the Fahrenheit degree in the ratio of 9:5. The point is that, if you program computers to regulate an oven in degrees per hour, a problem can ensue when converting degrees per hour either from or to centigrade. Most digital controllers used in the States are programmed to increase or decrease temperature as blocks of time or hours per degree(s), commonly referred to as "set points". The Libensky annealing chart on page 53 is an example of annealing and cooling using "set points" and "soaks." Using this system makes translating annealing charts to Centigrade or Fahrenheit relatively easy. Regardless of what system you choose, it still translates to degrees per hour.

The admissible stress in a glass casting is usually quoted in terms of 1/20 of the average glass strength. The total stress is composed of three components: the transition stress, the permanent stress, and the stress in the in-homogeneities of the glass. The transient stress is generated at heat drops or when the glass is exposed to mechanical stresses, and it vanishes as soon as the cause is removed. Permanent stress is generated within the transformation temperature range during annealing. Particularly undesirable is the stress in the glass in-homogeneities. The so–called cords are produced in places where two different glass kinds have been fused (even in a glass of one production batch and in-homogeneous composition may be observed), in the vicinity of mechanical impurities present in the glass, and in the cuts of the mold relief. Stress in the cords is most frequently responsible for cracks generated in the casting during the final cooling phase.

Stress in the glass can be measured as long as there is stress present in the glass. The latter behaves as an optically in-homogeneous matter. Due to interference, polarized light passing through glass is changed from white light into the so–called interference colors; the latter can be used to measure and estimate the amount of stress present in the glass. For a proper cooling of glass castings, we propose a path difference not to exceed 100 nm/cm. To estimate the stress in the glass in large castings after melting, two polarizing filters will do; the total stress can be estimated by the interference colors.

Cold working of glass castings

The first operation is a rough–grinding operation in which loose or bound abrasive grain size 60 to 120 is used. We use a silicon carbide abrasive and a grinding machine with a cast iron grinding wheel, or we do

Temperature Conversions

F = (C x 1.8) + 32
C = (F − 32) ÷ 1.8

the job by hand using a cast iron or glass plate and/or some shaping tools. Synthetic diamond abrasives could also be used for that purpose, but they are too expensive for rough grinding. The grinding operation produces a disturbed glass layer which is deeper than the surface relief layer after the application of abrasive. It is the task of the next operation to grind off this under-surface layer. It is, therefore, important to choose a proper abrasive grain size to obtain the required amount of glass to be ground off.

For smooth grinding, we use abrasive with a grain size of 400 to 600 in the form of loose abrasive, abrasive paper, or synthetic discs, respectively. The abrasive materials include silicon carbide, synthetic corundum, or synthetic diamond powder. To speed up the work we use a pneumatic grinding machine with a cast–iron grinding wheel, a rubber disc with an abrasive paper glued to it, or a special diamond tool. The individual facets of the sculpture have to be smoothed by hand with specially adapted glass or metal tools; the rounded shapes may be smoothed with abrasive paper on a soft pad. The smoothing operation is necessary to obtain a perfect surface finish of the sculpture before polishing. It is extremely laborious to remove even small imperfections on the surface by polishing.

> The total stress is composed of three components: the transition stress, the permanent stress, and the stress in the in-homogeneities of the glass.

For polishing, we usually use felt discs that are fixed to a grinder with a flexible shaft. The polishing materials are pumice and water. When polishing, the glass surface heats up and an inadequate quantity of the polishing material as well as water may cause excessive overheating and cracking of the glass, especially in the vicinity of the cords in in-homogeneous glass. An improper polishing of a poorly smoothed glass surface can also cause glass cracking. To complete the surface polish we use a mixture of the polishing material cerium oxide and water. This compound is applied to felt discs fixed to either a flexible shaft or and electric drill.

Jaroslav Zahradnik
Czechoslovakia, 1986 (The Czech Republic)

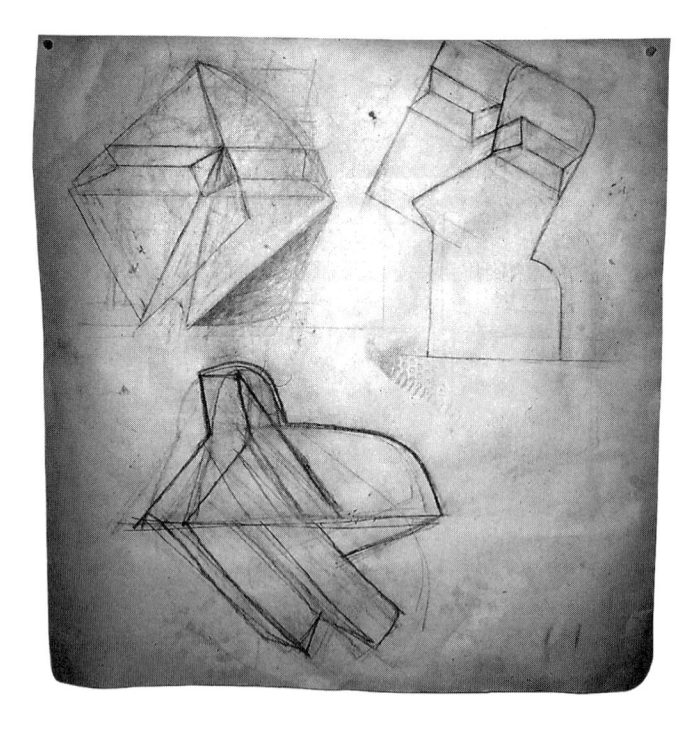

Libensky Drawing, 1987

Libensky/Brychtova Studio

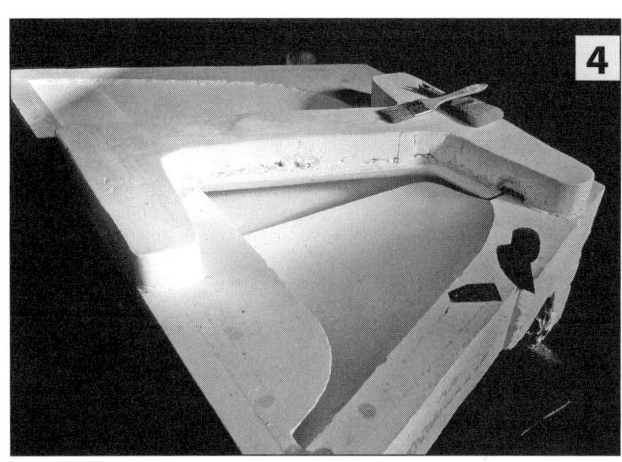

The Libensky–Brychtova studio : #1. Stanislav & Jaroslava in their basement studio. #2. Shows a clay model sculpted by Jaroslava from Stanislav's drawings. #3 Shows small models of work. #4 Shows a mold in detail. #5 Shows a few of their castings, circa the late 80's. #6 A casting on display at the Heller Gallery in NY, but interestingly this casting is also displayed at their studio in Zelezny Brod in a vertical position.

Libensky/Brychtova Casting Technique
Pilchuck 1986

Introduction

This section contains the notes as written by Ana Thiel at Pilchuck during a Libensky/Brychtova session and are included in this book with the permission of Ana and the Libensky's. My personal feeling is that Prof. Libensky's philosophy about the making of art is insightful and can be easily understood by all. His outline below on the Importance of Drawing and Composition is brilliant. His ideas are direct, clear, and fundamental to how one translates nature to creation.

If you read this chapter carefully, you will get some excellent tips on casting as well as an overview of Libensky's philosophy.

Presentation

The three principles of their work evolve first from drawing, then from transposing the drawings into clay models, and then finally transposing them to glass. Drawing is the single most important aspect of this design philosophy.

Overview

Importance of drawing, composition, and their relationship to glass.
Three-dimensional composition of drawing into clay:
- For transposition into glass.
- For problem solving in composition using clay or other materials.

Basic practice in mold-making for melting technique.
Melting glass in the mold and the relative time span used in melting and annealing the glass.
Glass cutting and its relationship to the final composition.

Importance of Drawing, Composition, and their Relationship to Glass

It is highly recommended to draw from nature in a large and a small scale. In a large scale, such as a landscape, one should take care to emphasize the different visual planes such as foreground and background.

In a small scale, we truly learn to see what is there; the play of volume and intersection, such as a branch intersecting a tree trunk, becomes the focus of interest. The human body is a figure of known proportions; for that reason, drawing it helps to train the eye and hand in the relationship of parts to the whole.

These drawings and studies can then be translated into reliefs and shapes in a more abstract form that still retain the original meaning and that remain recognizable.

Geometric volumes can also be studied by drawing, intersecting, cutting, or adding to them.

The key is to remember and discover simplicity in the lines and in the overall composition.

When a design has been selected, the drawing should be made to scale, especially when the piece will fit in a given architectural place or when it is formed of various parts.

The Libensky/Brychtova basement studio for painting and drawing. In the background are Stanislav's gouache paintings. Eventually Jaroslava will translate those paintings into clay models. One of those models can be seen in photo #2 and #3 on the previous page.

Clay Positive

For this example, we will use water-based clay to make our model.

On a flat waterproof surface build the model. If you're going to polish the surface of the finished casting make sure the clay positive is smooth. The better the quality of finish at this stage, the less work in subsequent stages.

Making the Mold Direct Negative

A mold for casting glass can be made directly from the clay model as shown on pg. 77, fig. 4 and 5. If you're going to cast more than one of the same model I recommend making a rubber positive from a plaster mold of the original clay model. Once a rubber positive is created you can make an edition.

To cast your mold, a box is needed to contain the plaster/silica while it sets. To build one that will accommodate different mold sizes, a set of boards can be adapted with "L" shaped metal angles, (fig. 1 pg. 76). For smaller pieces, the same principle can be adopted, but instead of boards one uses "L" shaped aluminum sheet ⅛" thick (fig. 3 pg. 77). These are clamped together with "C" clamps. The boards can then slide to make smaller or larger molds and can be reused. They are built around the positive with at least a 1 ½" space between it and the sides of the box (more if the piece is big).

The table where the mold will be cast should be level; it can have a marble top or be made of wood with a sheet of glass on it. The glass sheet should be of sufficient thickness to support the weight placed on it.

The clay positive is placed on the table and the boards clamped.

To seal the seams of the box, a small amount of plaster is mixed. Fill a plastic container less than half way with cool water; then add the plaster, sprinkling it until a plaster "island" is formed. Then mix it taking care to eliminate all lumps.

When the mixture starts to feel a little thicker, seal the edges by spooning it between the outer edge of the boards, the table, and between the corners formed by the boards (fig. 2 pg. 76). *Author's note: In most cases, pressing clay firmly around the boards will suffice.*

Cover the inside of the boards and bottom with mold separator using a brush.

*To make the mold, a mixture of dental plaster and silica flour is used. They are mixed dry in a proportion of 2 parts silica flour and 1 part dental plaster. If the mold is small, it is 1½ parts silica flour to 1 part dental plaster. In a plastic bucket, pour water, visually calculating ¾ the volume of the mold.

Author's Note: If you use U.S. dental plaster, use 1½ parts dental plaster to 1 part silica.

Add the dry mixture by cupfuls, sprinkling it on the surface of the water. Again, when a dry island forms and stays on the surface, start mixing. Mixing can be done by hand or by using a paint mixer attached to a drill and mixing it, making sure to move it up and down in the bucket as it rotates (fig. 11, pg. 79).

Author's Note: Before mixing, allow the plaster/silica mixture to hydrate for about 2 minutes. The drill method accelerates the time it takes for the mixture to set. When the mixture is uniform, place a plastic bucket close to the box and, with the hand, sprinkle the liquid on the positive, especially in edges or deep indentations, so that air bubbles will not get trapped. Then slowly pour the rest of the mixture into the box and into a corner, not on the positive, until it is completely covered. You should pour 1½" to 2" above the highest point. If there was not enough material to cover the model on the first pour, mix more and pour immediately. If plaster oozes out of the seams, immediately press clay into the place where the leak is occurring.

When the plaster has set for about ½ hour, open the box and taper all edges. If the upper surface is uneven, level it with a flat board by scraping the whole surface.

Take the clay out of the mold with care so as not to scrape its surface.

Let the mold air–dry for about 12 days. If you need it before then, it can be dried in an open kiln at about 220° F (104° C).

Casting The Glass

To calculate the quantity of glass to be cast, the specific gravity of the glass is needed. The manufacturer should be able to provide that information. If it is not available, you can determine the specific gravity of any glass using the following method.

Archimedes Lives

Make a sample of your casting glass about 3" long and about ¾" thick. Weigh the sample on an accurate gram scale and write its weight down to 2 decimal points.

A milliliter column is filled halfway with water. Make sure you fill to an exact line.

The glass sample is immersed in the water. Lower it carefully into the column. Make sure the sample is covered completely.

Record the amount of water displaced by the glass sample. For example, if you filled the column with 150 milliliters of water and the column of water rises to 183.2 milliliters after immersing the sample, then the displacement was 33.2 milliliters.

If your glass sample weighs 83 grams, do the following calculation: divide 83 grams by 33.2 milliliters. The answer is the specific gravity or 2.50.

The other measurement needed is the actual volume of the object to be cast.

Using a container that measures in liters, fill the mold with rice. Count how many liters it takes to fill the mold. Remember, accuracy counts.

Say that it takes 2.2 liters of rice to fill the mold. This volume is multiplied by the specific gravity. Our answer is 5.5 kilos

This is the amount of glass needed to fill the mold after it melts. Expressed in pounds, the answer would be: 12.13 lbs. The metric system is so much easier than the U.S. system of weights and measures.

$$\frac{83 \text{ gms. (weight of glass sample)}}{33.2 \text{ ml (water displacement)}} = 2.50 \text{ (specific gravity)}$$

2.2046 is the number of pounds in a kilo.

$$2.2 \times 2.50 = 5.50 \text{ kg. of glass}$$

$$2.2046 \times 5.50 = 12.13 \text{ lbs.}$$

Preparing the Glass

The glass may come in rods, chunks, or other shapes. It needs to be cut into pieces that will fit into the mold. Breaking the glass requires special protection. A plastic face shield is needed, as are heavy gloves. To cut big chunks or rods, the back of a mason's hammer is used. For smaller pieces, the chunk can be held in the gloved hand and cut with the same hammer.

The pieces are then weighed and thoroughly washed in soap and water.

Author's note: When putting the glass into the mold, it will seem that you are putting more glass into the mold than it will hold when the glass is melted. If you have done all your calculations correctly, the mold will fill exactly to the lip. Trust me, this calculation really works. I have used it many times and it has <u>never</u> failed me.

Indirect Negative, Plaster Intermediate

A plaster mold can be made from the clay positive the same way that the dental plaster-silica flour mold is cast. Instead of using these ingredients, however, only normal casting plaster is mixed with the water. Once the mold sets and the clay is out, the surface of the negative is covered with three coats of 6 lb. shellac. When the shellac dries, a mold release is brushed on the whole surface.

Bullseye glass has a specific gravity of 2.50

Author's note: The mold release is composed of 2 parts kerosene to 1 part Vaseline. Melt the Vaseline carefully in pot. When melted, remove from heat and add the Kerosene and stir.

The negative is then placed on the glass or marble table. The boards are placed snugly around it and sealed with plaster. A mixture of casting plaster is then poured into the mold to make the negative.

To open the mold, the union is cleaned with a spatula, the mold is placed vertically, and a spatula wedged in the union is gently tapped with a piece of wood or hammer.

All sides are so tapped, and then the mold is slowly opened. Both of these plaster molds can be worked on to correct surfaces or create textures before the final mold is made.

The surface is covered with shellac followed by mold separator after the shellac dries.
A dental plaster and silica flour mold is then made as in the direct negative method.

This plaster intermediate is useful when the piece has <u>no undercuts.</u>

Wax Intermediate

This method is recommended for pieces that have undercuts.

The clay positive is placed on the casting table, and the divisions for a two or three part mold are designated.

With tin snips, cut squares of a thin metal sheet (shims) such as flashing.

Press these squares into the clay where the mold division is to occur. Some of these may be bent to mark the proper fit of the two mold parts (fig. 4, pg. 77).

Prepare a mixture of casting plaster. While it is still liquid, cover one half of the positive up to the division; this will form a thin layer directly on the positive. Let the rest of the plaster set until it can be built up on top of the thin layer. With the aid of a spatula, the thick layer can be built from the bottom up (fig. 5, pg. 77).

Once this half is set, take the metal squares off the positive. Brush mold separator on that area which will become the union of the two mold parts (fig. 6a, pg. 78).

The second half of the positive is then covered with plaster in the same way that the first one was done.

Author's note: It is a good idea to put a dark dye into the face coat. This will act as an indicator for the seam line. It is not necessary to put indicator into the successive layers of plaster.

When the plaster sets, the top can be scraped to give the mold a flat bottom.

Take the clay out of the mold, and clean the mold with water and a soft brush.

The two halves are then put together with thick

rubber bands or wires (fig. 7, pg. 78).

Use sculptors micro-crystalline wax. Gently warm it in a container.

Author's note: For small quantities of wax, an electric deep-fat fryer works very well as you can control the heat. Once melted, wait until a thin film starts to form on the surface, and then pour it into the mold. Make sure the mold is wet before pouring the wax in. If it is not wet the wax will stick to the plaster (Fig. 7, pg. 78). If you pour the wax too hot, the shrinkage may cause the wax to crack upon cooling.

This wax positive can be worked on, smoothing the surface with a warm knife or clay tools. The positive is then used to make the final plaster/silica mold.

With clay, a reservoir can be added to the wax, uniting the clay and wax with copper wire (Fig. 8, pg. 78). A one-piece mold is made of the wax and clay reservoir. The clay is removed, and the wax is then steamed away by placing the mold upside down on bricks with a pan underneath to receive the melting wax (see pg. 65).

The Kiln

The floor and sides of the kiln must be protected in case a mold accidentally breaks and glass leaks out. The floor can be covered with ceramic kiln shelves and some sand.

The sides are protected by placing a steel band around the mold or in the inner cavity of the kiln.

A piece of sheet steel is bent (approximately 16 gauge) into a square or rectangle and the edge welded. This band is placed in the kiln, and the mold is placed within it. The mold must be level; if it isn't, move the mold around on the sand until it is. Use a bubble level.

Put refractory bricks around the mold to hold it together and then fill in with sand. If there is no space for bricks between the mold and the steel lining, just fill it in with sand (see pg. 79).

The kiln and the mold must then be vacuumed to eliminate dust and particles that will adhere to the glass when it is cast. After a thorough vacuuming, the glass pieces are placed in the mold.

Stanislav Libensky (The Professor)

Mold Box

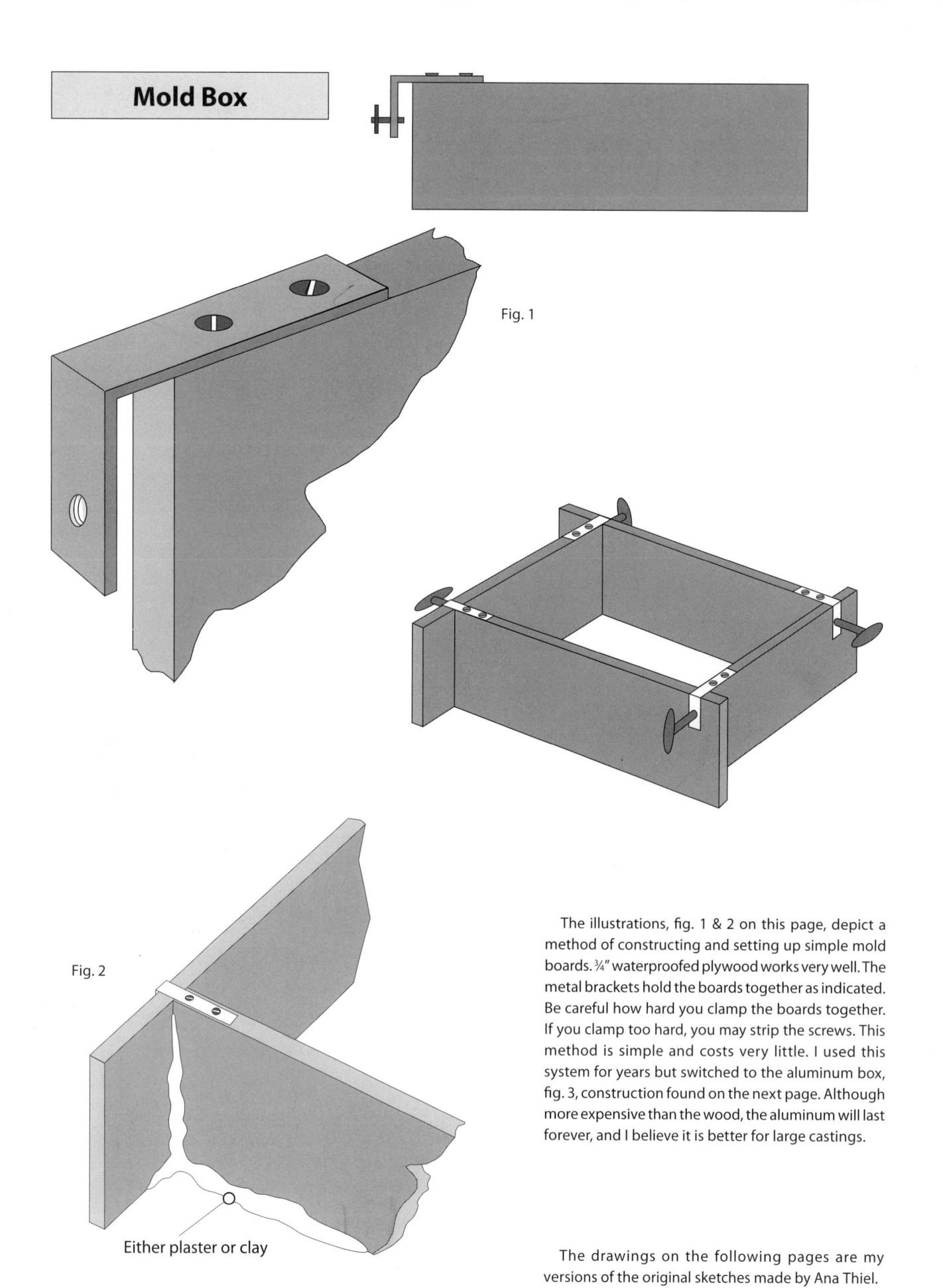

Fig. 1

Fig. 2

Either plaster or clay

The illustrations, fig. 1 & 2 on this page, depict a method of constructing and setting up simple mold boards. ¾" waterproofed plywood works very well. The metal brackets hold the boards together as indicated. Be careful how hard you clamp the boards together. If you clamp too hard, you may strip the screws. This method is simple and costs very little. I used this system for years but switched to the aluminum box, fig. 3, construction found on the next page. Although more expensive than the wood, the aluminum will last forever, and I believe it is better for large castings.

The drawings on the following pages are my versions of the original sketches made by Ana Thiel.

76 Glass Notes

Fig. 3

Photo of aluminum mold boards

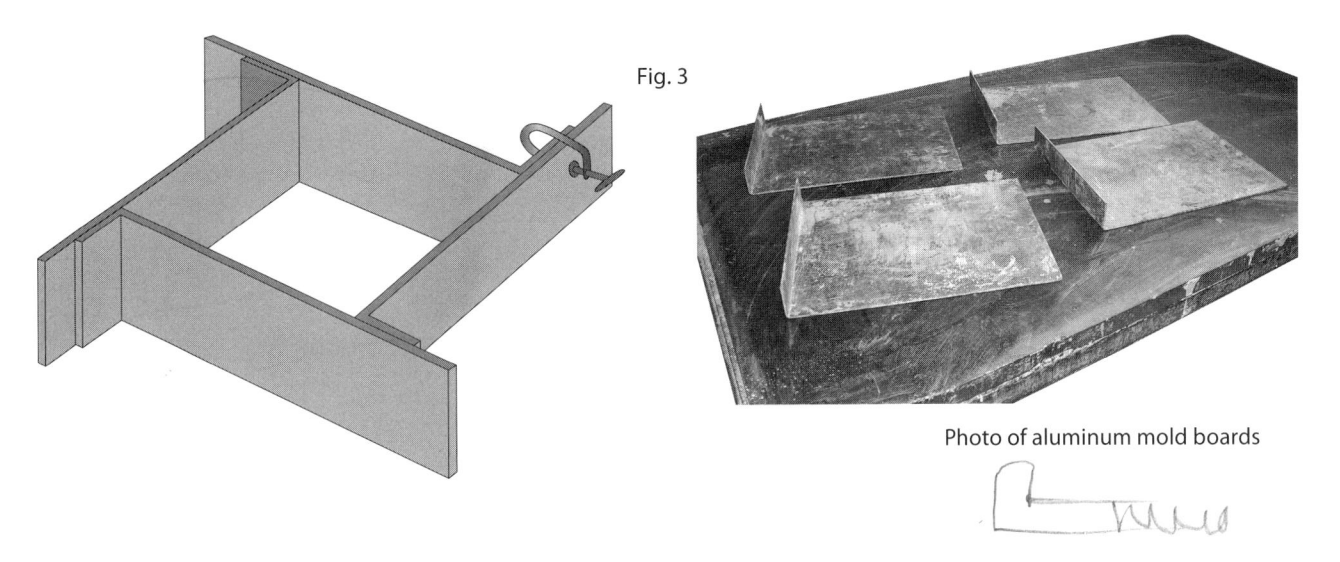

This is an aluminum mold box. The sides of this box are constructed from $1/8$" aluminum. The ends are bent at a 90° angle. To put the box together, merely "C" clamp all four corners as indicated. Make sure you have a machine shop put the bends in the aluminum. It is important that the bend be 90°. When making the mold, seal the bottom to the table with plaster or clay.

How to make a wax positive

Figs. 4, 5, 6, 6a, and 7 depict the making of a wax positive from the clay model. Fig. 4 depicts the clay model and the shims inserted. The shims divide the model in half. It is necessary to divide the model in half in order to facilitate the removal of the wax later in the process. Figure 5 depicts one half of the plaster mold. After making the first half, remove the shims and apply a good mold separator to the plaster. Make the second half (fig. 6). Don't try to mix all the plaster at once but instead build it in layers. It is also a good idea when doing the second half to add a water soluble dye to the first coat. This will indicate where the seam is. Separating the two halves is much easier if you know where the seam is. Iron Oxide or dark RIT fabric dye make good indicators.

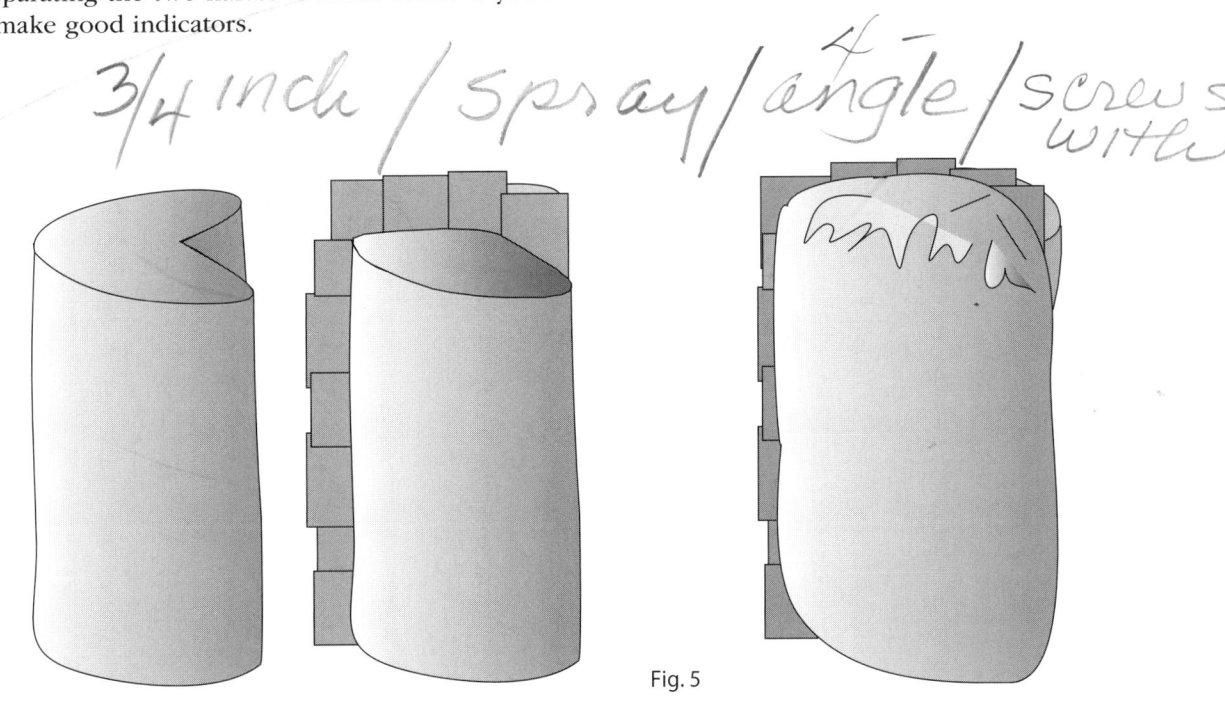

Fig. 4

Fig. 5

Glass Notes 77

Fig. 6 depicts the two halves of the mold separated and ready for removal of the clay model. After removing the clay, clean the mold off any residual clay. Put the mold back together and wire it together tightly. Before pouring the wax (fig. 7), make sure the plaster is good and wet. If you pour wax into a dry plaster mold, it will never come apart. Allow the hot wax to sit in the mold until the walls are about ¼" thick. Pour the rest of the wax out. Allow the mold to cool. You can put it in cold water to speed the process.

Remove the wax from the plaster mold. Construct a clay reservoir as indicated in figure 8. Place the wax model on top of the clay. Make sure you hold the wax model down when pouring the plaster/flint mixture; otherwise it will float. The reservoir should be at least double the volume of your model.

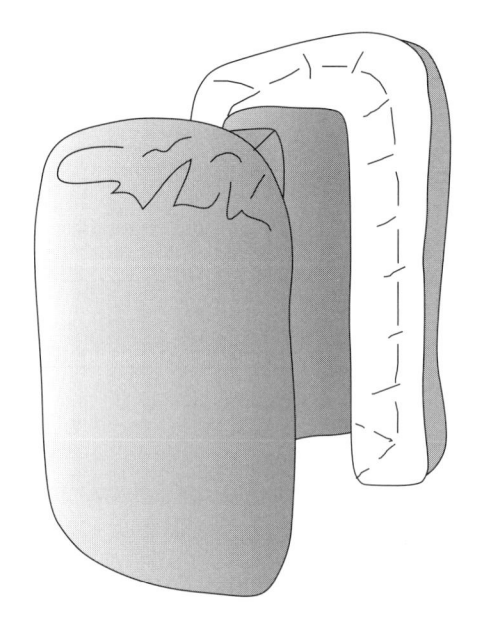

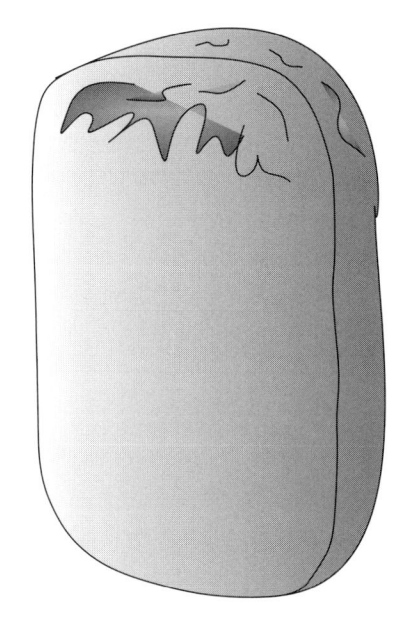

Fig. 6

Fig. 6a

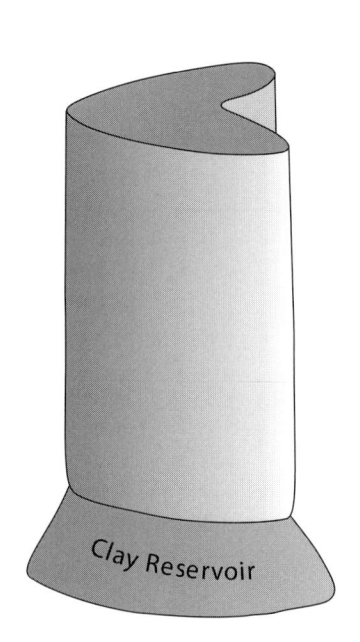

Fig. 7

Fig. 8

Making a Plaster Positive

Making a Plaster of Paris positive of your original clay is easy once you've constructed your two-piece mold. In this case, you pour plaster into the mold instead of wax. Make sure you use a good mold release on the surface of your mold to ensure that you will be able to remove the plaster model. It is also important to make sure that you have no undercuts. If you do, it will be impossible to remove the plaster model. You may wish to make a plaster model in order to work the surface of the sculpture. The Libensky studio uses this method exclusively in order to work and smooth the surfaces of their sculptures. They then construct a master plaster piece mold from this reworked plaster master. From this master they then make either a rubber positive or one from gelatin. The actual mold to be cast into is cast around either the rubber or the gelatin. The complexity of some of their pieces makes necessary the construction of piece molds. This is done in order to facilitate the removal of the rubber master. After removing the rubber or gelatin model, the mold is pinned back together.

Fig. 11 depicts mixing a large quantity of plaster using a power mixer. Don't use this method for quantities under 2 gallons. Fig. 12 shows leveling the plaster after filling the mold.

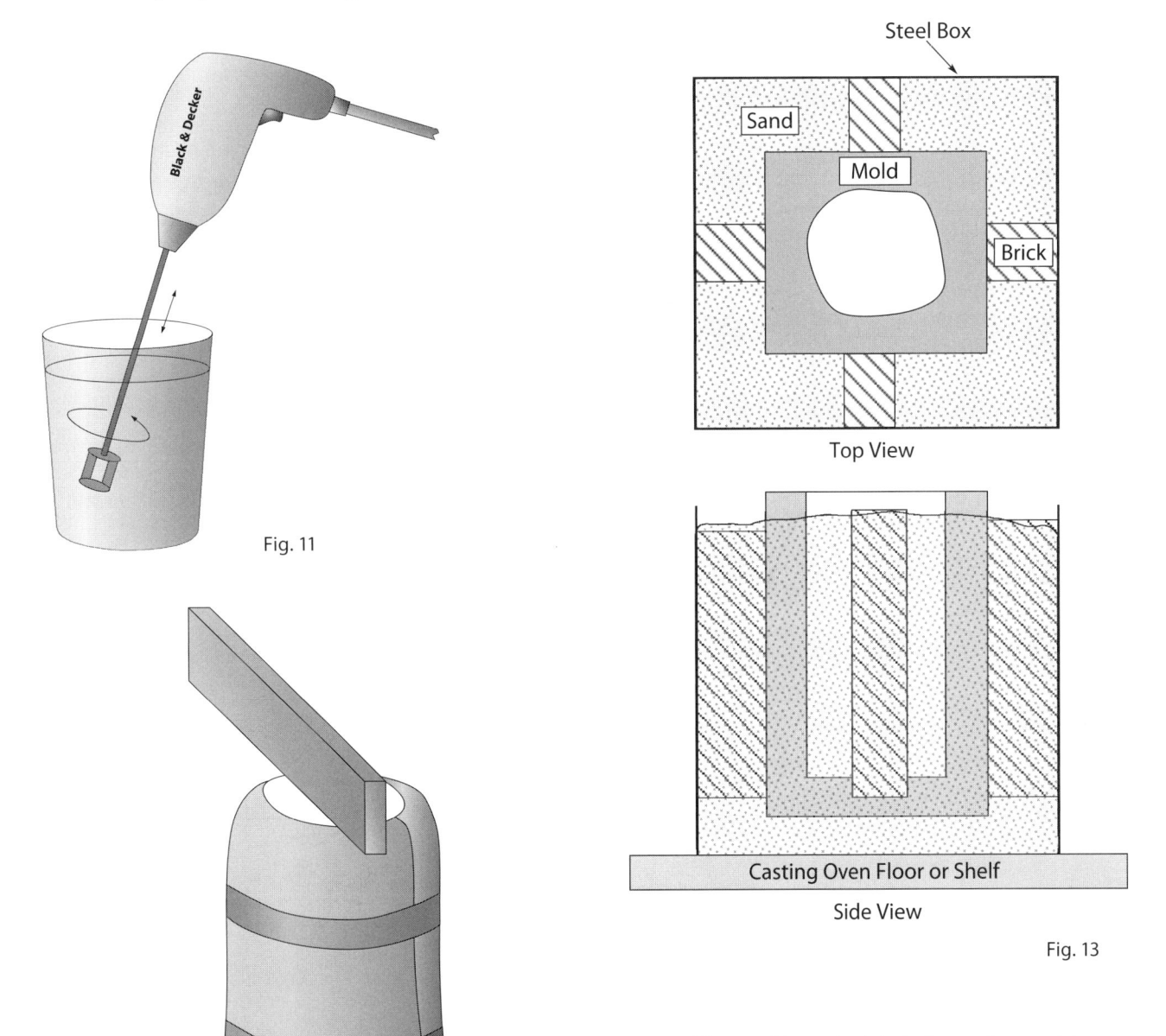

Fig. 11

Fig. 12

Fig. 13

The steel box, depicted above, does not have a bottom. It only has 4 sides. Do not construct the box from anything less than 16 gauge. Cover the top of the mold when placing the sand in the box.

Glass Notes 79

The Glass and Annealers

The Casting Glass

It is no longer difficult to find a good "off the shelf" casting glass in this country. The kinds of casting glass I'm referring to are those glasses that do not devitrify at casting temperatures. Most soda-lime glasses tend to devitrify as do some lead glasses. Just because a glass has lead in it does not mean it is suitable for casting. The companies that are producing excellent casting glasses are Bullseye, Uroboros, Gaffer, and Schott. Ordering information for these companies can be found in the vendors section at the back of this book.

Casting Ovens for Annealing

The best ovens for casting that I have found are ovens with elements in the floor as well as in the walls and crown. It is very important not to under power a casting oven. The more mass you put into an oven, the more energy it needs to attain and maintain casting temperature. In this case, mass refers to the materials of which your oven is constructed. One must also factor in the size of the molds you're casting into as well as the quantities of glass that you're casting. If your oven barely reaches casting temperature empty, it won't reach temperature when full.

It is important to build the casting oven as tight as possible to avoid drafts and thermal gradients. You may wish to put some vent holes in the back wall of your casting oven. The holes should be at the top just under the crown. Vents will permit steam to escape from the oven when heating and drying your molds. The placement of the electric elements will affect how even your heat is. Poor element placement will cause thermal gradation in your oven which in turn will cause uneven casting temperatures and very poor annealing characteristics.

Author's Note: A good rule of thumb for calculating the energy requirements for a casting oven with good insulation is to have 1000 – 1200 watts per cu. ft. To calculate the amperage, use Ohms law: Volts X Amps = watts. If you have calculated the watts, then divide the volts into the watts to determine amps.

Conclusion

There are many variations of mold formula and casting processes. Keep careful notes of what you do and the results. Try to analyze your mistakes so you don't repeat them. If you understand basic casting principles, you will have a greater chance at success. Look at historical as well as contemporary examples of castings to get an idea of their potential.

Sean Mercer's Skamol insulated top loading oven

Czech Casting Oven

Casting Calculations and Other Useful Information

When fabricating molds, it is helpful to calculate how much investment you will need in order to minimize waste. To accomplish this task, one must calculate the volume of the entire mold as well as the volume of the model being cast. Once you have this information, subtract the volume of the model being invested from the total volume of the mold. The mold is the plaster/silica mold.

Usually when fabricating a mold, you will pour into a regular geometric form of either a cylinder, rectangle, or square. To calculate these volumes, refer to the formulas below.

Converting cubic inches to cubic feet is very simple. Use the following formula to convert.
Cubic Feet = cubic inches ÷ 1728 (1728 is the cube root)

Calculating volume of invested pattern

If you're making your pattern from clay, it is relatively easy to calculate the volume as follows.

Take the amount of clay you will be using for the model, form into a square or rectangle, and measure the dimensions (length x width x height). This will establish the cubic feet of the model. This calculation will eventually be subtracted from the volume of the mold box.

Another Method

Weigh the clay and use the following formula to calculate volume. This method gives only an approximate volume, but it's better than nothing.
Cubic inches = ounces x .964

Hot Casting/Preheating the Mold

For molten glass casting, the mold is preheated to at least 1250° F (676° C). The mold should "soak" at this temperature for at least 2-3 hours depending again on the size of the mold. The reason for "curing" the mold is that the chemically-bonded water contained in the plaster will cause severe bubbling when the molten glass is ladled into it. Curing the mold drives out the chemically-bonded water. The drawback to this process is that the glass will have a mold film on its surface after casting. This surface will not clean off by simply washing it. One must sandblast it off. Once the mold is sufficiently preheated, it can be ladled into without fear of bubbling. After filling, the oven temperature can be increased to 1475° F (801° C) to allow the glass to smooth over. The glass is then annealed in the proper manner.

Hot Billet Casting

I first developed this technique many years ago. Discovering that Soda/Lime glass devitrifies at casting temperatures, and wanting clean castings, I devised the following technique for casting soda/lime glass into open face molds. Gather the glass on a ball gathering rod and drop it onto a heavy steel plate. Allow it to cool to the point where you could pick it up with diamond shears and carefully place it into the open face mold that is up to temperature (1475° F, 802° C). Once you carefully place it into the mold you cannot-- and I mean cannot-- move it. If you do, it will destroy your mold as it is very soft. You can add billets as needed. Close the lid and hold the temperature at the casting temperature and your glass will flow perfectly into all the nooks and crannies of your mold. This method allows you to use your furnace glass and it will not devitrify. A drawback to this technique is that you can only do it with open face molds.

Calculating Quantity of Glass to Fill a Mold

Water Displacement Method

Fill a bucket or container half full with water. Make sure that you will be able to totally immerse the model to be cast. The water level should be marked prior to immersing the model (mark 1). Immerse the model and mark where the water has risen to (mark 2). After removing the model, add your casting glass until the water level reaches mark 2. It is always a good idea to add a bit more glass to make sure that there will be sufficient glass to fill the mold (pg. 87).

Using Specific Gravity (once again)

Calculate as follows: Make a sample of your casting glass about 3" long and about ¼" thick. Weigh the sample on an accurate gram scale and write its weight down up to 2 decimal points. In this case, the glass weighs 83 gms.

Fill a milliliter column about half way with water, taking care to fill to an exact line. Use the bottom of the meniscus. Completely immerse the sample and record the displacement of the water (the rise of the water in the column). Example: if you filled the column with 150 milliliters of water and the column of water rises to 175 milliliters after immersing the sample, then the displacement was 25 milliliters.

Divide the weight of the glass (in grams) by the displaced water (in milliliters) to calculate the specific gravity.

Example: If the glass sample weighs 83 grams and the water was displaced 25 milliliters, the equation would look as follows:

$$\frac{83 \text{ grams}}{25 \text{ milliliters}} = 3.3 \text{ Specific Gravity}$$

Once the specific gravity is determined, the volume of the mold cavity needs to be determined. To do this, use a container that measures in liters. Fill this container with rice, and pour the rice into the mold cavity. Keep filling the mold until it is completely filled. Record how many liters of rice it takes to fill the mold. Multiply the number of liters by the specific gravity to calculate the weight (in kilograms) to fill the mold. Accuracy counts. You can use sand instead of rice if you wish, but make sure you clean your mold after using sand as it has a tendency to stick to a wet mold.

If it takes 2.2 liters of rice to fill the mold, multiply 2.2 liters by the specific gravity.

$$2.2 \times 3.3 = 7.26 \text{ kg. of casting glass}$$

This is the amount of glass needed to fill the mold after it melts.

To convert kilograms to pounds, multiply the weight in kilograms by 2.2046. The product is the weight in pounds.

$$2.2046 \times 7.26 = 16 \text{ lbs. of casting glass}$$

In case you didn't know, 2.2046 is the number of lbs. in a kilo

There you have it! Now you can weigh out your precious casting glass and know your mold will fill exactly. Best of all there will be no waste. It's really easy when you know how to do it.

And finally, here is a simple and quick method to determine the approximate quantity of soda/lime glass to fill a mold: First determine the square inches of the mold cavity, and then multiply the square inches by .085. Your answer is the approximate quantity in pounds.

Ratio of Plaster/Silica to Water

The proportion of plaster/silica to water is critical in order to fabricate a strong mold. If you don't add enough plaster/silica to the water, the ratio will be such that the mold will be soft and readily crack when subjected to heat. USG, a major manufacturer of plaster, recommends consistencies (proportions of plaster to water) and recommends that you weigh your materials. *Author's Note: The USG recommendations are for plaster to water and not for plaster/silica to water, but for our usage, we will use their calculations to estimate the ratio of plaster/silica to water. Weighing the plaster/silica to water defines the exact density of your mold.*

Once you've calculated the volume of investment you need, it is necessary to convert this information in weights of plaster/silica to water. It is assumed that you have subtracted the volume of the model to be cast from the volume of the mold box into which you will be pouring your plaster/silica into. Remember, we're working with cubic feet.

The next step is to select the consistency you will be using; low numbers equal higher density molds. The higher the number the faster the materials will set. It is really not necessary to go above 60 consistency. Most casters use 50 to 60 from the chart below. I use 55 and find this ratio quite adequate. Another important aspect of doing accurate measurement is that if you find it necessary to add more plaster/silica, the expansion and contraction of the different layers of your mold will be similar and you will not get any separation between those layers. For very large molds that require you to mix many batches of mold mix, this weighing method is very important.

Follow this Example

Multiply the cubic feet needed by the amount of both plaster/silica and water to give you the amount of each that you need. Example: The measurement of your mold box is 14" x 18" x 4". Using our calculation of length x width x height we find it to be 1008 cu. inches. This number is then divided by 1728, the cube root. Our answer is .5833 cu. ft. Now our model to be cast is 12 x 16 x 2; this calculation is 384 cu. inches or .2222 cu. ft. Subtract the model from the mold box and you get .3611. If we want a mold with a consistency of 55 we take .3611 and multiply it by 73 which gives us 26.3 lbs. of plaster/silica. Next we multiply .3611 by 40 which gives us 14.4 lbs. of water. If you have to divide up your final weights because it all won't fit into one bucket do it evenly. Divide the number of buckets into the weights of each. This may seem like a lot of effort, but it really takes all the guesswork out of making larger molds.

It is helpful when using this system to premix your plaster and silica in equal amounts. Both ship in 50 lb. bags.

Consistency	Plaster/Silica	Water	Total	
50	78	39	117	**Highest Density**
55	73	40	113	
60	68	41	109	
65	66	43	109	
70	62	43	105	**Lowest Density**

Plaster/Water ratio to make 1 cubic foot

Consistency	Factor	
50	2.3	**Highest Density**
55	2.0	
60	1.8	
65	1.7	
70	1.5	**Lowest Density**

If you use the eyeball system to calculate the quantity of plaster/silica mixture, this chart might help you calculate the weight of plaster/silica to water.

To use: multiply the weight of the water in lbs. by the factor. The answer is the weight of plaster/silica.

Casting into Plaster/Silica Molds
Introduction to Kiln Casting

The term "kiln casting" covers any number of methods of casting glass into plaster/silica molds as well as molds fabricated from other materials. It is a technique practiced by many glass artists today.

Before casting, one should dry the mold properly. The glass is then placed into the mold. Bring the mold and the glass up to temperature according to both the thickness of the mold and/or the thickness of the glass being cast. You do not want to raise the temperature so quickly that the mold will prematurely crack or the glass violently break and fly all over the annealer. (See Libensky annealing chart on pg. 53. This chart also has the drying time for molds.)

Once up to casting temperature, the mold is held at that specific temperature until the glass has flowed to all parts of your mold. The thicker the mold, the longer it will take. The temperatures needed to get the glass to flow properly is usually 1475° F - 1550° F (801°–843° C). I do not recommend going much past 1550° F (843° C) as the mold really begins to break down above that temperature.

Chunk casting is perhaps the simplest method of casting and is usually done with simple open faced molds or with the flower pot system. If you're using the chunk method for the first time, you may think that you've calculated the quantity of glass wrong as there will appear to be a great deal more glass than will comfortably fill your mold. Fear not, since half of what you have piled up in your mold is air spaces between the pieces of glass. The first time I used this process I estimated correctly the amount of glass needed but second guessed myself when I saw what looked like a huge amount of glass in the mold. I removed what I thought was an excess; after firing however, I realized my calculation was correct but my instinct was wrong. "Measure twice, cut once." See photo on page 87.

Flower Pot Casting

If a closed mold or a container form is being cast, other methods of filling the mold must be utilized. One of the cleverest methods employed is the following flower pot method. Expand the hole in pot to about an inch (2.54 cm). Suspend a terra-cotta flower pot over the opening of your mold to a distance of about an inch or so. Use pieces of brick or pieces of kiln shelf to suspend the pot. Fill the flower pot with casting glass. Use at least 10-15% more glass than you've calculated, for a good quantity of glass will adhere to the sides of the flower pot. When the mold reaches casting temperature, the glass will flow out of the flower pot hole and begin to fill the mold. If the flower pot does not hold enough glass to fill your mold, it will be necessary to add glass to the flower pot until the mold is completely filled. If the pieces you're adding are large, you should pre-heat the glass in order to avoid shattering the additional cullet. It takes quite a bit longer than you think for the glass to flow from the flower pot. I've taken up to 4 hours for a simple small mold at 1500° F (815° C) using Bullseye casting glass. If your mold is constructed well, and if you've put chicken wire in the mold, it will easily take extended casting times. The book: *Techniques of Kiln–formed Glass*, by Keith Cummings, published by Penn/Black, is okay and worth the read.

Plaster/Silica Mold with KS-4 Castable Jacket

Flower Pot Casting

Colored Frit
If you're British then it's coloured frit

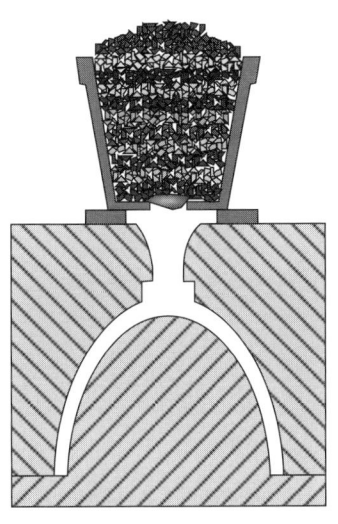

Layers of colored frit produce a color veiling effect

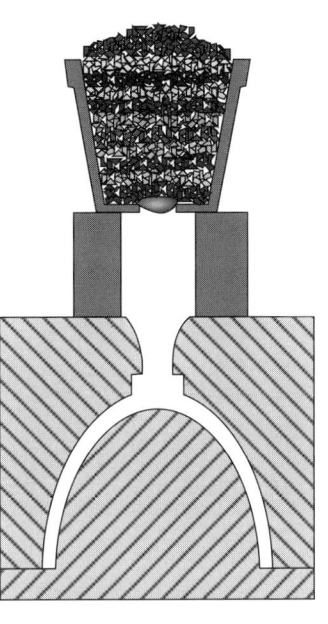

The farther the pot is away from the mold the greater the veiling effect

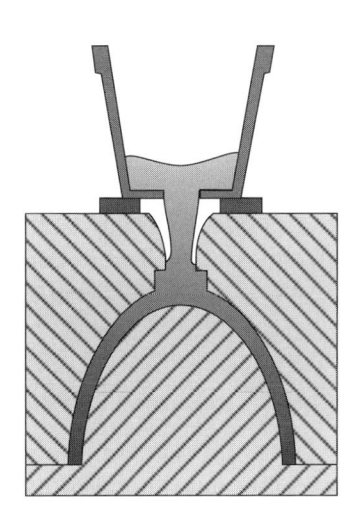

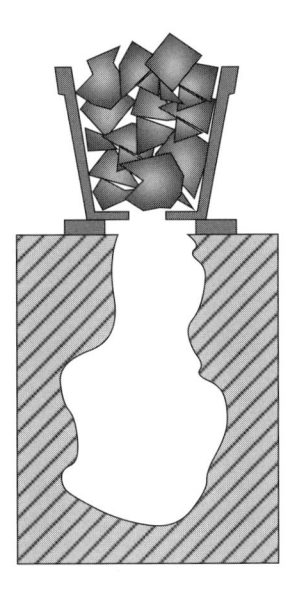

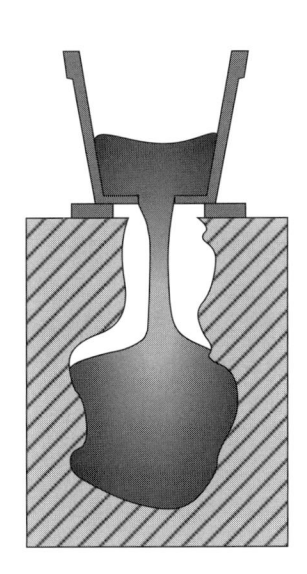

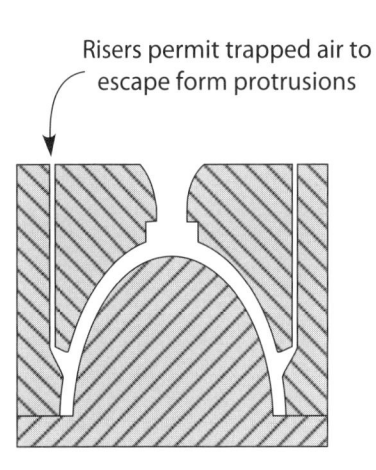

Risers permit trapped air to escape form protrusions

The diagrams on this page depict the application of the flower pot as a receptacle for the casting glass and shows what takes place when the oven is brought to casting temperature. The glass flows through the hole in the pot and fills the mold. The advantage to using this technique is: 1. Less trapped air bubbles, but that depends on the size of the pieces of glass used for the casting. 2. Various colored compatible glasses can be mixed or layered giving a veiled effect. One can use either chunks of glass or colored frits. Ann Robinson of New Zealand uses the flower pot technique to produce her beautiful vessels.

This photo depicts the flower pots suspended over the molds into which the glass will flow.

The oven depicted here is usually referred to as a "Bell" type oven. Its design allows for large castings. The lid travels in tracks and is opened and closed with a crank shown on the left. There are any number of variations of this design.

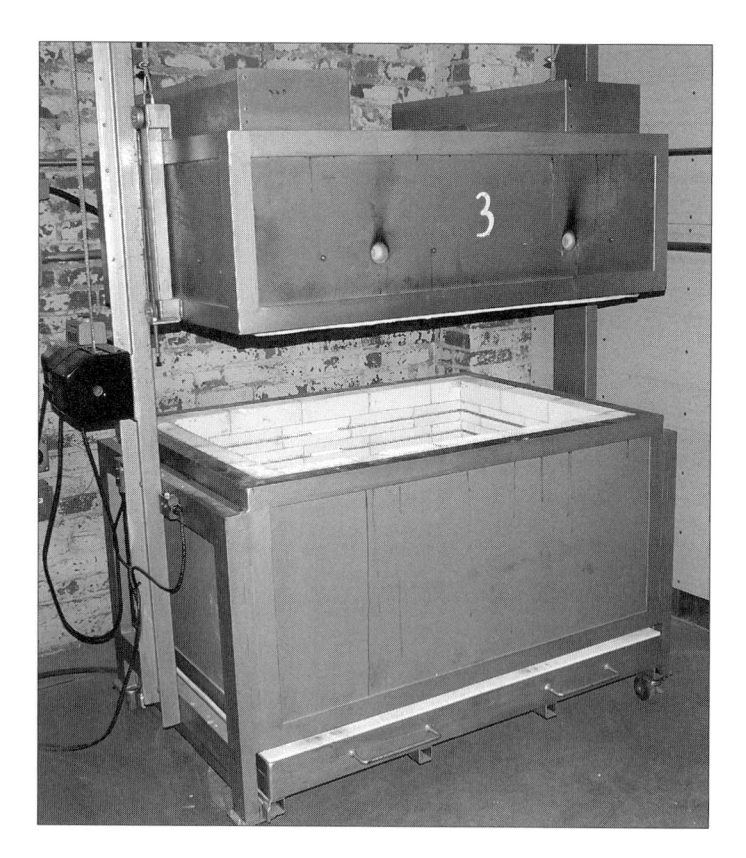

Flower Pot Casting

86 Glass Notes

Determining Quantity of Glass Needed for Casting

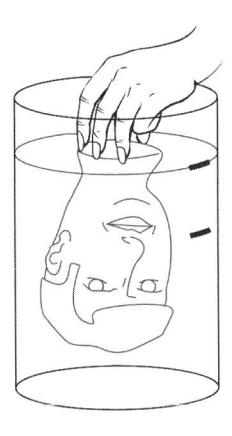

Mark #1 indicates level of water prior to immersing object to be cast. Mark #2 indicates level of water after immersing head.

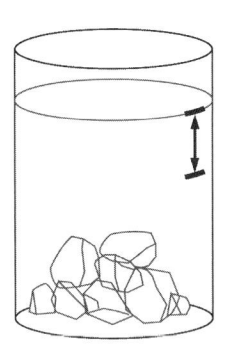

After removing object to be cast, put glass to be cast in water until the water level reaches Mark #2. This is the amount of glass needed to fill your mold.

Large open-faced molds ready for casting.

Glass Notes **87**

Ann Robinson's Mold Investments

The following was Ann's student handout at Pilchuck in 1996. Ann has revised it and included additional information. This is the 2006 edition. I have taken the liberty and translated her metric measurements into our archaic system of weights and measures.

It is generous of Ann to share information that has taken her years to develop. I am indeed grateful. Her work is quite beautiful and expressive of her surrounding in New Zealand. To view her castings, visit her Web site: www.annrobinson.co.nz.

Directions: All investment material is applied in separate batches; that is, the layers are built up by hand and shaped to the vessel. By shaping the investment to the vessel, you are assured of even annealing through the wall of the investment.

For large core vessels & Large Solid Castings

1st layer (should be ½" thick)
1 liter of water ------------------------ 1.057 quarts
1 kilo of plaster ---------------------- 2.2 lbs.
1 kilo of silica ------------------------ 200.0 mesh
½ kilo of fine grog ------------------ 1.1 lbs.
*100 gms of shredded paper ---- 3.5 oz. (can be made in a blender)
**fibreglass, chopped.

Backup layer (as thick as necessary)

1 liter of water ------------------------ 1.057 quarts of water
1 kilo of plaster ---------------------- 2.2 lbs. of plaster
1 kilo of silica (200 mesh) ------- 2.2 lbs. of silica
⅓ kilo fine grog --------------------- 10.5 oz. fine grog
⅔ kilo course grog ----------------- 21.1 oz. course grog
*100 gms. shredded paper ------- 3.5 oz. shredded paper
**fibreglass, chopped

Medium-sized vessels

1 liter water
1 kilo plaster
1 kilo silica
1 kilo fine grog
*100 grams chopped paper
**fibreglass, chopped

I recommend a high alumina refractory grog of the sort used in refractory cements for furnaces as it has less expansion and contraction when heated to casting temperatures.

*Paper: I recommend using PB 33 as sold by Eagle Picher (www.eaglepicher.com). It is pure wood cellulose. Look for this product on their web site under the main heading of Pre-co-Floc and listed under filtration. PB-33 has a short fibre length and mixes beautifully with no lumping. It aids in the venting of steam from within the mould. As you gradually heat up, it burns off from the outside in, leaving minute tunnels that vents the steam building up within, to the surface. If the steam cannot buildup pressure then it doesn't put pressure on any small cracks that may have initiated during the steaming out of the wax.

**Fibreglass is ½" (13mm) chopped. Chopped means just the individual strands of fibreglass. It can be purchased as individual strands or can be created using a chopper gun.

Other Mold Materials

Ransom & Randolph Glass-Cast™ Mold Materials

R&R is now marketing a line of mold fabricating products directly to the studio glass artist. They now offer their products under the heading of R&R Glass-Cast and have created a web site devoted to these products. Listed below are those products in their order of cost and quality.

R&R manufactures 3 products devoted to glass casting as follows:

- Glass-Cast 910
- Glass-Cast 400
- Glass-Cast 101

The 910 Investment is considered the strongest mold material commercially available. It can be used as either a complete mold product (large castings), or as a back-up for a fine grained face coat. Its strength allows for thinner molds, which translates to shorter annealing times.

The 400, although not as strong as the 910, has excellent mold integrity at elevated temperatures and is more economical.

The 101 is the most economical mold material offered by R&R. It is advertised as an, "all purpose mold material for kiln casting/slumping of glass." Its very fine particle size makes it ideal for detail.

I recommend you visit the R&R web site to get a better indication of the applicability of these products to your casting situation. These products are very different than the standard 1:1 plaster/silica mold materials and have very specific directions for water to material ratios as well as optimal setting times. The how-to manual is displayed on their website.

R&R Headquarters
3535 Briarfield Blvd.
Maumee, OH 43537
Tel: 419/794-1290
Fax: 419/865-9997
E-mail: dnixon@ransom-randolph.com
Web: www.glass-cast.com

Luminar™, Mold Mix 6

"ZIRCAR Luminar is Mold Mix 6 and is a refractory-molding compound designed to allow replication of three-dimensional objects in glass. It comes as a paste, which is applied to a suitably prepared pattern and hardens on drying. Properly prepared molds of Mold Mix 6 will resolve the finest details and possess good strength. However, it remains sufficiently friable to permit easy removal after annealing. Mold Mix 6 may be used for hot casting, kiln casting methods and slumping, all with excellent results. The greatest advantage of Mold Mix 6 is its ease of use."

The information above was taken from the Zircar website. Their site lists other applicable products for the glass caster as well. Mold Mix 6 is resold by a number of re-sellers at a considerable markup. I recommend buying direct form Zircar. Generally this product is used for making multiple castings from one mold as long as there are no undercuts. The mold should be kept on the small side and works best as an open mold, that is, where the piece is easily removed.

ZIRCAR Refractory Composites, Inc
P.O. Box 489
Florida, NY 10921
(845) 651-2200 Fax (845) 651-1515
www.zrci.com

Sodium Silicate Sand Casting

The sodium silicate/CO_2 process was first described in German and Eastern European journals published in the early 1950's. The process consists of coating sand grains with a sodium silicate binder. This mixture is packed into a box, packed around a form, and then gassed with carbon dioxide for approximately 15 seconds. This "hardens" the sand thus allowing removal of the model. It can be used immediately. This process has some advantages over the standard sand/molten glass casting process in use today.

The only disadvantages that I can think of are that a mechanical muller/mixer or cement mixer is necessary to get an optimum mixing of the sand and sodium silicate. After the start-up expenses, the cost of making molds is relatively cheap. Illustrations and further descriptions can be found on pg. 92.

Qualities

- excellent accuracy
- smooth finish
- no moisture gassing into the molten glass
- can be stored before use
- can be carved
- deep castings possible
- inexpensive to make
- molds can be preheated before casting (500° F maximum) (260° C)

Sand Preparation

Clean, clay-free sand is weighed and added to the mixer. It is important to weigh the sand as you will be making a percent addition of sodium silicate to it. Weigh out sodium silicate (3 to 5% by weight). Make sure you weigh out the sodium silicate accurately. Start muller or cement mixer, add sodium silicate, and pour in a gentle stream about 1" from the edge. Add all the binder in about 10 seconds or so. Mull for 2 minutes after adding the binder. Make sure the binder is not deposited on the sidewall of the muller instead of being mixed with the sand; scrape any sand mixture buildup from the sides using a scraping tool. DO NOT USE FINGERS. Remove sand after mixing and store in an airtight plastic bag. Clean muller or cement mixer before proceeding as the sand left in the muller will harden unless cleaned immediately.

Mold Preparation

Use a sturdy wooden or metal box to ram sand around the form. Using a sturdy box to ram into is important. The form that you ram around should have a flat top as you will be ramming the sand over the form. The box should also be about 2" taller than the form and at least the same on the sides. Make sure to ram the sand with a wooden or metal rammer as ramming by hand does not create the density of mold necessary for optimum mold making. Remember, you must use a form that can be removed from the sand after the gassing. If you're clever, it's possible to make a piece mold to facilitate the removal of complex forms. After you are finished with the mold making, smooth the sand level with the top of the box. Rap or vibrate the sides of the box before gassing as this will facilitate the removal of the hardened sand later on. Place a "lid" with a hole in it about the size of the CO_2 "mask" over the top of the box. Make sure the lid fits snugly. Gas with low pressure CO_2 (approximately 10 lb. pressure) for 10 seconds then gas with high pressure CO_2 (approximately 20 lbs. pressure) for 10 seconds. Turn off CO_2 regulator and cylinder valve. Remove cover from box and remove hardened sand from box. If your molds are big and thick, it might be necessary to gas them using a slightly different method. This method would entail your taking a rigid copper tube about ¼" in diameter and drilling tiny holes along the sides from the bottom to a few inches from the top. Seal the bottom of the tube and securely attach the top to the hose that goes to the CO_2 tank. After ramming the mold, take the perforated copper tube and carefully push it into the mold (avoid perforating your model). Turn on the CO_2 for about 10 seconds at about 10 lbs. pressure to gas the mold. Do this in a few places to make sure the sand is completely set. You are now ready to remove the model and cast the mold. It is not necessary to cast immediately as it can be stored indefinitely. (Alternate Methods follows).

Alternate Methods

CO_2 gassing equipment is the main expense for this process. A small muller would be highly desirable but is not essential. Small batches of sand can be mixed by hand or with a stirring device mounted in a drill press. The sand mixture, if kept in an airtight plastic bag, remains in a usable condition for a day or two. The integrity of the container in which the material is stored is critical, as CO_2 in the air will cause the mixture to harden. This disadvantage, however, can be used to your advantage. In the absence of gassing equipment, a sodium silicate sand mix could be rammed into a box, the sides rapped, and the mixture left to harden in the box (this can be hastened with heat). If your model is made from Styrofoam, be careful with the heat. Although this procedure would not accurately reflect the process, a usable sand mold would result.

Some Tips

- A good method for removing complex models from the hardened sand is to simply cut the hardened sand mold in half and carefully remove the model from the mold. The mold can then be "wired" back together and cast.

- The CO_2 molds are excellent for blowing into and, if you are careful, can be used more than once (a very good technique). Be careful to avoid thin edges as these edges will deteriorate easily. As in tip 1, cut the mold in half for two-piece blow molds. Try carving into the sand for different surface effects.
- Clean up your equipment before the sand hardens.

Assorted Information

Sodium silicate binders can be purchased from foundry supply houses. It is used as a de-floculent for making clay slips. It was also used as a preservative for eggs many years ago. Preserving eggs? For what? Ask great-grandma. A gallon of sodium silicate will produce 215 to 360 pounds of mold sand. Sodium silicate has an indefinite shelf life. The sand can be recycled, but it's easier to start with fresh sand. Sand and sodium silicate are cheap.

Author's Note: There is a self catalyzing additive for sand casting (see pg. 96, Chem-Bond).

Rigid Sand Molds for Casting
Sodium Silicate, CO_2 Method

By Ed Francis

Materials Needed

- Clean Silica Sand, lots of it, 80-100 Mesh (sand can be reused)
- Sodium Silicate 2.5% (foundry sand binder)
  Look in the yellow pages under "Foundry Supply"
  Comes in 5-6 gallon pail

The Injector

- Heat and forge one end of a ¼" copper tube (rigid copper) to a point, like a pencil. File it down smooth.
- Drill ¹⁄₁₆" or ¹⁄₃₂" holes every ½" along the length of the tube. Drill through the tube in two directions so there are four holes every ½". Tiny holes are preferable. The holes will have a tendency to clog if they are larger than the grain size of the sand.
- With ferrules and fittings, connect the tube to the petcock as shown below. Next connect the petcock to a 6' or longer high pressure hose and connect the hose to CO_2 cylinder and regulator. It's done.

Author's note: You may wish to make differently sized tubes for different size molds. A long tube is difficult to use on small molds. It's also nice if you can make the tubes out of something more rigid than copper, as the mold gets very hard and the tube may have a tendency to bend when you try to insert it into your sand mold.

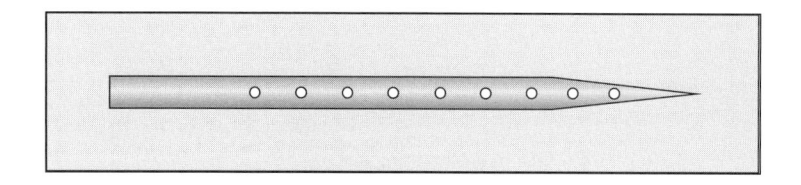

Sand Injector Tip

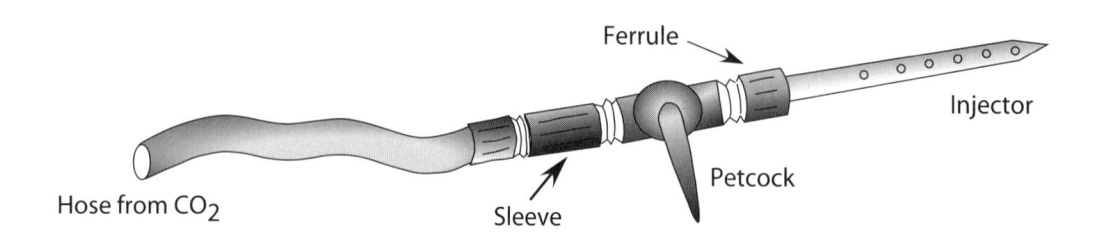

Ferrule
Injector
Petcock
Sleeve
Hose from CO_2

*Use a petcock that is made for use with CO_2. It can be obtained from a welding supply shop. The internal hardware of these petcocks is made from nylon and will not bind up like the ones from the hardware store.

Mixing the Sand

The easiest way to mix the sodium silicate binder into the sand is with a cement mixer. Hand mixing works okay, but it can be quite tiring if you are mixing large quantities. To mix, simply weigh out the sand and add the binder. Adding the binder (sodium silicate) while the mixer is turning helps to produce a greater homogeneity. Mix a few minutes or until the mixture feels uniformly "damp." It is important to screen the sand after mixing through a ⅛" mesh screen. This removes and breaks up any and all lumps of binder and sand that did not mix. The sand can be stored in airtight containers for a time, but the containers must be airtight. If they are not, the CO_2 in the air will set the sand before you have had a chance to use it. Do not add water to the sand as it will weaken the molds. Remember, it is CO_2 that causes the sodium silicate to get hard. A good mixture is 7% sodium silicate by weight for 80-100 mesh sand. Finer sand requires more binder for adequate strength. 150 mesh sand works best with 9 to 10% binder by weight. More than 10% binder should only be used in very large molds. If you use too high a percentage, the result will be very rough surface texture and possible cracking due to incompatibility. At the extreme, the sodium silicate will penetrate far enough into the casting and cause the surface to peel off in slabs.

About Sodium Silicate

Sodium silicate varies by manufacturer. A 2.5 ratio of sodium silicate seems to be the best. Foundry suppliers can mix different ratios for you, but it is not necessary. The 2.5 ratio is the off-the-shelf ratio. A 3.0 ratio will have more sodium and be stronger, but it will fuse to your glass at a much lower temperature. A 1.5 ratio will not fuse but will not make a very strong mold either. Make sure you get a sodium silicate with no additives. Additives tend to smoke in the annealer because they have organic binders. Look for a clear sodium silicate. If your glass sticks to the sand, you are using too much sodium silicate.

You may wish to use a graphite/alcohol mold release. Using this type of product can prevent any fusion of sand to glass. A mold release which is paintable or in an aerosol works very well. Sodium silicate will not smoke when subjected to high heat.

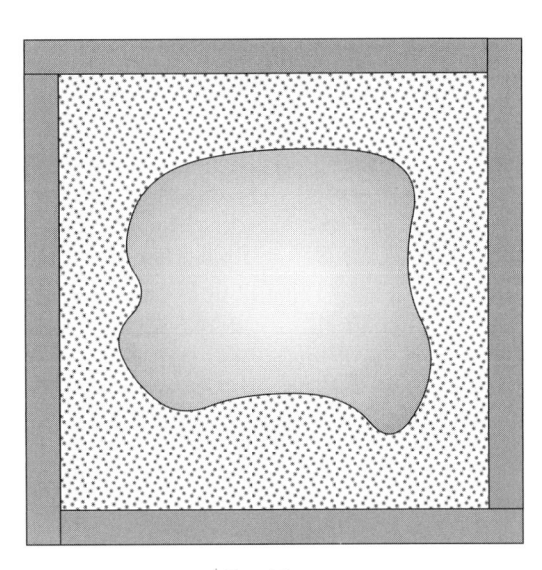

Top View

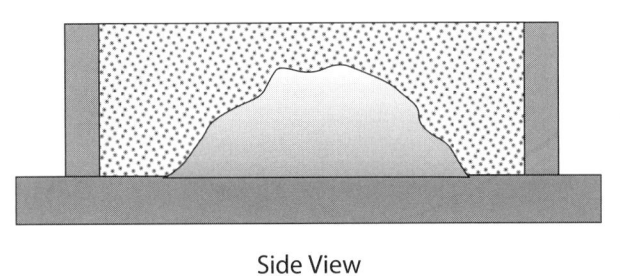

Side View

Leave at least 2" of sand around model for adequate strength.

Making the Mold

Any template used for sand casting can be used for making rigid sand molds. Templates can be wood, plaster, fired clay, Styrofoam, or found objects. Templates should have some draft and no undercuts. Multi-piece molds which can be removed one part at a time work well.

Lay the template face up on a table and construct a box or rigid form around it. For molds up to 16" x 20", leave at least 2" of space around the highest point. The larger the mold, the thicker the walls should be.

Fill the box with mixed sand. Pack it down fairly tight using a piece of wood. Level the sand to the top of the box. Remember this will be the bottom of the mold and should sit level.

You are now ready to inject the mold with CO_2.

Adjust the CO_2 regulator to 10 pounds pressure. Carefully slip the injector into the center of the mold at an angle. Try not to push the injector into the template. Open the petcock for about 10 seconds or more depending on the size of the mold. Carefully remove the injector.

Push the injector straight down in a corner of the mold and open the petcock for 10 seconds. Proceed around the edge of the mold, pushing the injector into the sand at intervals of 4-6". You will know each injection is done as the sand hardens and cools around these spots. Proceed to the next soft spot. When your mold is completely hard to the touch, you are done.

Remove the box or form from the hardened mold. Carefully feel around the edges for soft spots. If you find a soft spot, carefully insert injector and open the petcock for a few seconds. **When completed, allow the mold to sit for about ½ hour in order to completely harden.** Turn the mold over and carefully remove the template. Remember, this is a sand mold chemically bonded together, and it will break if you are not careful.

The mold is ready for casting as soon as it is made. A coat of acetylene carbon works well as a mold release. Small molds can be cast outside of the oven and then loaded into the hot annealer. Your mold will get weaker and have a tendency to crumble as the heat from the glass penetrates into the mold and breaks down the binder. Don't wait too long before loading it into the annealer. Large molds can get quite heavy.

It is easier to cast them in the oven. The molds can be brought right up to 500–700° F (260°–371° C) and cast. I found letting the molds sit at 500° F (260° C) for a couple of hours worked well. The molds soaked at this temperature were not affected. Cast all your molds and get the oven up to annealing temperature as fast as possible. If you cast the molds at annealing temperature, the sand and binder will fuse to the surface of your casting. If you are making very thick castings, the glass will raise the mold temperature above 1000° F (537° C) for a sufficient length of time, thereby causing the sand to stick to the surface of the casting. This effect can be quite interesting. There are other problems that can crop up depending on the types of shapes you are casting, but you will discover what they are and learn to avoid them. Cleaning the finished castings is quite easy; just wash the glass off with water and a tooth brush. Never use cold water on a casting. To be on the safe side, wait a few days before cleaning the casting with water.

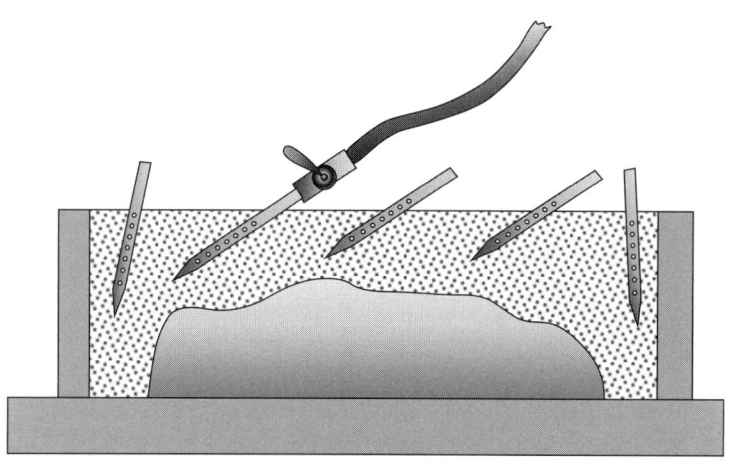

Sand injection
Various positions shown to completely harden the sand.

Observations

This mold process is ideal for producing many molds from a single template. Projects like wall tiles can be done quickly, efficiently, and cleanly. I have been successful in making blanks and carving into them. Screwdrivers, scrapers, and dental tools will carve the set sand very easily. It is still a sand–mold process and has its limitations on fine detail, but the textures are nice and the surfaces are bright. The sand can be reused in two ways. For example it can be ground up and remixed with new sodium silicate. The cooked sand actually works very well as it is free of organic material. The big chunks of cooked sand can be saved and used for inserts in castings. After heating and annealing, the sand is hard and durable. It can also be cut and carved cleaner than freshly made sand. Cores made from "used" sand will not gas and cause bubbles as fresh sand may.

The trick to successful use of CO_2 sand molds is to find the optimum sodium silicate to sand ratio as well as the correct mold temperature for casting. I do not recommend taking the mold above 500° F. (260° C) prior to casting.

Every process has its particular aesthetic. Don't let the process be a substitute for aesthetics. Keep notes on what you do, and share your information with others.

CO$_2$ Bonded Sand Casting

1. Ed pours the requisite quantity of sodium silicate into the mixer containing the sand.

2. After mixing, the sand is placed in the forms, covering the model to a depth of approximately 2" (5 cm).

3. The sand is tamped down.

4. The injector is inserted into the sand and CO$_2$ is pumped into the sand, hardening it.

5. The hardened sand is removed from the forms.

6. The model is removed from the hardened sand.

7. The hardened sand has been coated with a layer of carbon from an acetylene torch, and molten glass is then ladled into the mold. After the ladling is complete, the sand mold with the glass, is put into the annealer.

Chem Bond 4905 No-Bake Resin System

The previous section described the sodium silicate/CO_2 process of mold forming. The Chem Bond no-bake 4905 additive for sand precludes the need for CO_2 in order to "set" the mold. I saw this product in action when one of Gene Koss's students, Steve Durow, escaped from the Katrina disaster in New Orleans and set up shop at the Kent State Studio. Steve built very large sand molds using this product. After seeing this product in action, I'm convinced that the Chem Bond is the product of choice for this type of sand casting. There is little to no outgassing when the cast mold is placed in the annealer as there is when using chemically-catalyzed sand. What makes this bonding system so superior to the CO_2 process is that very large sand molds can be constructed and one does not have to inject CO_2 in order to get the sand to set. It is self catalyzing! It should also be noted that there are differing grades of catalyst corresponding to length of time for set (see table below).

"Normal mixing procedure is to add the catalyst to the sand and mix, then add the resin and mix. This will insure thorough wetting of the sand grains with both catalyst and binder."

"As with all no-bake binders, Chem Bond 4905 sands are very flowable and do not require ramming to produce high densities. However, the best density is produced by some mechanical means. This can be accomplished with hand ramming, or vibrating."

I could not find an e-mail address or a web site for the this company but I have listed their address and telephone number below.

Description and Operating Instructions (Provided by Chem Bond)

"Chem Bond 4905 no-bake binder is a two component liquid binder and catalyst (hardener) system. The Chem Bond 4905 binder system allows the end user to adjust the cure time without affecting the throughcure of the sand mass."

"Chem Bond 4905 no-bake binder system has a number of advantages compared to furan or oil no-bake binders. It is primarily inorganic; this results in very low gas and smoke emission in the studio. Mixed sand has very little, if any, odor and the cured sand mass releases easily from pattern or core box. Neither binder nor catalysts are toxic."

"Chem Bond Catalysts are used in the ratio of 10% by weight of the Chem Bond 4905 binder in the sand mix. Variation of the catalyst percentage in relation to the binder will not increase the cure rate of the mixed sand. In other words, 20% of the Chem Bond Catalyst by weight of binder will cure at the same rate as 10%. Reduction of catalyst level below 8% binder will result in lack of throughcure and subsequent collapse of cores and molds."

"Chem Bond Catalysts may be stored indefinitely under normal conditions."

"The following should be noted: Chem Bond 4905 cores and molds have a storage life of approximately two to three weeks under normal foundry conditions. As with all sodium silicate bonded materials, Chem Bond 4905 cores pick up moisture gradually and deteriorate in strength. Care should be taken not to store cores in direct contact with concrete floors, or under other conditions that would accelerate the deterioration process of the cured sand."

CATALYST	STRIP TIME ON 75° F SAND
Chem Bond Catalyst 210	75-85 min.
Chem Bond Catalyst 220	45-55 min.
Chem Bond Catalyst 230	35-40 min.
Chem Bond Catalyst 240	20-25 min.
Chem Bond Catalyst 250	10-15 min
Chem Bond Catalyst 260	6-10 min.

HA International LLC
630 Oakmont Lane
Westmont, IL 60559
Telephone 630/575-5700 Fax 630/575-5800

Plaster Blow Mold

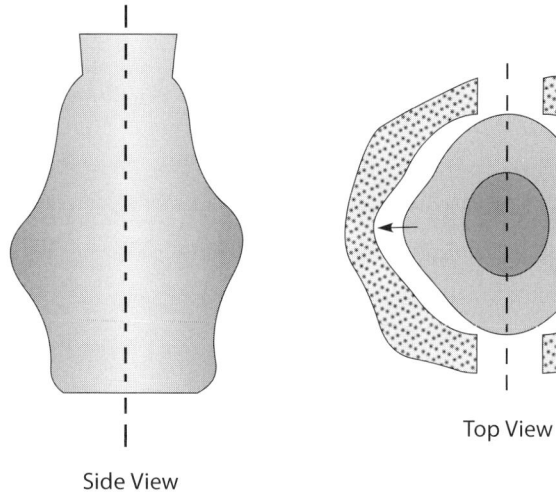

This diagram depicts the parting line for a two-piece mold. The parting line must be placed carefully in order to avoid any undercuts. Undercuts will prevent the glass from releasing.

Side View

Top View

This diagram depicts undercuts as well as how the two piece mold facilitates the removal of the glass from the mold. It also shows where to place vents for the release of air or steam.

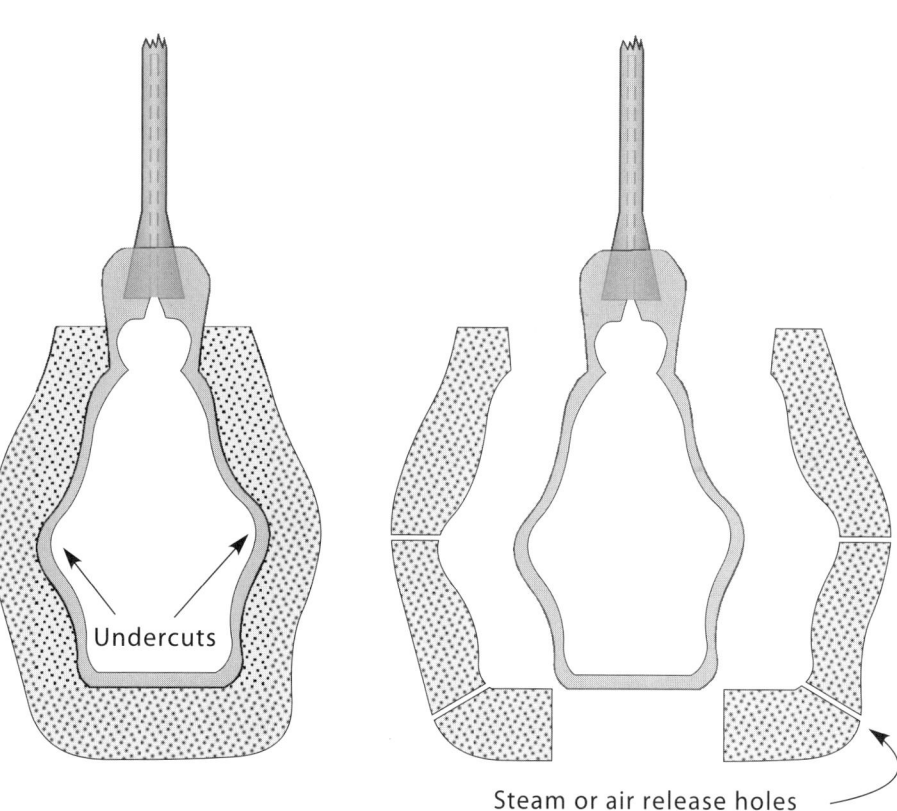

Undercuts

Steam or air release holes

Plaster blow molds for creating glass objects have several advantages: they allow the artist to create fairly complicated blown glass forms, they require minimal assistance, they allow for a limited number of editions of the same form, and they are relatively quick to make. The major disadvantage of plaster blow molds is that the plaster begins to break down from contact with the extreme temperatures of the glass after a short period of time; deterioration is usually noticeable within 4-8 uses. Thin edge protrusions are the first areas to deteriorate. Deterioration is also dependent on how hot the glass is when you blow the mold as well as how long you stay in the mold. Over the years some artists have used additives to the plaster blow mold as well as different surface coatings in an attempt to prolong the life of the mold. I've tried some of these treatments, but to be honest, I have never seen any of these additives extend the life of the plaster. If you want a mold that lasts without breaking down, I would recommend using a fine grain castable refractory.

I have used plaster blow molds on a number of occasions and really like them for their immediacy. A plaster blow mold will help you realize shapes that off hand blowing cannot. I have never made a plaster blow mold that was extremely complex or more than a two-piece mold. As in all molds, it is important to avoid any undercuts; If you do not you will not only be incapable of getting the glass to release from the mold but will also probably break the mold when trying to remove the glass. If you do have minor undercuts in the plaster, you can get the glass to release when it is still hot and has some viscosity. You can blow the plaster dry or wet but in either case, it is important to have steam-trapped air release holes at all the high points. At the most protruding areas of the form, drill small holes through the mold. These holes will release the steam or air build up from areas such as chins, noses, etc., which can prevent these protrusions from properly blowing.

For two-piece molds, quick release clamps are a convenient tool to hold molds together when blowing. Some artists I know build their plaster molds in hinged boxes so that an assistant can hold the box together while it is being blown. Mold blowing of any type exerts tremendous force, and holding a mold together is not always an easy situation.

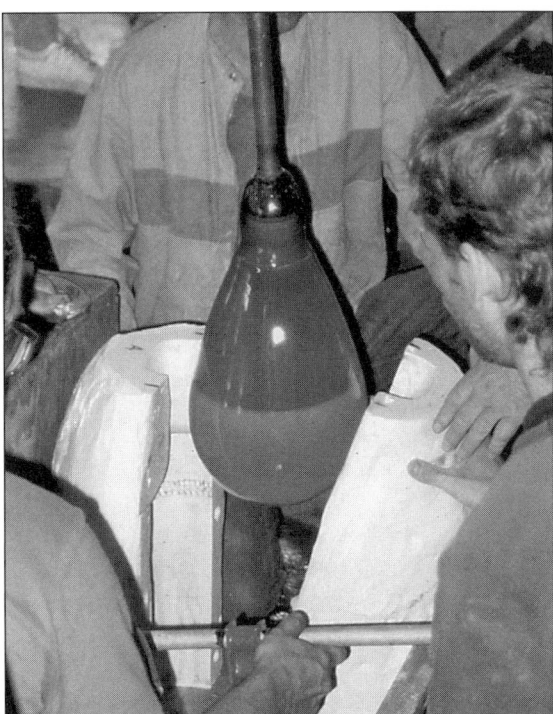

Plaster Mold Blow

Things to avoid when making plaster blow molds:

- Thin edges
- Thin molds
- Undercuts

Roman Mold Blown Vessels
Collection, The Corning Museum of Glass

98 Glass Notes

Sand Casting
Bentonite/Sand Technique

Sand casting for glass artists was first introduced in this country by Bertil Vallien of Sweden. Bertil, a great glass artist as well as a designer for Kosta Boda, is most famous for his sand castings. His castings are imbued with rich color as well as a mystical "Scandinavian" iconography and spirit. If you are not familiar with his work, you should seek it out as I think he is probably one of the most original artists working with glass today. Bertil first introduced the technique in this country publicly at the first Toledo GAS conference. Since that time the technique has been a strong focus at many university glass programs. Although the technique of sand casting is mastered fairly easily, few have defined what I would consider a mature aesthetic.

A simple description of the technique would be: an "artist" presses fairly rigid forms--wood, plastic, and/or plaster that have no undercuts--into a loose, damp mixture of sand and bentonite. The forms are removed, and molten glass is poured into the negative cavity. After cooling a bit, the hot casting is placed in the annealer. You are probably asking, "is that all there is to it?" The answer is, almost.

Preparing the Sand

It is possible to use almost any type of sand, but it has been found that one type of sand works better than others. As a matter of fact, the best type of sand to use is a mineral known in the foundry trade as Olivene. Olivene is not a pure silica product. It is a natural mineral composed of a solid grain of magnesium ortho silicate. Its actual composition varies, but the solid grain is about 45% MgO, 39% SiO_2, and 6% FeO. What is important to the sand caster, though, is not so much its chemistry as the shape of the Olivine crystal. The grains are angular and have sharp edges. The reason the shape is important is that, when the casting mixture is dampened and compressed, the grains attach themselves to each other, are not separated easily, and can render fine detail. Olivine is available through foundry suppliers. Olivine is used by foundries for core box metal casting as well as for sand blasting grain. Although it can sometimes be difficult to find, it is well worth obtaining as it gives excellent results when used for glass sand casting. A 50/50 mixture of 90 and 120 mesh Olivine has been found to give optimum results. Although plain builder's sand works for casting, the grains tend to be rounded and vary greatly in mesh size. Because of the variation in mesh sizes, the sand can have a porosity that can give a rough surface to the casting. If you use plain sand, try to find one that has a consistent grain size that is between 90 and 120 mesh.

Olivine or any sand by itself will not suffice for sand casting. A clay–like mineral called bentonite is added to the sand in order to give it the quality necessary for casting. We also add corn starch to this mixture to facilitate the release of the sand from the surface of the casting (more about corn starch later). This mixture of sand/bentonite/corn starch (in Europe corn starch is referred to as corn flour) will harden when subjected to high heat (molten glass). Bentonite is a type of clay that is actually a by–product of volcanic activity. It is a very fine greyish powder and, unlike the clays with which you are familiar, turns into a slimy goo when water is added to it. Bentonite is normally added in small quantities to clay bodies to increase plasticity. We add it to our sand to help it bind and harden when heated. Bentonite can be obtained from either a ceramic supply house or a foundry supplier. If you purchase it from a foundry supplier, they will ask you what kind you want. There are western and southern types. I don't think the kind you use makes much difference. The third part of our mixture is corn starch. Corn Starch is a recent addition to the traditional sand/bentonite mixture and, in my estimation, is one fantastic addition to the process. In a nutshell the corn starch mixed in with the sand and bentonite keeps the sand from sticking to the glass because it instantly carbonizes when the molten glass makes contact. It is still necessary to carbonize the surface with acetylene prior to casting, but it seems the combination of the acetylene carbon and the carbon produced by the corn starch keeps any-- and I mean any sand from sticking to the glass. I used this mixture, and I guarantee you it works. I was curious though to find out who introduced corn starch to the mix and sent an e-mail to the one person who I felt would have the answer, Bertil Vallien. Here is the answer I received from Bertil and I quote: *"I first heard about it when travelling in Mexico. Started to use it some years ago and it works well as you saw. Makes the sand not to stick. The shop smells like a bakery but the glass comes out really clean because of the carbon layer that is created when the fumes from the flour is escaping the easiest way towards the hot casting. The percentage I use is about 2% by weight. The drawback is that you can easily get a mat finish on the open surface + the smell from the annealers. When working in the factory I have to cast at night when using corn flour because the workers hate the smell and say they are not feeling well inhaling the smell. I can't see there should be any health hazards?????"*

Well, there you have it. An unknown caster in Mexico developed the process and Bertil gave it to the world. Way to go Bertil!

Preparing the Sand

The following steps will help you to prepare your sand for glass casting.

It is important to know by weight how much sand you will be using. I recommend you start with at least 100 pounds (45 kg.) of sand. *The reader should note that when I say sand I also mean Olivene if that is what you will be using.* You will eventually use a great deal more than 100 pounds of sand, but if you are just a beginner, 100 pounds will suffice. If you are using builder's sand from the local builder's supply, you will need to weigh it before adding the bentonite. It is also important that you begin with dry sand, as the bentonite or the corn starch will not mix with damp or wet sand. It will clump up and thus render it useless. It is much easier to purchase your sand in 100 lb. bags. You will also need a good sturdy box to hold the sand (see diagram below).

After the sand is weighed, add between 4 and 7 percent by weight of bentonite to it and from 2 to 6% corn starch. I know Bertil recommends 2%, but I found the higher percentage worked better. Experiment with the percentage to find what works best for you. We experimented with small quantities of the mixture prior to committing to the full weight. If you add too great a percentage of bentonite, the sand mixture will become lumpy and somewhat gooey when water is added. Foundry suppliers sell bentonite in 100 pound quantities only. If you want a smaller quantity, buy it from a ceramic supplier in your region or go to your local college or university ceramic department and beg for a few pounds.

If you do not have a cement mixer, then spread the sand onto a clean floor and sprinkle the bentonite into the sand as you shovel it around to disperse the bentonite. If you are mixing it in a barrel, try to layer it in as you add the sand and then roll your barrel around. Always wear a good filter mask when working with any product that creates dusts. I do recommend the cement mixer as it really makes life a lot easier. You can purchase a cheap mixer at through Harbor Freight (www.harborfreight.com). Just enter cement mixer in the search box and go.

After you have everything mixed, you are ready to add the water. It is easy to add water if you're using a cement mixer. Just add the water as the mixer is

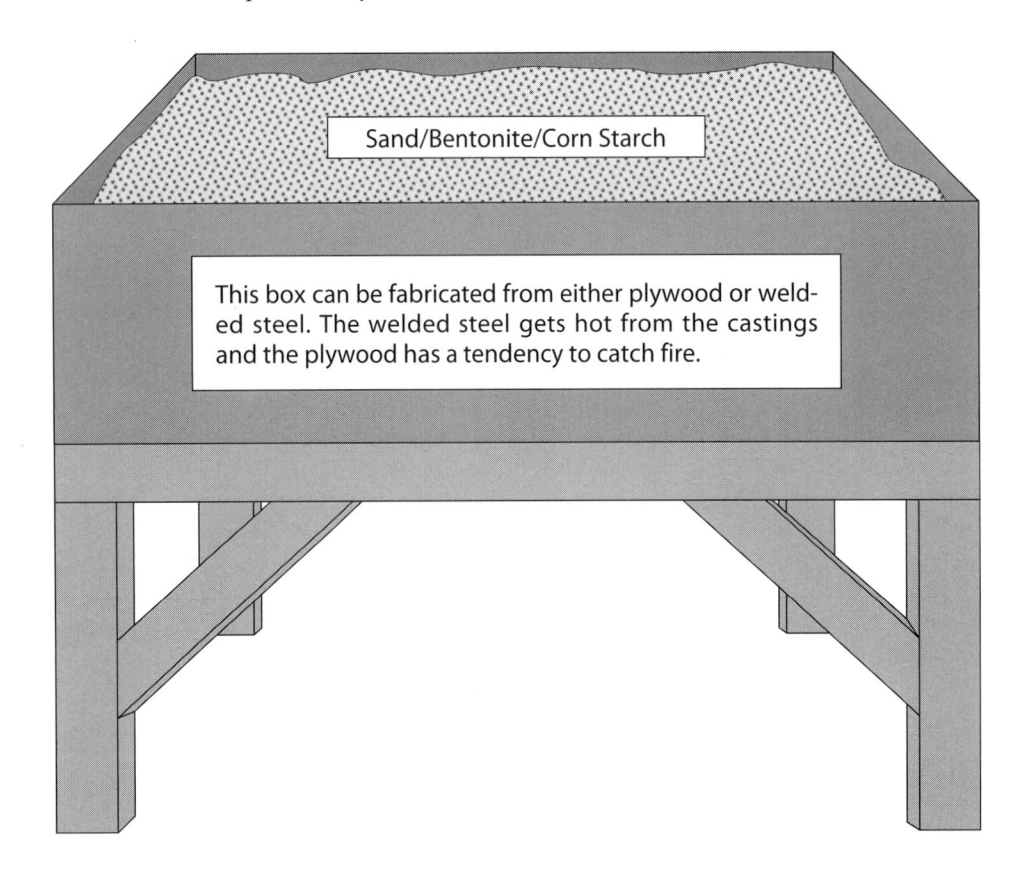

Sand/Bentonite/Corn Starch

This box can be fabricated from either plywood or welded steel. The welded steel gets hot from the castings and the plywood has a tendency to catch fire.

turning; add a little at a time as you do not want to get your sand too wet. If you're using the floor or a cement trough, add then sprinkle the water as you mix. It is very difficult to say how much water to add. The sand should be damp but not wet. You will notice that the sand will not wet evenly when using the floor or trough method. You will need to put your sand in a box and cover it with a plastic sheet and let it sit overnight. The next day all the sand should be damp and ready for use. It is possible to use too much water as well as not enough. It's more of a pain

> Sand that is too damp will create steam bubbles in the molten glass.

very quickly. A good-sized wooden scraper is used to push the sand through the screen. When screening, it is advisable to wear work gloves with leather palms. The reason for the gloves is that, eventually, your sand will retain bits of glass, and you don't want to jam pieces of glass into your hand. Okay, now we have our sand ready to go and as you've guessed, there is more to sand casting than just the sand.

The Ladle

You will need a ladle to scoop the glass from the furnace. The ladle is usually constructed from a very heavy steel pipe cap. These caps come in different sizes measured in inches. They are fairly shallow, have rounded bottoms, and are quite heavy especially after

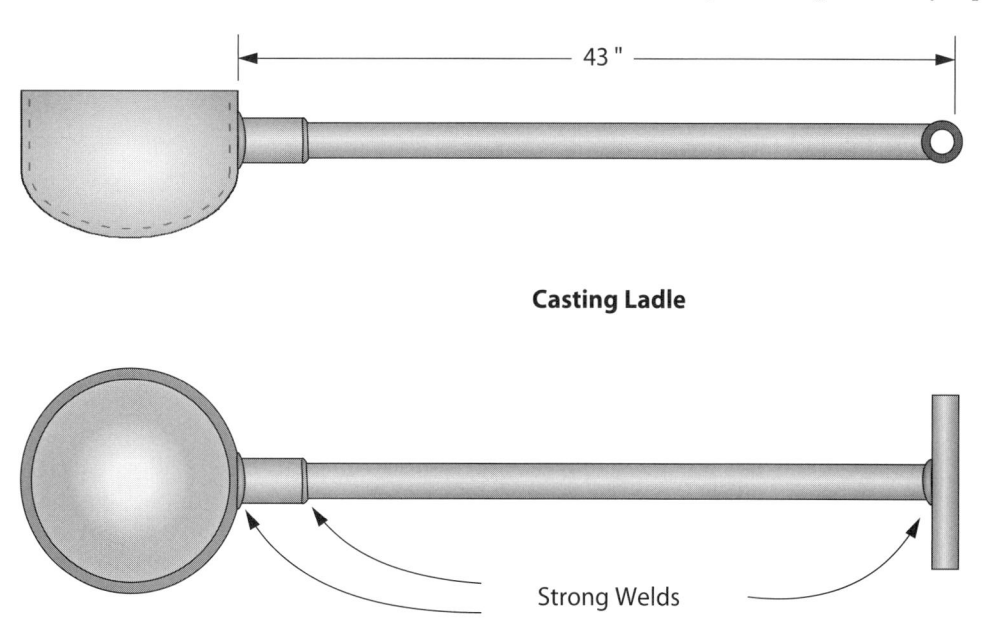

Casting Ladle

Strong Welds

if you add too much water as you will have to wait for your sand to dry a bit before you use it. You will know it's too wet if large bubbles form when glass is ladled into the sand. If it's too wet, spread it out on the floor and allow it to dry. However, if the sand is too dry, it won't hold the image pressed into it. You can sometimes use a spray bottle to moisten the sand as you're using it.

Before you can use the sand mixture, it must be screened so that all the lumps are removed and an even fluffy consistency is obtained. The screen can be very coarse. A window screen is too fine. We use a heavy duty screen that has holes approximately ¼" square. Build a box for the screen from 2 x 4's. The box should be at least two foot square and probably larger. It's a good idea to make your sifting box slightly larger than the box you're casting into. That way you can rest it on the box and screen

> Bentonite and corn starch should only be added to dry sand.

the handle is welded on. The ladle handle is made from double-walled black pipe (not galvanized). The small ladles use ¾" pipe and the larger ladles usually use about a 1" pipe for the handles. Make the handle long enough so that you can scoop the glass from the furnace without getting your hands and arms fried. Wearing gloves is essential. Weld a "T" onto the end of the handle so you can grip the handle without it slipping (see diagram). Pipe caps are available from plumbing supply houses and black pipe can be obtained from a good hardware store. For a price, the hardware store will probably cut the pipe to size.

Sand Mixture Percentages	
Bentonite	6 – 8
Corn Starch	2 – 6

Before welding the handle onto the ladle, grind the end of the pipe handle so that it fits the curve of the ladle. **It is of utmost importance that you get a good penetrating weld. The expansion and contraction of the ladle from heating and cooling will crack a poor weld.** If you are unsure of your welding skills, have a professional welder do it. It's not fun to have your crummy weld fail and your ladle fall into your big tank of crystal. Try pulling one of those puppies out. Again, get out your trusty yellow pages and look under welding. Ladles are not very expensive and, as I said above, they come in different sizes. Most glass casters I know have different size ladles.

The Process

Now that your sand box is built, ladles made, and sand prepared, you're ready to cast. Well, not quite. Forms or templates need to be created that can easily be pressed into the sand and removed leaving a definite impression. The templates themselves can be constructed from plaster, wood, or plastic parts such as dolls, fruit, etc. Any object that can be pressed into the sand and easily removed can be used as a template. I've seen students press their faces and other parts of their bodies into the sand. Don't try it! You'll get a bad cut.

All templates used will have one thing in common. They cannot have any undercuts. An undercut will prevent it from being removed from the sand after pressing. The diagrams should help explain what an undercut is.

As you can see, when the form is lifted from the sand, the undercut section will break that area of the sand. You must redesign your template to exclude any and all undercuts as shown in the second diagram. If you make your forms from plaster, it is a good idea to rub some graphite or dry silica flour onto the surface of the plaster. This will help it to release easily from the sand.

More Process

After pressing the template(s) into the soft sand, it is important that you firm up the sand around the template and shape it so that the edges don't break off and fall into the casting area. You will soon learn the art of pressing templates into sand. There really are no tricks, just common sense gained from experience.

At that point, you are almost ready to cast the glass.

Most casters do not want the sand to stick to the surface of their glass casting. To prevent this from happening, a "resist" is applied. A popular treatment is to "carbonize" the surface of the sand before casting. The first person I saw use this technique was Paul Marioni. Knowing Paul, he probably figured it out himself. A very clever fellow. Carbon is easily produced by igniting an acetylene torch without any oxygen. If you regulate the torch for a very lazy burn, you will generate a serious amount of carbon. You will know this when you see billows of black sooty smoke coming from the flame. After pressing your forms into the sand, run the torch flame over the sand, and it will deposit the carbon on the surface. Do this to all areas of your sand until you have a deep black deposit of carbon. This carbon will keep the sand from sticking to the glass. If you've put corn starch into the sand mixture, the combination of the carbon and flour will give you a pristine surface. A little experimentation will indicate how much carbon is enough. A thick layer of carbon will not interfere with the detail you've pressed into the sand.

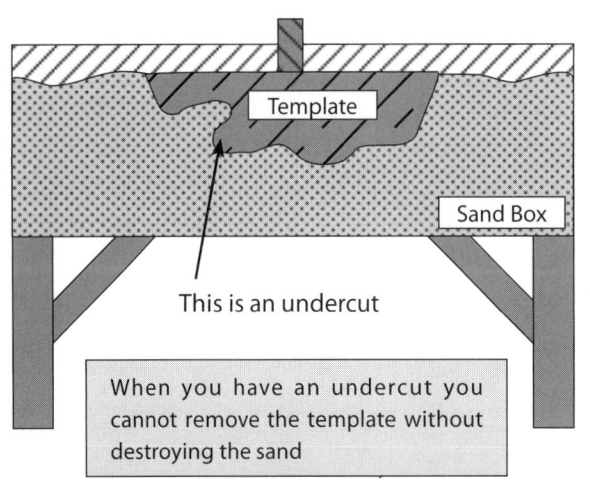

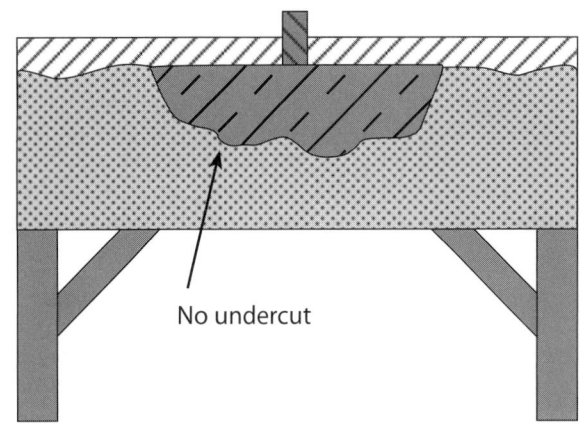

Another method I have used with some success is the Molasses spray technique. Buy yourself a bottle of Brer Rabbit Molasses (actually any brand will do but I like the Brer Rabbit label), and mix some with water until it is thin enough to go through a spray bottle. You want to get as much molasses into solution as you can. Spray this mixture onto the surface of your sand. The molasses, which is actually sugar, will carbonize when the molten glass hits it, thus preventing the sand from sticking to it. Be careful not to get the sand overly wet when spraying. You will know it's too wet if you're casting bubbles when the molten glass hits it. If your sand seems overly damp then I suggest you hit it with a bench torch. This will dry the sand and prevent bubbling. Another method is to screen fine graphite powder over the sand either before or after pressing the forms into the sand. Powdered graphite actually works the best of all; however, it is difficult to get an even coating in every nook and cranny of your casting.

If you want to create smooth "windows" in your casting, take pieces of solid graphite, press them into the sand, and leave them. When you pour the molten glass into the sand, the graphite will create a smooth "window" in contrast to the rough sand texture.

Ladling

Now we're ready to ladle some glass. This is real work and requires some serious upper body strength. The furnace should be full and very hot. The hotter the glass the easier it will flow and fill to the corners. Your glass should be soft and flow readily. Using bottle or window glass is rather counter productive as those types of glasses have very high viscosities and do not flow readily. You will need to have a 55 gallon drum partially filled with cold water. This will be used to quench the ladle before scooping out the glass and to cool the ladle after casting. The first thing to do is dip the ladle into the water. The ladle has to be as cool as possible to avoid having the molten glass stick to it. Remember if you dawdle with the ladle in the furnace as well as with the molten glass in the ladle, it will eventually stick to it. Trying to remove glass that has stuck to the ladle is a real pain.

When ladling you should wear a good pair of leather palmed gloves, a full face mask and perhaps a leather vest. These products can be found at welding supply houses. Using a strong scooping motion plunge the ladle under the surface of the glass and remove the full ladle from the furnace. Rest the handle of the ladle on a strong yoke and have your partner cut the strings and overflow from around the outside of the ladle. It is important that you use the right tool to trim the glass. There are some excellent casting trim tools on the market.

After trimming, carry the ladle over to the casting box and ladle the glass into the casting. You should pour from the side opposite from where it was trimmed. You will be required to move the ladle as you pour to make sure that the casting fills to the edges. If your casting requires more than one ladle of glass, you should have a second ladler pouring right after or at the same time you finish pouring the first ladle. Doing it this way will minimize any pouring seams. If your glass is not hot enough, it will not "run" and fill the mold. A glass that does not "set" quickly is advantageous. If your glass is cold or "sets" quickly, it will just sort of sit there without filling the mold. After casting, the ladle may have some threads hanging from the lip. Don't try breaking these off by pulling the ladle. Have your partner who is doing all the cutting trim these threads with the shears or burn them off with a torch. Now quickly take the ladle back to the furnace and, if you wish, dump all the glass that lines the ladle back into the furnace. Some people do this because there is usually a considerable quantity of glass left in the ladle. One of the problems with dumping the glass from the ladle back into the furnace is that you can get cool spots which might lower your furnace temperature. It always helps to have a second furnace for dumping. After cleaning the ladle, put it back into your 55 gallon drum of water to cool it and to prepare it for the next cast.

Everything that I have described above has probably taken considerably less than a minute. Now it's time to get back to the casting that you have just created.

The Casting

Everyone is now standing around looking at this clear, glowing mass of molten glass. The ohhs and ahhs slowly fill the air, but what is that there in the middle of the casting? It's a big fucking bubble rising to the surface. Your perfect casting now has a big gas pimple on its pristine glowing surface. What do you do? Fortunately, you thought ahead and have a beautiful new bench torch hooked up to a portable propane tank. You take careful aim at this obscene growth on the surface of your perfect casting. You quickly and deliberately squeeze the smooth chromed

> If you want to create smooth "windows" in your casting take pieces of solid graphite, press them into the sand, and leave them. When you pour the molten glass into the sand, the graphite will create a smooth "window" in contrast to the rough sand texture.

handle which sits perfectly in your hot sweaty palm. Your heart is pounding as the torch springs to life and you feel the full power of 150,000 Btu's roaring like the jets of the Space Shuttle. You aim the searing flame directly at this gaseous volcano. The bubble slowly peels back under the onslaught of the intense concentrated heat. Slowly this blemish, this insult to your anal retentiveness disappears and melts back into the surface, leaving only the faintest scar. A wry smile crosses your face and you shake your head knowing you've won this round. But, my friend, you must believe this is only round one. They will return.*

A few tricks

Eventually, you will grow tired of just casting molten glass into sand. The results can be quite boring and you will seek additional "tricks" to spice up the surface or interior of your castings. Some of the following techniques have been use by casters over the years.

After pressing your template into the sand, try some of the following techniques:

- Lightly sprinkle some color bar powder onto the sand. A light dusting will melt onto the surface of the casting. The color powders do not really melt or flow but only fuse to the surface of the casting. A light dusting is all that is needed. Anything more than a light dusting will not fuse and will only wash off. Course frit will fuse to the surface but will not melt or flow and will look like course frit fused onto the surface of the casting.
- Pull some colored cane and carefully lay or press them into the sand.
- Lay out some gold or silver leaf on the sand.
- Stick some copper wire into the sand. Make sure some of the wire protrudes into the glass. Copper has about the same expansion as glass and will not check when it cools. You can use the protruding copper wire to tie objects to the casting.
- Blow some colorful objects and keep them in an annealer. When you're ready to sand cast, quickly place them into the sand and then cast over them. Even if they check a bit, they will be held in place by the casting.
- Pull solid cane and push pieces into the sand with the ends protruding into the casting. For some reason, the cane doesn't check and anneals with the casting.
- When casting something thick, do it in cast layers. Put compatible objects between layers to be viewed from the clear top side.
- There are any number of other tricks that casters use. I'm sure once you've become familiar with the process you will invent a few of your own.

*If bubbles rise to the surface of your casting they can be smoothed out with a MAPP torch. The flame from a MAPP torch is very hot and will cause the bubble to break and smooth-out. Make sure you get the torch with the self start trigger.

Bentonite/Sand Casting

Rick Mills, University of Hawaii

This is about the best description of the sand casting process I have seen. Rick's descriptions of the process are accurate and to the point. I wish to thank him for allowing me to reprint this student handout and share it with you. Thanks Rick.

Pattern Making for Wet Sand Molds

Patterns for wet sand casting can be made from a variety of materials. The great advantage of this type of casting is that practically any type of material can be used to make an impression in the sand. However, the material should be relatively inflexible, strong, reusable, and have no undercuts. Found objects such as plastic doll parts, machine parts, and household items are all suitable for making an impression in the sand. Keep your eyes open for manufactured items which have interesting shapes or textures. Objects which have radically different thicknesses, or complex or attenuated forms will be nearly impossible to cast. Remember, you are only making an impression from one side of the form and will not be able to completely embed the form in the sand and then remove it! Multiple patterns can be pressed into the same mold to create unlimited combinations.

The following is a list of materials for carving and shaping your own forms from:

Foam Block: Either open or closed cell foam is easily shaped with the "hot wire," band saw, and belt/disc sanders. *Author's note: If you are using a hot wire you should wear a respirator as the fumes are dangerous, if you are using a sander make sure you have a particle mask on! Foam block is lightweight, rigid and may be glued together with rubber cement. A wood or foam handle glued to the back of your pattern will help remove it from the sand. No undercuts.*

Wood: Any type of scrap wood (that is free of nails) can be shaped by sawing, laminating, carving, turning, and sanding to create a durable, reusable pattern. Bare, unsealed wood is often hard to remove from the sand because it absorbs moisture and causes the sand to stick. Seal wood with a light coat of varnish. In addition to this, patterns can be covered with a light coat of spray graphite or talcum as a resist to prevent the sand from sticking to the pattern. All wood patterns should have a sturdy handle to permit removal from sand. No undercuts.

Plaster: Plaster forms cast into wet clay or latex molds make good patterns. Plaster blocks may also be carved to create additional patterns and textures. All plaster patterns should be sealed with gesso or varnish so they do not absorb moisture out of the wet sand and cause the sand to stick. Graphite or talcum are suitable mold releases, and handles may be attached by impressing a heavy wire with bent ends into the plaster as it is hardening. No undercuts.

Bisque Fired Clay: Because of clay's natural plastic quality, it is one of the easiest pattern materials to work with, unlike the previously mentioned materials. It is responsive, direct, and you do not have to hammer away with a chisel or dig the plaster from under your fingernails. However, unless the clay has been bisque fired, it is too fragile to use as a pattern for sand casting and will fall apart as you try to make an impression. Bisque–fired clay should be sealed and pattern released as mentioned earlier, and handles should be attached either in clay before firing. No undercuts.

"Pattern Materials that I have Known" (and do not work)

While you are free to try any sort of pattern materials you please, as long as they do not present a health or safety hazard, there are some that simply will not work. For example, fast food stuffs, thin tree branches, your head in a bag and pressed into sand, coins and other small objects with fine detail, foam rubber, large patterns which you cannot lift, and–yes– patterns with undercuts! I strongly recommend you use either found objects, foam block, wood, plaster, or bisqued clay as pattern materials before experimenting with alternative materials.

Sand Casting Process

There are two main approaches to sand casting: "in the box" and "out of the box." Mild steel flat boxes (mold boxes) can be filled with molding sand to pour glass into. These boxes are then loaded into the annealers, casting and all, to cool. The other approach is to pull the casting out of the box and load just the casting. Both approaches have their advantages. Loading in the box causes less distortion to the casting, and castings can be loaded hotter without thin sections getting too cold and checking. The disadvantage is that the boxes are heavy, take up valuable annealing space, and cool the oven down every time you load. Out-of-the-box loading allows you to cast larger forms because you do not have the box to contend with and more pieces can be loaded in the same oven without a drastic loss of heat. It does, however, create a problem with distortion and potential checking of thin sections.

Sand Mixture

The wet sand mix is made from a blend of 60 and 90 mesh silica sand with 5% bentonite added as a binder. The bentonite is a clay former and helps hold the silica sand together. All materials should be mixed thoroughly, screened, and moistened with water until the sand is just damp and "packable." Sand that is saturated with water will cause steam bubbles to rise up through the casting and render it useless in most cases. It is easier to err on the dry side and add more water with a spray bottle than it is to waterlog the sand and have to mix in more dry sand.

The theory behind sand mixtures is to produce a porous, sensitive sand body which readily takes an impression yet is strong enough to remove the pattern. The finer the grain of sand, the sharper your detail but the less porous the mold will be (which can cause outgassing). The sand should feel loose, loamy, and damp--not lumpy, packed, and soaked.

Process, Making a Single Impression

Once your patterns and sand have been prepared, you are ready to make an impression. Set your mold box on a level surface. If the table is not level, chances are your casting will be of uneven thickness because you will pack your pattern at an angle and the glass will only fill a level mold. Fill the box ⅔ full with damp sand by sifting it through a ¼" screen. This process is called "riddling" and loosens the sand so it will more readily take an impression. Take your pattern and firmly impress it into the loose sand. Make sure you have at least 1" between the pattern and the mold box on all sides and the bottom. Now, using your fingers and/or a ramming tool, pack the sand around your pattern. Add sand as needed until the top edge of the pattern is flushed with the sand, and continue ramming. A well-packed mold should fill the mold box to the edge, and the top of the pattern should be level with this. Strike off the top of your pattern to remove loose sand that may fall into your mold. Then take a wood or rubber mallet and tap the back side of your pattern into the sand (this does not work with patterns made of foam block). Use your handle to wiggle and move your pattern side to side and front to back to loosen the sand from the surface. After creating a little room around the pattern (³⁄₁₆"), gently and carefully begin to remove the pattern by lifting straight up without disturbing the walls. Removing the pattern from the mold is called "drafting." If you have difficulty drafting, it means either the pattern has undercuts, or the sand is sticking to the pattern. Remove any undercuts, and coat the pattern with release to help solve these problems. Do not be disappointed if your first several attempts do not yield a good mold. Each pattern will have its own unique problems. Small, incomplete impression areas can be resolved with careful touch-ups after the pattern has been removed. Use clay working tools to reposition and pack sand in incomplete areas. A water spray bottle will help selectively moisten areas to be repacked.

Surface Treatments

Once you are satisfied with the mold, spray graphite can be applied to prevent the sand from fusing to the surface. At least 2 even coats are required to completely cover the sand. Acetylene soot may be used if you are familiar with the Oxy/Acetylene torch operation. Colored glass powders, threads, frit, or copper additions may also be applied (after the mold release). Remember, the first color you lay down will be seen on the outside "front" surface of the casting; any additional colors, or the last color applied, will be seen from the "back" clear side of the casting. You should consider carefully the arrangement of colored layers and how they will be viewed in the finished sculpture.

Multiple Impressions

The multiple impression technique is perhaps the most open and free of all glass casting processes. By simply making an open, general impression or hollow in the prepared sand, smaller impressions may be driven down inside using wood patterns and tools. Undercuts may be created this way, which would not normally draft in a single impression approach. This gives you an incredible range of possibilities to use the sand like a three-dimensional drawing. When making multiple impressions, care should be taken not to disturb the initial impression by caving sand down into the mold. By reinserting the original pattern, you can re-establish your shape. Remember, each time you press something into the sand you are making a positive shape in glass. If you want to make negative impressions in the final casting, you need to build up positive sand shapes, or protrusions within the mold. This can be achieved by packing sand into another mold, removing it and dropping it into the larger impression. These are called "cores" and can also be made out of bonded sand.

Summary

Perhaps the wet sand's greatest advantage is its immediacy. Unlike lost-wax and investment mold casting, it is much more direct. Your casting will be a fossil record of the time and energy expended on the sand impression and the event of pouring the glass.

What one gains in a more raw, low technology process, one will lose in the casting as a platform approach in chorus with offhand inclusions, or manipulation, or mixed media. While sand casting is a relatively simple process, it is not without subtlety for which you must develop sensitivity. This is the nature of the process, and it should be reckoned with as you strive to find your voice as an artist.

Casting Ladles

Cast and Blow

One of my favorite techniques was "invented" in the early 70's by one of my former students, Tom Armbruster. The method involves pushing a form into a metal bucket filled with bentonite sand. Gather and form your glass as you would for blowing a mold. Before blowing into the sand, however, you can do one of two things: take a good, hot thick gather and motivate quickly over to the bucket. Let the hot glass run off the bubble into the cavity you pressed into the bottom of the bucket, being careful not to let the hot casting glass separate from the bubble. When the cavity has filled with hot glass, begin to blow the bubble into the upper cavity. When you pull the glass from the sand, you will have a sand cast bottom section and blown upper section. Another method is to simply ladle some glass into the bottom cavity and then take your blow pipe that already has a blown bubble of sufficient size and blow into the still-soft cast section. The latter technique might require that you work with a partner in order to coordinate the casting with the blowing. The problem with the second technique is that you run the risk of trapping sand between the casting and the blown form. If you've used the sand/bentonite/corn starch technique with an acetylene coating, the casting should come out clean and easily puntied. If you have sand stuck to the bottom of the cast section, you may have trouble puntying the piece.

I know it sounds rather strange, but I have seen some excellent stuff created using this method. I'm sure you can find variations of this technique that suit your specific aesthetic. I hope the accompanying illustration clarifies this technique.

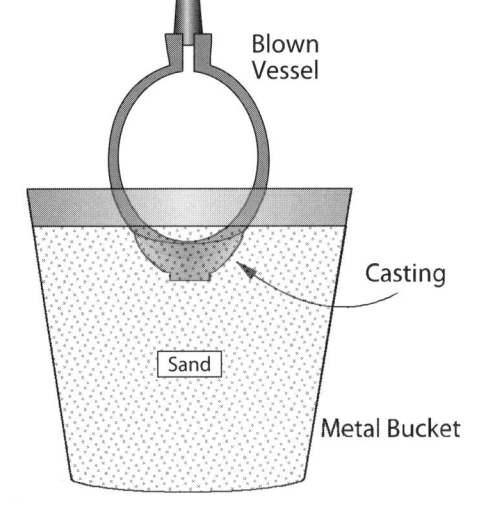

The Armbruster Bucket Blow

The José Chardiet Method of Sand Casting

José Chardiet is best known for his distinctive and elegant sand castings. His objects, infused with color, are both playful and formal in their presentation. His objects show a great deal of technical skill without being obvious. His combinations of colorful, hot worked forms combined with sand casting show a keen eye for juxtaposing diverse elements. The elegance of his objects is heightened by the many hours of cold working. Best known for his "Table" castings, Chardiet needed to develop a technique that would permit him to cast his long, attenuated forms. The technique he developed departed from the standard sand casting method in two distinct ways, as follows:

Chardiet does not cast at room temperature, nor does he cast into damp sand as described in the previous text on sand casting.

He takes a steel box, about 12 to 16 gauge, and fills it with the traditional damp bentonite/sand mixture. The model or models he is using are then pressed into the sand. The objects he usually casts using this method are table forms that have long legs (fig. 1, pg. 109). If he were to cast his table forms at room temperature into the damp sand, the molten glass would set before filling the legs of his pieces. After he presses the models into the sand, he preheats his formed sand boxes in an annealing oven to about 1100°

F (595° C). This accomplishes two things: it hardens and dries the sand mixture. Remember, the sand has bentonite clay in it. The high temperature causes the bentonite to fire, thus slightly hardening the casting sand and preventing it from deforming when the hot glass hits it. The one problem (if you can call it that) to this technique lies in the fact that you cannot use any carbon coatings on the sand to prevent sticking. Because the sand adheres to the surface of his castings, Chardiet sand blasts the surface to reveal the underlying glass. After attaining temperature, the annealer is opened, and the molten glass is ladled in while the sand mold is hot. Chardiet does not remove the boxes from the annealer to cast them but instead casts directly in the oven. If you intend to emulate this technique, it becomes important to design an oven that will permit you to cast in this manner. Because the sand is so hot, the glass stays viscous for a long period of time, thus permitting it to fill the deep pockets of his casting. Chardiet sometimes places decorative, preformed glass elements down the legs before preheating the molds. Slowly raising the temperature of the oven keeps these elements from checking.

After the piece is cast and before the lid to the annealer is closed, he presses preformed, dry plaster forms into the molten glass. It is very important to have dry plaster elements before pressing into the molten glass (fig. 1, below). If you press the plaster forms in at the right time, they sometimes penetrate through the casting, thus permitting the inserted form to poke through the bottom of the "Table." The plaster forms he uses are exact replicas of the bottoms of blown or solid-shaped forms already created. To replicate the bottom of these forms, he makes pressed clay molds of the bottoms of these pieces and then casts plaster into these clay molds. Before the plaster sets, a dry wall screw is pressed into the setting plaster to be used as a handle. The plaster forms anneal with the glass casting. After annealing, the plaster is easily removed, leaving an indentation that will hold his Table "inserts." After cooling, all the pieces are cold worked. Some surfaces may be gold leafed, others polished in preparation for final assembly.

Chardiet's techniques, although rather advanced, are certainly not complicated or difficult. I am rather amazed that more casting artists have not explored this very exciting method of sand casting.

It should be obvious to the reader that it is important to wear the correct clothing and heat-resistant gloves as well as a full face mask when trying this technique. It gets very hot working over an open, hot annealer. As they say on TV, this technique is being demonstrated by professionals and should not be tried at home.

I have produced a video of José demonstrating this technique. The video was shot at a workshop José gave at Kent State some years ago. It shows in fairly precise detail how his "tables" are cast. Anyone interested in obtaining a copy should E-mail or call.

Fig. 1

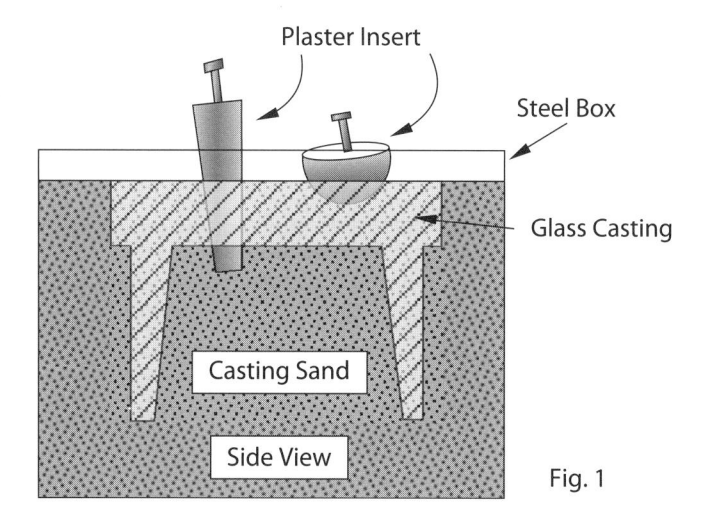

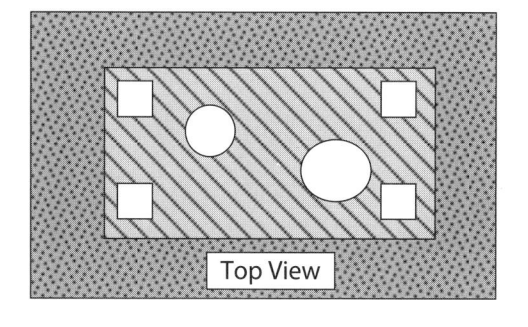

Fig. 2

"Havana Nights"
1998

Bob Carlson Break-Away Box

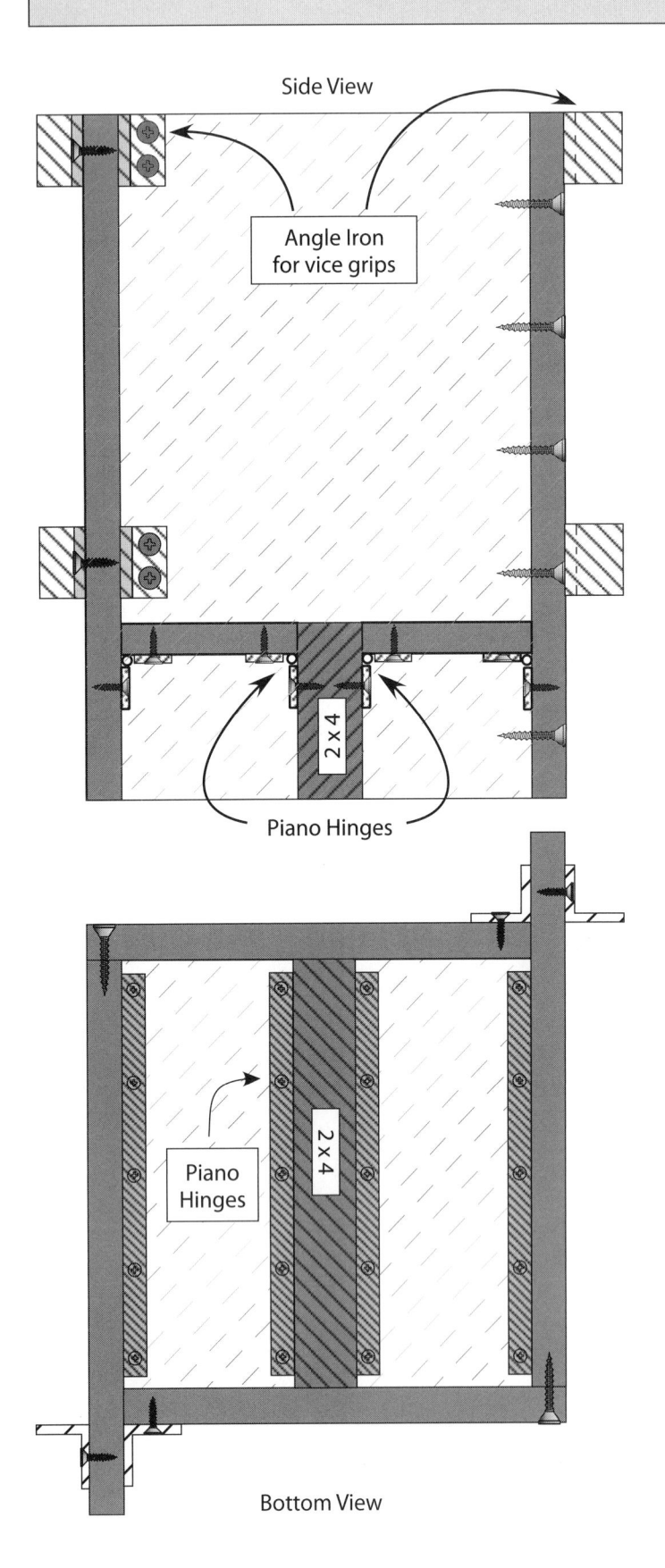

Side View — Angle Iron for vice grips — 2 x 4 — Piano Hinges

Bottom View — Piano Hinges — 2 x 4

In the early 90's, Bob Carlson presented a workshop at Kent State University and, at that time, introduced us to a very "clever" method of blowing into standard casting sand. The method is disarmingly simple once you know how to do it. Isn't everything? By using the break-away box described and shown on these pages, it is possible to create some unusual blown forms. I think this technique is a great contribution to the craft of glass blowing. It is one of the main techniques Bob uses to create the underlying glass forms upon which he paints his phantasmagorical images.

The box is constructed from ¾" plywood. In this version of his box, the angle iron is important as these are the points where you attach vice grips in order to keep the box from opening as you blow. After blowing the form, open the vice grips and rock the blown piece back and forth a bit to help it release from the sand. The rocking breaks the sand down a bit and makes it easier to lift out of the box although it still takes a bit of doing. Remember, you're not only lifting the glass but the sand as well. According to Bob, the easiest way to get it out of the box is to have an assistant open the box as you lift. Everything is easier if you have an assistant, Bob.

Bob Carlson Box Perspective

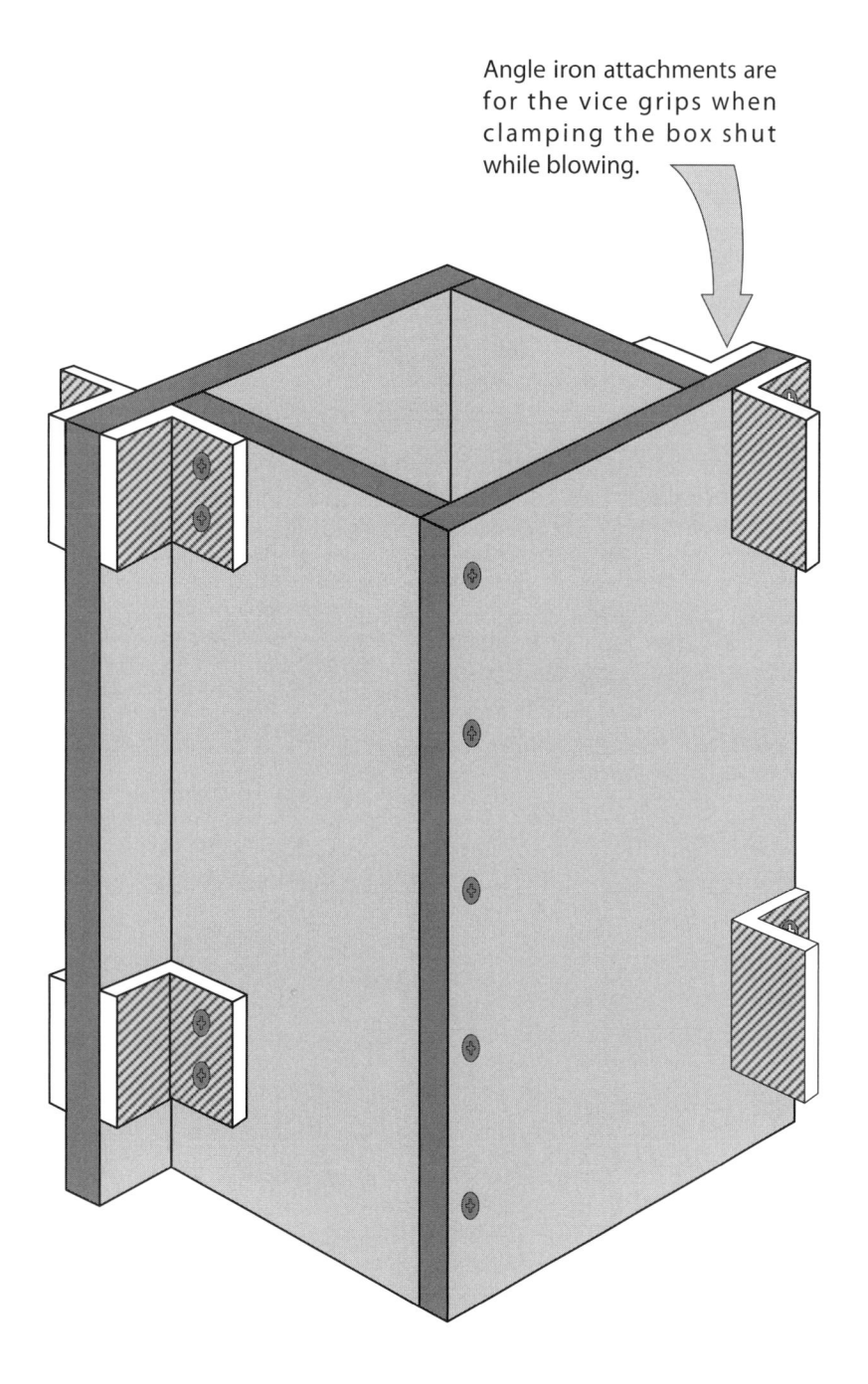

Angle iron attachments are for the vice grips when clamping the box shut while blowing.

The drawings on the following page are redrawn from Bob's own drawings found on his website and reprinted with his permission. The only real difference between the two versions is that Bob uses a simple hinged latching device to hold the box shut while blowing.

Glass Notes 111

Carlson Break-away Mold Box

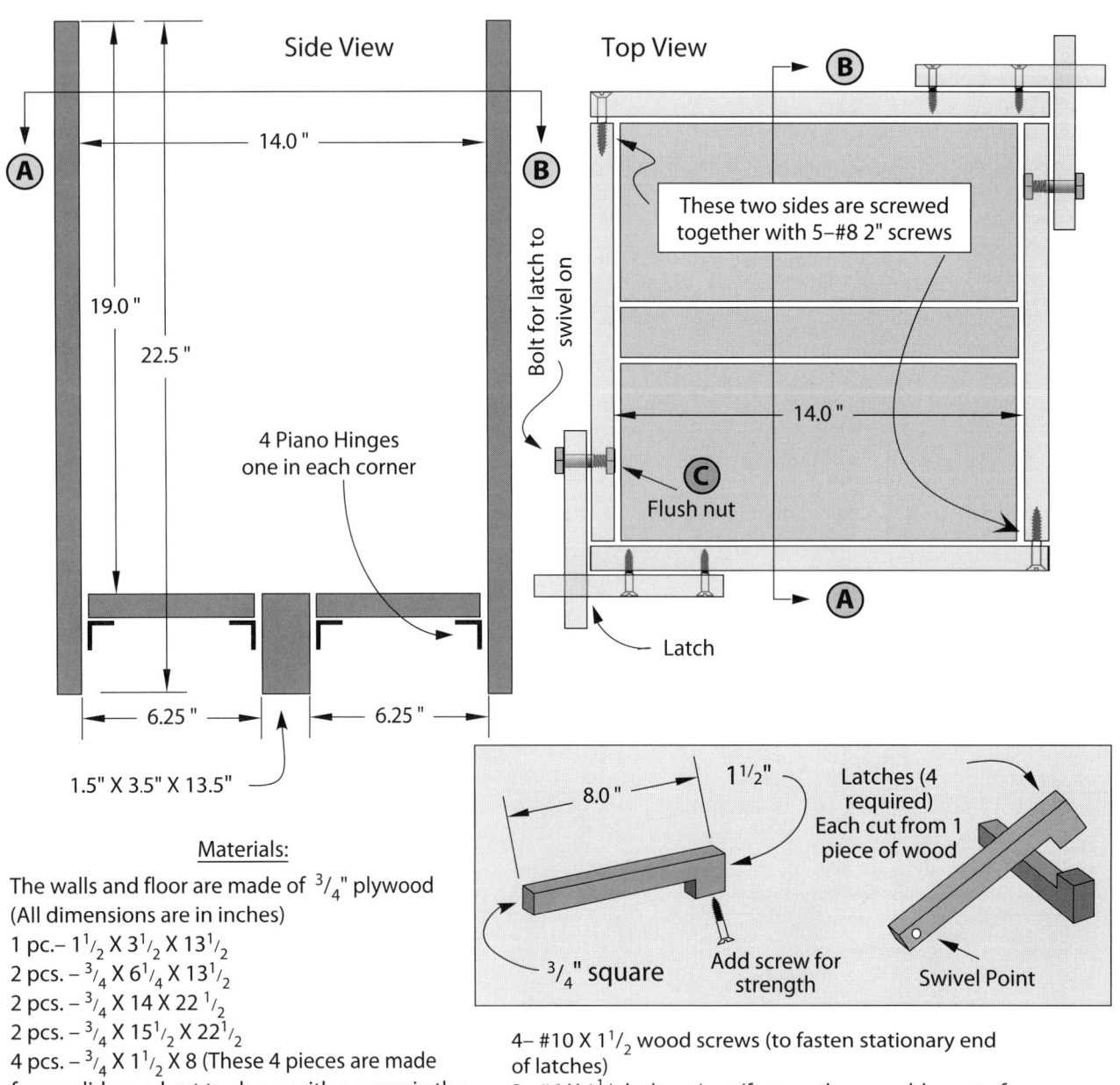

Side View

Top View

- 14.0 "
- 19.0 "
- 22.5 "
- 6.25 "
- 6.25 "
- 1.5" X 3.5" X 13.5"

A, B, C

4 Piano Hinges one in each corner

Bolt for latch to swivel on

These two sides are screwed together with 5–#8 2" screws

14.0 "

Flush nut

Latch

8.0 " 1½"

¾" square

Add screw for strength

Latches (4 required) Each cut from 1 piece of wood

Swivel Point

Materials:
The walls and floor are made of $^3/_4$" plywood (All dimensions are in inches)
- 1 pc.– $1^1/_2$ X $3^1/_2$ X $13^1/_2$
- 2 pcs. – $^3/_4$ X $6^1/_4$ X $13^1/_2$
- 2 pcs. – $^3/_4$ X 14 X $22^1/_2$
- 2 pcs. – $^3/_4$ X $15^1/_2$ X $22^1/_2$
- 4 pcs. – $^3/_4$ X $1^1/_2$ X 8 (These 4 pieces are made from solid wood cut to shape with a screw in the end for strength and makes 2 latches.)
- 4 – $^1/_2$ X $13^1/_2$ Piano hinges with $^3/_4$" screws for fastening. (the sturdier the piano hinge the better).
- 4– #10 X $1^1/_2$ wood screws (to fasten stationary end of latches)
- 2– #6 X $1^1/_2$ bolts w/nut (fastens the movable part of latches. I drill a blind hole slightly smaller than the nut and then hammer the nut flush with the inside surface; the bolt can then thread into it (see C in drawing above).
- 5– #8 X 2" screws

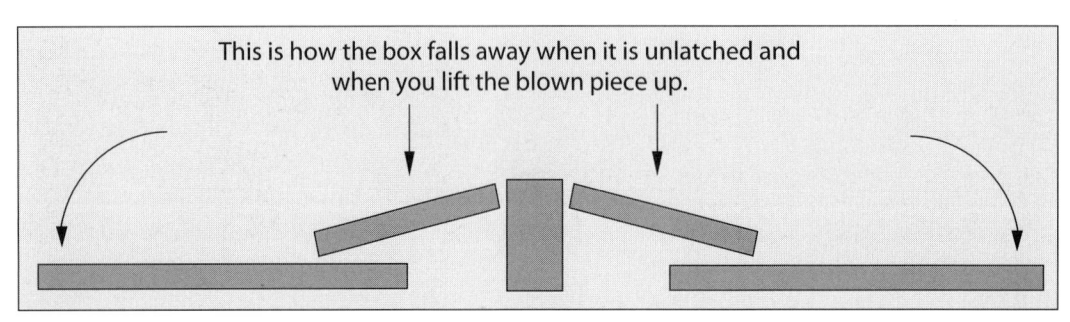

This is how the box falls away when it is unlatched and when you lift the blown piece up.

112 Glass Notes

The Set-Up of the Bob Carlson Blow Box

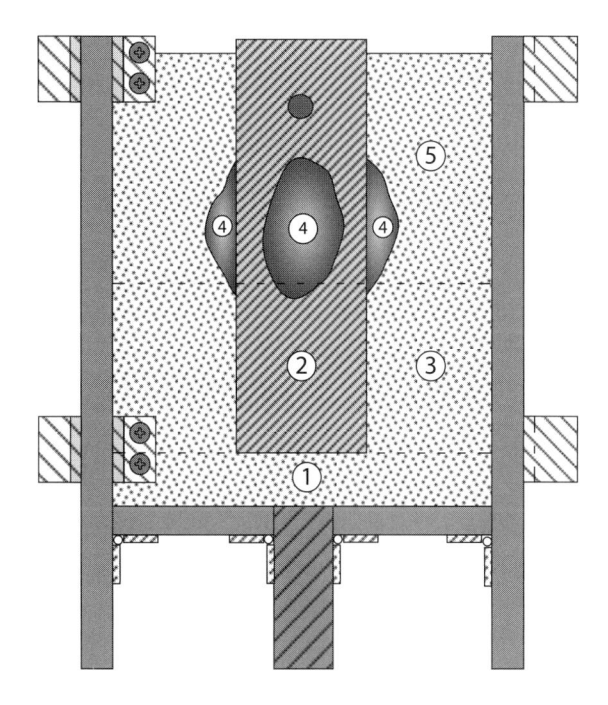

- Place a layer of damp casting sand into box as indicated.

- Place wooden form on this layer of sand.

- Fill with more casting sand as indicated. Make sure you tamp the sand firmly.

- Place wooden, plaster, or styrofoam form or forms against central wooden form and fill with more sand. Tamp the sand firmly. Make sure the additional forms don't move while putting sand into mold. It is the sand that holds the forms against the central wooden form.

- Fill to top with sand. Tamp firmly as you place sand into mold.

- After you have completely filled the mold with sand, carefully remove the central wooden form by lifting straight up. Notice the handle in the form. You may have to wiggle the form to remove it cleanly. If any of your forms have undercuts, you will not be able to remove them without disturbing the sand. It is a good idea to coat all the surfaces of the forms being used with graphite powder as this will aid in their separating from the sand. After removing the central wooden form, remove the additional forms carefully. It is a good idea to have a couple of screw holes in the forms to aid in their removal.

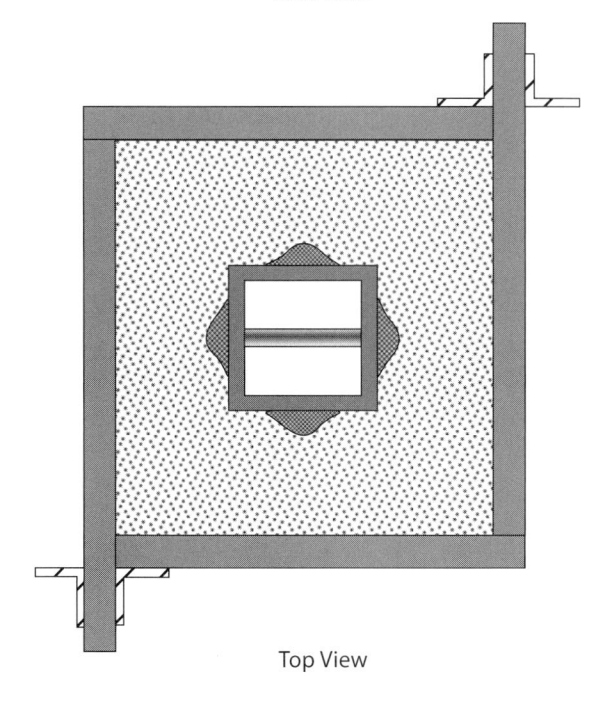

Side View

Top View

Mold Ready for Blowing

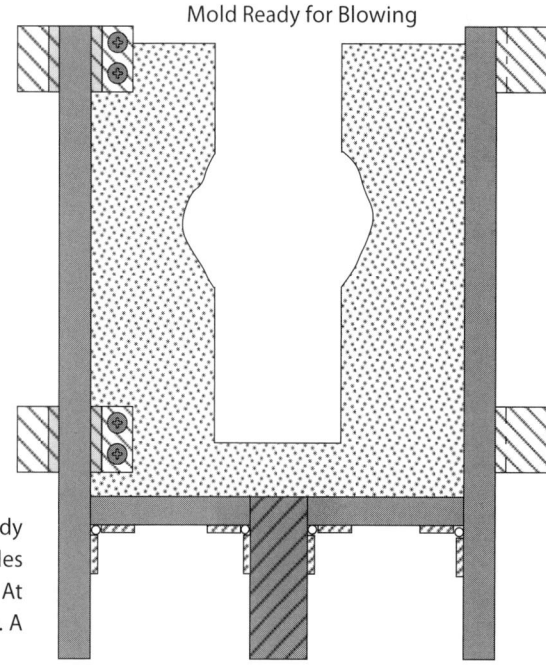

After the forms are carefully removed from the sand, the mold is ready for blowing. As you lift the blown object from the box, the hinged sides will fall away from the piece, permitting you to work it at the bench. At this point, it is a good idea to clean the sand from the blown piece. A wire brush works very well. The sand does not stick to the glass.

Robert Carlson

In his own words

I am at heart a three dimensional artist, and this is the reason I love using glass as my medium. While I spend a great deal of time and toil painting two-dimensional images on my glass pieces, the clear glass transmits these images through itself, allowing me to turn an object of surfaces into an object with both surfaces and an interior.

My pieces are three-dimensional narratives that are meant to be "grocked" (the term Robert Heinlein coined to express complete and immediate understanding) as opposed to "understood." Unlike a written narrative, where a linear progression of words slowly brings the reader to the story and ultimately to an understanding, my sculptures present an entire narrative experience in a unique and more immediate visual format. To me this is the beauty and allure of sculpture.

In my pieces, these images become truly grockable conceptions that burst into our consciousness and allow us to "understand" the original thought. Like dreams, they contain within them all the contradictions of wholeness. They combine reason with un-reason, form with formlessness, and comprehension with the incomprehensible. And much as we like to decipher our dreams, analyzing the bizarre juxtaposition of images and events into understandable segments, all we really accomplish is to separate an incomprehensible whole into bite size segments of understanding. But the dream is in its most complete form before we analyze it; it wants us to be mystified and awed.

Title: Axis Mundi, 1991
Artist: Robert Carlson
Dimensions: 6 x 13 x 32
Media: Blown Glass, Wood, Enamel Paint, Gold Leaf

Photo: Roger Schreiber

To learn more about Bob and his work, go to his website: http://www.robertcarlson.net/index.html

Kiln Casting

The Klaus Moje Method

I have always been a great admirer of Klaus Moje's work. I am attracted to the simplicity of his forms and their highly-charged colored surfaces. His shallow, slumped bowl forms are not unlike the simplicity of Japanese tea bowls. His work blends the container into a simple, colorful object, the essence of a decorative container. Only the color reveals their modernity. Unlike other glass objects that use degrees of transparency, his objects are usually opaque. I am often reminded of the color of Egyptian core vessels. Transparency and light seem to be such a consuming issue among many of the glass makers of today that one forgets that transparency was not introduced until the Roman era. Moje's issues seem to be the simple form blended with highly-charged color.

During the summer of 1995, Klaus Moje came to Kent State University to teach his techniques to a small class of enthusiastic students. I distilled the following notes and drawings from that workshop. Before printing the information, I submitted the document and drawings to Klaus for his approval. I have not introduced any of his aesthetic concerns but only his techniques in effecting the making of a "Moje form."

Making the Mold

Begin by constructing a plaster/flint mold. The mold is comprised of 2 parts potter plaster to 1 part silica. These proportions of plaster/flint are quite different from the mold mixture of 1:1. For this process the mixture is by volume and not by weight. *Author's note: Wear a good dust mask when working with plaster and silica.* To make the mold we first obtained a shallow bowl that had the shape of the area we would be slumping into. A box was constructed from ¼" (6 mm) plate glass by simply taping the four sides to a sheet of glass slightly larger than the glass object to be slumped. *Author's note: There are other ways to construct a mold box, but this method is so simple that I have included it.* The question arose in the class as to whether one could make a fired clay mold so that it could be used for unlimited firings. The answer is yes, but it must be able to withstand thermal shock and of course remain flat. Being an old potter, I would recommend that you carefully slab build one from a raku type clay. Trade a good potter a nice piece of glass for a mold. If you use a ceramic-type slumping mold, the surface must be coated with a kiln wash (1 part kaolin [EPK] to 1 part alumina hydrate and enough water to make a thick paint). A plaster/flint mold is much easier. It is possible to use the Moje style mold for multiple firing if you're careful not to move or touch it after it has been fired. As Moje says, "It must sit its whole life on a kiln shelf."

The glass mold box needs to be on a level table. Dry mix the plaster/flint and then add it to a sufficient amount of water that will comprise the total mold. You cannot make this mold in layers as they will separate when fired. It is assumed you are familiar with how the mixture is added to the water and how much plaster/flint is added as well. If you are not, familiarize yourself with these mixing techniques. After the mixture is poured and has begun to thicken slightly, lightly press a round-bottomed, metal mixing bowl or blown sphere into the setting mixture. Vibrate it slightly when placing it in the plaster mixture. This will ensure that the surface remains flat. It is held there until it has thickened enough that it will remain in place on its own. Let the mold "set" completely. After "setting," the mold will be quite soft. Allow the mold to dry completely in a warm place. After the mold is dry, it is placed in an annealer and heated at a rate of about 122° F (68° C) an hour for 12 hours (1465° F) (796° C). The temperature is then raised to 1545° F (840° C). The curing of the mold drives out all the chemically–bonded moisture and burns off all organic materials that can affect the glass when it is slumped. After curing, the mold will be lightly cracked. Do not attempt to move it as it will fall apart if you do. If you have done all of the above correctly, the mold is ready for the sheet that you will create.

Creating the Sheet

Before getting into Klaus' technique, it is important to know that, in order to realize this technique, you must use a glass that is fusing–compatible. Klaus uses Bullseye. Before Klaus started using Bullseye glass, he used Hessen glass which gave his work a dense opacity. It is my understanding that Bullseye owner Dan Schwoerer, after seeing Klaus's work, invited him to try Bullseye glass. Klaus obliged Dan, and the rest is history.

Bullseye glass is constantly tested for compatibility before it leaves the factory. If you know anything about glass and compatibility, you know Bullseye has solved one on the most difficult problems that exists in glass chemistry: color compatibility. The technology that they have perfected has made possible glass objects that have historically rarely been attainable. Thanks Dan!

Although this glass is tested compatible, be careful when fusing certain colors or using certain firing schedules. You should be aware that the colors made with cadmium and selenium (reds, yellows, and oranges) may change their expansion when taken to higher than normal fusing temperatures (i.e., 1500° F; 815° C) or fired for longer than usual times (i.e., 30 hours).

Author's note: Bullseye's testing method for cadmium/seleniums involves three separate firings (each firing being a full fuse to 1500°F with a 10 minute soak and a return to room temperature over a period of about 10 hours). Should the glass show stress on any of the three firings, it is not labeled as Tested Compatible.

Klaus' process sometimes involves times and temperatures outside of Bullseye's testing range. If you are pushing the limits of the material as Klaus sometimes does, test your particular color palette at the maximum temperature. I don't wish to scare you about this problem; I just wish to call your attention to the necessity of familiarizing yourself with the capabilities of the material. If you're exceeding the factory testing range be prepared to do the requisite additional testing yourself.

There are other reasons why your work may check that have nothing to do with incompatibility. It is assumed that you have some understanding of how glass is annealed. If you don't, you will need to obtain literature that explains the various technical rules that need to be observed before starting this process. The book you are reading now, *Glass Notes*, explains annealing and has an excellent chart developed by Jeremy Lepisto on pg. 122.

Begin

The first step is to create the glass sheet that will eventually be slumped. If you don't have two ovens, you will need to create the sheet before curing the mold. As stated previously, the mold cannot be moved once it is heat cured. Make the sheet first and then make the mold. Klaus began his introductory demonstration by first cutting his glass into strips. The strips are composed of various colors and are typically laid out in a simple striped pattern, usually no more than 3 layers thick. They are laid out on a flat kiln shelf that has a layer of fiber paper covering it. This paper will prevent the glass from fusing to the shelf. Although there are many patterns possible, he used the striped patterns to introduce us to the technique. His finished, "stacked" shape is usually a square or rectangle. As the diagram on the next page shows, the stack is bordered by stripes of fiber paper laid on top of each other creating a "dam." This fiber dam will help the hot, soft glass maintain its shape. If you wish to cut exact glass stripes, there are various gadgets on the market for doing this. One device I found that is rather well designed and reasonably priced is called *The Morton System*. A novel device, but it works. I'm sure your local stained glass supply store knows about this device. The diagrams that follow later in this chapter will help you understand the process being described.

Building the glass stack thicker than three layers can create problems in the slumping stage. All the layers can be composed of parallel stripes or placed randomly if you wish. It is important to lay the glass out in such a way that, when it softens and fuses, you do not create any thick and thin spots. This can eventually lead to uneven slumping. We also found that, if you attempt to lay a complete sheet of color as one of the layers and then lay strips on top, the piece will crack.

Klaus uses different patterns for laying down the glass stripes. Some stripes go in the same direction, and other layers lie perpendicular to each other. Sometimes the stripes lie next to each other; at other times, they lie partially on top of each other. Each technique used creates its own set of problems and its own particular aesthetic. If you follow the temperatures for fusing as stated in the diagrams, you can avoid some problems. One of the problems created is trapped air when the glass fuses. This usually happens when you use the method that has the strips lying partially on top of each other. When using this method, you will fuse at a significantly higher temperature than when fusing with the strips next to each other. The higher temperature permits the trapped gas bubbles

Moje Piece

to rise and break through the surface. The higher the temperature in fusing, the greater the chance the expansion of the cadmium/selenium colors will be affected and the greater the interaction one color has to its adjacent color. After laying out the glass strips, it will be necessary, as stated previously, to create a fiber paper dam around the perimeter of the glass. You will also do all your fusing on a flat kiln shelf covered with a sheet of fiber paper.

Follow the directions at each diagram, and you should be successful in creating a well-fused and slumped piece. Remember, this is merely an introduction to fusing. There are unlimited variations of this technique. It is not my intent to have you become a Klaus Moje clone but merely to introduce you to what I consider a very creative use of glass. The technique is rather simple to master. Making art with the technique should be what its mastery is about.

Henry & Klaus in the good ole days.

Opening the annealer. Moje workshop at Kent State University.

Strip Stacking

This diagram shows the technique that is perhaps the simplest of all the techniques that Klaus demonstrated. Narrow strips of glass are laid out next to each other in three layers. Fiber paper is cut in strips about an inch wide and long enough to totally enclose each side of the glass. The strips are stacked as high as the glass. When the glass softens and fuses, it will have a tendency to flow and thin out if the fiber dam is not in place. The fiber will remain in place throughout the firing.

Firing Procedure

Because the strips of glass are laid next to each other and not partially over each other (as shown in the diagram on the next page), the glass is less likely to trap air when it softens and fuses together. The temperature of the oven can be raised to 1540° F (840° C) as fast as your oven will go. 1540° F is the temperature for full fusing and is the temperature used by most kiln casters. If the temperature is lower, you will not get the glass to flow evenly. Holding the oven for 15 minutes at 1540° F is usually sufficient. If your oven is well insulated and cools slowly, the oven can be shut off and allowed to cool naturally. The natural insulation of the annealer is usually enough to give the proper cooling curve for glass of this thickness. If your oven cools extremely rapidly, you may run the risk of cracking the sheet. If this is the case, you will need to anneal the glass. After the oven is shut off, the door is usually opened and the temperature is dropped to about 1100° F (600° C) very quickly. Dropping the temperature back to this level will prevent devitrification of the glass surface. Although devitrification looks like a dull scum on the glass surface, it is actually tiny crystals that precipitate out of the glassy solution and form on the glass surface. If you drop the temperature below this level, you run the risk of warping the glass sheet or possibly cracking the sheet itself.

Stacked strips of Bullseye fusable glass (3 thicknesses)

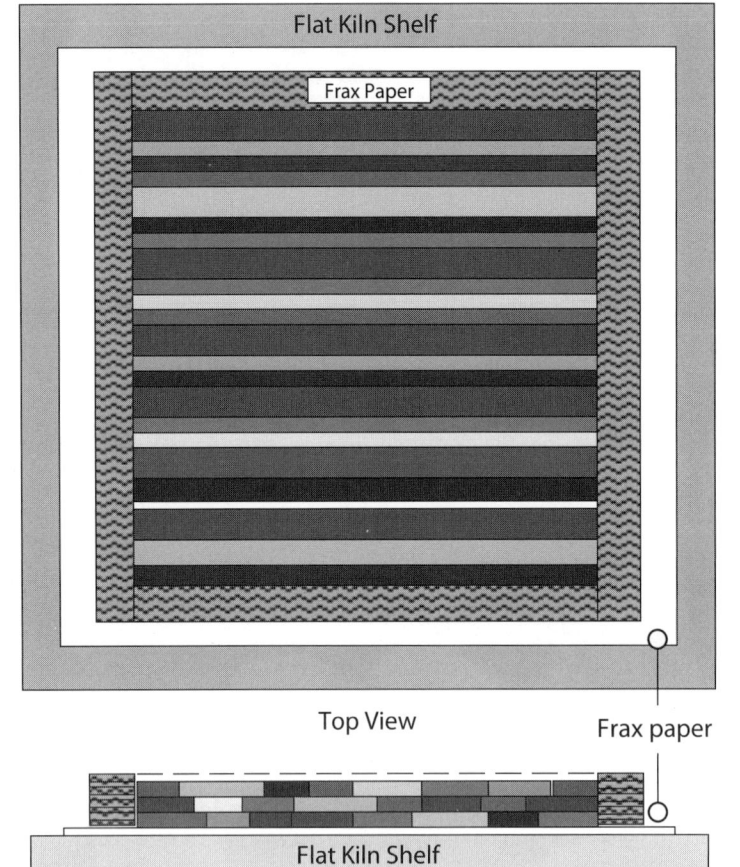

Flat Kiln Shelf

Frax Paper

Top View

Frax paper

Flat Kiln Shelf

Side View

Random Stacking, Fusing Procedure

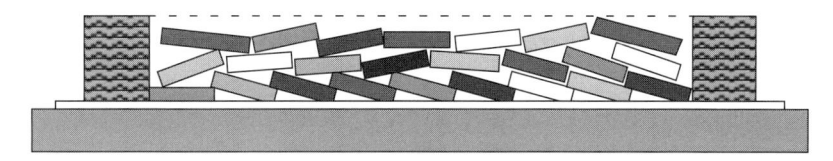

Side view of random stack

Because of the random nature of this stacking method, air will be trapped between the layers if we use the same fusing procedure described previously. To solve this problem, Klaus worked out the following procedure.

Raise the temperature of the oven to 1100° F (600° C) and allow the glass to slump slowly for about an hour or so. Then continue raising the temperature to 1700° F (925° C). At this temperature, the viscosity of the glass will be quite low and will thus permit the trapped air to rise to the surface and escape. The bubbles formed take some time to break, so you will need some patience to allow everything to smooth out. It is very important to have good side dams at this temperature as the glass is really flowing. At this temperature, one color will tend to flow into the adjacent color. If you have an oven that allows you easy access to the glass at this temperature, it is possible to go into the soft glass and manipulate the surface. This is an advanced technique and should not be attempted unless you really know what you're doing. At these elevated temperatures, 1700° F (925°C) is more than enough to set your clothes on fire and cause severe burns. You must wear heat–resistant clothing and a special face shield to attempt any hot kiln glass manipulation. After the bubble pock marks have sealed over, you can proceed to drop the temperature and cool as described on the previous page. You will notice that your glass surface will be quite shiny when taken to this temperature. This technique will eliminate most but not all of the trapped air. Don't worry about small air bubbles, they are part of the aesthetic. Once the glass sheet has been created, you're ready for the slump as described below and on the following page.

The Slump

Fig. 1

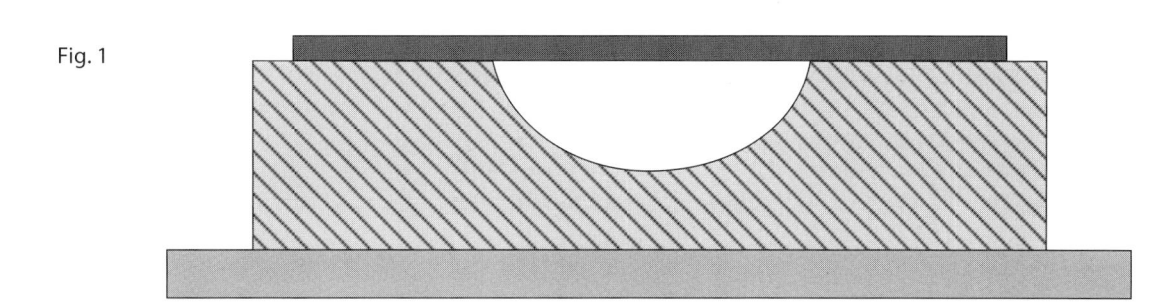

Fig. 1, above, depicts the cured mold with the completed glass sheet in place. After the sheet is placed onto the mold, the oven is closed and the temperature taken to 1115° F (600° C). It should take you overnight to reach this temperature. The next day, raise the temperature to 1200° F (650° C). At this point, the glass should begin to move slowly.

Fig. 2

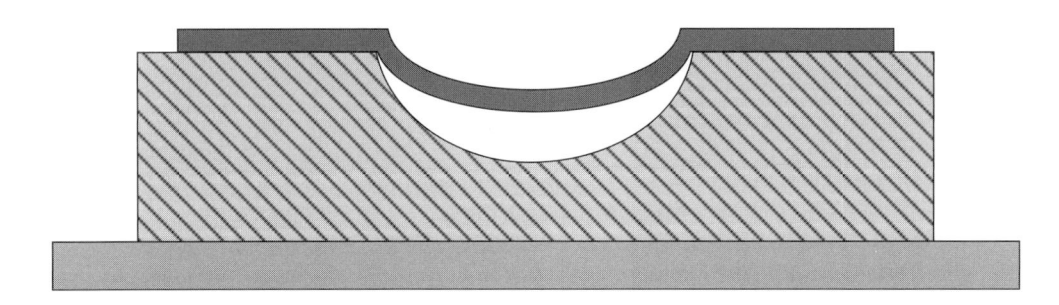

When the glass has slumped about ⅔ into the mold (Fig. 2), immediately raise the temperature to 1380° F (750° C). The glass will then completely slump and fill the cavity. It is important to go at full speed as it will avoid the various thicknesses of the sheet slumping at different rates. There are always slight variations in the thicknesses of the sheet regardless of how carefully they are fused together. These are slight variations in thickness that can cause the sheet to slump unevenly. When the oven is taken to 1380° F, the sheet will slump instantly (as long as it was ⅔ slumped before rising to that temperature).

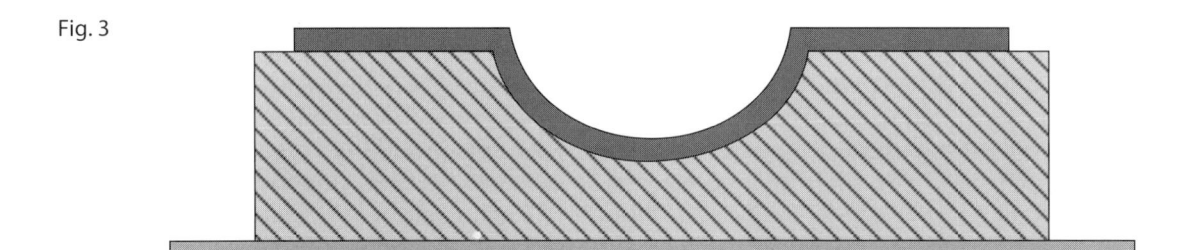

Fig. 3

Annealing

After the glass has been fused and/or slumped, you will probably need to anneal it. (For an explanation of what annealing is and does go to pg. 40.) For our purposes here, I will simply explain how to anneal your sheet of fused and slumped glass.

If the glass cools too quickly, stress created within the body of the glass will cause it to break. The glass must be held first at a temperature that will relieve it of all stress, and then it must be cooled at a rate slow enough that no new stress will be reintroduced. To accomplish this, your annealing oven should have a computer controller for the greatest accuracy.

If your glass is about ⅜" thick (9.5 mm) hold the temperature of your annealer at 975° F (525° C) for about 1 ½ hours. After this is done take 1 ½ hours to lower the oven to the strain point, 914° F (490° C). Hold at this temperature for about 15 minutes. If your oven holds heat well and takes at least 8 hours to get down to 400° F (204° C), you can simply shut your oven off. If the temperature of your oven drops like a stone, you need to adjust the cooling rate to fit an 8-hour curve. Annealing glass this thin and thinner is not that difficult, but it does require a decent annealer that is free of thermal gradients. If your glass is checking and you're convinced it's not being caused by incompatibility, then you need to adjust your annealing time and cooling rate.

That is the essence of the Moje technique. It is hoped that this small introduction to Klaus' technique(s) will stimulate you to find your own voice and not imitate what has already been done. Imitation is not always the sincerest form of flattery.

Kiln-Forming Temperature Ranges

OPERATION	TEMP. RANGE C°	TEMP. RANGE F°
Enameling	550 – 610°	1022 - 1130°
Bending (Uni-directional)	580 – 630°	1075 - 1166°
Curving (Multi-directional)	650 - 700°	1200 - 1290°
Slumping (No thickness change)	650 - 700°	1200 - 1290°
Fuse to Stick (Sintering)	680 - 720°	1255 - 1330°
Sagging (Cross section changes)	680 - 720°	1255 - 1330°
Tack Fusing (Edges soften slightly)	700 - 780°	1290 - 1435°
Strip Technique	800 - 840°	1470 - 1545°
Block Fusing	800 - 840°	1470 - 1545°
Full Fusing	820 - 840°	1510 - 1545°
Texture Fuse (Bas relief)	820 - 840°	1510 - 1545°
Combing	900 - 940°	1650 - 1725°
Casting Range	787 - 840°	1450 - 1545°

Chart created by Rudi Gritsch
Courtesy Bullseye Glass Co.

The above chart shows the temperature range of different kiln forming techniques when using Bullseye glass. One should not assume that this chart is applicable to other fusing glasses. It is recommended that you test other brands of fusing glass to establish accurate temperatures for the different kiln casting techniques.

Basic Fusing & Slumping Chart

By Jeremy Lepisto

Schedules 1 and 2 below can be used to fuse pieces that consist of 2 layers of 3mm (⅛ inch) fusible compatible sheet glass and that are approximately 12" (30.5 mm) to 16" (40.6 mm) in diameter.

Schedules 3 and 4 below can be used to slump pieces that are a pre-fused thickness of ¼" (6mm) of fusible compatible sheet glass and approximately 12" (30.5 mm) to 16" (40.6 mm) in diameter.

These schedules are only a point of departure for developing your own firing schedules. They should work for any and all fusing compatible glasses as long as the sheets to be fused are from the same manufacturer and have the same LEC.

For plate glass I only combine pieces that are from the same sheet and increase all temperatures by 100° F (55° C). I also always keep the tin side down.

AFAP = As Fast As Possible. When heating AFAP, different kilns will need different amounts of time to reach temperature. Therefore, you may need to program a controlled rate of rise or adjust a "Hold at Temp" to match the heat work between the two kilns. When cooling AFAP, I let the kiln cool naturally without crashing.

If you want to fuse or slump glass that is thicker than 6mm you may want to decrease your rates of rise up to the top temperature and increase your process temperatures, times, and rates coming down.

1. Basic Schedule for Full Fuse

Degrees per hr.	Temperature	Hold at Temp.
300° F (166° C)	1260° F (682° C)	45 minutes
AFAP	1450°/1500° F 788°/815° C	5-15 minutes
AFAP	960° F (515° C)	1 hour
100° F (55° C)	700° F (371° C)	0
AFAP	Warm to touch	0

2. Basic Schedule for Tack Fuse

Degrees per hr.	Temperature	Hold at Temp.
300° F 166° C	1000° F 676° C	0-30 minutes
AFAP	1300°/1425° F 704°/774° C	5-10 minutes
AFAP	960° F (515° C)	1 hour
100° F (55° C)	700° F (371° C)	0
AFAP	Warm to touch	0

3. Fast Slump

Degrees per hr.	Temperature	Hold at Temp.
200° F (93° C)	1200°/1350° F 649°/732° C	5-15 minutes
AFAP	960° F (515° C)	1 hr. 30 min.
100° F (55° C)	700° F (371° C)	0
AFAP	Warm to touch	0

4. Slow Slump
For thick pieces, ¼ inch (6mm)

Degrees per hr.	Temperature	Hold at Temp.
200° F 93° C	1080°/1150° F 582°/621°C	As long as it takes
AFAP	960° F 515° C	1 hr. 30 min.
100° F (55° C)	700° F (371° C)	0
AFAP	Warm to touch	0

I use the slow slump section above for bends that require greater precision and less mold texture.

The effectiveness of the glass to slump will be affected by the viscosity of the glass, the direction and temperature of the heat, the footprint of the cold piece in relation to the bend, and the weight of the piece.

The position of the glass on the mold will affect the rate of rise. Its relationship to the mold and final shape will affect the ability to anneal the glass.

How to calculate time to temperature :
Divide the degrees per hour into the desired temperature
Example: Degrees per hr. 300° F, temperature 1250° F
1250 ÷ 300 = 4.16 hours

Keeping accurate records is very important.

Author's Note: To calculate the corresponding temperature for degrees per hr. from the Fahrenheit system to Centigrade, divide the degrees per hr. by 9 and multiply by 5. The ratio is ⅝ . Since you cannot program parts of a degree, then you should either round up or down.

122 Glass Notes

Kiln Forming

By Jeremy Lepisto

I first met Jeremy in 2001 when I was teaching a class at Pilchuck and Jeremy was my assistant. Part of the class dealt with kilnforming. It became apparent that Jeremy knew a great deal more of this technique than I did, so I of course turned all the technical aspects over to him. The students benefited greatly from his vast knowledge of kiln forming techniques. I am very fortunate that Jeremy has permitted me to reprint his excellent and valuable chart on kilnforming times and temperatures as well as his introduction to some kilnforming basics. What is presented below, Kilnforming Basics, is only a very brief introduction to his presentation made at the GAS meeting in New Orleans in 2004. The complete text of his presentation can be found in the 2004 GAS Journal (pg. 78). If you wish to see Jeremy's work, it can be found on the Bullseye site, www.bullseyeconnectiongallery.com, the William Traver Gallery site, www.travergallery.com, and the Thomas R. Riley Gallery. His work is found in very prestigious collections throughout the world. Jeremy Lepisto co-owns and operates Portland's Studio Ramp LLC with wife and partner Mel George.

Jeremy Lepisto

Here is what Jeremy has to say concerning his work:

I am inspired by the many layered details that make an object or situation appear seamless.

In my work, I try to highlight the basic layers to capture the complex in the common. I strive to create my own objects that are inspired by the difficulty of construction, to yield a result of seamless simplicity.

For me, kiln working has unlimited potential. The simple combination of glass with time and temperature.

provides a city of avenues to explore. My very fortunate experience at the Bullseye Glass Company, working with other artists, running my studio, and making mistakes has taught me to take my time, double check, and always pays attention to "The Basics".

"The Basics" of Firing

1. Type of kiln

Special consideration should be given to a kiln's construction when figuring out whether it can perform the process you are asking it to perform. It is important to use the proper kiln for the exact kiln process you are attempting. Not all kilns are equal, so neither will be their results. The relationships between a kiln's amount of power vs. insulation, interior space vs. amount of thermal mass to be fired, and accuracy of temperature control vs. location of elements will help or hinder the success of firing for an effect.

2. Project placement in kiln

I only set up my kiln to fire one level of work at a time. I elevate my setup off the floor and as close to the thermocouple as possible. Fire similar setups together without overloading the kiln. I also try to have a bank of elements below or under my setup to assist with proper heating.

3. Program vs. Performance concerns

I have had great success following the annealing schedules provided by manufacturers for their glasses. Remember though, these schedules are only designed to anneal for the thickness of the glass in an accurate kiln, and may need to be adjusted for mediocre equipment, difficult shapes, multiple pieces, and also for the amount of shelving, dams, bricks, molds, etc in with, and around your piece.

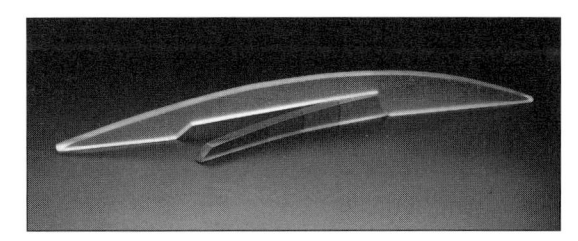

"End Transmission"
Span Series
5"h x 48"w x 5"d
2005

Pâte de Verre

by Alicia Lomné

It should be apparent to those that have spent any time looking at contemporary pâte de verre that Alicia Lomné is one of the finest exponents of the art. Her work is in the great tradition of a craft practiced by few. Her vision is personal and wholly original. Her work is delicate but with a strength expressed through her understanding of form and color.

It was a serendipitous that Alicia and I found ourselves at Penland during the summer of 05'. Since I was trying to find someone to write a section on pâte de Verre for *Glass Notes,* I naturally asked Alicia if she would share what she knew about the process with my readers. Lucky for us she readily accepted. Alicia has a great ability to describe this rather intricate process in terms that are readily accessible. What follows is a very detailed description of the pâte de verre process as she practices it.

If you're not familiar with Alicia's work, then go to the Bullseye Resource site, or better yet, find a gallery that sells her work and see the real thing: www.bullseyeconnectiongallery.com, click on Alicia's name, and take a peek.

In the Beginning

I was eight years old when my mom (Kéké Cribbs) first brought glass as an art medium into our home. I remember watching her on the porch brushing etching acid onto sheets of glass, wondering if it was really true that if it got on your skin it would eat away your bones. I always watched with a certain detached interest that only scientists and kids seem to have in common. I never had any great love of the stuff called glass until I was a teenager. As a graduation present, my mom and I took a class together at Pilchuck with Clifford Rainey. Seven years after that class and many jobs in between, I still remembered my love of casting glass. I decided to take a lost wax casting class at Pratt Fine Arts in Seattle. At the time, I didn't even notice or much care that the class covered one project in pâte de verre yet that one project changed the course of my life. For the last eight years, all I have done is experiment, and work in pâte de verre.

The first examples of pâte de verre methods being used date back to ancient Egypt. The term "pâte de verre" and its "fame" came about in the nineteenth century when a group of about six artists (mostly, but not all, French) were working in this method.[1] These artists and many subsequent artists were very secretive with their technical information. Because of this, very little written, technical information exists about the method. In the seventies and eighties, there were a handful of artists working in and teaching pâte de verre, but it is really only in the last ten years or so that pâte de verre has become a more popular and widespread method to work in. Now more than ever there is a demand for information.

Today, there are many different definitions and techniques, that fall under the term "pâte de verre." Literally translated from French it means, "paste of glass." Technically this term has come to describe a process in which powdered or granulated glass is mixed with water and a binder (some only use water), placed in a mold, and then fired in a kiln to fuse the particles together. Different versions of pâte de verre include: a glass paste being placed in thin layers within a mold to create hollow vessels, two part molds used to create hollow vessels, and molds that are filled with small granules to create solid forms. The processes I will describe are for creating thin-walled, hollow vessels, mainly using one part molds and concentrating on specific color placement.

The information I'm giving you is just one girl's version of pâte de verre. Each artist has his or her favorite glass, binder, mold materials, kilns, tools, firing schedules, and favored superstitions. This is by no means the end all, be all description of pâte de verre. I'm trying to provide as much information as I have and hope it will provide a nice, big stepping stone for other artists trying to find their way in the wonderful, strange, and sometimes fickle art of pâte de verre.

[1] Henri (or Henry) Cros, Albert Dammouse, Francois Décorchement, Gabriel Argy-Rousseau, Georges Despret, Almeric Walter.

Models

My favorite material for creating a model is water-based clay. I've used wax, plasticene (oil-based clay), plaster, Styrofoam, and various objects from buttons to bones. Hands down, water-based clay is my favorite material. The sculptural and textural possibilities are nearly endless: it is easily removed and cleaned from molds, it is reusable, and it is fairly inexpensive. The following descriptions will be of creating a mold from a positive form (model) of water-based clay.

Creating a model may be easy, but figuring out how you are going to successfully turn that into a glass object takes some consideration and planning. One of the first things you should consider is that the opening of the piece needs to be large enough for you to fit your hand and a tool into. As you are placing the glass within the mold, you want that interior space to be as accessible as possible. The next things to consider are what types of glass you're using and what kind of shape you have created. The easiest and most successful shapes to pack and fire in pâte de verre are vessels that are narrower at the bottom than at the top; the wider the mouth is the easier it will be. Generally speaking vessels on the smaller side are more successful as well (5" - 8"). If you have undercuts, you would be wisest to use an interior core of some sort which effects your firing time as well as the texture on the interior of your piece. You can fire pieces with undercuts in an open-faced firing, but if you do this, your packing has to be perfect and you probably will not achieve this by using straight 01 frit. When you use 01 frit (or any larger size frit) there is a certain volume of air between each particle; the larger the particle, the more volume of air in between. As the glass begins to melt, much of the air is pushed out; therefore, you loose some volume in your piece. You can account for this by adding an extra ½" to 1" on your actual model before pouring your mold. Another way to deal with this "shrinking" problem is to add powder frit to your 01 frit mix. The small particles of powder tend to fill in the air pockets and then you lose much less volume. If you want to fire a piece open faced that has a slight undercut it may also be helpful to add an extra flange of clay that opens out wider than the mouth of the piece. This creates a sort of shelf, which helps hold the glass in place, shown below. If you do this you will probably have to grind the excess glass off to get back to your original shape.

Once your model is complete, it is time to prepare it for pouring a mold. I like to use a sheet of clear Plexiglas (about 3/32" thick, .24 cm) to pour my mold on. These boards are easy to clean and can be reused thousands of times (*that's a lot of pâte de verre*). You can measure and mark a line around your model on the underside of your board that serves as a good visual reference to indicate your overall mold thickness. You can slide the sheet out over the edge of your work surface and look underneath to check the thickness of your mold. When you are finished pouring your mold and it has cured long enough, you can slide your board over the edge of your work surface and flex the board slightly, making it easy to pop the mold off the board.

To prepare for pouring a mold, take your finished model, turn it upside down, and attach it to your board. You can use a tool to seal your model to the board. What I usually do is roll out a rope of fresh clay, lay it on the board so that it fits the shape of my piece, place the model on top of that, and then use a tool to smooth it into place. This way, I ensure a tight seal between model and board. You do not want plaster running under your model. I usually use Murphy's Oil Soap as a release. I brush it on in a very thin layer with a soft brush. When you are using water-based clay, there is no real need to use a release, but I almost always do because it gives me a super clean mold. If you are going to use a release, you must make sure there are no bubbles or pools of excess release because it will make the surface of your mold crumbly and uneven.

Making a Mold

There are probably hundreds of different materials, recipes, and ways of creating a mold. I like to keep it simple. I use one-part molds, and I hand build my molds. This way, they use much less material and are generally thinner than a poured mold, which leads to a nice, even heating during your firing. You can get the materials to make this mold mix at any pottery supply store, and I've never found anything that works that much better.

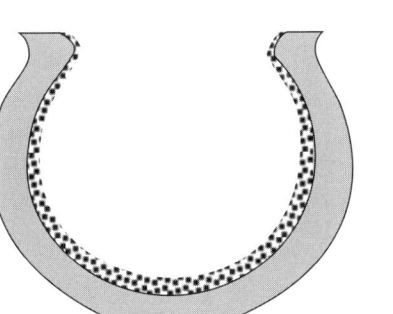

The first thing to do is set out all the materials you will be using. Timing is important, and it is best to have everything you will need at hand. My mold-pouring list goes like this: Respirator, rubber gloves (not necessary, but I find it saves my hands from becoming completely parched), buckets of water and 50/50 mix, sieve,

Mold with flange   Finished shape with flange removed

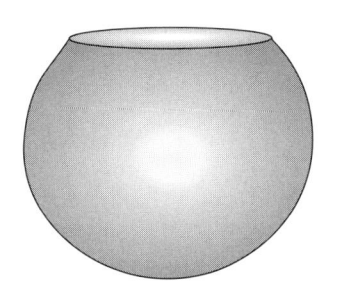

Glass Notes 125

spatulas, scraper, fiberglass, and a small square of ⅛" glass for creating a flat bottom on your mold.

Face Coat: I begin by applying a thin face coat to my model. I use:

50% # 1 Pottery Plaster
50% 200 mesh Silica

This will work just fine, but I usually use a mix that includes 1 cup of EPK (English Plastic Kaolin; any kaolin will work) for every ten pounds of 50/50 mix. In my experience, this mold has more elasticity and tends to crack less. 50/50 Plaster/silica is mixed by weight in a ratio of 1 lb. water : 1.75 lbs. pl./sil. I use the same measurement for my face coat with perhaps an extra splash of water. When adding this mixture to water, for the face coat, it is best to use a sieve to remove any lumps and ensure a smooth consistency. After you have finished adding your dry material to the water, let it sit undisturbed for two minutes. This procedure is called slaking; it ensures that the plaster has become properly re-hydrated, so don't skip this step. After you are done slaking, stir the mixture until it is creamy. I pour my mixture right over the top (what would actually be the bottom) of my model, letting it flow down the sides until the whole form is covered with a thin layer. If I have very defined details that are deep, I may use a straw to blow plaster into the crevasses. Some people use a paintbrush to get into detailed areas. After the 50/50 mix begins to set up a little bit more, I add more material using either a spatula (like icing a cake, but you have to be careful not to hit the model with your tool) or by hand. The thickness of your overall mold should be ¾" to 1" so this first layer should be about ¼" to ½".

Second outer coat: I use a 50/50 Plaster/Silica mix (same materials as above) with fiberglass. I use fiberglass matting, which I cut into strips and dip into my wet 50/50 mix and apply like a cast, starting at the bottom and moving to the top. In my classes, I always use fiberglass shorts (also called gun chop). These come in various sizes. I would recommend ¼" or ½" shorts (.64 cm or 1.27 cm) that you can buy from a marine supply store. In a way these are much easier to use. Once your 50/50 mix has slaked and been stirred, you can just add a handful of chop and stir it in. How much you add depends on how big your mold is. I can't offer a precise measurement, but you should be able to see it in your mix; it will take on the consistency of hot breakfast cereal. This provides extra strength to your mold and helps prevent cracking.

After you've added your dry material to the water, and while your mixture is slaking, it is a good idea to clean your board off with a scraper. Just before you add your second layer, spray the first face coat with water. I try to pour my second layer within five to ten minutes of the first layer. If more time has passed, you will notice that the water absorbs much more quickly into the surface of the mold. Spray it until it is saturated and then use a sponge to mop up the excess water at the base of the mold. This is done so that the first layer does not wick water away from the second layer and thus cause it to cure incorrectly. At this point, add your second layer. I always save a little bit of material in the bucket to put on the very top of the mold; then I place a piece of glass on top of that and level it. You can use a level, but usually eyeballing it works fine. This creates a flat bottom on your mold, which makes life a lot easier later, especially when it comes to loading your kiln. Once your mold is poured and hard enough that it can not be dented with your fingernail, pop it off the board. After removing the mold from the board, dig out your clay. It may come out cleanly or you may have to dig a bit (be careful not to dig into your mold walls). Use a Surform to clean and shape the outer edge of your mold. This prevents small chips of plaster from falling into your glass later. Clean your mold carefully making sure all the clay has been removed. As a final step, I usually rinse out the entire mold in the sink under running water.

The next step is to wrap your mold so that it will retain its moisture. You want your mold to be wet when you pack it with frit. Some people use cloth for this; some people soak their molds before they use them. I use paper towels that have been moistened (I wet them thoroughly and then wring them out lightly) to completely cover the exterior of the mold (usually just one layer thick). After the paper towels are in place, I add a layer of plastic wrap and then tape that in place. Once that is done, you can cover the opening of the mold with a paper towel and sheet of plastic, which acts like a lid. I have found that I can keep a mold wet for days like this. If you think more than three days are going to pass before you can work on your mold, put an extra layer of paper towels or plan to soak your mold. If the mold is drying out while you're working on it you can use a spritz bottle with water to re-hydrate. Pull the plastic wrap away from the mold body and squirt water on the outside of your mold. Sometimes I use an atomizer to moisten the inside of my mold with a fine mist; never do this to your frit powder layer. The moisture in your mold is important because it helps hold the glass in place while you are packing it. **A mold, if too dry, may become a nightmare to work on**. I try to start packing my mold the same day I pour it.

Glass: When I first started trying to experiment with pâte de verre, I tried several different glasses without much success. I then found Bullseye glass and had immediate success. Other companies make a similar line of products with a slightly different palate of colors. These are probably just as good, but I prefer to use Bullseye partly because it has my favorite palate of colors. I only work with 01 frit and 08 powder.

Binder: There are many different binders that can be used. CMC and wallpaper pastes are commonly used glues. CMC comes in a powdered form and can be mixed to different viscosities as can some wallpaper pastes. I have tried a few of these but for some reason I seem to always prefer Gum Arabic. If you choose to use this I recommend the premium grade, 100% Gum Arabic. It is a little more expensive, but a little goes a long way.

Mixing glass: Working with compatible glass is a treat because you can create your own colors by mixing glass or layering it to form new colors. **Being able to create a homogenous blend without lumps of unmixed color is important.** I use clear plastic containers with tight-fitting lids (food storage containers like Rubbermaid or Zip lock). These are great for mixing and storing excess color; they are easily labeled, cleaned, and then reused. First, add your 01 frit, say the container is ½ full, spray it with water (use a spray bottle; three or four sprays will do), put the lid on and shake vigorously. Then add your 08 powder, perhaps ¼" put the lid back on, and shake again (it works like Shake'n' Bake, the smaller particles coating the larger ones). Make sure you take the lid off and clean around the edges to get any unmixed parts knocked back in and then remix. After this is done, the mixture will be barely wet and well blended, and then you can add your binder and more water. Most of the containers I use are fairly small 3 ¼ cups. For a container this size filled ¾ with glass, I would add a little more than 1 tablespoon of Gum Arabic. After I add my binder, I would spray some more water in and then mix it by hand with a spoon. You want your mixture to be wet but not soupy. The amount of water you use is personal, but it also affects how the glass compacts. If your mix is very dry, you tend to get more air between the particles. If it is too wet, it may compact nicely, but excess water will collect in the bottom of your mold and eat away at what you've already laid in.

If you are doing a large project and want the glass to be the same throughout, it is a good idea to mix your glass in a large batch or measure the amounts you are using. There is nothing worse than being almost finished, running out of glass, and then discovering you cannot match what you mixed previously.

Testing Colors: This process is essential. You can do this in a very precise, measured way: mixing one color with clear by ratio 1:1, 1:5, 1:10, 1:15 etc. to 100 by weight. If you do this, it is best to use a wedge-shaped tile so that you can see how tile color changes from the thin to thick area. This gives you valuable information, but it is a very tedious process. I like to mix my colors like paint or a chef creating a new sauce. I put in a bit of this, a pinch of that, a few sprinkles, add some more ,and stir. You can see why sometimes I have to mix in large batches since these are not exact measurements. The best part of this is that I am able to create my own color palate. I've also been working with the same glass for a long time, so usually I know exactly what I'm going to get. However, even I get a surprise sometimes. That's why I am constantly making test tiles and encourage color testing.

Packing a mold: There is an endless number of possible ways to pack a mold. This is the most exciting part of creating a piece in pâte de verre, and it may also be the most difficult. It pays to be patient and take your time to do it right. The success of your piece has everything to do with the way you pack it. When I refer to "packing" a mold, I am speaking of the process of laying glass in the mold and tamping it down to the surface of the mold with a tool. Ultimately, this part of the process comes through practice and finding what works best for you. I will cover a few different techniques in which I work, but if one has the time to experiment, there are many other techniques still to be discovered.

General rules of packing: Start laying in glass at the bottom of your piece and work your way out to the edges. You can work in concentric rings or in sections that run from bottom to top. The tool I use most frequently is a spoon. I have spoons in all sorts of sizes, with different length handles, bent to conform to the shape of my piece. I also make my own tools from copper or wood. You want a tool that fits the shape of your mold well so that you can get the

Tools for Packing Mold

glass to form a nice, even layer over its surface. Use a spoon to pick up the glass and lay it in the mold. Use the edge of the spoon to gently push or "chop" (very gently) the glass so that it spreads out in an even layer across the mold surface. Once you have done this a few times, you will have a small area covered in glass and you can begin to tamp it in place. To do this use the back of your spoon, angle it slightly upward toward the lip of your vessel, and use an up-and-down motion to "hit" the glass. You are compressing the glass to the surface of your mold. I work in a side to side motion like a typewriter or printer, making sure to compact everything as I work my way upward. The angle of your spoon drives any excess glass up toward the lip of your vessel and then out. When you are done tamping and you go to lay in your next area of glass, make sure the edges of your old work and new work overlap each other slightly. You want to create an even layer with out "low spots." A low spot in a firing can turn into a dent or even sometimes a hole. Your goal is to make one uniform layer of glass over the entire surface of your mold. It is especially important to pay attention to the first two inches beneath the lip of your vessel (less so if you are firing with an inner core). If you create areas that are thicker than the rest surrounding it, during the firing it may act as a weight and drag down a section of your vessel wall. Oftentimes I will taper my glass out to the edges.

I always put three layers of 01 frit in my mold. The thickness of a piece will vary widely from person to person. The overall thickness of my pieces before they are fired ranges from 1/8" (very thin) to 1/4", generally speaking, there are always exceptions. You should complete one layer entirely before starting the next. If you are using the same color for all your layers, it may become hard to tell the difference between your first layer and the second. I used to just add a little powder or color so I could tell the two layers apart, but Deborah Horrell taught me a great trick, which was to add a few drops of food coloring to your mix. This way, you have a clear visual difference between layers.

Controlling exterior textures: Your exterior texture comes first from your model and then by your choice of frit size. To create a rough granular texture, you would use 01 frit. You can use it straight from the jar (if you are using pre-crushed glass), sieve it, or mix in powder.

The more powder you add, the subtler the granular effect will be. Pieces using 01 frit fired in an open-faced mold, without a core, tend to be the most translucent.

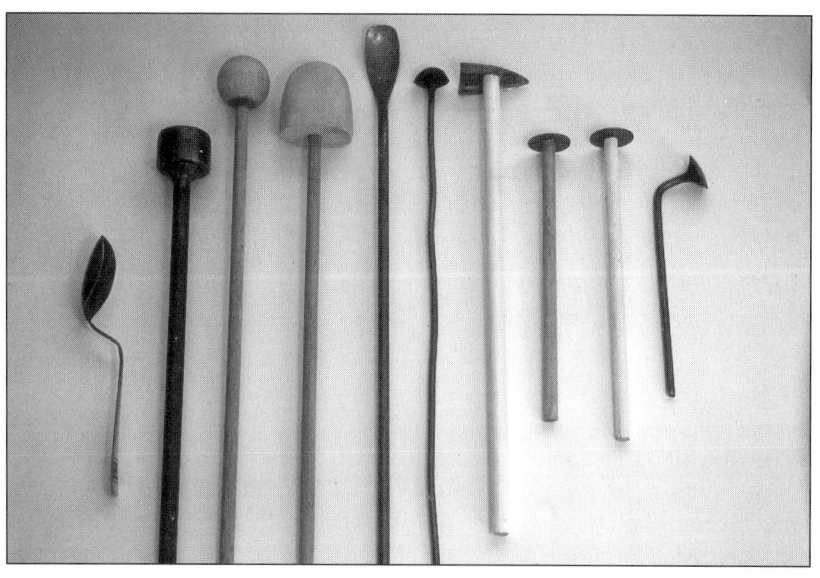

Tools for Tamping

The smaller the particles of glass are, the smaller the air bubbles are, and the less translucent the piece is. You can also control how granular your piece is with the firing schedule.

To create a smooth, rock-like surface, your first layer would be 08 powder. Sometimes you can mix your powder into a paste and use that as a first layer. I have never found satisfactory results this way. I use small sieves (sold at ceramic supply stores for enameling) to apply powder to my mold surface. The powder is dry and sticks to the surface of your mold because it is wet. The powder layer is very thin, maybe a few sheets of paper thick, and 1/16" at the thickest. You will know when your powder layer is too thick because it will not absorb water from the surface of your mold, and it will be too dry to stay in place. After I finish my powder layer I pack the piece with 01 frit the same as I would any other piece (three layers thick).

Inlay: I create my inlay by carving a design in relief on my model surface. I would suggest that the depth of your relief be about 1/8" and not deeper than 1/4", or it will not fire solid but pull in on itself, creating an uneven surface with holes. When your mold is poured, what was convex on the surface of your model is now concave on the interior of your mold. This concave area makes a perfect channel to lay your glass into. You can use 01 frit; I would sieve it (through a small kitchen sieve) to get the smaller particles for better control. When you are doing inlay, generally, you

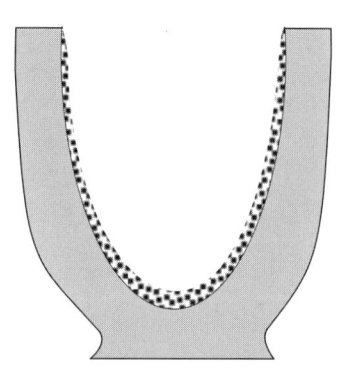

Mold with tapered edge

don't use as much material so you can mix up a small amount in a plastic cup. You have much more control doing inlay with a wetter, almost soupy mix. When you have finished filling your inlay area, let it sit for a few seconds to make sure the water has absorbed, compact it, and then clean up any loose bits of glass with a paint brush. When you are choosing colors to inlay with, keep in mind that it will be affected by the color behind it (especially if it is translucent). It is usually best to choose a color, one that is very bold, or dense, or opaque.

To use powder as an inlay, you can either mix it with water, making a paste to inlay with, or sieve it in dry. Once again, I have not had much success using the powder as a paste unless it is in very shallow details; then this works fine. I would sieve the powder into my relief, not worrying about filling the relief with powder, and then clean the edges with a paintbrush. After that I would pack the piece normally or back fill with 01 frit.

Working with powders: Powders are my favorite to work with. You can get subtle gradations in color and design that you can't get any other way. There are two reasons I don't like working with the powder in a paste form. Within the powder are smaller and larger particles. When water is added and this mixture is placed on the mold surface, the mold acts like a sponge, absorbing the water, as it does this, the smallest particles migrate to the surface of the mold causing what I call a watermark. This mark is visible after firing and impossible to get rid of. I am absolutely sure there is another way to mix the powder so that this does not happen, but I have never taken the time to figure it out yet. The other trouble with thick layers of powder paste is that they tend to either trap air or not get completely compressed. Either way during firing it tends to pull in on its self and sometimes cause holes or uneven surfaces. Sieving in your powders seems to give the best results. You can sieve in a line of color and then use a paintbrush to give that line a defined edge, or even make a pattern. I use medium bristle paintbrushes in varying sizes. Usually I end up chopping off the handles so that I can have better access to the interior of my mold. By using different amounts of water in your brush, you can manipulate the glass in different ways. You can shape lines by using a wet, but not dripping, brush (drips could destroy a design). You can "vacuum" particles up using a medium dry brush. You have to rinse out your brush and then blot it on a paper towel frequently between picking up particles. You can use a water-loaded brush to splash small amounts of water over a pre-powdered area and then put another layer of a different colored powder over that. This creates the affect of speckles or spots of another color. There are so many possibilities just using a paintbrush that I think I can't go into it all here, but it is very exciting.

Inclusions: An inclusion would be the process of incorporating a pre-fired element into your mold. I've only done this a few times, so I'm not going to pretend I'm an expert on the subject but it is really rather simple to do small inclusions. You would begin by having a small element of glass, for example a pre-fired tile or lamp worked ball. Make sure it is clean, and of course it should be made from the same glass you will use to pack your mold with. Take this element and gently press it into the surface of your clay model or attach it with some fresh clay. You want a good seal so that your 50/50 mix doesn't run behind it and separate it from the model. Once this is done, you can pour your mold. When you dig your clay out, you will see the exposed surface of your object on the interior of your mold. Now pack your glass right over the top of it as if it were part of the mold surface. Remember that if this element is very thick you need to account for it in your annealing cycle.

Collaboration
1999
Alicia Lomné & Ké Ké Cribbs (Alicia's mom)
Pâte de Verre, steel, mosaic, reverse fired enameled glass

Firing Your Piece

Loading your kiln: often when you put your mold into the kiln, it is still wet. To prevent cracking your kiln shelf and for better heating, you should put something between the bottom of your mold and your kiln shelf. I use small strips or squares of fiber frax, but sand works just as well. You should place your mold so that it is as level as possible; you want gravity to be pulling evenly on all sides. If you are loading more than one piece into your kiln leave at least a 1 ½" space, if not more, between the molds. This will allow the air/heat to circulate evenly between the molds.

Firing: After eight years, sometimes I feel like I'm still figuring this part out. Firing a piece in pâte de verre is not like fusing, and it is not like solid casting. The glass is very thin, but it is held within a mold so the temperature can vary greatly within the piece from top to bottom. Because the glass is thin, it is more sensitive to quick changes in temperature. I have cracked more than one piece, even student pieces, trying to rush a schedule. It pays to slow down a little. Most of my schedules are still fast compared to some other peoples. I can't offer a-one-stop-meets-all firing schedule or a perfect formula for concocting one. I can however offer a schedule that will work and some of the questions you need to ask to come up with your own schedules.

First, you should consider what colors of glass you used to pack your mold. Most (but not all) opaque colors are harder and will need to stay at your high melting temperature for longer. Most transparent colors are much softer and won't take as long to go glassy in an open-faced firing.

This first schedule is for an open-faced firing (no core). I tend to fire high at 1400° F. For a first project, I would say try 1375°-1380° for 20 - 25 minutes. Program #1 is written for an Orton Controller or any controller that programs in degrees per hour. Program #2 is written for standard time/temperature controllers. You'll have to test your own kiln to see how fast it goes up, how quickly it loses heat, what temperature it is actually at, etc.

#1	Open - Faced Firing (Degree Based Program)		
	Degrees per hr. F	**Temperature F**	**Hold**
	Degrees per hr. C	**Temperature C**	
1	110°	220°	3
	61°	104°	
2	250°	1100°	1
	139°	593°	
3	600°	1400°	15 min.
	333°	760°	
4	*9999	960°	2 hr.
	9999	516°	
5	50°	700°	1 min.
	28°	371°	
6	80°	500°	1 min..
	44°	260°	
7	100°	80°	1 min.
	56°	27°	

To convert degrees per hr. to hours per degree, divide the degrees into the temperature. Example: Step 1, 220° F ÷ 110° F = 2 hr. then hold for 3 hours.
*9999 = As fast as Possible.
This chart is for annealing Bullseye fusing compatible glass. Substitute the annealing temperature for whatever glass you're using.

Note: When calculating degrees per hr. from F to C use a 5/9 ratio. Example: If you're raising the temperature 110° F per hr. it would equal 110° F ÷ 9 x 5 = 61° C.

Degrees per hr.: how many degrees per hour.
Time: The length of time to reach temperature.
F & C: (Fahrenheit & Centigrade) the temperature you are going to.
Hold: how long you stay at temperature.

In step 1, you are drying out your mold. I am going up quite quickly at 110° p/h; some go as slowly as 50° p/h. If cracking is a problem, try going up at a slower rate. You want to drive as much water out of your mold

#2	Open - Faced Firing (Time Based Program)		
	Time	**Temperature F**	**Hold**
		Temperature C	
1	2.5 hr.	220°	3 hr.
		104°	
2	4.5 hr.	1100°	1 hr.
		593°	
3	2.5 hr.	1400°	15 min.
		760°	
4	*AFAP	960°	2 hr.
		516°	
5	24 hr.	300°	off
		149°	
	*AFAP = As Fast As Possible		

as possible. I dry my molds for a very short period of time, between 2 and 3 hours; generally my molds are very thin. Some people dry their molds for as much as 6 hours. During this time you should vent your kiln (leave the door open a couple of inches or so). The water should be escaping and not settling into your kiln bricks. In the long run, it is best for the kiln if you install a mechanical vent.

In step 2 you are bringing the temperature up to 1100°. You don't want to do this too quickly or it will cause mold cracking. This is when the chemical waters are released, and again, it is wise to vent your kiln. At 1100° the glass begins to relax. I find that if I soak (stay) at 1100° for an hour before shooting up to my high temperature, my final melt is much better.

In step 3 you are shooting up to your high temperature, your melting point. I am very comfortable firing at 1400° F, but most are not. This "high temperature" can very from 1250° F to 1410° F. I wouldn't go any higher than 1410°; you'll end up with a puddle. You can choose to fire at a lower temperature and hold for longer; for example, 1350° for 40 minutes, 1370° for 30 minutes, and 1400° for 20 minutes give you almost the same results. You can fire at a lower temperature for a shorter amount of time (1350° for 20 minutes) and get a piece that is rough and granular inside and out and completely porous. At melting temperature, you can open the kiln and visually check your piece. Usually I do not have to do this, but when I do, I use a flashlight so I can see what the interior surface of glass looks like.

In step 4 you are dropping as fast as possible to your annealing rate; that's what 9999° means. You may want to vent (crack the door open a couple of inches, not too much or you may shock the mold) during this time to help the kiln drop in temperature. You shouldn't vent beyond 1100°. Certain colors are more likely to devitrify in this temperature range, and crash cooling can help to avoid that. 960° is the annealing temperature for Bullseye. The length of time you stay here depends on the thickness of your piece. I am on the safe side here with two hours; if your glass is really ⅛" you could go with an hour and forty minutes but I prefer to be on the safe side.

In steps 5 through 7, bring the piece down to room temperature slowly. In step 5 I have gone down in temperature as fast as 70° F per hour (39° C), but at that rate, even a tiny breeze coming through an open peephole might crack your piece. After cracking a lot of pieces that way, I do not recommend it. 50° to 700° is a little conservative, but I've never cracked a piece that way.

Firing with a core: Talc is most commonly used as an inner core. I've done some experimentation with sand and had some interesting results. When you are using talc, it is best to dry your packed piece at 212° (I always go a few degrees higher at 220°) first and then fill it with talc. After the piece has dried, you would remove it from the kiln and use a funnel or a small container to fill the interior of your mold to the brim. After you put the piece back in the kiln, you would continue your normal firing cycle. In section three of your firing cycle, you would fire at 1400° for an hour or as long as an hour and forty minutes. If you do not pre-dry your molds, the talc sometimes absorbs the water coming out of the mold and cakes up like a dry

#1	Firing with a Core		
	Degrees per hr. F	Temperature F	Hold
	Degrees per hr. C	Temperature C	
1	100°	212°	4
	56°	104°	
2	250°	1100°	*1
	139°	593°	
3	600°	1400°	1
	333°	760°	
4	**9999	960°	2 hr.
	9999	516°	
5	50°	700°	1 min.
	28°	371°	
6	80°	500°	1 min..
	44°	260°	
7	100°	100°	1 min.
	56°	56°	

*Vent – When this cycle is finished take the mold out and fill with talc.
**9999= As Fast as Possible

#2	Firing with a Core		
	Time	Temperature F	Hold
		Temperature C	
1	2 hr.	220°	4 hr.
		104°	
2	4.5 hr.	1100°	*1 hr.
		593°	
3	2.5 hr.	1400°	1 hr.
		760°	
4	**AFAP	960°	2 hr.
		516°	
5	24 hr.	300°	off
		149°	

*Vent
**AFAP = As Fast As Possible

river bottom and may pull a layer of glass with it.

I have tried filling a mold with sand and got great results, but there have also been some problems with this on larger pieces. I think the sand holds too much heat which causes the piece to crack because it cannot cool properly. I loved the look and quality that the sand left on the interior of my piece though. The next time, I tried wetting my sand and packing it into my mold like another layer of glass (about ½" thick). Once this was finished, I filled the remaining void with vermiculite. I put a little bit of sand on the top to weigh everything down. I've tried firing this way about eight times now and have had good success with it. When firing with this sort of core, the heat passes through much more efficiently. I have found that I had good result firing at 1400° for thirty minutes or 1380° for forty-five minutes.

A Few Tips

I have elements on the sides and ceiling of my kiln. If you are firing small pieces, 6" to 8", having both top and side elements on works great. I have fired pieces as tall as 13"; if you are firing anything above ten inches, it's best to turn off the top elements. It is too much direct heat on the top lip of your vessel. If you're firing with a core, this is not as much of an issue.

You can cover the mouth of your mold with a sheet of fiber frax or a kiln shelf. This creates a more even heating throughout the mold. If you want a granular piece, this may work very well for you. I have never gotten a piece with a glassy interior this way, but I also haven't tested for that.

Most commercial kilns have peepholes; keep them out while you're venting, but put them back in after you've hit your high temperature. If your oven does not have a vent, it is a good idea to put one in.

To anyone who reads all of this, thank you, and good luck!

Alicia

House of One
2003
20" x 7.25" x 9"
Alicia Lomné
Pâte de Verre, wood base with copper

The Pâte de Verre of Alicia Lomné

Alicia working in her studio

Stacking #9, Blue Ridge
2005
22.5" x 6.25" x 6.25"
Alicia Lomné
Pâte de verre, steel, carved & painted wood

Two Take Flight
2001
13" x 19" x 9.5"
Alicia Lomné
Pâte de Verre, steel, painted wood

String Vessel
2003
8.5" x 6" x 6"
Alicia Lomné
Pâte de verre, wood, wire

NOTES

Refractories, Furnaces, Recuperation

Chapter Contents

Refractories	136
Understanding Insulation	142
Furnaces and Pots	144
Building a Day Tank	145
AZS Liner & Base	148
Day Tank, Korundal XD, High Alumina Liner	150
Steel Support System	154
Front of Furnace with Door	155
Cast Crown Construction	156
Building the Invested Pot Furnace	158
Pot Furnace with Dimensions	160
Invested Crucible Pot Furnace	161
How to Make the "Beehive Crown"	162
The Sled Template	163
Freestanding Pot Furnace	166
Freestanding Crucible Furnace	170
Two Ways to Lift a Cast Crown	172
Recuperation	175
Recuperators and Glass Furnaces	177
The Basic Principal of Recuperation	179
Three Ways to Power Recuperators	180
Two Stack Designs	181
The Hub Recuperator	186

Refractories

Refractory= The ability to withstand heat

In the dim dark past there were many companies that manufactured and sold refractory materials, but in today's world there are only a handful left. Some have gone out of business, and the three mainline companies, A.P. Green, North American Refractories Co., and Harbison-Walker, have been absorbed by ANH Refractories Co. (www.hwr.com). Although ANH sells most of the products manufactured by those companies, there are still a number of independent refractory manufacturers that produce excellent refractory products for the glass studio. The names and contact information for those companies can be found in the Vendors section at the back of this book.

Before building any piece of studio equipment, familiarize yourself with the many different types and uses of refractory materials that exist. Many but not all refractory companies with which I am familiar have a vast array of bricks, castables, and insulation materials. Just surf on over to **www.hwr.com** and click on **products>data sheets** to get an idea of just what is available. Most of the independent refractory companies have Web sites that list their products. If you are a beginner, it can be mind boggling to try to understand the uses of these products. I hope the following information will help you understand the types and application of refractory materials used in the glass studio.

Firebrick

Firebrick is primarily composed of alumina and silica in the proportions of approximately 40% alumina to 50% silica. The low–end quality brick is formed by extrusion, and the higher quality is produced by dry press. Dry press brick have higher densities and greater dimensional stability than extruded brick. There are many "standard" dimensions of firebrick, but the size referred to as the "standard" size is 9" long x 4 ½" wide x 2 ½" thick or 3" thick, depending on your preference. There are other standard sizes available such as 9" long x 9" wide x 2 ½" thick or 3" thick as well as 9" x 12". The type of firebrick used in most studios is the Hi-Duty variety. The A.P. Green "Empire S" brick is good to a temperature of 2500° F; the Clipper DP is good to 2650° F; the H–W (Harbison-Walker) "Alamo" super-duty is good to a temperature of 2600° F; and the B & W (Babcock & Wilcox) "80" is good to 2800° F. For studio applications using firebrick, I have always found A.P. Green's "Empire" or "Clipper" brick work well. Firebrick is never used for direct glass contact. It is almost always used as a backup brick for the furnace liner as well as for the foundation brick for the furnace itself. If your regional or local refractory dealer does not have what you're specifically requesting ask if they have a comparable product.

Insulating Firebrick (IFB)

Insulating firebrick, commonly referred to as IFB, is probably the most common type brick found in the glass studio. It is very versatile and can be used as the primary brick for the construction of glory holes, annealers, and a host of other studio equipment. It is used for backing up and insulating most day tanks and pot furnaces.

IFB is made from clay. When fired, small air pockets form throughout the brick. These air pockets and the refractory quality of the clay give the brick its insulating quality. When I was a potter, we made our own IFB by mixing coffee grounds or fine saw dust with the clay; when bisqued, the grounds or sawdust burned out, leaving a poor man's IFB. IFB are unusually light when compared to a firebrick of equal size. They can be cut with a hand saw and can be grooved easily in order to hold electric elements. Like firebrick, they are made in standard sizes. The usual size used by the studio glass artists is a standard 9" long x 4 ½" wide x 2 ½" thick. They are also available in 2" as well as 3" thicknesses. The temperature designations are similar regardless of the brand. The designation usually used when ordering is by temperature range. The lowest temperature range is 1600°–2000° F, followed by 2300°, 2500°, 2600°, 2800°, 3000°, and 3200°. Not all companies (and there are very few) make IFB in all these ranges. The mainline company that manufactures IFB is BNZ at www.bnzmaterials.com/zelienople.html.

When building equipment that uses IFB, it is wise to establish the highest temperature usage for that particular piece of equipment and use IFB that will service it. For example, if your annealing/casting oven is only going to reach a maximum temperature of 1700° F (927° C), you would use brick in the 1600°–2000° range. The same holds true if you were building a glory hole from IFB. Since glory holes can get extremely hot, you should use 2800° IFB. IFB should not be taken above their rated temperature. If you go beyond their range, you run the risk of destroying their insulating value. Don't use IFB in excess of the high end temperature of the equipment or you will be wasting energy because the insulating value for IFB decreases as its temperature range increases. That

> **Build it right the first time**

is, 2000° IFB has a higher insulating value than 2300° brick, etc. A glory hole constructed from IFB takes longer to heat than one constructed from fiber, but it retains its heat whereas fiber does not. **IFB stores energy--fiber does not.** See The IFB Glory Hole found on page 198. Although some glass artists build fiber glory holes, I prefer IFB.

High Alumina Block

High alumina block or brick has many uses in the glass studio. They are usually used as liners for glass furnaces. As a tank liner, they are much lower in price per cubic foot than a tank of equal size constructed from AZS refractories. Notice I didn't say more cost effective. An AZS liner will last at least 5 years or longer, while a high alumina tank will usually last about 2 years, less if you're batching. Alumina block are much and I mean much lower in initial cost than AZS. If you're going to build a day tank, I recommend AZS over alumina. What you build your day tank from really depends on how you're going to use the furnace and what your budget will support. The percent of alumina in the brick varies from a low of about 49% to a high of 99.3%. The alumina block sometimes used above the tank liner is an alumina/mullite block. Tamax is the trade name. Not all alumina block can be used inside a glass furnace or for direct glass contact. It is important to match the usage for which the block was designed. Using the wrong brick can create disaster. Some alumina type brick will spall terribly when used in a glass furnace. Spalling is when the face of the brick peels away in sheets. Not much fun when you've spent lots of money and time building your dream furnace. Just because a block is high alumina does not mean it can be used as a tank liner.

Years ago, all our furnaces were constructed from a block called "Crystalite." This high alumina brick was manufactured by A.P. Green, was inexpensive and filled our needs at that time. The block that I have used as a substitute for the Crystalite is the Harbison Walker Korundal XD. It is reasonably priced (a relative term) and good for about 2 years in a school, if you're lucky and only using "cullet." As stated earlier, I don't think high alumina block will hold up well if you're melting batch at elevated temperatures.

Most studios today build crucible furnaces. The crucibles are high alumina and, if taken care of, can last a good length of time. The advantage of the crucible furnace is that, when the crucible goes, all you need to do is replace the crucible. When a day tank fails, you need to replace the complete furnace. Day tanks usually outlast crucibles by a factor of at least 2 : 1, and cracks in alumina liners are not, in the short run, a serious problem. If you're using a very active glass, that is, one that has a very low viscosity, it will attack your liner and produce stones in short order. As temperature rises, glass viscosity goes down. Remember, the hotter you get your furnace the shorter the life span of your block if it's alumina. This is not such an issue for AZS. So why use alumina block as a glass liner? The only reason is that they are relatively inexpensive and fairly easy to build with.

AZS Block

AZS stands for Alumina Zirconia Silicate. These blocks are also referred to as "fused cast refractories." AZS is the ultimate in tank liners. If treated properly they will last many years under the harsh conditions of glass melting. The caveat is "if treated properly," but more about that later.

A great deal has happened to the companies that manufactured AZS block in the last few years. At one time it was possible to purchase this block from two mainline manufacturers, Carborundum and Corhart. Over the last few years both of these companies have been absorbed by other companies. Corhart has been absorbed by St. Gobain/Sefpro, and Carborundum is now part of the Cookson Group/Vesuvius. It is difficult to obtain block from St. Gobain, but as of this writing one can purchase block from Vesuvius/Monofrax.

AZS block is produced by melting pure alumina, zirconia, and silica in a giant, water-cooled electric arc crucible and pouring the mixture into graphite molds. The AZS block is then annealed for weeks. The resulting block has the highest density of any existing glass tank liner block. Don't try to pick up one of these blocks if you have a bad back. When I say these beauties are dense, I mean dense.

After they are annealed, they are diamond cut to size and then the sides diamond ground to ensure a perfect fit for construction. The high refractory nature of the materials, plus the density of the block, make them ideal for direct glass contact. Since the cost of manufacture is high, the retail price is also high; however, AZS block will last longer than any other type of glass liner you will use and are very cost effective in the long run. AZS works best at elevated temperatures. The downside to AZS is that it is very prone to thermal shock. They need to be maintained at temperatures above 1800° F (982° C). If they fall below that temperature, they have a strong tendency to crack. One must take that into account when charging, as cold cullet or batch can drop the temperature quite suddenly and possibly crack the line. Small charges can help mitigate thermal problems. Regardless of how carefully you maintain the proper temperature, your AZS liner will eventually crack.

When lighting up, it is imperative that you raise the temperature very--and I mean very--slowly to above 1800° F. It is not unheard of to take at least one week to bring them up to operating temperature. I've constructed four AZS furnaces and have never had anyone of those furnaces last less than 7 years. If you're going to build a day tank, I strongly recommend the AZS liner. If you order a liner, the designation that accommodates soda/lime glass would be CS-3. Within the named designation are a series of different types and mixtures of fused cast products with specific applications. Ask the sales person for other AZS block designations that might fit your needs.

Using fused cast refractories as a furnace liner has many advantages. They last longer than all the other types of liners, do not break down under high heat, are not attacked as readily by corrosive glasses, can be heavily insulated, and can be purchased in monolithic shapes, thus avoiding "seams" or joints. Glass block seams are more readily attacked by molten glass. Look in a one-year-old day tank constructed from alumina block, and you will see corroded seams. As stated earlier, the only downside to AZS refractories is their high initial cost and their sensitivity to thermal shock. You can't change the cost, but you can guard against thermal shock.

If you wish to receive further information or order, you can e-mail Bud Davis at bud.davis@us.vesuvius.com or Stephen Graham at steve.graham@US.vesuvius.com. One last note: there is usually a delay of 10 to 12 weeks for delivery when placing an order.

In the furnace building section you can find an AZS designed furnace (pg. 147) that might help you in construction. My design is not the beginning and end all of day tank design and construction but is one that has worked for me in the past. As of this writing, Fred Metz has a great web site depicting the construction of an AZS day tank (www.spiralarts.com).

The Poor Man's AZS

Other companies manufacture a type of fused cast block that are less prone to thermal shock. These products are not solid AZS block but are manufactured by grinding fused cast material into a course "gravel" and pressing it into a block. They are also expensive and to my knowledge are not superior or equal to straight AZS. As I said, they do not thermal shock as readily as straight AZS. The AZS composite block is called "Vision" and the other is called "Vista." To get information on where to purchase these products as well as information sheets in .pdf format, go to ANH Refractories Company (www.hwr.com). Their Website is filled with information.

Castables

Castable refractory materials come in many forms, and each product serves a specific purpose. All castables fall into one of three categories: light-duty, medium-duty, and heavy-duty. It should be noted that within each duty range there are levels of insulating value. Some castables have higher insulating value than others. As the castable density increases, insulating value decreases. Recent advances in castable chemistry, if we can actually call it that, has produced some high temperature castables with excellent insulating value. The light-duty castables fall within a temperature range of 1400° to 2000° F (750°–1095° C). Most of the castables that are in this range are of the high insulating variety and are usually used as backup material to increase the insulating value of the unit. Medium-duty castables fall within a temperature range of 2200° to 2600° F (1200°–1425° C). Heavy-duty castables are in the range of 2800° to 3400° F (1535°–1875° C). The high heavy-duty castables are usually used as glory hole liners, glory hole doors, crucible pedestals, pot furnace liners, and pot furnace and furnace superstructures.

Within these temperature ranges, there are a variety of castable products that have many different applications. Without castables, life in the glass studio would be difficult.

Basically, a castable is a coarse, dry, refractory material that hardens when mixed with the correct proportions of water. It is important to use the correct proportion of clean cool water to castable when mixing. If you use too much water, your castable will not set correctly; not enough water will create a similar problem. Always use the manufacturer's recommendations when mixing. It takes a lot less water to mix a castable than you think. Most if not all castables have a data sheet that specifies the correct ratio of water to castable. Castables give you the ability to construct small as well as monolithic refractory forms that are not possible with bricks. Castables have a versatility not found in any other refractory product. The downside to using castables in the construction of monolithic forms is that, eventually, they will tend to crack. It is important to take that into account before designing what it is that you're going to cast. With experience you will come to understand the shortcomings that each product presents.

If you are going to use a castable as a replacement for some product you are already using, make sure it is a superior replacement for the product being replaced. Does it insulate better, or is it equal to the product being replaced at a similar thickness? It is important that you do not exceed the temperature limit of the castable. To be on the safe side, stay at least 100° F (37° C) below the nominal rating of the castable. Castables like A.P. Greens "Mizzou" or Narco's "Super Noxtab F" are excellent as crucible pedestals or for casting around crucibles. Again, be careful of what you use this or any castable product for. While "Mizzou" may make an excellent pedestal for a crucible, it may be a disaster as a crown for a day tank. Just because a product can withstand the heat doesn't mean it belongs in the kitchen. Match the product to its usage. I find A.P. Green's Kast-O-Lite 30 is an excellent 3000° F (1650° C) insulating castable. It makes an excellent glory hole liner as well as furnace and glory hole doors.

Other prefer Mizzou for glory hole doors. Before using a product for a specific application, try and get some feedback from others who have used the product you're considering. The Internet is a great source of information. There are any number of message boards where one can ask a question and get some excellent educated answers; on the other hand I've read some bogus ones as well. The one board that seems to be the most professional (most of the time) is the CraftWeb (http://talk.craftweb.com).

Some refractory companies that manufacture castables have products that are comparable and sometimes superior to other refractory company products. Your dealer can recommend a comparable product.

If you live in the boonies, you will either have to travel to the nearest city to get the products you want or have them shipped. What glass blower doesn't own a pick up? We're not known as the truck drivers of the art world for nothing. If you have to have your materials shipped in, you will pay freight charges on top of the cost of the material. If you purchase excess quantities of castable, make sure you store them in a warm dry location. They have a limited shelf life, depending on how you store them. If you live in a rain forest, don't buy more than you need. Sometimes price is misleading. Check how much of one company's material it takes to make 1 cubic foot as opposed to another company's comparable product. You may pay less per pound of product for one but get less volume. Some companies' products have comparable products, but conversely, some do not. Read the directions and always measure your water to castable ratios carefully.

Plastic Ramming Mixes and Patch Mixes

Plastic ramming mixes are actually refractory materials in the wet–clay state that are capable of being formed into different shapes. After forming, they can be fired like any ceramic material. Although plastic ramming mixes are not used that much in the glass studio, they serve an important purpose and are usually reasonably priced. The rammable is quite stiff and, when used, is rammed into place with a hammer. Hammering it into place shapes it. The density of the material in the wet state is so great that it must be formed by hammering. I've used a high alumina (80%) rammable around the outside edge of invested pot furnaces and also to angle the sill blocks of furnaces. I've also made furnace doors from plastic rammable fireclay with good results. After forming the door, we dry it and fire it in an annealer to red heat. Rammable doors can really take thermal shock. High alumina rammable makes excellent burner blocks.

Patching Material

When furnaces age, the seams of the glass tank sometimes open up and allow glass to seep into the backup block and insulation. There is a patch mix that can seal up the seams and give the furnace a little extra time before it gives up the ghost. The material that I have used with great success is manufactured by Narco and is called Zirmul 160 Patch. It is a ram/patch composed of alumina-zirconia-silicate. To use it, cool the furnace down and ram the Zirmul 160 into the seam, making sure to fill the void completely. Allow it to dry and restart the furnace. This patch mix is specifically designed for direct glass contact.

Fiber Insulation

Ceramic fiber insulation is often referred to as Fiberfrax or just plain frax. Fiberfrax is actually a trade name coined by the now defunct Carborundum Co. The name Fiberfrax has become so common that we use it to describe all fiber insulation regardless of its manufacturing company. It is primarily composed of alumina and silica. The high temperature variety has zirconia added to it. It is probably one of the most important products found in the glass studio. I know of no studio that does not use this product in some way, shape, or form. The most commonly used forms of Fiberfrax found in the glass studio is either blanket, board, or paper. It comes in many other forms as well.

Fiber blanket is manufactured in different temperature ranges, thicknesses, and densities. The temperature range, thickness, and density that the studio artist uses depends on its specific application. If you use it as a backup insulation, you will probably use it either 1" or 2" thick, 4 lb. density, and rated at 2300° F (1260° C). If you are using it as a liner for a glory hole, you would use it either 3" or 4" thick, 6 to 8 lb. density and rated at a high temperature range of approximately 2700° F (1500° C). See pg. 190.

I could ramble on for two pages and relate to you all the applications for this product. The tiles on the space shuttle are a form of Frax. Nick Labino helped develop the external re-entry fiber tile for the space shuttle. Nick had a secret little area in his studio where he worked on it for the space agency. Every time I visited him he made sure I didn't go into that secret little room. Like I would have known what I was looking at anyway! He said he'd have to kill me if I went in that room. I think he meant it. Nick's place was really something. Everything he ever worked on or invented was squirreled away in some corner of his studio. He never hesitated to whip something out and ask you if you knew what it was. I never did. But you could be sure it was something he invented or improved. Ask me or Fritz sometime to tell you about his motor in a walnut shell. He was an irascible guy but great fun on his good days. He shared a lot of his knowledge with me and others but only if he felt we had done our "homework."

There are some things you should know about Fiberfrax before using it. Fiberfrax does not store heat like brick does. It reflects most all the heat back that it is exposed to. A fiber oven needs less energy to achieve operating temperature than one made from IFB, but that same oven requires more energy to maintain its temperature. Less energy to achieve temperature, more energy to maintain temperature. IFB will radiate heat back into the oven when annealing and cooling. To fully understand this, try shutting off a fiber oven and see how fast it drops to 200° F (93° C). It will drop like a stone. Some production studios use fiber in order to get their ovens to cool quickly. Anneal and cool at night, ready the next morning. Brick ovens don't give you this attribute. If you have a studio in a location that has many power failures, you might

> **We're not known as the truck drivers of the art world for nothing**

consider building an IFB annealer. Another problem with fiber insulation is that the fibers become easily airborne and are not healthy to breath. The fiber should be encapsulated to avoid this problem.

There is another convenient form in which fiber insulation can be found: vacuum–formed fiber block. Some companies take the raw fiber and vacuum form it into a modular size block and at different densities. I've used 40 lb. density cast fiber with great success. Density = weight per cu. ft.

The company that will cast to your specification, for a price, is the Danser Corp. (www.danserinc.com/vacuduct.htm). I've seen vacuum cast fiber panels with Kanthal A-1 elements cast into the block itself. By using it in this form, it's possible to build an instant annealer complete with elements. It can be drilled, screwed, and glued. In this form, it is quite expensive, but think of the convenience!

Fiberfrax can also be purchased as a moldable material. That is, the fiber blanket has been soaked with colloidal silica and, when molded and dried, becomes quite rigid. This can be quite convenient if you have an odd shape that needs this type of insulation. It is sometimes sold as "Moist-Pack".

Another popular style of frax is fiber paper. The fiber paper comes in different thicknesses and is fairly tough before it is fired. The toughness comes from the starch binder. When it dries, the starch give the paper some rigidity. When fired though, the binder burns off and the paper no longer has anything holding it together and will dust quite readily if handled. If you leave it in place, however, it can be reused. The paper is quite popular with the kiln forming, fusing crowd. Normally, and unlike kiln wash, glass does not stick to it; if it does stick, it can easily be washed off the glass surface.

When used correctly, frax is an insulation that can be and often is indispensable. Although it can be expensive, the energy savings realized will more than pay for itself in a short time.

Semi-rigid Board (Mineral Block)

Semi-rigid board or mineral block is an excellent backup insulation. It is usually a dark grey green and fairly soft. It is generally used as backup insulation for annealing ovens. Its rigidity and modular size make it easy to use. It cuts quite easily with a saw but also sheds its fibers easily. Always wear a good dust mask when using this product or any fiber product for that matter. It has a very high insulating value. An annealing oven constructed from one layer of brick should be backed with 2 to 3" of mineral block. In the annealing oven section of this book, I refer to this product and its application for annealers. Never use this material as the hot face for an annealing oven, even if it is rated within the heat range of the oven. Never leave it exposed. Back it with sheet metal to prevent the fibers from becoming airborne. A lot of stuff we use in the glass studio is nasty. Get smart and practice safe glass studio.

Vermiculite Board & Calcium Silicate Board

Vermiculite Board is manufactured by the Skamol Corp. of Denmark. It is a material that has excellent density and strength. It is used to construct annealers. The MDS sheet does not indicate any negative health problems that one finds with fiber boards. It can be purchased in sheets 24" w x 36" l x 1 - 4" thick (see Skamol Annealer, pg. 261). What I really like about this product is that the slabs can be cut and shaped using ordinary wood working tools. The material can be routed to allow for easy installation of element wires.

As a back up to the vermiculite board you can use any standard back up material or their Calcium Silicate Board. "Calcium silicate slabs are designed for the application as backup insulation of all refractory constructions--dense firebrick, insulating firebrick, castables, plastic refractories, etc." I have seen this product used in annealing ovens; and I believe it to be an excellent product and I highly recommend it. The product is available from:

Skamol Americas, Inc.
8318 Pineville-Matthews Rd.
Suite 267
Charlotte, NC 28226.
Tel: 704/544-1015
www.skamol.com

Re-wettable Fiberglass Cloth
Alpha Maritex

The re-wettable fiberglass cloth is good to 1000° F (538° C). When wetted it can be molded to conform to compound curves. It is an excellent product for encapsulating fiber insulation. The company that sells this product also sells a full range of other encapsulating products that can withstand higher temperatures than the fiberglass cloth.

Great Lakes Textiles, Inc.
Web: www.gltproducts.com
Tel: 800/874-1748

Alpha Associates, Inc. sells a number of products that (www.alphainc.com) might be of service for encapsulating fiber. If you're interested I recommend you call them directly. The product I used was Alpha Maritex Style #84215/9485 but I think they have added any number of new products to their line. Thomas Chapman of Dayton, Ohio told me about this product.

Author's Note: All fiber insulation should be considered hazardous to your health and handled accordingly.

The First Toledo Museum Glass Studio, circa 1970,
Artist Unknown

Understanding Insulation

By Charlie Correll

There are few (if any) hot-glass artists that will argue with the fact that heating expenses are far and away the most significant they encounter. In the last decade alone, artists (depending on location) have seen their fuel bills rising anywhere from 3 - 10 orders of magnitude. This single **operating expense can be crippling** to many businesses, universities, and individuals like you. The remainder of this article will shed some light on the factors effecting these costs and real-life examples of how they can be avoided. Until now, the rapid increase in fuel costs have not been matched by a rise in consciousness of ways to combat this expense. The problem demands a new awareness of and attitude toward the economics of glass making.

Let's start by breaking things down into their simplest constituents. Your furnace is the backbone of your glass shop and has a few basic characteristics. It's essentially a box with a burner going in and a flue going out. Obviously the burner introduces the combustible gases that eventfully bring the load up to temperature. The flue facilitates the exhaust of the heated, non-combusted by-products into the atmosphere. Simple enough. Now lets improve on the process.

There are only two ways that the heat your equipment generates can escape. First, and probably most obvious, is through the flue with the exhaust gases. The second major loss of heat is directly through the walls of the furnace itself. For many years, the standard design parameters associated with insulation variables has consisted of one course of hard brick, for the furnace liner, followed by one course of soft brick and maybe a layer of ceramic fiber. This has been deemed sufficient to maintain interior temperature long enough to heat the load. This will make good glass but at a cost!

Consider the nature of insulating materials. Heat passes through a given material at a given rate per unit of time. The slower the rate, the greater insulating quality of the material. We can easily assign an arbitrary number (standard) to a insulating material of known efficacy. For comparison purposes we will issue hard brick a value of "one." By using multiples of one, insulating materials can now be compared to other know materials and expressed as **E**quivalent **I**nches of **F**irebrick or (EIF).

Authors Note: The above reference to EIF and the following tables are partial excerpts of A.P. Green's, Calculating Heat Transfer Through Refractory Walls. This book is unfortunately no longer published but can be found in the North American Refractories Handbook.

Table 1 on the following page shows the basic equivalents of various materials as compared to the standard.

Tables 2 & 3 shows the difference in EIF and relative heat loss in BTU / hr. / ft^2 at a temperature constant of 2400°.

Now let's evaluate the traditional furnace constituents, both with and without the additional 1" of ceramic fiber, as they relate to the parameters listed above. As you can see, Table #2 shows a Total EIF value of 20.70 for the furnace constructed with one course of hard brick and one course of soft brick. Conversely, Table #3 depicts a furnace constructed with an additional layer of ceramic fiber yielding a Total EIF value of 32.70.

As you can clearly see, the addition of just one inch of ceramic fiber insulation is responsible for a 34.5% reduction in heat loss. Considering that a single inch of fiber is "theoretically" capable of decreasing heat loss by ⅓, one could be led to believe that the problem is solved. Unfortunately the life of a glass worker isn't that simple. We still need to consider another basic property of these materials, that being density.

True, fiber does appear to be a wonderful insulator…within a closed system. All of the above comments are valid, as long as you never open the door of your furnace! This holds particularly true with top-loading units such as many kilns used by potters. Regardless of the style, the second you open the door to your furnace, heat retention becomes more a function of the density of the insulative material.

Essentially, ceramic fiber and vermiculite (both with similar EIF's) are very porous. In other words, they have lots of empty spaces. Actually, they are filled with air. Anyone that has ever opened the door to a glass furnace knows that unconfined air isn't a very good insulator. The moment you open the door, you're hit in the face with a blast of hot air. However, air confined within the matrix of a solid (that is, ceramic fiber or vermiculite), does have **limited** insulative characteristics.

Insulating Values

This table shows the basic equivalents of various materials as compared to the standard of one issued to heavy Firebrick	
Material	(E.I.F.)
Heavy Firebrick	1.00
Heavy Castable	1.00
3000° Insulating Castable	2.92
2500° Insulating Castable	2.92
2200° Insulating Castable	4.80
2000° IFB	4.30
2600° IFB	3.70
2800° IFB	3.15
1900° Block Insulation	12.00
1600° Vermiculite Castable	12.00
2400° Ceramic Fiber	12.00

The Tables below show the difference in E.I.F. and relative heat loss in KBTU/hr./Ft2 at a temperature constant of 2400° F.

Table 2

Material	Thickness	EIF	Product
1 Course Hard brick	4.5"	1.00	4.50
1 Course 2600° IFB	4.5"	3.60	16.20
Totals	9.0"	4.60	20.70

Total EIF = 20.70 Units = Heat loss of 840 BTU/hr./ft²

Table 3

Material	Thickness	EIF	Product
1 Course Hard brick	4.5"	1.00	4.50
1 Course 2600° IFB	4.5"	3.60	16.20
Ceramic Fiber	1.0"	12.00	12.00
Totals	10.0"	16.60	32.70

Total EIF = 32.70 Units = Heat loss of 550 BTU/hr./ft²

Furnaces and Pots
A Few Things to Know Before Starting

For the beginner, building any type of glass furnace can be a daunting task. Perhaps the following diagrams and descriptions can remove some of the "unknowns" from that task.

It is important to understand what materials to choose in building the furnace and also to understand why. A knowledge of refractory materials is paramount to building the furnace or annealing oven. To the beginner, understanding refractories may seem, difficult, especially given the quantity and types of refractory materials offered. It is not as difficult as it may seem however, because the glass artist uses a relatively narrow range of these materials. When I first wrote this book, there were many refractory companies to choose from, but in recent years most of the mainline refractory companies have been swallowed up by one company. In some ways, life is easier when choosing a product as all one has to do is go to the Internet and go to www.hwr.com. There you will find all the products made by A.P. Green, N.A. Refractories, and Harbison/Walker. Hundreds of products under one roof. Not only will you find the products you seek, but you can also download the specification sheets on how to use the product. Once you find the product that your after, you will need to find the link for the distribution center closest to you. Yes, that information is on the HWR site as well. If you do not have access to a computer and you wish to purchase a refractory product, then I suggest you go to your yellow pages and look under refractories. Familiarize yourself with the product you wish to use and make sure you're using it for the application intended. There are still any number of independent refractory companies that sell excellent products. You will find a list at the back of the book. It should be noted that some companies claim to manufacture products comparable to another company's product. In some instances that's true, but not always. That's why it's a good idea to find out from someone with experience what they recommend, but before doing that make sure that person has more that 5 minutes of experience using refractories. In some instances you may wish to use a particular refractory product in a way that is not recommended by the manufacturer; check first before going out on a limb as you may come to grief.

Research what you're building, develop a design, and then find the right product(s) for the job. Castable refractories have a rather short shelf life; so only purchase what you'll need for the job.

At this point in time, the Internet can provide information on products and their application, but in some cases you may not find a Web site for a company that sells the product you're looking for. I have tried to list those companies that sell refractory products for the studio artists and where they can be contacted, but there may be a few missing. If you have a manufacturer that you've purchased product from and it is not on my list, please E-mail me with that name and I'll try and include it in any future updates. Remember, the Internet and search engines are your friends. Oh yes, I almost forgot, in order to build a furnace you're going to need to know how to weld. If you can't weld, find someone who can. A welder is a very important resource if you're going to build equipment. Now make your plans and get to work.

My First Furnace, 1968
Vermillion, South Dakota

144   Glass Notes

Building a Day Tank

The furnace depicted on the following pages is not much different than the one originally built by Nick Labino for Harvey or the one Fritz built in Toledo in the late 60's. Everyone who has ever built a day tank has different detailing, but they are all basically the same. I hope the following drawings give enough information to get you started. For the beginner, the best advice I can give is for you to start small, say a 150-200 pound melt. The smaller the tank, the smaller the problems, big tanks, big problems. It is important to engineer the furnace well (precision counts). Everything must fit snugly. The external angle iron frame is very important. It is the frame that holds everything together. A hot furnace exerts tremendous pressure against this steel frame. The steel frame depicted on the following pages has evolved from many years of furnace building. While it is not the only way to configure a furnace frame, I have found that it works very well. It requires a little extra effort but, believe me, it is well worth it. Pay attention to details. For example, the quality of your weld is extremely important. If you do not create strong penetrating welds, it will be apparent when you fire up that beauty. I have built many day tanks and have had my share of disasters.

A flue is extremely important. If you do not build one, you will get serious "sting out" as well as internal pressure that will open the seams of your furnace and render it useless. "Sting out" is when the flame vents from the front of the furnace. How do I know about these problems, you ask? I've been there! A good formula for determining the flue size is: 1 sq. inch for every 10,000 btu's.

How you choose to fire your furnace is very important. Burners and systems can be found on pg. 223. If you know little to nothing about burner systems contact, Wet Dog Glass (www.wetdogglass.com), Abell Combustion Inc. (www.abellcombustion.com/glassblowing.htm), or The HUB Consolidated, Inc. (www.hubglass.com). As far as flame retention burner tips are concerned you have a choice between the Giberson, Wilton, and Spiral Arts. In today's glass furnace world nozzle mix burners seem to be the burner of choice. In the early days of furnace building, we top fired our furnaces, but in today's world the nozzle mix side fired furnace is standard. Regardless of the style or type of furnace you choose to build, make sure you have an understanding of what you're doing. The furnace depicted on the following pages is one I've built. The furnace foundation is important, so make sure you build a strong base from heavy-duty steel. Furnaces are heavy. Triangulate the legs for added strength. After building the base, cover the top with a heavy piece of sheet steel (⅛" is sufficient). Make sure it's flat and level. Before building the furnace, determine the height of the lower lip of your gathering port and then build your base to accommodate this height. Don't make the lower lip too high or you will have difficulty gathering. I find that 36" from floor to lip is fine. If you're very tall, you may want it somewhat higher. Make sure your furnace is comfortable to gather from. Draw accurate diagrams of the furnace you wish to build before you build it. Photograph its construction. Keep records of all the materials you use and their cost.

There is a Zen to building furnaces. Recommended reading: *Zen and the Art of Motorcycle Maintenance* by Robert M. Pirsig.

Day Tank

> **To determine the flue size of any furnace:**
> 1 sq. inch for every 10,000 btu's
> 6.45 sq. cm for every 2,520 kg-cal.

The Day Tank
List of Materials

	Material	Quantity
For Furnace Foundation	For Base Super Duty Fireclay Brick KX-99 or Clipper (straights)	50
	IFB 2300° (straights)	50
For Sidewalls	IFB 2600° (straights)	250
	[1]Tamax or Gen-Sil Silica Block (straights) If you use 3" straights reduce the quantity by 20%	60
	[2]Board insulation	28 sq. ft.
Liner Back-up	[3]Tamax (2 ½" straights)	30
Tank Liner, Vesuvius/Monofrax	CS-3, 21" x 15" x 3"	4
	CS-3, 18" x 9" x 3"	2
Sill Block	[4]Tamax, Korundal XD, UFALA XCR, 10" x 9" x 3"	1
Crown & Port Block	[5]Tamax or Gen-Sil Silica Block	45
Crown Insulation	2" 8 lb. density, 2600° fiber	40"
	2" 8 lb. density, 2300° fiber	80"
	[6]Excelfrax, ½"-1" or 1" of 2300° fiber	60"

1. Tamax is a mullite block and has been used with excellent results above the glass line, but it is very expensive. At this writing, about $17.50 per straight. What I offer here is not an alternative to Tamax but a brick that is fabricated specifically for superstructures and less expensive than Tamax. This brick is a crystalline silica brick (Gen-Sil) and is manufactured by Utah Refractories (www.glassonline.com/utah/ Tel: 412/851-2430). The sales representative is Tom Mulholland. They also manufacture crown arch brick and the mortars for installation. I have used this brick and recommend it highly. There are two minor caveat's to using this brick; it is prone to thermal shock but so is your CS-3 liner. If you use Gen-Sil in a furnace that is cycled often you may find it problematic. The other problem is that the Gen-Sil block cannot have direct contact with AZS refractories. There are a few solutions to avoid direct contact as suggested by Bud Davis of Vesuvius; the one I find easiest to use is a Zircon-based mortar buffer between the AZS and the first layer of Gen-Sil silica brick. The suggested mortar is NARCO 702 heat set or NARCO 150 patch.

2. Some furnace builders use two layers of IFB as their total insulation, and that works just fine, but in this case I recommend using 2" of a good rigid insulating board like the Skamol Calcium Silicate board. It is a bit thinner and gives greater insulating value for its thickness. It is also possible to use any of the frax boards manufactured by any number of companies. I've used Thermal Ceramics M board with great success as well. Your call.

3. For below the glass line, there are two ways to effect a sturdy back-up for the AZS liner. One method is to use a dense AZS castable. I have built 4 furnaces using the AZS castable method and it worked fine, but it means you will have to build a very sturdy, and I mean sturdy, form. Your casting has to be extremely accurate in order that the rest of the furnace goes together accurately. I can tell you from experience that it is no fun having to cut dozens of IFB because my casting was off by one quarter inch. The other method for back-up is to use a mullite type block such as Tamax or Tamul or UFALA XCR. It is quick, easy, and accurate when using block. The backup block should be mortared to each other but not to the liner.

4. The sill block needs to be a high alumina block as it will have to withstand the drips from gathering. Again, either of the block mentioned above will suffice.

5. I recommend building the crown from either Gen-Sil silica brick (see crown construction illustrations on pg. 153) or Tamax crown brick. The Gen-Sil is less expensive block than the Tamax.

6. Most of the heat loss from any furnace is through the gathering port, flue, and the crown. The Unifrax Corp. has a fairly new insulation that is really fantastic insofar as insulating value to thickness is concerned. The product is called Excelfrax Microporous insulation. 1" of this product is equal to 3.9 inches of fiber. It comes in two forms: 1800 board and 1800 Flexliner. The 1800 designation references the temperature limit of the product. It is not a product that you want to sandwich close to the furnace as you can easily exceed its temperature limit. I would recommend it as the last layer of insulation. The board cannot be bent into curves, and it is quite friable when handled. If you plan on using this material as the last layer of your crown, I would recommend you call the Unifrax Application Engineering Department at 716-278-3800 and ask about the Flexliner and its ability to contour the curve of your crown. I've used the board and found it to be a fantastic advance in insulation.

A Few Words About Building a Day Tank

In the 3rd edition of *Glass Notes* I listed the price of materials used to build the furnace. In this edition, I have not done this as the price of materials changes from week to week. It behooves you to contact the sales office of the companies that sell the products you're interested in and obtain their latest pricing. Remember, when getting prices be sure to get shipping costs. These products have substantial weight and will be quite expensive to ship. If the point of shipping is close enough, I recommend you gather up your dog, grab a Rolling Rock, hop in your old beat-up 350 V-8 pick-up, crank up the tunes on the ole 8 track, and go get the stuff. It might save you a lot of money. Oh yes, make sure you're not going to haul 2 tons in a one ton pick-up, Ouch!

The furnace presented in this edition of my book uses an AZS liner instead of the high alumina liner in the previous edition. It is now my opinion that if one is to construct a day tank it should be from a material that will give high quality service over a long period of time. That material is AZS Monofrax/Vesuvius refractory block. Although this block is initially expensive, in my opinion it will, if taken care of, more than pay for itself in the long run. If you wish to go the inexpensive route, the Korundal XD will make a decent furnace but has a very limited life expectancy if run 24/7. The Korundal XD, if taken to the elevated temperatures of batch melting will be attacked by the low viscosity of the glass whereas the AZS is a lot less prone to this type of attack. The lower the viscosity of your glass, the faster it will attack your refractory. IMHO only build with Korundal if money is an issue. Don't be penny wise and pound foolish. The design of the furnace will only vary in the configuration of the glass tank block; the dimensions remain constant. The pavers for the AZS furnace will go inside the sidewall whereas the pavers for Korundal XD furnace will go under the sidewalls. There was a time when one could easily purchase an AZS tank liner from Corhart, but easily is is no longer possible. There is a block that is a step down from the pure AZS and cheaper and sturdier than the Korundal XD. That type of block is called Vision or Vista block. The Vision has a slightly higher Al and Zr content than the Vista. This formulation is fabricated from granular AZS and pressed into a dense block. The idea in fabricating from granular AZS is that one avoids the thermal shock one gets when using a pure AZS block; it is also less expensive. I have used this block and found it initially spalled when in direct glass contact, but after the initial spalling stopped, it gave good life under constant usage. Block density translates into the expected life of the particular block being used. The order of density would be as follows: Pure AZS (Monofrax CS-3), Vision and mechanically pressed high alumina (at least 92%) Korundal XD. As you can surmise the cost of each of these materials is in the same order.

The number of tank liner block calculated for this furnace is exact; the number and quantity of the other materials is approximate but hopefully fairly accurate.

All the drawings are to scale; that is, all the proportions are accurate. The diagrams on the following pages will tell you what bricks go where.

If building a day tank seems like a daunting task, and for many it is, I recommend purchasing one from one of the fine companies and/or individuals that build this type of equipment.

One of the early furnace's I built in 1972. Notice the lack of insulation on the crown. What was I thinking you ask? At the time I thought that since I could put my hand on the crown fiber and not burn myself, it must be well insulated. I had a lot to learn, which I eventually did.

The Furnace

The furnace depicted on the following pages is a generic design for a day tank. The dimensions depicted for this furnace will give a nominal capacity of 360 lbs. (163 kg) of glass and an actual capacity of about 300 lbs. (136 kg). Although I recommend AZS as the liner of choice, you can use Vision composite AZS block sold by ANH and found at www.hwr.com. You will notice that the paver block for this design are inside the sidewalls and not under the sidewalls. The reason for this is that the density of AZS and Vision are greater than than soda/lime glass and therefore will not float. I do not recommend this design if you're going to use high alumina block as there is a possibility for a loose block to float. I have drawn an alternate plan for a high alumina block liner on pg. 150. Otherwise, the rest of the furnace is built in the same fashion as depicted in these drawings.

AZS Liner & Base

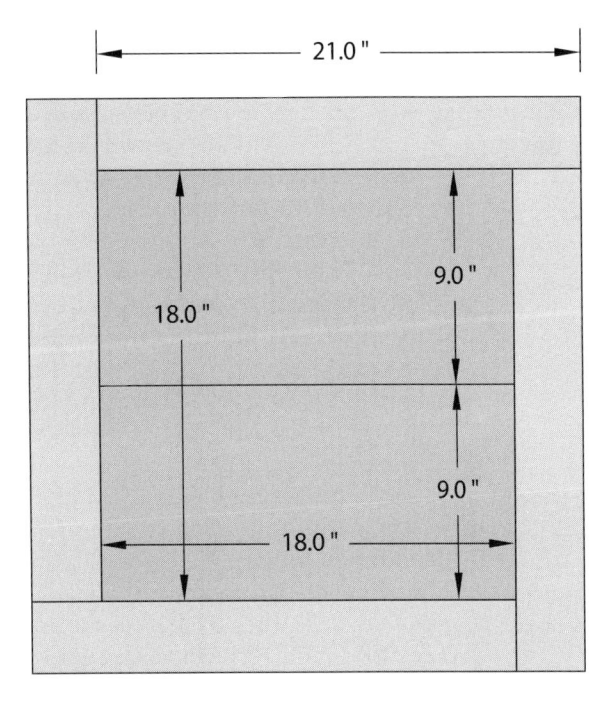

These two views depict the configuration of the AZS liner. It should be noted that the paver blocks go inside the sidewalls. As noted in the construction notes, this configuration will hold approximately 300 + lbs. of soda/lime glass. Soda/lime glass weighs about 160 lbs. ft.[3]

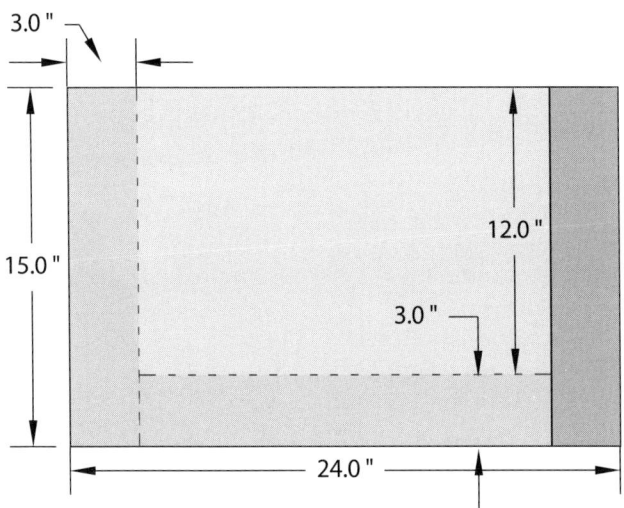

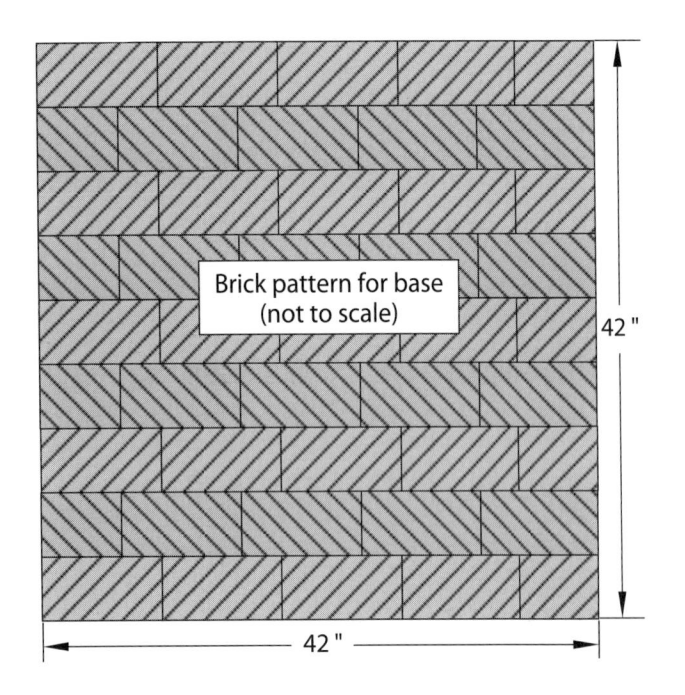

This view depicts the brick pattern that will be the base for the furnace. There are two layers, 2300° IFB and heavy-duty hard brick. The furnace liner will sit on the hard brick. When putting down the second layer of brick, make sure the brick pattern is opposite that of the previous layer; that is, you do not want the seams to line up.

Remember, the furnace will be quite heavy, so you will need to build a very--and I mean very--sturdy base for the unit.

Furnace Liner

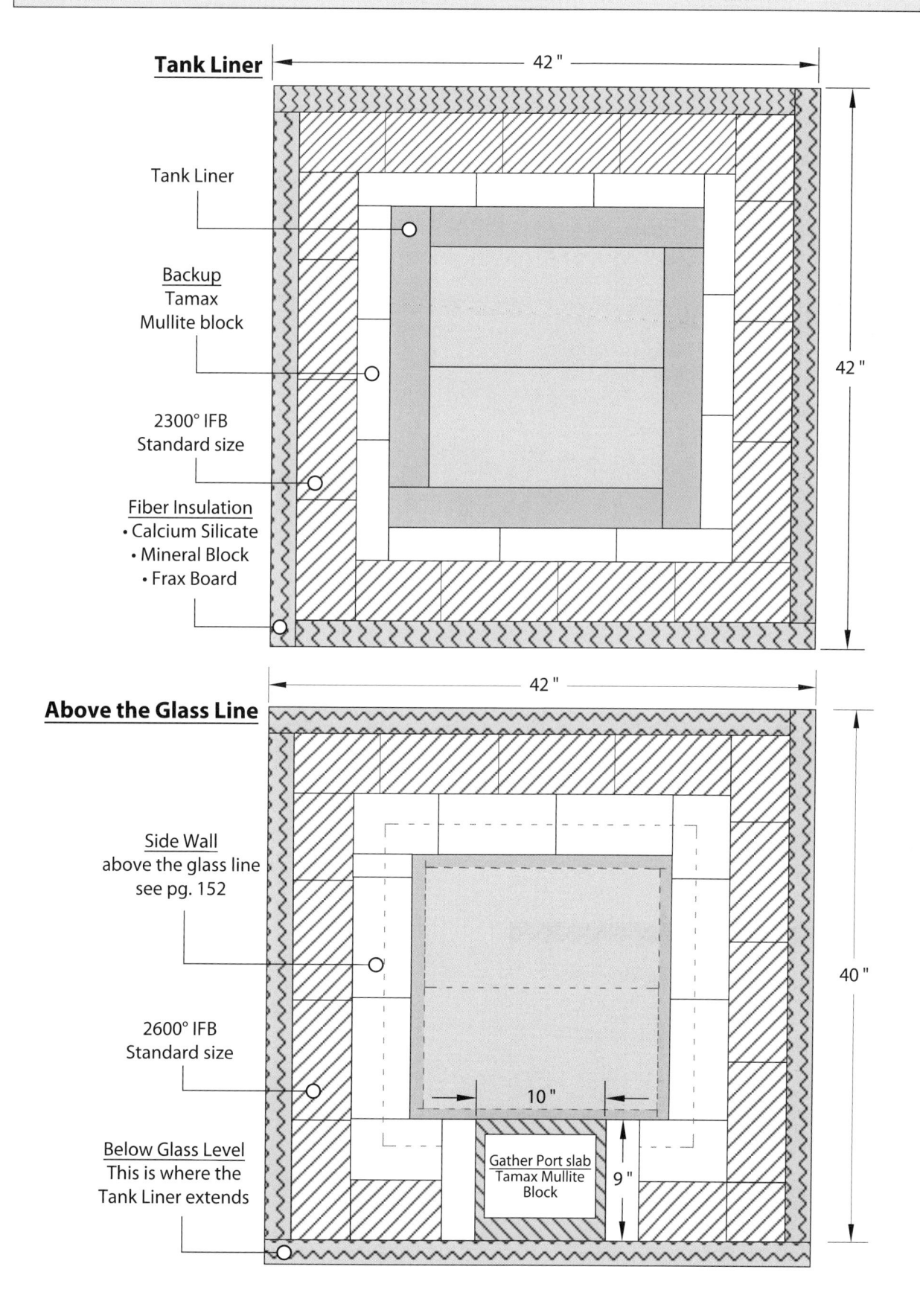

Tank Liner

42"

42"

- Tank Liner
- Backup Tamax Mullite block
- 2300° IFB Standard size
- Fiber Insulation
  - Calcium Silicate
  - Mineral Block
  - Frax Board

Above the Glass Line

42"

40"

- Side Wall above the glass line see pg. 152
- 2600° IFB Standard size
- Below Glass Level This is where the Tank Liner extends

10"

Gather Port slab
Tamax Mullite Block

9"

Glass Notes 149

Day Tank, Korundal XD, High Alumina Liner

If you choose to create a day tank using Korundal instead of the AZS, this is how the liner is configured. It has exactly the same dimensions as the AZS and is built the same way as indicated in these plans.

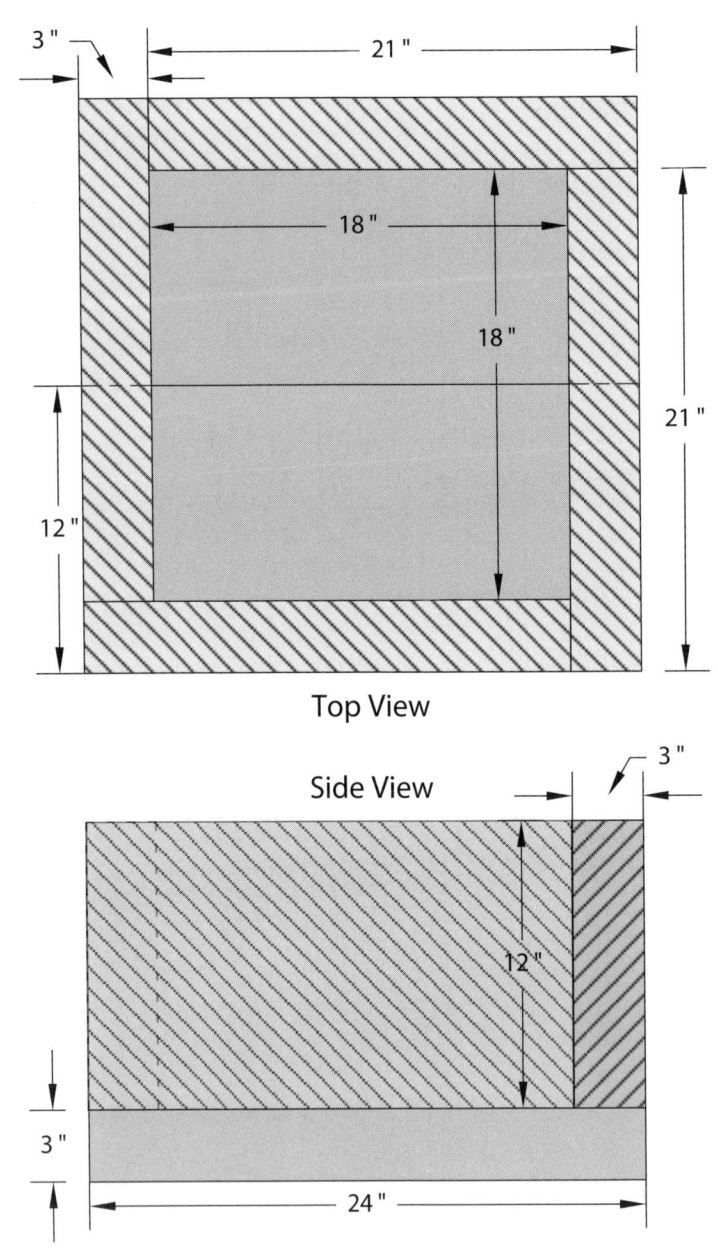

Top View

Side View

All block are Korundal XD
The sidewall block always goes on top of the pavers

This view illustrates how the block are configured when building a day tank from Korundal XD. It is imperative that the sidewalls go on top of the pavers.

Korundal XD   4@   21" x 12" x 3"
                   2@   24" x 12" x 3"

The Day Tank, Front View

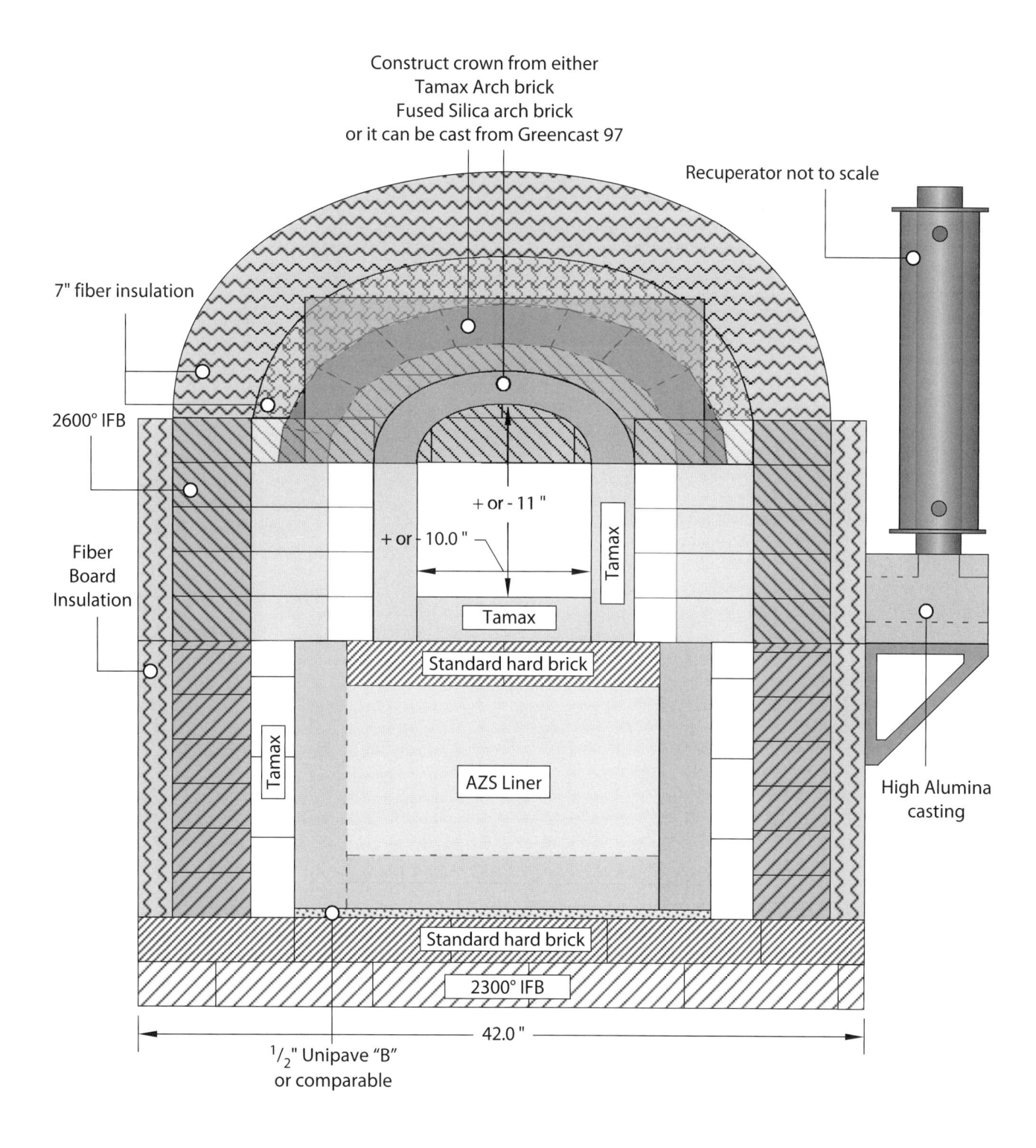

Construct crown from either
Tamax Arch brick
Fused Silica arch brick
or it can be cast from Greencast 97

Recuperator not to scale

7" fiber insulation

2600° IFB

Fiber Board Insulation

+ or - 11 "

+ or - 10.0 "

Tamax

Tamax

Standard hard brick

Tamax

AZS Liner

High Alumina casting

Standard hard brick

2300° IFB

42.0 "

$1/2$" Unipave "B" or comparable

Side View

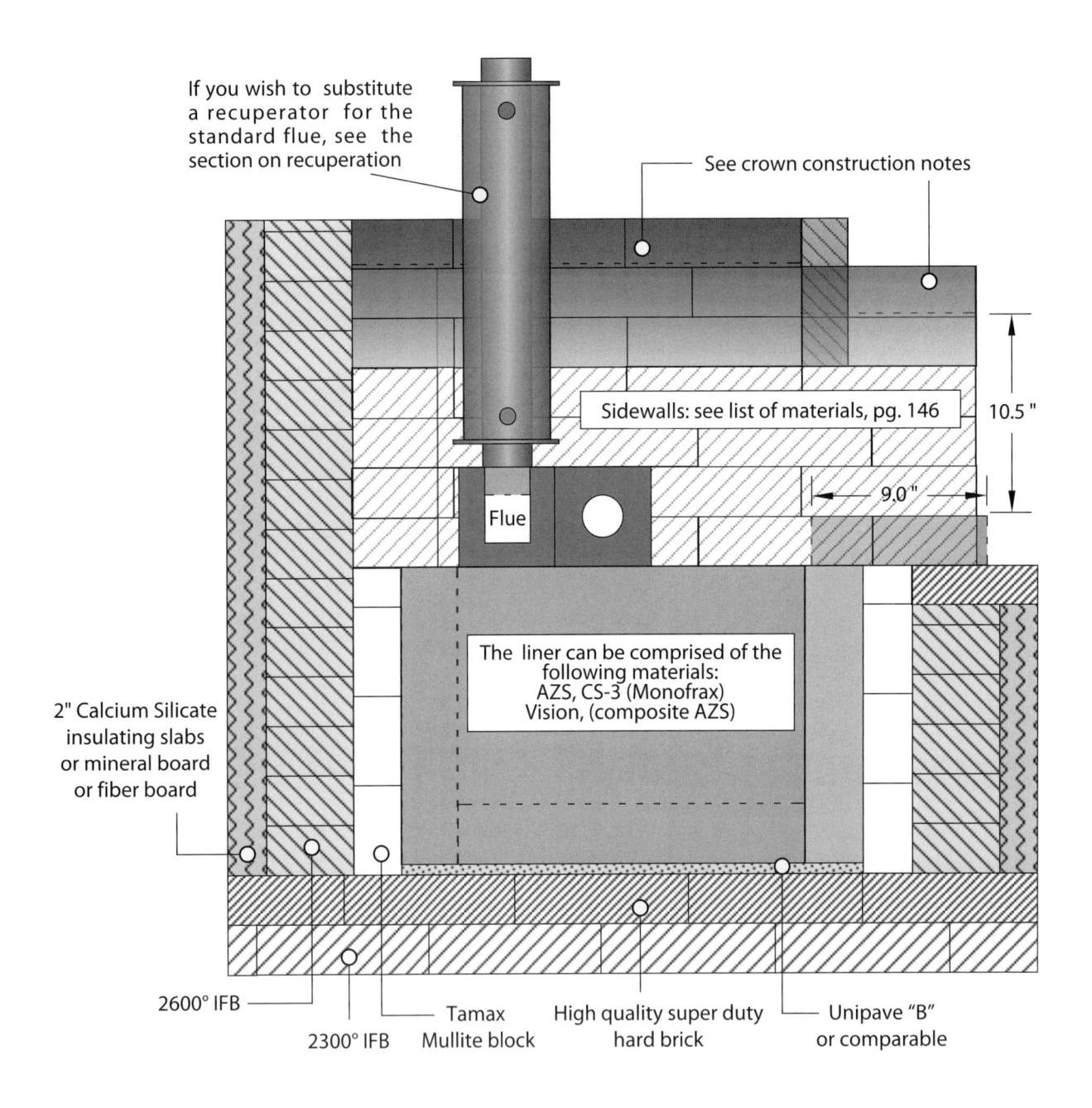

If you wish to substitute a recuperator for the standard flue, see the section on recuperation

See crown construction notes

Sidewalls: see list of materials, pg. 146

10.5 "

9.0 "

Flue

The liner can be comprised of the following materials:
AZS, CS-3 (Monofrax)
Vision, (composite AZS)

2" Calcium Silicate insulating slabs or mineral board or fiber board

2600° IFB

2300° IFB

Tamax Mullite block

High quality super duty hard brick

Unipave "B" or comparable

152 Glass Notes

Front View with Sprung Arch Crown

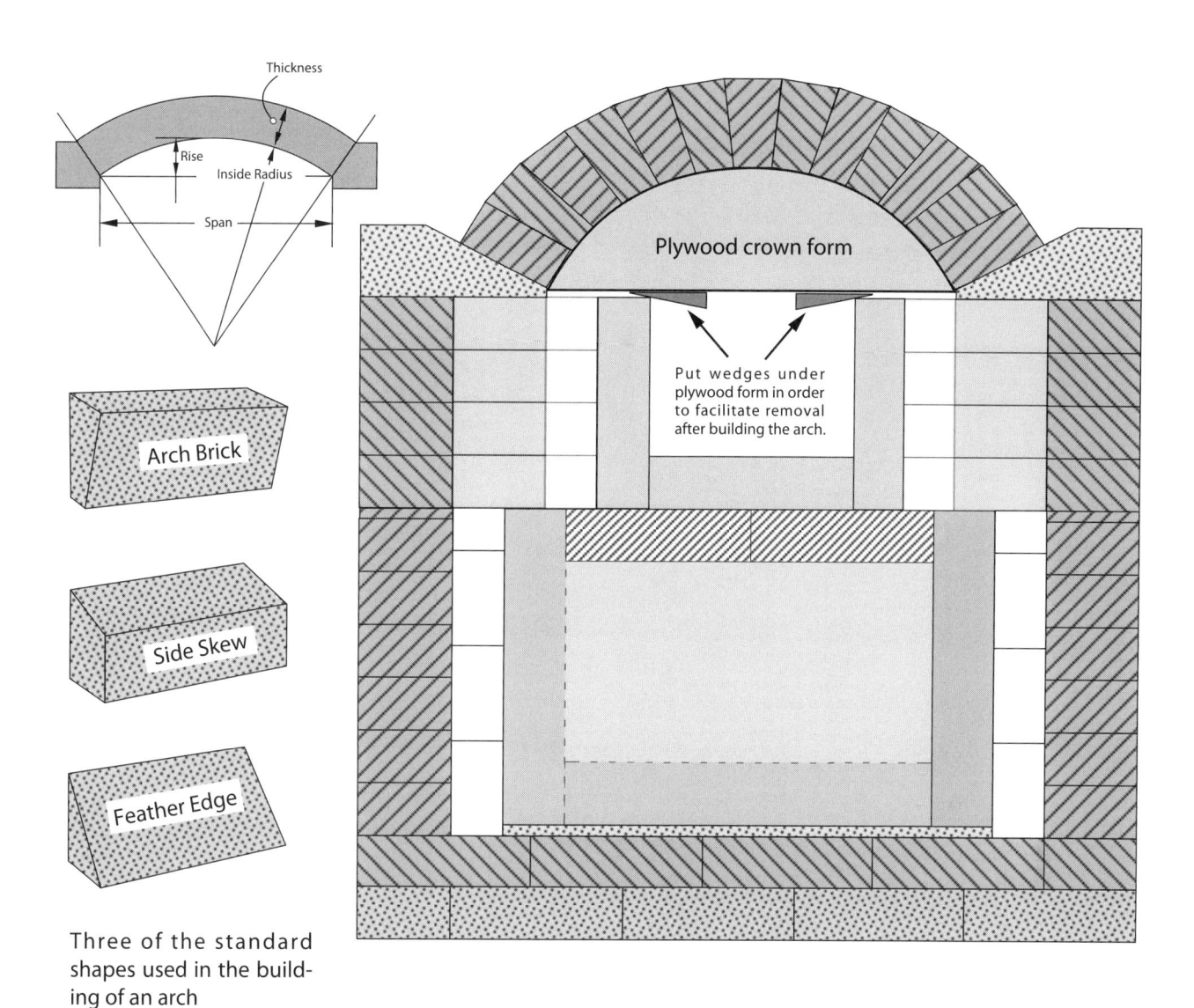

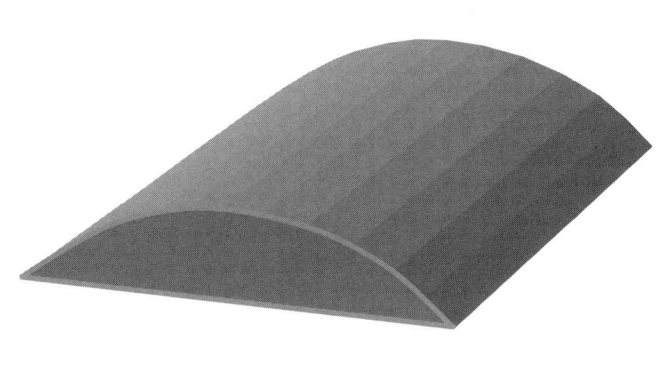

Thickness
Rise
Inside Radius
Span

Plywood crown form

Put wedges under plywood form in order to facilitate removal after building the arch.

Arch Brick

Side Skew

Feather Edge

Three of the standard shapes used in the building of an arch

Crown Form

In my opinion, a sprung arch crown is a superior to a cast one, although I have cast many a crown without any problems over the life of the crown. Although building a sprung arch crown requires a bit of skill, the satisfaction one gets from constructing one is indescribable.

At one time, A.P. Green printed a pocket reference guide that listed all their products as well as a chart that listed the number and type of arch brick necessary to build a sprung arch for most any size span. This guide is no longer in print, but I'm sure this information is available when you call to place an order. Arch brick come in 3 angles, #1, #2, and #3, the #1 brick having the greatest angle. The arch springs from a skew brick or a feather edge. The gathering port is built in a fashion similar to how the crown is built. When building the gathering port crown, it may be necessary to cut your own side skew brick.

Glass Notes 153

Steel Support System

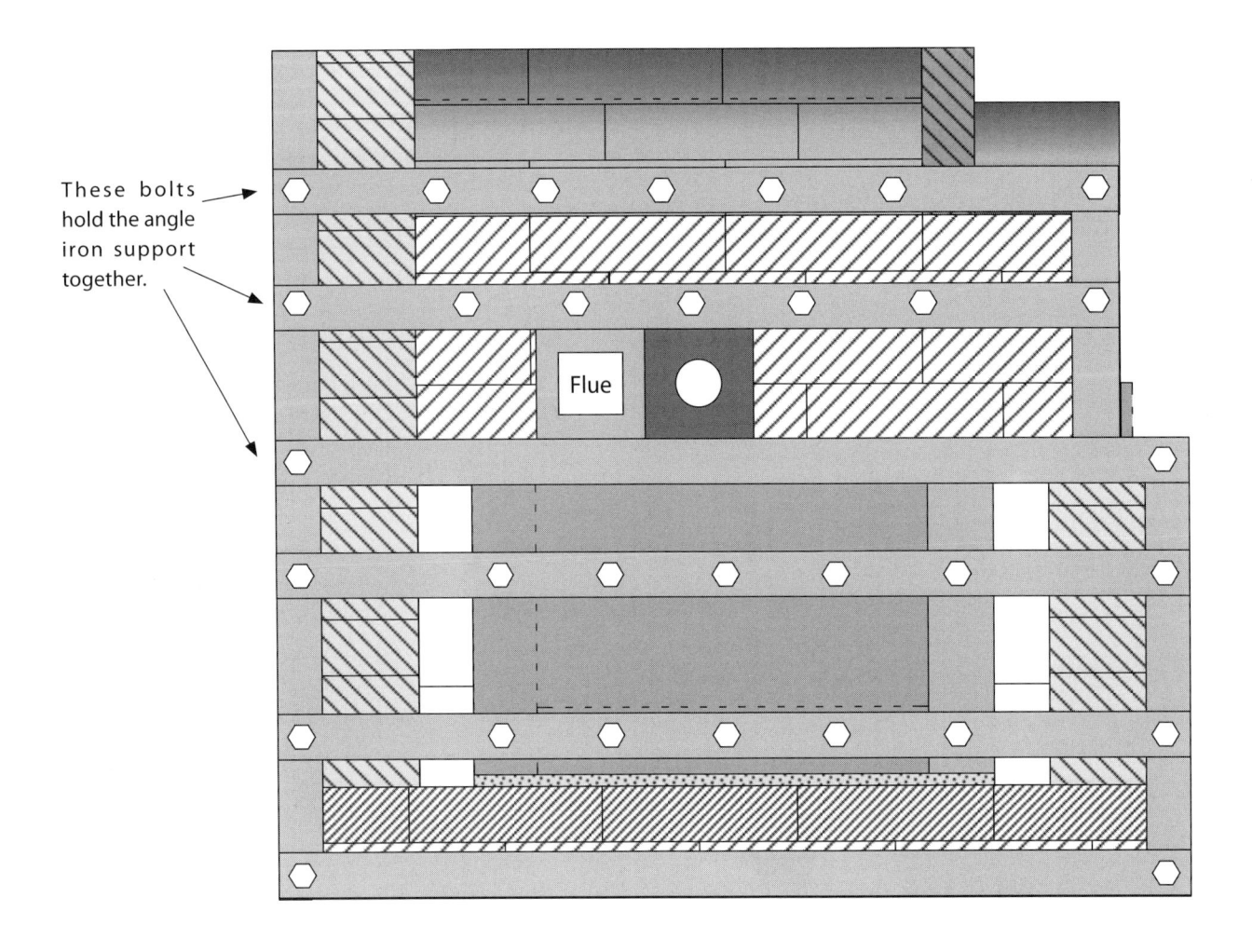

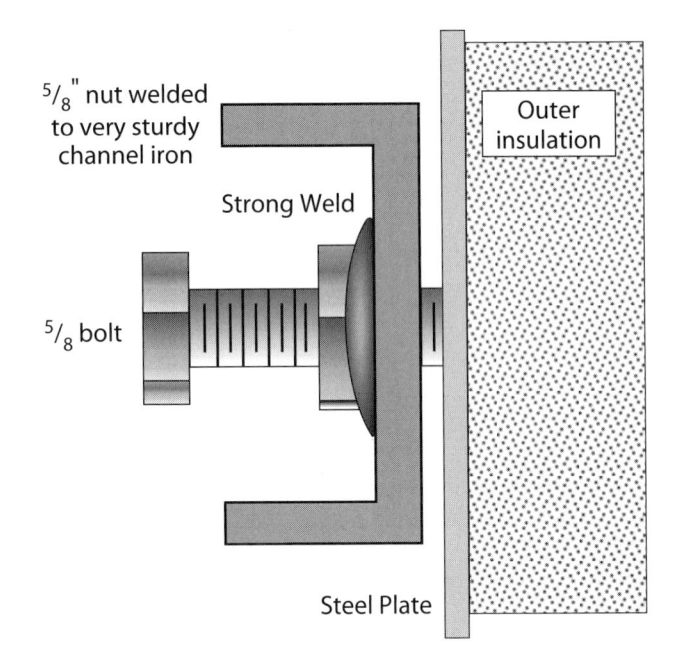

These bolts hold the angle iron support together.

5/8" nut welded to very sturdy channel iron

Strong Weld

5/8 bolt

Outer insulation

Steel Plate

These diagrams show the angle iron support system that holds the furnace together. It is very important to construct these supports on all four sides of the furnace. It is important that a steel plate, at least 14 gauge, be between the furnace and the bolts. The pressure from the bolts will be properly distributed. This nut and bolt system keeps the internal combustion pressure from opening up the seams of the tank liner. The liner block are shown to help you understand where to locate the support system.

Flue

154   Glass Notes

Front of Furnace with Door

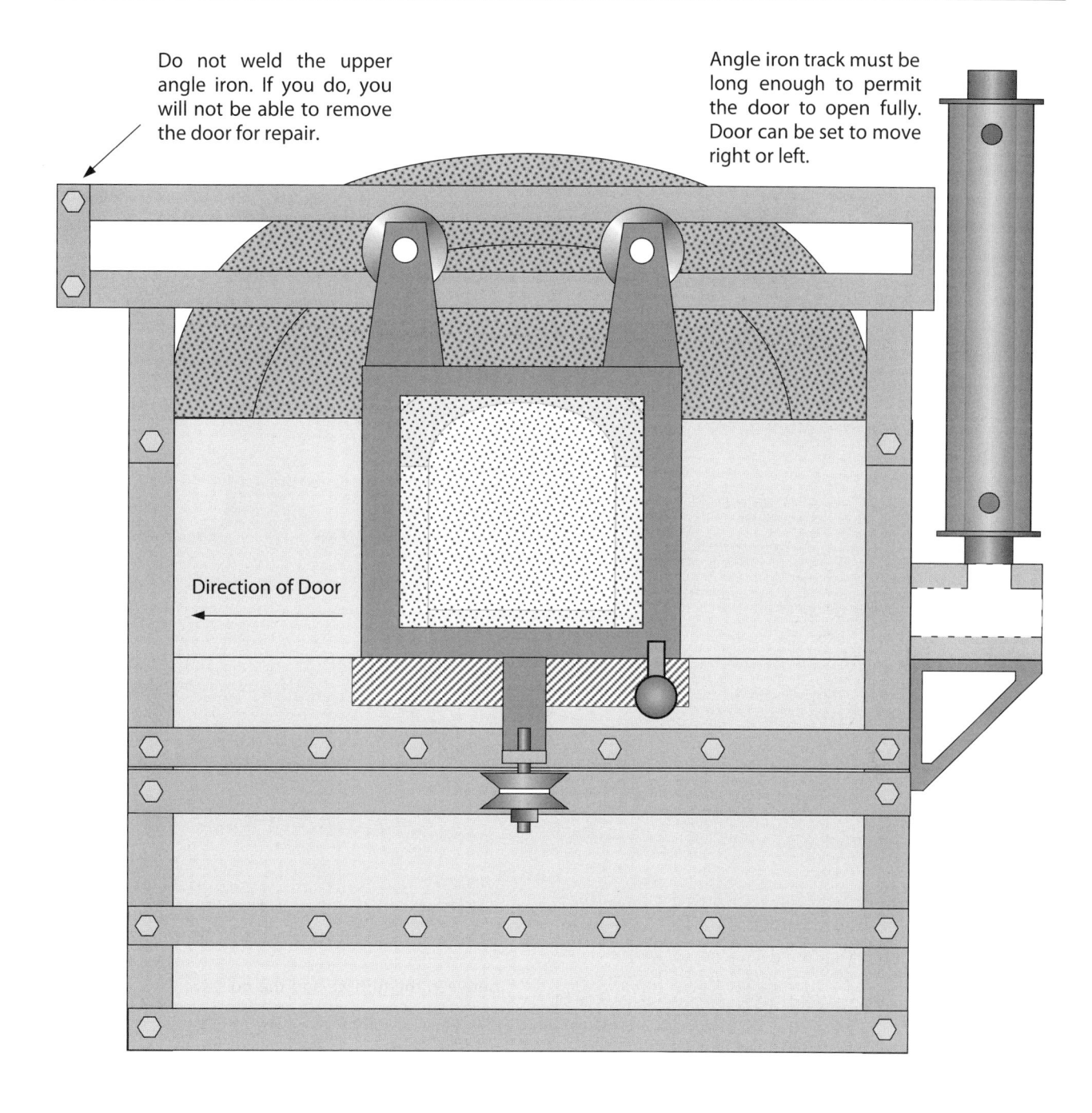

Do not weld the upper angle iron. If you do, you will not be able to remove the door for repair.

Angle iron track must be long enough to permit the door to open fully. Door can be set to move right or left.

Direction of Door

This front view of the furnace shows the door in place. The lower wheel is adjustable in order to keep the door at the proper distance from the gathering port. Use a good quality wheel. All of the steel used is ⅛" thick or greater angle iron. The upper wheels are high quality "V" groove wheels with roller bearings. The wheels run smoothly on the lower angle iron. The upper angle iron does not touch the the wheel but is close enough to keep the wheels from jumping the track. It is also far enough away from the heat so that it will not bind. The front of the door should be about as close as possible to the gathering port. The gathering port is the greatest area of heat loss along with the flue. The lower wheels are far from any heat. The upper track should act as your door stop.

The door is made from a heavy-duty castable and is cast in place. There are many door configurations. This is one I have used and find to work quite well.

Glass Notes 155

Cast Crown Construction

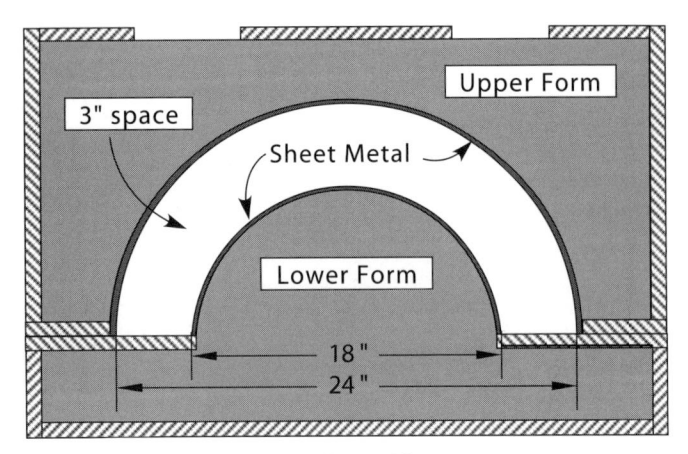

Fig. 1 Front View

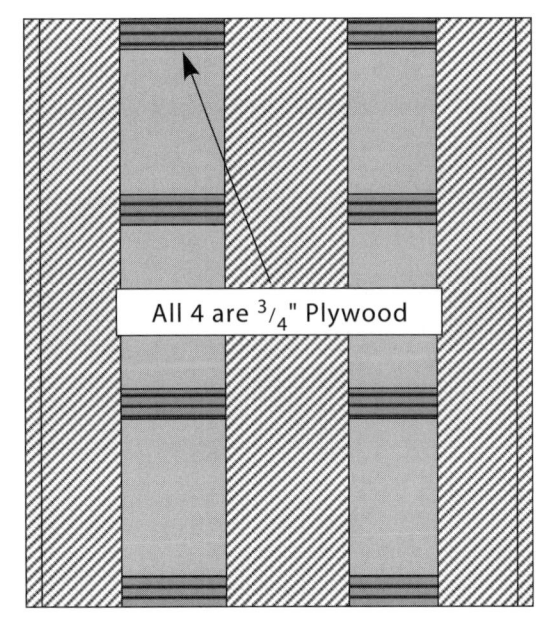

Fig. 2 Top View

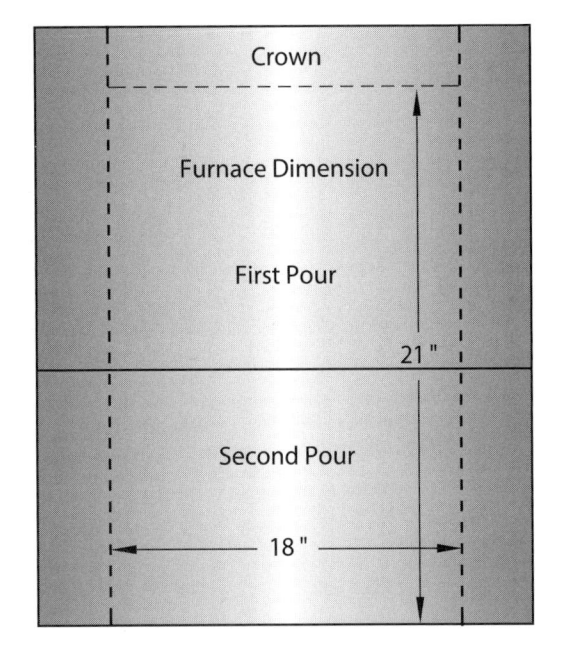

Fig. 3 Top View, Cast Crown

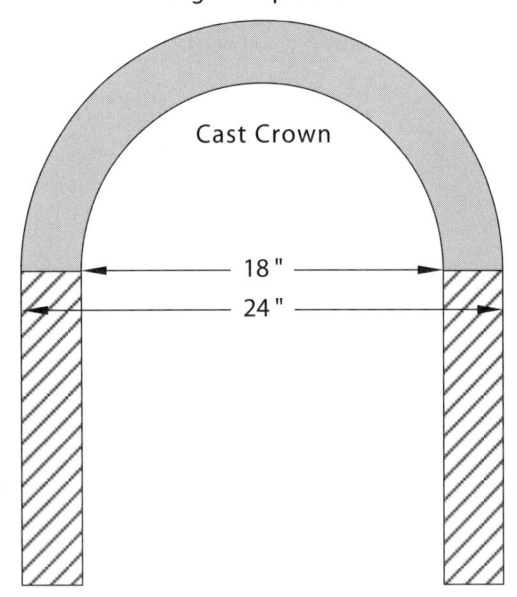

Fig. 4 Crown in Place

    This plywood and sheet metal form is constructed in a fashion similar to the one found on pg. 162. A sash chain inscribes the arc, and the upper form is cut from ¾" plywood depicted in Fig. 1. You will cut 4 of these forms shown in the top view, Fig. 2. With sheets of plywood, you will box in the upper forms. Press thin sheet metal into the curve and nail in place. You will probably need a sharp, pointed punch to make a hole through the sheet metal. If you try and use the short nails to make a hole you will smack your fingers. The lower form is the same arc as the upper form but 3" smaller. Cut 4 of these forms and construct the box in fashion similar to how you built the upper form. Make sure the boxes fit together and that they are the size of the full arch that you will cast for your furnace crown. You will cast it in two pieces of unequal sizes as shown in Fig. 3 if you're going to top fire the furnace. In top fired units, I like to have the burner slightly forward of center. If you're side firing you can cast them of equal size. Fig. 4 depicts the front of the furnace with the crown in place.

156   Glass Notes

Casting a Crown

1. Crown Mold: Fabricated from plywood and sheet metal.

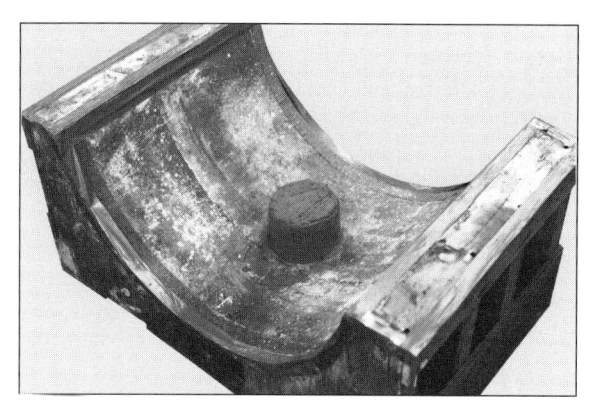

2. Burner Plug: Fabricate from clay. Place forward from center.

3. Assemble Mold

4. Cast crown in two sections, divide at center of burner.

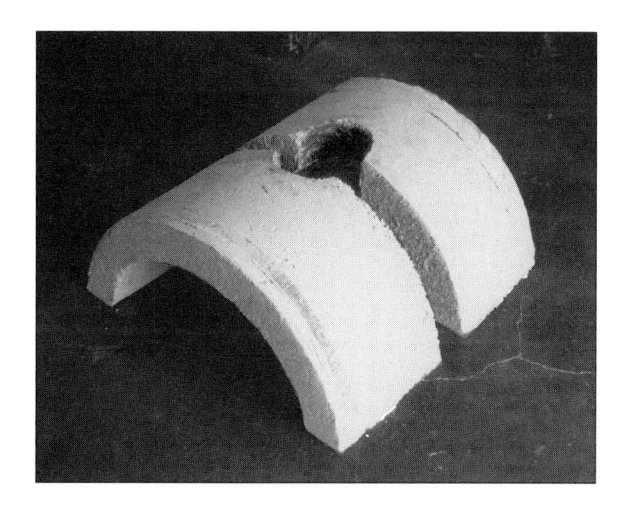

5. Finished Crown, 2 Parts

These five pictures depict how a crown is cast for a day tank. The mold is fabricated from plywood and sheet metal. The curve is established by holding a sash chain at the outside diameter of the crown and letting it hang (pg. 162). Trace the curve and cut the plywood as indicated in step 1 on the preceding page. Cut four or more pieces of plywood exactly the same and assemble as indicated. The inside curve of the crown is drawn onto plywood and is 3" smaller than the outside of the crown. The crown is cast in two parts divided at the burner hole. If you're going to side fire your furnace, leave the burner plug out and cast in two equal sections. The reason for casting the crown in two parts is that a monolithic, one piece crown is apt to crack; a two piece is less prone to cracking. The burner hole is not in the middle but about 2" forward. Cast the first half of the crown and wait 24 hours before casting the other half. Use Vaseline as a separator. Let the crown set under plastic. Use Greencast 97 or a comparable product. Allow it to set for a couple of days to insure a good, hard set. When setting in place, mortar the two sections with a high alumina mortar.

Building the Invested Pot Furnace

Before you decide to build an invested pot furnace, I should make you aware that this type of furnace is not the most economical to run, but it can under some circumstances serve a purpose. An invested pot furnace is actually a day tank in disguise. The pot in this situation is not really a pot but merely a liner. Crucibles by nature are thinner than day tank liners and, because of that, will wear faster--especially if you're melting batch. The invested pot furnace is usually built by studios that work intermittently as in working a day job during the week and blowing glass Friday, Saturday, and Sunday. The great fear is that if one builds a free standing crucible furnace, the crucible will crack in short order and the glass will leak all over the place and it can get expensive replacing pots; you know the drill. No problem with an invested pot, though if it decides to crack, it is backed with a heavy-duty castable and all will be well with the world. The seepage through the crack will eventually "freeze" when the glass reaches the cooler zone of the backup material. Keep in mind, however, that when the invested pot furnace wears out you have to throw the whole unit out or at least a good part of it. Now if I haven't talked you out of building an invested pot furnace, then you can read on. If you're feeling brave and think you can maintain a free standing pot furnace, you can skip this section and proceed to pg. 171.

The invested pot furnace described in this section uses a 60-pound capacity crucible. Some, but not all of the dimensions are applicable to any size pot furnace you wish to build. The dimensions applying to most invested pot furnaces would be the distance from the pot surface to the crown as well as the castable surrounding the crucible itself. Obviously, larger capacity crucibles have a greater diameter and are taller. It is important to diagram your pot furnace design before beginning construction. Pencil in all your dimensions so you will have an understanding of how much space it will occupy. If you are building it directly on the studio floor, you will still need to use at least two layers of insulating brick as a base for the furnace. If you are building a low steel stand, your dimensions for the stand will be generated by the drawing you make. Always double check your dimensions for accuracy. I like the steel stand design because, if built correctly, it will permit you to lift it with a good pallet jack and move it to any location you like.

To build the pot furnace, you will start from the inside and work out. The first thing needed will be a flexible cylinder that will allow a 3" space around your crucible. A sheet metal ring bent to the diameter needed works fine. You will need to cut it to the correct height as well. Some studios build with a Sonotube. If you use a Sonotube, it is much easier to get one larger than you need and make one lengthwise cut. Bend it in on itself to the desired diameter. It can be held together using sheet rock screws (see drawing this page). Cutting the tube makes removing it very simple. A Sonotube is a heavy-duty coated cardboard tube used in the construction trade. They come in various dimensions and are available through construction firms.

It is critical that you put a piece of sheet plastic that has no holes over the insulating brick before setting the sheet metal or Sonotube ring on it. If you do not, the insulating brick will absorb all the water from the castable and render it useless. Make sure you center your ring.

Put a 3" piece of firebrick in the center of the ring and place the crucible on it. You will now need some weight in the crucible to prevent it from floating when you pour the castable. Put several hard bricks into the crucible (or something as heavy) and tape a piece of cardboard over the top of the crucible to keep it clean when pouring the castable. Make sure the crucible is centered and level. A good bubble level should help. Start pouring the castable around the outside of the crucible until it gets to about 2" below the lip. Check to make sure it's level before you leave the studio.

Sonotube cylinder being assembled

After the Mizzou castable has set (at least 24 hours later) you may remove the Sonotube or sheet metal ring. The next ring of castable will be made from Kast-O-Lite 30 (A.P. Green) or a comparable product. It will be about 3" thick. This ring, as shown in the diagram on the following page, will be about 4" higher than the rim of the pot. This is the ring that the crown will sit on. Before putting your next tube in place, you need to cut a short ring from the first tube about 6" wide and place it over the Mizzou that you have already cast. This ring should fit snugly and will allow you to cast the next ring to the desired height. Place the outer ring and pour your castable.

158   Glass Notes

After this has set, you may remove the outer tube and the inner ring. Fill the 2" space at the top with Greenpak 80 ramable (A.P. Green) or a comparable product. Angle the Greenpak slightly back toward the crucible. This angle will prevent any pools of glass from forming behind the crucible. You are now ready to cast the crown.

I know it is not easy to follow written directions, so to avoid confusion please refer to the diagrams on the following pages.

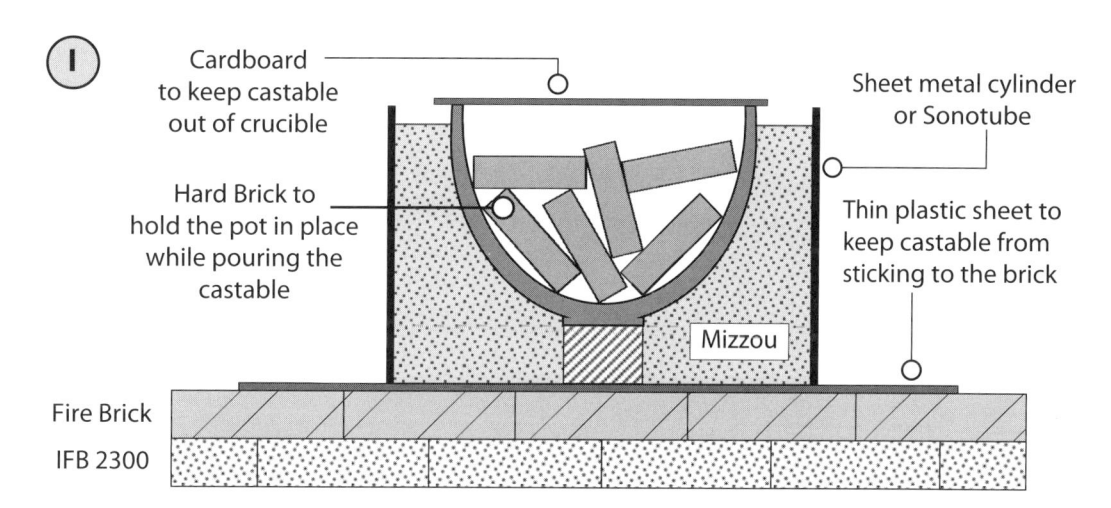

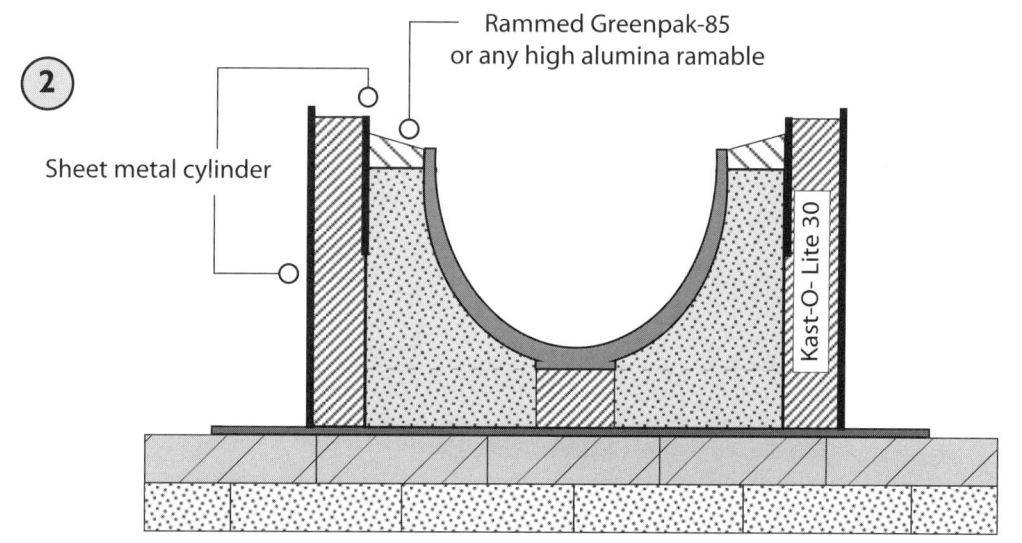

1
- Cardboard to keep castable out of crucible
- Sheet metal cylinder or Sonotube
- Hard Brick to hold the pot in place while pouring the castable
- Thin plastic sheet to keep castable from sticking to the brick
- Mizzou
- Fire Brick
- IFB 2300

2
- Rammed Greenpak-85 or any high alumina ramable
- Sheet metal cylinder
- Kast-O- Lite 30

Getting the Sonotube ready to cast outer insulating ring

Outer insulating ring after casting

Glass Notes 159

Pot Furnace with Dimensions

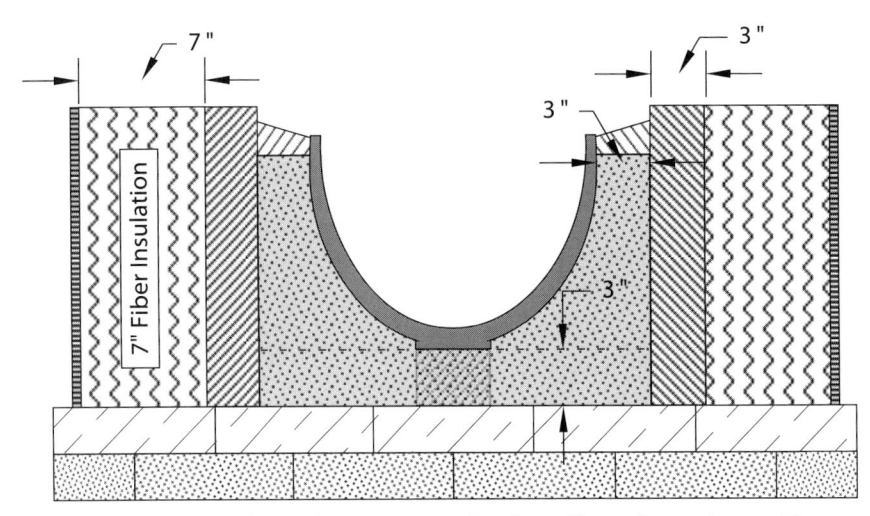

The dimensions shown here are not absolute. Your dimensions will vary depending on the amount of insulation you choose to use and the size of the crucible.

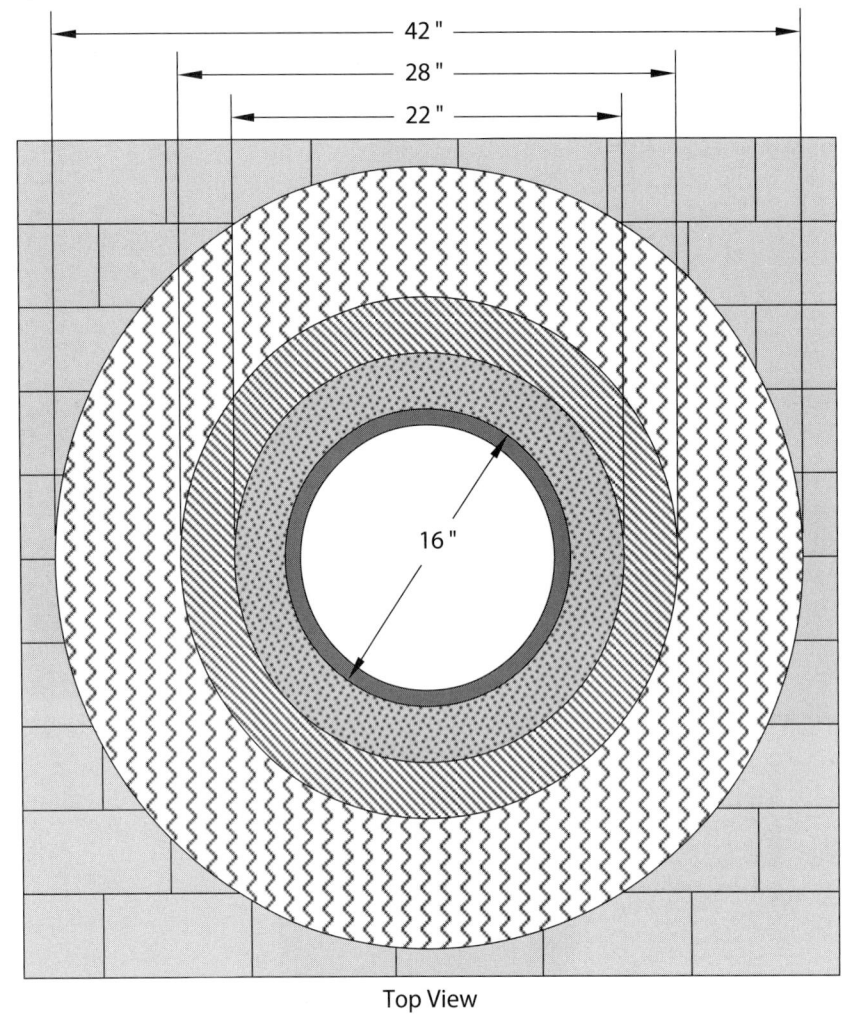

Top View

Invested Crucible Pot Furnace

This is a front, cut-away view of tangential-fired, invested pot furnace. Since the furnace is round, the flame swirls around the interior similar to the way the flame circulates in a free-standing pot furnace. If you were to build a top fire furnace, the crown should be a few more inches from crown to the glass surface.

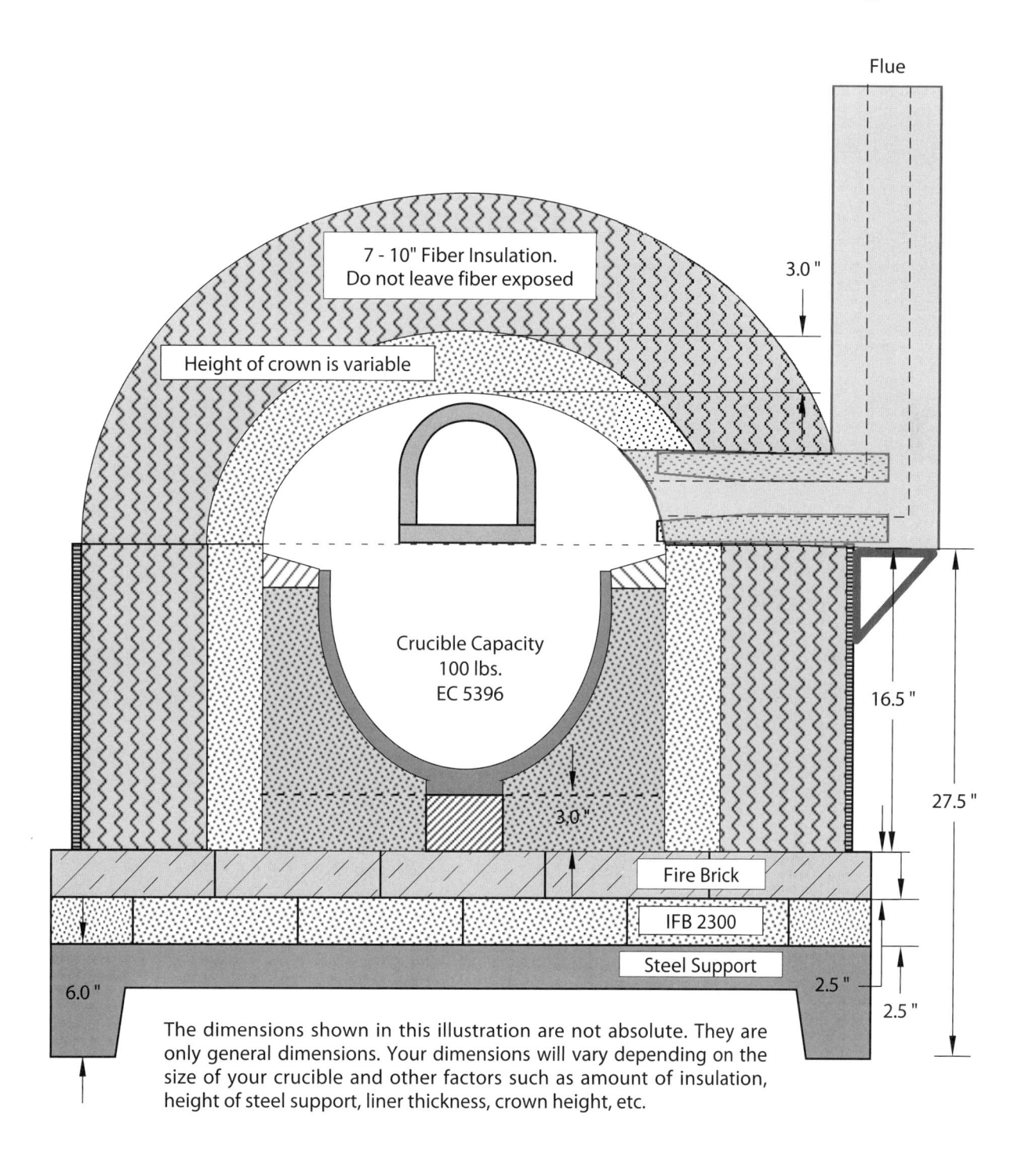

Flue

7 - 10" Fiber Insulation. Do not leave fiber exposed

3.0 "

Height of crown is variable

Crucible Capacity
100 lbs.
EC 5396

3.0 "

Fire Brick

IFB 2300

Steel Support

16.5 "

27.5 "

6.0 "

2.5 "

2.5 "

The dimensions shown in this illustration are not absolute. They are only general dimensions. Your dimensions will vary depending on the size of your crucible and other factors such as amount of insulation, height of steel support, liner thickness, crown height, etc.

The flue on this furnace is next to the burner as depicted in the top view on page 173.

Glass Notes **161**

How to Make the "Beehive Crown"

Creating the "beehive" crown for the invested pot furnace or for any pot furnace for that matter takes some ingenuity, but once the technique of construction is mastered, it will serve you well. The following pages show in detail how to construct the molds in which you will cast the crown. The term "beehive" is obviously derived from the shape. I first came across this technique for making molds in my ceramic mold-making class at the Rhode Island School of Design in the 50's. The mold-making technique is usually referred to as a "Sled Template." This technique, among others, is described in literature produced by the U.S. Gypsum Co. All I did was adapt it for pot furnace crowns.

The form of the beehive is basically a catenary curve. The catenary curve is quite familiar to ceramic kiln builders. The ceramic kiln is simply an extruded catenary curve while our furnace assumes a beehive shape. It can be made to almost any scale and, once the plaster molds are made, a crown can be cast very easily. An unlimited number of crowns can be cast from your molds. It might be wise to attempt making one on a small scale to work out the bugs. For those of you who are mathematically inclined, a catenary curve is a hyperbolic cosine. The great thing about using the catenary curve is that it is self supporting. If cathedrals were built using the catenary curve, they would not need flying buttresses.

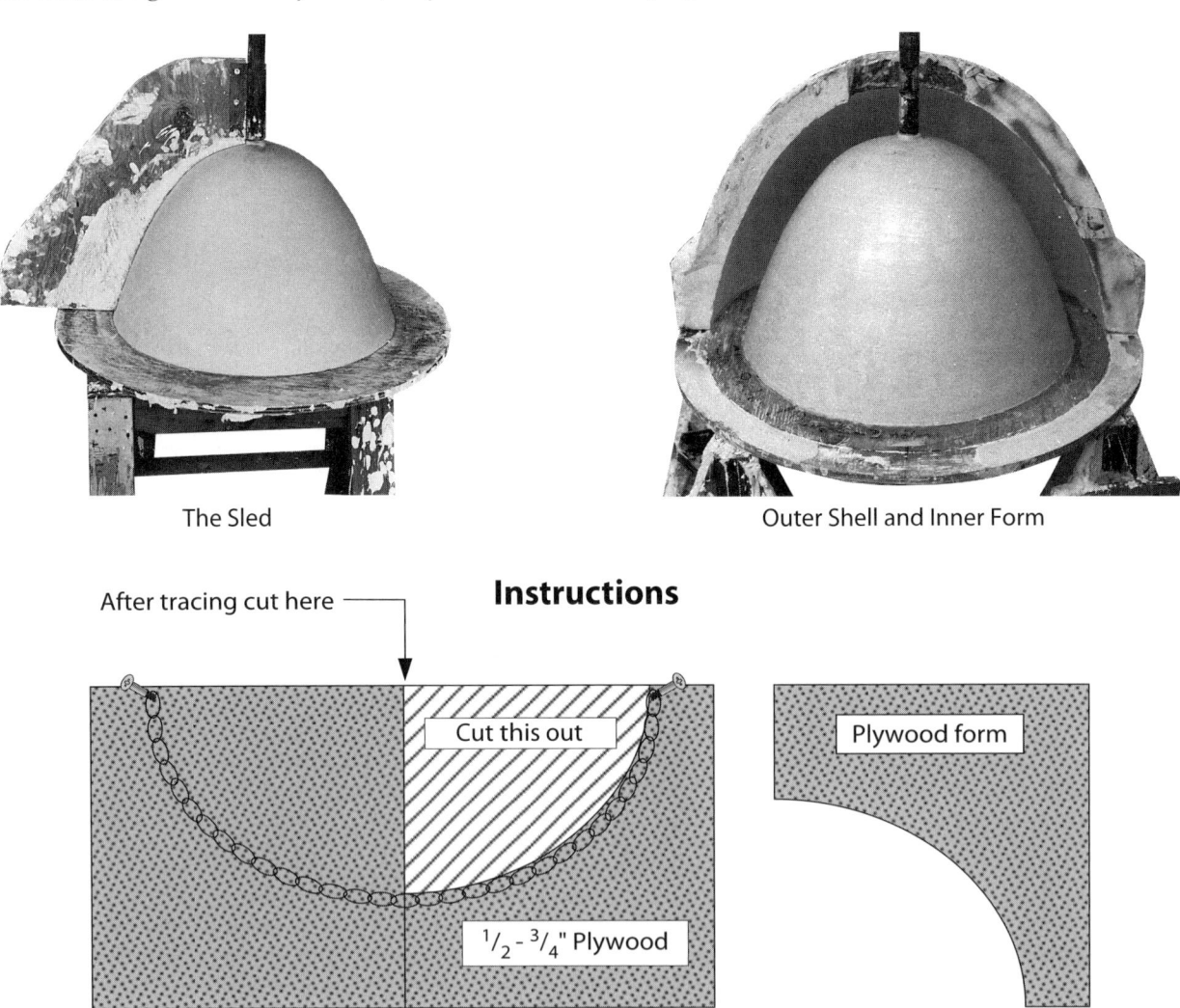

The Sled

Outer Shell and Inner Form

Instructions

After tracing cut here

Cut this out

1/2 - 3/4" Plywood

Plywood form

On a ½ to ¾" piece of plywood, you will establish two points. The first is the inner diameter of your crown. Hammer a nail at each point as indicated above. The second is the height of crown. Hang a sash chain from the nails and let it hang to the exact inner height of the crown as shown in the illustration above. Make sure the chain hangs free. The curve established by the chain is known as a catenary curve. Trace this curve and cut out the inner shape as indicated. Make sure the plywood is wide enough because you will have to cut the form two more times as indicated in the drawings on the following pages.

162 Glass Notes

The Sled Template

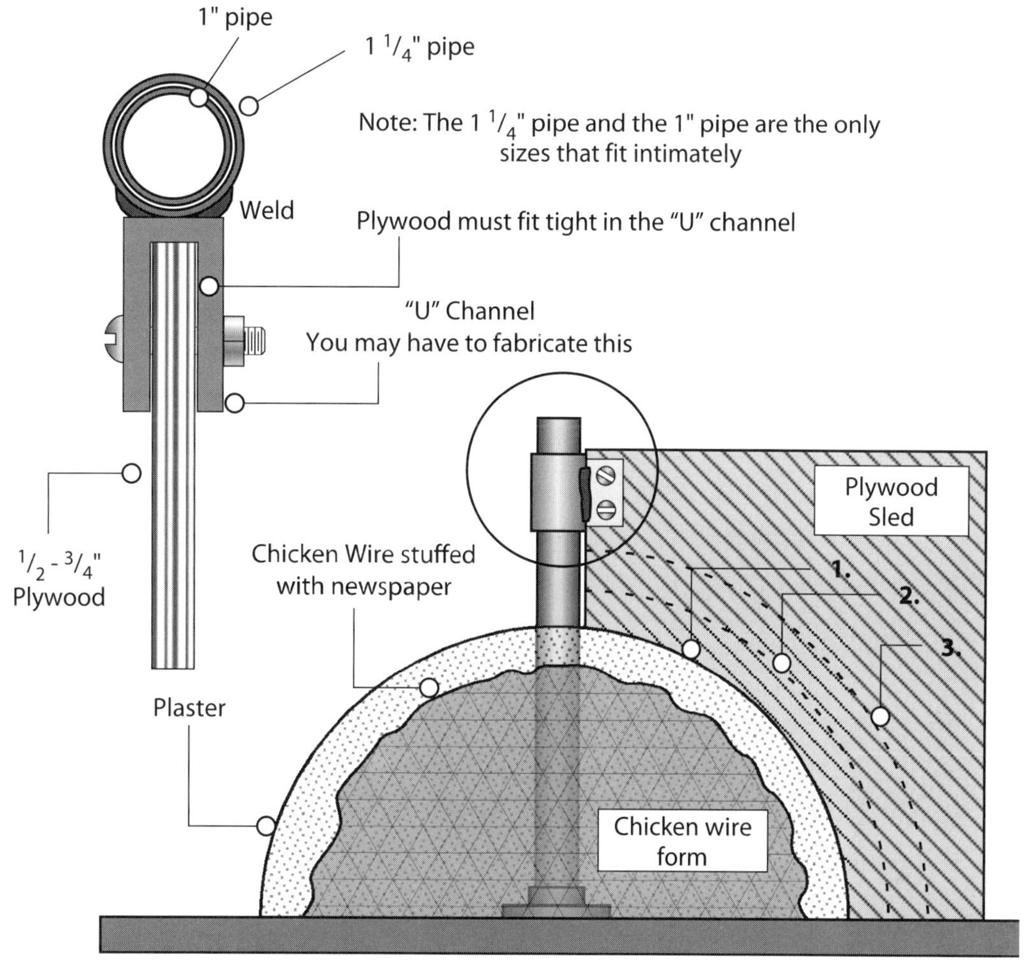
1" pipe
1 1/4" pipe
Note: The 1 1/4" pipe and the 1" pipe are the only sizes that fit intimately
Weld
Plywood must fit tight in the "U" channel
"U" Channel
You may have to fabricate this
1/2 - 3/4" Plywood
Chicken Wire stuffed with newspaper
Plywood Sled
1.
2.
3.
Plaster
Chicken wire form

The sled template will create the two plaster forms needed to create a "beehive crown." The plywood sled (template) rotates 360° around the chicken wire form. There is a 1" to 2" gap between the newspaper/chicken wire and the sled. Plaster is built up between the chicken wire and the sled. When the plaster has reached the sled, begin to rotate it. The rotating sled will smooth and spread the setting plaster, eventually creating a perfect "beehive" form. This is the inner part of your two–part crown mold.

After creating the inner form, shellac it (3 coats). Re-cut the plywood about 2 ½ to 3" as indicated above. The curve should be the same as the inner form. You will fill the new space with either soft clay or plaster and rotate the sled as you did for the inner form. Eventually this section will be discarded. If you use plaster, make sure you use a good mold release over the shellaced plaster. A good mold release is 2 parts petroleum jelly to 1 part kerosene. Heat the mixture in a double boiler. Keep the kerosene away from the flame.

Re-cut the plywood sled again. You only need to make it 1 ½ to 2" wide this time. If you have used plaster for step #2, you will have to once again use a good mold release to ensure this outer section will release. Again, build up the plaster as you rotate the sled. After the form from #3 is created, you can discard the part created in #2. The space between #1 and #3 is where your castable is poured to create the "beehive crown."

Clay Beehive Crown

Soft water base clay | **Sled**

After soft clay is in place and formed, cut sled along dotted line. Fig. 2 shows sled after being cut.

Inner plaster form

Fig. 1

Top View — shim in place on center

Fig. 2a

Shim — Cut shim to just fit under the sled

Sled

Fig. 2

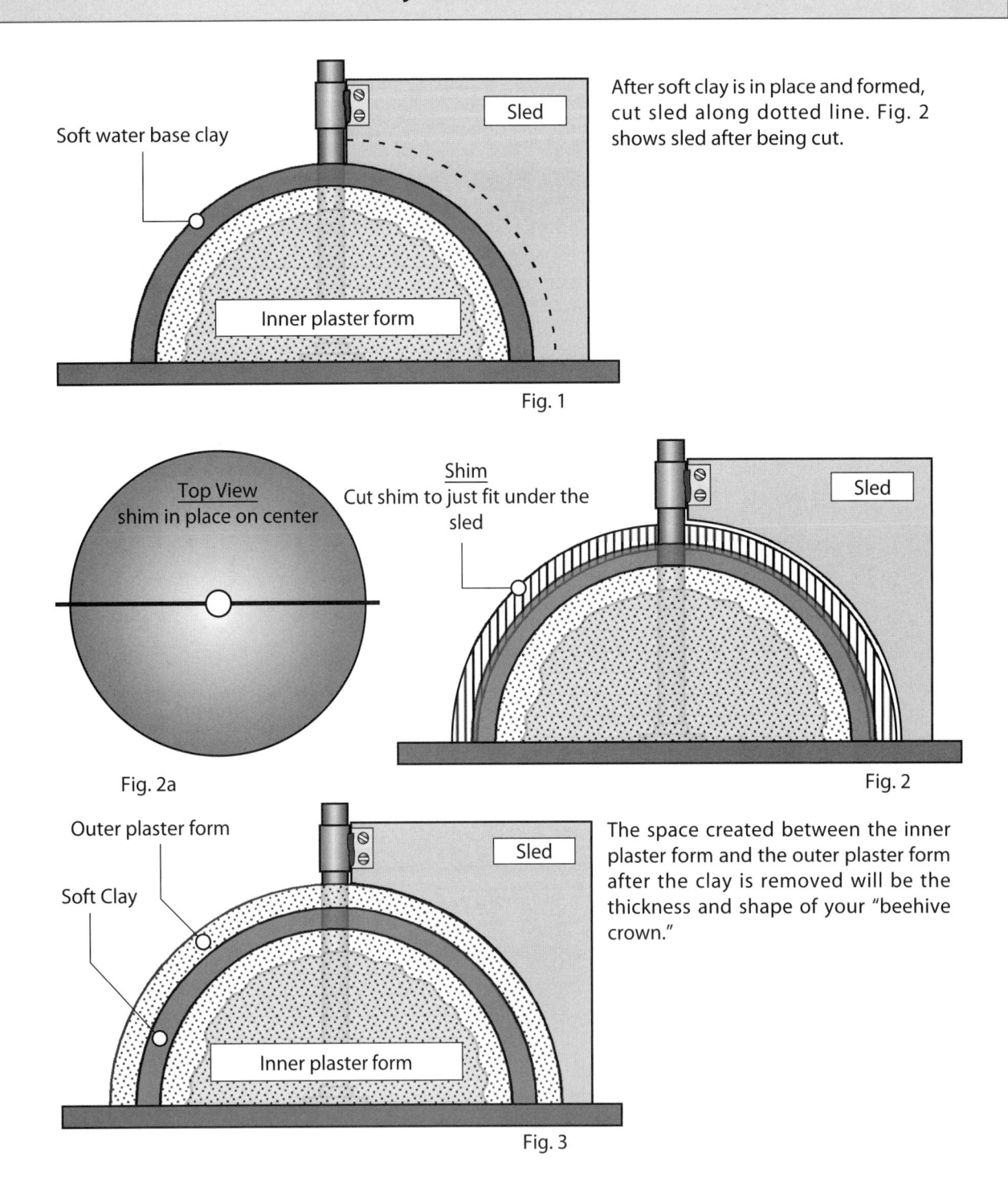

Outer plaster form
Soft Clay
Sled
Inner plaster form

The space created between the inner plaster form and the outer plaster form after the clay is removed will be the thickness and shape of your "beehive crown."

Fig. 3

Fig. 1. Depicts the inner plaster form with the soft clay in place and formed by the sled.

Fig. 2. Depicts the shim inserted at the center point. The shim is used so that the outer plaster form can be created in two sections. This will facilitate the removal of the outer plaster form after the castable crown has been cast.

Fig 3. Spread plaster over the entire clay form. It will take a fair number of plaster batches to create the outer shell.

After the plaster shell has set, remove it as well as the shims. Remove the clay. You now have the two forms needed to create the "beehive" crown.

164   Glass Notes

Casting the Beehive

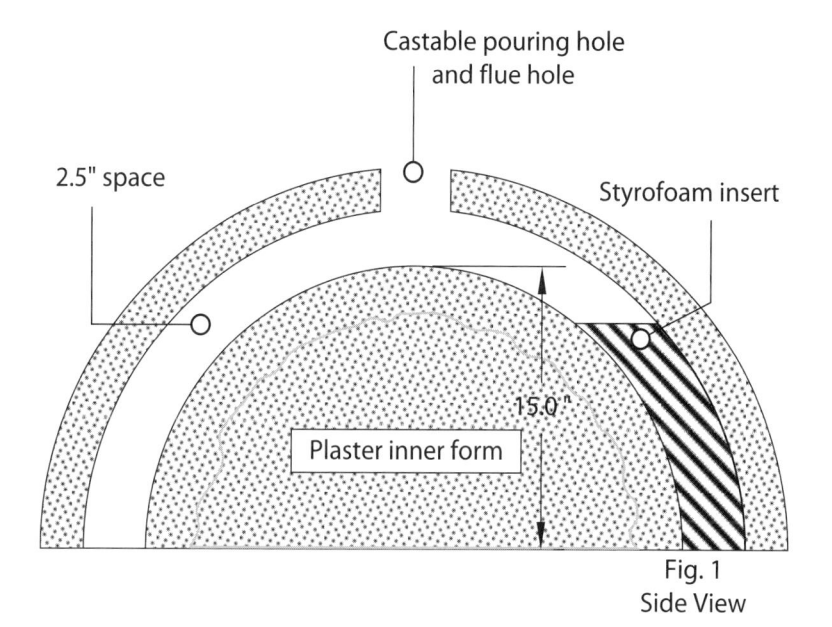

Fig. 1 Side View

- Castable pouring hole and flue hole
- 2.5" space
- Styrofoam insert
- Plaster inner form
- 15.0"

Before casting the crown, align the inner form to the outer form correctly. If you do not, you will not get an even wall thickness.

A Styrofoam insert in the shape of the gathering port is inserted between the outer plaster form and the inner plaster form. Make sure the Styrofoam form is adhered firmly to the inner form. When the castable is poured, creating the crown, the gathering port will automatically be created by this Styrofoam insert.

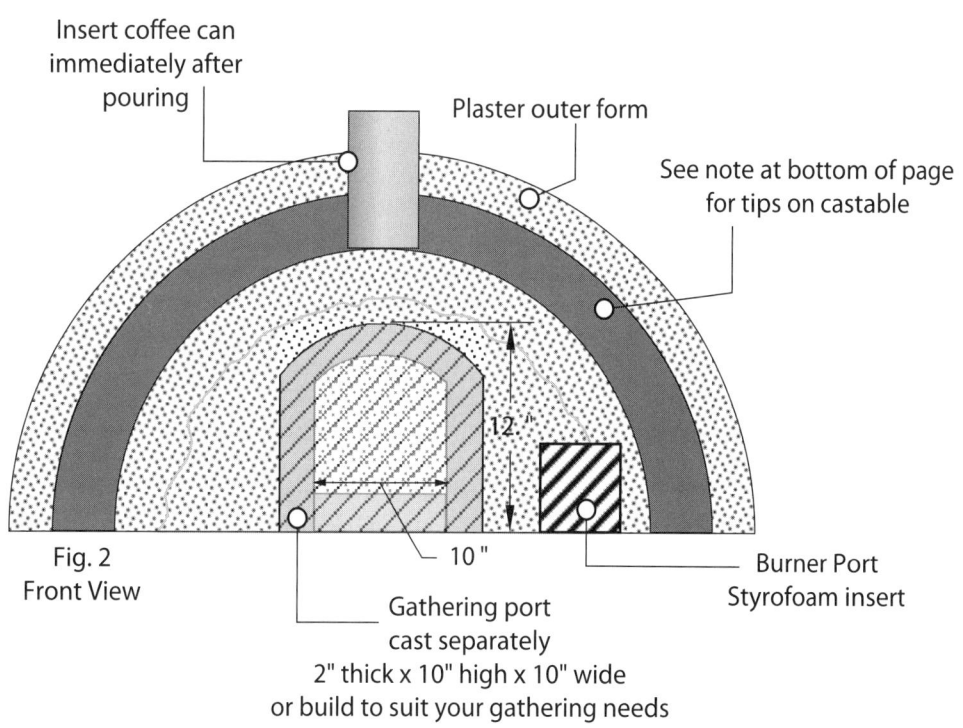

Fig. 2 Front View

- Insert coffee can immediately after pouring
- Plaster outer form
- See note at bottom of page for tips on castable
- Gathering port cast separately 2" thick x 10" high x 10" wide or build to suit your gathering needs
- 10"
- 12"
- Burner Port Styrofoam insert

If you wish, you may cast the beehive in two sections using the shim method as described in fig. 2 pg. 164. It is advantageous to have the separation at the gathering port as indicated. Large, monolithic crowns tend to crack. The pouring hole in the top should be large enough so that a curved tamping tool can be inserted to tamp the castable into place. This will ensure that you obtain a good casting free of air bubbles. Be careful not to disturb the Styrofoam inserts. If you're going to recycle the crown, it is recommended that you use a good high alumina castable such as Morcocast 95 or Monrox C. The Monrox is a self leveling castable which, in this situation, might be ideal. I have also used Kast-O-Lite 30 with good results.

Freestanding Pot Furnace

The pot furnace is probably the most popular style of glass furnace in use today. They are fairly easy to construct, easy to maintain, and economical to build and run if insulated properly. Most private glass studios use some variation of the basic design outlined in this chapter. The invested and freestanding furnaces share a few similar building techniques. One is the construction of the ring that comprises the container in which the crucible sits and another is the "beehive" crown. If you choose to construct this furnace, please reference the section starting on page 156. In order to build this, or any pot furnace for that matter, it is important to familiarize yourself with the refractory materials that go into the building of glass equipment.

1. The crucible pedestal should be either cast from a heavy duty castable or constructed from hard brick. The floor should slope toward the clean-out drain. You may need a small portable burner to keep the glass hot and flowing when it comes through the drain tube. It's a mess and a pain when it happens. I recommend putting sand between the pedestal and the crucible. Sand sometimes helps in getting the crucible to release when it needs to be removed. Sometimes a sledge hammer is needed to remove the pot.
2. The sloping floor is very important because it directs the glass to the drain tube. Make sure you slope the floor to a slight channel directed toward the drain tube. Obtaining a good slope can be facilitated by using a good, super-duty high, alumina plastic ramable. You may wish to ram your floor, slope it, and lay in the drain tube before you cast the ring. It makes setting up the ring a bit tricky, but it can save you an aching back. If you set the floor after the ring is cast, make sure you leave a hole in your sidewall mold for the drain tube, or cast the drain tube first and then cast the ring around the tube. Casting a drain tube should not present any problem. If you cast your own burner port and drain tube, try to fire them in a kiln before setting them in place. Plastic ramable is merely a special clay formula that, when dry, is somewhat brittle. Firing hardens it the same way as bisque firing a pot.
3. When insulating with fiber blanket, make sure the first 2" are 2600° F, 8 lb. density blanket. Beyond that you can use the 2300° F, 8 or 6 lb. density blanket. To avoid airborne fibers, I recommend encapsulating the fiber.

The Care and Feeding of Crucibles

One of the most common complaints from people using pot furnaces is that the crucible that they paid big bucks for cracked after being used about one week. There are many reasons why crucibles crack before their time. The following information concerning the care of crucibles was supplied and written by John Bartel formally of The Laclede Christy Crucible Company. The information presented here is applicable to EC crucibles as well.

The change of the glass melting crucible composition from the clay flux type to the more resistant, high alumina, zirconia materials, has introduced a new factor into the successful thermal management of the crucible. This factor is referred to as "down shock"—a phenomenon wherein the differential temperatures between the inside wall of the crucible and its outside surface are of sufficient differences to develop a destructive stress force that will result in cracked refractory crucible walls. Normally, these cracks are not destructive to the point they render the crucible useless, but they do establish a condition whereby corrosive forces associated with glass materials have a more favorable environment for accelerated deterioration in the crack zones. Ultimately, this results in a destructive hole through the structure of the crucible. The cracking described accounts for the majority of premature failures. There are other factors which can cause this type of cracking, but the largest contributor is the manner in which the filled material, batch–cullet is added to an active crucible. The addition of batch, cullet, or combinations thereof introduces the mechanism for lowering the interior surface temperatures of the crucible. The amount, frequency, and temperature of the charge are the key contributors to the development of forces severe enough to crack the crucible's surface. The addition of clod charge, in contact with the walls of the crucible, can drop the temperature, in the area of contact, to a 1000° F (537° C) in a matter of a few minutes. This results in the interior wall, or that portion of contact, wanting to shrink while the other, hotter surfaces want to expand. It is this heat differential between the inner and outer wall that creates enough stress to sometimes crack the crucible. There are ways to moderate these forces.

The temperatures of the charge material should be as warm as your operation will permit. In addition, the material must be dry. You can help yourself if, at the very least, you bring the material in and allow it to sit in the warm surroundings of the furnace prior to its introduction into the crucible. Some people place their batch into an annealer and raised the temperature to 500–700° F. The hotter charge will lower your heat differential and cut your melt time.

The amount and frequency of charging is another key element. Small charges minimize the degree of temperature drop and the duration of time the contact surface remains at the reduced level. The amount of the charge is dependent upon your operation, the length of time you allot for the filling sequence, and the size and configuration of the crucible. A shallow, wide crucible affords the best receptacle for charging; it affords the least amount of wall space for potential material contact. It is recommended that the amount of each charge be limited to about one fourth of the volume of the crucible. The interval between fills should be of a duration that allows the interior wall of the crucible to return as near to temperature equilibrium as possible. The minimum point for this occurs when the pile of the charge softens and flattens out. The sequence is repeated until the crucible is filled. The increased time between charges ensures a greater equilibrium between the inner and outer walls.

The next area of concern is crucible corrosion resulting from the batch charge as well as the relative corrosiveness of the batch glass itself. Keep in mind that the lower the viscosity of the glass the faster it will attack the liner. The higher the alkali and lithia the more corrosive the glass. Lithia is very popular as a batch addition because, in small amounts, it decreases glass viscosity appreciably.

Temperature is an important contributor to influencing the effects of corrosion upon refractory surfaces of a crucible. Temperature is an accelerator; its excessive use in combination with the alkali and other aggressive components in glass will destroy or disrupt the contact surface of the crucible to a point whereby unsatisfactory properties such as stones, seeds, and cords are imparted into the glass. Melt at the lowest temperatures possible because excessive temperatures will ultimately compound your problems. The correct temperature has to be determined by each operator; it is dependent upon factors related specifically to your operation, such as batch composition, desired glass properties, furnace design, etc.

The use of batch, cullet, or combination is a factor for consideration. The easiest to melt and handle is cullet; however, glass quality, flexibility, and control are not as good as that obtained from batch. If price is a factor, cullet may be cheaper to use. When you factor in the shipping costs of cullet, however, batch may prove to be a viable alternative. Making your own batch can be very problematic and dangerous if the right precautions are not taken. Chemical storage can be a problem. Conversely, if you understand the care and handling of these chemicals, the resultant glass quality and flexibility will be far superior to cullet. Cullet has two great advantages over batch: it has an unlimited shelf life, and it won't attack your crucibles quite as harshly as batch will. A crucible under optimum conditions will have a life expectance of about 90 – 100 campaigns, possibly longer when using cullet.

It is important to thoroughly mix the batch prior to its addition into the crucible––this assures homogeneity in the melt, and it reduces the tendency of destructive corrosive elements of the batch to come in direct and sole contact with the refractory surface of the crucible (resulting in pitting and subsequent related glass defects). If you are able to pelletize your batch or purchase a pelletized batch, you will be able to minimize the corrosiveness of alkali because it will be encapsulated. Heat penetration of pelletized batch is very good and allows a more rapid temperature equilibrium. A similar effect can be enhanced in batch by adding pea-sized cullet.

The proper position and placement of the fill inside the crucible is important. It is not a good idea when charging batch to leave a mound in the center of the charge as the alkali will melt and run down to the periphery of the charge where it will then contact the crucible and "eat" into the surface. Flatten the charge to prevent this from happening. It would also aid in the protection of the crucible if a glass residue, referred to as "heel," could be left in the bottom of the crucible. Heel serves as an insulator between the surfaces of the crucible and the elements of the charge. It protects the bottom, is pushed to the outer surfaces when new, and flows upward to offer a protective barrier between the effects of the batch and the refractory nature of the crucible. Proper application of these practices provides favorable results in several areas: it reduces thermal shock influence and minimizes the corrosive attack on the crucible.

The use of cullet presents its own set of problems when charging into a crucible. When charging cullet, it is wise to avoid throwing large, cold, heavy chunks into the crucible. You should not fill the crucible to the top with cullet because the temperature differential will crack the pot for the reasons explained earlier. If you follow the directions outlined, you will minimize your risks.

The majority of crucible failures occur for all the stated reasons (as well as others that are impossible to cover) as related to the placement of cullet and batch materials into a crucible. The problems and possible solutions stated above seem to be the ones that affect the studio artist the most and should be followed as closely as possible.

Crucibles are not indestructible. Proper furnace management, common sense, and patience will provide you with an economical medium and quality glass.

Summary

When lighting up, start with a small, soft flame and build the temperature gradually until you get above red heat. At that point, you can raise the temperature more quickly. Many crucibles crack during start up. Crucibles are like a piece of glass: if you heat them too fast, they crack; if you cool them too quickly, they can also crack.

- Use dry, warm, and, if possible, preheated material.
- Make multiple fills in small quantities, allowing adequate time between additions for temperature equilibrium.
- After charging, make sure to flatten out the charge. You do not want a peak.
- Keep a residue, or heel, amount of glass as an insulator against initial fill addition.
- Use a percentage of cullet with raw batch if possible. Your glass will melt faster.
- Minimize the use of temperature. Excessive temperatures create excessive crucible wear.
- Make sure your batch is thoroughly mixed and not agglomerated, meaning, that if you have a clumps of soda ash, they will deteriorate the crucible at the points of contact when they melt. If soda fluxes sand, it will definitely flux your crucible.
- Keep tramp metals and foreign materials out of cullet or batch. Metals can drill holes through crucibles.
- Remove glass from the crucible and reduce the temperature if the operation is placed in an idled or holding pattern for a prolonged period of time.

There are other reasons for pots breaking in addition to the ones stated. Of course, you can crack a crucible if you hit the pot with your blow pipe or a mongo ladle. It is also possible that your pot was cracked before you put it in the furnace. Check your pot carefully; it may have cracked in shipping. If it has, refuse the shipment and fight it out with the shipper. Do not store pots inside each other to save space. The weight of the top pot will crack the one below. If your pot happens to crack after being used one week and you call the company, they'll give you a hard time and for good reason. They have no way of knowing how you treated your pot after setting it; they have no way of knowing if heated it too quickly; they have no way of knowing who is at fault. I know of situations where Pete VanderLaan replaced pots that broke prematurely but that's Pete, not the company. Pots also crack due to thermal gradients in the furnace itself. Don't put a cold pot in a hot furnace. Again, don't drop huge chunks of cullet into the pot. Use common sense; pots are very fragile when they are hot. The bottom line is this: baby your pot, heat it slowly, cool it slowly, and don't use a very active glass. The lower the viscosity of your glass, the faster it will eat the crucible. Your pot may last a year if you're lucky. Again, the average life of a crucible is estimated to be about 90-100 charges if you're using batch. Your crucible will last longer if you use cullet.

It is a fact, though, that freestanding crucible furnaces are a much more economical than day tanks. The advantage to day tanks is that they can take a great deal of abuse. If you do a lot of sand casting and use big, heavy ladles, you might consider building a day tank.

Laclede Christy

Laclede Christy is a subsidiary of Emhart Glass. To obtain a catalog of their glasshouse crucibles go to their Web site (www.emhartglass.com). You will have to register your name and pick a password in order to obtain the .pdf catalog download. Ordering instructions are on their site.

The Laclede Christy Clay Products Company makes their crucibles from a number of different formulations. Following is a brief description of the two formulations most commonly found in the glass studio.

- FOMLAC. This is a common crucible found in the glass studio. Over 70% of the crucibles sold by Laclede Christy for studio glass use are this formulation. It is very good for melting soda lime flint glasses in either batch or cullet.
- LC-833. This is an AZS formulation and is designed for melting a wide range of corrosive glasses. It is rarely if ever used as a freestanding crucible because of its inability withstand thermal shock.

At the 2006 GAS meeting in St. Louis, John Bartel (our salesman at Laclede Christy), announced he was retiring from the crucible sales business. He is now kicking back and enjoying whatever comes his way. John was and is a friend to all who know him. Who can forget his hospitality suite at some of the GAS conferences. John, we wish you all the best in your retirement. The best is still in front of you.

Laclede Christy – www.emhartglass.com

Engineered Ceramics

Although we have known about this company for many years, very few studios used the EC crucible until Pete VanderLaan became a distributor. The EC brand seems to be the crucible of choice for most of the U.S. studios. It is also less expensive than the corresponding Laclede crucibles. Both EC and Laclede fabricate many different capacity crucibles. Pete VanderLaan has a page on his Web site that displays the EC crucible configurations as well as their glass capacities. Olympic Color Rod also distributes EC crucibles for Pete.

EC – www/guadalupeglass.com
Olympic – www.glasscolor.com

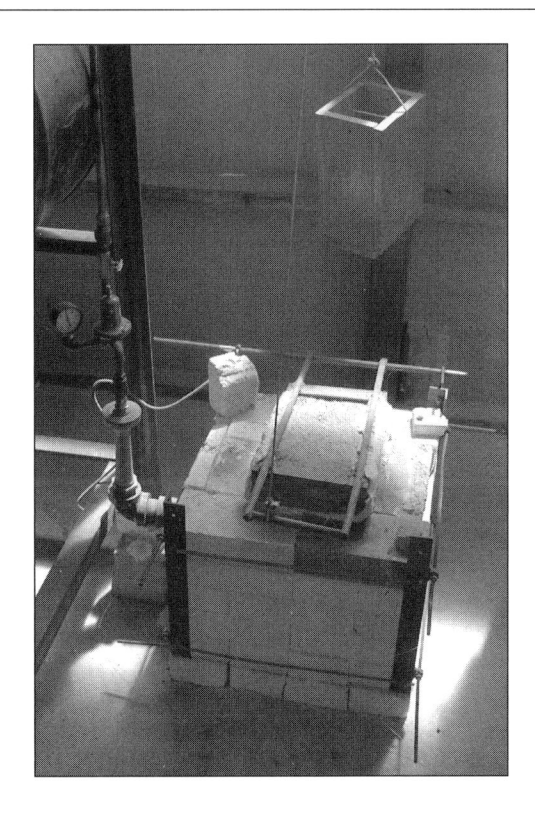

Pot Furnaces, 1972 - 2006
Can you tell which is which?

Freestanding Crucible Furnace
Tangential Fired

Furnace size is determined by crucible capacity

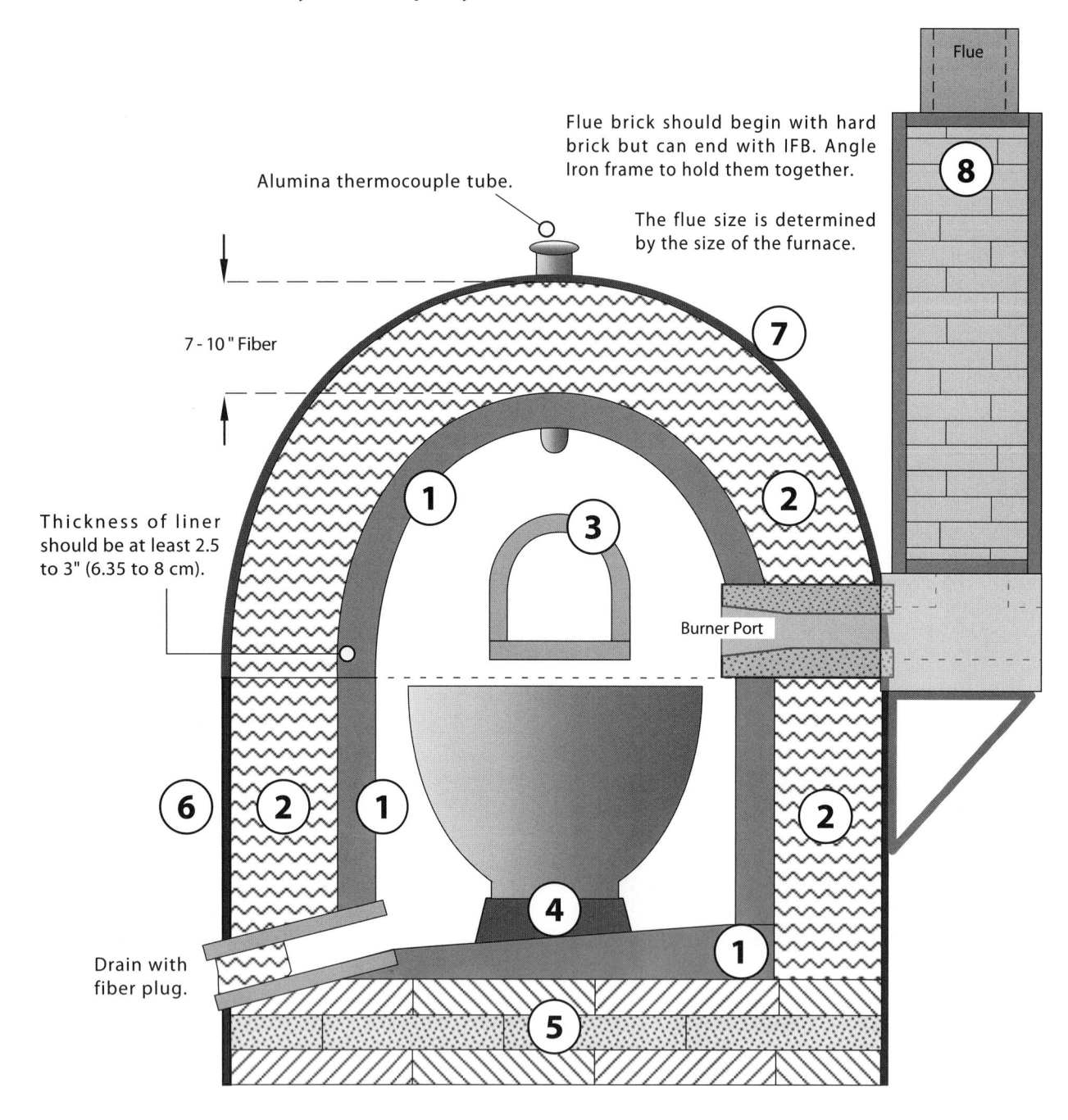

Alumina thermocouple tube.

Flue brick should begin with hard brick but can end with IFB. Angle Iron frame to hold them together.

The flue size is determined by the size of the furnace.

7 - 10 " Fiber

Thickness of liner should be at least 2.5 to 3" (6.35 to 8 cm).

Burner Port

Drain with fiber plug.

1. High alumina castable (1, Monrox C, or Phlocast 33, or Greencast 97)
2. At least 7" of fiber insulation; 10" is even better.
3. Gathering Port
4. Crucible Pedestal, hard brick or high alumina castable
5. Brick foundation, hard brick, 2300° IFB, Hard Brick
6. Sheet metal skin, encapsulates fiber
7. Re-wettable fiberglass cloth. see pg. 140
8. Flue or recuperator

The Freestanding Pot Furnace

The freestanding pot furnace depicted on page 170 is a general design that has many variations and configurations. This one I have chosen to depict is round in design and not all that difficult to build. Construction is not unlike the invested pot furnace as shown on page 158. A round furnace has less thermal mass than a square furnace and is consequently more economical to run. A round furnace can also be fired tangentially. Fining in this manner gives the flame an opportunity to fully develop as it swirls around the perimeter of your furnace. This is important as you want to get every last btu available from your burner flame. Tangential firing also is much easier on your refractories as you do not have a flame impinging against the refractory on the opposite wall as you have in square furnaces.

The size of your furnace is determined by the size of your crucible. I would recommend you build your furnace so that it is capable of accepting two different sized crucibles. A 200 lb. capacity crucible is not that much smaller than the 300 lb. capacity crucible. If you build to accept the 300 lb. capacity crucible but start blowing from the 200 lb. crucible, at some point in time your skill will improve to the point where you will want that extra 100 lbs., and voila, your furnace will easily take that larger crucible without having to build a new furnace. Whatever size crucible you choose, make sure you leave about 2 to 4" of clearance from the edge of the pot to the sidewall.

The interior liner of this furnace #1 includes the floor, sidewalls, and crown. There are any number of products one can use that have been proven to withstand the caustic atmosphere of the furnace. Some of the products I would recommend are: For sidewalls, Kast-O-Lite 30. For the crown and base, Morcocast 95, or Greencast 97. Some people have used Kast-O-Lite 30 for the crown and have had good luck with it. I also know that Pryor Giggy makes some excellent castables, and their Monrox M might do the trick for you. For the burner block, I would use Morcocast 95 or any of the high alumina Greencast products, that is, if you're going to cast it. The 95 stands for the alumina content. If you wish to have a really solid, long lasting burner block, you might consider ramming it from a high alumina rammable such as Greenpak 80. If you do ram it, I would pre-fire it in your annealer to around 1500° F. Casting is much easier than ramming.

The #2 in the illustration depicts about 7-10" of fiber insulation. I do not recommend using less than 7". It is important that you layer your fiber as follows. The first layer that is up against the liner and crown must be 2" of 2600° F, 8 lb. density fiber, the next 3" can be 2300° F, 8 lb. density fiber. Do not put the 2300° F fiber up against the furnace liner. If you do, you will have problems when you're melting batch at 2350°. If you exceed the temperature limit of the fiber, you will destroy it. It is important that you encapsulate the fiber as you do not want it exposed. Fiber insulation is a known carcinogen. Eventually, the little fibers will begin to splinter off and float in the air and find their way into your lungs. Not a good thing. The vertical side of the furnace can easily be encapsulated with sheet metal #6. Pop riveting holds it together nicely. The crown fiber can be encapsulated with re-wettable fiberglass cloth. I know some furnace builders who just spray the fiber with colloidal silica and claim it works fine for encapsulating the fiber. Not true. Although it toughens the surface of the fiber a bit, it does not stop the fiber from becoming airborne. Remember, you want to make your shop as healthy as you possibly can as you will be spending a great deal of time there. No one wants to develop weird lung, stomach, or throat diseases. If you're a smoker and you have a poorly constructed studio, chances are about 100% you'll eventually develop some illness that will do you in, as in, dead before your time.

The last point in this construction is to make the crown so that it can easily be removed when you need to change out the crucible. The illustration on the next page depicts two methods of installing a monolithic crown. It's actually easier if you make the crown in two equal sections and mortar them together when installing. If you give it a bit of thought, I'm sure you can come up with some clever ideas of your own.

Glass Notes 171

Two Ways to Lift a Cast Crown

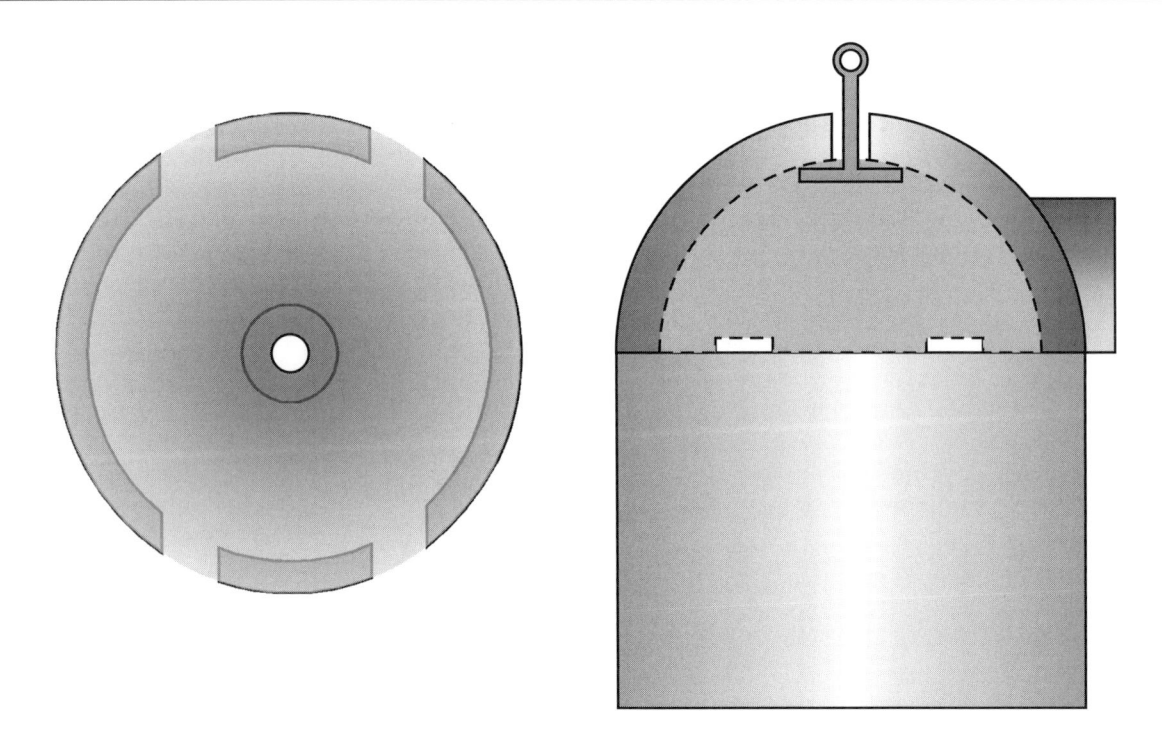

Both of these illustrations depict two methods of lifting the crown in order to change a crucible. One method is to cast in 4 slots that can hold engine block lift straps, and the other depicts a hole in the crown through which one can insert a sturdy steel "anchor" and lift the crown with the ever popular engine block lift. There are any number of methods one can devise in order to lift the crown. If you cast holes or slots in your crown, it should go without saying that they should be plugged when the furnace is in use and unplugged when you're ready to do the heavy lifting.

Corning model of a typical early American glass factory. The furnace is a "bottle" style furnace. It has about 12 monkey pots filled with glass. The burner is in the center of furnace and shoots a flame from the floor straight up the flue. Not very efficient.

Crucible Furnace
Burner and Gathering Port

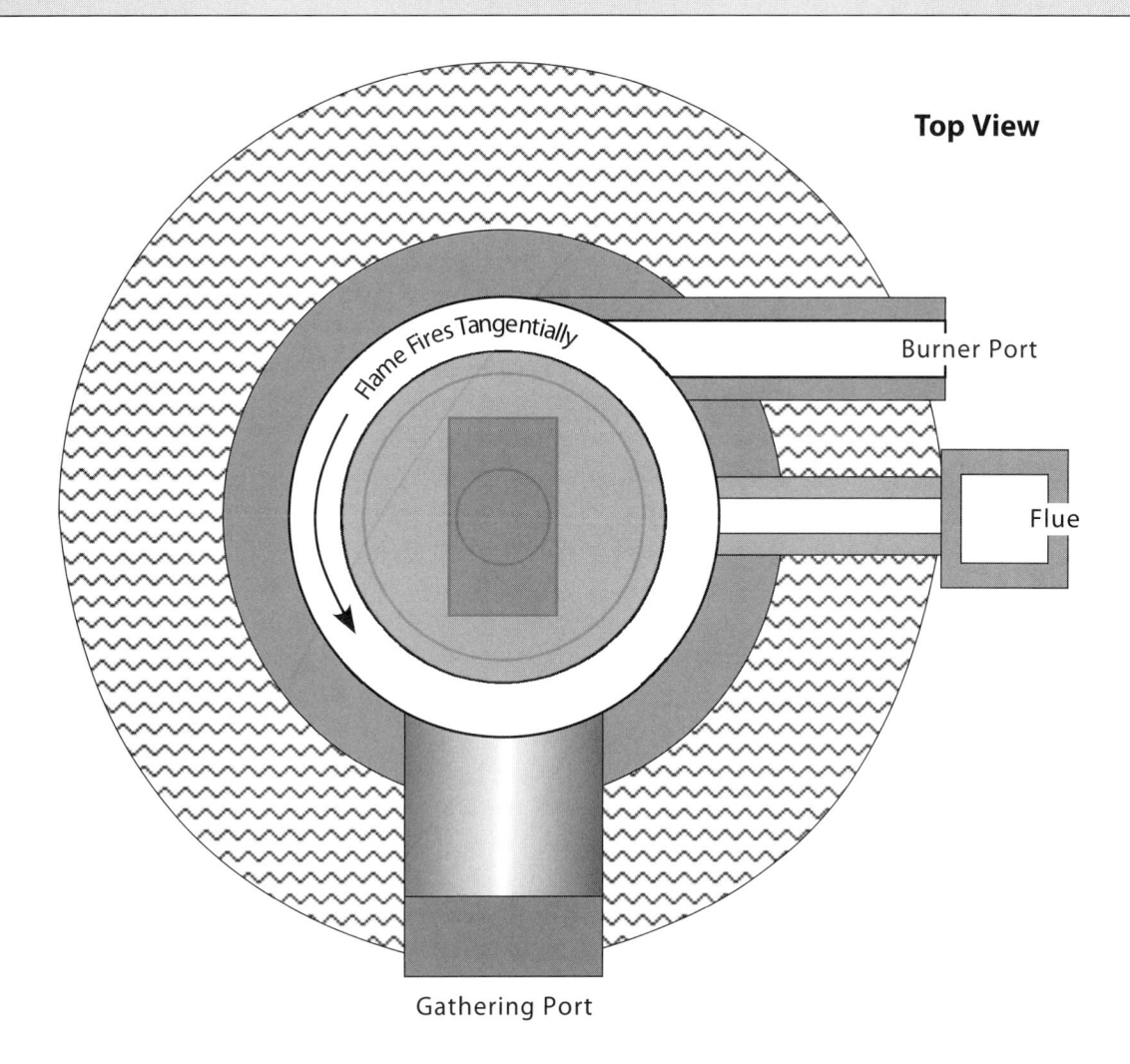

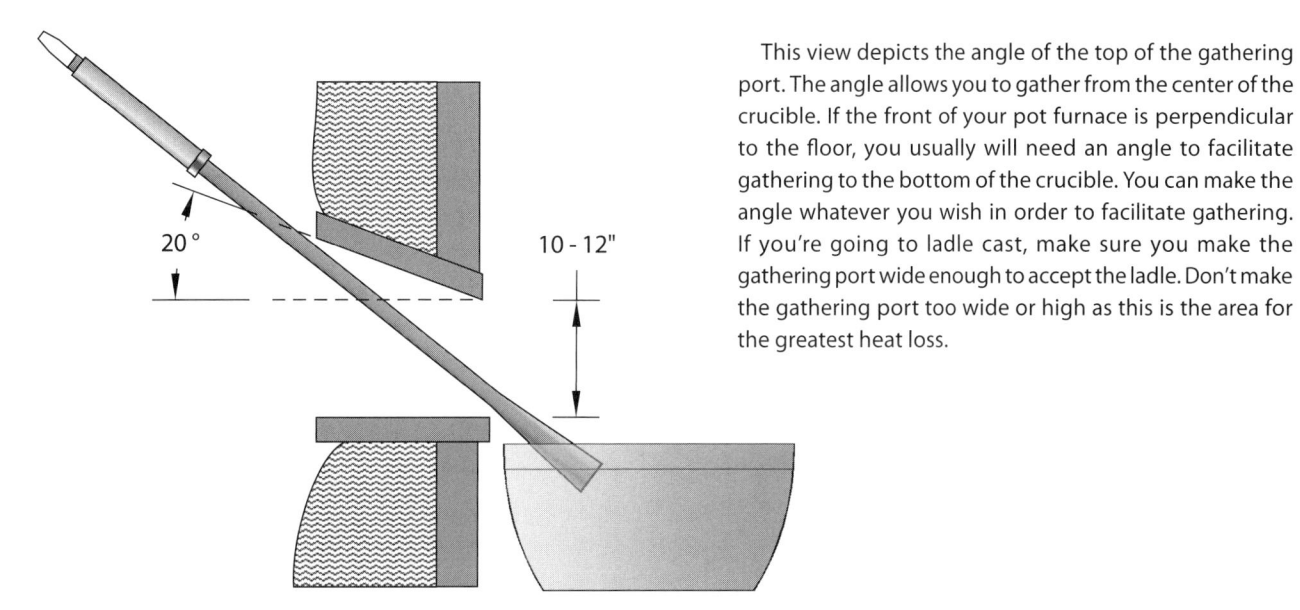

Top View

Flame Fires Tangentially

Burner Port

Flue

Gathering Port

20°

10 - 12"

This view depicts the angle of the top of the gathering port. The angle allows you to gather from the center of the crucible. If the front of your pot furnace is perpendicular to the floor, you usually will need an angle to facilitate gathering to the bottom of the crucible. You can make the angle whatever you wish in order to facilitate gathering. If you're going to ladle cast, make sure you make the gathering port wide enough to accept the ladle. Don't make the gathering port too wide or high as this is the area for the greatest heat loss.

Pot Furnace Door

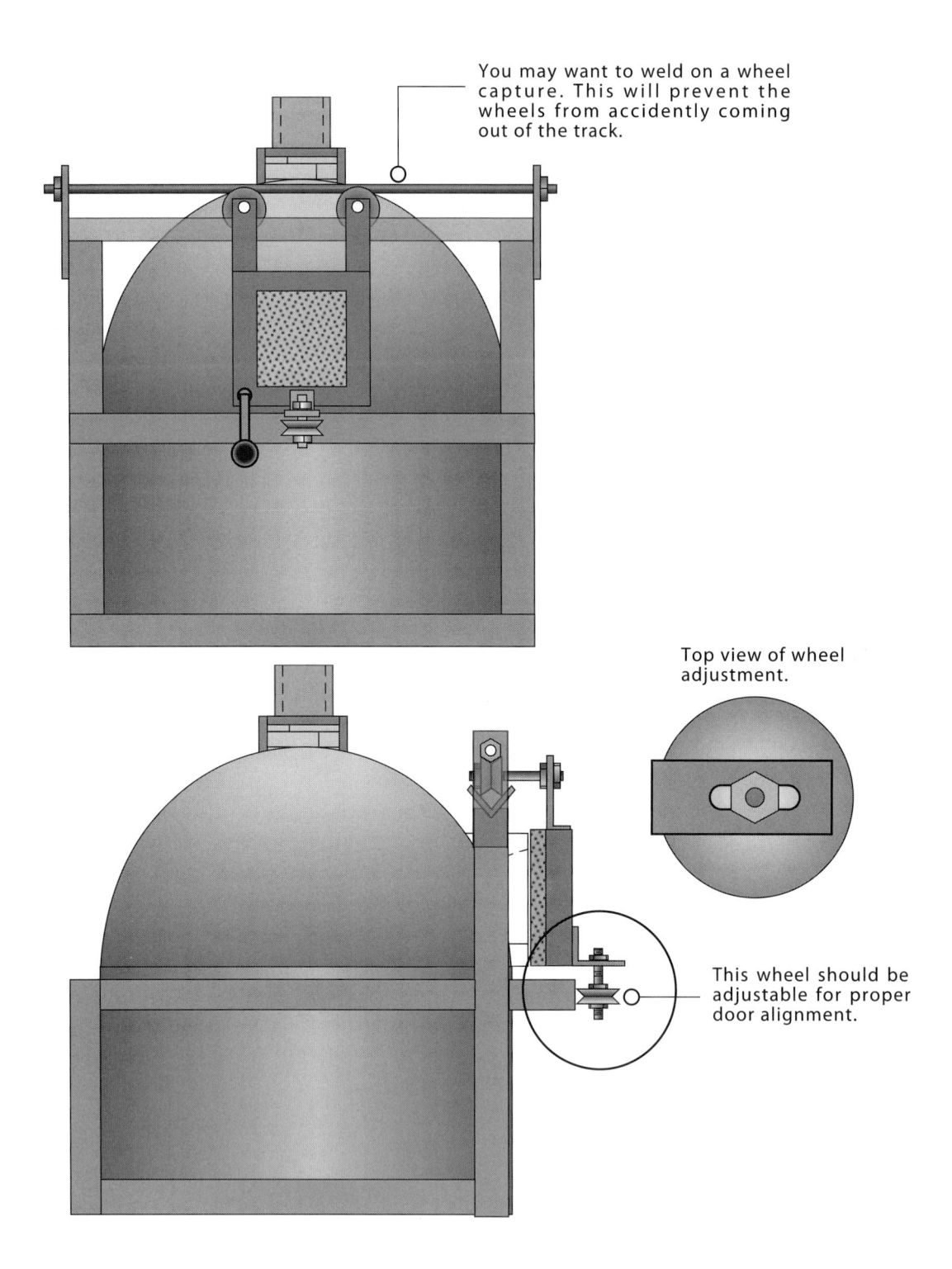

You may want to weld on a wheel capture. This will prevent the wheels from accidently coming out of the track.

Top view of wheel adjustment.

This wheel should be adjustable for proper door alignment.

The door depicted here is just one style of door. There are other styles that furnace builders use. This one seems to be one of the more popular styles. It should be noted that the upper track should be set behind the gathering port so that it is out of the heat zone.

Recuperation

by Charlie Correll & Hugh Jenkins

High fuel costs make it imperative that the studio glass artist employ systems to their furnaces that will make them more efficient. We all know that adequate insulation and tuned burners help in that respect, but not many understand the savings one can realize with recuperation. If you, the reader, are like me, we know what recuperation is but little about how to effectively employ such a device on gas fired furnaces. So, who ya gonna call? Gas busters! Hugh Jenkins in Hawaii and Charlie Correll in Massachusetts. The information they provided will hopefully answer your questions about recuperation. The drawings in this section were originally provided by Hugh and Charlie. After reading what Hugh and Charlie have to say, I'm sure many of you will, on your next furnace rebuild, employ some form of recuperation.

Charlie Correll

Hugh Jenkins with Crew

In case you're not aware of it, Charlie builds and sells recuperated crucible furnaces as well as many other high class products for the glass studio. He and all that equipment can be found at www.correllglassstudio.com. I would be remiss if I didn't tell you that Charlie and Hugh are first-rate glass blowers as well as recuperator gurus. Hugh Jenkins' beautiful glass can be found at www.bigislandglass.com.

Glassmakers have been trying to conserve the energy expended on melting glass for decades. Many ingenious methods have been tried, refined and discarded, from moving furnace heat to annealing ovens to moving it to hot tubs. Almost anything that conserves the eternal fuel consumption is worth the effort. This article will concentrate on the methods used to keep as much of the heat that would otherwise be dissipated into the atmosphere, in the furnace, be it by insulation, or transferring the exhaust heat into the combustion air and returning it to the furnace. What follows is an abstract of the paper I presented at the Los Angeles GAS Conference in 1985. It is as pertinent today as it was then. Following that is a discussion of the history of heat reclamation and some rather novel approaches to the problem. Some drawings of different recuperative systems are included as well as some theoretical considerations on the design and construction of these systems.

The first serious attempts to reclaim this heat involved the use of regenerative systems. These involved the use of a dual exhaust/dual burner system. Huge chimneys were built with an arrangement of brick checker work contained in them. The exhaust would exit the furnace via one chimney, heating up the bricks. When the bricks were hot, the exhaust port was closed, and combustion air for the burner was fed through the brick checkers, picking up the stored heat and returning it to the furnace. In the meantime, the exhaust port on the other chimney was opened, allowing the gasses to flow out where previously the incoming air had flowed. Cycle times were in the several minute range. Modern regenerative systems have very compact arrangements of ceramic balls to absorb the heat, and cycle times dropped to as low as six seconds.

Recuperative systems are simpler and much more manageable for the studio glassblower, involving only the recuperator and one burner. The first studio recuperator I heard about consisted of an old VW Bug air-cooled engine head hung up above the door of a furnace. The fins on the oil cooler picked up heat and air was forced through the "device" to the burner. I have seen flexible exhaust pipe for the air wrapped around glory holes. Anything to grab the heat.

There are several factors to consider when designing recuperators. The geometry of the system is very important. It is important to maximize the surface area to volume ratio. A circle contains the most area relative to its perimeter for any geometrical shape. This theoretical consideration makes the tube the worst possible shape for a recuperator. We want to maximize that ratio. A rectangle of infinite length and infinitely small area contains the least area in relation to its perimeter. This of course, doesn't work. So a series of reasonably-sized, rectangular-shaped "envelopes" will provide the highest ratio of surface to volume. The limits to this are practical. One is sheer size. Another is the size of the spaces inside the envelope and the spaces through which the exhaust gasses escape. If the inside space is too small, it takes too much pressure to get the combustion air through. If the exhaust spaces are too small, the recuperator clogs up easily with batch residue or soda volatilizing off the glass. It is necessary to reach that practical geometry which allows for efficient recuperation while allowing a typical blower to be able to move enough air through the system.

Hugh has come up with another concept meant to keep a recuperative system going in the event of a power failure. Recuperators require forced air to overcome the inherent friction in a recuperator. When I went to install the first recuperator in Penland, I arrived with the work well under way by Hugh and Bill Worcester. I looked around and saw my stainless recuperator lying on a table with a venturi screwed into the air intake. I wondered what I was getting into and who I was dealing with. I soon found out that I was looking at a GREAT idea. Venturis use the energy from high pressure gas going through a very small orifice to pull in the combustion air at ratios of up to 25 to 1. Hugh's idea was to use an air compressor to force air into the venturi, thus entraining additional air to go in with it. Then it all fell into place. In the event of a power failure, the compressed air already in the tank provides a "battery" of energy to keep the combustion air flowing. A large tank will provide a lot of time for the power to come back on, thus saving a pot, the glass, and the furnace. There is always more than one way to get the job done.

Charlie Correll

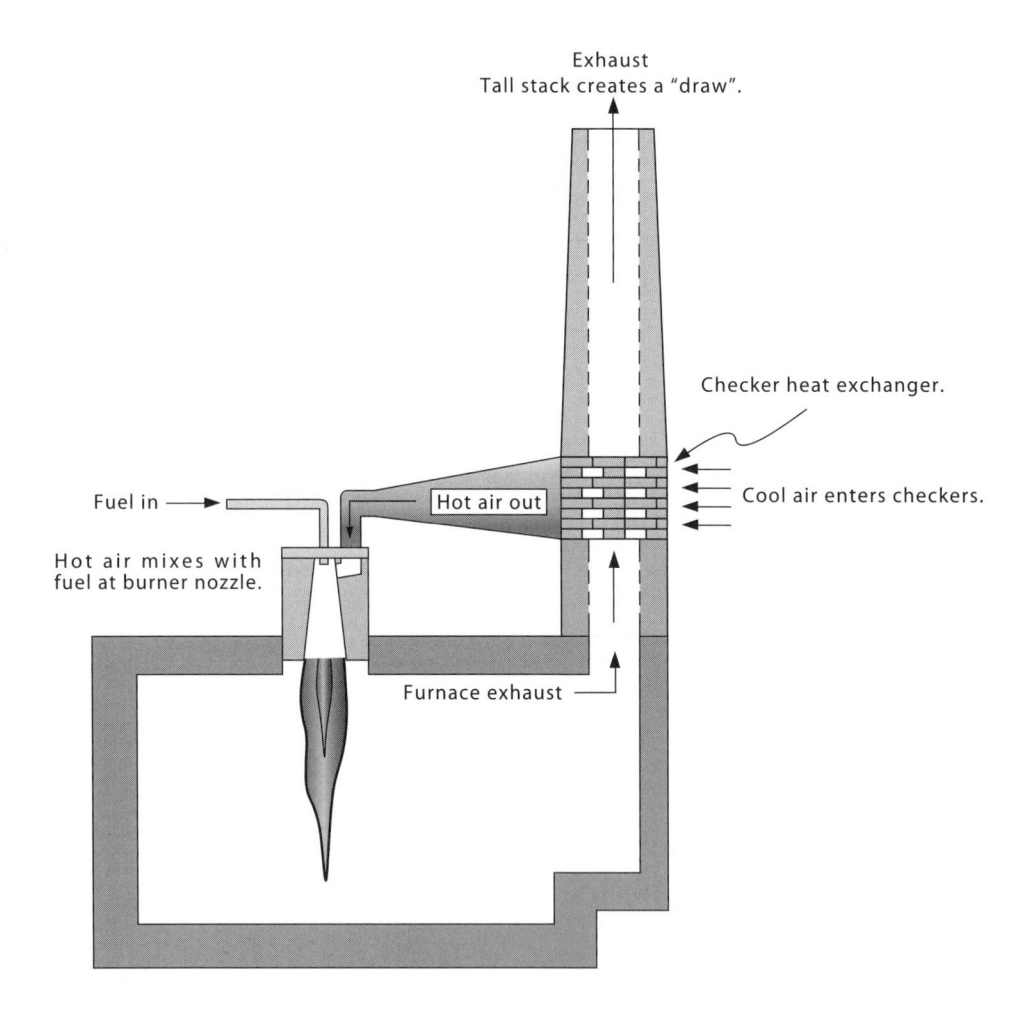

Regenerator Recuperator
Closed Furnace System

Recuperators and Glass Furnaces
An Overview
by Hugh Jenkins

Glass shops have always been high energy consumers. The common early fuel was wood, and whole forests were consumed near glass furnaces. Though the fuel was cheap, the labor cost of harvesting and hauling it was relatively high. Early in the industrial revolution, energy recovery became a serious issue. The design of exhaust stacks allowed a lot of the heat to be recovered and returned to the combustion chamber, thus recouping the heat. Since then, recuperation has been the norm in industry. Early in the American studio glass recovery, energy costs were fairly low. For a few hundred dollars a month, you could run a furnace and a glory hole. The cost to melt per pound was not the issue that it was in industry. Nonetheless, by the late seventies, there was a growing interest in making more efficient furnaces, and the interest in recuperation started. The prices for fuel were not even close to what they are today, but the need to control cost was still apparent.

Early studio experiments with heat recovery were presented in the "Hot Glass Information Exchange" papers (John Bingham, 1979). Ingenious uses of radiators, Volkswagen cylinders, cast clay helixes, and double wall furnaces all worked to recover heat. Since essentially all shops were using premixed gas/air systems, there were some inherent limits on the upper air temperatures that could be reached without pre-ignition ("popping", backfire) occurring in the burners. During the 80's Charlie Correll developed a sophisticated stainless alloy heat exchanger that could handle high heats and a nozzle mix system that kept the gas and air separate until in the burner throat. These were designed using blowers as the driving force and have been available on order with or without his furnace ever since; though somewhat expensive, with fuel costs going up, these became economically sound investments, saving 35-40% or more of the gas used. School programs such as Penland School of Crafts in North Carolina and Punahou High School in Honolulu installed them in 1990 and 1991. The systems returned their cost within the first eight months and lasted as much as seven years. It was not hard to convince these schools that any investment that would pay back in less than one fiscal year made good sense. The case had been made and proven for recuperators in glass studio furnaces.

The basics of a recuperated system are an excess of recoverable waste heat, a heat exchange structure to pass the heat from the spent air to fresh air, and a means of reintroducing the heated air back into the burner. Recuperation is applicable to low temperature systems such as grain dryers and laundries and to almost all high temperature processes such as metal smelting, ceramic firing, and of course glass melting. All recuperators need a force to move the air through the system. Tall industrial stacks create a draw that can be used in sealed furnaces to pull air through a heat exchanger such as stacked brick "checkers" and into the combustion chamber. Most smaller systems applied to kilns or studio glass furnaces use pressure from blowers. A venturi using compressed air can be used in place of a blower. In systems where the temperature approaches or exceeds the gas combustion temperature, separating the heated air from the fuel until it is in the combustion chamber, removes the possibility of pre-ignition.

Whereas the use of stacks and blowers have a history in recuperated systems, the use of venturis for this purpose has had little attention. As a way to get around fairly common power interruptions with concurrent safety system shutdowns, compressed air can be used as a driving force. The principle of venturi action is that a high pressure jet of gas entrains a much larger volume of air. If high pressure air is used through the jet, very high air flows can be achieved using relatively little compressed air. A large capacity compressed air tank can keep the system operating even through several hours of power outage. In addition, using the example of a venturi driven vacuum cleaner, the venturi can be used to pull heated air from the heat exchanger and then push it through the burner. Casting the venturi shape into a block of refractory creates a heat proof system for very high temperatures. Comparison of the operating cost of an intermittent compressor cycle to that of a continuous running blower does not indicate that compressed air used in this way is expensive.

The ideal measure of efficiency for a recuperator would be the percentage change in fuel used from before to after installation. Retrofits, though possible, are not common, since most recuperator installations are done on new equipment.

The main factors that determine the efficiency of a recuperated furnace are:
- The percentage of the waste heat actually passed through the heat exchanger.
- The surface area of the exchanger.
- The passage time of the fresh air in the exchanger.
- The conductivity of the exchanger material.

The measure of heat change in the exhaust from entry to the exit of the exchanger is also an indication of the effectiveness of the exchanger. Reductions of stack temperature from 2100° F to 700° F are being achieved today, and efforts to get higher efficiencies are being made. Changes in several factors at once can result in dramatic improvements in efficiency. In the case of the ceramic lined stack, increase of length from two feet to three feet, increase from six channels to eight, and use of a more conductive refractory improved the return from 40% to about 65%.

The issues controlling the amount of waste heat going through the recuperator are the insulation of the furnace and the fit of the door. Well built furnaces recuperate much better than those with loose fitting doors and hot exterior surfaces.

The heat must go up the stack to be reclaimed by the recuperator. The surface area of the heat exchanger is a factor of the length of the air passages, the number of passages and the configuration of the surface.

Increasing the length, number, and complexity of the passages, will increase the efficiency.

Irregular surfaces will transfer heat more effectively than smooth surfaces will.

With increased length of the stack the return is based on a percentage formula. If the first foot gives a 30% return, the second foot would give a 30% recovery of the remaining 70%, or another 21%. The third foot would give a 30% return on the remaining 49%, or another 15%. Another foot would return about an additional 10% (30% of the remaining 34%).

Various materials and configurations have been used for heat exchangers. There are big differences in the durability and effectiveness of these alternatives. There is a cost to be considered in the construction or purchase of the system to determine the value of return vs. expense. Some are not too complicated to be made by the do-it-yourselfer, college prof., or studio artist. Others require precise fabrication methods.

The stack heat exchanger that has been most available is the Correll unit. It is comprised of multiple stainless steel channels with the fresh air flowing on the inside and the exhaust passing over the outside. An input manifold brings air from the blower to the passages. Stainless can handle temperatures up to 2000° F fairly well, but the exhaust can be hotter than that especially during a melt cycle. To deal with this, a section of the stack has silicon carbide slabs as the heat conductor between the exhaust and fresh air. Over the years, these have been modified with baffles to extend the life of the stainless section. With proper care they have been known to operate well for many years.

Recent development of the multiple channel, refractory-lined stack by the author has shown that a technically simpler fabrication can have excellent results (see pg. 181). Using standard insulated wood stove stack pipe, a series of passages are cast around a central exhaust channel. A higher number of channels and denser refractory has improved the response of these stacks. The first one that was made in 1997 has no apparent damage and has been used many times while other stacks were in the making for new installations.

More stack would always seem to be better, but there are diminishing returns. Theoretically you can recover close to 100% of the heat with enough stack surface. Heat flows from hot to cold, so there must always be at least a small heat differential between exhaust and fresh air entry temperature. It might be best to consider another use for the remaining heat, such as heating water, when the stack temperature is reduced to a few hundred degrees. The best stack temperature that has been directly observed is 700° F, so there is still heat available. A three foot refractory stack gets heavy and cumbersome. Adding another foot would make the stack difficult to handle. Combining the refractory stack with a lighter metal section for the lower temperatures is an area to be explored to approach optimum returns.

Most of the work with recuperators has been concentrated on furnaces. Since they are on full time, furnaces are usually the main energy consumer in the shop. Glory holes, however, can use as much or more gas in a work day than a recuperated furnace. A large glory hole uses over two gallons of propane per hour. There is a lot of room to improve the fuel efficiency in glory holes. The initial retrofit of a glory hole with a refractory stack is presented in the comparison chart with a 35% to 40% reduction in fuel consumption. A side benefit is a much cooler studio. The fact that glory holes operate with some degree of door opening almost all the time means that some heat will never be available for recovery. Still, well-fitting door faces and well-insulated walls create a much better situation for installing a recuperator. Ribbon burners are becoming a popular choice for glory holes because the heat distribution is favorable compared to spot heating for many types of work. Development of a long profile recuperated burner for glory holes would make this more attractive for many studios.

The Basic Principal of Recuperation

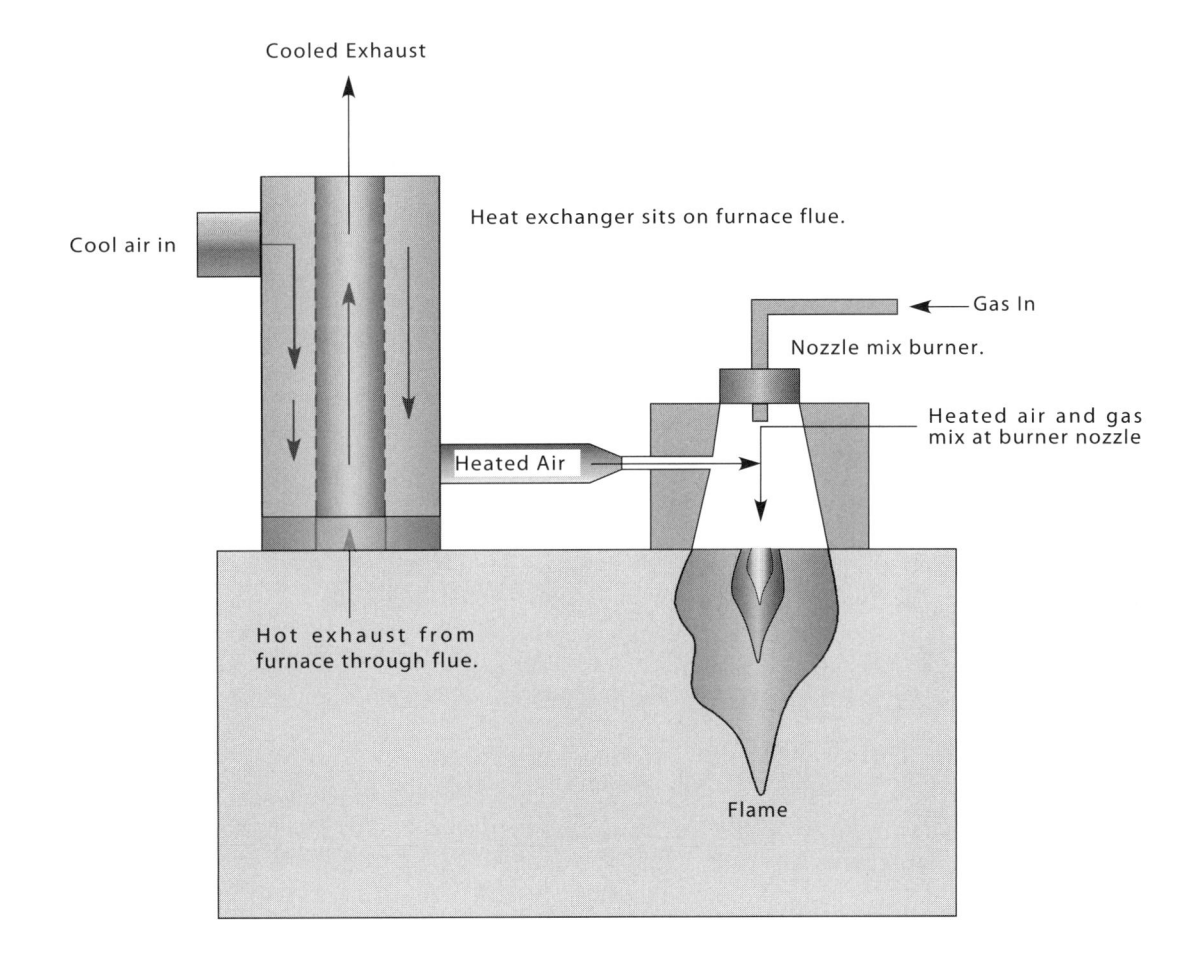

Cooled Exhaust

Cool air in

Heat exchanger sits on furnace flue.

Gas In

Nozzle mix burner.

Heated air and gas mix at burner nozzle

Heated Air

Hot exhaust from furnace through flue.

Flame

The basics of a recuperated system are an excess of recoverable waste heat, a heat exchange structure to pass the heat from the spent air to fresh air, and a means of reintroducing the heated air back into the burner. The less energy needed to heat the combustion air amounts to more energy saved.

The above diagram depicts a basic recuperator system. The heated air is introduced into the burner system at the nozzle where it mixes with the gas and ignites.

Three Ways to Power Recuperators

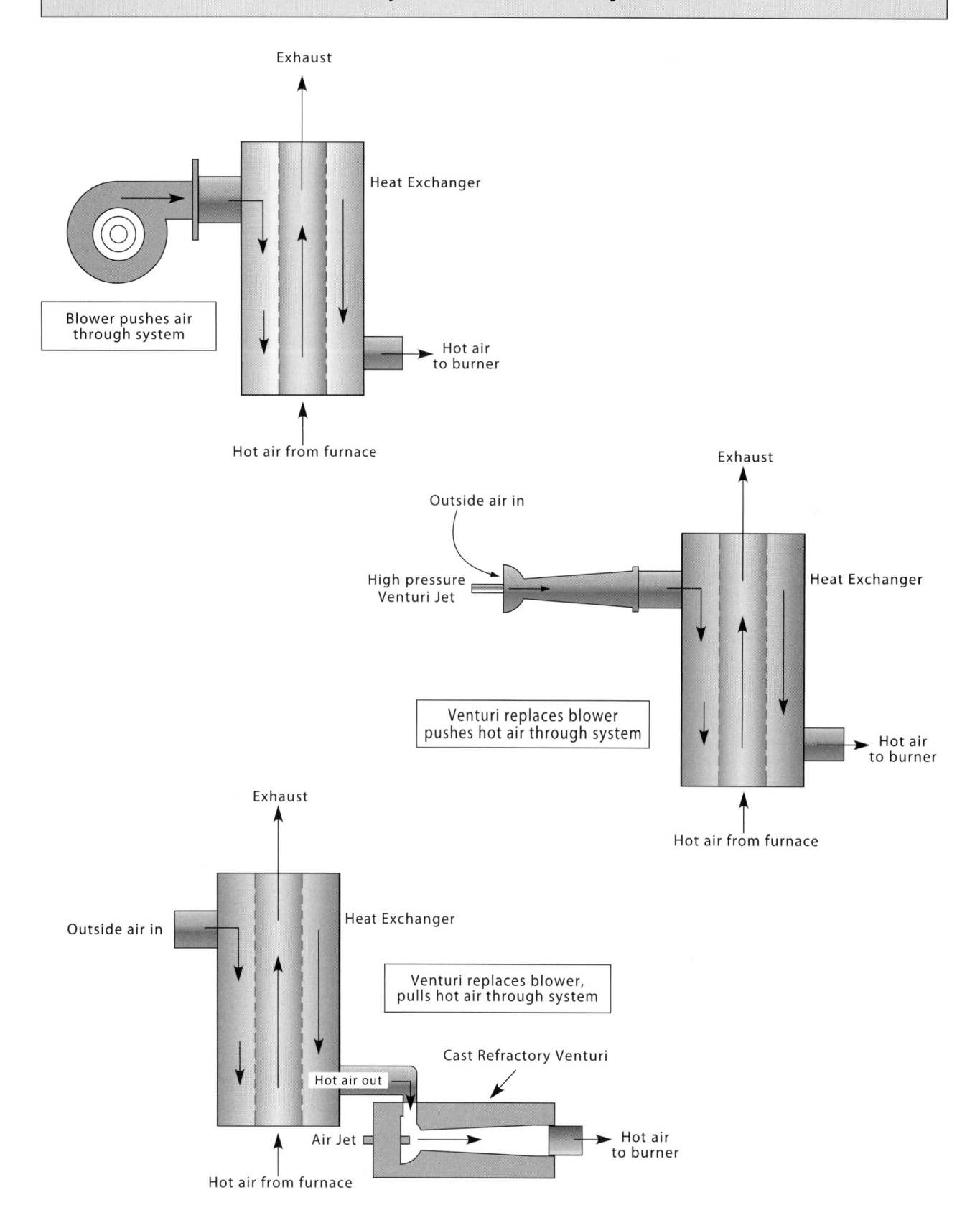

Blower pushes air through system

Exhaust
Heat Exchanger
Hot air to burner
Hot air from furnace

Venturi replaces blower pushes hot air through system

Outside air in
High pressure Venturi Jet
Exhaust
Heat Exchanger
Hot air to burner
Hot air from furnace

Venturi replaces blower, pulls hot air through system

Exhaust
Outside air in
Heat Exchanger
Cast Refractory Venturi
Hot air out
Air Jet
Hot air to burner
Hot air from furnace

180 Glass Notes

Two Stack Designs

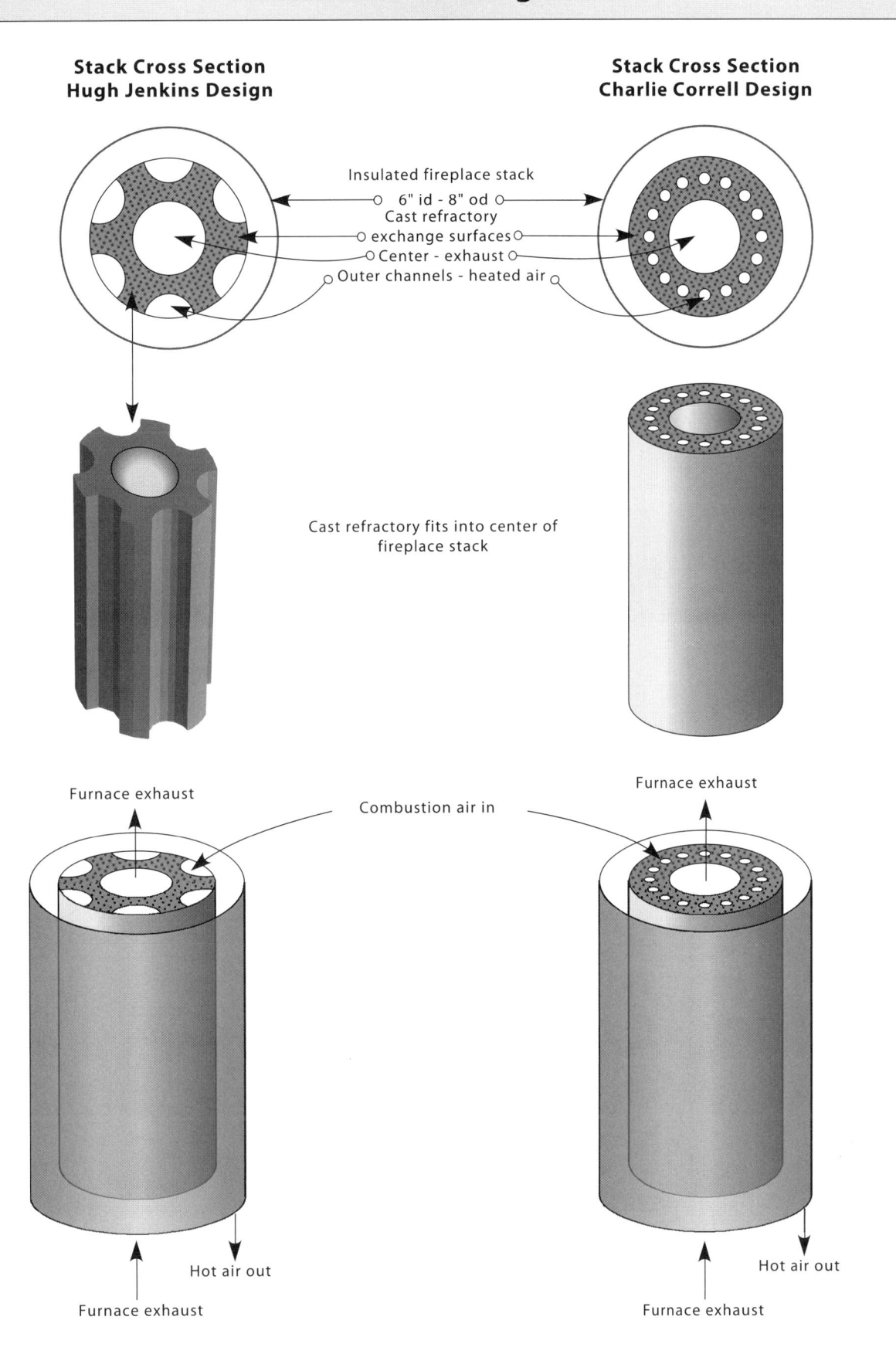

**Stack Cross Section
Hugh Jenkins Design**

**Stack Cross Section
Charlie Correll Design**

Insulated fireplace stack
6" id - 8" od
Cast refractory exchange surfaces
Center - exhaust
Outer channels - heated air

Cast refractory fits into center of fireplace stack

Furnace exhaust

Combustion air in

Furnace exhaust

Hot air out

Furnace exhaust

Hot air out

Furnace exhaust

Glass Notes 181

Stainless Tube Recuperator

1

Spiral Recuperator

Forced Air

2

Air

To Burner

Exhaust

Correll Recuperator

Air to burner

Exhaust through outside channels

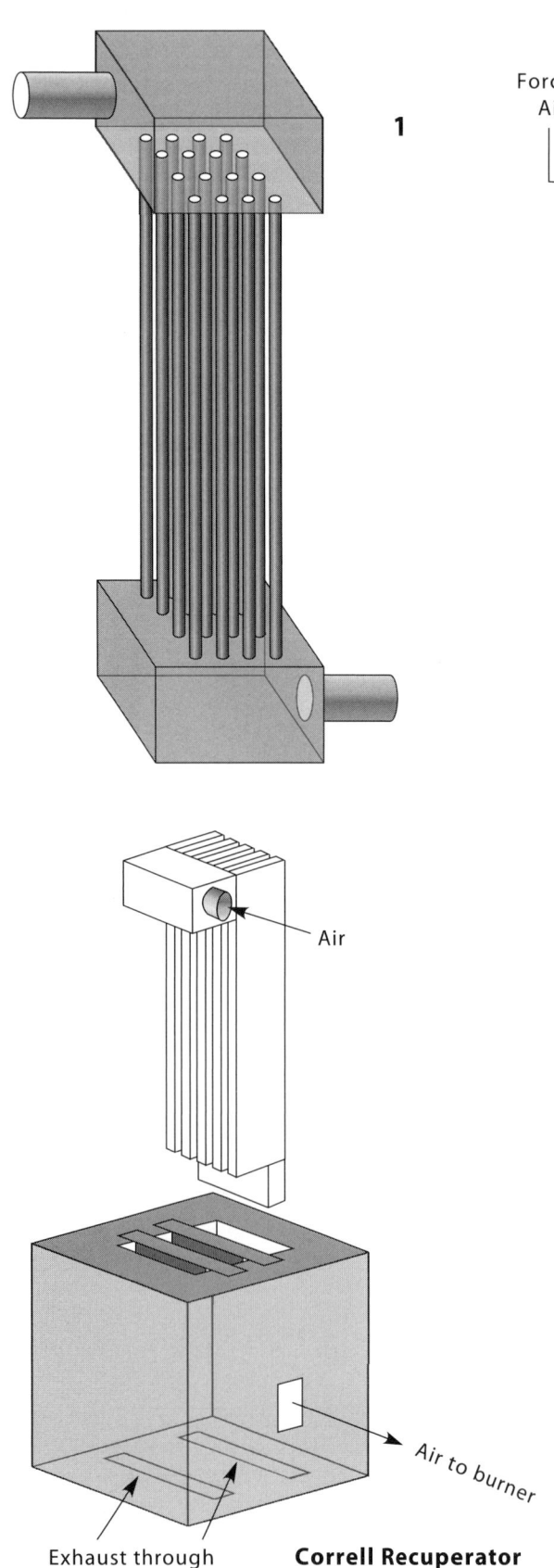

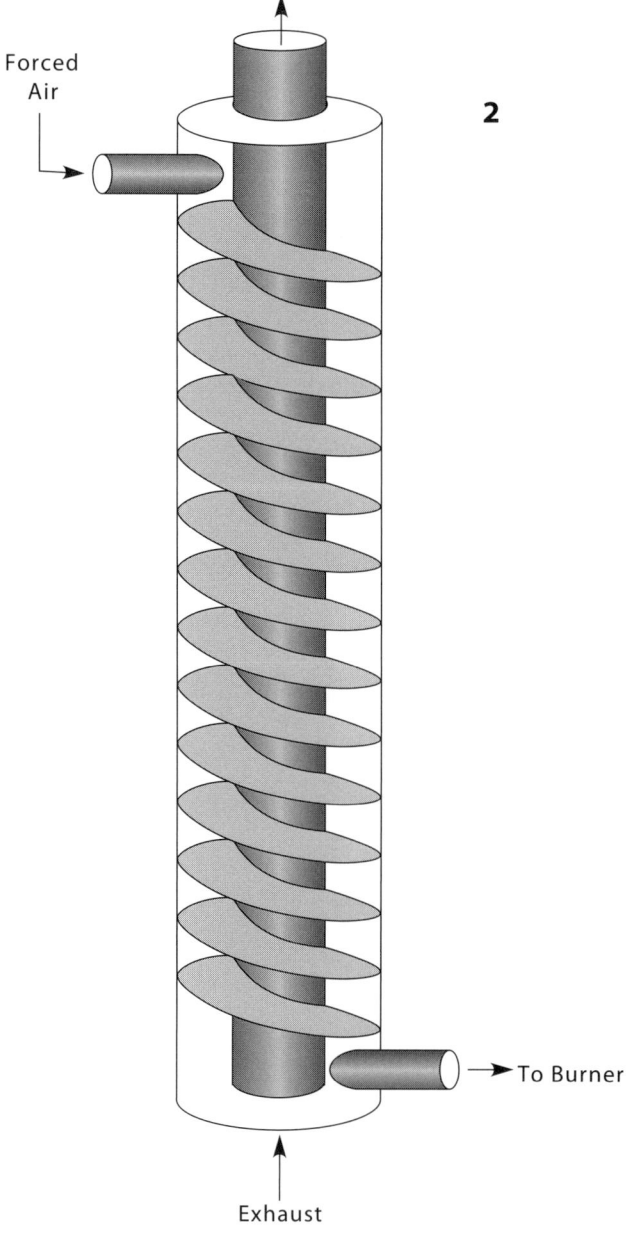

These are three Charlie Correll recuperator designs. It should be noted that design #1 and #2 can easily be used as heat exchangers as well as high heat recuperators. Outside air powered through the main body can be used to heat a room. Either of the two designs can be suspended under your furnace hood where the tubes in #1 or the fins in #2 will pick up the radiant heat that collects in the hood. If you use #1 as a heat exchanger, it can be fabricated from aluminum. Electrical conduit works well. I saw a design similar to #1 at Nick Labino's studio many years ago.

Comparison of Installed Refractory Stack Recuperators for Propane Burners

By Hugh Jenkins

The following table shows the jets, gas pressure, and propane consumption for several recuperator installations. Two comparisons are for pre and post retrofit. The others are for similar capacity furnaces. In comparing different furnaces, some caution is advised. Older furnaces always show a change in fuel consumption. More significantly, regular, over-the-counter pressure gauges are not very accurate. At low gas pressures, a pound or two of inaccuracy can be significant. When possible, the fuel consumption should be determined by using a dedicated tank or calibrated flow meter. Otherwise, use a standard industry chart of orifices and pressures to estimate fuel flows.

Furnace type	Jet	PSI	BTU	Gal/hr.
Two side by side 140# invested				
pot furnaces without recuperator	#59	12 psi	65k	0.74
with VW cylinder exchanger	#64	12 psi	50k	0.56
Retrofit of 80# invested pot furnace				
before recuperator	#61	5 psi	39k	0.43
with 2 ft. refractory stack	#65	5 psi	31k	0.35
80# free stander with 3 ft. stack	#67	5 psi	25k	0.28
Comparison of two 300# furnaces				
invested pot no recuperator	#58	12 psi	72k	0.80
with 3 ft. refractory exchanger	#65	10 psi	44k	0.49
Comparison of 140# furnace with changed stacks				
with 2 ft. refractory stack	#66	10 psi	40k	0.44
with 3 ft. refractory stack	#67	8 psi	32k	0.36
40# free stander with 2 ft. stack	#68	4 psi	22k	0.24
Retrofit of 14" diameter glory hole				
before recuperator	#60	24 psi	90k	1.00
with 2 ft stack	#61	16 psi	70k	0.77

Operation and Maintenance of Recuperators

In the operation of recuperated furnaces, there are a few things that are different from a straight gas/air burner. Recuperated furnaces have what is referred to as a "flywheel effect." Once they get hot they tend to stay that way since the exhaust heat is recycled rather than lost. Also, once they get cold, they are a bit stubborn to heat back up. This is because the "new energy" supplied by fuel is only a percentage of the heat passing through the burner. If the recuperator is cool, then the heated air is also cooler. It takes a strong fuel boost to recover from a major "cool down." Once the stack is heated up again, the recuperation increases and recovery accelerates.

Another result of recuperation is that as the furnace heats up during a melt, the recycled heat increases, and the fresh air is more expanded than at idle setting. Since this is a dynamic change, the more the furnace is heated the more the air is expanded. The result is that the flame gets less oxygen and may go over into reduction. Discovery of an air setting that will compensate for this thinning of the air, or regular adjusting of the air over the last few hours of the high melt, is necessary.

It isn't realistic to think that once installed, recuperated furnaces need no maintenance. Maintenance is minimal but necessary. Small jets are subject to interference by condensation, dust, and entrained pipe residue. The stack itself condenses the evaporated batch components. These can reduce the efficiency of the system. As recuperators become even more efficient, they use less fuel and less air, and the jet sizes are proportionately smaller. As the stacks work to regain more of the heat, more evaporated material will condense. Fortunately, the furnace response is a good reminder of the need for maintenance. Cleaning the jets is a necessary routine in all high pressure gas furnaces. Natural gas jets are considerably larger and not so easily disrupted. Regular blowing out of the stack takes only a few minutes before charging. It is well worth it.

Another area that needs emphasis is protection of any metal parts. Over the years the Correll stacks have had widely variable life spans from six months to seven or more years. This is primarily due to method of operation. At the end of the high heat phase of melting, the exhaust exiting the furnace could be 2400° F or higher. Reducing the air flow at this point leaves the heat exchanger quite vulnerable. Continuous excess air setting is one method prescribed to counteract overheating the exchanger. **Forcing a shorter melt cycle with high burner settings may be necessary for certain shop work schedules but has a negative impact on the life of the heat exchanger.** A few more days of work per month may well make it worth replacing the metal unit more frequently. Under normal use with care, and cleaning, they can last a long time before warping or burning through.

In the refractory stack recuperators which use a cast refractory venturi block (pg. 180), there is a steel spud with an air jet in the hot air stream. The constant flow of cool air through these parts keeps them from being damaged. Once again it is at the end of the melting cycle when the gas and air are turned down that these parts can get hot. That is when the exhaust is hottest. Regulating the gas and air separately helps to reduce this. To protect the system and to help it cool down, the gas can be reduced to below idle pressure, but the air flow kept at a raised level for a few hours. For example, melt with the gas at 18 psi and the air jet at 32 psi. At turndown, lower the gas to 3 psi and the air to 15 psi. The idle setting when the glass has cooled is gas 5 psi and air 8 psi. The spud and jet are inexpensive parts and easily replaced, but with care, that is not necessary more than once a year.

In general, operating a recuperated furnace is no more complicated than any other gas furnace. Understanding that the gas and air volumes are greatly reduced from non-recuperated systems is the main shift. Charging cycles can be adjusted by using more or less fuel. Filling a free-standing pot in eight charges, melting for 8 hours and cooling to gathering temperature over 4 to 5 hours is a normal schedule. Safety systems and automatic controls are applicable as required or desired.

Conclusion

Recent experience indicates that there is a great savings to be gained from recuperating any gas-fired furnace or glory hole. Further experiments should lead to even higher percentage returns. The cost of installation can be returned in a few months, and the savings continue for years. In fact, glory holes may be the biggest future application since even electric furnace shops operate gas-fired glory holes. Adapting to different burner formats and exhaust locations keeps there from being an easy off-the-shelf solution that works for everyone. Installations have been very effective for units ranging from 30 to 300 pound capacity and there should be no limitations for larger or smaller size furnaces.

Hugh Jenkins

Hugh's Original Drawings

Glass Notes 185

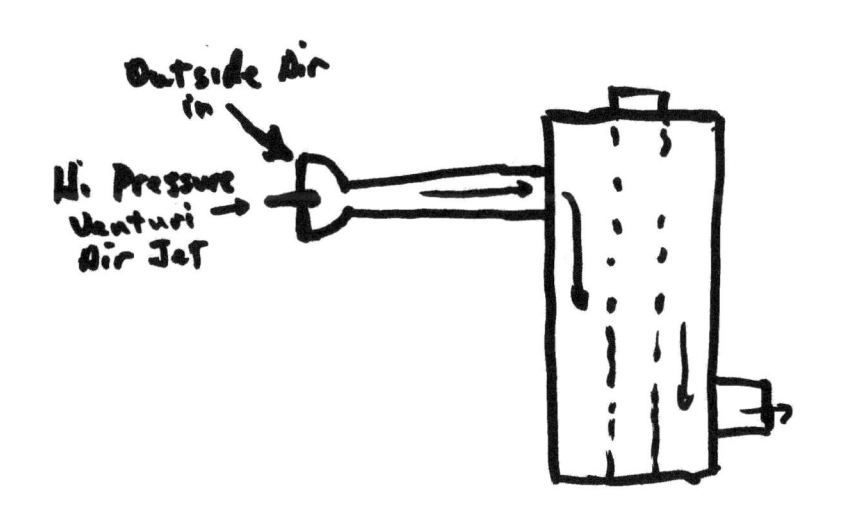

The Hub Recuperator

While talking with John Chiles about the glory hole plans that were included in *Glass Notes,* he mentioned that he had a recuperation design that was part of his furnace system or could be retrofit onto an already existing furnace.

Building one of these units is not all that easy as one needs skills that go beyond simple welding; nonetheless it can be done. My personal recommendation is to purchase one of these units from Hub Consolidated and get it right the first time.

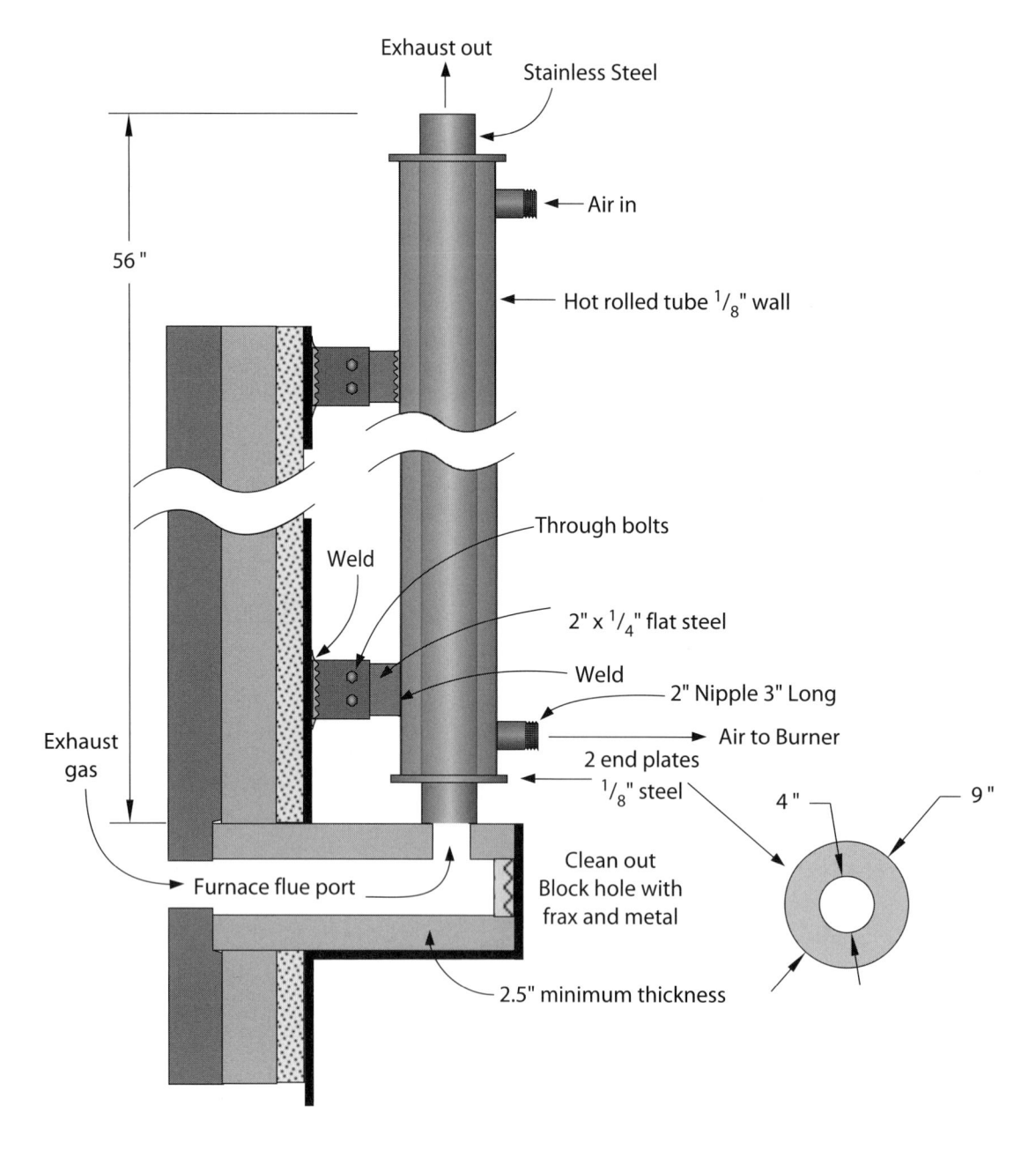

The placement of the recuperator is at the outlet of your flue. The illustration above is only to give you a general view of how the unit works and how to affix it to your furnace. If your flue is at the top of your furnace, the recuperator will be placed at that point.

186 Glass Notes

Hub Recuperator Details

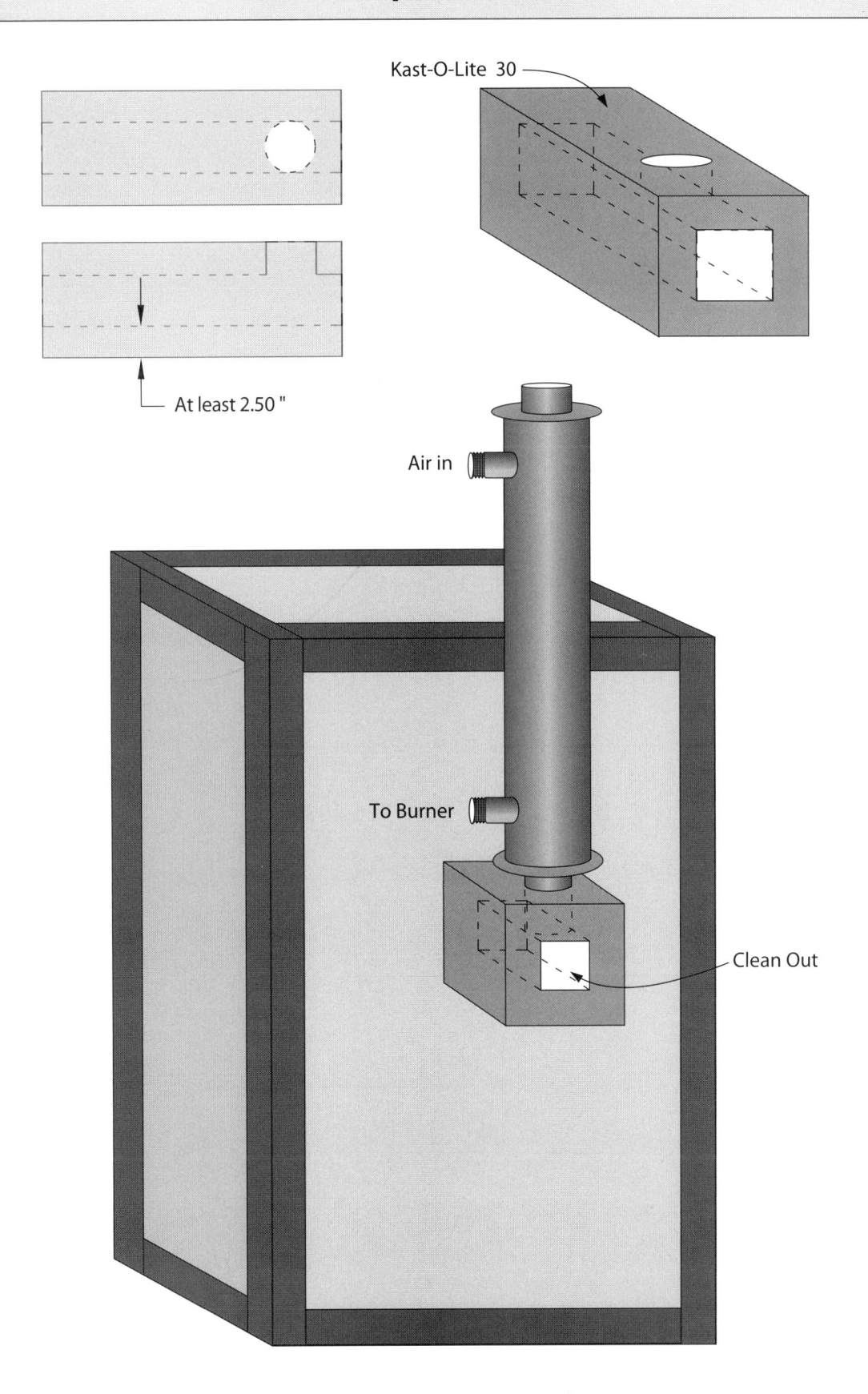

Kast-O-Lite 30

At least 2.50"

Air in

To Burner

Clean Out

Glass Notes 187

NOTES

Glory Holes & A Garage

Chapter Contents

The Fiber Glory Hole 190
The Hub Consolidated IFB Glory Hole 198
Construction Techniques 201
Casting the Heat Retaining Ring 203
Materials Needed for Doors and Stand 204
Frames 205
The Glory Hole Stand 206
The Doors 209
Molds for Cast Door 211
The Hinges 212
Final Assembly 214
Pivot Hinge and Door Stop 216
Door Openers and a Burner Block 217
Another Burner Block 218
The Pine Ridge Square Glory Hole 219
Pine Ridge Parabolic Rolling Door 221
The Garage 222

The Fiber Glory Hole

Before we built glory holes, furnaces were used for reheating. Unfortunately, our furnaces were not very hot, and reheating took forever. It was not uncommon for someone to lose a piece off the punty into the furnace; however, no one really cared that much at the time. The thrill of making the piece was all that mattered. A little color in the "crystal" only made things nicer.

The first real glory holes I remember were built for Fritz at the Toledo Museum in the very early 70's. They were large factory designs with four opposing openings and one huge burner fired from the bottom. Fritz told me the studio was being designed and built by old factory engineers, and that's the way it was done in the factory. The studio the museum built for Fritz looked more like a milk pasteurizing plant than a glass studio. It was very funny to see those tiny blown vessels being reheated in huge glory holes. As you might guess, the first piece that dropped off a punty went straight into the burner. Needless to say, those glory holes didn't last long.

Story has it that the name "glory hole" is originally derived from the gold rush and had nothing to do with hot glass. A prospector would yell "glory hole!" upon discovering a vein or hole filled with nuggets of gold. Apparently the earth took on a golden glow from the reflection of the gold lying in the dirt. Early glass blowers felt the color of their glory holes had a similar golden glow. Although the truth of this story has never been determined, it makes a good legend. Building a glory hole is somewhat easier than finding gold, but it's not as much fun. Hey, if you can think of a better story, I'll listen.

A Word of Warning

The fiber glory hole described in this section is not as common as it once was as we are all very aware of the health issues attributed to fiber. To be honest, I do not recommend the use of fiber glory holes because of those health issues. It is a known fact that the fiber used for high temperature insulation is a carcinogen and, I quote from the MSDS sheet, "In October 2001, the International Agency for Research on Cancer (IARC) confirmed that Group 2b (possible human carcinogen) remains the appropriate IARC classification for RCF (Refractory Ceramic Fiber)." It should also be noted that fiber turns into Cristobalite when heated to 2100° F (1149° C) and is also a known carcinogen. I strongly recommend that you read the MSDS sheets for this product before proceeding. You have been sufficiently warned, and if you still wish to build one, proceed at your own risk.

Pros and Cons

The advantage of a fiber glory hole is that it takes less energy to reach working temperature than an IFB or a cast GH and it can reach temperature very rapidly. It also requires less energy to maintain temperature. The disadvantage is that it will lose heat very rapidly if you're required to open the door for large pieces. Fiber does not store energy, IFB does. Fiber only reflects heat back into the firing chamber, and, when the doors are opened, the internal heat plunges rapidly. One should also understand that if you exceed the maximum temperature rating of the fiber, it will rapidly deteriorate, rendering it useless.

Building the Glory Hole

Basically, the standard fiber GH is a 55 gallon drum lined with hi-temperature fiber sometimes referred to as HTZ. The first thing needed for construction is a clean, 55-gallon or 30-gallon (208 or 115 liter) drum. Make sure the drum is clean. Sometimes the drum looks clean but has a residual chemical clinging to the lining. *Author's note: Don't torch a drum that has had any flammable materials stored in it. You may create an explosion or fire.* To be safe, wash the inside of the drum with soap and water or a nontoxic solvent. In the long run you're probably better off to have a drum rolled to your specific dimensions. A good weld shop can usually do this for you. It might cost a bit to have this done, but you will have a drum rolled to your specifications and fabricated from a much sturdier steel.

Fiber Information

It is important to know what type of fiber insulation you will use to line the drum, as fiber insulation comes in two heat ranges, standard and high temperature. Standard fiber insulation has a maximum temperature of 2300° F (1260° C) which is not sufficient for glory hole construction. You will need to use a fiber blanket rated at 2600° or 2700° F (1425° or 1480° C) as most glory holes exceed 2300° F. The standard width of fiber blanket is 24" and 1" or 2" thick. I prefer the 2" thick blanket. The blanket is also manufactured in different densities. Higher density means a greater density of fiber per cu. ft. Density is measured in pounds (lbs). Low density is 4 lb. High density is 8 lb. There is also a 6 lb. density. You should use at least 6 lb. density for your GH, but 8 lb. density is better. The higher the density the higher the price; you get what you pay for. 1" thick fiber has 50-square feet to the box and 2" thick fiber has 25-square feet. It will take at least 2 boxes (maybe more) of 2", 8 pound density to construct one average glory hole. The diagrams included in this section demonstrate how the glory hole should look when completed. If you buy name brand fiber insulation, you will pay top dollar. Some companies charge significantly less for the same quality fiber. Look in the Suppliers list for the names and addresses of fiber companies.

Begin

Because you wet the fiber before placing it in the drum, you should punch some holes into the bottom of the drum to allow it to drain.

The first step is to lay some plastic sheeting on the floor and unroll a section of blanket. Using the drum as a guide, cut a circle of fiber to line the bottom or back of the drum.

The Pleat Fold

To create a fiber liner that will be at least 3" to 4" (7.5–10 cm) thick, do the following:

1. Cut a length of fiber slightly longer than the drum. If the lining is to be 3" long, then cut a 7" wide

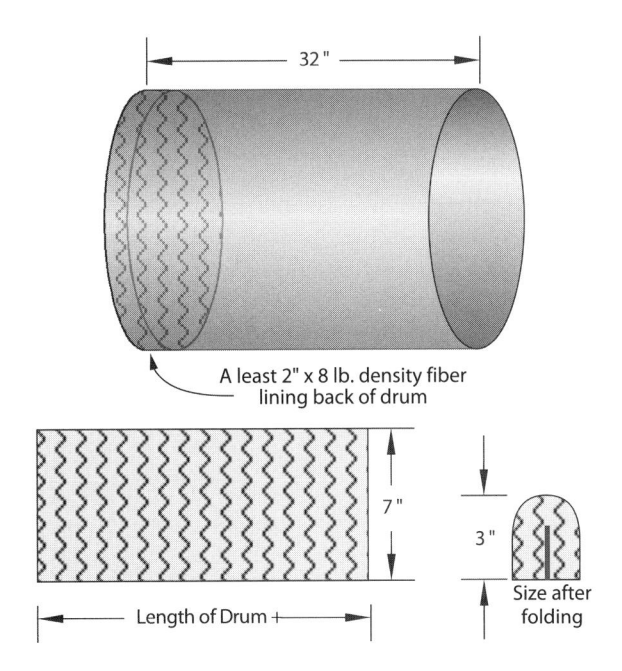

   [Diagram: 32" drum with A least 2" x 8 lb. density fiber lining back of drum; 7" width, 3" size after folding, Length of Drum]

   section. The extra inch is to compensate for the fold. Soak this section of insulation with water. If you add colloidal silica to the water or use the colloidal silica by itself, the fiber will become rigid when dry and be less apt to deteriorate. I recommend wetting the fiber with colloidal silica because of its rigidizing properties. Wetting also keeps the fibers from becoming airborne. Carefully fold the wet insulation into a pleat. The diagram on the following pages should give you an idea of how the pleats look. After you have made the pleat, place it in the standing drum. Continue making your pleat sections until the drum is fully lined. You may find it easier to fold the pleat over a thin, metal straight edge. When the wet fiber dries, it expands slightly and exerts a bit of tension. This tension is what permits it to hold itself in position. It is amazing how strong the fiber gets when it dries. Do not lay the drum down until it has dried.

2. When you have completed all the pleats and they are in place, cut another circular piece or two of fiber to fit into the back of the glory hole up against the first circle of fiber. This piece will provide extra insulation and prevent any flame from getting between the lining and the back fiber panel. Wear a good particulate dust mask. Wear a Tyvek jump suit with a hood. You do not want to get the fibers on or in you.

Height

After the glory hole has dried, it can be placed on the stand you have constructed. *Author's note: See the glory hole table construction diagrams beginning on pg. 206 for details.* Hopefully, you have estimated the center of the glory hole to be about stomach height (32" to 36", 80 to 90 cm). If it is too high, you will strain yourself getting heavy pieces off the yoke. Since we come in all sizes, estimating the relative height of glass blowing equipment in a school situation is difficult. When I was a student at the University of Wisconsin, I had to stand on a cinder block to gather from the furnace, but then again, I'm vertically challenged.

The Heat Retention Ring

If you wish to create a cast heat retention ring as shown on pg. 203 (and I recommend that you do), carefully cut a 2" to 2 ½" section off the front of your pleats to accommodate the ring. If you choose to cast the heat retention ring separately, make sure you fit the ring snugly to the fiber. I recommend you cast the ring in place. Casting the ring in place ensures a snug fit. Make sure you weld some tabs on the drum to hold the ring in place (see pg. 194). The purpose of the ring is to hold the heat in the glory hole when it is fully open. The glory hole will lose heat very rapidly when the doors are fully open. The lip of the cast ring tends to hold the heat in for a greater length of time. Fiber insulation loses heat very quickly when there is nothing to keep it from escaping.

Preventative Maintenance

It is not uncommon to drop a piece off the punty into the bottom of the glory hole. If the glass is not removed immediately, it will eventually eat through the fiber insulation and render it useless. If this is going to be a problem at your studio, I recommend you replace the fiber insulation at the bottom of your glory hole with a cast section. You can do this after the glory hole is in place. Simply cut and remove a section of pleats and cast into the cavity. It is also important to remove any glass that pops off your punty and sticks to the fiber insulation. This can be done in the morning before you light up. It is not a good idea to clean your pipes and punties in the glory hole. The glass that pops off will eat through the insulation. It is a good idea to maintain the integrity of your fiber glory hole. If you do, it will last a long time. Some studios apply a thin zircon wash to the surface of the fiber to prevent glass from eating into the fiber. The zircon wash has to be renewed every so often.

The Burner

The location of the burner depends on your style of working. If you like to reheat directly in the flame, then you will locate the burner port in the center side or center top of the GH. If you wish to have the flame swirl around the GH, then it will be located off to the side (see burner positions, pg. 194). Once you locate where the burner will go, cut a hole in the drum with a cutting torch. The size of hole is depends on the size of your burner block, and I do recommend a burner block. If you think ahead, cut the burner port prior to lining the fiber pleats into the GH. Locate the burner slightly front from the center of the GH. Locating the burner toward the front will permit you to heat up the lip of your work without overheating the body of the piece or the punty. You can use a Giberson, Wilton, Spiral Arts or the Ribbon burner (see section on burners). If you use the Ribbon burner, follow the installation directions that come with it. Retro fitting a glory hole with a new burner system is difficult but not impossible. If you've got a used fiber glory hole, you may find it difficult to cut the fiber. Fiber gets somewhat brittle with usage.

If you are using a separate blower for your glory hole, I recommend the Maxon pre–mix blower. For their address, see the Vendor List at the back of this book. Safety equipment on your gas line is very important. In most states, you will not be able to get fire insurance for your studio if you do not have state approved safety equipment on your burners. Safety equipment may be expensive, but it can save your studio and your life. Check with your local burner representative for this type of equipment. Most studios do not have safety on their glory holes as they consider them to be supervised; that is, someone always is there when the GH is running, and they are shut off at the end of the day.

The Doors and Hinges

After completing the glory hole, you must build a table and doors. Doors are a very important component of the glory hole and should be engineered carefully. If you are sloppy, you will waste a considerable amount of energy, and your doors will never operate properly. There are usually two sets of doors. Each set presents a larger access hole that permits the glassblower to warm in differently sized pieces. I have always used cast doors for my glory holes. Doors usually have to be replaced every couple of years. I've always cast my doors from Kast-O-Lite 30 or any strong, high-temperature castable. For best results, cast them directly into the welded angle-iron frames. For the opening, we usually use a can that has the diameter of the hole we are casting. *Author's note: I strongly recommend you follow the directions beginning on page 209 for constructing the doors as well as the hinges.*

Make sure your doors are in perfect alignment before welding. Doors that are not aligned will not close correctly. The extreme heat of a glory hole can do strange things to doors. Weld tabs to the top of each door so that it can be "hooked" open as necessary.

That just about covers the construction of a simple fiber glory hole. There are lots of little details that are impossible to cover in this chapter. You will have to discover some of those things yourself. I am sure you will find many variations on building your glory hole as you go along. My motto for building most equipment is "keep it simple."

Observations

Here are some observations on glory holes (not in any particular order of importance).

- Brick and castables store energy, fiber does not. The denser the insulating material (IFB and castables), the longer it takes to heat up, but the hotter it will stay with the doors open (but only if you have a heat retention ring). Fiber glory holes, if constructed well with correctly-sized burners, will heat up very quickly and be somewhat more economical to run than IFB or castable ones (although I have no scientific proof of that).
- Fiber will deteriorate if molten glass sits on it. Some glass artists put a Zircon wash on fiber to prevent bits of molten glass, that pop off punties and blow pipes, from "eating" the fiber. Zircon wash will not stop a large piece of molten glass. If you lose a piece in the glory hole, remove it immediately. Zircon wash must be renewed constantly, and the glass that sits on it must be removed before lighting up in the morning.
- I have seen many excellent drum glory holes constructed from hi-temperature IFB as well as castable. We had fiber glory holes for years at school but eventually switched to IFB ones. The level of heat necessary for quick reheats was easier to maintain with IFB, and an IFB GH will outlast a fiber hole.

Author's note: When I suggest a piece of equip-

ment is "easy" or "straight forward" to construct, I assume you know how to weld, can drill holes in steel, know how to use castables, know where to obtain materials, and have all the other necessary skills to develop the designs found in this book. If you do not, you will have problems carrying out some of the tasks that are necessary in constructing glassblowing equipment.

Your glory hole should be built to the size of the ware that you are making. If you make small goblets, there is no reason to have a large glory hole. It may be more economical for you to have two different sizes and types of glory holes. Light the one that serves your need for the day. The energy saved will more than compensate for the cost of a second glory hole. When I was in Germany, I visited the Eisch glass factory in Frauenau. Each goblet maker had his own small glory hole at the bench to reheat lips and feet. The interior size of their glory holes was not much bigger than a large coffee can (see photo below). If you were a marble maker, what would you reheat in?

If you build a glory hole on wheels, make sure they are lockable. It's no fun to have to chase a hot glory hole in the middle of an earthquake. Some states have laws against flame–operated equipment on wheels. Most glass blowers I know do not equip their glory holes with flame safety because the glory hole is always attended. It's not good to leave a glory hole unattended if it is not equipped with safety.

If you have problems constructing your glory hole, find someone to help you. Strong welds are your best friend. A hot glory hole puts a great deal of stress on all your metal supports. If you do everything correctly and size your burner accurately, you will find this glory hole to be will give excellent service. Good luck.

Eisch Factory in Frauenau, Germany
Small glory hole, lower left, for reheating dropped foot
Can you find the glass of beer?

The Fiber Pleats

A word about the fiber pleats

I've built this fiber glory hole with the folded end, as well as the cut end, facing the hot zone; both systems work. See the diagrams below.

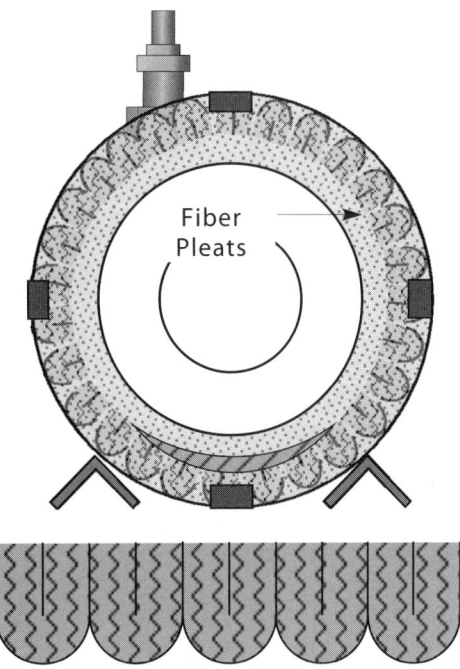

The cut end faces the hot zone.

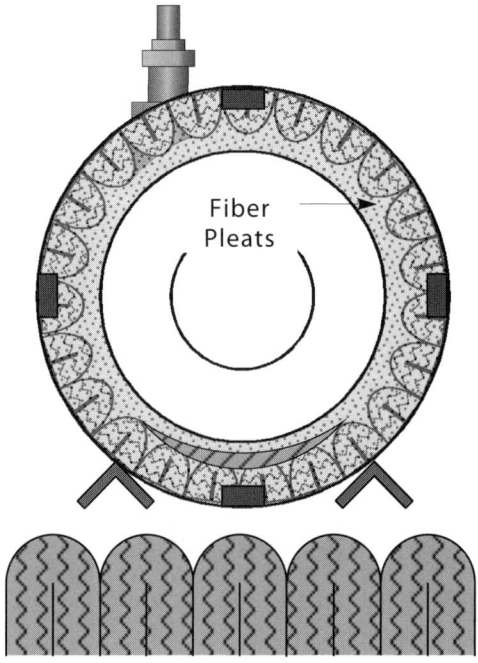

The folded end faces the hot zone

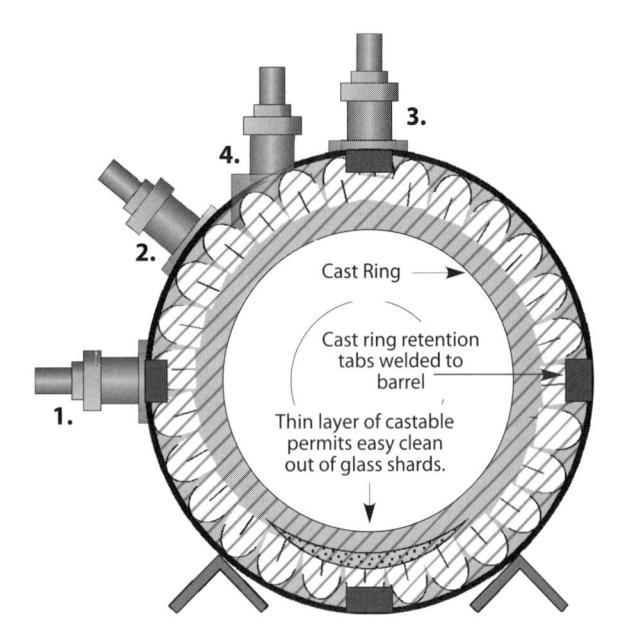

Burner placement is a personal choice. Some glory holes have the burner placed in the center top, and others have the burner placed as a side fire. The type of burner is also a personal choice between a retention tip or a ribbon burner. Your style of working will dictate what type of burner you will use as well as its placement.

1, 2, and 3, are similar placements; that is, they fire in the center of the GH. 4 fires tangentially.

Ribbon burners can be placed in the same manner as depicted here.

194 Glass Notes

The Glory Hole

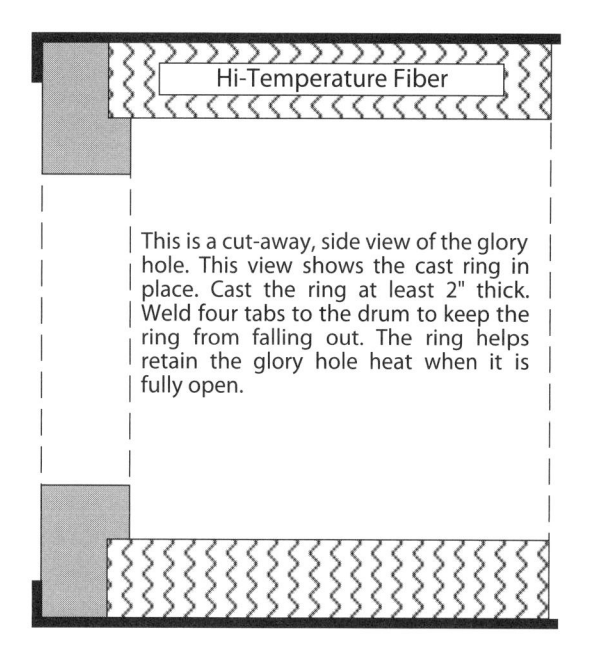

This is a cut-away, side view of the glory hole. This view shows the cast ring in place. Cast the ring at least 2" thick. Weld four tabs to the drum to keep the ring from falling out. The ring helps retain the glory hole heat when it is fully open.

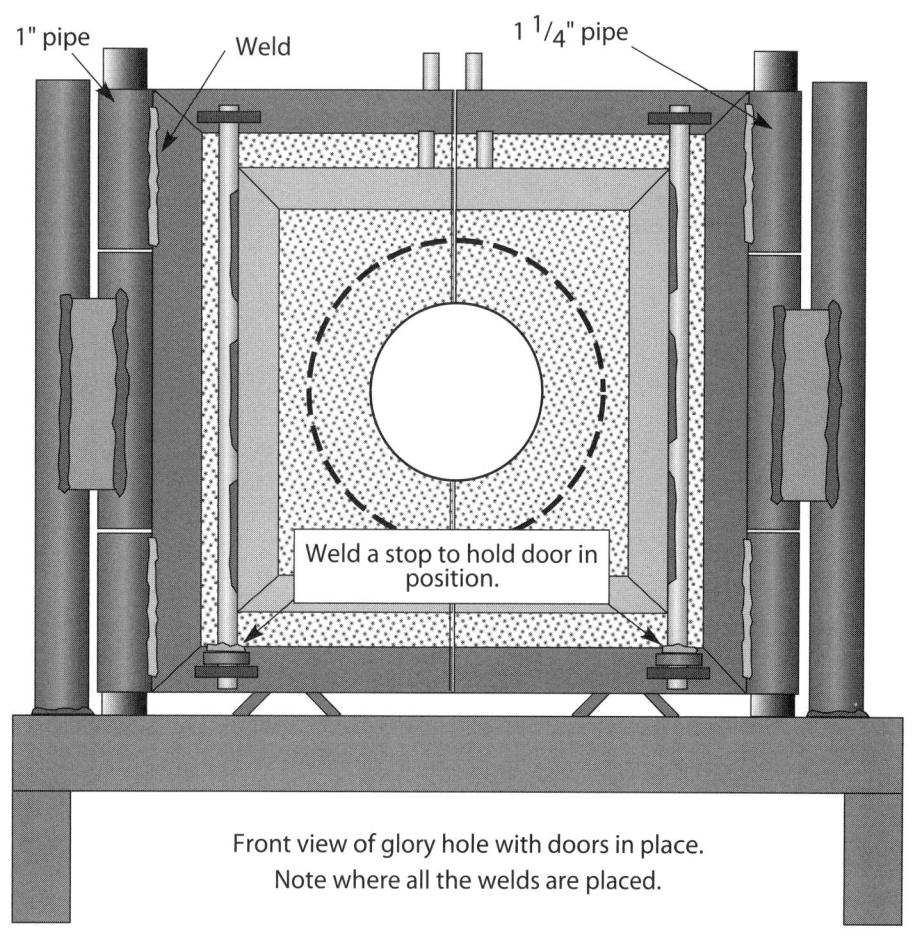

Hi-Temperature Fiber

1" pipe   Weld   1 1/4" pipe

Weld a stop to hold door in position.

Front view of glory hole with doors in place.
Note where all the welds are placed.

Glass Notes 195

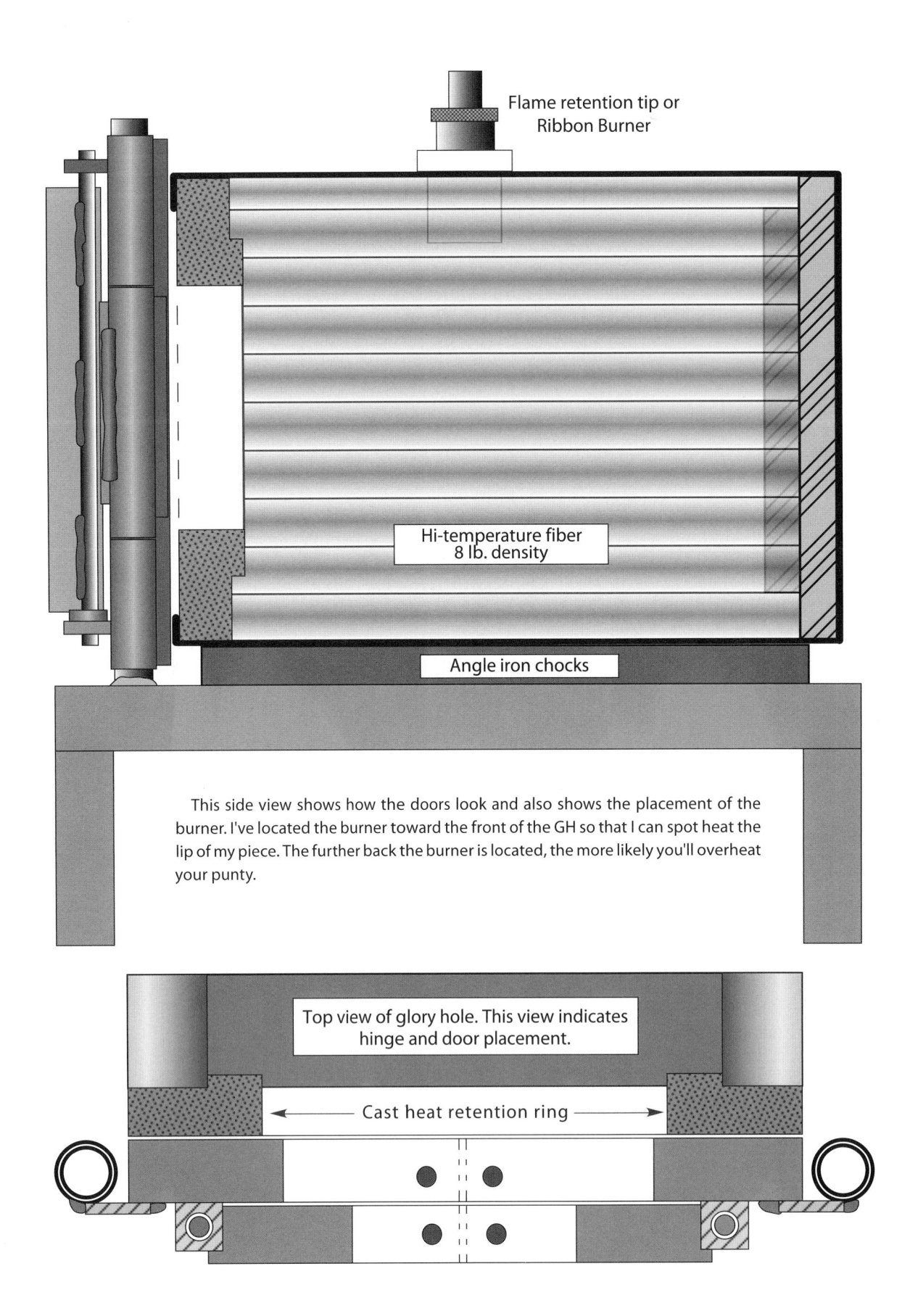

Flame retention tip or Ribbon Burner

Hi-temperature fiber
8 lb. density

Angle iron chocks

This side view shows how the doors look and also shows the placement of the burner. I've located the burner toward the front of the GH so that I can spot heat the lip of my piece. The further back the burner is located, the more likely you'll overheat your punty.

Top view of glory hole. This view indicates hinge and door placement.

← Cast heat retention ring →

Specifications and Price for Fiber Products

ETS Schaefer

This company does not have local distributors. You must buy direct. The fiber products sold by this company are high grade and priced lower than all the other mainline companies.

8050 Highland Pointe Parkway
Macedonia, OH 44056
Tel. 330/468-6600
Toll Free: 800/863-5400
E-mail: sales@etsschaefer.com
Web site: www.etsschaefer.com
Contact: Nancy Malee

*K-Lite HTZ 2600° F fiber insulation
1" x 24" x 8 lb. density --------------------------------- $1.82 per sq. ft.
2" x 24" x 8 lb. density --------------------------------- $3.66 per sq. ft.
1" x 24" x 6 lb. density --------------------------------- $1.48 per sq. ft.
2" x 24" x 6 lb. density --------------------------------- $2.96 per sq. ft.

*K-Lite 2300° F fiber insulation
1" x 24" x 8 lb. density --------------------------------- $1.23 per sq. ft.
2" x 24" x 8 lb. density --------------------------------- $2.49 per sq. ft.
1" x 24" x 6 lb. density --------------------------------- $.94 per sq. ft.
2" x 24" x 6 lb. density --------------------------------- $1.90 per sq. ft.

*Bulk Fiber (2300° F)
30 lb. cartons --- $1.10 per lb.

*Fiber Paper 2300°
1/16" -- $2.00 per sq. ft.
1/8" --- $3.91 per sq. ft.

*IFB (Insulating Fire Brick) Boxes of 25, Standard size, 9 x 4.5 x 2.5
2000° --- $54.00
2300° --- $56.00
2600° --- $67.00
2800° --- $73.00

*Colloidal Silica
Per 5 gal. pail $60.00

There are other companies that manufacture fiber insulation. Check your area for distributors.

Prices as of 2006

The Hub Consolidated IFB Glory Hole

A few words before proceeding

The glory hole and table depicted in this section were designed by John Chiles and are produced by his company, The Hub Consolidated, Inc. The drawings and information were also provided by John Chiles. If all you want to do is blow glass and don't wish to waste your energy on building equipment, then buy one. If you would like to build one but you're mechanically challenged, buy one. Time is money! Call John and buy one off the shelf. Hub also fabricates everything for the glass studio. I have heard nothing but great things about his construction expertise. As you will see, his descriptions are very detailed and leave little to chance. When I was teaching, we built two of these beauties using John's plans; I can tell you firsthand that they are on the money.

The barrel we used for our GH was fabricated for us to our specs. and from heavy duty 14 – 12 gauge steel. If you're considering using a 55 gallon drum for your GH remember they are rather thin and, because of that, do not weld easily. Another reason to have a barrel rolled for you is that the weight of this glory hole when completed is quite substantial and requires you to weld lifting handles to it.

If you've never built a glory hole before, this set of drawings should be a big help. What I like most about John's glory hole is the fact that it is very simple and straightforward.

It is quite easy to build any size IFB glory hole if you follow the calculations and plans on the following pages. The dimensions of this glory hole are for a 16" opening. That dimension can also vary depending on your needs. John's glory hole is 38" to center. This is not a bad dimension for the average-sized glass artist. Obviously, if you are height challenged, you may wish to build your glory hole lower. With this set of plans you can vary any and all of the dimensions.

The cost of materials has gone up considerably since the last edition of this book. Once you establish your bill of materials, brick, steel, and castable, call the companies that sell those materials and get a price quote; remember to include shipping. Of course, price depends on the size you're building. On the average, I price castables at about $50 to $100 per bag. Do not use anything less than 2800° F (1540° C) IFB. Another thing to consider is whether to mortar the IFB joints or not. The choice is yours as I have seen both types and both methods seem to work just fine, but I prefer the mortared joint, and John thinks it's always best to mortar them. Remember, craftsmanship really counts when building studio equipment. If you can't build it right the first time, buy one! For information on all their products, contact Hub directly:

The Hub Consolidated, Inc.
690 Route 73
Orwell, VT 05760
Tel. 802./948-2209, Fax 802/948-2215
E-mail: info@hubglass.com
Web: www.hubglass.com

Interior of Hub Glory Hole with Ash Ribbon Burner installed. Notice the fiber packing around the burner and the burner block that it is set into. The burner block maintains the same curve as the interior shape.

The IFB Glory Hole
Creating the layout

The insulating fire brick (IFB for short) glory hole is not difficult to build. An IFB glory hole has advantages and disadvantages over a fiber one. The one advantage above all others is its ability to store and retain heat when working with the door wide open. Fiber does not retain heat and cools immediately when working in this manner. A slight disadvantage, if you can really call it that, is that brick takes longer to achieve working temperature. The cost of running an IFB GH is probably a bit higher than a fiber one.

The reader should note that, since the publishing of these working drawings in 1996, the construction of this GH has essentially stayed the same.

Calculating the number and angle of brick

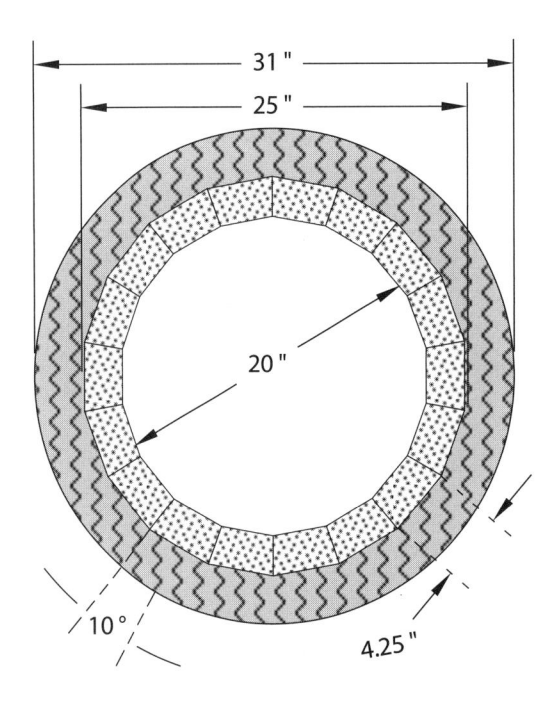

The diameter of the steel barrel will be 31" (20" diameter of opening) + 5" (brick thickness) + 6" (insulation) = 31".

To calculate the angle of the cut

- The actual **diameter (D)** of our opening or circle is 20".
- To determine the **circumference (C)** of a circle, multiply the diameter by Pi (π) (3.14) as follows.
- 20" + 5" x 3.14 = 78.5 is the circumference of the outside of the brick IFB ring.
- To find the number of bricks around the circle, divide the width of 1 brick into the circumference. The width of a standard insulating brick is 4 ½", but we will be trimming about an ⅛" from each edge of brick (making the actual width 4 ¼").
- The number of bricks: 78.5 ÷ 4 ¼" (4.25) = 18.47 bricks.
- To find the angle to cut on each brick, divide the number of bricks into 360°. Divide the answer by 2 (2 sides to each brick). 360° ÷ 18.47 = 19.49 ÷ 2 = 9.74°. For our purposes a 10° angle will work.

$\pi = 3.14$ $C = D \times \pi$

200 Glass Notes

Construction Techniques

To begin building this glory hole, you will first need to cast a disc from Kast-O-Lite 30 or a comparable product 2 ½" thick x 25" wide. If you are building a smaller glory hole, cast a smaller disc. Whatever size glory hole you build, leave 3" between the sidewall and the edge of the cast ring. Cast the disc on a hard flat surface. Place a plastic or tar paper barrier underneath where you will be casting. To make the ring mold to cast into, laminate some plywood to the correct thickness and cut your ring mold from this. You may wish to cut the plywood ring mold in half before casting to facilitate its removal after the castable has set. Wait at least 48 hours before de-molding and placing the disc in the barrel. Kast-O-Lite takes a long time to reach full strength.

As indicated in the following illustrations, place 4 or 5 stilts (insulating brick) 3" high into the bottom of the drum. Pack bulk fiber around the stilts with the disc on top. You are now ready to start placing the 2800° IFB. The IFB will be mortared as you place them.

Use Sairset mortar manufactured by A.P. Green or any comparable product. Before using the mortar, you will need to thin it down. Upon opening the mortar, use a good strong electric drill with an industrial paint mixer to mix it. You will not need much mortar–about 2 gallons should suffice. After it is thoroughly mixed, remove half the mortar and place it in a bucket. As you mix this half, slowly add water until the mortar is about the consistency of ketchup and mustard (yellow ball park).

Put the first ring of bricks that you have cut to the proper angle on your Kast-O-Lite 30 disk. Pack bulk fiber around the brick as you build. Wet the fiber before packing it. This will keep it from dusting. Even if you wet the fiber, it's a good idea to wear a good dust mask. Drill some holes into the bottom of the drum to allow the water to drain. Keep building the rings and packing the fiber until you reach the top of the barrel. If the bricks are tight, tap them with a rubber mallet. It's a good idea to use a standard brick pattern as indicated in the side view diagram. This pattern will lock the brick in place.

When you reach the top of the drum, you should leave a 1 ½" space from the top of the last row to the top of the barrel.

Weld a hook to the barrel. This hook can be important as an aid in lifting the finished glory hole into place. Make sure you weld it very securely. If you are welding onto a commercial drum, you may find it difficult to weld. Have someone with welding experience do the welding. Weld it 2" toward the back to compensate for the extra weight in the back of the barrel. You may wish to have your glory hole barrel fabricated at a good welding and machine shop. If you do, have it fabricated from substantial sheet metal (11 gauge is best).

Author's note: The GH can also be lifted in place using straps and a portable engine block lift. Two sets of straps around the GH works fine.

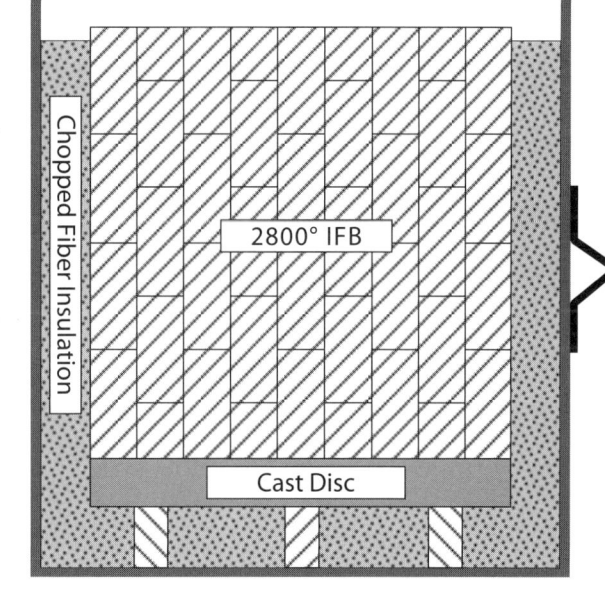

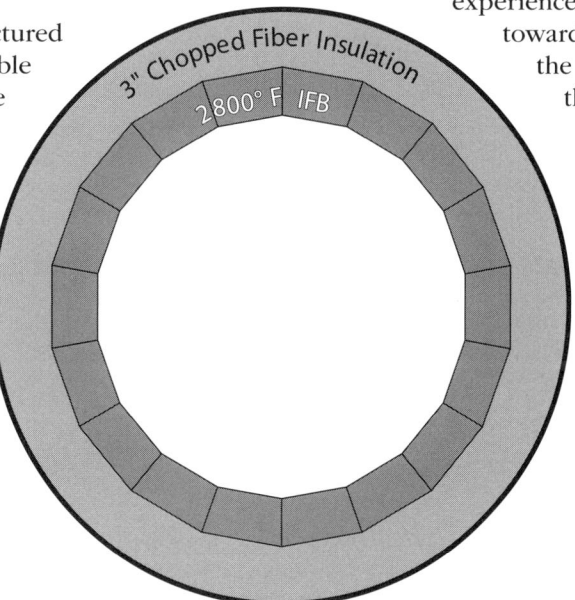

Glass Notes

Side View

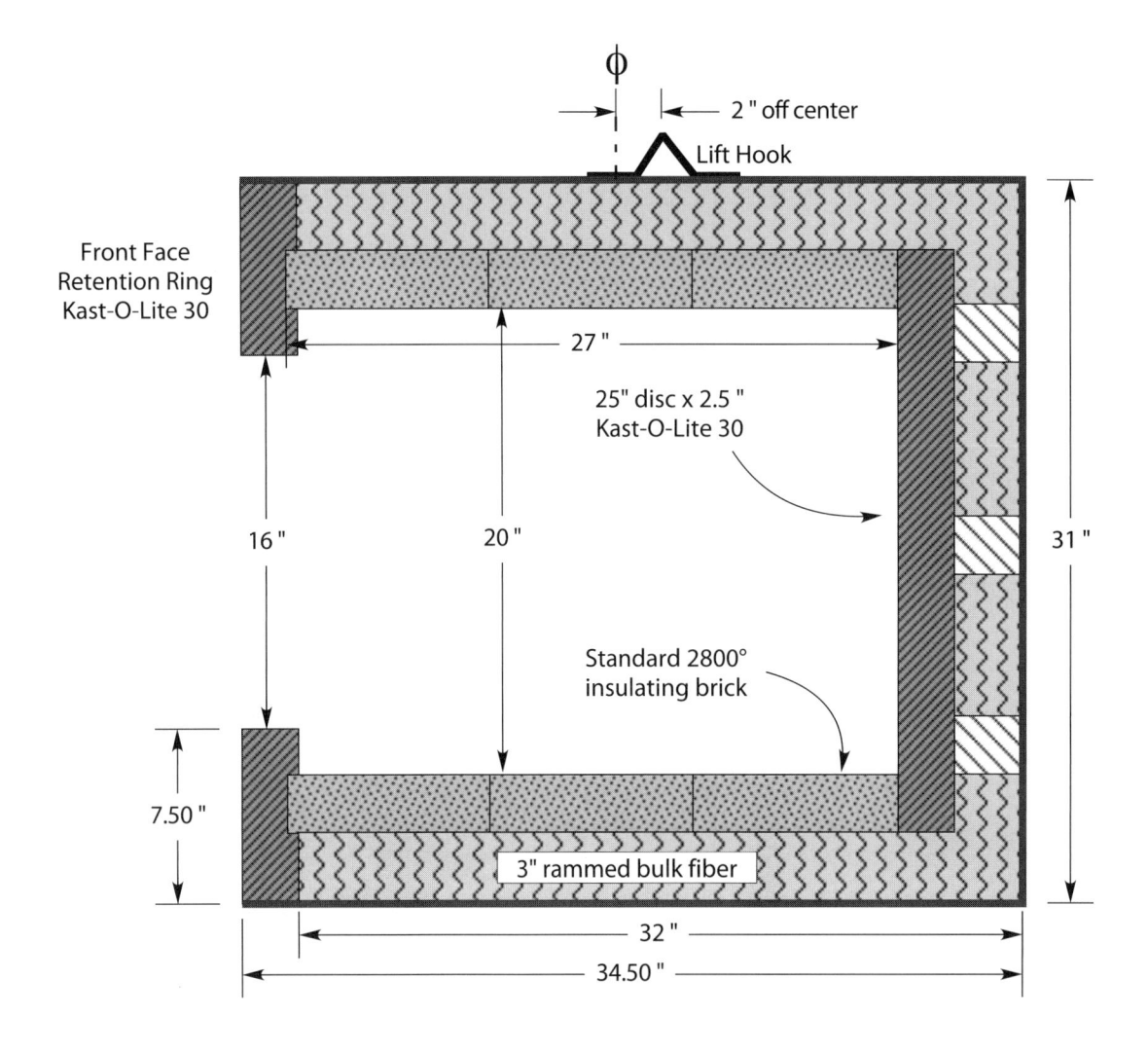

Diagram labels:
- 2" off center
- Lift Hook
- Front Face Retention Ring Kast-O-Lite 30
- 27"
- 25" disc x 2.5" Kast-O-Lite 30
- 16"
- 20"
- 31"
- Standard 2800° insulating brick
- 7.50"
- 3" rammed bulk fiber
- 32"
- 34.50"

This diagram depicts the side view of the glory hole. It gives you an idea of how the glory hole looks front to back. Pay particular attention to the front face ring. This ring helps the glory hole retain its heat when it is fully open. The ring should be at least 2" thick. Cast it in place after laying the brick. If cast correctly, it should lock itself in place. See the next page for casting the front heat retaining ring.

Casting the Heat Retaining Ring

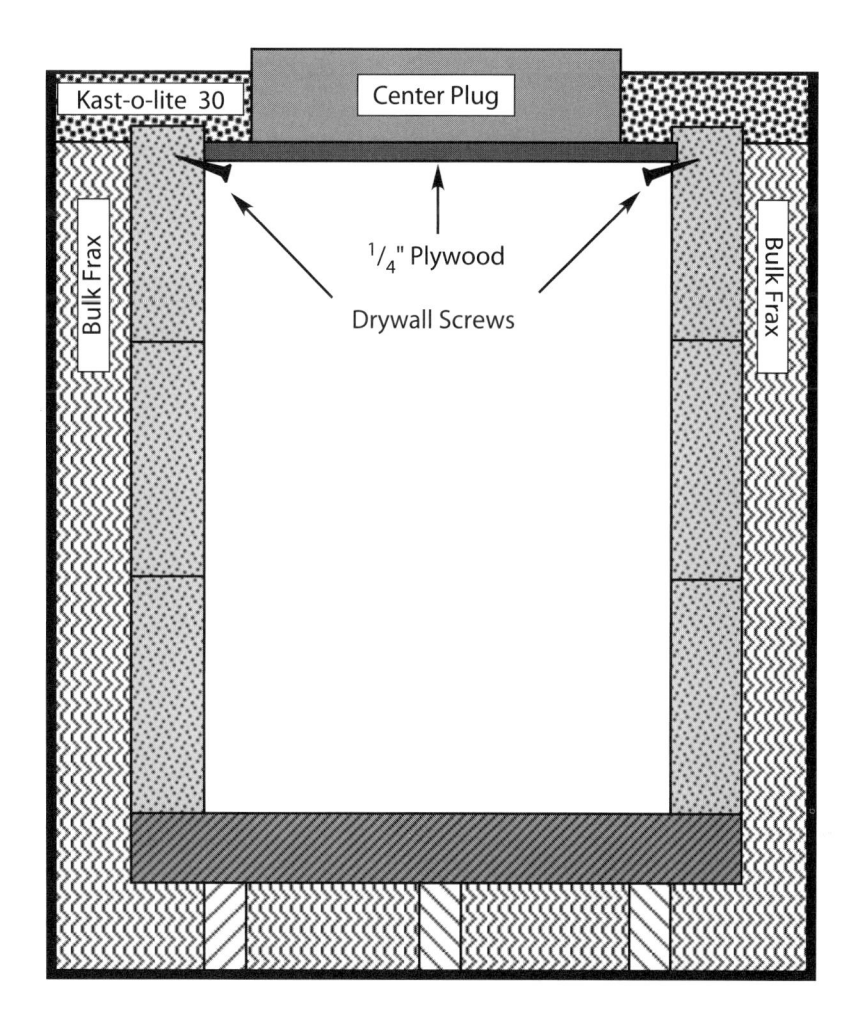

(Diagram labels: Kast-o-lite 30, Center Plug, Bulk Frax, Bulk Frax, ¼" Plywood, Drywall Screws)

The next and last step after building the body of the glory hole is to cast the front heat retaining ring. This is actually very simple to do.

Take a straight edge and put it across the drum, measure down about 2 ¼", and put a mark on every other brick. Put a 1 ½" drywall screw into the bricks at each mark. Allow the screw to stick out about ¾". Cut a piece of ¼" plywood to fit down inside the bricks. The plywood should sit on the drywall screws. Next, place a styrofoam plug 16" in diameter by 2" centered and on top of the ¼" plywood. Before casting the ring, make sure the fiber and IFB are wet. Dry absorbent materials will suck the water from the castable and make it rather weak. Finally, cast the front disc in place with Kast-O-Lite 30. The diagram above is fairly clear concerning this process. When the disc has set (24 hours or more) remove the center ring and carefully cut away the plywood. Don't force it!

Materials Needed for Doors and Stand

From W.W. Grainger

- 4 Castors (4X783)
- 4 Castor Brakes (4X825)
- 4 Lock Collars ⅝" i.d. (2X569). Sold in packs of 3 -- 2 packs needed.

From assorted sources

- 16 - ⁵⁄₁₆" x 1 ¼" fine thread bolts w/nuts and lock washers
- 80' - 2" x 2" x ³⁄₁₆" angle iron
- 10' - ½" solid round rod
- 18" - 3 ½" x ¼" flat stock
- 2 bags of Kast-O-Lite 30

Making a Stand

Cut from 2" x 2" x 2" x ³⁄₁₆" angle iron

- 5 pcs. 35" long
- 6 pcs. 33" long
- 2 pcs. 50 ½" long
- 2 pcs. 17" long

The first thing to do is lay out 2 of the 35" pcs. with 2 of the 33" pcs. on a flat table or floor to make a rectangle 35 ½" x 33 ½". Overlap the ends as indicated. When welding, it is important that everything is square. Use a good steel right angle to check yourself and make sure you only tack weld everything before doing the final welds. The tack welds will permit you to change things if they are not square or if you make a mistake. This is very important. Good craftsmanship and good technique do count.

Frames

1.
Tack weld the front as indicated

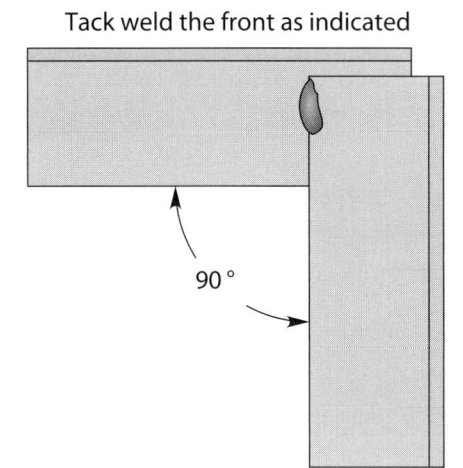

90°

2.
Flip frame over and weld the top sides

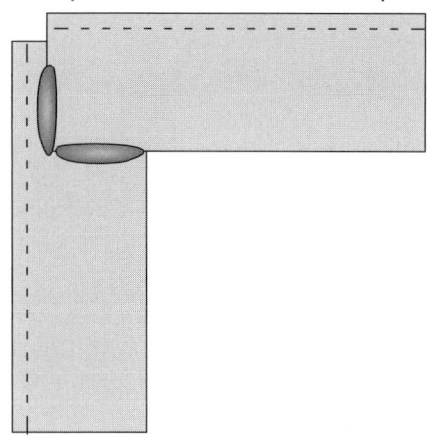

3.
This is the back of the frame

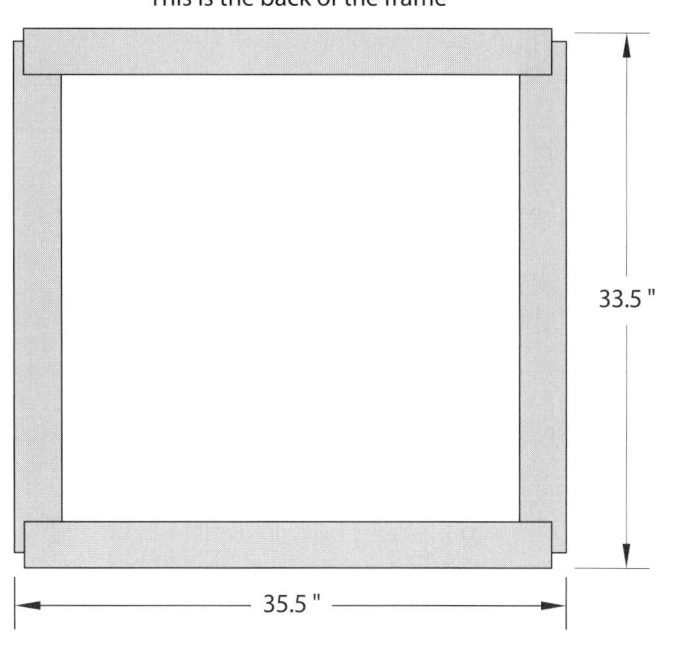

33.5 "

35.5 "

The Glory Hole Stand

Weld the legs to the two frames. Clamp and tack weld one side at a time and then make sure it is all square. When you are sure it's square, weld the stand completely. Always visually check your work.

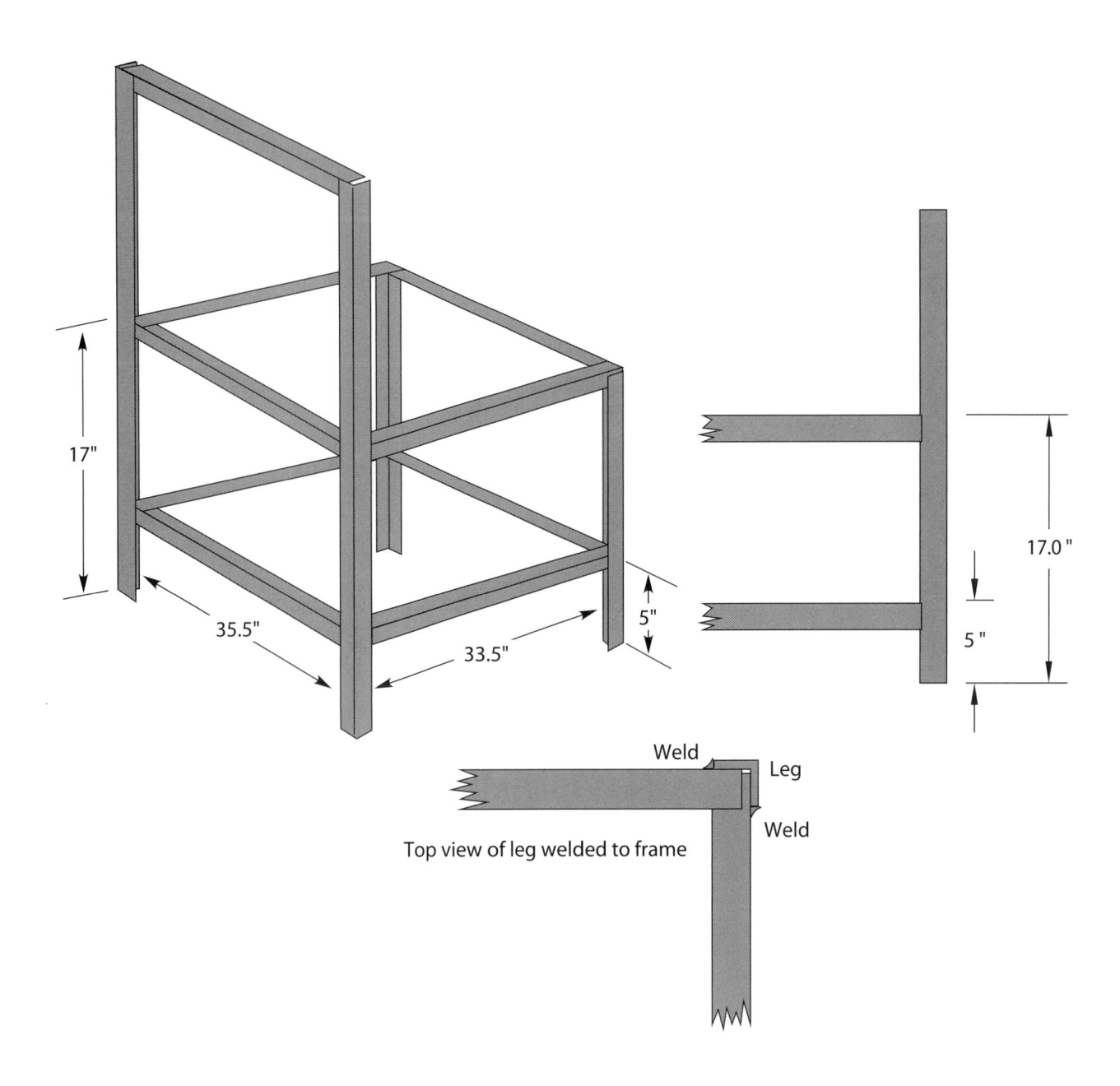

17"

35.5"

33.5"

5"

17.0"

5"

Weld

Leg

Weld

Top view of leg welded to frame

Cut 4 pcs. from 3 ½" x ¼" flat stock 4 ½" long and drill 4 ⅜" holes in each. Weld these to the bottom of the legs. Bolt on the wheels with the 5⁄16" x 1 ¼" bolts and lock washers.

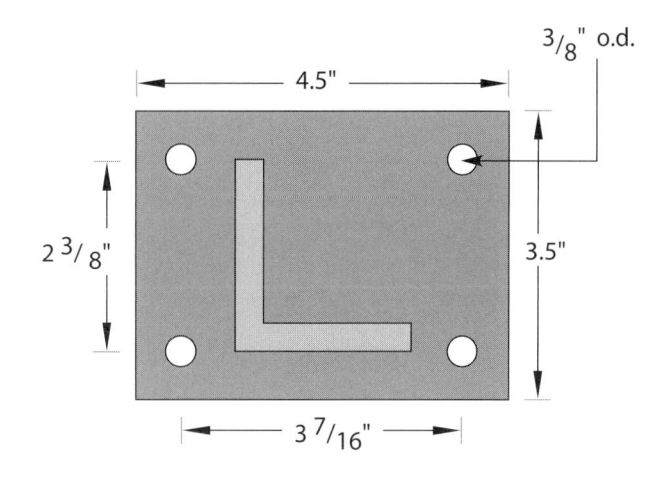

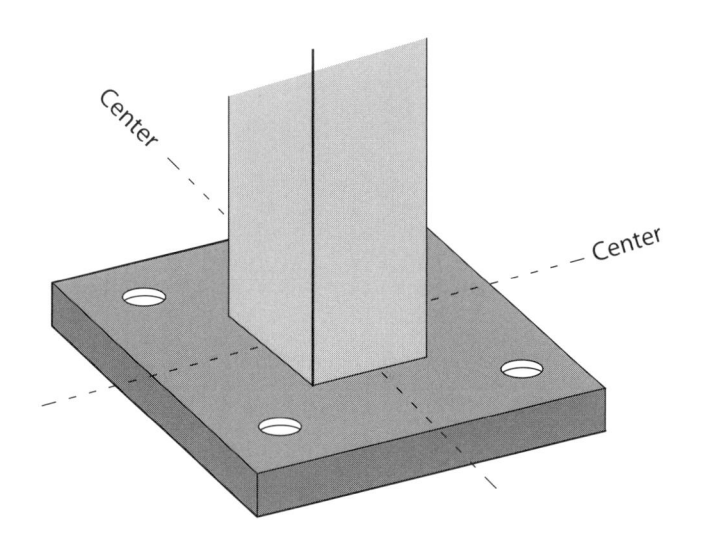

Lift the finished gloryhole drum on the stand. Be careful--the drum is very heavy, especially if it is still wet. The front face of the glory hole should stick out past the front legs about ½".

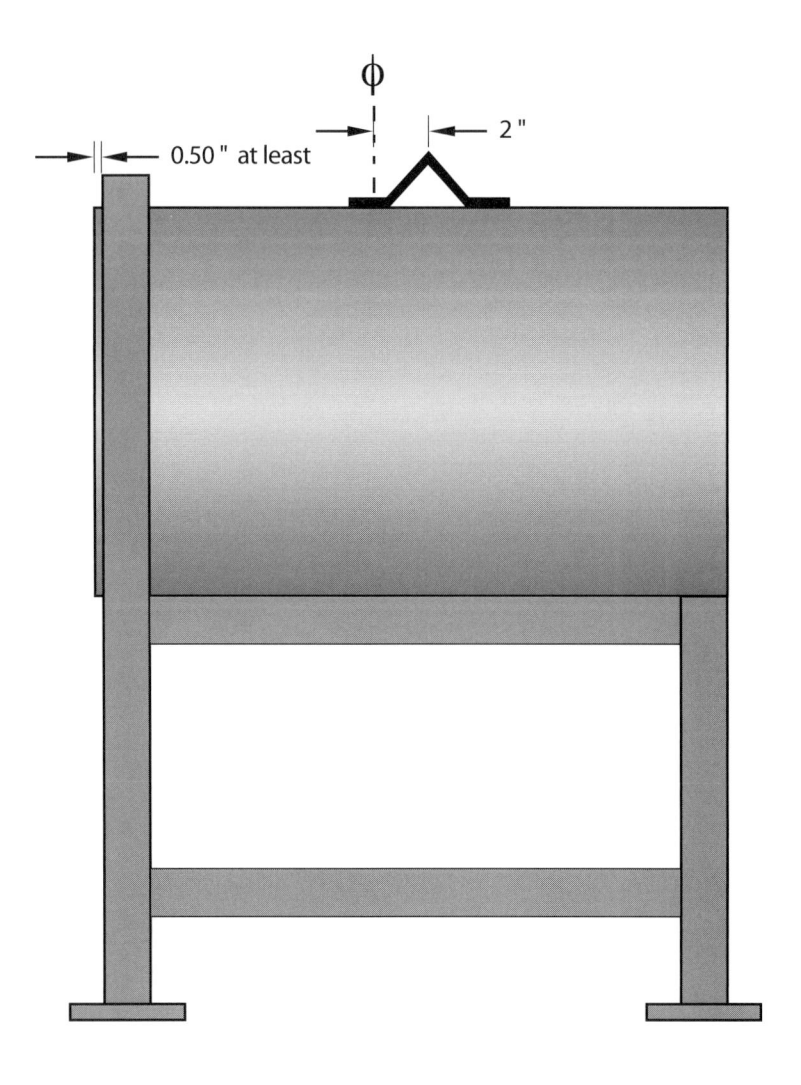

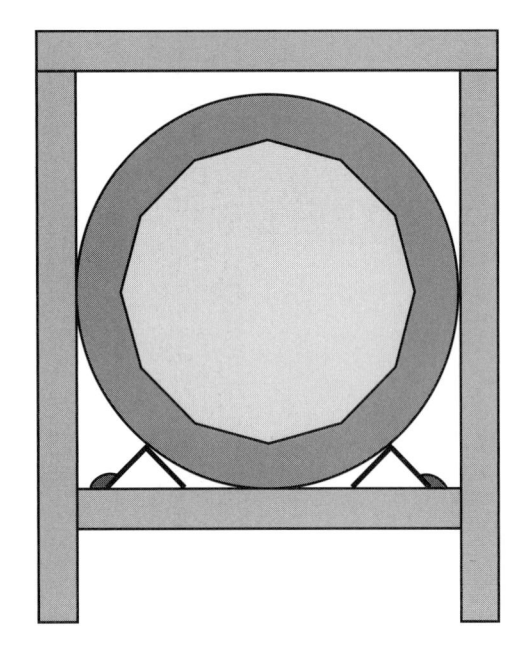

Weld the last two 33 ½" pieces of angle to the stand, one on each side of the drum, as chocks to keep it in place. Don't weld the chocks to the drum until the drum is properly lined up and centered.

208 Glass Notes

The Doors

Use 2" x 2" x 3/16" angle iron

- 4 pcs. 11" long
- 2 pcs. 22" long
- 4 pcs. 8" long
- 2 pcs. 16" long
- 2 pcs 16 3/8" long
- 2 pcs. 22 3/8" long
- 8 pcs. 3" long

The corners need to be mitred. Cut the pieces to length and then cut the mitres with a good cut-off saw.

Author's note: A good 14" cut–off saw is a necessity in any shop. It is really the best tool for making accurate cuts in steel. A power hack saw will do the job as well, but they are very expensive.

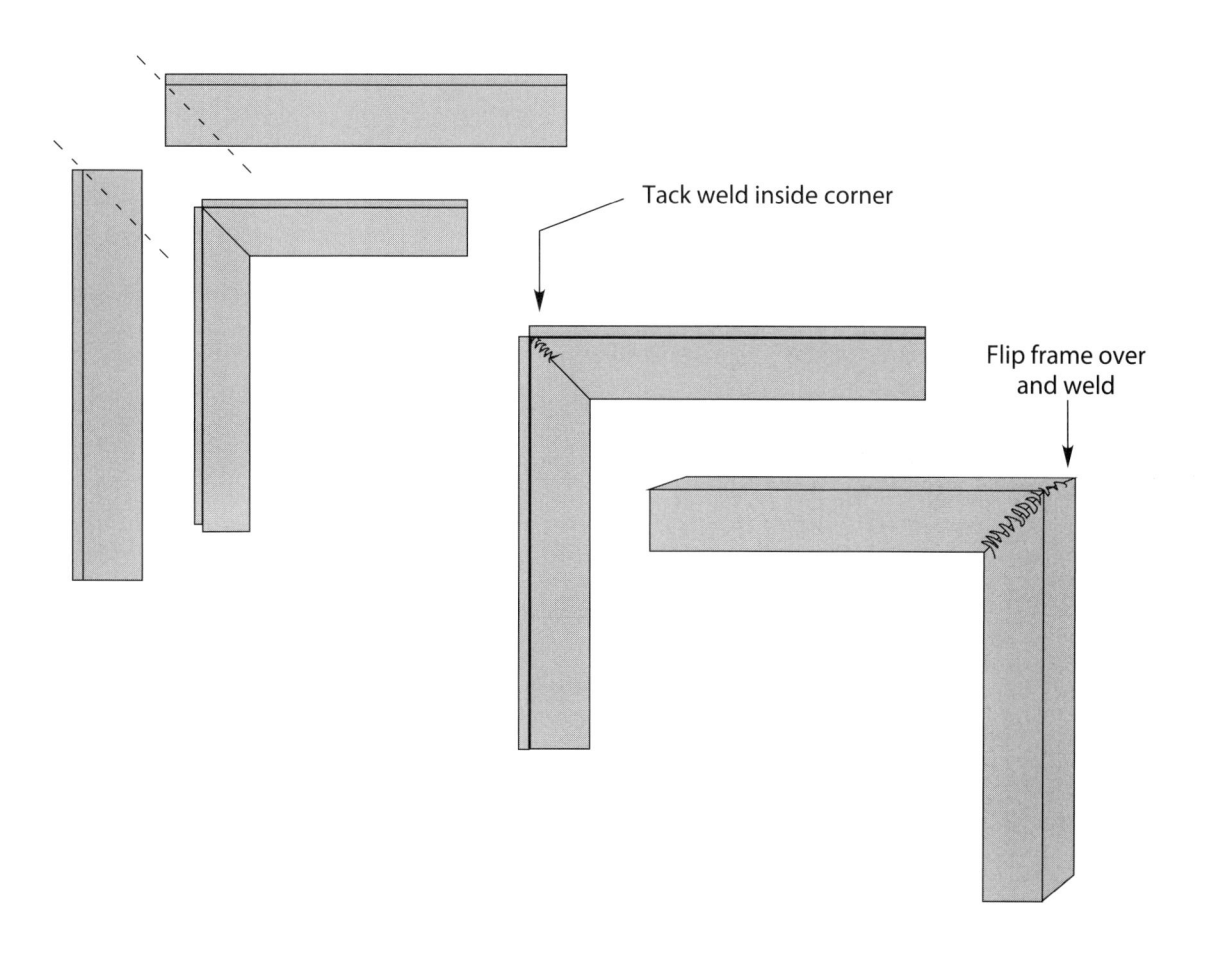

Make two each of the following frames.

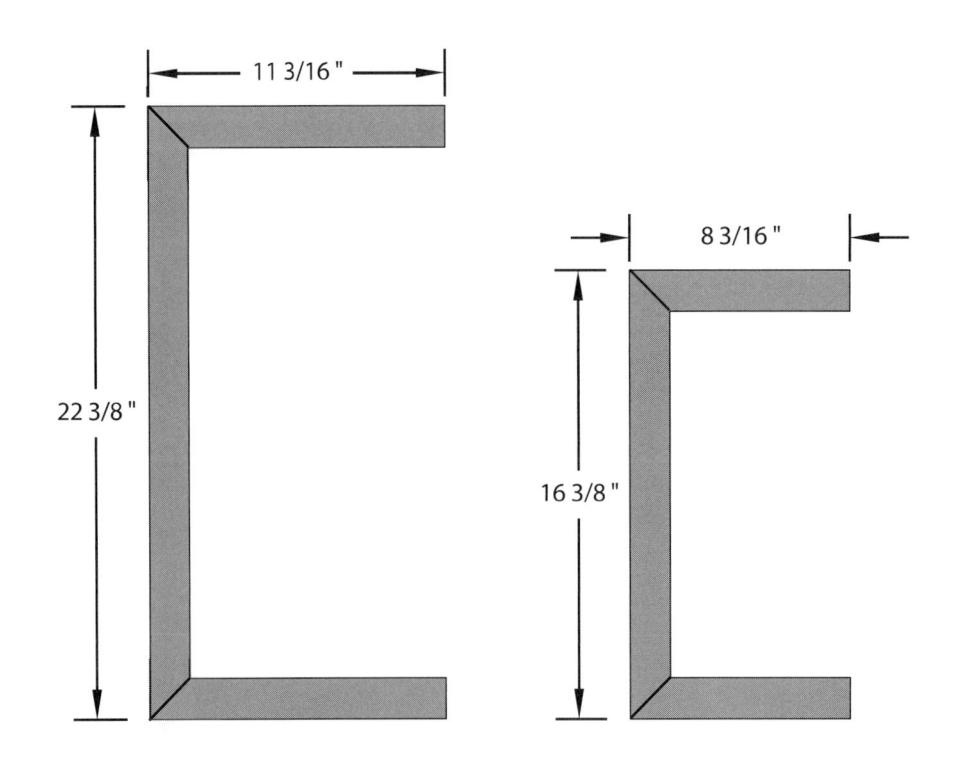

11 3/16 "

22 3/8 "

8 3/16 "

16 3/8 "

Stainless rods welded into the frame keeps the glory hole door from falling out.

Cast Door

Front

Cutaway view of cast glory hole door

This view depicts the glory hole door frame with the ½" s.s. rod welded in place. When the door is cast, the rods hold the casting in place. There are other methods for holding the castable in place, but I found this to be a very simple solution.

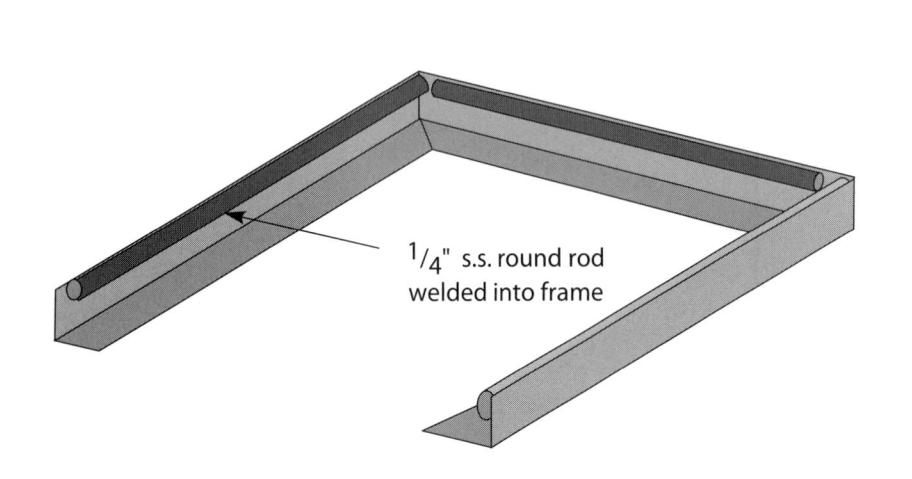

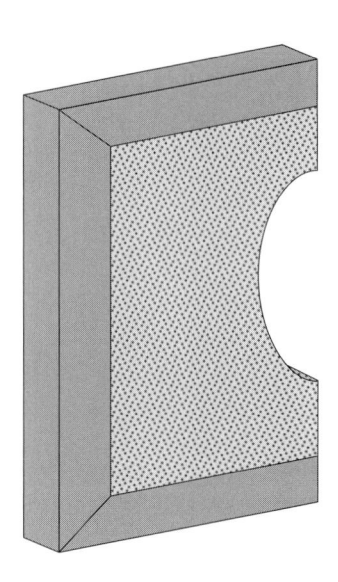

¼" s.s. round rod welded into frame

210 Glass Notes

Molds for Cast Door

Stack and laminate plywood to about 2" to 2 ½". Cut out 2 circles, one 10" and one 4". Cut these circles in half. Cut 2 pieces of angle iron 22 ⅜" long and 2 pieces 16 ⅜" long. Drill holes through the angle iron near the center of each. Screw the plywood "half moons" to the angle iron.

Put at least 4 layers of 2" tar paper strips on each half moon. Tack weld the molds to the door frames that you constructed. Make sure you only lightly tack them. They will be removed after the castable has set. You are now ready to cast the doors. Put some plastic or tar paper under the doors before casting. Make sure you do the casting on a flat surface. Cast the doors from Kast-O-Lite 30 or a comparable product. After the Kast-O-Lite 30 has set (at least 24 hours) cut through the tape holding the tar paper and grind through the tacks. Carefully remove the molds.

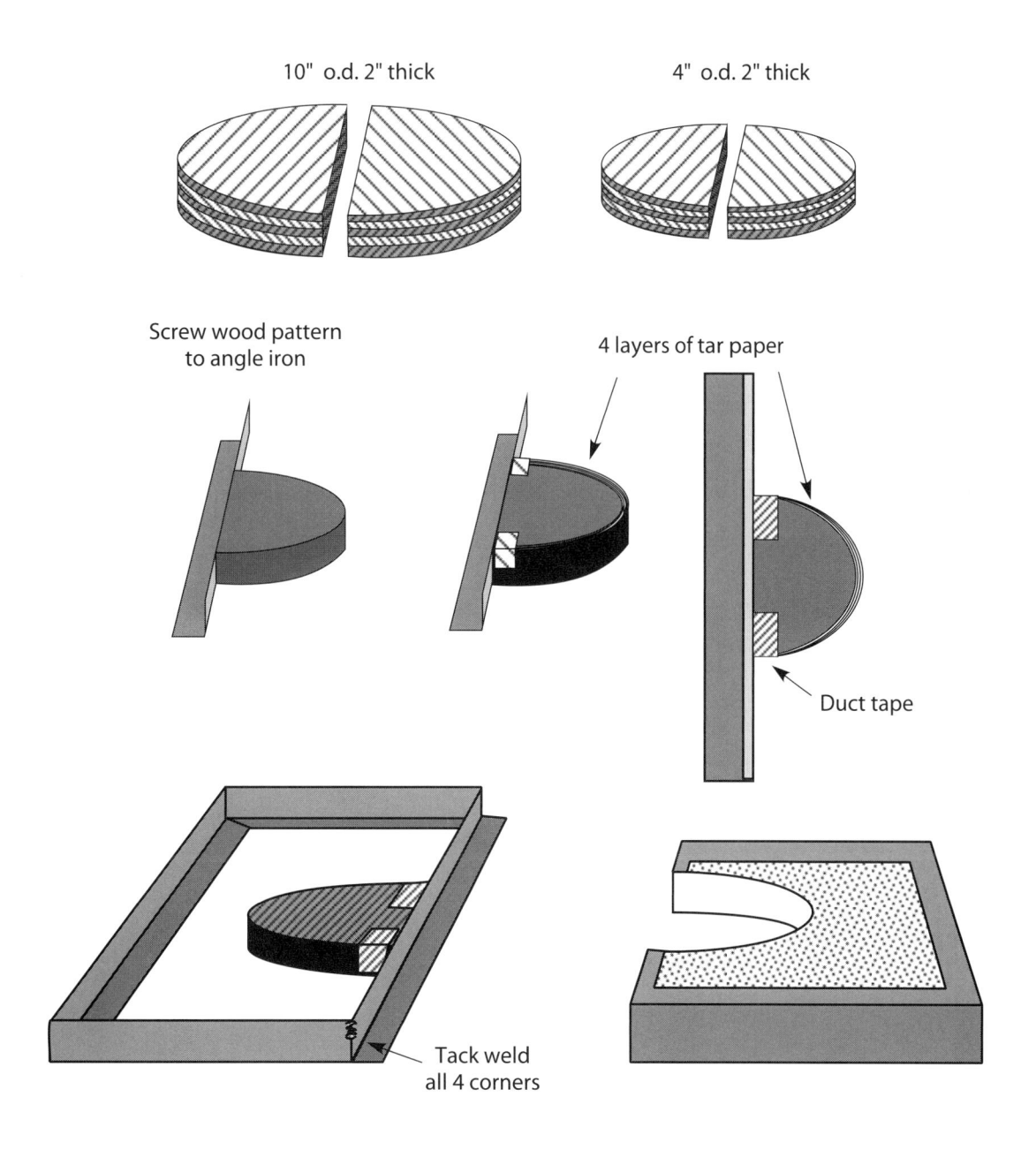

10" o.d. 2" thick

4" o.d. 2" thick

Screw wood pattern to angle iron

4 layers of tar paper

Duct tape

Tack weld all 4 corners

Glass Notes 211

The Hinges

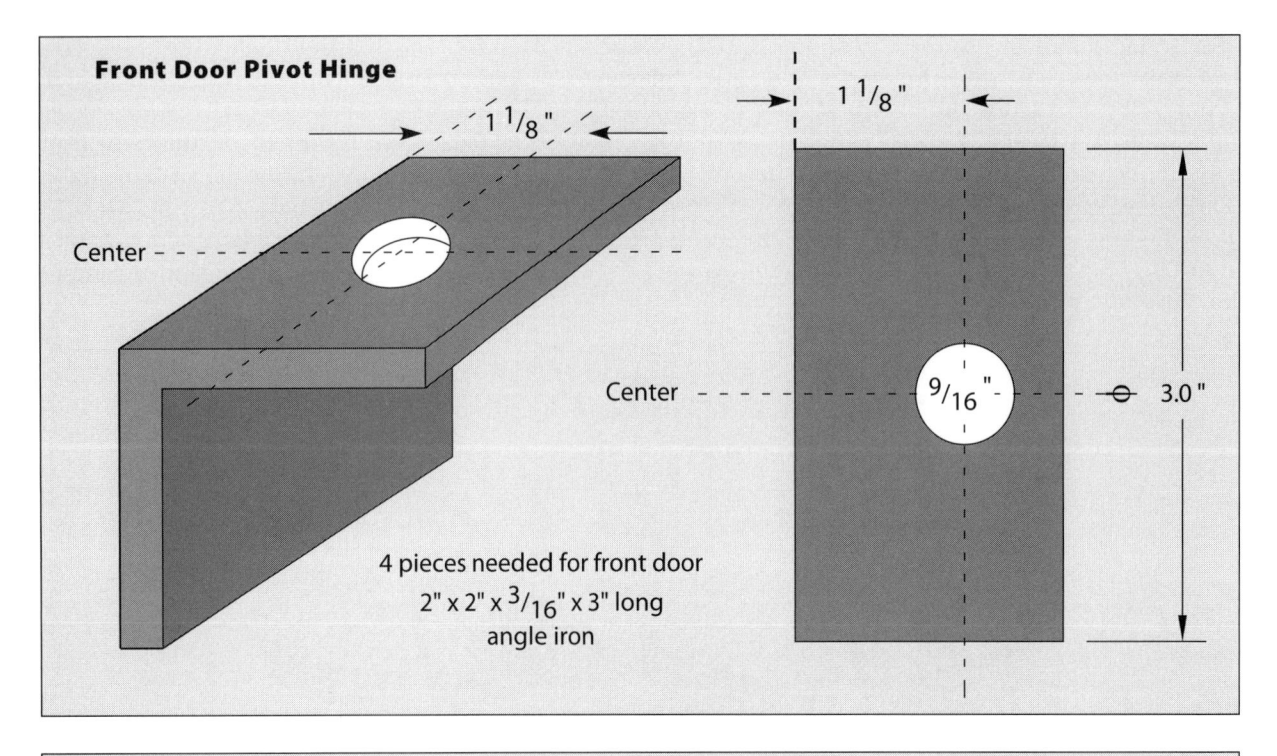

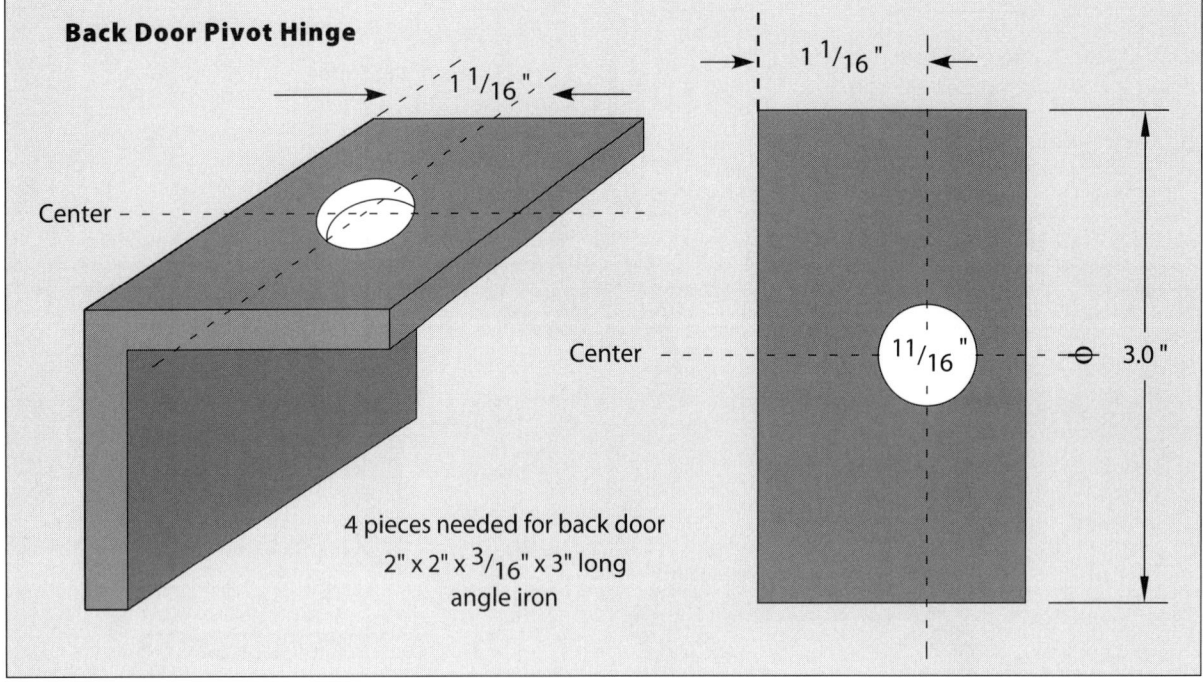

Front Door Pivot Hinge

1 1/8 "

Center

1 1/8 "

Center

9/16 "

3.0 "

4 pieces needed for front door
2" x 2" x 3/16" x 3" long
angle iron

Back Door Pivot Hinge

1 1/16 "

Center

1 1/16 "

Center

11/16 "

3.0 "

4 pieces needed for back door
2" x 2" x 3/16" x 3" long
angle iron

Cut from angle iron and drill as indicated

Cut from ½" solid round steel rod:

- 4 pcs. 10" long
- 4 pcs. 6" long
- 4 pcs 1 ½" long

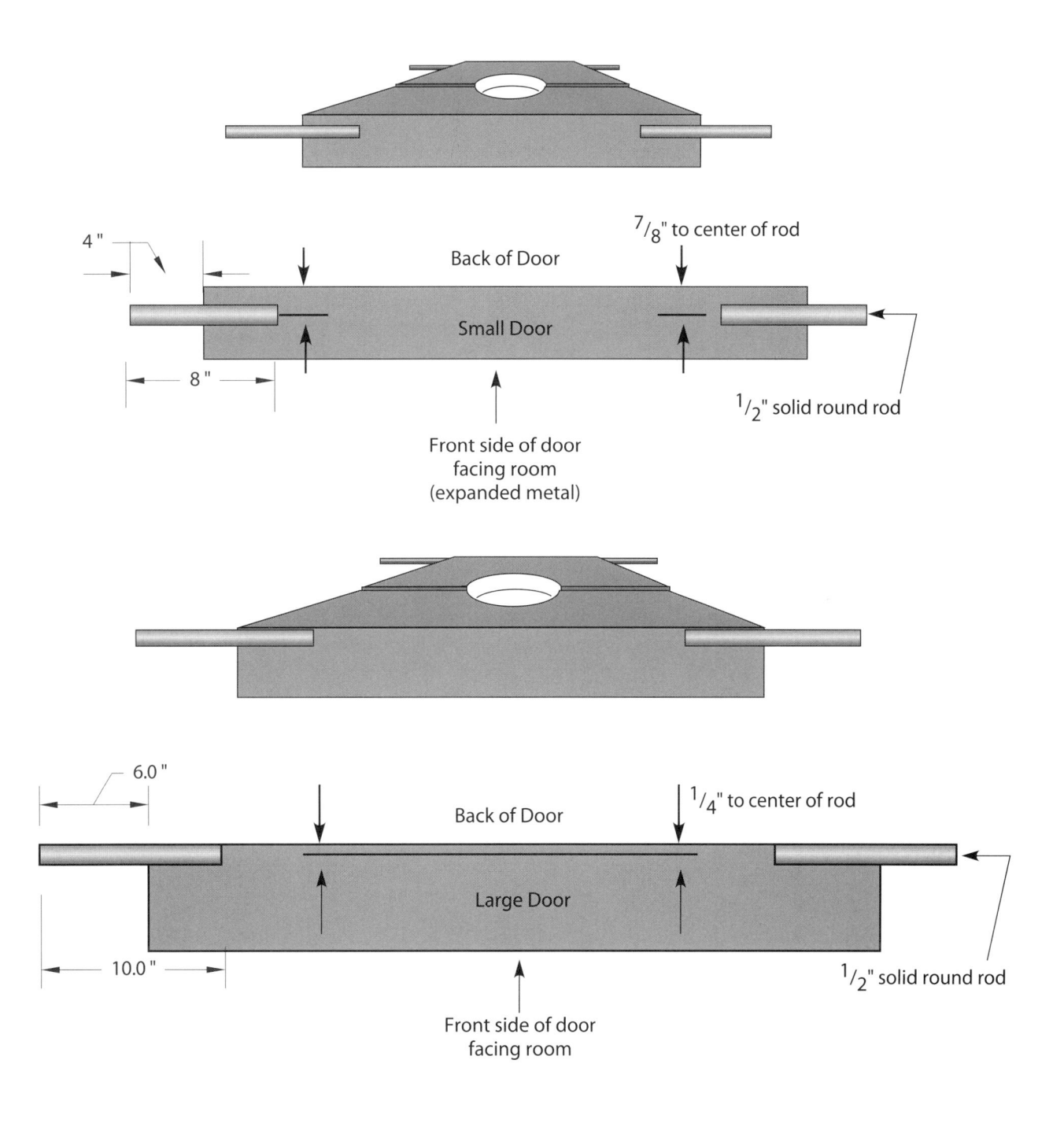

4"

Back of Door

$7/8$" to center of rod

Small Door

8"

$1/2$" solid round rod

Front side of door facing room
(expanded metal)

6.0"

Back of Door

$1/4$" to center of rod

Large Door

10.0"

$1/2$" solid round rod

Front side of door facing room

Glass Notes 213

Final Assembly

Lay the two large doors on a flat surface with the outside surface up. Lay the two smaller doors on top of the large ones. Slide one of the pieces of angle that you cut and drilled over each rod of the small doors. Make sure the doors are lined up correctly. Weld the angle iron in place. Lay the bottom hinges in place and weld in place.

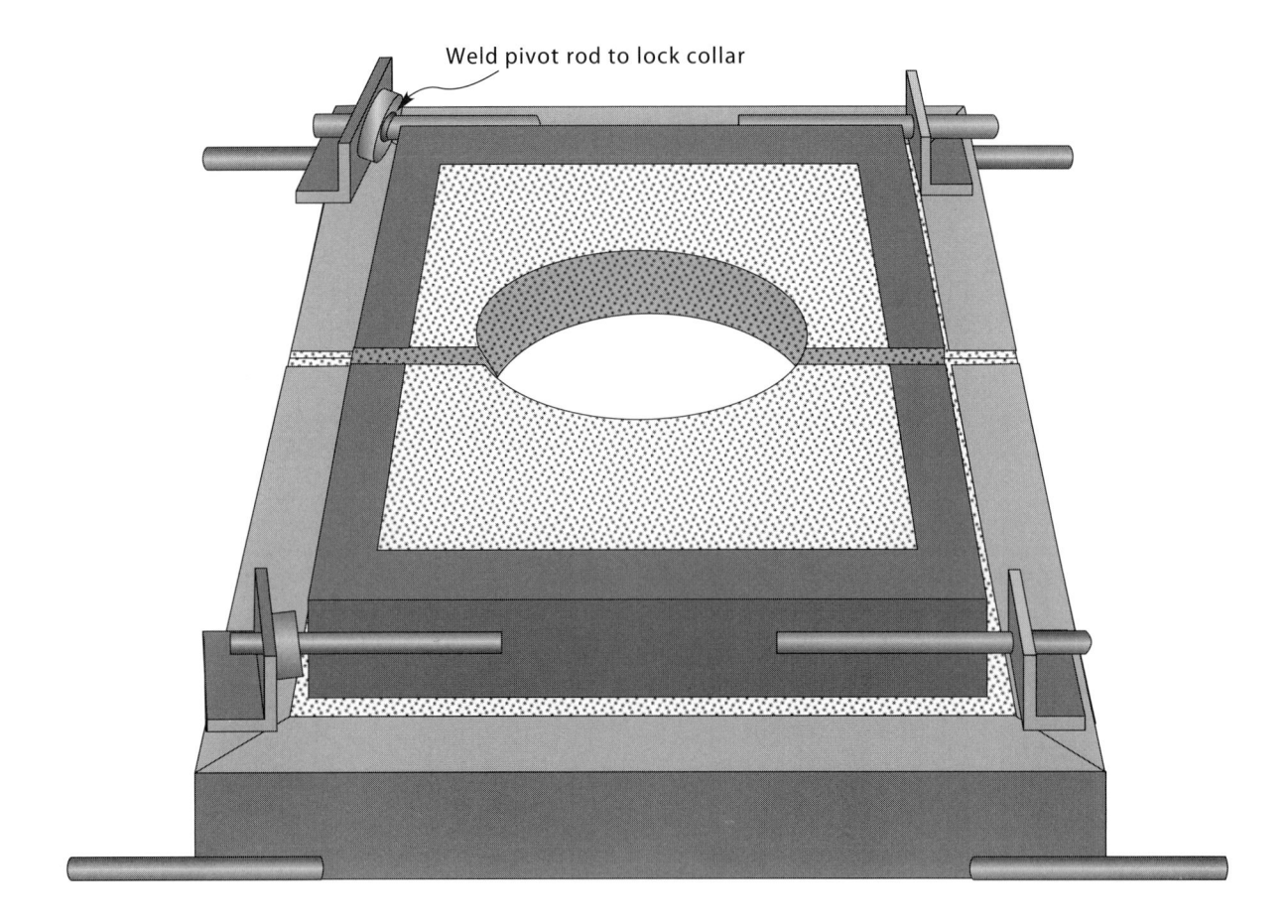

Weld pivot rod to lock collar

Hanging the Doors

It is now time to hang the doors on the stand. Use sturdy clamps to hold the angle iron "hinges" in place. Make sure your placement of the doors is exactly where you want them. Do not make your final welds before you're sure of the door placement. When you're sure you have the correct door placement, make good sturdy welds. Because of the angle of the lock collar, you may have to ream it out slightly. The angle of the lock collar creates friction so that the doors will stay open or closed. Details of circled objects on next page.

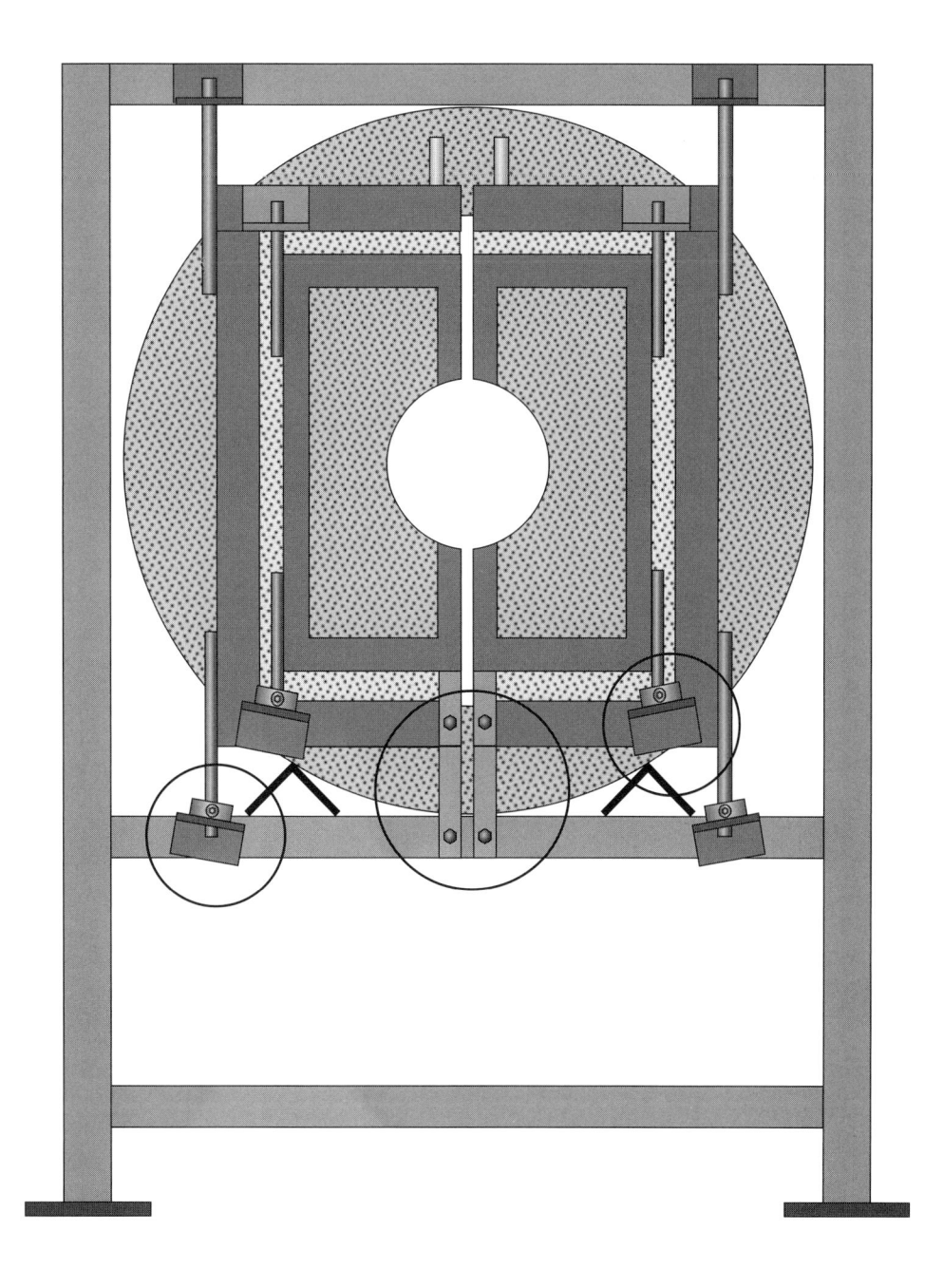

Door Pivot Hinge & Door Stop Spacers

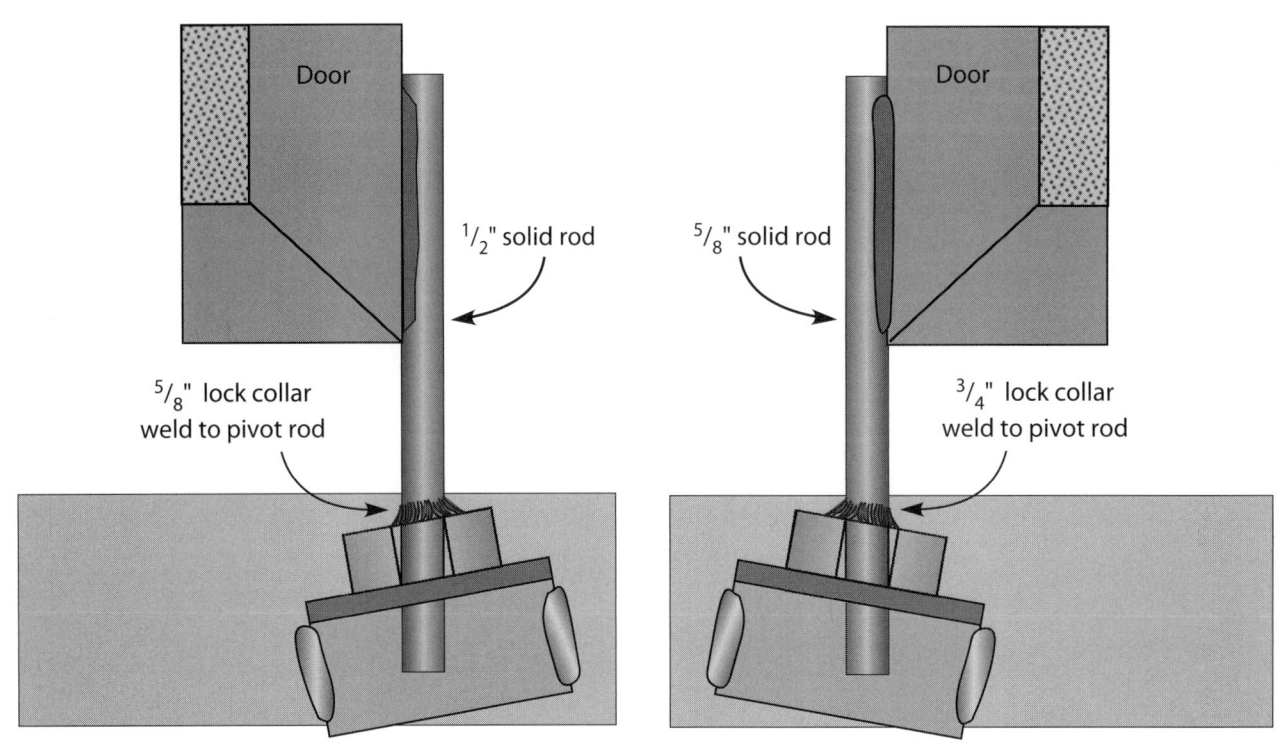

Door — $1/2$" solid rod — $5/8$" lock collar weld to pivot rod

Door — $5/8$" solid rod — $3/4$" lock collar weld to pivot rod

Front Door Pivot Detail

Back Door Pivot Detail

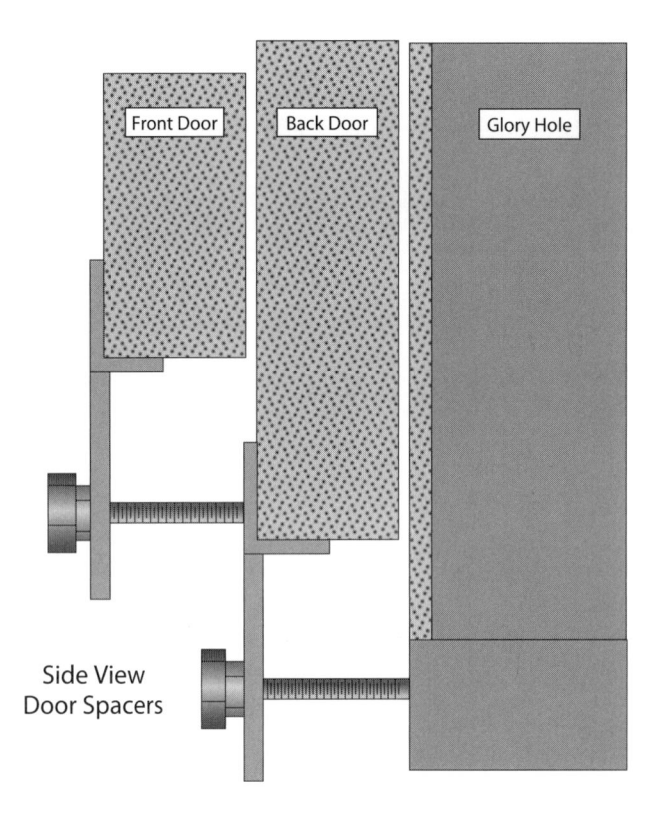

Front Door | Back Door | Glory Hole

Side View
Door Spacers

These drawings are not to scale

216 Glass Notes

Door Openers & a Burner Block

The last step is to weld the four 1 ½" x ½" solid steel rod pieces to the top of each door. Weld them about 1 ½" from the center.

You're now ready to fire up this beauty. It is very important that your first heat is slow. If you go too fast, you may crack your doors. There is a great deal of residual moisture in the glory hole. "Slow and steady wins the race."

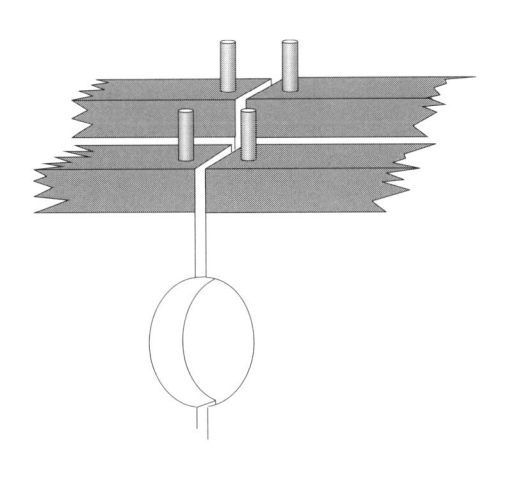

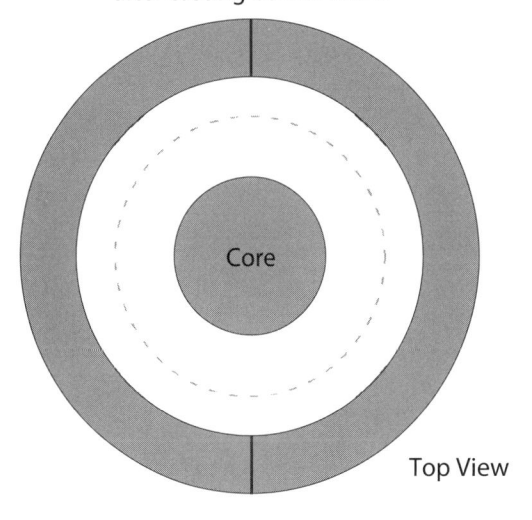

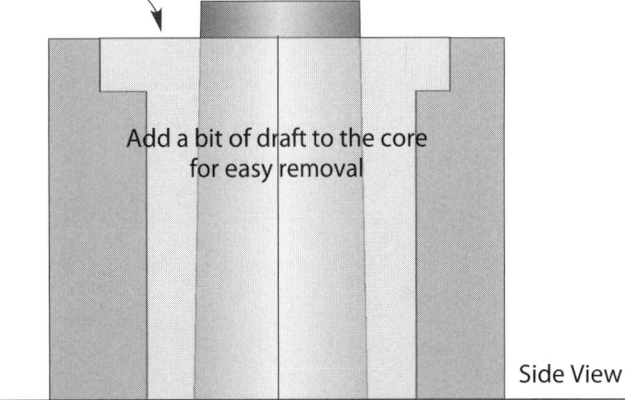

This burner block mold is fairly simple to construct and is designed for a retention style tip (Giberson, Wilton, Spiral Arts). Turn the core model as well as a full sized model of the burner block on a wood lathe or create from hard foam. The next step is to make a plaster cast of the burner block model. Make sure you cast it in two sections as indicted in the diagram. The core is placed in the center of the outer form. Make sure to secure the outer mold and core in place so that they do not move when casting.

Cut a hole through the barrel and through the brick in the side of the glory hole where the burner is to be placed. The burner block should fit snugly, and the flange should sit on the steel barrel. You're now ready to place the retention tip.

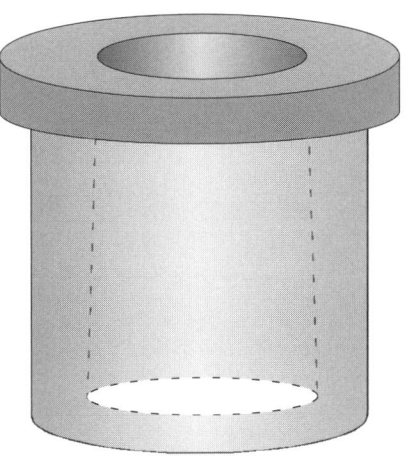

Outer form split to facilite removal after casting burner block

Top View

Castable goes in here
Core
Add a bit of draft to the core for easy removal
Side View
Attach mold to board to prevent shifting when pouring

Burner block for retention tip

Glass Notes 217

Another Burner Block

The drawings below show how to construct a wooden form for casting a burner block for the IFB Glory Hole. This burner block will only take up the room occupied by two bricks.

1. Place two bricks that have been cut to the same angle as the brick that comprises the liner on a piece of plywood, and trace around them (fig. 1, below).
2. Cut out two of these; they will be the ends of the burner block mold.
3. Assemble the sides and bottom as indicated in fig. 2 below. You now have a mold that will take the place of 2 bricks.
4. Make a plug for your burner from clay, foam, wood or clay (fig.3). Place the plug in the wooden form (fig. 3) and cast with a good high alumina castable.

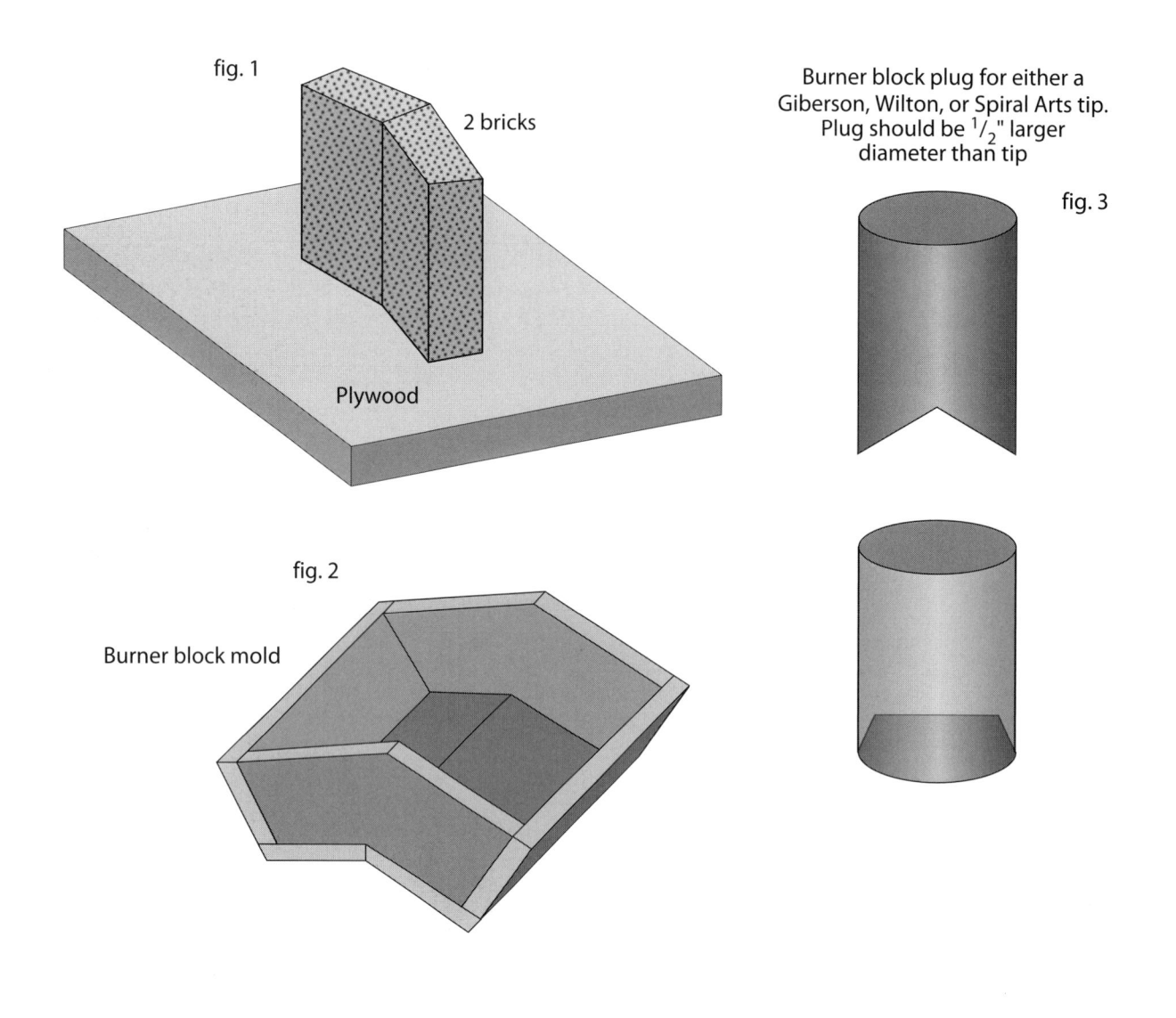

fig. 1

2 bricks

Plywood

Burner block plug for either a Giberson, Wilton, or Spiral Arts tip. Plug should be $1/2$" larger diameter than tip

fig. 3

fig. 2

Burner block mold

The Square Glory Hole

According to Tom Ash

Tom asks the question, "why a square glory hole?" Conventional wisdom has said to build a round glory hole, mount a high velocity burner head on the tangent, and use the resulting vortex action to spread the flame along the length of the hole. This approach does work, but it has a few drawbacks. First, the turbulent vortex action creates an objectionable amount of noise. Second, it tends to push a good deal of heat out the front of the hole. Third, it rarely heats the hole evenly. Finally, if one part of the structure fails, the entire glory hole must be rebuilt.

The ribbon burner has allowed the designer to take a new look at glory hole construction. Since this burner introduces heat into the hole at low velocity over a wide area, it does not need a vortex action to heat the hole evenly. In fact, if the wall opposite the burner is flat, the vortex action is almost eliminated. The result is a very low noise level with a minimum of heat pushed out the front opening. Another advantage of the square glory hole is that it is built in a modular fashion, using a variety of different materials. All materials have strong points and weak points when used in glory hole construction (refractory castables have excellent strength but aren't great insulators; frax and insulating board don't take glass contact well; square firebrick do not lend themselves to round construction, etc.). The square glory hole allows the builder to use a number of different materials, placing each where their strong points are used to best advantage. This modular approach also allows the components of the hole to be repaired or replaced individually. If the floor wears out, or the door degrades, or the roof arch fails, they can be fixed as a separate component -- without having to rebuild the entire glory hole. See page 236 for information on the Ash Ribbon Burner.

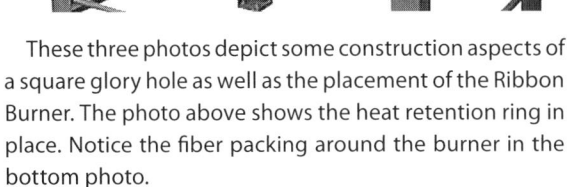

These three photos depict some construction aspects of a square glory hole as well as the placement of the Ribbon Burner. The photo above shows the heat retention ring in place. Notice the fiber packing around the burner in the bottom photo.

Contact info:
Pine Ridge Enterprises
PO Box 121
Paradise, CA 95967
Tel. (530) 877-9793
Email: pineridge@earthlink.com

Pine Ridge Square Glory Hole

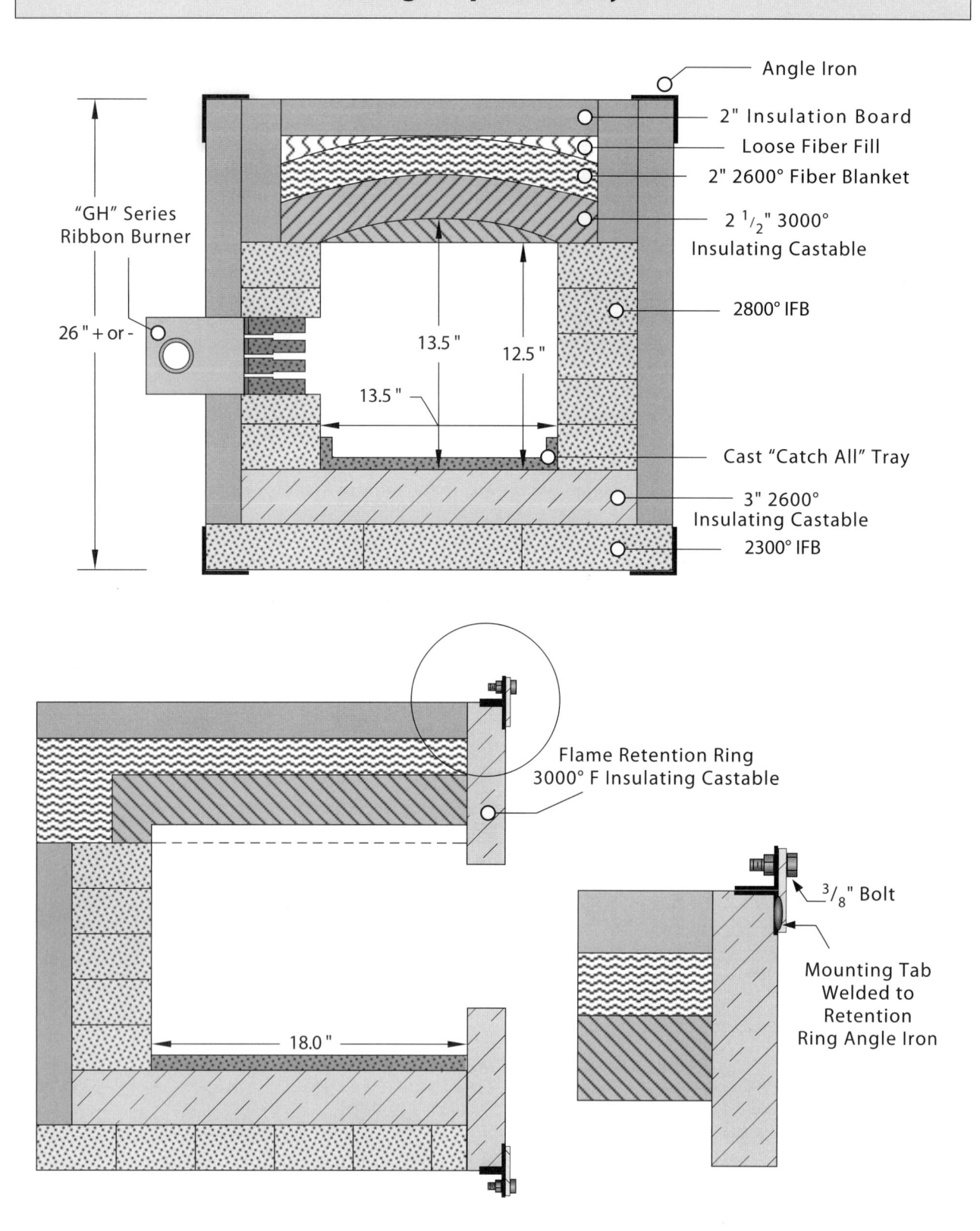

- Angle Iron
- 2" Insulation Board
- Loose Fiber Fill
- 2" 2600° Fiber Blanket
- 2 1/2" 3000° Insulating Castable
- 2800° IFB
- Cast "Catch All" Tray
- 3" 2600° Insulating Castable
- 2300° IFB

"GH" Series Ribbon Burner

26 " + or -

13.5 "
13.5 "
12.5 "

Flame Retention Ring 3000° F Insulating Castable

18.0 "

3/8" Bolt

Mounting Tab Welded to Retention Ring Angle Iron

The original plans for this glory hole came from Tom Ash. I have made a few changes to the refractory materials, but essentially the drawings are accurate to Tom's dimensions and layout. It should be obvious that this glory hole can be scaled to meet your particular needs. It is fairly easy to build, and as Tom says, " If the floor wears out, or the door degrades, or the roof arch fails, they can be fixed as a separate component--without having to rebuild the entire glory hole."

Pine Ridge Parabolic Rolling Door

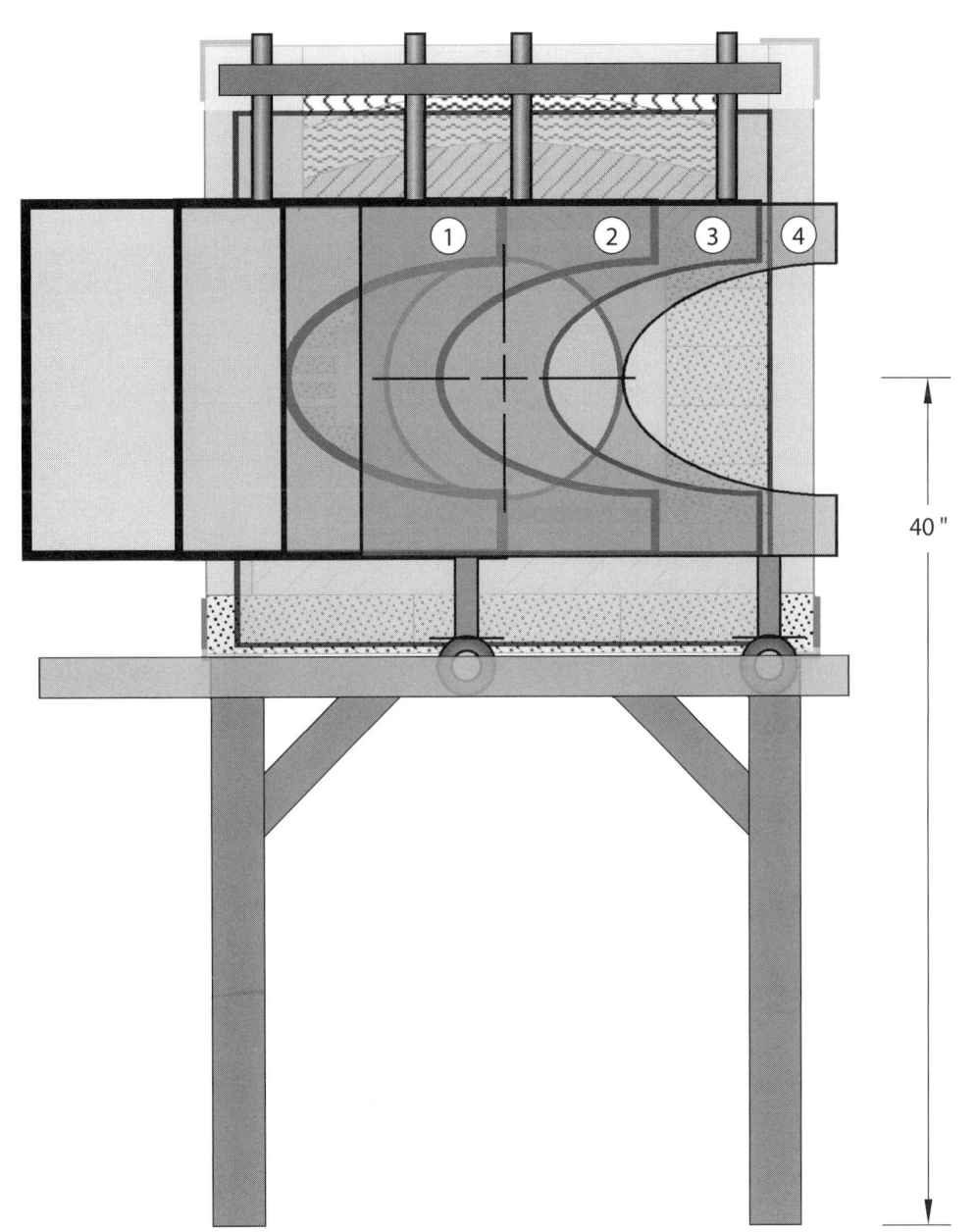

The height from the floor to the center of the glory hole I have placed at 40" (102 cm) but can obviously be varied to suit your needs.

40 "

The door depicted here operates on almost the same principal as a camera shutter. The door has an endless variety of positions capable of suiting the exact size opening needed. I've depicted four positions: full open, ¾ open, ¾ closed, and fully closed. There is one problem with this door system as I see it: when using a rolling yolk, the center of the door opening will move from right to left as you work the piece from small gathers to a larger piece. You should be on center when your piece is large. I have placed a cross hair to show true center. If this is a problem, then I would recommend the standard double glory hole door.

For this transverse door, it would be simple to create a pneumatic system to regulate the door position using a foot pedal. An advantage to this system is that the door can be fully closed prior to use, which in turn builds up heat at a quicker rate than the standard type of hinged door.

A variation to this style of door that does maintain true center would have the same shutter type system but the door would move vertically rather than horizontally. I have seen a foot-operated pneumatic vertical system on the glory holes at the Pittsburgh Glass Center.

The Garage

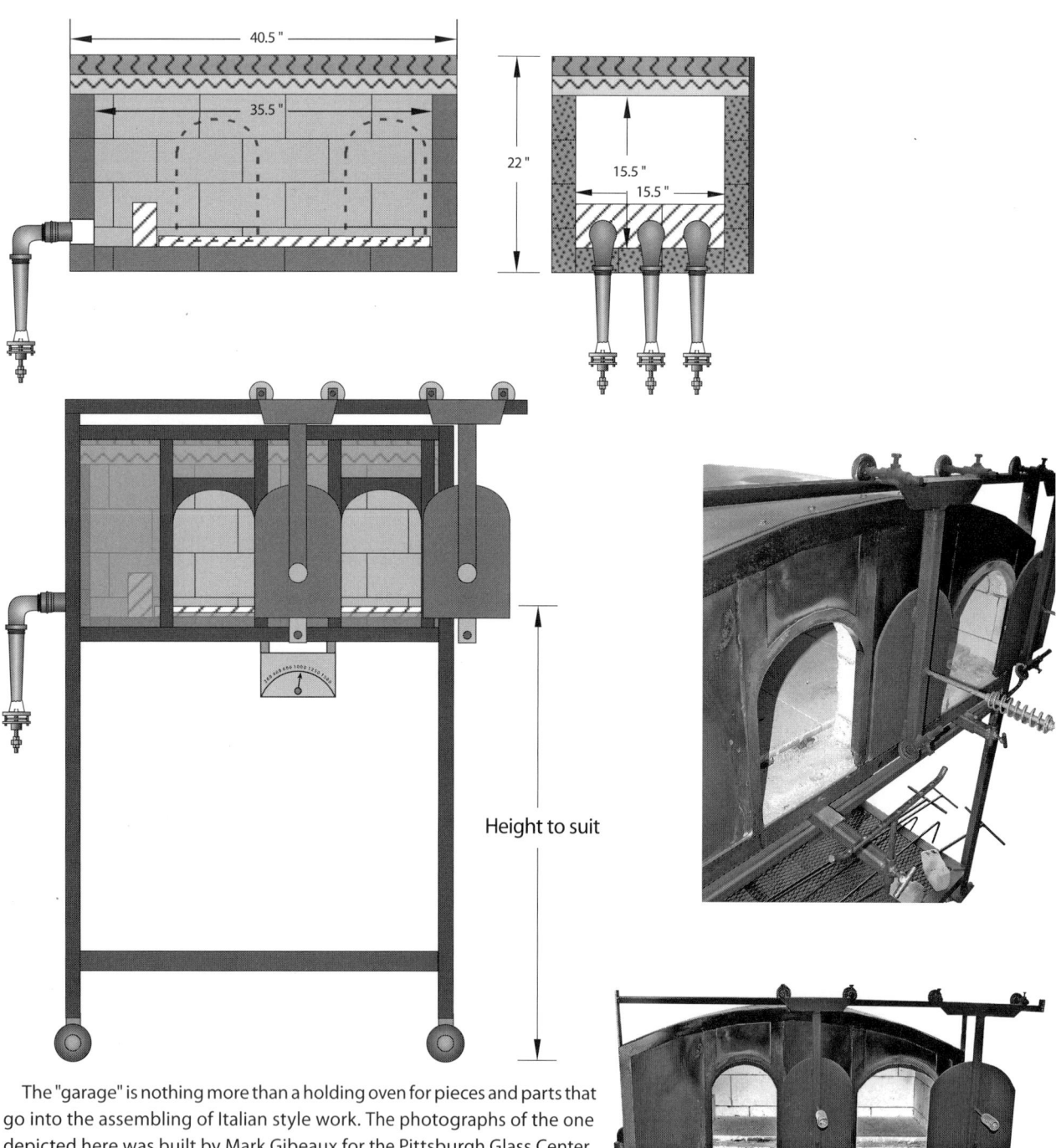

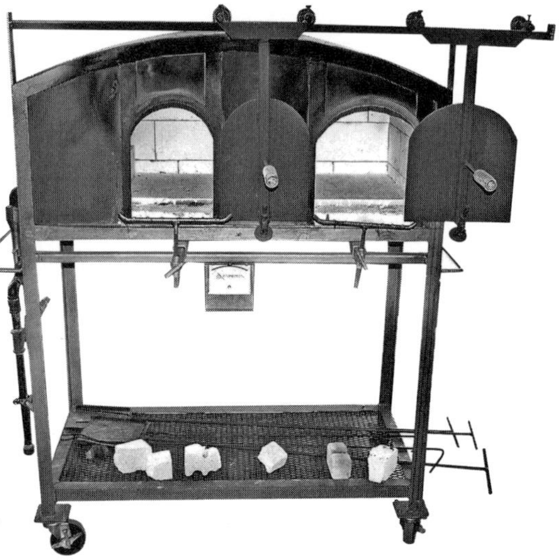

The "garage" is nothing more than a holding oven for pieces and parts that go into the assembling of Italian style work. The photographs of the one depicted here was built by Mark Gibeaux for the Pittsburgh Glass Center. His design is fairly typical. I have modified his crown design from an arch to a flat roof. The oven is constructed from 2000° IFB. The crown can be a good dense grade of fiber board or Skamol Vermiculite Board with a backup of Skamol Silicate Board. I recommend using hangers (pg. 251, 275) to hold the crown in place. This particular model is propane fired and has three small burners. It can be fired with natural gas as well, with the appropriate burner. The doors slide and are used to balance the heat. There are usually two heat zones; one zone has a holding temperature and the other a slightly higher temperature where the piece is moved prior to removing for placement.

Burners & Flame Safety

Chapter Contents

Burners	224
About Burners	225
Combustion of Fuel	226
Atmospheric Regulator with Premix Aspirator Mixer	233
Alfred Style Burner	234
Giberson Style Burner	235
Ribbon Burner	236
NFPA Requirements for Gas Burner Systems	237
Piping Schematic Drawing of Burner System	238
NFPA Approved	238
Flame Safety	239

Burners

The information on the following pages will hopefully help you understand burners and burner systems. We have come a long way from our crude "Labino" burner system to our Eclipse side-fired, nozzle-mix, recuperative-ultra safe, computer-controlled systems. To some degree sophisticated systems existed at the beginning of the studio glass movement, but it has taken us many years to apply them to our studio furnaces. With the cost of energy rising to new heights every month, it is imperative that you find a burner system that will save you money in order to keep your studio operational. The following pages will outline different types of burners and systems as well as where they can be purchased or, if you're handy, how you can construct them.

Although the drawing below was done in the early 70's by Fritz, this system is still used by many studios today. There have been advances in flame safety since Fritz penned this drawing. Although the "purple peeper" is expensive to install, it is approved in all 50 states as part of a safety system for what is known as "open flame" safety (see pg. 237-238 for up-to-date flame safety information). What is not approved in Fritz's drawing are the wheels on the furnaces. Earthquakes come to mind. Safety is your responsibility. Check with your burner engineer or local fire inspector for your code requirements. Every state has different fire safety codes for open flame equipment. If you do not follow the codes in your state, it may void your fire insurance.

The Dreisbach Toledo System as Drawn by Fritz

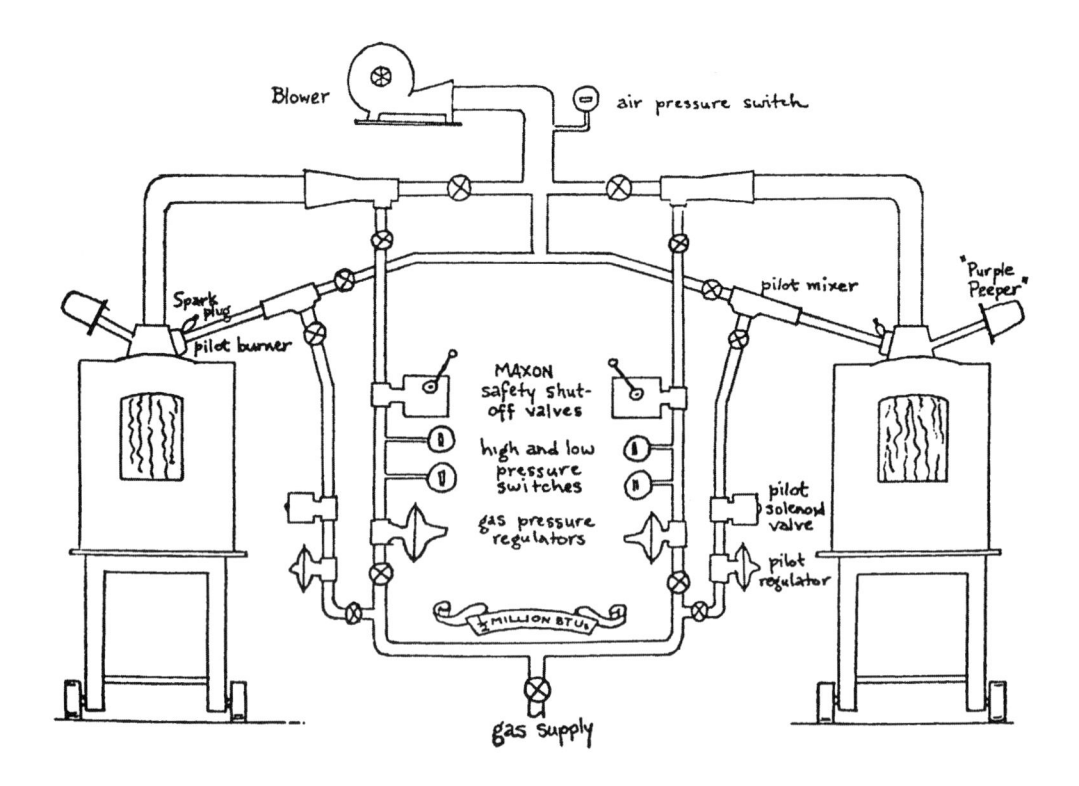

About Burners

Now that your furnace or glory hole is built, it needs a burner system. Not just any burner, but a burner that is just right for your particular furnace or glory hole. This section should help you to understand how burner systems operate as well as how they are configured. I have used, with permission, information contained in *The North American Combustion Handbook*. This 500-page book is considered by many to be the definitive text on combustion and burner technology. For those of you who want more information on combustion, I recommend this text (pg. 233). I have also used specific product information to explain different parts of the burner system. My main focus is on systems that are most applicable to the studio glass artist. Burner systems seem to be the least understood aspect of the glass studio. In the long run, it is the energy consumed by your burner that comprises your greatest single overhead expense. A poorly designed burner system will eventually cost you a great deal of money. I must admit it took a lot of research to compile accurate information for this chapter. However, there is a considerable amount of complex information concerning burner systems that is not contained in this chapter. What you will find is a general overview of information that should help you engineer the correct burner system for your application.

What is Combustion?

Combustion, or burning, is a rapid combination of oxygen with a fuel resulting in release of heat. The oxygen comes from the air, which is about 21% oxygen and 78% nitrogen by volume. It is an established law of science that matter is neither created nor destroyed in the process of combustion and that the heat given off in any combustion process is merely excess energy that the new molecules are forced to liberate because of their internal makeup. Perfect combustion is obtained by mixing the right proportions of fuel and oxygen so that nothing is left over.

If too much oxygen is supplied (excess air) we say that the mixture is lean and therefore is oxidizing. This results in a flame that tends to be shorter and clearer. If too much fuel (or not enough oxygen) is supplied, we say that the mixture is rich and therefore is reducing. This results in a flame that tends to be large and sometimes smoky. For the glass artist, there are circumstances that require either an oxidizing or reducing flame. The oxygen supply for combustion usually comes from the air. Because air contains a large proportion of nitrogen, the required volume of air is much larger than the required volume of pure oxygen. The nitrogen in the air does not take part in the combustion reaction--it just goes along for the ride.

Here are some important points to remember about burner combustion. *Primary* air is that air which is mixed with the fuel at (or in) the burner. *Secondary* air is usually that air brought in around the burner. *Tertiary* air is usually that air brought in downstream of secondary air or through other openings in the furnace.

Combustion of Fuel

Good combustion requires:

1. Proper proportioning of fuel and air.
2. Thorough mixing of the fuel and air.
3. Initial and sustained ignition of the mixture.

These, together with flame positioning, are the functions of a combustion system.

What does a good burner system control? Basically, 1, 2, and 3, above.

Liquid fuel (propane) is usually evaporated, and the resulting combustible vapors when combined with air burn as a gas. Natural gas is supplied as a vapor and when combined with air will burn. Oil is atomized. Atomization of the liquid oil produces millions of tiny liquid particles, thus providing a large amount of surface to combine with oxygen and combust. This section will not deal with oil or oil burners.

Ignition: Made possible by the combining of our fuel, in this case gas, with oxygen. This is commonly referred to as oxidation. Ignition occurs by the addition of an external source of heat (flame pilot light) until the reaction itself releases heat faster than heat is lost to the surroundings.

The heat released by the chemical combination of a fuel with air:

1. Heats up the combustion products and the incoming fuel–air mixture.
2. Radiates to the surroundings.
3. Is carried away by direct contact with the surroundings.

Naturally, the flame temperature is highest when the losses to the surroundings are smallest. Additions of excess air or excess fuel only provide more material to absorb the heat of combustion so that the flame temperature cannot go as high as with a perfect fuel–air mixture. This is similar to a home heating furnace which will heat a small house to 68° F (20° C) but a large house to only 60° F (15.6° C). Remember that an efficient burner system will only be as efficient as your glass furnace. High fuel bills may be the result of poorly insulated or poorly constructed furnaces and not a inefficient burner system.

It is also possible to over insulate. Over insulation below the glass line will result in premature wearing of the liner, except in the case of AZS refractories. The *Combustion Handbook* states very clearly that a small amount of excess air to excess fuel can greatly reduce the flame temperature. The table provided in the book shows us that 16.2% excess air lowers the flame temperature by 262° F (145° C). If high flame and furnace temperature is desired, accurate fuel/air ratio control is most critical.

Different types of fuel contain various amounts of energy measured either in Btu's or kilocalories. In the U.S.A. we usually measure in Btu's (British thermal units). A Btu is the quantity of heat required to raise the temperature of one pound of water one degree Fahrenheit. A kilocalorie is the quantity of heat needed to raise one kilogram of water one degree Celsius. A furnace that has a glass capacity of 200 lbs. requires fewer Btu's to achieve temperature than a furnace with a 400–lb. capacity. The 400–lb. furnace, however, will not necessarily require twice the number of Btu's to achieve the same temperature.

Another area of concern is flame speed. In stable burner flames, the flame front appears to be stationary. This is because the flame is moving toward the burner with the same speed that the fuel-air mixture is coming out of the burner. If the fuel-air mixture is fed into the burner at too fast a rate, the flame may blow off. If the fuel–air mixture is fed into the burner at too slow a rate, the flame may flashback into the burner. **Flashback can be very dangerous if the proper safety equipment is not installed.** The flame may flashback as far as the mixing point, or it may be quenched by the cool burner wall.

All the proceeding information could be considered a very basic primer on combustion. You should now have an understanding of what burners are designed to do and how they do it. Some burner systems are more efficient than others. It does not pay to be stingy when constructing a burner system There is more to a burner system than just the tip. I have seen many studios using *efficient burner tips* on very inefficient burner systems and vice versa. All parts of a burner system must be balanced in relation to your energy requirements. In the days of cheap energy, many people didn't care how much energy their burners consumed. A good example of this is the West Virginia glass factories. Most of them are out of business, because among a number of reasons, they did not modernize their burner systems and furnaces. Couple that with a poorly designed product and you have a recipe for disaster.

Nick's Burner

The first burner system we were introduced to was designed by Nick Labino. His design consisted of a black iron pipe inserted into a high temperature soft brick that had been crudely carved into a primitive venturi style burner block. A small blower, usually bought from the local W.W. Grainger store (part number 2C781 and still available), was attached to a flange bought at the local hardware store. I remember the part number because I bought so many of them to replace the burned out ones. We screwed a 1 ¼" pipe into the flange and attached a pipe "T" somewhere along the run. The gas line went in one end of the "T" and the burner tip at the end of the run. As I recall, they were very difficult to light. Nick used this type of burner to his dying day. He swore by them. They were quiet and, to be honest, I think they were rather efficient in their own crude way, although I can't prove it. Nick said they were. The next discovery we made was the flame retention tip. This tip design revolutionized our burner system because you only had to screw one of these beauties onto the end of your burner system and it lit and got hot as hell--no burner block required. Unfortunately, they are noisy, inefficient, and burn up if they get too close to the furnace. They are inefficient because they depend on secondary air for proper combustion. The Giberson, Wilton, and Spiral Arts burner tips are flame retention styled tips that differ from the cast iron variety. These tips are constructed from high temperature castable refractory and do not depend on secondary air for proper combustion.

Insulation and Heat Transfer

Many questions arise that pertain to furnace insulation. Although this has nothing to do with burner systems, it certainly impacts the efficiency of your burner. Depending on the type of liner you melt glass in, it is possible to over–insulate if using alumina type tank liners (over–insulating below the glass line causes premature erosion of the refractory) and under–insulate (under–insulating creates a very inefficient furnace). It is no longer difficult to recommend the kind and quantity of insulation necessary to build an efficient furnace as there are computer programs that can calculate the efficiency.

Many schools and studios still build day tanks and pot furnaces without any knowledge of heat transfer through refractory walls. Most of us learned by trial and error. Technically, heat transfer is accomplished in the following manner. Heat flows into a furnace wall by a combination of radiation and convection from the flame and hot gasses. After the heat gets to the furnace wall, it may be:

1. Stored there, causing the wall temperature to rise;
2. Re-radiated to the load in the furnace; or
3. Transferred to the outer wall surface by conduction and then to the surroundings by convection and radiation.

After a wall reaches equilibrium (steady state, no more temperature change at any point) additional energy input is needed to heat the load in the furnace and balance losses through openings. The rate of heat absorption by a wall is greater at the beginning than when it is approaching equilibrium.

Btu's

Estimating the Btu requirement of a glass furnace is no easy task. There are some very complex formulas dealing with this issue. Most of us have determined Btu requirements through trial and error. The bottom line is: size your burner system to your Btu requirement. If your burner is undersized, you will never reach temperature; if you do manage to reach temperature, your recovery rate will be very poor. If your burner is oversized, it will consume more energy than is necessary and result in higher than normal fuel bills. On the next page is a good "seat of the pants" formula for estimating the Btu requirement of your furnace.

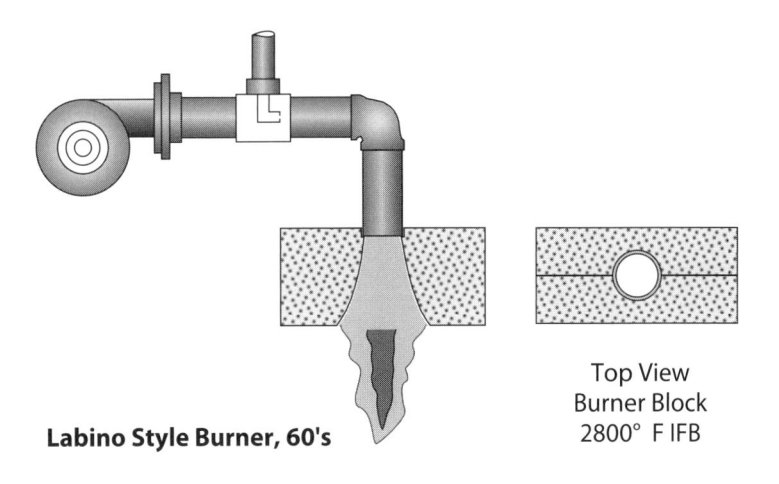

Labino Style Burner, 60's

Top View
Burner Block
2800° F IFB

Burners

The primary functions of a burner are flame positioning and continuous ignition maintenance (without a pilot). Many "burners" also perform a variety of other functions such as mixing the fuel and air, proportioning the fuel to air, supplying fuel and air at the proper rates and pressures, and facilitating the previous functions <u>with safety</u> at any rate required for the process. One of the major factors to consider when designing a burner system is its stability. This characteristic (stability) of burners is very important for safe, reliable operation. A stable burner is one that will maintain ignition, even when cold, throughout the range of pressures, input rates, and fuel/air ratios ordinarily used. No burner is considered stable merely because it is equipped with a pilot. Some burners

Determining Btu's
Our furnace dimensions are:
18" long x 18" wide x 12" deep

18" L x 18" W x 12" D

$$\frac{L" \times W" \times D}{1728} = 2.25 \text{ cu. ft.} \times 100,000$$

2.25 cu. ft. x 100,000 = 225,000 Btu's

will function satisfactorily under adverse conditions (particularly in cold surroundings) only if the mixture is rich and if the flame is burning in free air. With such unstable burners, it is necessary to keep the furnace door open from light-up until a stabilizing temperature develops in the combustion chamber. If the doors are not open, the free air in the furnace will be used up quickly, and an unstable burner flame will be extinguished. It is under these conditions that the presence of a pilot may be a potential source of danger because combustible gases will accumulate rapidly after the flame goes out and they will be ignited explosively by the pilot as soon as a pocket of the mixture in the combustion chamber enters the range between the flammability limits.

Burner Systems: Two major burner systems are worth examining. The first is the premix system. This system is the most common type of burner system found in the glass studio. The second type system is the nozzle mix system. In premix gas systems, the primary air and gas are mixed at some point upstream from the burner ports by an inspirator mixer, an aspirator mixer, or a mechanical mixer. The burner "nozzle" serves only as a flame holder, maintaining the flame in the desired location. The nozzle mix system does not require a premix as the gas and air are mixed in the burner assembly itself. *Author's note: It is important to understand the difference between a burner and a burner system. A gas burner is also referred to as a tip, burner and/or nozzle. A burner system is everything that is upstream from the nozzle. The burner system is what delivers*

| 100,000 Btu's of gas for every cubic foot of glass. |

the properly proportioned gas/air mixture.

Large port or pressure type gas burners permit a high rate of heat release within a relatively small space. There are many designs for this type of burner, but it is generally characterized by a single mixture port or "nozzle" that produces a short, intense flame. Most of the burners used by the studio glass artist are burners of this variety. They may be open or sealed in type. Air for proper combustion is usually supplied by a properly sized blower. The burner or tip, when used without a burner block, often includes a flame retaining feature (the ubiquitous Giberson Tip as well as the flame retention nozzle). All burner companies manufacture nozzles of this design. This flame retaining feature consists of a number of small bypass ports feeding into a recessed piloting ring encircling the main nozzle. These bypass ports have a greater resistance to flow than the main port, so the velocity in their exit ring is lower, and consequently, the tendency for the flame to blow off is greatly reduced. If any irregularity should cause the main flame to be blown off, the ring of flame, fed by the bypass ports, serves as a pilot to relight the main flame. This style tip is referred to as a flame retention burner or a self-piloting burner. The stability of this style nozzle makes possible a large range of turn down ratios. That is, small lower temperature flames are achievable without flame out. This is important when preheating a furnace. Let us examine some of these systems.

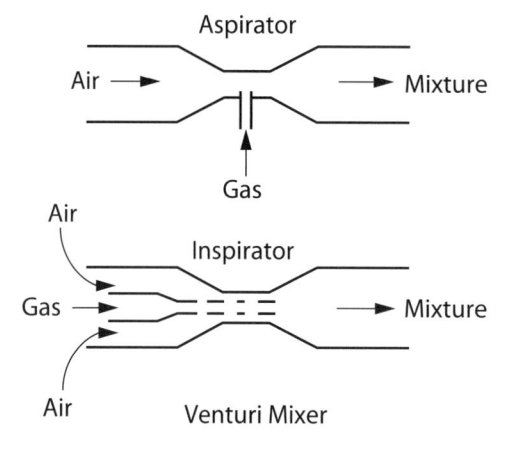

Inspirator: The first is an inspirator (or gas-jet venturi mixer) which utilizes the energy in the gas to induce primary air in proportion to the gas flow. This is the only type of mixer with which no air blower is required. The use of these burners in industry (which includes our glass furnaces) is limited to cases where high pressure gas is available, the reason being that for this style burner to operate efficiently, propane gas pressures above 5 psi are necessary and 10 psi are needed for natural gas. Studios using propane might use this type of mixing system. Most studios I know do not have natural gas pressures above 1 lb. If you had high pressure natural gas available, you would be required to install special gas lines to meet safety codes. The inspirator mixer on the preceding page demonstrates the function of an inspirator mixer. Inspirator mixers are not commonly used by glass studios.

Aspirator: The most common type of burner system used in the glass studio is the aspirator (or air-jet) mixer. This device mixes and proportions low pressure air (3 to 24 psi) and "zero gas" (gas at atmospheric pressure). The air flows through a venturi recent times, the nozzle mix burner has become rather common in studios as well as the university system. It is the nozzle mix system that permits the usage of recuperators. The Eclipse Burner Co. has a series of nozzle mix burners sized for the studio glass and university programs. Their system is called ThermJet. According to the "Combustion Technology Manual," the nozzle mix burner can be evaluated as follows: A Nozzle Mix Burner differs from a Pre-Mix Burner in that the air and the fuel are kept separate until the **point of ignition**. A Pre-Mix burner would require the mixing of the fuel with the combustion air prior to its' entrance to the burner head (Giberson, Wilton, Spiral Arts, Ribbon, etc.).

With a Nozzle Mix Burner it is virtually impossible for flashback or backfire to occur in the burner housing and supply system. The design allows for wider turndown, greater stability, more variety of

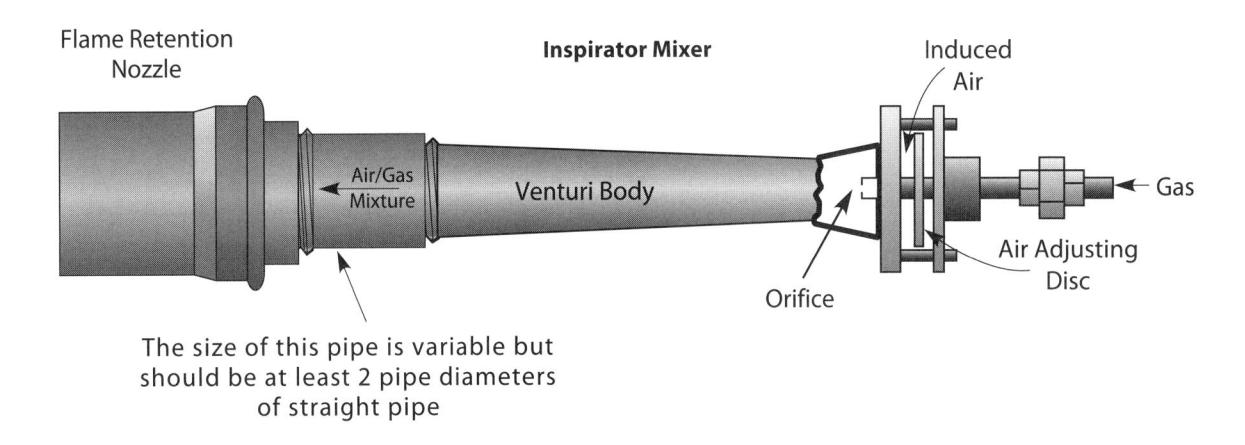

Inspirator Mixer

Flame Retention Nozzle — Air/Gas Mixture — Venturi Body — Orifice — Induced Air — Air Adjusting Disc — Gas

The size of this pipe is variable but should be at least 2 pipe diameters of straight pipe

so that the low pressure at the throat of the venturi induces gas into the air stream in proportion to the air flow. Controlling the air flow thus controls the gas flow, giving proper proportioning with single (air) valve control. An adjustable limiting orifice permits manual setting of air-gas ratio.

Mechanical: The next is a type of mixer known as a premix system (or mechanical mixer). In this type mixer, gas is admitted to the air inlet of a turbo–type blower. Such units may include controls for proportioning the air and gas. Any mixer is susceptible to flashback (gas ignition upstream from burner tip), but it is more detrimental in a blower/mixer system because a greater length of piping as well as the blower housing are filled with a combustible mixture. Because of this problem, I would not recommend this type of mixer for any unsupervised equipment.

Nozzle Mix: As the name implies, gas and combustion air do not premix until they leave the ports of this type of burner. This type of burner system can be very efficient; however, it requires a fairly substantial burner assembly. They are usually side-fired only. In flame shapes, and variation in combustion volume. This design will produce a relatively short, intense flame, thus increasing the mixing rate. This allows higher heat transfer to the glass because of the higher velocity that is achieved with the Nozzle Mix design. This all translates into fuel savings.

Nozzle Mix Burners offer a better turndown range than pre-mix burners because the flashback point is eliminated, thus allowing a lower rate of input at low fire.

Regarding energy conservation, the Nozzle Mix Burner more readily adapts to the use of pre-heated Air with temperatures up to 700° F for a standard burner. You cannot use preheated air on a Pre-Mix Burner.

Turbo Blower: Most of the burner systems that are used by studio glass artists fall into one of the systems described. It is assumed that your system will use a turbo type blower to provide the air for the system. A turbo blower is capable of holding nearly constant pressure while delivering any volume within their rated capacity range. The blower's function is to supply combustion air to your burner system. Although capable of providing a great volume of air, the air delivered is low pressure and is usually measured in ounces. The volume of air provided is controlled by a simple butterfly valve. A butterfly valve in a one-burner system does not appreciably affect pressure within the line. It simply controls the quantity of combustion air feeding the mixer. A butterfly valve should never be used as a tight shut-off valve. Similarly, a blast gate can be employed to control the flow of low pressure air (up to 5 psi).

A turbo blower is usually purchased from companies that manufacture burner systems. As stated previously, it is important to size the blower according to your needs. The static pressure within your air line should remain constant when all the equipment hooked up to that line is on. The company that sells you your burner system should be able to estimate the size blower that will best suit your needs. An undersized blower will not provide enough volume of air for proper combustion, and an oversized blower will waste energy. In order to properly size your blower, you will need to know the Btu requirements of all your equipment. You will have to use the proper size piping for all your air and gas lines. It is important not to over-engineer your system. It has been my experience that burner systems engineers often recommend turbo blowers that are rather large (over-engineered) for our systems. You should probably engineer your blower to meet your eventual energy needs. For example, if you are presently burning 250,000 Btu's's per hr. and plan to add equipment within a year that will add another 250,000 Btu's, buy a blower that will satisfy your eventual needs. Sometimes all you will need to do is purchase a higher horsepower motor for the same turbo blower. Stay with a simple burner system. If you are going to operate a glass studio, it is important to understand how to melt glass and how your burner system works. I recommend you send for a handy little pamphlet titled: *Practical Pointers: Industrial Burner Control Systems*. This pamphlet and the *Combustion Handbook* is put out by the North American Mfg. Co. 4455 E. 71st St., Cleveland, OH 44105.

Gas Pressures: All burner systems depend on specifically proportioned quantities of gas and air. To combust properly, natural gas needs 10 parts of combustion air to 1 part of gas; propane requires 24 parts of combustion air to 1 part of gas. For efficient burner operation and safety, it is extremely important that the volume of gas and air be constant. If you are using a turbo blower as your source of air, it is a simple matter to supply a constant volume and pressure as the pressure in the air line is always constant and volume is regulated by a simple butterfly valve. Although natural gas is metered, it is prone to line fluctuations. That is, the line pressure during the course of a day can fluctuate from a low of 4 w.c. (gas pressure is measured in water column inches) to a high of 1 psi. The numbers used are arbitrary, but you get the point. If the gas pressure is not regulated in some way, burners will fluctuate wildly. In some instances, one can even have a flameout which can create a very dangerous situation. In order to overcome gas line fluctuation and supply a constant volume and pressure of gas, we are required to install a gas pressure regulator. Gas pressure regulators provide an efficient means of reducing or stabilizing the line pressure of any clean commercial fuel gas. The regulators that are most commonly found in the glass studio using natural gas

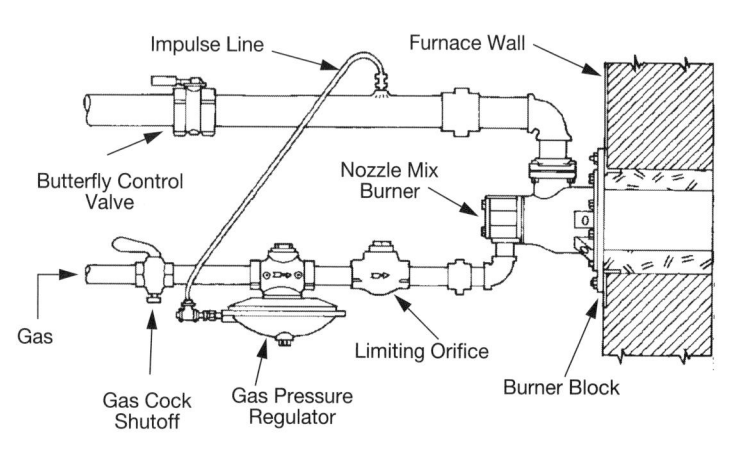

Nozzle Mix Burner System

are referred to as **atmospheric regulators**--sometimes known as zero governors. This type of regulator does not supply gas to your burner under pressure but reduces low pressure gas to "zero" atmosphere. These types of regulators are normally used in proportional air/gas mixing systems to ensure that an exact amount of gas flow is maintained for constant air/gas ratios. It is important to size the regulator to your specific needs as well as to follow the installation procedure as outlined in the directions that come with the regulator. It is also important to maintain the regulator, as they can and do wear out from usage and from the caustic effect of the gas itself. If you have high pressure gas, you will need an additional type of regulator. This additional regulator should probably be hooked up to the main gas line that feeds your total system. Once the pressure is reduced, it becomes possible to use a zero governor regulator. Most small studios do not have high pressure gas; if you do, stay away from using it. The lines are difficult to maintain and any problem can have catastrophic results. It is recommended that each burner system have its own independent regulator. Pilot lights also may require a small regulator in order for them to maintain a constant flame.

Not to be overlooked as part of your burner system is the **Supervising Gas Cock**. Locate your Supervising Gas Cock or main shut-off in a convenient location in case of any problems that might arise. Not only should you have a main gas shut-off, but each and every separate burner system should have its own gas cock. Do not use a shut-off valve that is not designed for gas. A gas valve is not designed to regulate gas flow and should not be used for this purpose. Adjustable limiting orifices were designed for this purpose. They can be purchased separately for nozzle mix systems and are contained within the body of the aspirator mixer. The adjustable orifice is simply a mechanically (screwdriver) adjustable needle-type valve. By turning it with a screwdriver, you can adjust the flow of gas to the mixer. Most glass artists have different settings for a specific temperature needed. You can visually make adjustments if you use a high-quality pressure gauge.

An important aspect often overlooked is the location of the piping, valves, and all the other parts and pieces that comprise the burner system. Locate your system so that it is easy to make adjustments. Avoid placing it where you will klunk your head when gathering or fry your hand when turning it up or down. The regulator needs to be in a cool location so that it doesn't overheat either. The main supervisory gas cock needs to be easily accessible in case of an emergency. Locate your pipes so that they don't interfere with your heat shields. It's a good idea to design your complete studio on paper first. It might prevent having to retro fit later.

The last consideration when installing a burner system is noise. All burner systems and the devices associated with them generate noise. A quiet studio is a happy studio. You can blow more glass in a quiet studio than a noisy one. There are any number of things you can do to keep burner noise to a minimum. First locate the turbo blower in another room or house it in a sound dampening box. Every company that sells blowers also sells mufflers for them. A muffler can make a big difference in the decibel output of a blower.

Flame turbulence is also a source of noise. For premix flames, I recommended that you locate orifices, valves, and fittings far upstream to allow the turbulence to decay before the stream enters the flame. The noisiest burners are those using the cast iron, flame retention type nozzle. These nozzles need secondary air to operate properly. The inrush of secondary air around the tip creates a great deal of turbulence and, consequently, a great deal of noise. It is recommended that you use a tip that does not require secondary air to operate adequately. These types of tips are usually constructed from some type of refractory material and can be inserted into the crown or wall of your furnace. In this case, the furnace acts as a muffler.

One of the best muffling systems is to have your furnace and glory holes contained within an exhaust hood that has insulated baffles hanging in front of all the equipment.

Well, you now have everything you ever wanted to know about burner systems and how they operate. It is up to you to design an efficient and safe system to fire your furnaces and glory holes. I must stress that along with your investment in a burner system that you also invest in full safety to go along with that snazzy new system. It's no fun to burn your studio down because you were penny wise but pound foolish. In other words, don't cheap out.

Centrifugal Turbo Blower

Eclipse Nozzle Mix Burner

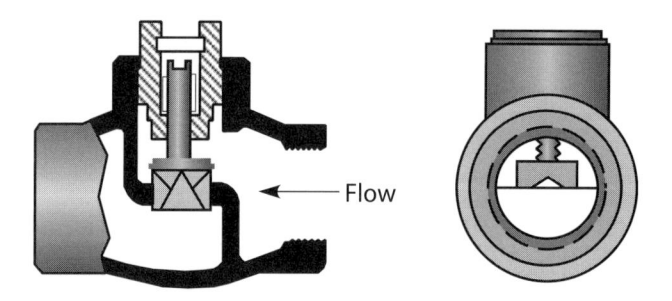

This is a cutaway of a limiting orifice. Although this particular one is designed for a nozzle mix burner, it operates on the same principal as the one found in the aspirator mixer. As the central needle and seat assembly is screwed out, it permits a greater amount of gas to enter the mixing chamber.

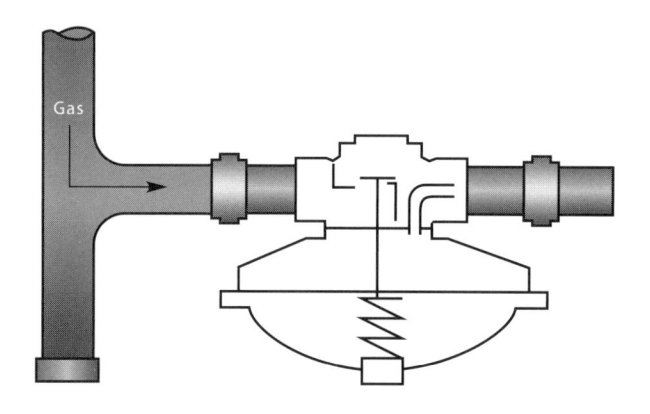

Gas Pressure Regulator

Please read: Hopefully, this chapter helped you understand burners and how they work. I would like to add a word of caution: I do not recommend the installation and operation of any burner system without proper safety equipment. Although burner systems can get quite expensive, and the installation of safety equipment can be more expensive than the burner system itself, don't get cheap when it comes to safety. Your life and the lives of others are not worth your being foolish. You may find it difficult, if not impossible, to get insurance if you do not have proper safety measures in place. Safety is a must. Just ask those whose studios have burned down because they "couldn't afford" proper safety.

Atmospheric Regulator with Premix Aspirator Mixer

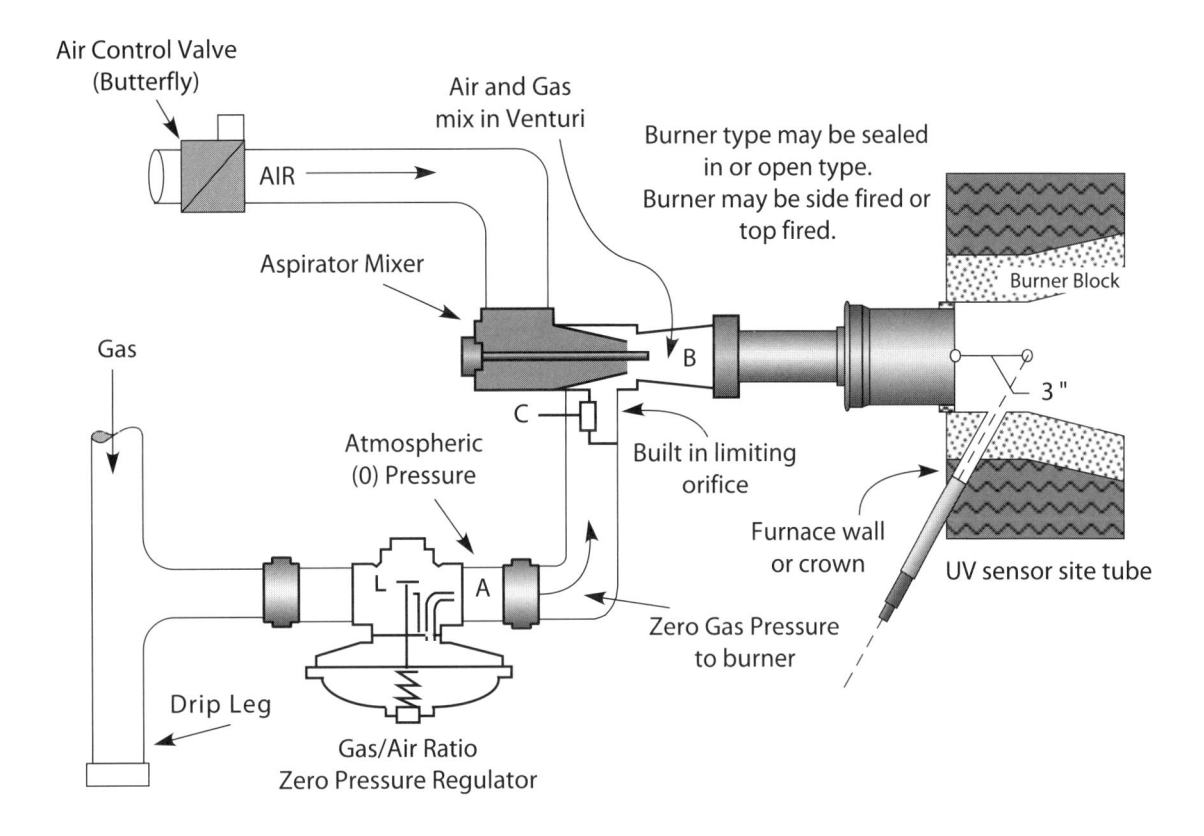

Air Control Valve (Butterfly)
AIR
Air and Gas mix in Venturi
Burner type may be sealed in or open type. Burner may be side fired or top fired.
Burner Block
Aspirator Mixer
B
3"
Gas
C
Atmospheric (0) Pressure
Built in limiting orifice
Furnace wall or crown
UV sensor site tube
L   A
Zero Gas Pressure to burner
Drip Leg
Gas/Air Ratio Zero Pressure Regulator

This type of system is very common and is probably the simplest of all the burner systems. You are not required to have high gas pressure (1 lb. or above) to use this type of burner system. The system works this way: As air flow through the venturi increases ("B"), increased suction causes more gas flow through the limiting orifice valve ("C"). This in turn slightly reduces the pressure at ("A") which causes the regulator to open and allows more gas to flow and maintain the atmospheric or "zero gauge" outlet pressure.

I wish to thank the North American Mfg. Co. of Cleveland, Ohio for giving me permission to use sections of text from their excellent book, *The North American Combustion Handbook*, as well as their *Practical Pointers: Industrial Burner Control Systems*. If you wish to purchase these books and receive information concerning their burner systems, write or call the North American Mfg. Co., 4455 E. 71st St., Cleveland, Ohio 44105, Tel. 216/271-6000.

Alfred Style Burner

This type of burner was originally used to fire ceramic kilns but has proven to be very adaptable for glass furnaces. Although it is referred to as the "Alfred Style Burner," I cannot say for sure that it was invented at Alfred University. It has proven to be rather adaptable for various furnace and kiln configurations. This burner was recommended to me by my late friend Bill Wyman. There are other styles of this burner, but I have found this one works well for glass furnaces. If you do not have the bucks to purchase a decent premix aspirator burner and all that goes with it, this little beauty can be assembled from parts picked up at your local hardware store. Use black iron fittings, as the zinc–coated variety are not approved for gas line. This style burner has been described by Dave Gruenig in his publication, *The Independent Glassblower* (issue #34 June/July/Aug. 94). In this set of drawings, It is similar in concept to the Giberson Burner on the next page.

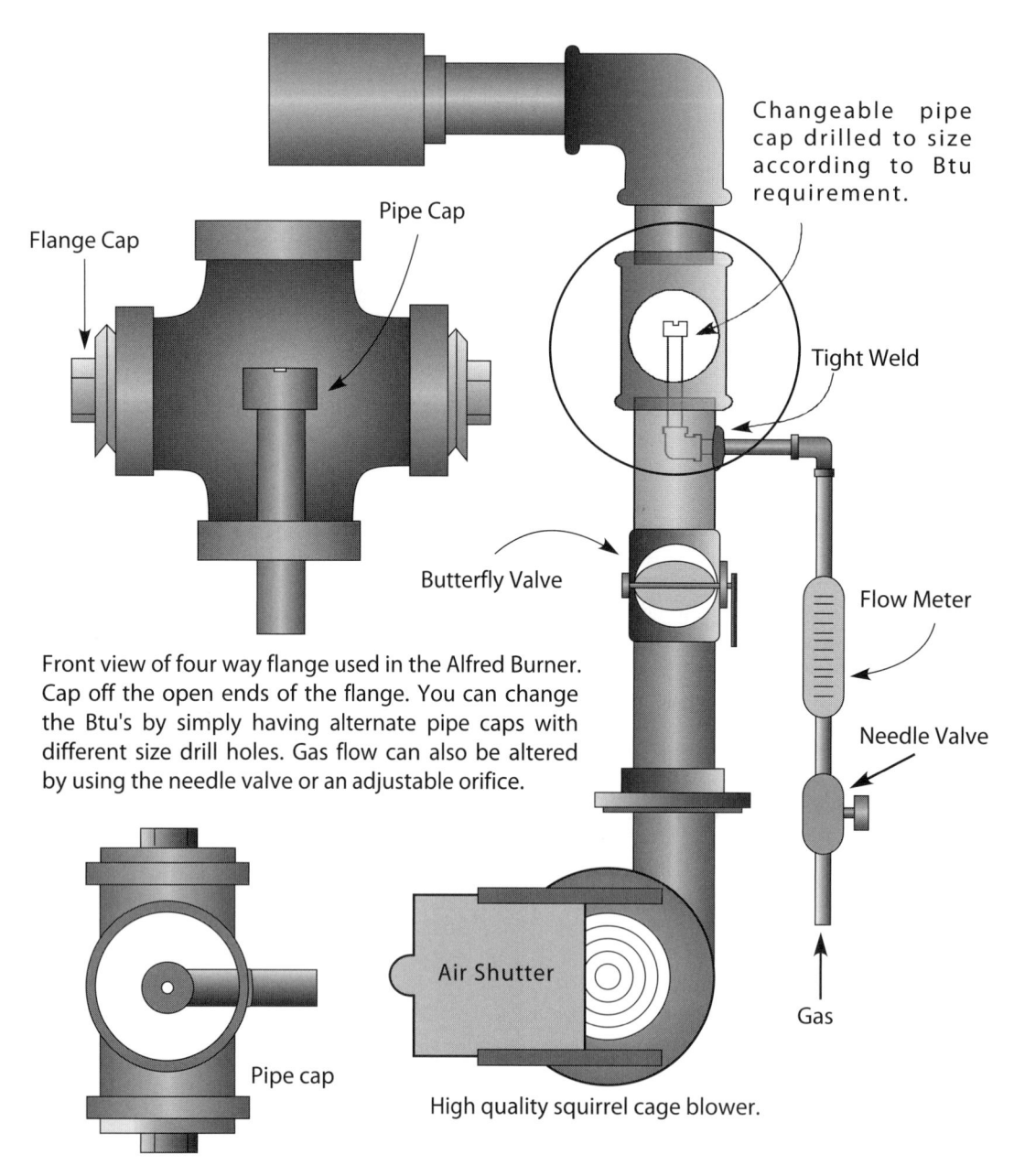

Changeable pipe cap drilled to size according to Btu requirement.

Pipe Cap

Flange Cap

Tight Weld

Butterfly Valve

Flow Meter

Needle Valve

Front view of four way flange used in the Alfred Burner. Cap off the open ends of the flange. You can change the Btu's by simply having alternate pipe caps with different size drill holes. Gas flow can also be altered by using the needle valve or an adjustable orifice.

Air Shutter

Gas

Pipe cap

High quality squirrel cage blower.

View of pipe cap looking into flange from the top.

234 Glass Notes

Giberson Style Burner

This burner is similar to the Alfred style burner. It is a bit easier to construct, compact, and designed specifically for glass furnaces. It can be used for side-fire as well as top-fire. I would replace the Grainger blower with a higher quality one. If you only use this on weekends, this blower will suffice.

Squirrel Cage Blower

Refractory Retention Burner Head

Make sure you use correct orifice size.

Air

Weld

Needle Valve

Gas

Pressure Gauge

Glass Notes 235

Ribbon Burner

This burner tip is considered by many to be the best ever developed for glory holes. As you see in the drawings below, it is not shaped like any other tip. This particular style burner was developed in Sweden and eventually found its way to these shores. All the information concerning this burner tip comes via Tom Ash of Pine Ridge Enterprises in Paradise, CA. According to Tom:

"The original Orrefors Glassworks ribbon burner was designed in conjunction with a square" glory hole (pg. 219). Unlike other burners that concentrate their heat in one spot and need a round glory hole to swirl the heat throughout the interior, the ribbon burner delivers heat evenly along the entire length of the hole. This dispersed, low-pressure approach eliminates the roar associated with burners that rely on high pressure and a vortex effect to transmit heat throughout the glory hole. Although our burners work quite well (and quietly) in round holes, the flat opposing wall of the square hole serves to further reduce the swirling effect of the hot gases. This and the acoustic nature of the insulation bricks serve to reduce the decibel level even further. After over 20 years of experimentation, I believe this design is the quietest, most efficient glory hole burner available today.

There is no doubt that working with a ribbon burner requires a somewhat different "feel" than working with other burners, and a small bit of re-learning is required. But to my knowledge, no one who has made the switch has ever gone back."

Bottom View

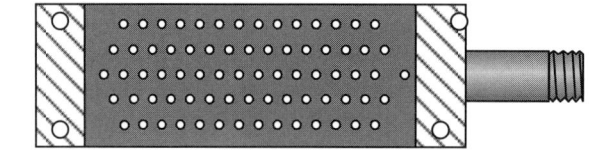

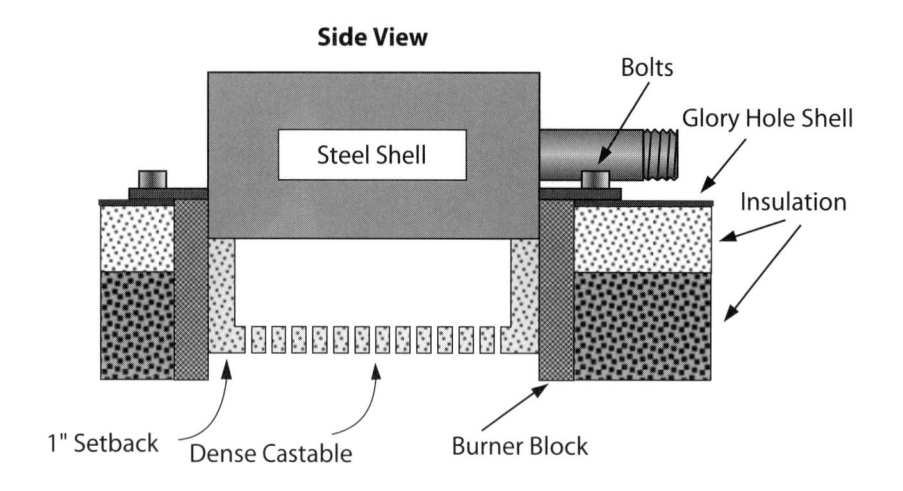

Side View

This burner is available from: Pine Ridge Enterprises, P.O. Box 121, Paradise, CA 95967, tel. 916/877-9793. It is available in 3 sizes, designated, GH390, GH590, GH890. Call or write for information.

NFPA Requirements for Gas Burner Systems

Over the years I have had numerous phone calls from artists that have built studios and are in need of information pertaining to flame safety. In any number of instances, the call was from an artist who had built a furnace and glory hole and had failed inspection because they did not have approved flame safety or, sadly, no safety at all. I have even had phone calls from inspectors that did not know the open flame safety codes. Hopefully the information on the following pages will bring you up to speed on what goes into the building of a burner system that is approved and will fulfill all code requirements. What you will find is the optimal system requirement as outlined by the National Fire Protection Association. (NFPA) Be advised, however, that the system described may not be necessary for all installations. It is your responsibility to familiarize yourself with what safety system to employ in order to keep you safe and meet the requirements for the code in your location.

The schematic and notes on the following page condense the gas burner system requirements of National Fire Protection Association (NFPA) 86 into an easy-to-use format. They should provide most of the engineering information required to lay out burner air and gas trains.

In addition to the requirements shown on the schematic on pg. 238, NFPA 86 also requires that the combustion control system have the following features:

1. Safety control circuits must be single phase, one side grounded, with all breaking contacts in the "hot," ungrounded, circuit-protected line not exceeding 120 Volts.
2. Prior to energizing spark or lighting pilot, a timed pre-purge of at least four standard cubic feet of air per cubic foot of heating chamber volume is required.
   a. Airflow must be proven & maintained during the purge.
   b. Safety shut-off valve must be closed, and when the chamber input exceeds 400,000 Btu/hr (117 kW), it must be proved and interlocked.
3. Exceptions to a re-purge are allowed for momentary shutdowns if (any one):
   a. Each burner is supervised, each has safety shutoff valves, and the fuel accumulation in the heating chamber cannot exceed 25% of lower explosive limit.
   b. Each burner is supervised, each has safety shutoff valves, and at least one burner remains on in same chamber.
   c. The chamber temperature is more than 1400° F (760° C).
4. All safety interlocks must be connected in series ahead of the safety shutoff valves. Interposing relays are allowed when the required load exceeds the rating of available safety contacts or where safety logic requires separate inputs, AND the contact goes to a safe state on loss of power, AND each relay serves only one interlock.
5. Any motor starters required for combustion must be interlocked into the safety circuit.
6. A listed manual reset excess temperature limit control is required except where the system design cannot exceed the maximum safe temperature.
7. The user has the responsibility for establishing a program of inspection, testing, and maintenance with documentation performed at least annually.

The scope of NFPA 86 extends to all the factors involved in the safe operation of ovens and furnaces, and anyone designing or building them should be familiar with the entire standard. Copies can be purchased from:

The National Fire Protection Association
1 Batterymarch Park
Quincy, MA 02269-9101
800-344-3555
508-895-8300 if outside U.S.
Web: www.nfpa.org

Piping Schematic Drawing of Burner System
NFPA Approved

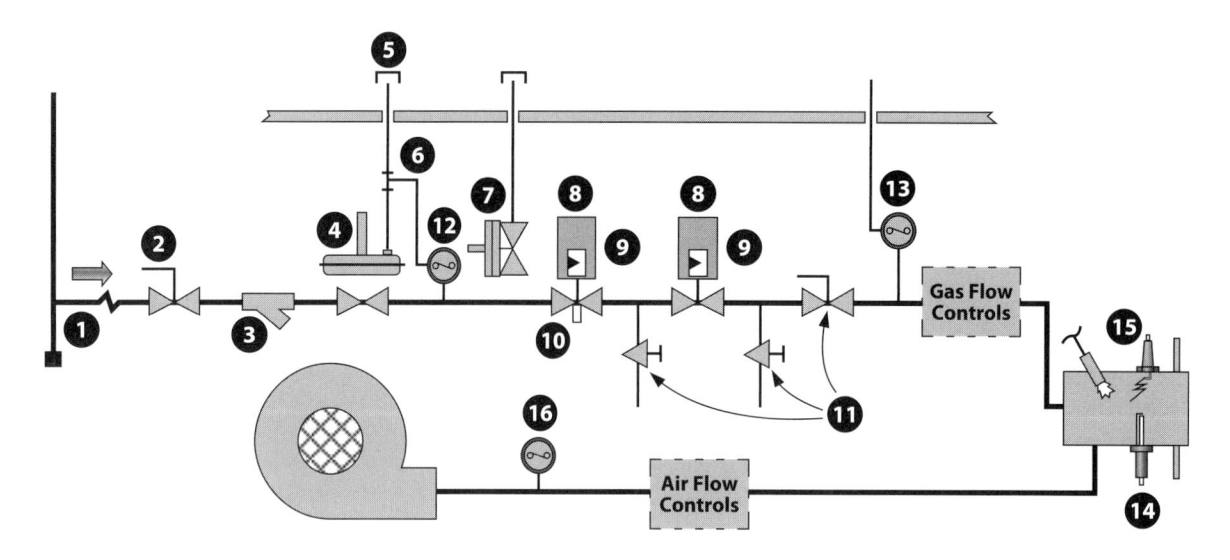

1. Facility to install drip leg or sediment trap for each fuel supply line. Must be a minimum of 3" long.
2. Individual manual shutoff valve to each piece of equipment. ¼ turn valves recommended.
3. Filter or strainer to protect downstream safety shutoff valves.
4. Pressure regulator required wherever plant supply pressure exceeds level required for proper burner function or is subject to excessive fluctuations.
5. Regulator vent to safe location outside the building with water protection & bug screen.
   - Vent piping can terminate inside the building when gas is lighter than air, vent contains restricted orifice, and there is sufficient building ventilation.
   - Vent piping not required for lighter than air gases at less than 1 psi, vent contains restricted orifice, and there is sufficient ventilation. Vent piping not required for ratio regulator.
6. Gas pressure switches may be vented to regulator vent lines if backloading won't occur.
7. Relief valve required if gas pressure at regulator inlet exceeds rating of safety shutoff valve.
8. Safety shutoff valves required for each main and pilot gas burner system.
9. Position indication (not proof-of-closure) required on safety shutoff valves to burners or pilots in excess of 150,000 Btu/hr (44 kW).
10. For capacities over 400,000 Btu/hr (117 kW), at least one safety shutoff valve must have a closed position switch to interlock with the pre-purge.
11. Permanent and ready means for checking leak tightness of safety shut-off valves.
12. Low gas pressure switch (normally open breaks on pressure rise).
13. High gas pressure switch (normally closed breaks on pressure rise)
14. Flame Supervision:
    - Piloted burners
        Continuous pilot: Two flame sensors must be used, one for the pilot flame and one for the main burner flame.
        Intermittent pilot: Can use a single flame sensor for self-piloted burners (from same port as main, or has a common flame base and has a common flame envelope with the main flame).
        Interrupted pilot: A single flame sensor is allowed.
15. Spark Ignition:
    - Except for explosion-resistant radiant tube systems, direct spark igniters must be shut off after main burner trial-for-ignition.
    - If a burner must be ignited at reduced input (forced low fire start), an ignition interlock must be provided to prove control valve position.
    - Trial-for-ignition of the pilot or main must not exceed 15 seconds. An exception is allowed where fuel accumulation in the heating chamber cannot exceed 25% of the lower explosive limit and the authority having jurisdiction approves a written request for extended time.
16. Combustion air flow or pressure proving switch (normally open, breaks on pressure rise).

Glass Notes

Flame Safety

The objective of a combustion safety system is to stop the flow of fuel if the flame should happen to be extinguished. If the fuel flow is not stopped, the combustion chamber (or an entire building) may be filled with an explosive mixture of fuel and air.

A pilot is not enough protection. It may go out or become inadequate to relight an extinguished main flame promptly. In addition, a pilot may be unable to relight the main flame if the fuel/air ratio is too rich or too lean, or if the feed rate is too fast or too slow. The old idea that a constant pilot was helpful because it was always there to relight an extinguished flame has fallen into disrepute. Too many pilot flames have been unable to light a main flame when needed but have later served to ignite an explosive accumulated fuel-air mixture. An interrupted pilot with its programmed trial–for–ignition period is the best way to avoid a pilot–ignited explosion. To prevent an accumulation of unburned fuel in a combustion chamber, flame monitoring devices should be used to govern automatic fuel shut–off valves. A flame supervising system (combustion safeguard) senses the presence of flame and causes fuel to be shut off in the event of flame failure. A glass studio is not complete without some sort of flame safety. Although safety equipment can get rather expensive, it is worth the investment; some flame safety equipment is not as expensive as you might think. You don't need me to tell you how devastating a studio fire can be. With proper safety, you will sleep much better. There are other reasons why flame supervision is necessary. Before you can purchase fire insurance, your fire and insurance codes may require you to have a specific type of flame supervision. One problem you may run into is that there are city as well as state codes concerning open flame safety––these may conflict with each other. I have heard a number of stories concerning insurance inspectors who have little to any understanding of open flame combustion systems and are unable to make any recommendations in this area. **It is your responsibility to research flame safety.** You're not fooling anyone if the inspector permits you to "get away" with inadequate flame supervision. Although most insurance agents are only familiar with homeowner's fire insurance, some insurance companies will offer a discount on your rates depending on the type of flame safety you have. When buying insurance, make sure you understand what you are buying and what is specifically covered. Fire insurance can be very complicated. *Author's note: Those of you who avoid inspection by building a studio in a garage not zoned for open flame run the risk of voiding your homeowner's insurance. In good conscience I cannot recommend building a gas–fired glass studio in a residential neighborhood.*

To fully understand flame safety, it is imperative that the manufacturer's representative explain how your safety equipment works.

Some of the information here was gleaned from *The North American Combustion Handbook*. Although flame safety equipment can be pricey, there are safety systems for every budget. There are companies that will package a burner safety system to meet your needs. The companies that address the needs of the glass studio are: Wet Dog Glass, the Hub Consolidated, Inc., and Abell Combustion, Inc. The prices of safety equipment will vary from company to company. If you are shopping for safety equipment, educate yourself about flame safety. I hope the following guide will help you understand the different levels of safety. Remember, "it's better to be safe than sorry."

Automatic Fuel Shut-off Valves

"Safety shut-off valves shall be utilized as a key safety control to protect against explosions or fires. Each safety shutoff valve will shut off the gas to the burner system after interruption of the holding medium (such as, electric current or fluid pressure) by any one of the interlocking safety devices, combustion safeguards, or operating controls.

There are different automatic safety valve requirements depending on the total Btu's of the combustion system. The higher the Btu's the more safety is required i.e., visual position indication, proof of closure, valve proving system, valve seal, overtravel, and interlock." *

The prime requisites of any fuel shut-off valve are that it cannot be manually locked open, that it shut tightly, and that it be sensitive to any possible failure in the system. In addition, it is desirable to have a manual shut-off arrangement, high mechanical advantage for easy opening, and an auxiliary switch. A manual reset fuel shut-off valve works in the following manner: when the control circuit is interrupted (electrical power failure), the electromagnet no longer holds the valve open, and a strong spring snaps it shut so fuel flow is stopped quickly. When the trouble has been eliminated so that the circuit is again closed, the valve can be opened by the action of the hand lever. If, however, the trouble has not been satisfactorily corrected, the

---

* NFPA Bulletin 86 section 7.7 "safety shutoff valves." Note: These regulations change frequently, and a competent combustion engineer can guide you through this maze of information.

circuit remains open and the valve cannot be opened by moving the hand lever because the valve stem remains disengaged from the handle. This is termed *a manual reset fuel shut-off valve*. The manual reset type is used wherever the presence of an operator is required to assure a safe, low–fire relighting of the burners.[1]

Although a manual reset fuel shut-off valve does not offer flame supervision (UV sensor) it does offer a modicum of safety. Many power failures are extremely brief and can be a nuisance, especially if you live in an area that is prone to brief power outages (a few seconds or less). A trip delay unit can be installed to mitigate power failures of 4 seconds or less. A trip delay unit assures continued operation despite momentary power interruptions but must be ordered separately and requires mounting in an electrical enclosure.

Pressure Switches

A combustion system that is in compliance with NFPA 86 guidelines would have an air pressure switch and a high gas and low gas pressure switch if a turbo blower is used. An air pressure switch would not be required on a venturi burner system. The high and low pressure switches are wired in series prior to the manual reset valve for added safety. This will protect you in the event that there is a rise or fall in gas pressure. The low gas pressure switch makes electrical contact on pressure rise. If there is a loss of gas pressure in the gas line, the unit would sense it and break the contact thus resulting in the main gas valve(s) closing. A system shut down would then occur.

The high gas pressure switch breaks the electrical contact on pressure rise. If the gas pressure in the gas line rises above the desired set point, the normally closed contact would open, break the electrical circuit, and result in the main gas valve(s) closing. A system shut down would occur.

Ultraviolet Scanner, Loss of Flame

An ultraviolet detector is sensitive to the ultraviolet (UV) radiation emitted by all flames in small amounts. Since they are completely insensitive to infrared and visible radiation, they cannot be fooled by radiation from hot refractory. When UV radiation impinges on the cathode within the detector tube, electrons start to flow toward the anode, ionizing the gas within so that it can conduct a d-c current as long as a voltage is applied to the terminals. To make such a system fail–safe, an interrupter, such as a shutter, ensures that the tube will conduct a current only while receiving the UV radiation that repeatedly re-establishes its conductivity. In short, an ultraviolet detector will supervise the gas line if your flame should fail or deteriorate for any reason.

Speak to a local flame safety representative concerning your needs. You should design your safety system when designing the burner system. It is more expensive to retro fit an existing burner than to include it in the initial burner package, but it is not impossible. The quote below should be read and heeded.

"The irony of safety controls is the fact that they sometimes are used so rarely that they easily fall into neglect and become unsafe. An essential corollary of a safety equipment investment is a safety maintenance commitment—regular checking of safety circuits and mechanisms to make sure that there has been no tampering, jumping, clogging, galling, wearing, corroding, or other irregularity. If an interlock or valve has not been actuated for months, there is a chance that it never will be—even when needed." [3]

I would like to thank Steve Abell of Abell Combustion, Inc. for providing the information on Gas Burner Systems as well as the NFPA schematic with accompanying information. Contact information for Abell Combustion, Inc. can be found in the Vendors section of this book.

Disclaimer: Flame safety and decisions concerning safety are the operator's responsibility. Situations dangerous to personnel and property can develop from incorrect operation of combustion equipment. The author urges compliance with National Safety Standards, adherence to Insurance Underwriters recommendations, and care in operation.

[1,2,3] *North American Combustion Handbook*, Second Edition, North American Mfg. Co., Part 7, Combustion Control.

Annealing Ovens, Electricity

Chapter Contents

The IFB Annealing Oven 242
Building the Oven 250
Lid, Lid Support, Counter Weight, and Hinge 251
Annealing Oven 252
Creating the Element Slot 253
The Elements 257
The Lid 258
The Hinge 259
Materials for Annealer 260
The Skamol Annealer 261
Standard Sizes for Skamol Slabs 262
Hot Face/Cold Face Calculations for Skamol Annealer 262
Tips on Building the Skamol Front-Loading Annealing Oven 263
The Skamol Front-Loading Oven 264
The Roll-Out Casting Oven 266
Detail of Air Seal 271
Elements & Stainless Crown Supports 272
Crown Details 273
Another Type of Air Seal 274
Flat Crown Construction 275
Rigid Panel Installation 276
The Convection Oven 277
Designing Electric Elements 278
Currents for Resistance Heating Loads/Amperage Conversion 280
Using Ohms Law to Make an Element 281
About Three Phase 282

The IFB Annealing Oven

This chapter should help you understand some basic principals of annealing ovens and the materials used to construct them. Before beginning, I think a bit of history and a brief reminiscence would be nice.

Historians tell us that the Egyptians did little to anneal their glass. I believe they either buried the pieces in hot sand and let them cool naturally or placed them in a waste heat chamber. Regardless of how the pieces were annealed, you can bet their methods were not very sophisticated but were sufficient for American studio glass artists were very simple and unsophisticated, but were sufficient to anneal most of our crude objects. Given the type of controls we employed to run our annealers, I don't think they would have been capable of annealing much more than blown objects. Sophisticated temperature controllers were still a long way off. Robert Barber introduced us to the first "controller" at GAS 1 held at Penland. Bob came from a physics background and was very clever technically. His device was soldered together from resistors and other electronic devices. I don't know if

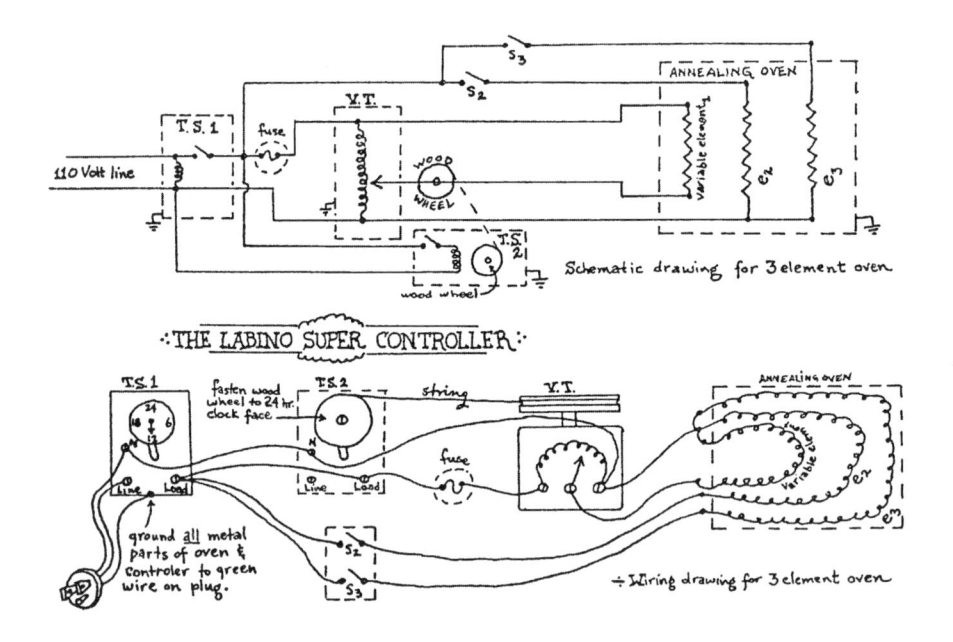

Fritz Dreisbach drawing of the Labino Controller, circa 1972

survival. Later, as the technology became more sophisticated, wood and coal-fired annealers were constructed. These ovens had a fire box and a series of baffles to control the temperature. To tell the temperature of the annealer, the glass blower simply threw a piece of wet, wadded paper into the hot annealer to see how long it would take to catch fire. If the proper time elapsed before the paper caught fire, he knew the temperature was right for annealing. If it caught fire too soon, he would adjust the baffles to change the temperature. *Author's note: There is a wonderful shot of this type of annealer in the Maurice Marinot film at the Corning Museum Library. This is a "must see" film. The sound track alone is worth the price of admission.* The same method of annealing continued well into the 20th century. Since the advent of electricity, many types of sophisticated devices have been introduced to take the worry out of annealing.

The first annealing ovens constructed by the it actually worked, but he claimed it did. Nick Labino invented a clever annealer controller from a 24–hour timer purchased from W.W. Grainger coupled with a Variable Auto Transformer sometimes referred to as a Variac. Nick's device--with its wheels, gears, and cams—automatically turned the transformer wheel so that the temperature dropped at a rate slow enough to allow the glass to anneal properly. Nick had many different cams, depending on the thickness of the pieces he was annealing. Those of us clever enough to understand how to build one of those devices did so but most used Range Controllers. A range controller is the same controller found on electric stoves. They were about the cheapest controllers money could buy. Ovens that used these controllers had to be constantly monitored, as the temperature had a tendency to rise beyond the softening point of the glass. Many "great" objects were melted into puddles because of these controllers. Those of us who had some money used a

242 Glass Notes

Set-Point Controller. These devices, still in use, solved part of our problem, as they allowed us to set the high-end annealing temperature. Once set, it would maintain this temperature. A set point controller is maintained by a thermocouple which in turn is controlled by a relay. When the temperature is reached, a signal is sent from the controller opening the relay, shutting the power off. When the temperature drops a few degrees, the relay closes and power is sent back to the elements. On/off, on/off. The major problem with a set-point controller is that you have to lower the temperature by hand, similar to the range control, but with a great deal more accuracy. I can recall in the early 70's trying to anneal castings using simple range controls. Annealing those pieces required me to sleep in the studio in order to turn the controls down by hand.

The introduction of the digital controller has taken the worry out of annealing and has allowed me to get a good night's sleep. Our only worry now is a power failure, but that has always been a problem regardless.

Today, most of us use some type of digital device to control our ovens, and we have learned to build more sophisticated annealers. With the advent of the digital controller and our abilities to build larger and larger ovens, the scale and complexity of our work has increased as well. Our ability to conquer the technical problems presented to us has helped to produce large–scale glass works as well as work of great complexity. Because of this we can now realize an aesthetic that challenges architectural space on a scale never before possible.

The first annealers at the University of Wisconsin were simply constructed from bent galvanized sheet metal and lined with fiberfrax which was pinned to the sheet metal with element wire. The floor of the annealer was fiberfrax with a layer of vermiculite covering it. The door was cut to the same shape as the annealer, lined with frax, and hinged at the bottom with a piano hinge. They looked like mailboxes and were in fact called mailbox annealers. The only insulation these annealers had was about two inches of fiberfrax. If the power shut off, the temperature of the ovens would drop like a stone.

As stated earlier, an annealer is simply a box that holds heat. Beyond that, the heat must be controlled in order for the glass to be annealed and cooled properly. It can be constructed from either fiber-board, fiberfrax, insulating brick, or other types of insulating materials. An annealer can be a top loader or a front loader. It can be a car-kiln design or the lid can roll, lift, or drop. In my travels, I have seen many different types of annealing ovens, some bordering on the bizarre and some ingenious in concept and design.

Annealers serve many purposes beyond just annealing glass. An annealer is also a casting oven, slumping oven, fusing oven, and can be used for just about any other glass processes that require controlled temperature.

The term oven and annealer are interchangeable and are often used together. An annealer should not be confused with a lehr. The differences between the two are that the lehr is usually gas fired and has a moving belt. Essentially, the belt moves the glass from the "carry in" through zones that anneal it, cool it, and finally transport it to the finish end of the lehr where someone is removing the ware, packing it and shipping it to Wal-Mart. At one time we had many factories in the U.S. producing many different types of glass, but since we have become a global economy, very little of anything is actually produced in the U.S. The U.S. has become a nation of consumers and very little else. Well, that's my little political rant; after all, this is a book for those that make things. Back to the lehr. The glass goes in hot and comes out cool. Quite handy when you're making hundreds of pieces in a day. The cool end of the lehr has some minimum wage, non-union person grabbing those tchotchkes before they hit the floor. Hey, what's a tchotchke you ask? "Tchotchke" is a borrowing from the Eastern Yiddish tshatshke, which came from the obsolete Polish czacko, meaning "knickknack, trinket, toy." The current Oxford English Dictionary gives the origin as the Russian tsatska, and defines it as "a trinket or gewgaw." (But nobody says "gewgaw" anymore--it's one of those words you see in dictionaries.) William Safir writing in the N.Y. Times, quoting Sol Steinmetz, author of the 1986 *Yiddish and English" A Century of Yiddish in America*. Now wasn't that fun?

The Annealer

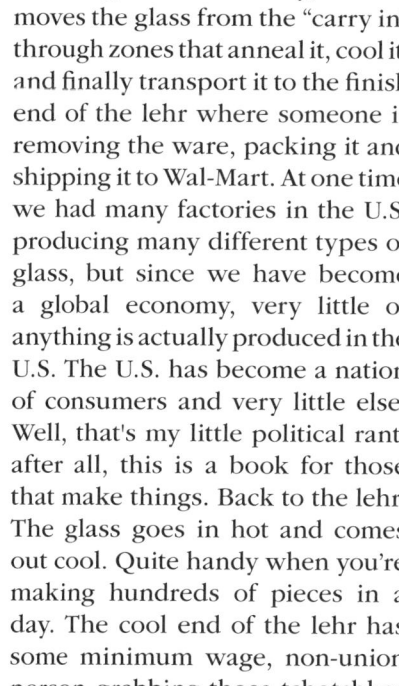

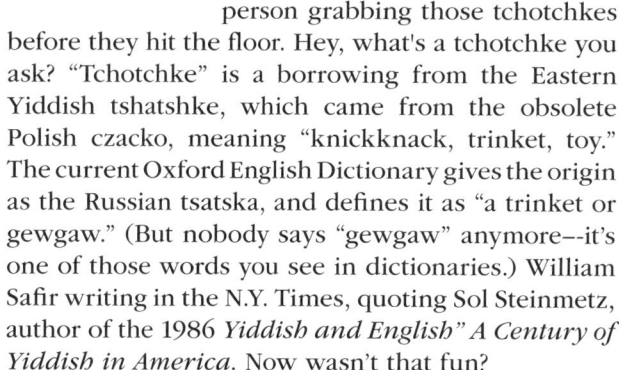

For purposes of this book, I have chosen to build and depict what I consider to be a fairly simple annealer of average size and top-loading. There are many different types of annealers: top-loading, front loading, roll out, bell types, and other types still being invented. These annealers can be fabricated from many different types of refractory materials. Before you set off to build your annealer, it is a good idea to know

Kent State Controller, 1972

what type of usage it will get as the type of ware and style of work being annealed will dictate what you will build it from and how much insulation will be required. For instance, if you're going to be blowing production, and the work is fairly thin and coherent in wall thickness, you will probably build from some form of fiber as fiber cools very quickly and usually a fiber annealer can be unloaded the next morning. Fiber annealers also get up to temperature very quickly. If you doing very thick pieces such as castings and or thick blown ware with prunts, handles, and additions, you might wish to build from IFB as insulating brick stores energy and cools to a gentle downward curve. Because IFB stores energy it can also protect the work in case of a power failure. To get an idea and description of different types of refractory materials see page 136. To suit your needs, annealers can be constructed from many combinations of refractory insulating materials.

Power to the Annealer

As I said earlier, annealers serve many purposes beyond just annealing. If you provide sufficient power to the annealer, you will be able to achieve temperatures sufficient for plaster/silica mold casting (1550° F, 843° C), fusing, slumping, and a host of all the other glass forming processes with some room to spare. The temperature your oven is capable of achieving is a function of the power provided in relation to the insulation.

In today's glass world, proper annealing of any type of glass requires you to have some type of programmable digital controller; there are many types available for the studio glass artist.

Before beginning construction on your annealer, there are questions you should answer: Will the annealer be used for blown ware only? Will it be used for annealing castings as well? Will I make pizza? Broil a chicken? You think I'm kidding about broiling a chicken? When I went to an event at the Bullseye Glass Co. in Portland, Oregon some years ago, Danny Schwoerer, the owner and brains behind the operation actually broiled 100 or so chickens in their lehr (and they were fusing delicious). Anyway, the answers to those questions that get at the function of your annealer will help you to design your annealer.

The diagrams on the following pages explain how to construct a simple top-loading annealing oven. Building this oven requires some knowledge of bricklaying (sans mortar), welding, and other mechanical skills. I hope the diagrams help clarify some of your questions. Remember, when building any

$E = mc^2$

and all studio equipment, craftsmanship counts.

If you use it only for annealing blown glass, it need only reach about 1000° F. If you use your oven for casting as well, it needs to reach about 1500° F but be capable of achieving 1700° F. The size oven I have chosen for demonstration will operate at 75 amps, 220 volts single phase and will be capable of reaching 1700° F (926° C).

I will ask the rhetorical question: How did I arrive at 75 amps? There is a simple formula to employ when calculating your energy needs depending on the type and quantity of insulation. This simple calculation informs us of the Amperage draw of our annealer at a specific Voltage. Since we're building an annealer for a professional glass studio, we will need at least 208 – 240 volts single or three-phase. It should also be noted that one can build an annealer to run at 120 volts, but 120 volts does not have enough oomph to permit us to build an annealer of any scale.

Further note that our 75–amp oven will actually be engineered to draw only 60 amps at 220 volts for the following reason. As elements age from use, they begin to oxidize and their resistance decreases. A decrease in resistance means that the element will begin to draw more energy than it was engineered for. After some usage, your oven that was calculated to draw only 60 amps will begin to draw in excess of 60 amps. The excessive current draw will trip your breaker. If you've engineered your elements correctly, they should last for quite a few years as the surface temperature of the element is insufficient to age it prematurely. Engineer the electrical need of your oven at 80% of the full capacity of the circuit breaker to avoid this problem, and have your elements wound accordingly. Always use a circuit breaker rated for the full capacity of your oven. Wire sizes must be engineered accordingly as well.

Another problem connected with elements that age and oxidize is that they begin to lose their ability to achieve optimum temperature. Although old elements may still be capable of achieving optimum temperature, they will take longer and longer to do so. Eventually they will fail. Replace your elements when it becomes a struggle for your oven to achieve temperature. Elements become brittle as they age and can break without our knowing it. If your oven suddenly is not achieving temperature, check to see if any of the elements are broken. It is wise to replace all the elements at the same time. New elements produce a greater heat than old elements. If you mix old and new elements, you may create serious heat differentials in your oven. These heat differentials will prevent you from annealing or cooling your ware correctly. Like people, elements fail as they age, but elements unlike people can be replaced. It is important to engineer your elements correctly and choose your friends wisely.

Some Electrical Talk

In order to calculate the Amperage requirement of your annealer, you will need to calculate the watts needed to achieve temperature. The formula that I find helpful in this respect is simple and varies with the type and quantity of insulation used in the annealer.

Most studios use 220 volts, single-phase power, and for our purposes, our oven will employ single-phase. There are conveniences found with three-phase but single phase is easier to understand and, under most circumstances, can be understood by the novice. Your voltage will remain constant. If you're using 220 volts to power an annealer, it will always remain at 220 volts. You will need to increase the amperage if you want more power. It is possible to do this as long as the additional amperage is available in your main panel and the wires that carry the power to your annealer are sized correctly. Bear in mind that, if you change the size of the breaker at the main panel, all the wires carrying the increased load must be sized accordingly. You will also have to replace your elements with ones capable of handling the increased load. If you increase your oven's electrical capacity and keep the same elements, you will not get any increase in heat. The elements will only draw the amount of energy for which they are rated. That is, if all the elements combined are rated at 45 amps and you increase your load to 75 amps, the elements will not suddenly draw 75 amps but will continue to draw the 45 amps at which they were rated when purchased. You must order new elements capable of handling the increased load. Before increasing the load of your oven, check to see if the wires are sized to handle a larger breaker. If you increase the size of the breaker and your wires are too small to carry the increased load, they, like the elements themselves, will get hot and can under the right circumstances burn your studio down. Get the point! Don't fuck with electricity. Always check with a licensed electrician when determining your electrical needs. Electricians are expensive, but they are a hell of a lot cheaper than building a new studio. Find one that collects glass.

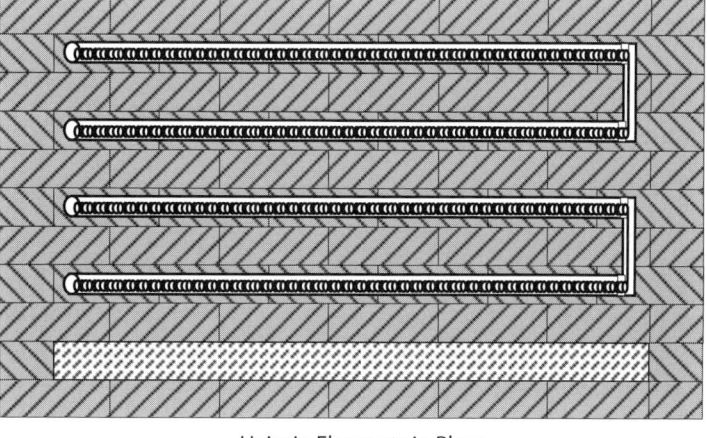

Hairpin Elements in Place

The Oven

The interior dimension of the oven is 49 ½" long x 31 ½" wide x 22 ½" deep or about 20 cubic feet. If this oven was to be used for annealing blown ware only, you might be able to power it with 30 amps at 220 volts. If you wish to do some casting, you would need at least 50 to 75 amps. If we apply our 80% rule, the 50-amp annealer would actually draw 40 amps and the 75-amp oven would draw 60 amps.

30 amps at 220 volts or 6,600 watts (volts x amps = watts) may heat an oven of 20 cu. ft. to a temperature of 1000° F, but 6,600 watts may not heat that same oven to 1500° F. Casting ovens require more energy than simple annealing ovens. The higher the temperature, the more energy required. The more mass you put into an oven, the more energy required to bring that mass to the temperature needed. The following formula should help you calculate the energy required to run your casting/annealing oven. The general rule of thumb is to allocate 1000 – 1200 watts per cu. ft. for an oven constructed from 4.5" of IFB with 1 – 2" of board insulation. An oven with this wattage will achieve 1700° F. when fully loaded.

Every object you put in an oven takes on energy. The brick in the oven and the casting molds have to absorb energy in order to heat up. If your oven is underpowered, it will never produce enough energy to heat the mass in the oven sufficiently. All the insulation in the world will not help an underpowered oven. For those of you interested in a scientific explanation of the laws of thermodynamics, take a course at your local community college. If you are really smart, get a text and teach yourself. If you wish to learn more on this subject, I suggest you get a copy of *The North American Combustion Handbook*.

A good point to mention is insulating brick (IFB) versus fiber insulation for the construction of annealing ovens. My personal preference is to use IFB if you're going to be casting as IFB stores energy and gives a gentle cooling curve. Although fiber makes a wonderful oven, it has its drawbacks when used for annealing ovens. Fiber insulation heats up very quickly and requires less energy in the heat-up phase. It is easy to construct an oven from it, and it keeps the space shuttle cool upon re-entry. Fiber ovens are good for blowers as they can be cooled at a much faster rate than an IFB oven. This is advantageous if you need to empty the oven in the morning and get it back up to temperature quickly. All the ovens I have built over the years were constructed from insulating brick; they are still operational and have taken many years of abuse. Fiber insulation, like many materials in the glass shop, can also be a health hazard if not handled properly. If you're going to use fiber I recommend using a hard fiber-board or Skamol Vermiculite board and not fiber blanket. The fiber-board offers a greater degree of safety. The fiber blanket releases its particulate readily, and you do not want to breath those particles.

About Digital Controllers and Relays

Every annealer needs a device capable of turning it on and off as well as maintaining accurate annealing temperature and controlled cool down. Fortunately, there are many such devices on the market for us to choose from and the prices are very reasonable. A programmable digital controller is actually a dedicated minicomputer. It is dedicated to maintaining a pre–programmed time/temperature profile. Most commercial programmable controllers can do a great deal more, but usually glass artists needs are slight compared to industry needs. The digital controller, coupled with the proper thermocouple, is capable of accurately sensing the temperature of your oven and sending signals to an electric relay to turn your oven either on or off. The cycling of the relay is what maintains the oven's heating and cooling rate. Every oven must have a relay of some sort to turn it on or off. The programmable digital controller is the brains behind the relay. A simple explanation of how the relay and computer work is as follows: Your computer receives information from your annealer's thermocouple in the form of a millivolt. The controller translates this signal into information that relates to the temperature that you have programmed. If the information received is a temperature lower or higher than the one programmed by you, the computer will send its own electrical signal to the relay and either turn it on (heat) or off (cool). There are different types of relays to choose from. The simplest is called a mechanical contactor. This type of relay, although reliable ages quickly and usually fails at the most inopportune time. They are noisy and need maintenance. There are other more sophisticated relays (SSR's) on the market that can regulate temperature much more accurately than the simple mechanical on/off type, and they are not as expensive as you might think.

If you are still using a noisy mechanical contactor, you should switch to a mercury displacement relay (MDR). Although still considered to be a mechanical relay, they are more reliable, are capable of cycling more frequently than the mechanical ones, and are quiet. The only problem they pose is that they contain a considerable quantity of mercury and if replaced must be disposed of according to EPA standards. For those of you wishing something more sophisticated, you should investigate solid state relays (SSR's) as well as SCR relays. It might soon come to pass that MDR's will no longer be manufactured in this country since they contain mercury. Mercury like lead is toxic to all living things.

Element and IFB Placement

Before building the oven, you must groove some of the insulating brick. The special grooves will hold the elements in place as well as get them out of the way of the glass you will put in the annealer. There are two ways to put the properly shaped grooves in an insulating brick (pgs. 253, 254, and 255). The method you use is up to you. I have depicted two methods using a router. The first method is to mount a carbide tipped router in a good drill press. Build a wooden jig at a 30 to 45° angle to hold the brick and clamp it to the drill press table (pg. 253). When pushing the brick through the router, do not push too quickly. Set the drill press for high speed. Wear a good pair of work gloves when doing all of the above. Dip the brick in water to prevent dust. For those of you who cannot afford a drill press you can affect excellent grooves using Jack Schmidt's "Poor Boy" groover depicted on page 255.

Regardless of the method employed for grooving, the groove created in the brick will be perfect for your element wire to sit in (pg. 257). After the annealer is constructed and the metal frame is in place, you will need to drill a ¼" hole at the end of each groove through the insulating brick as well through the sheet metal on the exterior of the oven. This is where your element pigtail will exit the oven. Make sure you locate the holes accurately. I recommend drilling the holes with a drill press prior to installation. It will be necessary to increase the size of the hole in the sheet metal where the pigtail exits to prevent the element from grounding itself and causing an electrical hazard. Special sheet metal drills are made for this purpose. When you have drilled all your holes, place the elements into the grooves and push the pigtails through the holes you have drilled. After seating all the elements, it will be necessary to pin the elements to the brick behind them. If you do not pin them, even though they are sitting in the grooves they will eventually begin to sag out of the grooves. They should be pinned about every 6 to 9". An element pin is about 2" long; it is made from extra heavy element wire and shaped like a bobby pin. *Author's note: When ordering elements, ask for pin wire.* The pins are pushed around the element and into the IFB as indicated in the diagram on page 257.

The coiled elements used for annealers are made from Kanthal A-1 and not nichrome. A description of how to design the elements as well as how to order a pre-made element is described in this section (pg.

278-280). Because you want the annealer to heat up and cool down evenly, it is important to locate the annealer elements correctly. Placing them in the two long side walls of our oven seems to be the most logical location. The heat has less distance to radiate in the sidewalls than if you were to place them in the endwalls. If your oven is small or if you have a sufficient number of elements, you may be able to place them in all four walls. The best casting ovens have elements in all four walls, the crown, and the floor. If you ever get a chance to visit The Czech Republic, take a look at their casting ovens. They are the finest studio ovens I have ever seen.

Insulation

The annealer must be insulated sufficiently so that heat loss through the side walls and crown is minimal. Since studio annealers do not go beyond 1700° F (925° C), we can use 2000° F (1095° C) IFB backed up with 2" of mineral block insulation. The completed oven will be held together with sheet metal and angle iron. The lids, in this case, are constructed from a good rigid fiber-board, 1 or 2" thick and backed with 1 or 2" of mineral board. Over time and with constant movement, the fiber-board is apt to crack and fall into the oven. To mitigate this problem, we will support the fiber top-loading doors with stainless steel supports, (see pg. 251 for photographs of the s.s. supports). The lid operates with a simple counterweight system. There are many different ways to open annealer doors and lids. I have chosen a very simple and inexpensive method as shown in the lid and hinge diagrams (pg. 251, 258, and 259). Locate your oven near your work area and away from any obstructions. Build it on a level floor and allow at least 3' of space behind it.

The dimensions I have chosen for the annealer are not arbitrary but work dimensionally in relation to the size of standard insulating brick. If you stay with standard brick dimensions, you will have less brick to cut and less waste. A standard insulating brick is 9" x 4 ½" x 2 ½".

2000° F (1095° C) IFB insulates better than 2300° F (1260° C) IFB. Insulating value decreases as the temperature range of the IFB increases. Use IFB with the lowest number that meets your requirement. When building the annealer, it is important to always wear a good dust mask. I cannot stress good health and safety practices enough. I shudder when I recall how careless we were in the early days of studio building. At that time, I think we all thought we would live forever. I believe many of us are still careless in how we handle some of these refractory products.

Beginning

When I first built annealing ovens, the frame was not welded but used a threaded rod system as shown in Fritz's illustration above and in the photo of the oven on page 250. Over time this system proved to be less than adequate. Eventually I came to understand that a sturdy welded frame was needed. Initially we built the oven and then built the frame to fit the oven. In some cases this method will suffice, but I believe it is best to construct the frame first and then fit the oven materials inside the already constructed frame. Doing it this way ensures that your angles will be welded perfectly square. I have a good illustration on page 262 of how a front loading annealer frame looks. A top loading annealer frame would be constructed in a similar manner (pg. 249).

I also recommend a sturdy set of lockable wheels attached to each corner of your oven for obvious reasons. It's not a good idea to build your oven directly on the floor.

Horizontal angle iron supports on your bottom section of frame is a good idea as they will help to keep the sheet metal underneath the oven nice and flat. You're now ready to build the oven.

Author's Note: Prior to building the oven, it is important to establish where the elements will exit the interior of the oven so that holes can be accurately drilled in the sheet metal and the insulation. Drilling holes after the fact can lead to holes that are not square to the unit. In order to do this it is necessary to route the element grooves into the hot face board or IFB. Once you've established the location of where the element pigtails will be located, holes can be drilled using a drill press. Make sure you accurately mark the sheet metal. Drill the sheet metal holes larger than the holes for the pigtails through the insulation. You do not want the element pigtail grounding out on the sheet metal.

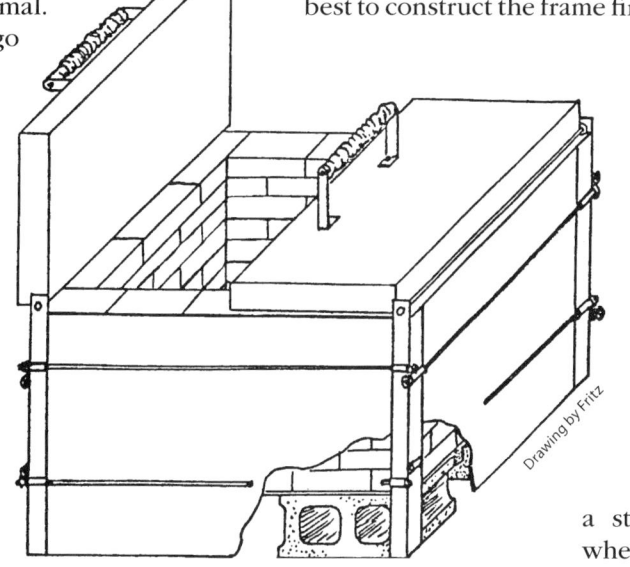

Dreisbach top loader, circa early 70s
The handles were hand carved.

If it does, you will have a very shocking experience. I've used mullite tubes, inserted through the drilled annealer wall, to keep the element pigtail secure.

The First Layer

Start with the sheet metal. It is assumed that your holes have been drilled prior to building the oven. Clamp and tack weld all the sheet metal around the sides and bottom.

Place the block insulation on all four sides and the bottom. I used a 2" layer of mineral block insulation. Any backup insulation will suffice.

The next layer is IFB or Skamol Vermiculite board and will be the material that is the hot face.

Author's Note: Build the sidewalls, then build the floor inside the walls. This creates an excellent heat lock. It also permits you to easily repair when it wears out (see the order of construction on pg. 250).

Regardless of what material you use, make sure the hot face board is at least 2" thick. If you have to piece together two or more boards for the hot face I recommend cutting a lap joint where the boards butt up to each other. Doing this will create a good heat lock (pg. 263).

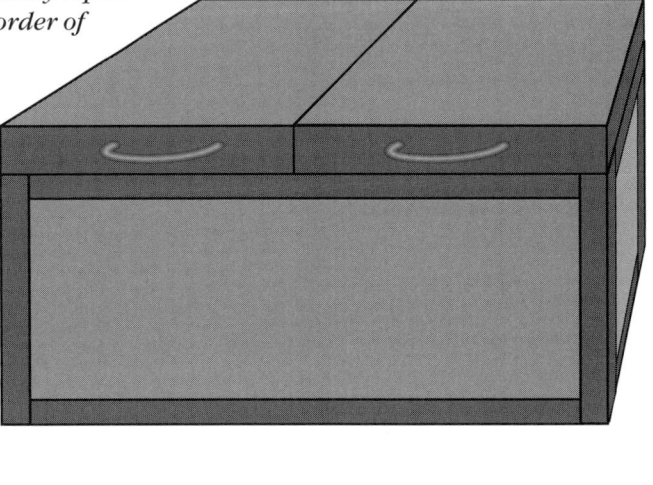

It may be necessary to cut brick or board as you build. IFB and board cuts easily. To facilitate cutting IFB accurately, you may wish to construct a small wooden mitre box. The best and most accurate way to cut IFB, is to use a 14" tile saw. A tile saw is water cooled and cuts square. Water cooling will minimize dust. Use a masonry blade designed for this purpose and not a diamond blade. After the first row of wall brick is in place, you should put the first row of grooved brick next. Make sure the grooves all face in the same direction with the angle of the groove facing down. Make sure you stagger each row of brick as shown on page 252. If you do not stagger each course of brick as indicated, your annealer walls will not be stable or secure. After a short time you will get quite good at laying brick. It's easy when you don't use mortar. You will have 4 grooved courses per side (a total of 8 grooved courses). The elements should start low in the annealer as heat rises. If your elements are close to the top, you are liable to have a cool floor. The brick portion of our oven will be finished at the 11th course.

The final course of brick should have a countersink carved into it. This is done to insure that the top metal frame is below the lip of the oven. If the metal at the top is exposed to the heat of the oven when the lid closes, it will warp (See illustration on pg. 249).

The Lid(s)

After completing the annealing oven body and welding the top steel framing in place, you're ready for the doors. If you want to use your annealer for casting, I recommend using a single lid. The drawings that follow describe how to construct a simple fiber-board lid. It should be noted that fiber-board comes in many forms and densities. If you're going to use a soft low-density fiber-board, I would recommend you soak it with colloidal silica. The colloidal silica will help keep the soft fiber particles from dusting. I used a garden size sprayer to soak the fiber after it was installed. The drawings show in detail how I constructed the lids. When using any monolithic board, I highly recommend using Inconel hangers to support the board. If you do not, your lid will eventually sag and crack. The lid shown is a single, counter-weighted one, simple to construct and very sturdy. It should be noted that some annealers have two lids. The two-lidded top-loading annealer is usually for blown ware. The single lid is for a casting oven. The elevated temperatures used for casting will cause any steel exposed to the heat to deteriorate. Annealing temperatures do not readily affect steel angle iron as long as they do not exceed 950° F. Over time the heat will affect the steel; that's why I recommend using stainless.

The lids are essentially angle iron frames into which you place your fiber-board cut to size. *Author's Note: All welding of handles and the like should be done before installing the fiber-board.*

Although my oven is constructed from IFB, my lids are constructed from 1" of Thermal Ceramics™ "M" board and 2" of mineral board as insulating back-up. The "M" board is somewhat expensive but is a rigid density board that does not need to be sealed with colloidal silica. The top of the lid is backed with 16 gauge sheet metal. For obvious health reasons, I do not want any fiber products exposed. Skamol Vermiculite board also works very well in place of the "M" board.

Counter Weights and Hinge

Although I mentioned that all the welding should be done prior to constructing the lid, the hinges should be welded in place after the lid has been placed on the annealer. Make sure your lid(s) are aligned accurately. The hinge must run absolutely parallel to the annealer. If it does not, your lid will not open correctly. The diagrams on pages 251 and 259 should be explanation enough as to how these systems work and are constructed. There are numerous methods for hinge and opener devices.

I have, in my travels, seen many different types of lids. Although I have tried to cover many of the details for constructing a simple annealing oven, it is impossible to describe every detail. There are other methods for constructing annealers, doors, hinges, etc. If you have never built this type of equipment, my advice is to visit other professional studios that maintain this equipment to familiarize yourself with how others construct equipment. I would offer one caveat. Many studios have annealers that work but are not built well, are not safe, and are not efficient ($). Be careful. Grunge may be cool for some but not for you. Do it right the first time!

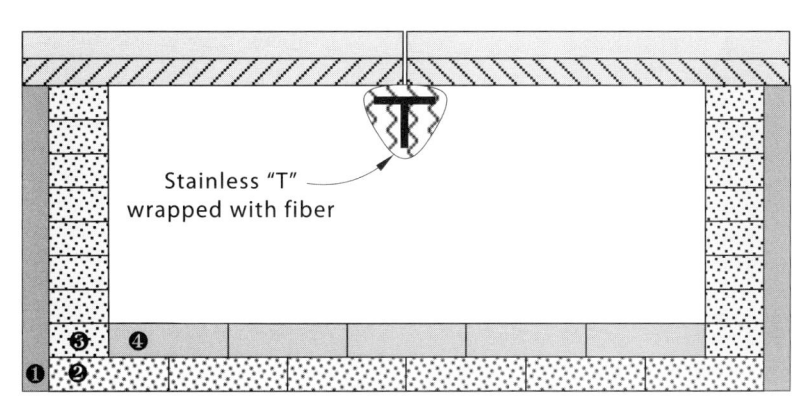

Stainless "T" wrapped with fiber

The order of construction
1. Outer wall insulation
2. Floor insulation
3. Wall
4. Floor

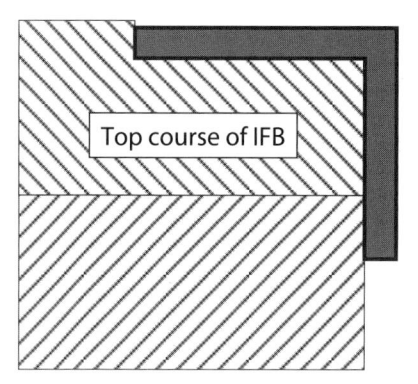

Side View of Angle Iron Frame

Top course of IFB

Building the Oven

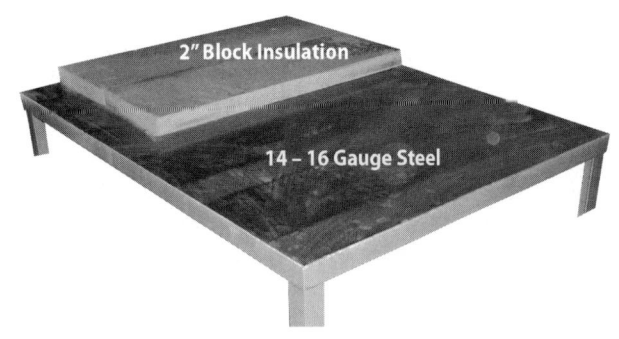

After building the table cover it with a good flat sheet of either 14 – 16 gauge steel. Don't weld it in place.

The first layer is 2" of mineral block insulation. This type of insulation has excellent insulating properties and is inexpensive. It is only good as a back-up insulation and should never be used in a heat zone.

This view shows the fiber-board insulation in place. I then pinned the board to the IFB and removed the clamps. The oven is now ready to have the steel sides welded into place. The angle iron and sheet metal are then put in place and welded.

Building the oven is fairly easy, but note how the IFB are laid above. In the case of this annealer, I've grooved the IFB on the long sides of the oven as indicated above.

This is one of the first top loading ovens we built at school in the early 70's. It lacked everything except enough energy. The temperture was adjusted with range controls shown on the left. The lid was cast from castable block insulation (not recommended). This shot is only to show how not to build and annealer.

The photos above depict how I built an oven a few years ago. If I built this oven today I would construct the frame first and then build the oven inside the frame.

250   Glass Notes

Lid, Lid Support, Counter Weight, and Hinge

View of the inside of lid with Inconel supports

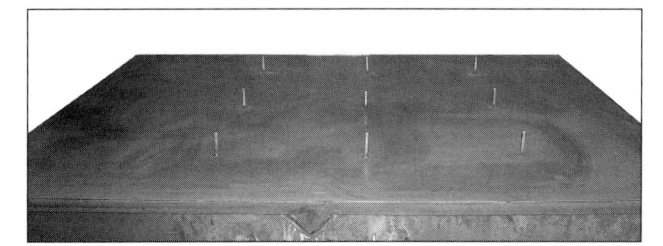

Top of Lid showing Inconel hanger supports welded in place

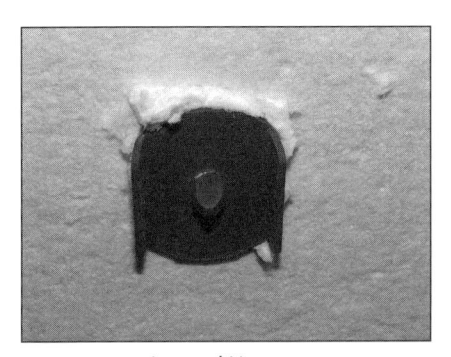

Inconel Hanger

Close-up of hinge

Annealing oven built by HUB

PVC pipe counter weight--sand or cement filled

Glass Notes 251

Annealing Oven

Top View

Side View

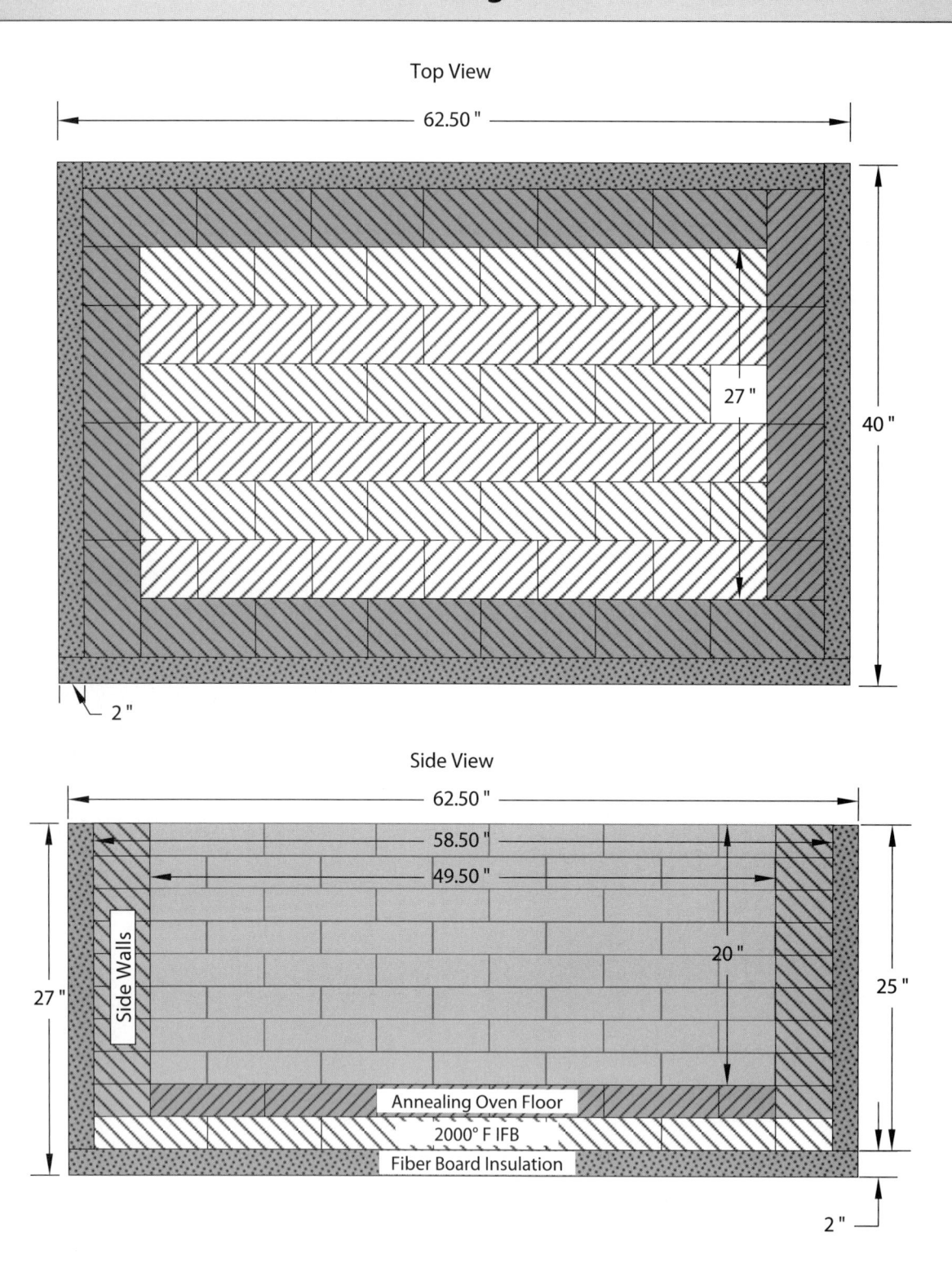

These are the actual dimensions of the annealing oven described on the previous pages. The drawing is to scale. Remember, If you substantially increase the cu. ft. of the interior, you will have to increase the power needed to run it. If you make the annealer smaller and use the same amount of power, your annealer will get hotter faster. It is better to overrate than underrate the oven. Remember, the elements will only draw the amount of energy for which they are engineered.

When building a studio, always plan for the future and install more power than you think you need. It is very expensive to run extra power lines. Halem's law says that you will eventually need twice the amount of electricity you think you need the first time.

Creating the Element Slot
Router Method 1

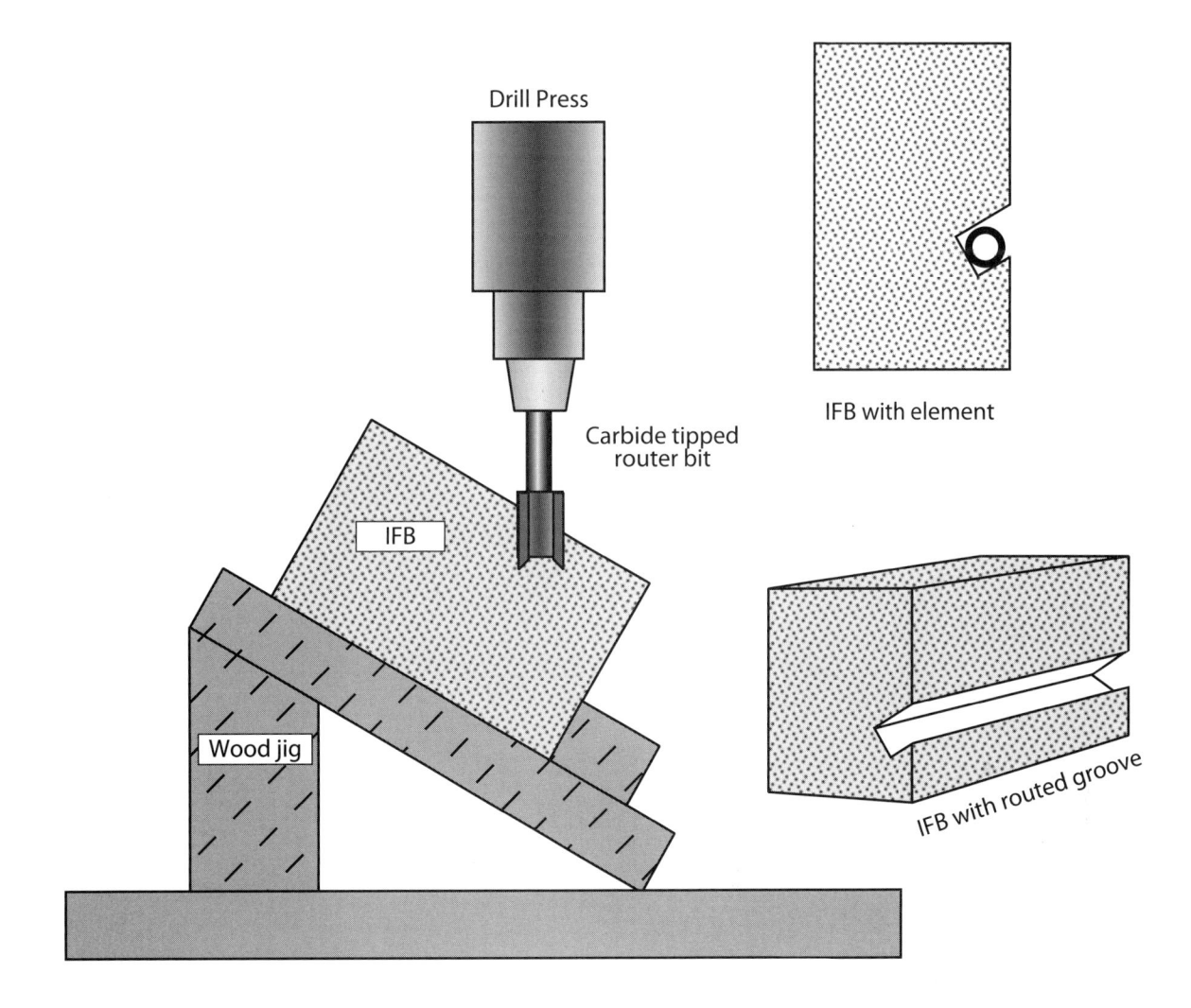

Drill Press

Carbide tipped router bit

IFB

Wood jig

IFB with element

IFB with routed groove

This diagram demonstrates how to make the groove in the IFB using a carbide-tipped router bit. The groove you create will hold the electric element. Although the groove created in the brick will make a nice "seat" for the element, it will still be necessary to pin the elements every 6". To groove the brick, you will need a good drill press. It is very important that you set up a guide for the brick so that the groove will be exactly parallel to the edge of the brick. Construct a wooden guide that will hold the IFB at about a 30° angle. Make sure the guide is parallel to the router bit. Once you've established the position of the guide, affix it to the table with clamps. Before routing the groove, dip the brick in water to minimize any brick dust. Using a couple of scrap brick, test your guide to see if it is absolutely parallel. Once you've set the guide correctly, you can run your brick through the router bit. Simply push the brick. Do not push the brick quickly or it may bind. Use your drill press at a very high speed to create the groove. Wear a high quality dust mask, heavy leather gloves, and a good, sturdy face shield. Grooving brick is dangerous work.

Creating the Element Slot
Router Method 2

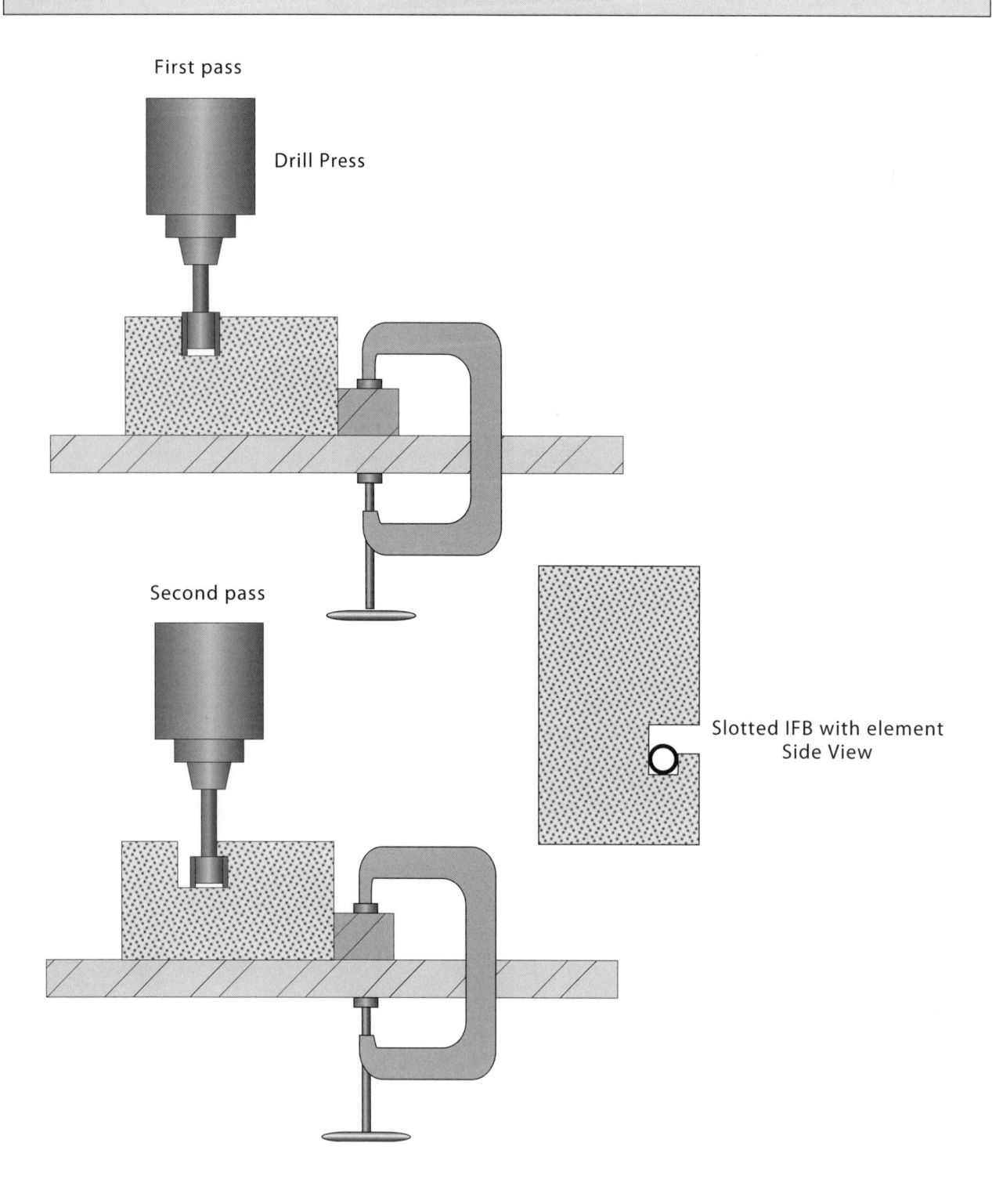

First pass

Drill Press

Second pass

Slotted IFB with element
Side View

Here is another method of slotting IFB. This slot requires two passes with carbide-tipped router blades. The first pass is about ½" wide. The second pass is about 1" wide. Although it takes a bit more time to make these slots, I think the groove holds the element more securely and out of the way. This slot design can prevent the dreaded element droop.

Jig for Grooving IFB

By Jack Schmidt

Make the jig long enough so that the brick can be moved back and forth to file groove into brick.

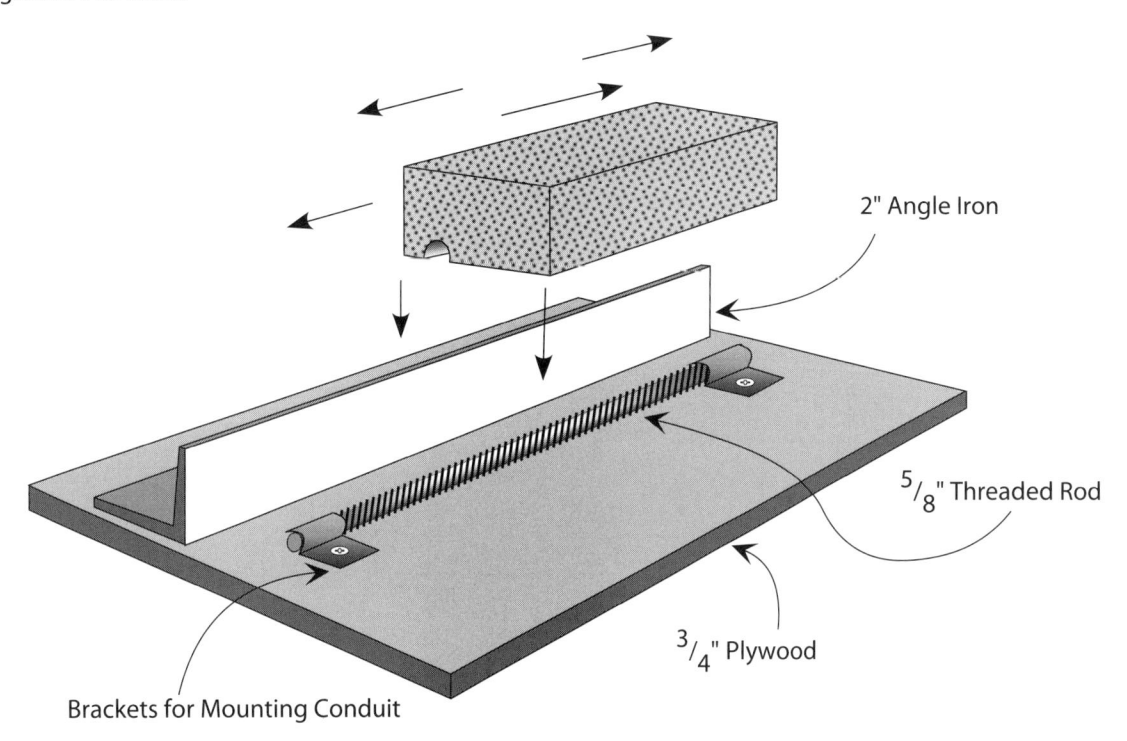

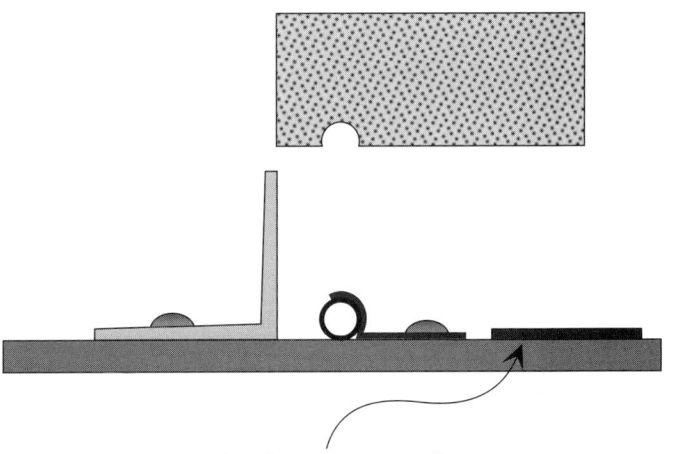

2" Angle Iron

5/8" Threaded Rod

3/4" Plywood

Brackets for Mounting Conduit

Depth of groove can be adjusted by placing thin pieces of metal or wood on plywood surface

These drawings are based on drawings sent to me by that great artist from Toledo, Ohio, Jack Schmidt. Thanks Jack!

Continued on next page

Glass Notes 255

Power Hack Saw Blade

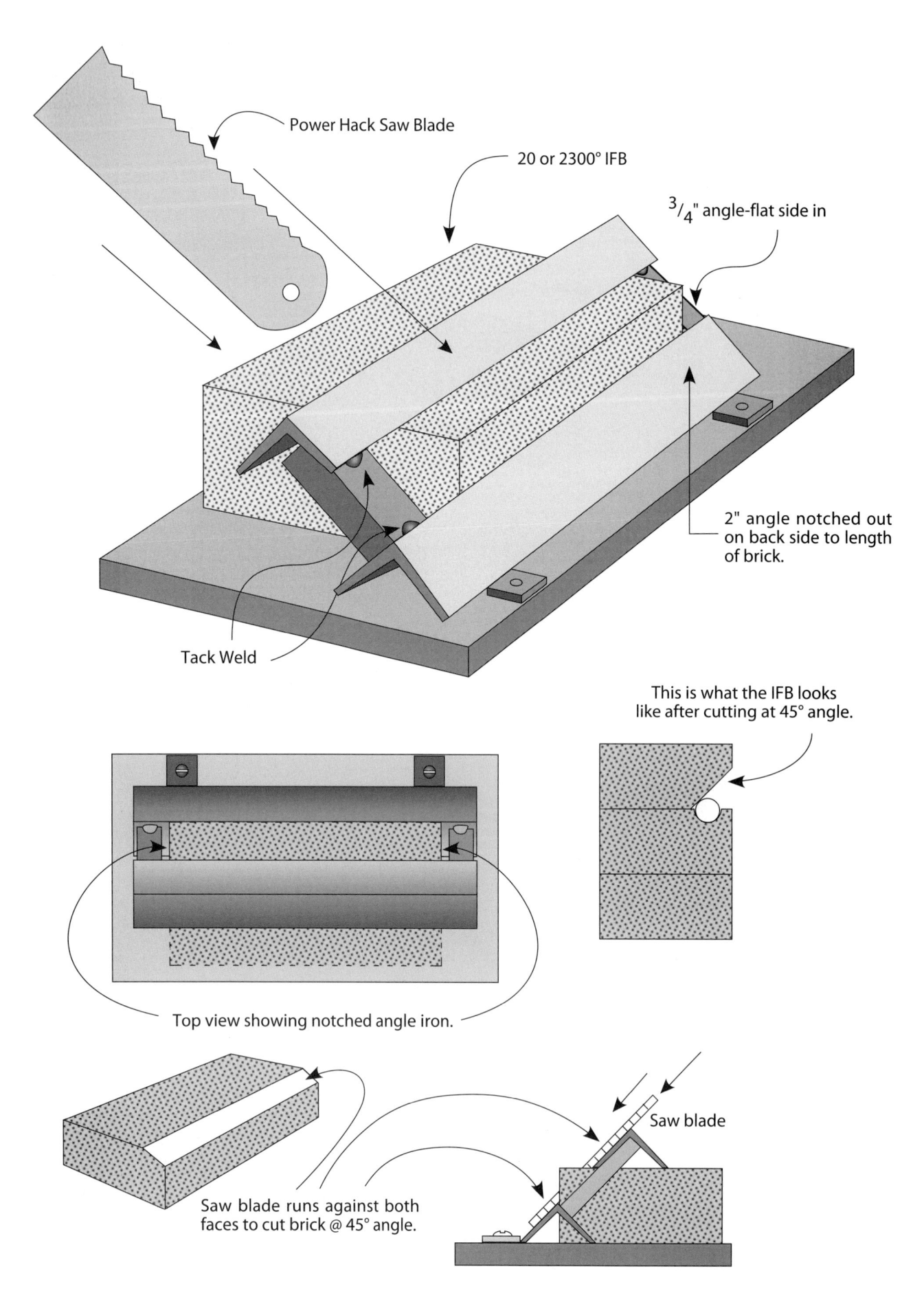

20 or 2300° IFB

3/4" angle-flat side in

2" angle notched out on back side to length of brick.

Tack Weld

This is what the IFB looks like after cutting at 45° angle.

Top view showing notched angle iron.

Saw blade runs against both faces to cut brick @ 45° angle.

Saw blade

256 Glass Notes

The Elements

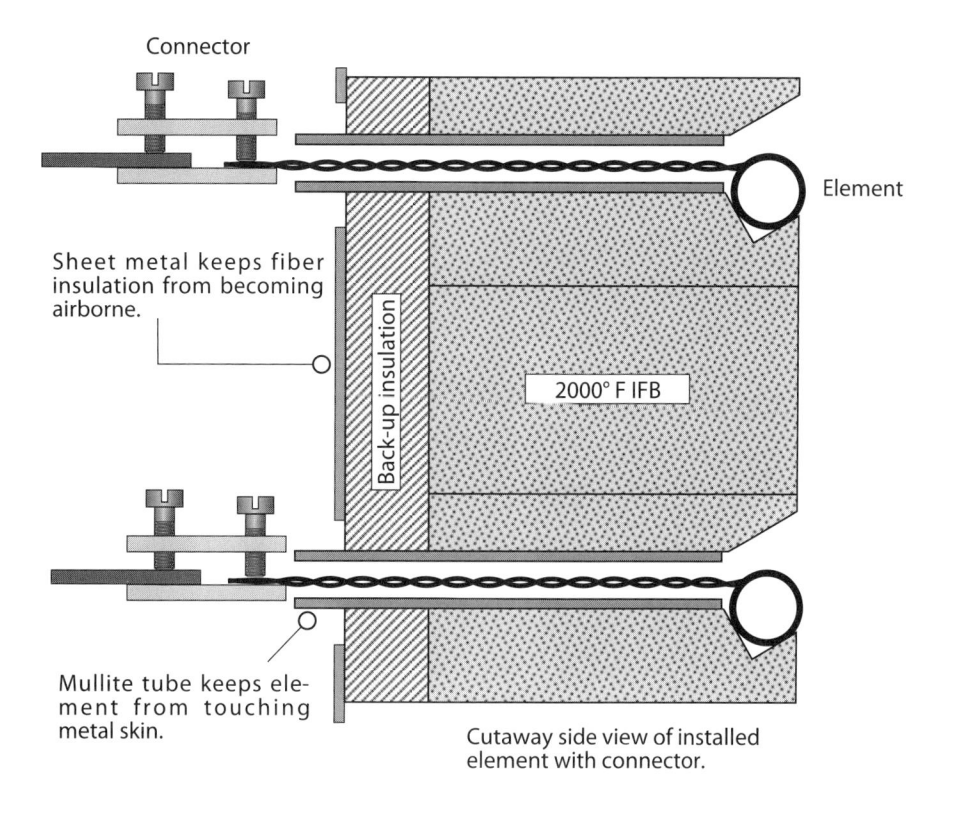

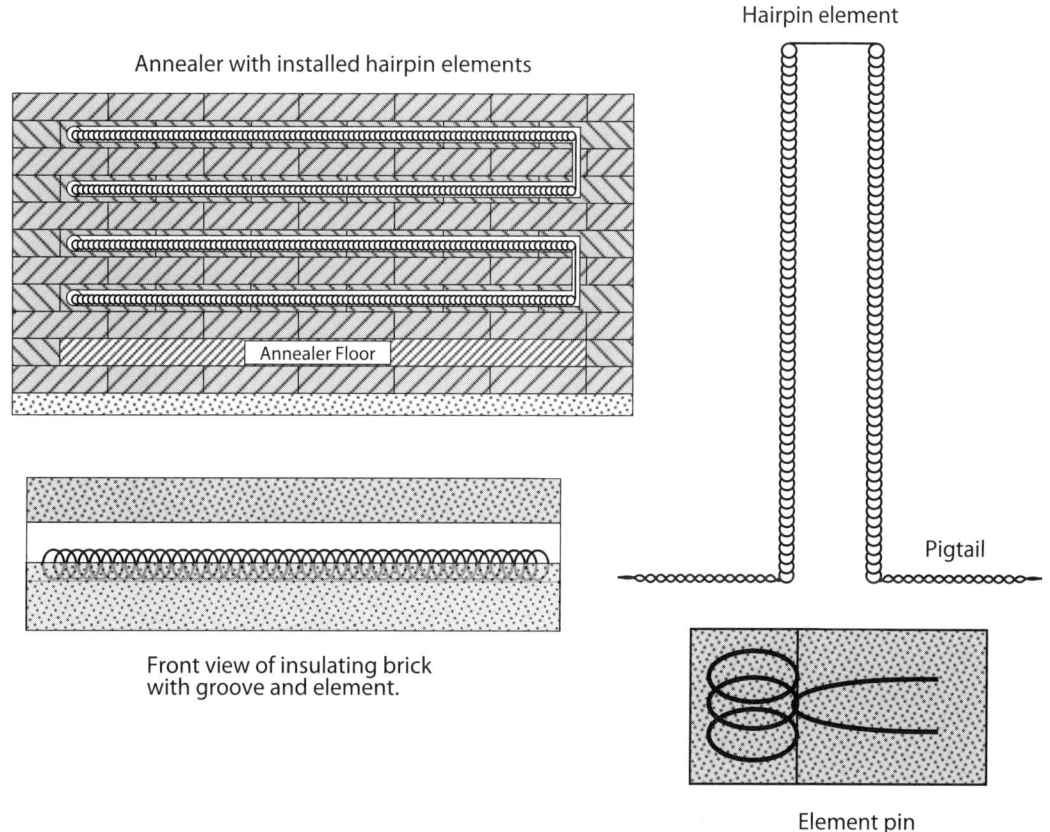

Connector

Sheet metal keeps fiber insulation from becoming airborne.

Back-up insulation

Element

2000° F IFB

Mullite tube keeps element from touching metal skin.

Cutaway side view of installed element with connector.

Annealer with installed hairpin elements

Annealer Floor

Front view of insulating brick with groove and element.

Hairpin element

Pigtail

Element pin

Glass Notes 257

The Lid

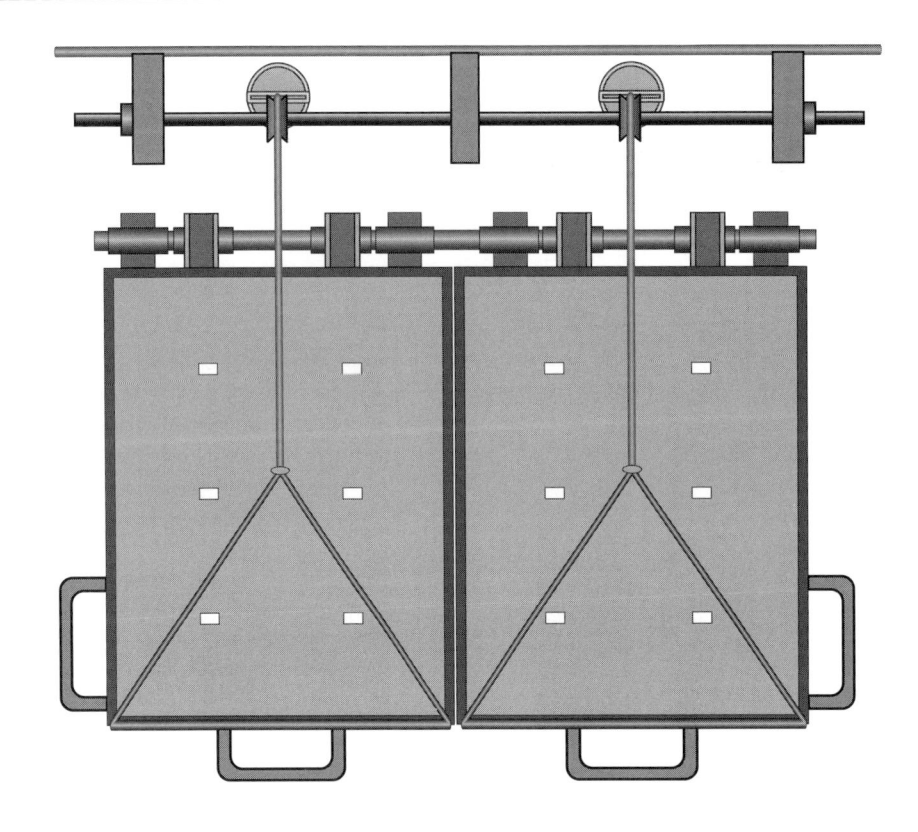

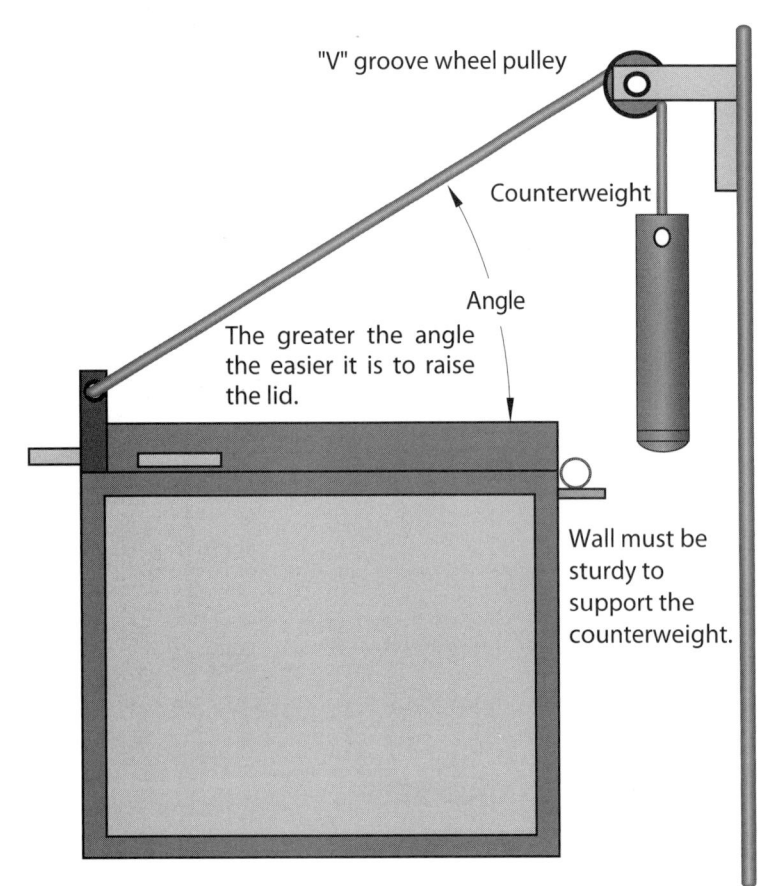

"V" groove wheel pulley

Counterweight

Angle

The greater the angle the easier it is to raise the lid.

Wall must be sturdy to support the counterweight.

These diagrams show the lid system in place. Aircraft wire is used to hold the counter weight. Use a "V" groove wheel instead of a pulley to operate the counterweight system. This type of wheel has roller bearings in the bore and is very smooth.

Use a 3" to 4" plastic pipe with a cap on one end as a counterweight. Fill the pipe with concrete until your lid moves easily. If you use too much counterweight, your lid may not close properly. The greater the angle, the less weight needed.

If your oven is not near a wall, then construct an "A" frame to hold your "pulleys." Make sure you lag bolt the frame into the floor. If you are clever, you can attach the counterweight system directly to the oven's angle iron frame.

The Hinge

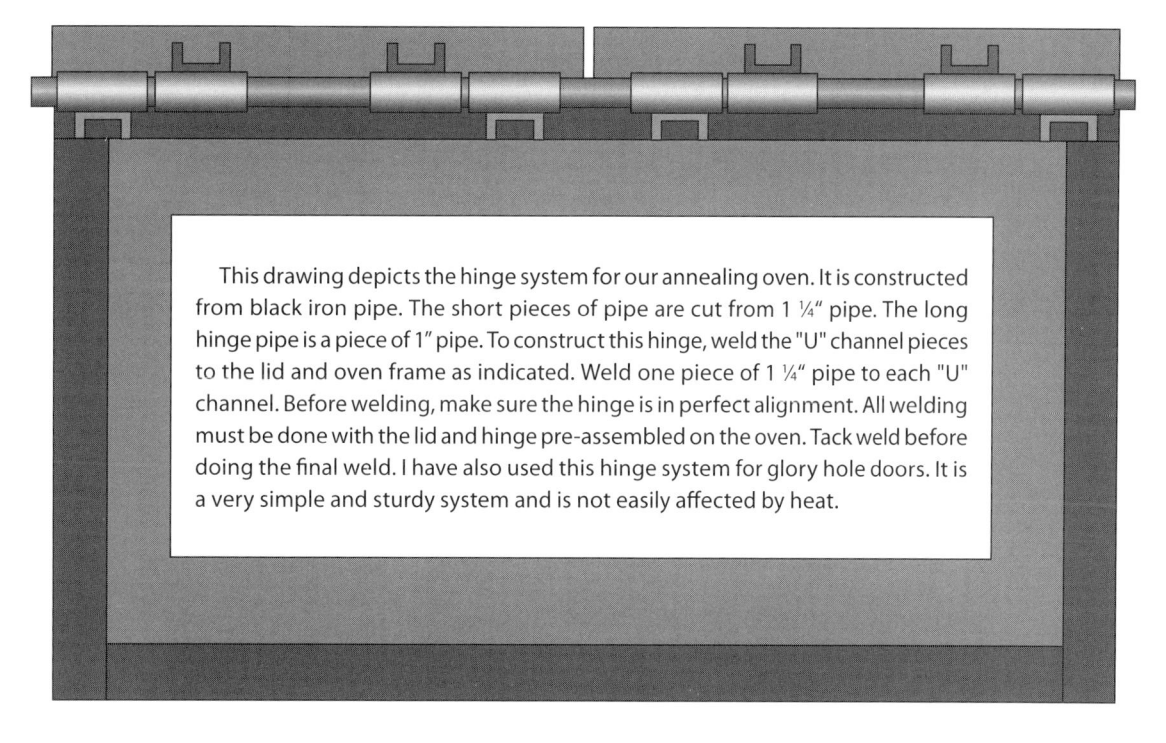

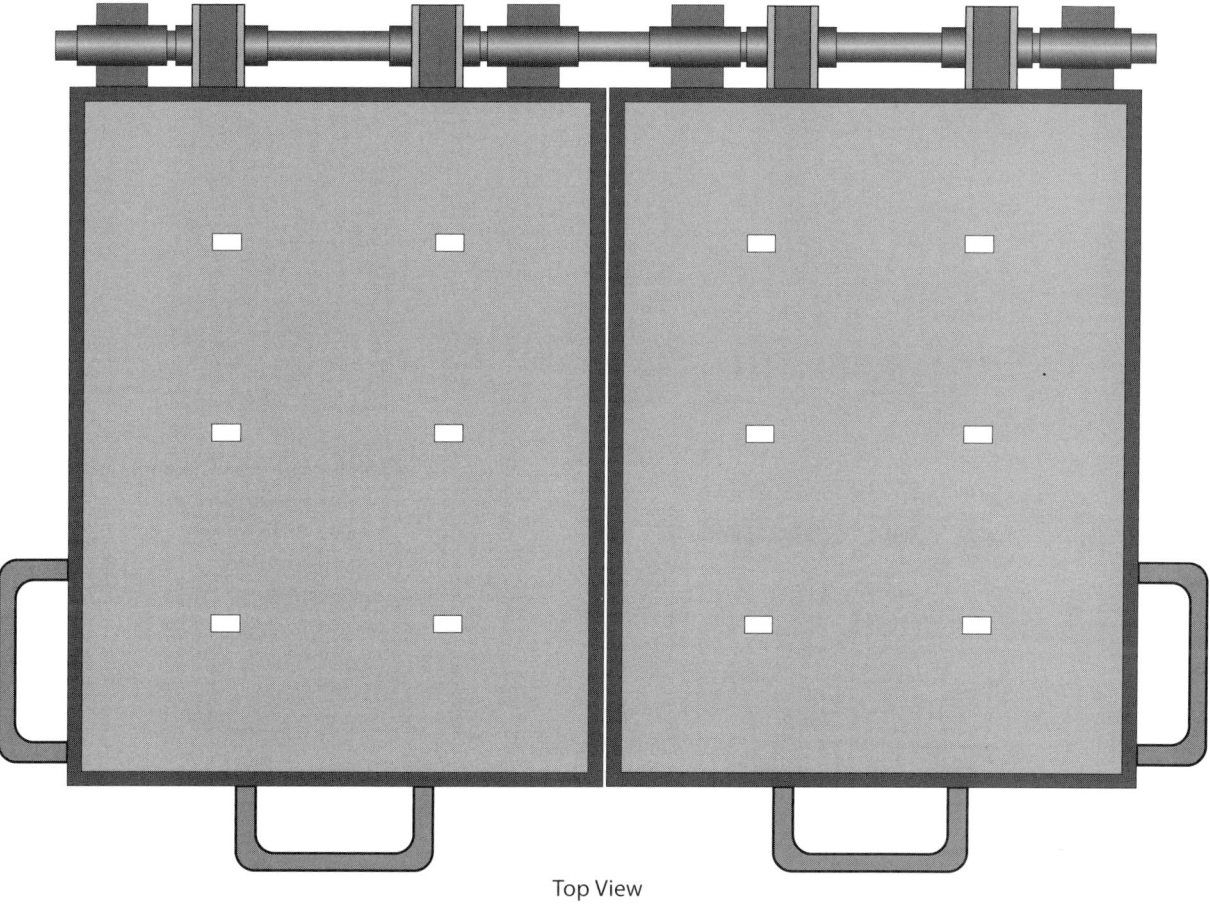

This drawing depicts the hinge system for our annealing oven. It is constructed from black iron pipe. The short pieces of pipe are cut from 1 ¼" pipe. The long hinge pipe is a piece of 1" pipe. To construct this hinge, weld the "U" channel pieces to the lid and oven frame as indicated. Weld one piece of 1 ¼" pipe to each "U" channel. Before welding, make sure the hinge is in perfect alignment. All welding must be done with the lid and hinge pre-assembled on the oven. Tack weld before doing the final weld. I have also used this hinge system for glory hole doors. It is a very simple and sturdy system and is not easily affected by heat.

Top View

Materials for Annealer

- 2000° F (1093° C) Insulating Brick (IFB), ------- 325 pcs. (13 boxes)
- Mineral Block Insulation, 2" thick, --------------- 40 sq. ft.
- Electric heating elements ------------------------------ 4
- 2" Fiberboard (each lid requires approximately 9 sq. ft. of board)
- 2" Mineral Board, (each lid requires approximately 9 sq. ft. of board)
- Angle Iron, 1 ½" x 1 ½" x ⅛" ----------------------- 75' linear feet
- 1" black iron pipe -- 5'
- 1 ¼" black iron pipe ------------------------------------ 4'
- Inconel Hangers, 18 for ea. lid
- Digital controller, MDR or SCR or SSR relay, 1 of either
- Assorted materials for counter weight system (see drawing)
- The above materials will vary depending upon the size annealer you build. Use the materials list as a starting point.

At today's prices, you can expect to pay $1,500 to $2,000 to build this annealer. This price does not include the cost of your controller, relay, thermocouple, or electrician. If you purchase a digital controller, you can expect to pay between $300 and $500 depending on the controller you purchase. The cost of relays can be a bit pricey as well.

An electrician will charge for time and materials. Shop around for an electrician and make sure you get a written estimate. Remember, an estimate is only an estimate. If the electrician encounters problems, that $2,000 estimate can rise appreciably. Know exactly what you want the electrician to do and make sure the electrician knows what he's doing. If you make changes after accepting the estimate, your costs will rise appreciably. After adding all the expenses, this annealer might seem expensive; in reality it is very inexpensive when you consider that, with minimal maintenance, it should last as long as your studio. Your annealer is your best friend. Build it right the first time.

This drawing of the "mailbox" annealer by Dudley Giberson is exactly what we used at the U. of Wisconsin in the 60's. The only difference is that our door was bottom-hinged and not-side hinged. Half the time when we opened the door it would flop down and create a cloud of fiber dust. Oh, my aching lungs.

The Skamol Annealer

The Skamol line of Vermiculite Insulating slabs and the Calcium Silicate Insulating slabs for the construction of annealing ovens is in my estimation an ideal product. What makes these products ideal is the fact that they have none of the health problems one associates with fiber and also have high hot face values, excellent insulating values, are rigid, strong, and do not break down over time. What more can you ask for? The slabs can be purchased in various lengths, thicknesses, and densities. At the present time, many studios are rebuilding their annealers with these product. The products that seem most applicable for building annealing ovens are the Vermiculite Insulating Slab V-1100 (475) or the V-1100 (600). The Calcium Silicate Super-1100E is the back-up insulating slab of choice as well. Skamol manufactures other refractory products that you may find applications for in your studio. Skamol is a Danish company, but they do have U.S. and worldwide distribution. To obtain information about the Skamol line of refractory products, go to their Web site--www.skamol.com--or call Kevin Keeler at 503/698-3998 to find a distributor.

Vermiculite Insulating Slabs
For hot face insulation, up to 2102° F (1150° C)

V-1100 (375) • V-1100 (475) (30 lb.^{3}) • V-1100 (600) (37.5 lb.^{3}) • VIP 12

SKAMOL V-1100 is a vermiculite-based, high-temperature, energy-saving, and cost-effective insulating slab designed for a maximum service temperature of 2012° F (1100° C). It combines good strength with low thermal conductivity and is highly resistant to thermal shock. The slabs are clean to handle and easy to install. If using jointing mortar, use: SKAMOL FL-06

The SKAMOL V-1100 vermiculite slabs cover several grades in various combinations of bulk density, insulation properties, and compressive strength. The product composition allows for easy cutting and shaping of both slab types on site using ordinary wood-working tools.

SKAMOL VIP-12 is a high-density slab characterized by good insulation value, very high mechanical strength, and excellent abrasion resistance. A 1" layer of VIP - 12 makes an excellent floor for annealers. See the illustrations on the following pages.

Calcium Silicate Insulating Slabs
For backup insulation, up to 2012° F (1100° C)

SUPER-ISOL • SUPER-1100 E • SUPER-1100 ET

The SKAMOL SUPER calcium silicate slabs cover a range of extremely lightweight insulating slabs with excellent insulating value, high mechanical strength, and good heat resistance. The Super-1100 E slabs are designed for maximum service temperatures of 1832°F (1100°C), are light grey, and have smooth, rigid, and non-dusting surfaces. The recommended grade for the backup of annealing ovens is Super-1100 E.

SKAMOL SUPER calcium silicate slabs are designed as backup insulation of all refractory constructions, dense firebrick, insulating firebrick, castables, plastic refractories, etc.

See pg. 333 for contact information on purchasing the Skamol line of products.

Standard Sizes for Skamol Slabs

Standard Sizes Metric Vermiculite Insulating Slabs		
V-1100 (375) V-1100 (475)	1000 x 610 mm 1000 x 305 mm	25 through 75 mm
V-1100 (600)	Same as above	25 through 75 mm
VIP 12	1000 x 305 mm 610 x 305 mm	30, 40, 50 mm 25, 30, 40, 50, 60, 75 mm

Standard Sizes US/British Vermiculite Insulating Slabs		
V-1100 (375) V-1100 (475)	36" x 24" 36" x 12"	1" through 4"
V-1100 (600)	Same as above	1" through 3"
VIP 12	36" x 12	1.25", 1.50", 2"
	24" x 12	1", 1.25", 1.50", 2", 2.5", 3"

Standard Sizes Metric Calcium Silicate Insulating Slabs	
mm length x width	Thickness
1220 x 1000 1000 x 610 1000 x 305	25 through 100

Standard Sizes US/British	
inches length x width	Thickness
48 x 36 36 x 24 36 x 12	1" through 4"

Hot Face/Cold Face Calculations for Skamol Annealer

Hot Face Temperature 1700° F (927° C) Lower Hot Face = Lower Cold Face		
Skamol Vermiculite V-1100 (600)	Super 1100° F Calcium Silicate Thickness in inches	Cold Face Temperature Degrees F
1" (25 mm)	3	176° (80° C)
2" (50 mm)	2	187° (86° C)
2"	3	164° (73° C)
3" (76 mm)	1	211° (99° C)
4" (101 mm)	1	196° (91° C)

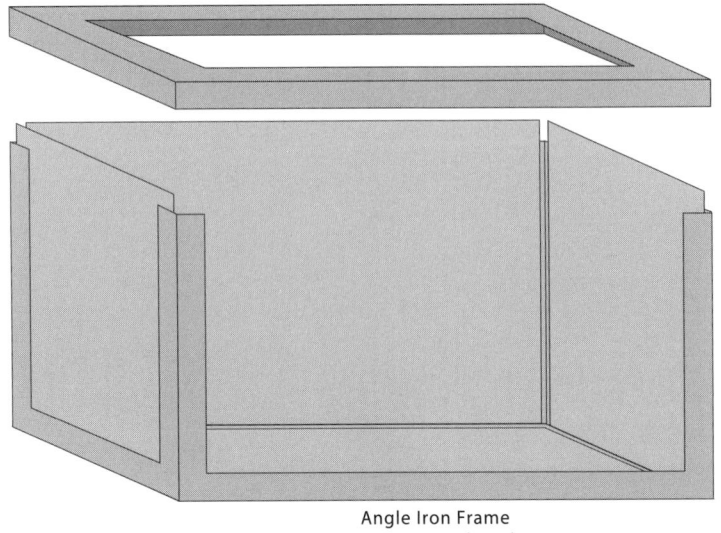

Angle Iron Frame
with sheet metal in place

Tips on Building the Skamol Front-Loading Annealing Oven

- Develop a drawing with dimensions of your oven. If you're building the oven depicted on the following pages, all the drawing is done for you. Before you begin to build using Skamol Vermiculite board, note the following:
    - Skamol Vermiculite board has the same coefficient of expansion as steel, and as a result, it will expand and contract each time it is fired. Because of this characteristic, I highly recommend when building with Skamol Vermiculite board that you at least build in a 1" lap joint when two boards meet. It is not necessary to do this to the Calcium Silicate backup boards. (See lap joint illustration below.)
- Using the outer oven dimensions, build your angle iron frame but do not attach the top angle iron. Only build the bottom and side angles. After making sure all the pieces are square, firmly tack weld the frame together. If you make an error in your measurements, you will be able to easily break the tack weld. I recommend you use sheet metal to contain the oven. It's not necessary to weld the sheet metal in place. I also recommend you cut the sheet metal a bit smaller so that it has some room to expand when it gets warm.
- A word to the wise: Do not cut the insulating slabs prior to welding the frame as your dimensions may differ somewhat from the drawings.
- Assemble the pieces and parts starting with the bottom and then the sidewalls. The drawings are very clear as to how the oven goes together. The crown goes in last.
- Make sure you've routed the element grooves and pre-drilled the holes for the element pigtails prior to installing the Skamol.
- You may wish to use the recommended cement for the joints to insure a tight fit. Install and pin the elements prior to putting the crown in place.
- Once the crown is in place, carefully weld the top angle iron frame. When welding the top angle iron, only tack weld so that it can easily be taken apart at a future date and rebuilt. If you've measured twice and cut once, all should fit perfectly. Now you're ready for the doors.
- Weld the door frames, assemble the insulating panels, and weld up the Inconel studs. These studs are very important as they are what holds the door in place. If you think friction is enough to hold the panels in place, you're mistaken as eventually they will fall out from constant opening and closing.
- Carefully lay the oven on its back and lay you're doors in place.
- Weld your heavy-duty hinges in place and your finished. Oh yes, figure out a good latch and put that in place. Your latch should be easy to open with one hand, and remember: that hand may have a very thick glove on it.

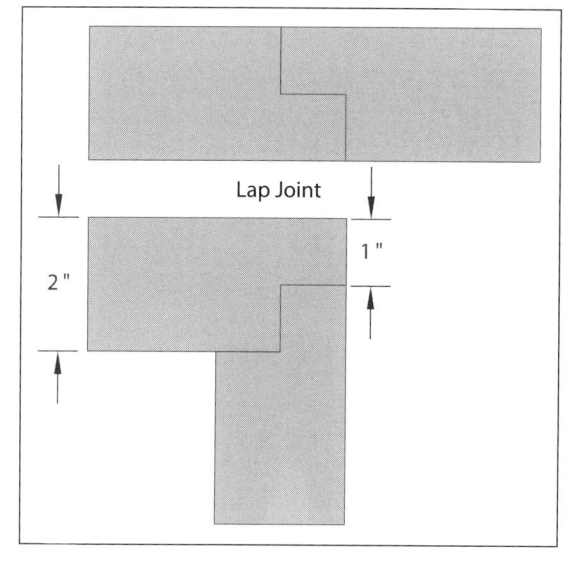

Materials Needed to Build the Annealer

You will be required to cut and route the boards to fit the dimensions shown in the drawings but there is little surplus material. I recommend you purchase a couple of extra pieces just in case. It is important that you use good tools and have sharp blades.

- Interior of oven, Skamol Vermiculite V-1100 (475), 5 @ 36 x 24 x 2
- Doors, 2@ 36 x 24 x 2
- Floor, VIP 12, 1@ 36 x 24 x 1
- Back-up Insulation, Super 1100 Calcium Silicate, 5@ 48 x 36 x 2
- Doors, 2@ 36 x 24 x 2
  All dimensions in inches

The Skamol Front-Loading Oven

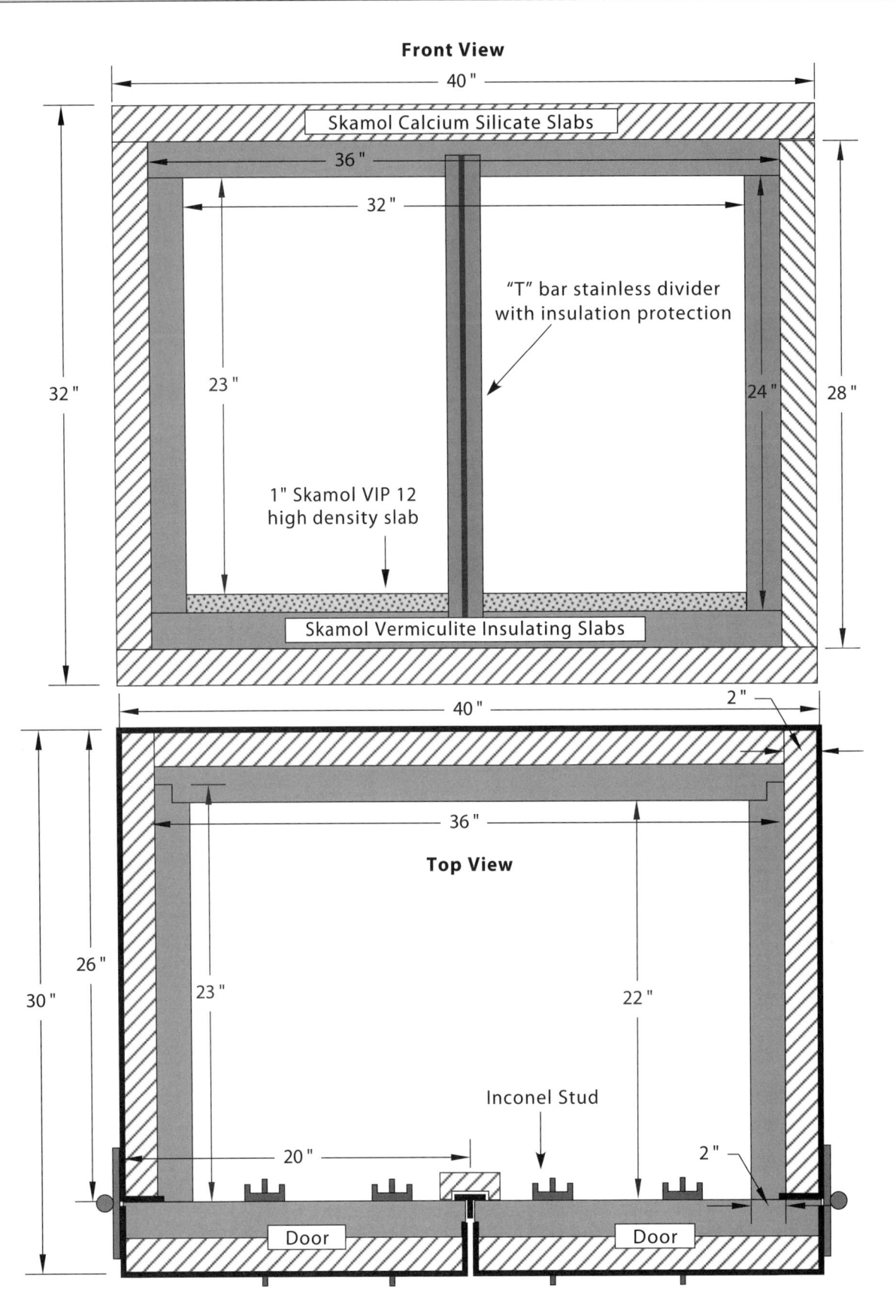

Front View

- 40"
- Skamol Calcium Silicate Slabs
- 36"
- 32"
- 32"
- 23"
- 24"
- 28"
- "T" bar stainless divider with insulation protection
- 1" Skamol VIP 12 high density slab
- Skamol Vermiculite Insulating Slabs

Top View

- 40"
- 2"
- 36"
- 26"
- 30"
- 23"
- 22"
- Inconel Stud
- 20"
- 2"
- Door
- Door

264 Glass Notes

Skamol Oven Side Views

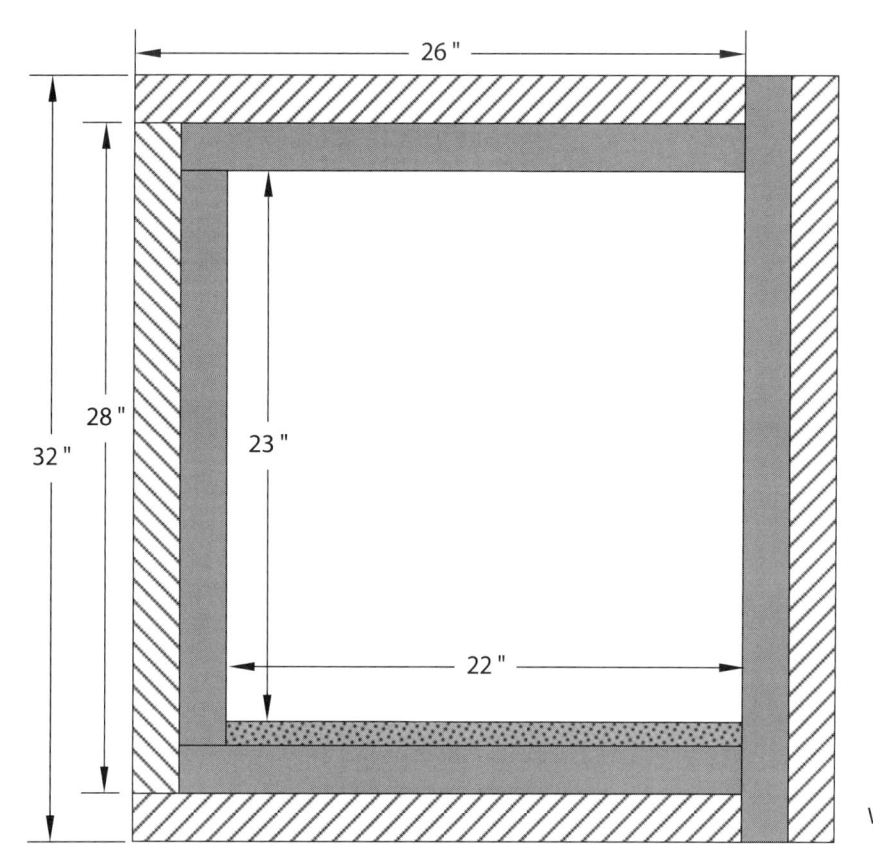

When building an annealer with these products, remember that the Skamol Vermiculite Insulating slabs are used for the hot face and and Calcium Silicate Insulating Slabs as the backup. These illustrations give a general idea of how to construct an oven using Skamol Vermiculite Board and the companion Calcium Silicate Insulating slabs. I have sized this oven to fit the standard sizes of the Skamol Slabs. You can size your oven to any dimension that suits your need.

Side View
With Dimensions

I recommend a floor composed of Skamol VIP 12 and placed on top of and inside the Skamol Vermiculite Board. The VIP 12 is a high density board and very abrasion resistant. If and when the floor wears out, it can easily be replaced without having to tear the oven apart. The Skamol board on the sidewalls can easily be routed to accommodate the elements. To be on the safe side, you may wish to support the crown with Inconel studs and washers. Although the board is strong, over time it might crack. The Inconel studs will prevent that from happening.

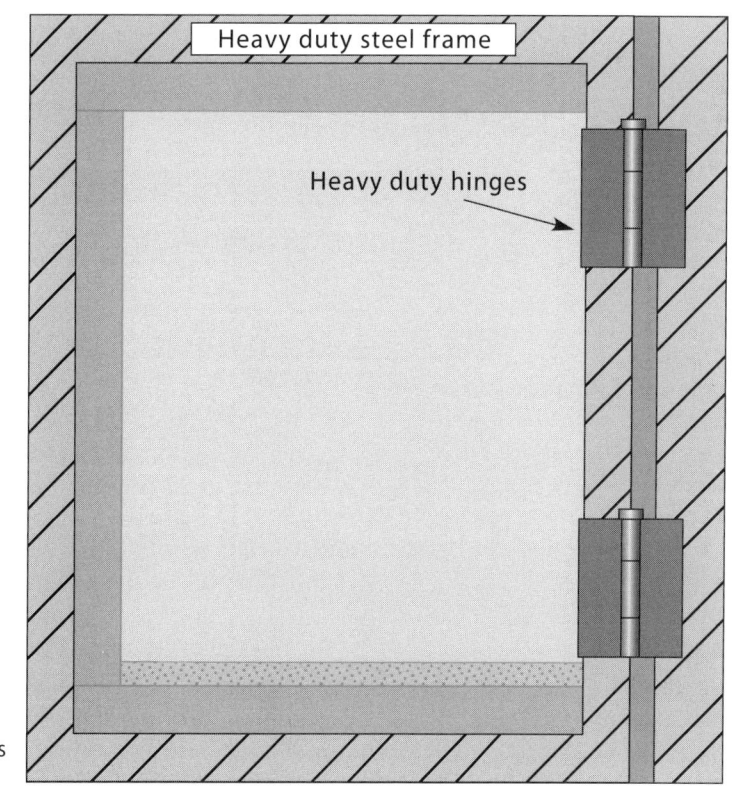

Side View
With Frame & Hinges

Heavy duty steel frame

Heavy duty hinges

Glass Notes 265

The Roll-Out Casting Oven

The "roll–out oven" is probably the one major contribution that I have made toward the technical advancement of glass casting. I introduced this style oven in the early 70's, first as a small pickup oven and then as a larger version for casting. For those of you familiar with ceramic kilns, it is not unlike a car kiln. The glass version is similar in every way except it is fired electrically. The advantage of this style oven is that it allows the artist to open the oven by rolling out a "car" thus permitting you to easily manipulate your casting, slump, fusing, pâte de verre, etc. It is particularly handy if you're doing large sand castings and need to cast while the molds are in the oven. It is also very handy if you're doing large kilncastings and have very heavy molds. Loading the mold in the roll-out is quite easy. Our students have done sand castings that have weighed over 100 pounds (50 kg) in one of these ovens as well as 100 pound kiln casting molds. The roll-out can be built to most any dimension to accommodate either low flat castings or high vertical castings. I have recently built 2 roll-out ovens each measuring 6' x 4 ½' x 2 ½' high (1.8 m x 1.3 m x 61 cm high).

When building one of these ovens, it is important to engineer it well. The following drawings should give you some idea how this oven is built. Before building the oven, I would like to make some observations concerning the construction of various elements of this style oven.

Brief Overview

The first thing to construct is the car. The size of your car will dictate the dimensions of the cinder block wall foundation (Fig. 1). The car will hold the floor and the door. You will also need to weld sturdy cross members onto the car in order to hold the brick floor in place (Fig. 1). Once the car is constructed and the wheels are put in place, lay the track and affix it to the floor (Fig. 1, pg. 270). You will need to drill into the cement floor and affix the track with expandable fasteners (wedge anchors). A good hardware store should carry them. If you cannot locate these fasteners, you can obtain them from W.W. Grainger. Their order number is (3A445). Under no circumstance do you want the track to shift. Make sure you locate everything on a smooth, level floor. Lay the cinder block, leaving about 1" clearance around the perimeter of the car. The cinder block must be square to the car. It should go without saying that the car must be constructed from heavy– duty steel and welded absolutely square. If you cannot weld, find someone who can. This is not a project for a novice welder. The height of the cinder block should be at least one brick plus ½" to 1" lower than the steel top of the car bed. Once you have completed all of the above, you are ready to begin the brick work.

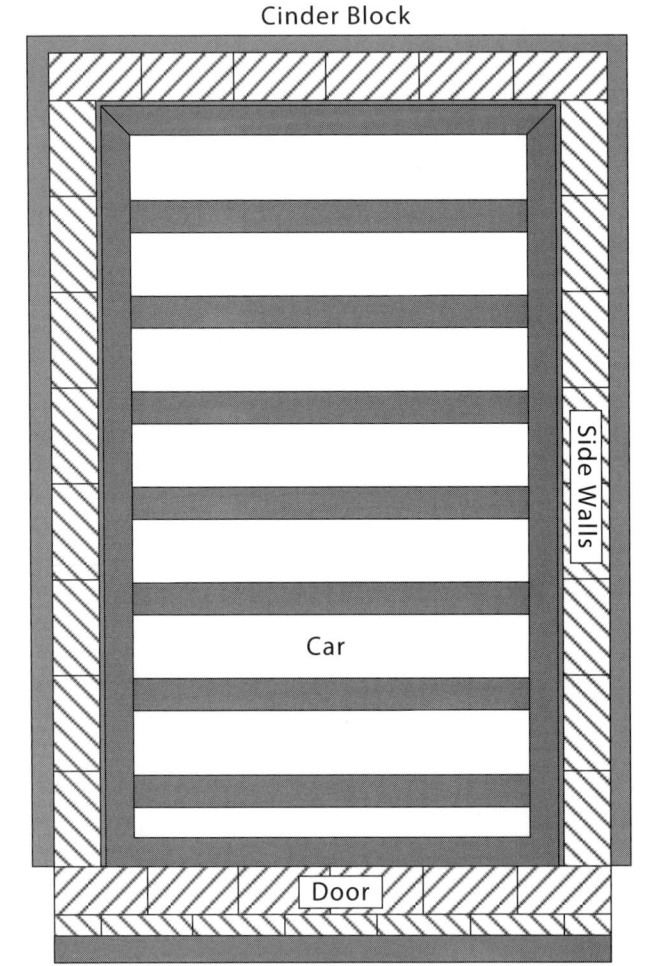

Details

The Car: The car should be constructed from ¼" (6 cm.) steel. It must be square, have strong welds, and roll smoothly. The car dimensions will generate the oven wall dimensions. Always use a good steel square to assure accurate angles. Tack weld before doing the final weld. It's easy to break a tack weld if you make any errors. Weld all cross members for the floor when you are absolutely sure where they are located. The car wheels should be square to each other. If they are not, the car will not roll accurately. Use a high quality "V" groove wheel––one that has roller bearings in the hub. The wheels need to run smoothly and handle some serious weight. These

Top View, Steel Car in Oven
Fig. 1

266   Glass Notes

types of wheels are expensive but are well worth the investment.

The Track: Once the car is built, and before you do any brick work, you need to construct the track, affix it to the floor, and place the car on it. If you have engineered everything well, your car should roll smoothly and accurately. The track that the car runs on should be made from heavy–duty angle iron. Once the track dimension (width of the car wheels) is established, it should be welded with steel strap so that its dimension won't change. It should then be placed accurately between the cinder block and bolted to the floor; the car should then be placed on it. It is worth noting that the car will be quite heavy; if you push too hard after the oven is built, the inertia of the car can destroy all your hard work. You may wish to weld a small car stop at the front of the track before building the walls of the oven. To prevent the car from rolling off the track, weld a stop on the back of the track as well. Take your time when calculating dimensions. Mistakes can be costly.

The Cinder Block: After you have finished the car and located the track, you can lay the cinder block. The mason that lays the block may not be able to lay the block with the car in place, so it is important to draw the lines on the floor where the block will sit. The height of the cinder block should be at least one brick plus ½" to 1" lower than the steel top of the car bed. Once the block is in place and set, you can put your car back on the track. Make sure the mason lays the block square and the top of the block is absolutely level. If it is not, the walls of your oven will "lean." Refer to Fig. 1 to understand the relationship between the cinder block and the car.

The Air Seal: Once all of the groundwork is done, you are ready to do the brickwork on the oven. Perhaps the single most important aspect is engineering the air seal. The air seal is used in ceramic car kilns as well as our glass roll-out, and it prevents any outside air from entering the oven during the annealing and cooling cycles. The principal is that air and heat do not readily move around right angles. The seal must run the length of the two sides and the front (pg. 271) The air seal slot should have a ½" to 1" space (1.25–2.5 cm.) all the way around it. To totally seal the groove from any outside air, pour sand on the lower lip of the of the car seal. If you have not constructed your car accurately or located everything on a level surface, you may find the brick that fits into the slot will bind. If this happens, try to locate the source of the problem and, if it is not too out of square, shave a bit from the slot until it rolls smoothly. The drawings concerning the air seal are very accurate and should help clarify this important detail.

The Walls: Before constructing the walls of the oven, it will be necessary to build the oven bed and the door first. You will build the oven walls to fit the door. If you build it this way, your oven will always seal accurately. The tolerance of the space between the wall and the brick on the car is usually no more than ½" to 1" (1.25–2.5 cm). The walls of the oven need to be perpendicular to the floor of the car. If your oven walls are not perpendicular, it may be because the cinder block was laid poorly.

The walls will be 4 ½" (11.5 cm) of 2000° F (1095° C) IFB insulating brick and 2" (5 cm) of block insulation behind that. Sheet metal covers the completed outside. The sheet metal accomplishes two things: it keeps the block insulation fibers from becoming airborne, and it holds the oven together. To keep the block insulation in place when installing it, take some thin nails about 2-3" long and push them through the block and into the insulating brick. You can leave them in when building the angle iron frame. It is important to weld an angle iron frame around all the edges of the oven. To do this, you will need a serious number of bar clamps to tighten and keep the angle iron in place while welding. Make sure everything is as square and plumb as possible before welding. Be careful how hard you clamp the angle iron. Your walls can buckle easily if you clamp too hard. Remember, you have only 3 walls to this oven. An oven with 3 walls is not as sturdy as one with 4. Tack weld all the angle iron before committing to a permanent weld. Tack weld the sheet metal sides to the angle iron to prevent it from slipping. If you make any mistakes, a tack weld is easy to undue. Building this type of oven is not for the novice. I recommend you build a standard type oven before attempting one of these beauties.

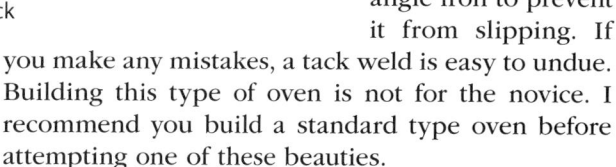

Element location: If this is to be a casting oven, it is important to have elements in the floor. Elements in the floor can really facilitate kiln casting.

It is assumed that you are familiar with how much energy it will take for you to power your oven. I recommend using three-phase power (if you have it). It may be a bit tricky to wire, but the benefits far outweigh any wiring inconvenience. To determine what your requirements are for three-phase power as well as to understand the different wiring methods of three-phase, I recommend you call Mark Jesson at The Duralite Company. If I haven't mentioned it, Mark Jesson is very knowledgeable and gives fantastic telephone help. The floor elements will sit in a groove, and all the connections for power will be done on the underside of the car. It is important to put 2 layers of silicon carbide kiln shelves over the elements. Silicon carbide offers very little insulating value and permits the heat from the elements to pass through quite easily. The silicon carbide will prevent sand from getting into the elements and will also prevent abrasion or molten glass from making contact with the elements. The second layer of shelves should be dimensioned differently than the first layer so that there is no crack leading to the elements. If there is, sand can get into the elements. While the sand won't hurt the elements, it can shorten the life of the element. Olivine sand, used by many casters for sand casting, has a low fusion temperature and, if it sits in the groove with your elements, can shorten their lifespan. The iron content of builder's sand is quite high and can also shorten the lifespan of your elements if not regularly cleaned out of the element grooves. If you use sand as a bed for your castings, use a good, clean, "white" sand. It is good to vacuum out your floor elements occasionally if you're doing sand casting. A clean oven is a happy oven.

The rest of the elements are located in the sidewalls and ideally in the crown as well.

The Crown

The flat-roof construction described in this section is simple to construct and, if done correctly, should last the life of the annealer. The advent of lightweight, space-age materials has made the job of constructing a crown much easier than in the "stone age" of my youth.

How to Build the Crown

Dense fiber-board and Skamol Vermiculite Board, make flat roof construction very easy. If you use any of these materials you should use the Inconel 601 supports to help maintain the rigidity and integrity of your crown. Regardless of how rigid your crown is, over time, it is apt to crack if it is not supported in some way. Reference the drawings on the following pages to understand how the crown is built and supported.

More Elements

I'm very partial to ovens that have elements in the crown as well as in the bed of the car. I like this design very much because the floor elements, and crown elements seem to complement each other. The heat seems to be fairly even throughout the oven. Just as an aside, Danny Schwoerer of Bullseye glass once said, "you can never have enough thermocouples." This means that, if you really want to know what the actual front to back temperature of your oven is, you should place thermocouples in many different locations. Good advice, Dan. If your oven has serious thermal gradients, you may never be capable of adequately annealing your castings without introducing some method of convection. For those of you wishing to use crown elements, use the directions that follow.

Mullite rods: In order for the coiled elements to maintain their integrity, it is necessary to insert mullite tubes down the center of them. Using mullite rods will permit you to suspend the elements from the top of the sidewalls. The mullite tubes must be longer than the stretched element and longer than the width of the annealer. If sized properly, they will slip into grooves cut into the top row of insulating brick (Fig. 3 and 3a, pg. 272). The tube that you purchase should fit down the center of your wound elements. I recommend tubes at least ¾" (2 cm) in diameter since narrow mullite tubes tend to warp.

The stretched length of your elements may be greater than the width of your oven and you will need to use a "hairpin design." I have used this design many times and find it works quite well. The larger diameter electric coil will also make for a shorter element.

After slipping the tubes down the center of the elements, lay them on top of the oven in their permanent location. Groove the brick deeply enough so that the lid will not crush the tube or the elements. You should make the groove long enough so that the element and tube can be moved and dropped out when they need replacing. You will have to measure carefully where the pigtails exit the crown and drill small holes to accommodate the pigtail. If you have made the grooves correctly, the elements can be put in place after the crown is placed on top of the walls of the oven. When the elements wear out, replacing them is an easy task. It is assumed that you know how to hook the elements to the power source.

The end: I believe I have covered most of the salient points in constructing the roll-out oven. Before attempting to build a huge roll-out, I recommend you construct a small one to get a "handle" on all the details of its construction. My explanation of how to build one of these beauties can be confusing at times. I hope the drawings included with this text will help you.

This oven is a great example of elements with Mullite rods running down the core of the element. I have no idea where to obtain the vertical and crown hangers shown in these photos. Marian Karel built this oven at his studio in the Czech Republic. It's a really nice touch having ovens of this scale open from the front and the back. When the Libensky's were teaching at Pilchuck, an oven similar to the one shown above was built for them. This is one fantastic casting oven.

Side View of Roll-out Oven

Fig. 1

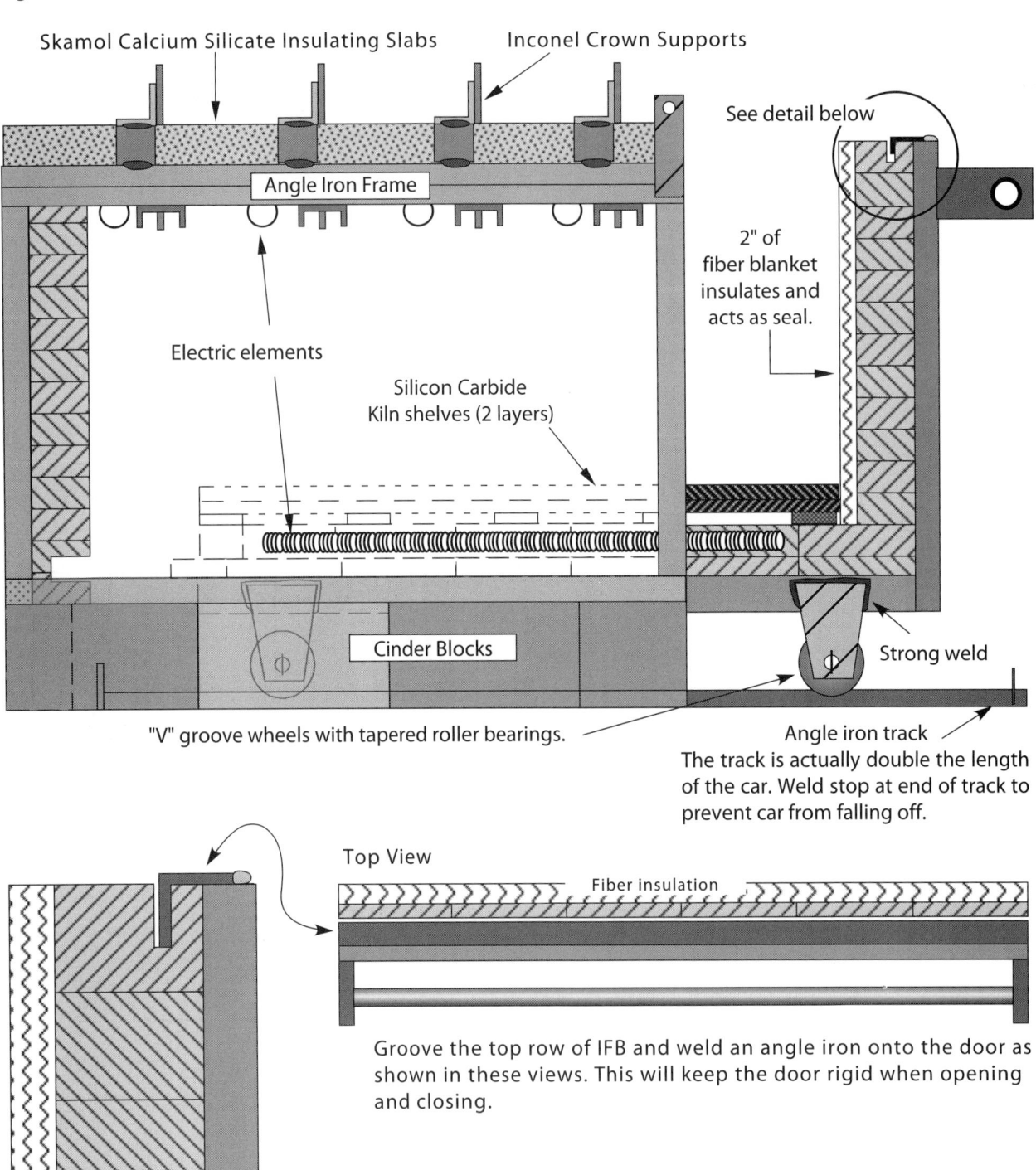

Skamol Calcium Silicate Insulating Slabs

Inconel Crown Supports

See detail below

Angle Iron Frame

2" of fiber blanket insulates and acts as seal.

Electric elements

Silicon Carbide Kiln shelves (2 layers)

Cinder Blocks

Strong weld

"V" groove wheels with tapered roller bearings.

Angle iron track
The track is actually double the length of the car. Weld stop at end of track to prevent car from falling off.

Top View

Fiber insulation

Groove the top row of IFB and weld an angle iron onto the door as shown in these views. This will keep the door rigid when opening and closing.

Side View

Front View of Roll-out Oven
Detail of Air Seal

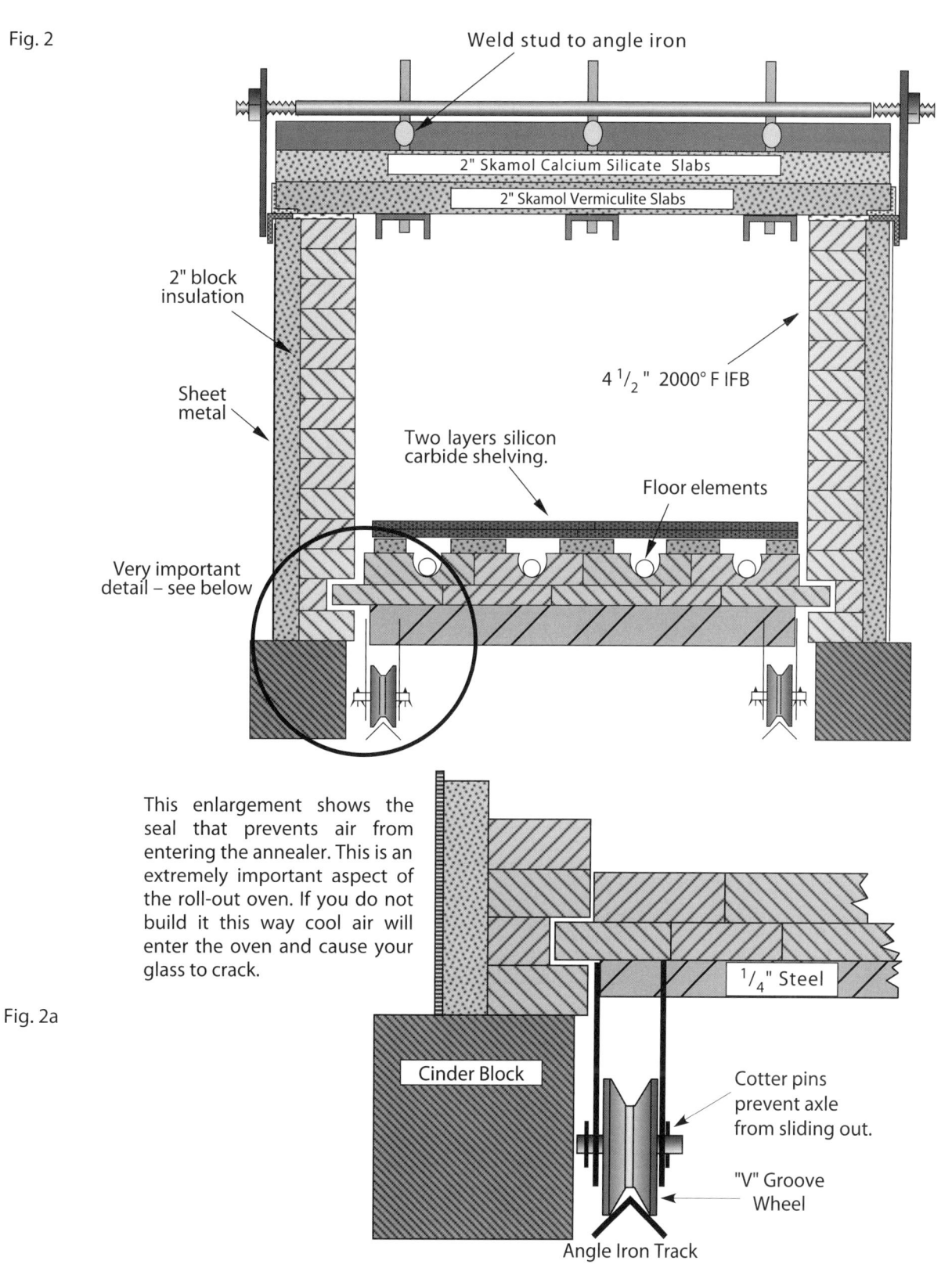

Fig. 2

Weld stud to angle iron

2" Skamol Calcium Silicate Slabs

2" Skamol Vermiculite Slabs

2" block insulation

4 $1/2$" 2000° F IFB

Sheet metal

Two layers silicon carbide shelving.

Floor elements

Very important detail – see below

This enlargement shows the seal that prevents air from entering the annealer. This is an extremely important aspect of the roll-out oven. If you do not build it this way cool air will enter the oven and cause your glass to crack.

Fig. 2a

$1/4$" Steel

Cinder Block

Cotter pins prevent axle from sliding out.

"V" Groove Wheel

Angle Iron Track

Elements & Stainless Crown Supports
Top View

These top and front views demonstrate how the elements and stainless steel supports are installed in the crown. A groove is cut in the top row of brick sidewalls, as indicated. The mullite tube is dropped into this groove. To replace the element after the crown is in place, simply slide the mullite tube to the side and it should drop out.

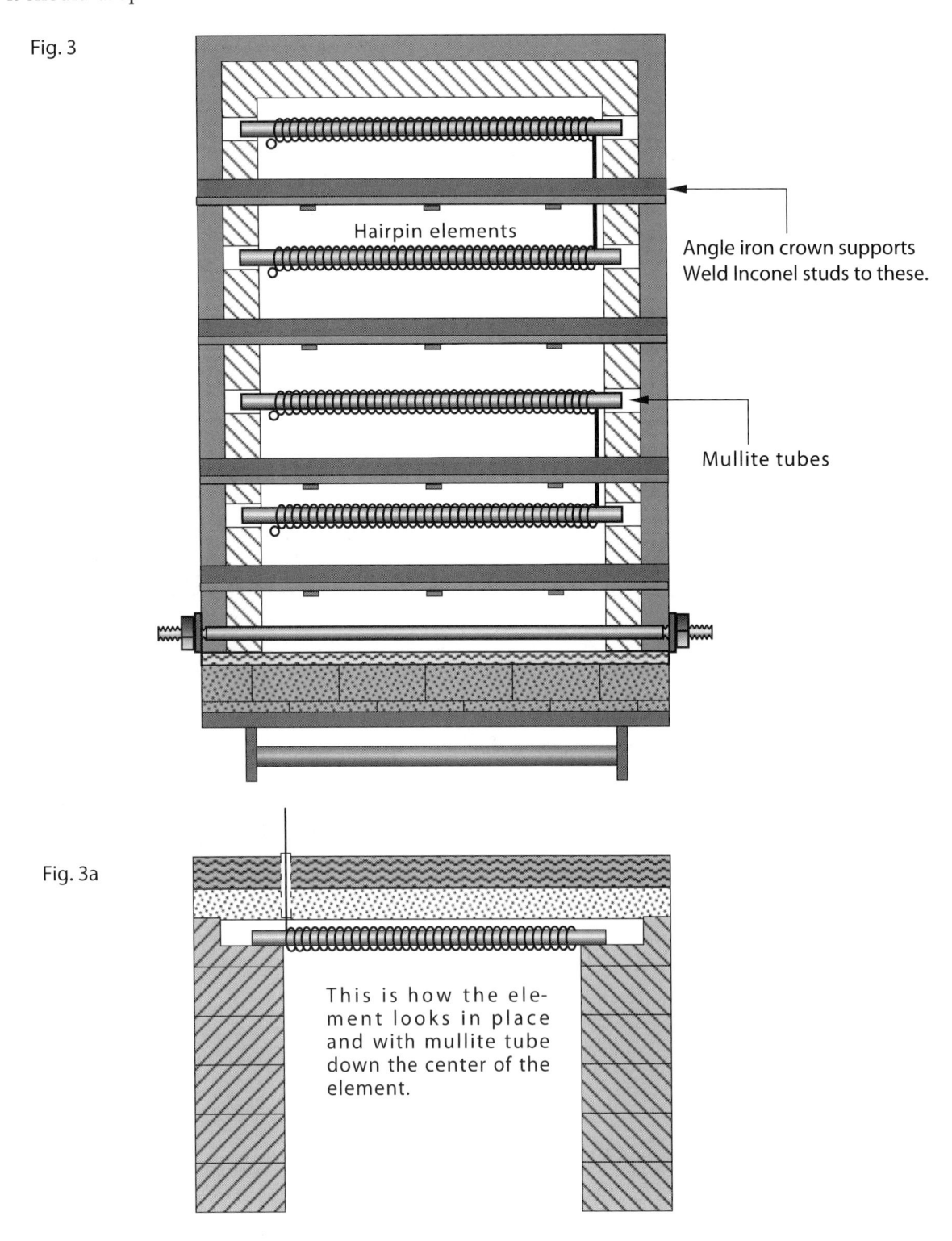

Fig. 3

Hairpin elements

Angle iron crown supports
Weld Inconel studs to these.

Mullite tubes

Fig. 3a

This is how the element looks in place and with mullite tube down the center of the element.

272   Glass Notes

Crown Details

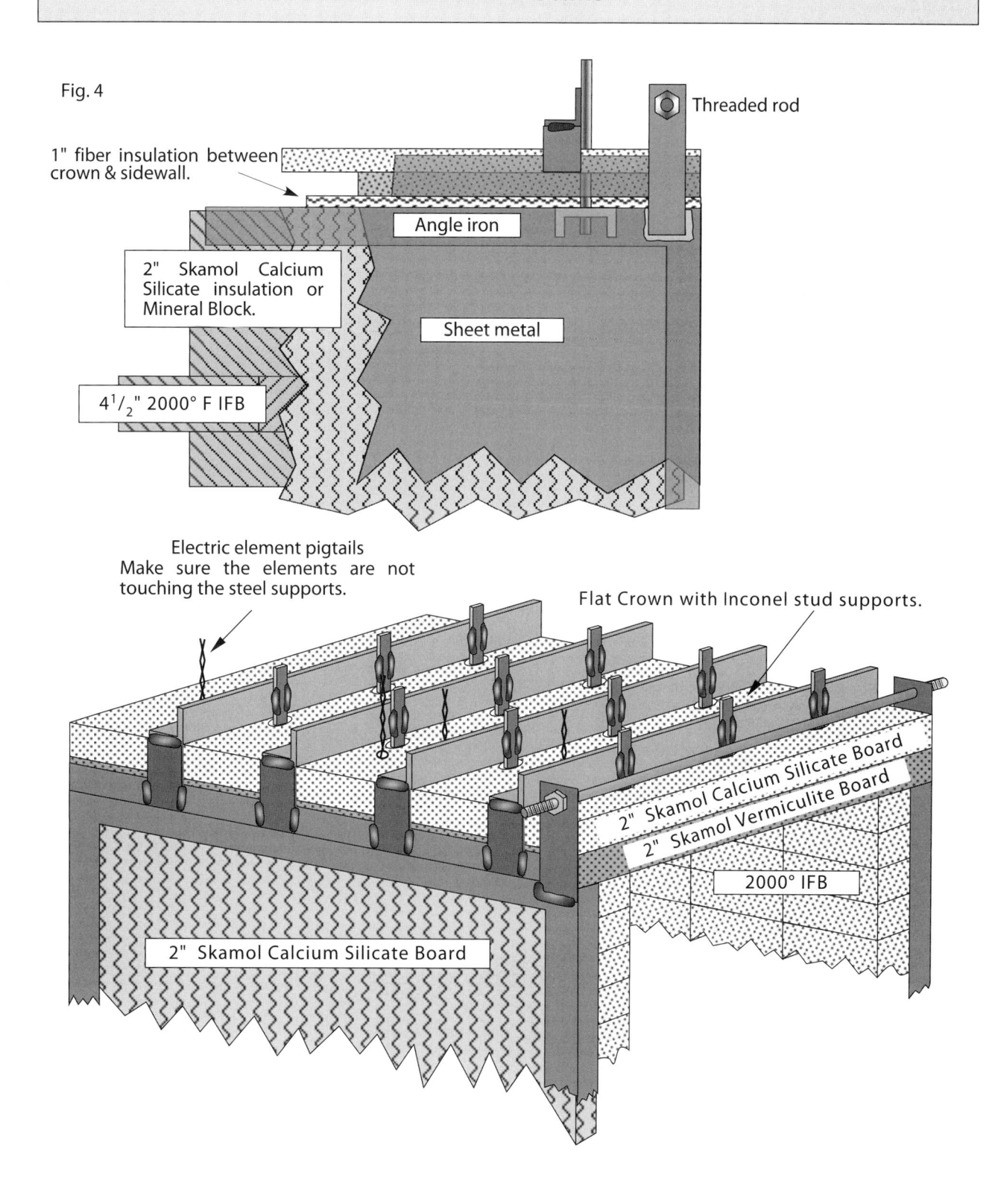

Fig. 4

1" fiber insulation between crown & sidewall.

Threaded rod

Angle iron

2" Skamol Calcium Silicate insulation or Mineral Block.

Sheet metal

$4^1/_2$" 2000° F IFB

Electric element pigtails
Make sure the elements are not touching the steel supports.

Flat Crown with Inconel stud supports.

2" Skamol Calcium Silicate Board

2" Skamol Vermiculite Board

2000° IFB

2" Skamol Calcium Silicate Board

Glass Notes 273

Another Type of Air Seal

While reading *The North American Combustion Handbook*, I came across a drawing of a industrial–type car kiln. The drawings below are simplified from the originals but demonstrate another method of creating an air seal for a car kiln. What you are looking at is a steel trough attached to the underside of the car kiln. The trough contains sand. An angle iron is attached to a plate that runs the length of the kiln wall. One side of the angle iron extends into the sand and preventing any air from entering the kiln. I think it is an excellent alternative to the air seal on the preceding page and is very applicable to our needs. It shouldn't be too difficult to fabricate a trough from some heavy duty "U" channel. The rest of the steel work seems straightforward. Although I've never built a car kiln annealer using this style of air seal, I can see advantages to this design in relation to the one on page 271. The only similarity to the one I've constructed would be the "tongue" at the front of the car.

The wheels on this car are an industrial type used on large ceramic car kilns. I recommend using the "V" groove wheels instead of these.

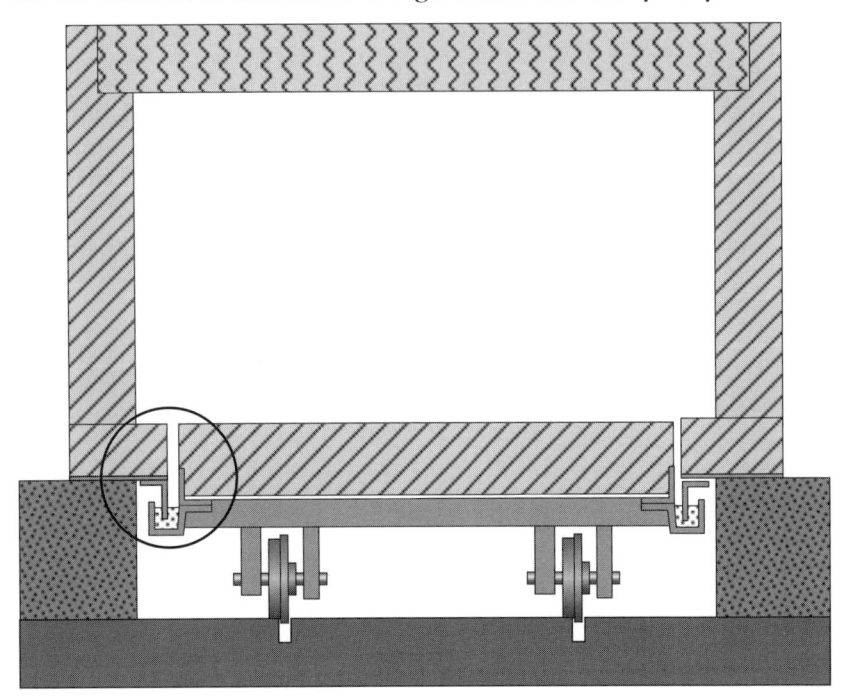

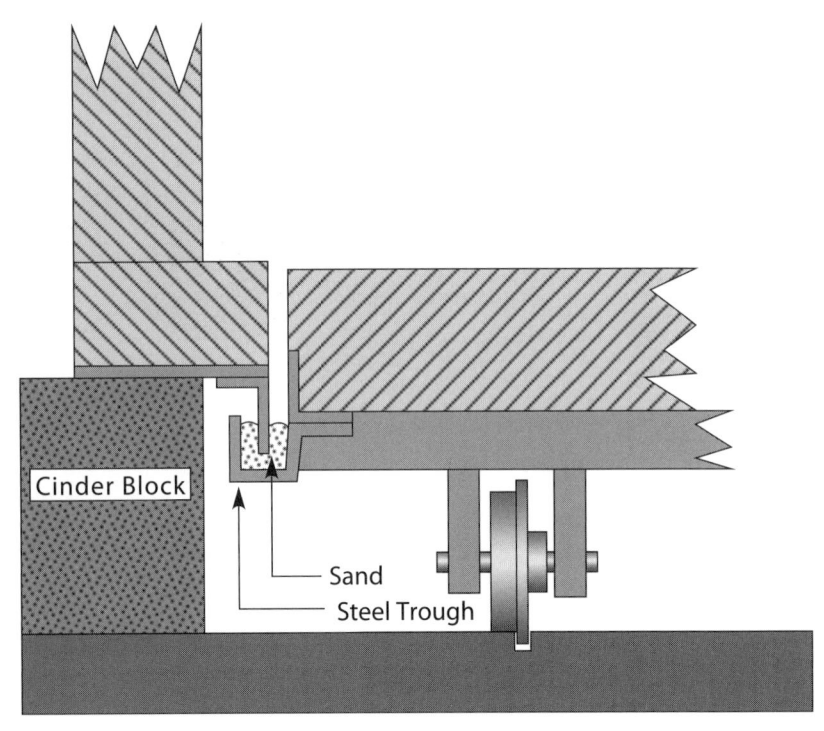

274 Glass Notes

Flat Crown Construction

The easiest and simplest way to construct a flat-roof crown is to use a fairly dense fiber-board or Skamol (see Skamol annealer). Fiber panels can be obtained in standard sizes from any number of companies, but the Skmol must be obtained from a Skamol distributor (www.skmol.com). If the annealer you have designed is wider than the standard sizes available, it will be necessary to use two or more panels to complete the span. The following diagrams show how the panels are installed and how the hangers are placed to support the crown. The hangers are made from Inconel 601 and are capable of withstanding extremely high temperatures. They can usually be obtained from one of dealers of refractory products found in your area. To find a location, go to www.hwr.com and click on *locations*. They are or were called Ins-Twist. A set includes the stud and the anchor washer. The stud comes in different lengths. The 6" or 8" lengths should suffice depending on the thickness of your crown. If you use these hangers, make sure you weld the Anchor Washer to the stud to be extra secure and weld the back end to angle iron as indicated in the following diagram. Make sure you use stainless steel welding rod. Standard, mild steel rod will not work. Installing these panels is not as difficult as it appears, but it does require you to be resourceful. I have constructed two very large roll-out casting ovens using this crown technique. The ovens are now 9 years old and are as good as the day they were created. These Inconel studs can be used for any oven configuration that has a flat crown. I have also used these studs for front loading doors that have fiber panels. The stud keeps the door permanently in place. My oven at home is a top loading oven with a fiber-board crown and is held in place with these studs.

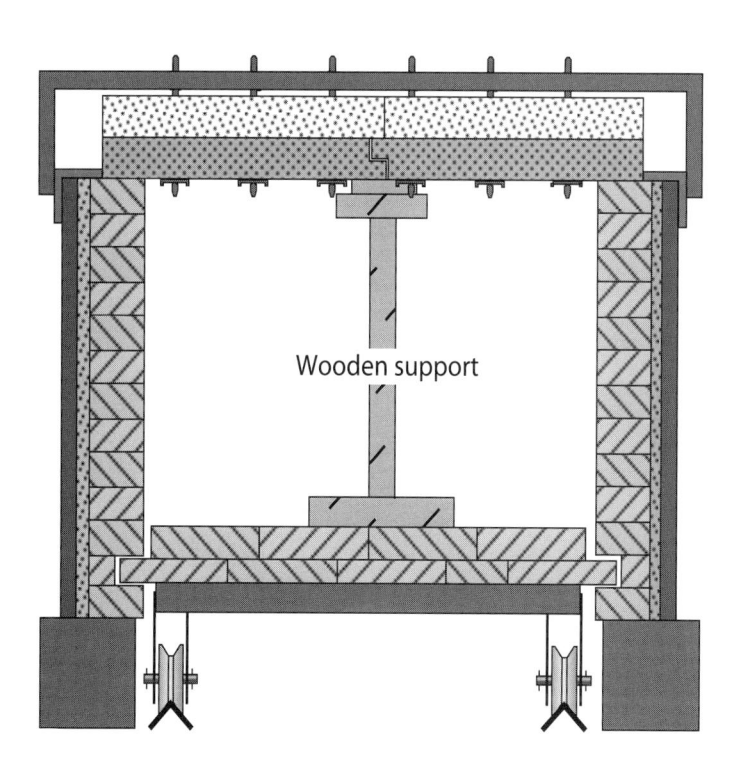

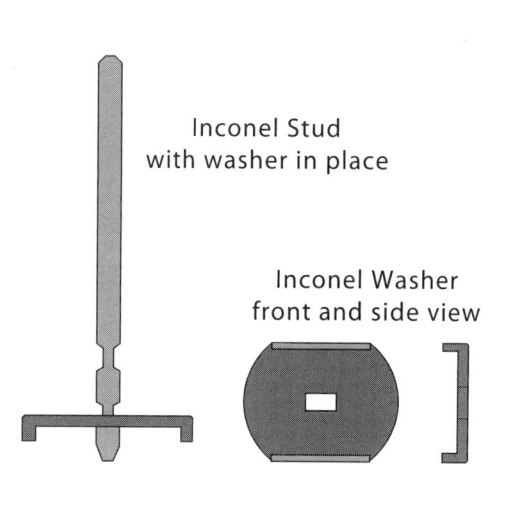

This view depicts the wooden form in place holding the crown panels while installing Inconel 601 crown supports.

Inconel Stud with washer in place

Inconel Washer front and side view

Rigid Panel Installation

The fiber panels come in standard sizes. If you cannot find a size that will completely span your annealer, it will be necessary to combine two panels to complete the span as depicted in these drawings. Even if you can span the width of your oven, I strongly recommend supporting the crown using this method. If you do not, your crown is apt to crack over time and possibly fall into the oven. If you're using fiber panels, I recommend pre-firing the panels to burn off the binder. I used a table saw and cut the heat lock running the width of each panel. I recommend doing this as it will prevent heat from escaping. It really isn't necessary to do this, but I like to be on the safe side. If you don't do this over time you may find the crack will widen. I installed the fiber panels in the manner pictured on this page. It is not as difficult as it appears to be. When installing these panels, it is important to keep the sections aligned.

Top View

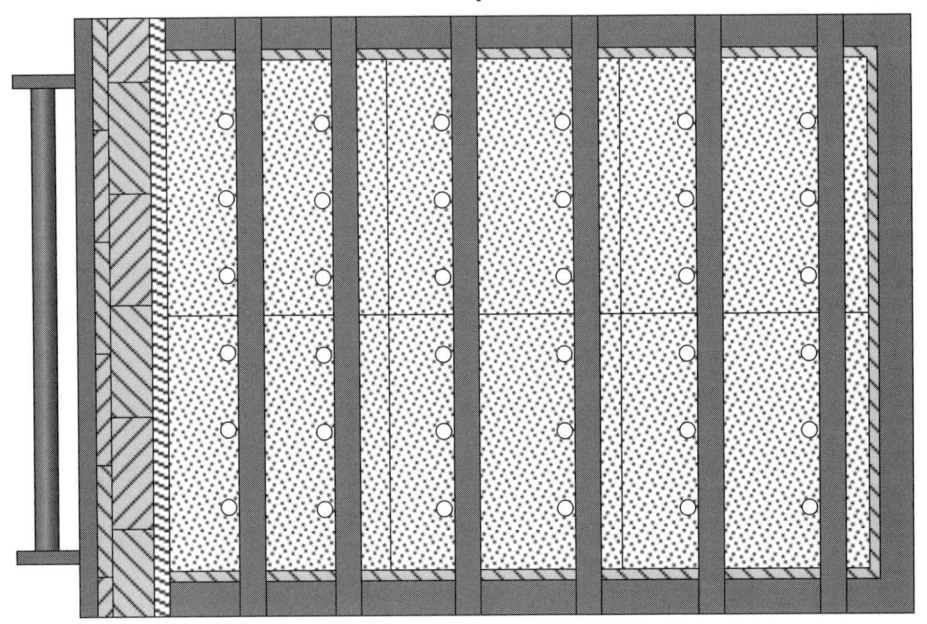

Weld Inconel hangers to angle iron with stainless welding rod.

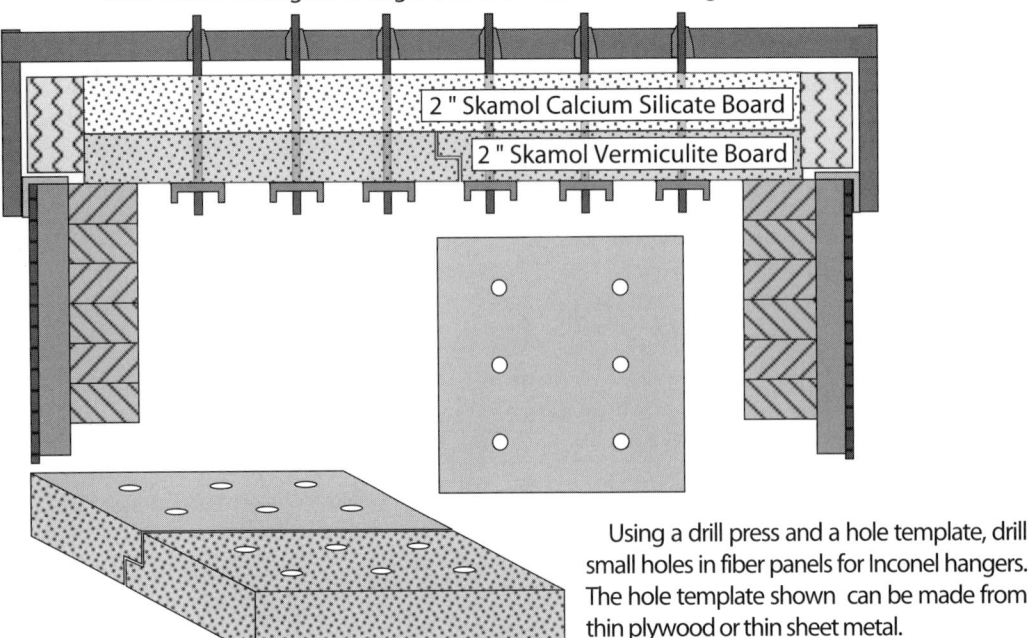

2" Skamol Calcium Silicate Board
2" Skamol Vermiculite Board

Using a drill press and a hole template, drill small holes in fiber panels for Inconel hangers. The hole template shown can be made from thin plywood or thin sheet metal.

276   Glass Notes

The Convection Oven

Years ago I built two large casting ovens and erred when placing the elements. Because of poor element placement, the oven had serious thermal gradation. It was recommended to me that I convert my ovens to a convection type oven, similar to the ones diagramed below. The slight movement of air during the casting, annealing, and cooling cycles equalizes the temperature throughout the oven. The system depicted requires a good compressor, ½" stainless tubing, an open-close valve, and an-in line air and oil filter.

The ½" stainless tubing has small holes drilled every inch or so. The tubing should be angled so the holes point at a 20 to 30° angle toward the side walls as shown in the views below. The air pressure is set for about 3 to 5 lbs. pressure. You do not want great quantities of air blowing through the oven, but you should be able to feel the air blowing from the holes. The air will be at temperature when it exits the tube, and contrary to what some believe does not blow dust. Make sure you seal the ends of the tubes.

Numbers 1 and 2 below depict two different systems. System 1 has the air emanating from the bottom of the oven, and system 2 has one tube at the top of the oven. They both work, but I prefer system 1.

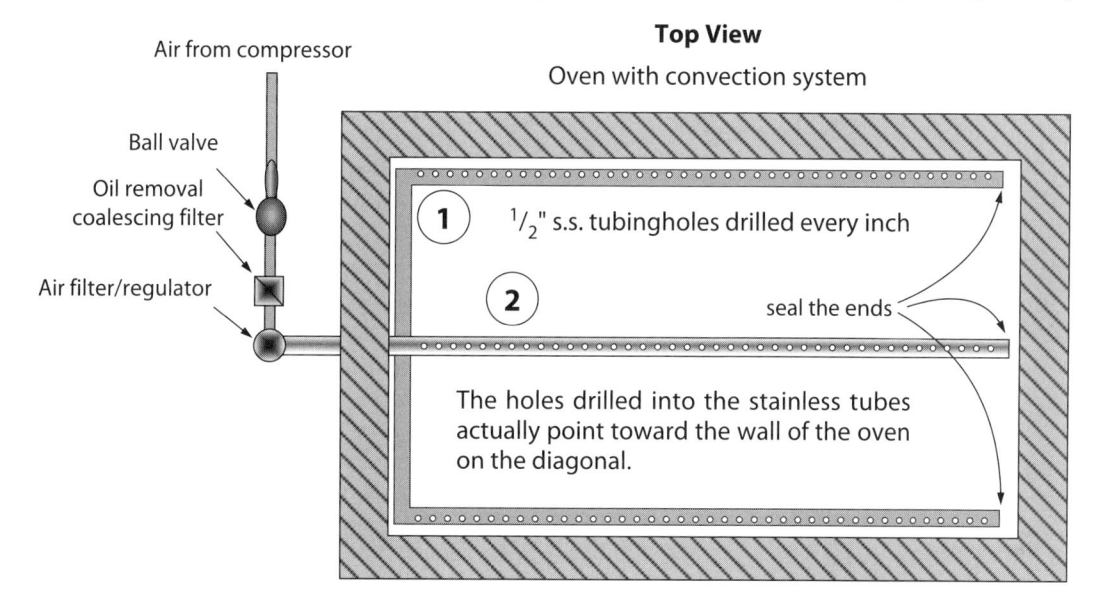

Top View
Oven with convection system

Air from compressor
Ball valve
Oil removal coalescing filter
Air filter/regulator

1 ½" s.s. tubing holes drilled every inch
2 seal the ends

The holes drilled into the stainless tubes actually point toward the wall of the oven on the diagonal.

Front View
The holes that are drilled into the stainless tubes actually point toward wall of the oven on the diagonal.

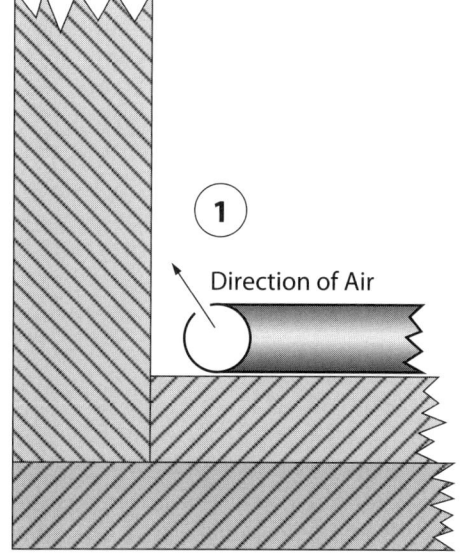

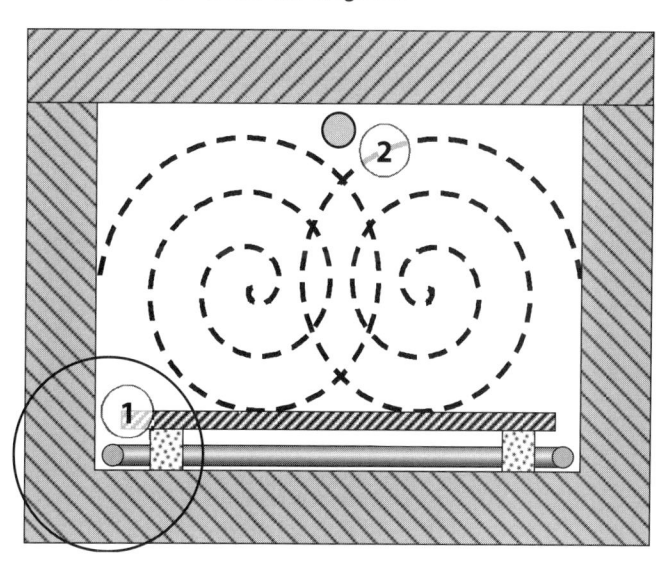

1 Direction of Air

Glass Notes 277

Designing Electric Elements

Designing electric elements remains a mystery for many glass artists. I hope these few pages will help de-mystify this aspect of annealing-oven building.

In the preceding chapter, we determined that we will be using four elements to power our annealer. To determine the power consumption of each element used in our annealer, we need to answer some questions.

Q. What is the total power requirement of our annealer?
A. 45 amps at 220 volts, single phase. It will produce a total of 9,900 watts.

Q. What are the total number of elements used in our annealer?
A. We will use 4 elements.

Q. How thick is the annealer wall?
A. Our annealer is 6 ½" thick. 4 ½" of brick plus 2" of mineral block insulation.

Q. What is the maximum temperature our annealer will achieve?
A. Our annealer will achieve 1500° F (815° C).

Q. How are our elements to be hooked up?
A. Our elements are to be hooked up in parallel.

After answering these questions, you can now design the elements using the following calculations.
45 amps. (total amps. of all 4 elements) ÷ by 4 (to determine amps. of 1 element) = 11.25 amps.
45 ÷ 4 = 11.25

To determine the wattage produced by each element using ohms law:
E x I = W (Volts x Amps = Watts)
220 x 11.25 = 2,475 watts or 2.475 kilowatts
Each of our 4 elements is now designed to draw the following amount of current:
11.25 amps at 220 volts with a rating of 2.475 kilowatts
Although our total amperage is divided equally into each element, voltage stays constant.

Some things to know about resistance elements

Calculating the correct size and type of element needed for your oven is not an easy task if you're unfamiliar with electricity. When I first started building annealing ovens, I knew little to nothing about calculating the specific energy needs of the ovens I was building. To make a long story short I located Duralite, Inc. in Riverton, CT. They took the time and walked (actually talked) me through what information I would need for them to provide the correct elements for my ovens. Duralite is still at it today providing elements for every conceivable annealer and kiln throughout the world. They have an excellent Web site with lots of very helpful information, (www.duralite.com). Some of the pertinent information you will need is on the following page and should help you to determine your needs.

It is important to know how to install your elements, because if you install them incorrectly, they will not give adequate service and can cause a great deal of trouble. It is assumed you've grooved your sidewalls correctly so that the elements will fit snugly and not easily fall out. The elements once fitted into the grooves should be pinned in increments of 6 to 9".

- If the elements make a 90° bend in the corners, make sure to pin them tightly into the corner. If you do not, they will eventually droop, and you will not be able to "undroop" them.
- Keep your thermocouple away from the elements. If an element touches the thermocouple when it is powered up, you run the risk of frying your controller.
- You cannot bend an element after it has been heated. It becomes brittle and will break if you attempt to re-bend or straighten it. Sometimes you can re-bend a used element by heating the area to be bent with a torch and then carefully bending it while it is still glowing.

After installing your elements, you are ready for the final hookup. If you are not familiar with how to do the hookup, I recommend you find an electrician who is familiar with your electrical needs. Electricity is not something to fool with.* Your electrician will need to know how your elements are to be hooked up (parallel, series, phase). Your electrician will provide all the necessary hardware to do a safe hookup.

It is very difficult, if not impossible, to anneal correctly without a digital microprocessor controller. There are many on the market these days, and the prices have come down dramatically. The GB series from Digitry has been on the market for many years and is reliable. I use a GB-1. If you need a more sophisticated controller, I recommend a (Proportional) Profiling Controller.

The next page can help you figure out what information you will need to order your elements.

Quartz Tubes (highly recommended)

Quartz tubes are a viable means for mounting heating elements inside kilns. The quartz tube provides a relatively easy and stable means of mounting elements and has many other benefits. The heating element is inside the tube and thus provides electrical insulation. Quartz is an electrical insulator, yet it passes IR heat with very little absorption. The heating element is also protected from contamination which is one of the greatest causes of premature element failure. Heating element flaking and spalling are contained inside the quartz tube thus protecting your product from falling debris. Quartz tubes will operate at temperatures to 2100° F.

I have my elements in quartz tubes and recommend their use. They are easy to mount, and they prevent the dreaded element droop. That in itself should be enough to convince you to use them.

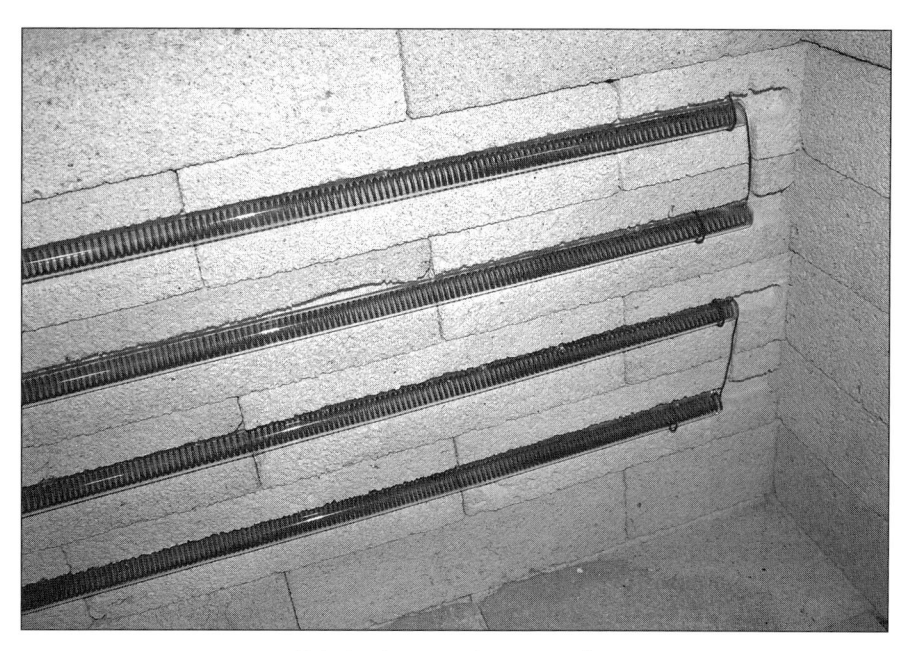

Hairpin elements in quartz tubes

* If you are not familiar with how to hook up your elements to the power source, have a licensed electrician do the work. If you do it wrong, you run the risk of receiving a serious electrical shock; destroying an expensive controller; and, at the extreme, burning your studio down. Don't (insert four letter word here) with electricity.

Duralite Inc.
15 School St.
Riverton, CT 06065
toll free: 888/432-8797
tel. 860/379-3113
web: www.duralite.com

Currents for Resistance Heating Loads/Amperage Conversion

When you're ready to order elements for your annealer, it is important to have the answers to any number of questions. The chart below will help you establish the current draw of your oven. The chart will pinpoint the Kw, Volts, and amps.

Kw= kilowatt. A kilowatt is equal to 1000 watts.

	Single Phase					Three Phase Balanced Load			
KW	120V	208V	240V	440V	480V	208V	240V	440V	480V
1	8.4	4.8	4.2	2.3	2.1	2.8	2.5	1.4	1.3
2	16.7	9.7	8.4	4.6	4.2	5.6	4.9	2.7	2.5
3	25	14.5	12.5	6.9	6.3	8.4	7.3	4	3.7
4	33.4	19.3	16.7	9.1	8.4	11.2	9.7	5.3	4.9
5	41.7	24.1	20.9	11.4	10.5	13.9	12.1	6.6	6.1
6	50	28.9	25	13.7	12.5	16.7	14.5	7.9	7.3
7.5	62.5	36.1	31.3	17.1	15.7	20.9	18.1	9.9	9.1
10	83.4	48.1	41.7	22.8	20.9	27.8	24.1	13.2	12.1
12	100	57.7	50	27.3	25	33.4	29	15.8	14.5
15	125	72.2	62.5	34.1	31.2	41.7	36.2	19.7	18.1
20	167	96.2	83.4	45.5	41.7	55.6	48.2	26.3	24.1
25	209	121	105	56.9	52.1	69.5	60.3	32.9	30.1
30	250	145	125	68.2	62.5	83.4	72.3	39.4	36.2
50	417	241	209	114	105	139	121	65.7	60.3
75	625	361	313	171	157	209	181	98.6	90.4
100	834	481	417	228	209	278	241	132	121

Annealer Heating Element Design Questions

Prior to ordering elements for your annealer you will need to have the answers to some or all of the questions listed below.

Line Voltage -------------------------------------- three-phase or Single PHASE?
Voltage--- 110, 220, 440
Amperage Available ---------------------------- (Check the fuse rating for the annealer)
Dimensions -- Length, width, and height. Is it a top-loader or a front-loader?
Construction--------------------------------------- IFB Brick, Ceramic fiber; board, or blanket, or combination?
Element Mounting------------------------------- Size of grooves in brick, hung on hook in wall, mounted in or on ceramic or quartz tubes? Hung from roof, mounted in grooves. In floor and walls only?
Electric Connections --------------------------- What length for tails? Twisted pig tails or welded terminals?

This page supplied by Duralite Inc.

Using Ohms Law to Make an Element

For those of you who wish to fabricate your own elements, here is some information that might be helpful. As you can see from the preceding pages, there is a lot of information needed before one can wind elements. If you're going to wind a lot of elements, you may wish to make the investment in the materials for the job, but if you're winding only a few it is not worth the effort or the investment.

E– Volts ---------------- The pressure which causes the current to flow is measured in volts.

I– Amperes ------------ The current of electricity is measured in amperes which state the quantity passing through a conductor in one second.

R– Ohms -------------- The resistance which a conductor offers the current is measured in ohms.

W– Watts --------------- A unit of power equal to one joule per second: the power of a current of one ampere flowing across a potential difference of one volt.

Kilowatt --------------- A unit of power equal to 1000 watts.

To determine watts use the following formulas

$$\text{Volts} \times \text{Amps} = \text{Watts} \quad \text{or} \quad \text{Watts} = \frac{\text{Amps}}{\text{Volts}}$$

Problem: An element rated at fifteen (15) amperes is desired.
E or volts to be standard 220 volts AC.
It is necessary to determine the length of element wire that will furnish the required resistance.
(The ohms resistance per foot is supplied by the manufacturer of the element wire.)

Solution: Use the equation: R = E over I (ohms = volts over amps)
Thus R equals 220 divided by 15 or 14.666 ohms resistance.

Suppose a Kanthal A-1 wire of 14 gauge is used and has a supplied factor of .212 ohms per foot.

Divide the ohms resistance needed by the ohms resistance per foot, or 14.666 ÷ .212. This gives as the answer 69.179 feet or the length of the element wire needed for an element of 15 amperes on a 220 volt circuit. 69.179 feet is the actual length of the wire, not the coiled length.

To find the wattage of the element using ohms law: E x I = W or 15 x 220 = 3300 watts, or expressed as kilowatts.

$$\frac{15 \text{ amps} \times 220 \text{ volts}}{1000} = 3.3 \text{ kilowatts}$$

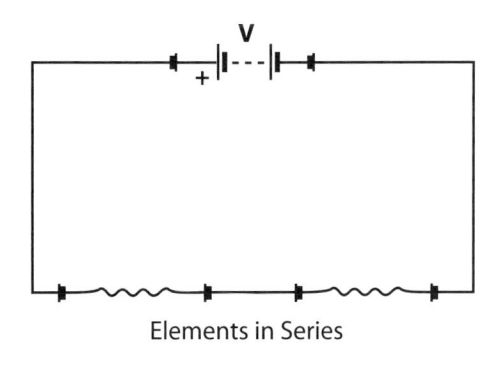

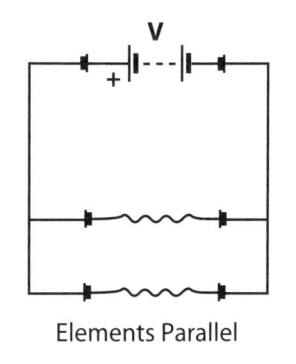

Elements in Series

Elements Parallel

Single Phase Wiring

A series circuit is one that has a single path for current flow through all of its elements.

A parallel circuit is one that requires more than one path for current flow in order to reach all of the circuit elements.

About Three Phase

Some of the following information on three phase is reprinted from the Wikipedia Web site, http://en.wikipedia.org

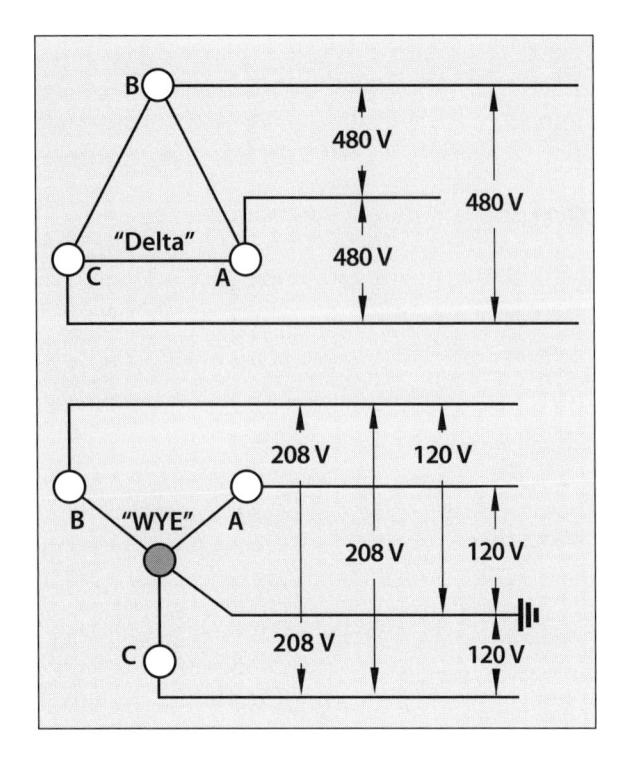

Most alternating-current (AC) generation and transmission, and a good part of use, takes place through three phase circuits. If you want to understand electric power, you must know something about three-phase. It is rather simple if you go at it the right way, though it has a reputation for being difficult.

Phase is a frequently used term around AC (alternating current). Electrical phase is measured in degrees, with 360° corresponding to a complete cycle.

Three-phase refers to three voltages or currents that differ by a third of a cycle, or 120 electrical degrees, from each other. They go through their maxima in a regular order, called the phase sequence. The three phases could be supplied over six wires, with two wires reserved for the exclusive use of each phase. However, they are generally supplied over only three wires, and the phase or line voltages are the voltages between the three possible pairs of wires. The phase or line currents are the currents in each wire.

When you connect a load to the three wires, it should be done in such a way that it does not destroy the symmetry. This means that you need three equal loads connected across the three pairs of wires. This looks like an equilateral triangle, or delta, and is called a delta load. Another symmetrical connection would result if you connected one side of each load together and then the three other ends to the three wires. This looks like a Y and is called a WYE load. These are the only possibilities for a symmetrical load. The center of the WYE connection is, in a way, equidistant from each of the three line voltages, and it will remain at a constant potential. It is called the neutral and may be furnished along with the three phase voltages. The benefits of three-phase are realized best for such a symmetrical connection, which is called balanced. If the load is not balanced, the problem is a complicated one whose solution gives little insight, just numbers.

A casting/annealing oven run on three-phase will have elements in multiples of 3. If you want more than 3 elements, then the next step up would be 6 elements, etc.

Many studio artists believe that it is cheaper to run ovens using three-phase power. That is not the case when it comes to resistive load. Kilowatts is kilowatts as far as the power company is concerned, and they do not care if you're using three-phase to run your oven or single phase. Your oven will still need the same number of kilowatts to run at either phase. You will save money though when you get to large capacity ovens as the wire sizes are smaller for high energy ovens. Less copper, smaller wires (see below). There is a saving in energy consumption when running three-phase motors as a three-phase motor at, say, 2 h.p. is smaller than a single-phase one with equal h.p.

Some basic factoids about three-phase: Most of the electric power in the world is three-phase. The concept was originally conceived by Nikola Tesla and was proven that three-phase was far superior to single phase power. Three-phase power is typically 150% more efficient than single phase in the same power range. In a single-phase unit, the power falls to zero three times during each cycle; in three-phase it never drops to zero. The power delivered to the load is the same at any instant. Also, in three-phase the conductors need only be 75% the size of conductors for single-phase for the same power output.

282 Glass Notes

General Information

Chapter Contents

Adhesives	284
Enameling on Glass	290
Pick-up in Paradise	293
Resist, Wax, Scavo, Separator, Rubber Mold, Crucible	294
How to Print a Photograph Inside a Bottle	297
Iridizing (Fuming)	298
Iridizing Sprayer	302
Lusters and Bright Metals	303
Converting Silver Nitrate to Silver Salts	304
Niijima Element Configuration	305
Precious Leaf Pick-up Table	306
Color Bar Breaker	307
The Penland Bar Breaker	307
More Color Bar Breakers	308
Pipe Cooler, Battery Powered	309
Fritz's Original Bench	310
Blowing Bench	311
Bench, Side View	312
Make-Up Air	313
Sizing Your Exhaust System (CFM)	314
An Inexpensive Make-Up Air System	315
Sam Scholes Fudge	316
Diamond Drilling in Glass	318
Diamond Drill Speeds	319

Adhesives

As a youngster, the only glue that I was aware of was LePage's mucilage, but it has been quite awhile since I was a youngster and glue has come a long way. It is no longer fashionable to call it glue; it is now called adhesive. One could say that the product is an adhesive and that the parts you use the adhesive on are glued. Modern chemistry has given us a host of adhesives to choose from, and those that are applicable to our industry have extraordinary characteristics and strength.

The glass artist generally uses three types of adhesives: Silicones, epoxy's, and UV adhesives. Each of these adhesives serves a very specific purpose, and each has specific characteristics that differ from each other. This section will list the most common of each type as well as how they are used and in what situations.

Adhesive companies manufacture a large range of products that serve the purpose of different types of industries, so it is important to know the specifics of the adhesive that you intend to use. It should be understood that when you use the correct adhesive for your specific application in an approved manner they will have a very extended life span. It should also be understood that no manufacturer will claim their adhesive, even when used correctly, will last forever. Forever is a relative term though. In my estimation, there are some adhesives that will last a lifetime. Lifetime is also a relative term. Since I am now in my late 60's, I believe any adhesive I use will last my lifetime. If I were in my 20's, I wouldn't be so quick to make that statement.

It is important to read the directions on how to use any and all adhesive products. It is also important to know that if you're gluing an object that is to be displayed indoors, you might use one type of adhesive; if it is to be displayed outdoors, you might choose another. Moisture, temperature, and sunlight can affect the adhesive bond, so before you install that big outdoor commission that is held together with 5 minute epoxy, you better check to see if it will survive sitting in the sun as well as freezing and thawing.

Epoxies

Epoxy is stored in two parts because once the two parts are mixed, the chemical reaction that hardens the epoxy begins and cannot be stopped or reversed. Consequently, if you want to work with a batch of epoxy for a while rather than constantly mixing up new, small batches, make sure it has a long pot life.

Setting and Curing Time

Two-part Epoxies "set" (the time for them to begin gripping) and then "cure" (the time for them to reach maximum strength). Be sure to investigate these characteristics before mixing.

Generic Two Part Epoxy **Available at most hardware stores**	
Advantages	• Various cure rates • Low shrinkage • Fills gaps • Good strength
Disadvantages	• Yellows • Weakened by UV light • Difficult clean-up

---

HXTAL NYL-1
Available from:

Conservator's Emporium, 100 Standing Rock Cir., Reno, NV 89511
Tel. 775/852-0404 · fax. 775/852-3737
http://www.consemp.com/catalog/b.html
Email: consemp@consemp.com

Restorer Supplies, Inc., P.O. Box 387, Golden, CO 80402-0387
Tel. 303/384-9121
http://www.tias.com/stores/restorersupplies/

Talas, 20 West 20th Street, 5th Floor, New York, NY 10011
Tel. 212/219-0770, Fax: 212/219-0735
http://talasonline.com/
Email: info@talasonline.com

His Glassworks, Inc., 91 Webb Cove Road, Asheville, NC 28804
Tel. 800/914-7463 toll free or, 828/254-2559 fax. 828/254-2581
http://www.hisglassworks.com/
Email: info@hisglassworks.com

Advantages	• Clearest of all epoxies • Low Shrinkage • Excellent optical quality • Good for large surface • Bonds well on glass surface • Not affected by solvents • Long pot life
Disadvantages	• Needs to be heated for best set • Must be degassed to remove bubbles • Expensive • Difficult clean up

About Hxtal NYL-1

Hxtal NYL-1 is unlike other epoxies that were made for hobbyist, home, and industrial uses. Hxtal was designed especially for restoration and conservation and has been used for many years by glass artists who laminate layers of glass and also bond parts that require extreme strength. Besides having great strength, Hxtal NYL-1 has an index of refraction that approaches that of fine crystal. Examples are found in the work of Jon Kuhn, Michael Taylor, Pete Vanderlaan and Bill Carlson to name a few.

How Hxtal NYL-1 is described on the manufacturers Web site:

Hxtal is a two-part epoxy resin system. The resin (Part A) and the hardener (Part B) are mixed 3:1 by weight. The unused mix can be kept for 4 to 5 days in the freezer. It is most important that the container be tightly closed. The cured resin does not embrittle with time and is very resistant to yellowing and surface degradation, even after prolonged exposure outdoors. Hxtal's initial yellowness index is 6 to 8, which is unchanged after 1600 hours of Weather-ometer exposure, rising slowly to 13 to 14 at 3,000 hours. The best competitive epoxy adhesive has an initial Yellowness of 9 which rises to over 40 after 800 hours in the Weather-ometer. After 800 hours exposure, the coating begins to erode.

This exciting new epoxy cures in about 1 week at 75° F or in 2 days at 95° F. Cure times can be cut sharply by preheating the mix to 100° F for 15 to 20 minutes before use; and for even faster cure, immediately after mixing raise the temperature to 140° F - 170° F for 1 to 2 minutes. After cooling, such preheated resin has a viscosity similar to the viscosity of the epoxies commonly sold in tubes, and the cure time is just a few minutes. The cure time can be shortened by heating the cemented object up to 140° F.

The cured resin can be removed from hard surfaces with Epoxy Resin Dissolver, but prolonged soaking may be required to soften joints.

It is used most often as an adhesive for bonding glass, dries clear, and can be thinned with aromatic or ketone solvents, thus enabling the application by air brush. It is soluble in Methylene Dichloride.

In order to use Hxtal for laminating, it is important to de-gas it using a vacuum pump and bell jar. If you do not de-gas it is prone to developing bubbles in the laminate.

As you can see using this epoxy is not for the amateur and requires patience and a thorough knowledge of how it is applied and cured.

Epoxy Resin Dissolver

This compound has been formulated to remove thermoset resin compounds (including epoxies and polyesters) AFTER CURING! Simply immerse the resin to be removed until it softens and falls away. If you cannot soak the object, try putting the object in a closed metal can (not plastic!) with a few ounces of Epoxy Resin Dissolver. Usually the vapors will crumble the cured epoxy resin in a few days. On larger objects, try soaking a cloth in Epoxy Resin Dissolver and holding it against the joint to be separated by a few wraps of aluminum foil. Epoxy Resin Dissolver will not react with most metals, linen, Teflon, nylon, ceramics, or molded phenolics. It's also reusable.

UV Adhesives

UV (Ultraviolet) adhesives are extremely easy to use and provide very strong, clear, and long-lasting bonds between glass substrates and many other surfaces. UV adhesives only cure when they are exposed to ultraviolet light, so the user can get the materials in position before they begin to bond. UV adhesives are a one-part system that permit the glass artist to glue and laminate pieces and parts in seconds. To use this product one must have an adequate source of UV light (more on that below).

For the studio glass artist, there two companies that manufacture UV adhesives that serve our purposes. Those companies are Loctite (www.loctite.com) and Dymax (www.dymax.com). Although these two companies maintain extensive Web sites, it is impossible to purchase products directly from them in small quantities. Their Web sites have lots of information on their lines of adhesive products. It is not easy finding your way around their respective sites, but persistence will pay off. Both have downloadable .pdf files describing each of their products. I have listed on the next page some of the UV adhesives that are applicable to the studio glass artist. Loctite has many distributors throughout the world, and Dymax has one distributor that caters to the studio glass artist: Dewey Associates (www.glassbond.com). I have used products from both companies, and for my purposes, I find them to work as advertised. Personally, I like dealing with Dewey as they are familiar with how we use their line of Dymax UV adhesives. They give terrific telephone help and will send free samples of their Dymax line of UV adhesives if requested. You can't go wrong with either Loctite or Dymax.*

What is UV Light?

In the literature, UV light is simply described as follows: Ultraviolet (UV) light has shorter wavelengths than visible light. Though these waves are invisible to the human eye, some insects, like bumblebees, can see them!

Scientists have divided the ultraviolet part of the spectrum into three regions: the near ultraviolet, the far ultraviolet, and the extreme ultraviolet. The three regions are distinguished by how energetic the ultraviolet radiation is, and by the "wavelength" of the ultraviolet light, which is related to energy."

For UV adhesives to work, they require an adequate UV light source. There are any number of companies that sell UV light sources for industry, but only one, Spectronics, has a line of lights suitable for the studio artist. The least expensive UV light source is the sun, but using the sun for your project can and usually is difficult to effect. The UV light source that I used for years with great success was a black light purchased from a head shop. At one time it sat next to my Lava lamp and illuminated my Dylan and Doors posters, but that was long before UV adhesives were invented (1972). A black light works just fine for curing UV adhesives, but at some point in time, you might wish to find a UV light that is a bit more convenient to use and closer in wavelength to effect a quicker cure. For about $100 you can purchase a Spectroline E series light from Dewey Associates. It is a small, florescent unit that fits easily into the palm of your hand. I recently purchased one and really enjoy its convenience. My old black light is now back in my den illuminating those old Doors and Dylan posters from the 60's. Can't find that Lava lamp though.

*Some of the information has been provided by Dewey Assoc. International.

General Guidelines for Successful Adhesive Performance

Bond to clean surfaces--typically an isopropyl alcohol wipe will provide the best surface for bonding. Chlorinated solvents are also suitable. Most petroleum–based solvents leave residues that can interfere with optimum performance. Ketone–based solvents (acetone/methyl ethyl ketone, MEK) will inhibit/retard curing. Always check your cleaning process for best results. Parts must fit well for the adhesive to work optimally. UV adhesives do not "jump gaps" very easily, so it is imperative that the parts being glued fit intimately.

Use only the amount of adhesive required to do the job. Over–application adds nothing to the performance of the joint.

Once assembled, do not disturb the parts until full cure has been achieved. Proper fixturing is very important.

Should a failure occur, don't be too quick to blame the adhesive... the adhesive usually is not the cause of the failure.

When curing with UV light through a transparent surface, the surface must transmit the light for curing to occur. Ensure that the transparent material doesn't contain UV inhibitors which could slow or prevent the UV adhesive from curing. ALL resins must be completely exposed to UV light in order to cure. The adhesive must be exposed to the UV source until it is fully cured. I once tried affixing some opaque glass to a piece of clear laminated glass and could not get the adhesive to work. It eventually dawned on me that the material used for the lamination filtered UV light. It was another one of the those learning experiences.

Author's note: If the glass you are UV bonding has color and does not bond, it may be because the color is inhibiting the UV light.

Dymax UV Adhesives – Light-Weld 401, Light-Weld 425, Ultra Light-Weld 424
Available from:
Dewey Assoc., International. 459 Main St. Suite 102, New Rochelle, NY 10801
Email: deweyint@glassbond.com
Web: http://www.glassbond.com
Note: Call Dewey for advice on which UV adhesive is applicable.

Advantages	• Excellent optical clarity • One-part system • Instant set with UV light • Easy to use • Good for large and small areas • Easy clean up
Disadvantages	• Glass must be clear to permit UV light penetration • Glass surfaces must be intimate

Henkel/Loctite– UV Adhesive #3491
Available from:
Call 800/Loctite (562-8483) for a local distributor
Web: http://www.loctite.com/int_henkel/loctite_us/

Advantages	• Same as above
Disadvantages	• Same as above

Silicone Adhesive

What would we, no, what would the world do without silicone adhesives? Silicone will bond just about anything to anything. Every high rise, curtain-walled glass building in the world is held together with silicone adhesives as is every aquarium. The development of silicone adhesive is right up there with the invention of the wheel. Well, maybe that's a bit of an exaggeration, but you get the point. Under most conditions it will last forever or at least as long as you will last; after that, someone else answers the phone. UV light has little effect on silicones which makes it an ideal adhesive for outdoor use. Silicones can be purchased from just about any hardware store. Silicones can also be purchased in a range of colors. The literature describes silicone adhesive as follows:

"Silicone adhesives and silicone sealants are based on tough silicone elastomeric technology. Silicone adhesives have a high degree of flexibility and very high temperature resistance (up to 600 degrees F), when compared to other adhesives. While silicone adhesives and silicone sealants have a high degree of flexibility, they lack the strength of other epoxy or acrylic resins. Silicone adhesives and silicone sealants are available in two-component addition or condensation curing systems or single component RTV forms. Room temperature vulcanizing (RTV) forms cure through reaction with moisture in the air and give off acetic acid fumes or other by-product vapors during curing. Silicone Adhesive Sealant is a non slump paste-like, one part material which has excellent resistance to extreme temperature, moisture, ozone, vibrations and weathering. Silicone Adhesive Sealant will skin over in approximately 30 minutes. All tooling should be completed within 20 minutes of application. Also, because of the cure process, thickness over 1" should be avoided."

Silicone Adhesive: Dow Corning, GE, Somaca Available from: Most hardware stores, Somaca, Grainger Supply and others	
Advantages	• Flexible • Jumps gaps • Strong if use over a broad surface • Bond does not deteriorate or become brittle with age • Bonds to most substrates • Resists chemicals, moisture, UV, thermal shock, and vibration. • Can be applied at temperatures from -35°F (-37°C) to 140°F (60°C) • Retains adhesion and flexibility -67° F (-55°C) to 500° /f (260° C) • Comes in colors
Disadvantages	• Clear is actually hazy grey • Difficult Clean-up • Long cure time • Gives off acetic acid fumes when curing
Types	• Dow Corning 3145 • GE 1200 Construction grade • Somaca 88R • Other grades and types of silicone are too numerous to list

Enameling on Glass

Most glass enamels are a two-component system composed of a clear, colorless flux and a coloring oxide or pigment. The addition of tin oxide and zirconium oxide to the flux will add opacity to the flux.

Fluxes are made by mixing and melting together lead oxide, boric oxide, and silica, plus lesser amounts of soda, titanium dioxide, zirconium oxide, and cadmium oxide. Titanium dioxide helps to improve acid resistance, and zirconium oxide aids alkali resistance.

As the flux melts during the process of manufacture, a thin stream is allowed to run into water which breaks it up into a size suitable for grinding. This process is usually referred to as fritting, water-cracking, or water-quenching. With the advent of lead laws, most enamels are no longer made with lead (although some still are).

The water-cracked flux, along with a suitable quantity of coloring pigment, is charged into a ball mill and water ground until it can pass a 325 mesh screen. This ground and dried product is a finished glass enamel. Soft glass enamels begin to mature at about 1050° F (565° C) and fully mature at about 1120° F (604° C). They contain about 64% lead (PbO), 14.5% Silica (SiO_2), 18% Boron (B_2O_3), and 3.5% Cadmium (CdO). Soft enamels are not recommended for any food-bearing surfaces nor will they survive the dishwasher. The lead and cadmium free enamels require a temperature of 1120° - 1160° F (604° - 626° C) to mature.

Before application to glass, these powdered glass enamels must be mixed with a liquid vehicle such as pine oil, squeegee oil, turpentine or ethylene glycol. After application to the glass, the liquid vehicle is burned out during the firing process and the flux is melted, which causes the color to adhere firmly to the glass.

Technique

Before using enamels, you should practice good safety procedures. Glass enamels that are lead based also have additions of Cadmium, Selenium, and other dangerous materials. A good exhaust fan is necessary as is a good filter mask. The type of enameling described should not be confused with traditional glass painting. Glass painting is used by glass stainers. The techniques used by glass stainers is described in a wonderful book *The Art of Painting on Glass*, written by Albin Elskus. His book is filled with wonderful technical descriptions and is highly recommended reading for anyone interested in glass enameling and glass staining. Albin's exceptional work is shown throughout. This book had been out of print for some time but has been re-published and is available from Amazon.com. as well as Whitehouse-Books.com. Most enamels come dry. To use an enamel, a medium is added to the dry material and mixed. You can use a mortar and pestle, or use a pallet knife on a flat piece of plate glass. Glass enamels are available from Reusche enamels as well as Beldecal.com. I have never used the Bel enamels, so I cannot vouch for their quality. The Reusche enamels are of very fine consistency and make a nice paste for applying to the glass surface. There are a number of mediums you can use. Oil-based enamel painting mediums (oil of lavender, pine oil, or squeegee oil) have a rather noxious odor but make a very smooth buttery "paint." These painting mediums can be purchased from Reusche as well. Ethylene glycol (antifreeze) can also be used a medium. The advantage to using ethylene glycol is that it is water soluble and has no odor. I personally use it almost exclusively. It is also possible to use turpentine or water as mediums. They impart their own particular consistencies. Experiment with all of them to find the one or ones that best suits your style. Ethylene glycol is dangerous if ingested. It will kill animals if they ingest it. If you spill any, clean it up as your pet dog or cat will lick it since it is sweet to the taste. Ethylene glycol should never be used as a diamond saw coolant.

Enamel painting on glass is quite easy. Making art is difficult. All that is required is a clean, dry, glass surface and something with which to apply the enamel. Brushes are ideal, although I've used small pieces of sponge, cloth, and pallet knives as well. It is important that you avoid applying the enamel too thickly, as it will have a tendency to "orange peel." If you wish to draw on the glass before applying the enamel, use a fine line marker. The marks will burn out when fired. When the enamels are applied to clear glass, they look quite opaque before firing but can get somewhat washed out when fired. The Reusche enamels have excellent opacity when applied to clear glass. If you want a more opaque quality to your enameling, you might consider laying on a white ground and firing it prior to doing your painting. It is possible to use thin color washes over a white ground to achieve beautiful effects. I have used this technique quite frequently. Some of my pieces are fired 4 or 5 times. Multiple refiring does not seem to affect the colors either. Running one enamel into the other when wet creates some striking effects. There is no limit as to what one can do with enamels. Mastering the technical intricacies of enameling is quite easy. Being creative with them is the problem. I have seen the most mundane glass objects come alive when enameled.

Enameling on vertical surfaces is no problem as long as your enamel has sufficient viscosity to keep it from running. Heating the piece will not cause the enamels to run, as the mediums listed above dry when heated. When doing multiple firings, you must have patience. The glass you enamel on should have a form that will not readily slump when fired to enameling temperatures. 1050° F (565° C) to 1120° F (604° C) are the usual firing range for soft enamels. It is not necessary to dry the piece before firing.

Firing

To fire the enamel, place it in the firing oven and raise the temperature to the strain point. Be careful to raise the temperature at a rate slower than you cooled the piece from the strain point. If you do not know the strain point, raise the temperature to the annealing temperature slowly enough that it will not crack. If you have a piece of glass with different thicknesses, it is important to go slowly so that the piece heats evenly. Once above the strain point and/or the annealing point, you can fire very quickly. As fast as your computer or oven will go is fine. It is important to fire very quickly to the maturing temperature of the enamel after you reach the annealing point. The firing range of soft enamels is usually somewhat above the softening point of all the standard blowing glasses, and going too slowly might cause the glass to slump. Actually, glass moves quite slowly at the firing range of enamels, and I have never had a piece slump. I usually hold the piece for about 5 minutes at the firing temperature and then lower the oven to the annealing temperature as fast as possible. Anneal and cool the work in the standard way. You should test your glass every so often for its softening point. The softening point of glass is usually 50° above the high annealing point.

Unused enamels can be saved. If you use the oils as a medium, you must keep all the unused enamels from drying out. If you've used ethylene glycol, there is no problem if they dry, as adding fresh EG will reconstitute the enamel. If you have your enamel on a plate glass pallet, cover it with Saran Wrap. When enameling, it is important to keep your fingers out of your mouth, cut your nails, refrain form smoking and eating, and don't fool around with your significant other until you've showered.

Decalcomania Transfer

Decals are simple to use and can be applied on practically any piece of glass in any location; well not quite any location since water slide decals are not flexible and will not adjust to a compound curve, as in a round bottle. Decals work best on flat surfaces.

The transfers are made up of a piece of un-sized paper coated with a water-soluble size (starch). Colored enamel suspended in a decal medium is silk-screen printed onto this sized surface and then overprinted with a clear, transparent decal cover coat film which holds the design together during transfer.

To use a decal, dip it in water for about 30 seconds and then slide the colored impression off onto the glass in the proper location. After transfer, the decals should be pressed down or rolled down to remove water and air bubbles from underneath. A worthwhile precaution in the use of decals is to allow them to dry for a period of 12 to 24 hours at room temperature before firing. After careful drying, they are fired in the usual manner.

Decal paper is available from BelDecal.com. I recommend you visit their Web site and look at the products they sell for fabricating glass decals. They also do custom glass decal work.

Fill-in

In days gone by, a popular method of marking glass was to fill etched lines on the surface of the glass with enamel color. This was usually accomplished by mixing the color to an almost–dry paste with turpentine and then filling the etched lines by rubbing the color over them and wiping off the excess. The color was then fired in the usual manner.

Writing Pen

Perhaps the simplest way to draw on glass is with an ordinary steel nib writing pen. Nibs can be obtained in any art-supply store. Enamel is mixed with ethylene glycol (antifreeze) or pine oil, picked up with a writing pen, and applied to the glass just as ink would be applied to paper during writing. For best results, the mixture should be thin enough to flow off the pen nib, and the color and medium should be ground in a mortar and pestle to disperse any lumps. After drawing on the glass, it is fired in the usual manner.

Fun Trick

Here is a little trick I tried with success after seeing it demonstrated by my late Czech friend Bohumil Elias. What a super guy he was. Paint an enamel on a glass surface and, while wet, sprinkle some sand onto the enamel. Shake off the superfluous sand and fire the enamel in the usual manner. The enamel will "glue" the sand to the piece. This is a nice technique to create enameled textures.

Paradise Paints

David and Shari Hopper market this material through their company "Paradise & Co." To use these enamels on blown vessels, you might try the following as a good starting point.

Blow a fairly thick blank, and anneal in the usual manner. After the vessel is annealed, enamel it with Paradise Paints and place it in the annealer. *Author's note: The pine oil medium in which these enamels are suspended is very noxious and will cause a major headache if not used in a properly ventilated room.* Bring the temperature of the annealer up above the annealing temperature by about 50°. Allow the blank to soak for awhile. Pick the blank up by either blowing a bubble into it or on a hollow post (see illustration on pg. 293). Fire the enamels in the glory hole before your next gather. If you don't fire the enamels sufficiently in the glory hole, you will get outgassing (bubbles) when you gather over the enamel overlay. After firing sufficiently, allow the glass to cool to the point that it can be gathered over. It should be obvious that if you are gathering over a blank it will need to be thick enough so it won't collapse when gathering. After gathering, blow in the usual manner. This technique lends itself to heavier blown objects. You will need to experiment with these enamels to develop the technique that suits you. I have seen some excellent and some conceptually poor pieces that employed these enamels. If you can't paint well to begin with, what makes you think you can paint well on glass? For information visit the Hopper

Web site: www.paradise-co.com/paints

Everett "Shorty" Finley blowing a mold at the Blenko Glass Factory, 1976
Shorty was the best mold blower around. In the mid 70's he came to our school to teach the students to blow into wooden molds as well as mold blow pieces for our annual Christmas sale. He and his assistant blew out a 400 lb. capacity furnace in about 3 hours.

Pick-up in Paradise

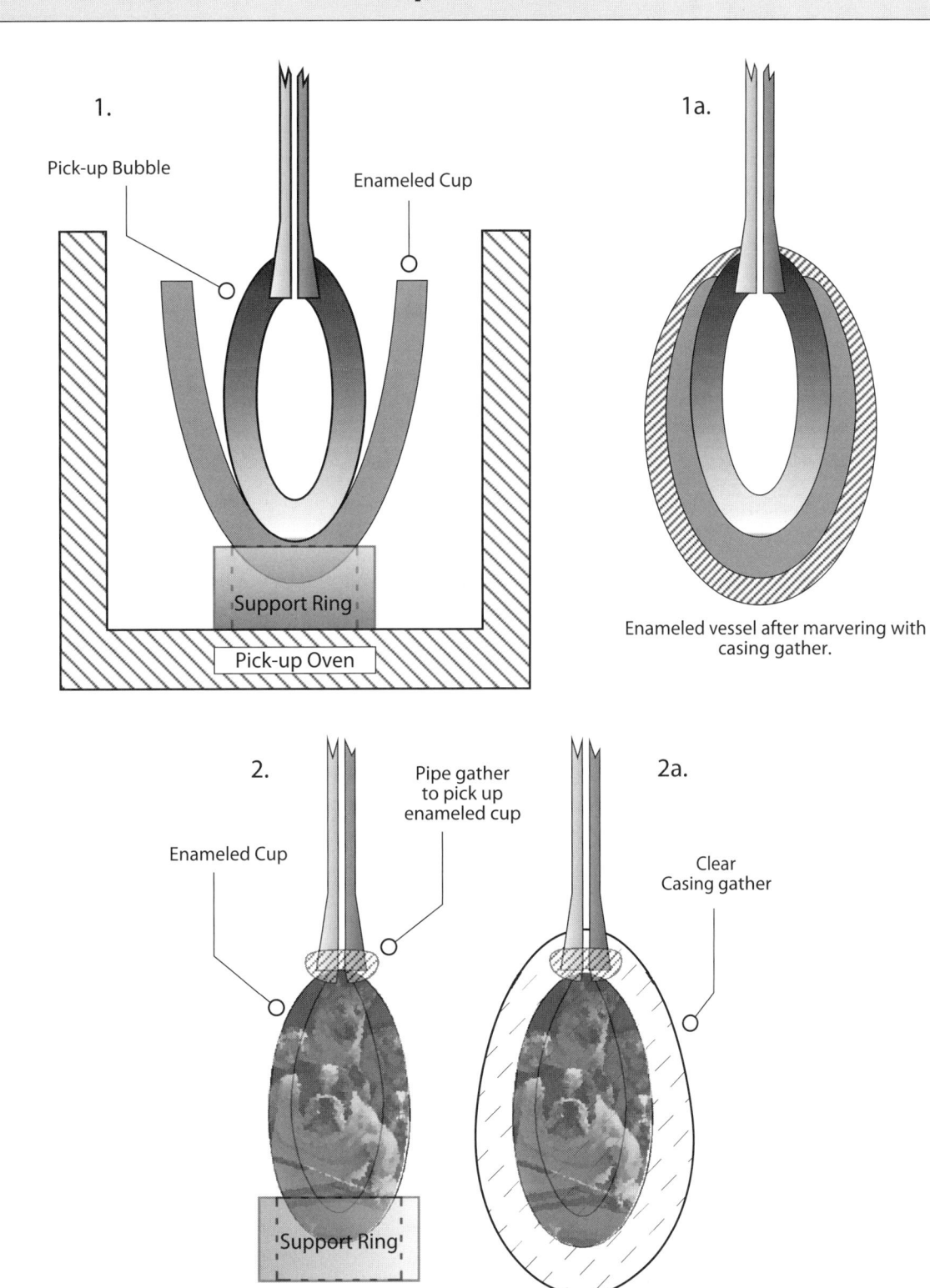

1.
- Pick-up Bubble
- Enameled Cup
- Support Ring
- Pick-up Oven

1a.

Enameled vessel after marvering with casing gather.

2.
- Enameled Cup
- Pipe gather to pick up enameled cup
- Support Ring

2a.
- Clear Casing gather

#1 & #1a depict a technique similar to the Swedish Gral. In this case, a bubble is made and carefully placed into the enameled cup that has been brought to a temperature slightly above annealing. The cup is worked into the pickup bubble prior to making the casing gather.

#2 & #2a depict the enameled vessel being picked up on a ring of glass. This technique requires a narrow vessel and is tricky when making the casing gather.

Glass Notes   293

Resist, Wax, Scavo, Separator, Rubber Mold, Crucible

Czech Sandblast Resist

I discovered this resist while visiting Czechoslovakia in 1987. One of the glass teachers at Zelezny Brod High shared this formula with me.

This resist is for curved surfaces and works quite well for deep blasting. What follows is a direct translation from the Czech. It is to be used warm and can be heated in a double boiler. If heated directly use a low heat. The heat is what keeps the mass liquid. *Author's note: The carpenter's glue used is actually horsehide glue. I assume any animal hide glue will suffice.*

Makes 3-4 liters (A liter is slightly more than a quart. 1 liter= 1.0567 qts.)

- 22 oz. (630 gms.) Horsehide glue (dry) sometimes referred to as carpenter's glue
- 12 oz. (350 gms.) Technical Glycerine (available from any pharmacy)
- 10 oz. (280 gms.) Whiting (Calcium Carbonate)

Let the horsehide glue soak in cold water for 24 hrs. Use 3 or 4 liters of water. On the second day or so, put the dissolved mass through a strainer or sieve and add the glycerine and (later) thicken with whiting. If you want a thinner resist, add more water. If it is too thin, either add more whiting or let the water evaporate. If you add too much whiting, the resist will lose its flexibility. You can either paint this resist on or dip your pieces in it directly. Very fine lines can be cut into it after it has hardened. Handle pieces carefully after applying. Once mixed into a liquid, the resist will not have a pleasant odor. Add a few drops of formaldehyde to keep the mixture from becoming rancid.

Milton Mud (Jack Wax)

This is the original formula used by the glass blowers at the Blenko Glass Factory in Milton, WV. Joel Phillip Myers shared this formula with us many years ago. It is much better than beeswax alone; that is, it hangs onto your jacks a lot longer. The original name for this wax was "Milton Mud." It is a pain to get the wood charcoal into the mixture. Be patient and keep stirring.

- 2 ½ - 3 ½ lbs. Beeswax.
- 1 lb. Wood Charcoal-- you <u>must</u> use wood charcoal.
- 3 level teaspoons Rosen; this is the same stuff used on violin bows.
- 3 sticks Pink Bubble Gum. Yes, that's right, bubble gum. Fleer's double bubble works best.
- Heat the whole mess up; stir until all the wood charcoal mixes in.
- Although it's not called for, you may wish to add some carnauba wax.
- Pour into small paper cups.

Scavo

Please read: Scavo is a hot technique. After applying, you <u>must</u> fire it in a glory hole to "set" it. Scavo dust can be very dangerous if not used properly. Always apply it in a well–ventilated dust booth that has the proper filters installed. Do not vent it into your neighbor's yard or window. Keep it out of the reach of children and pets. The surface of any piece that has had Scavo applied to it must be washed with a good stiff brush in warm soapy water after annealing.

Base Formula

Potassium Nitrate, 3 parts

Whiting (Calcium Carbonate)----1 part
Wood Ash -------------------------------1 part

Additions for color spots

- Tin Oxide
- Manganese
- Potassium Carbonate
- Lead (very dangerous and toxic)

Add only one of each to the above formula. Use these in small quantities at first and observe the results. Alter the formula for desired effect.

Other chemicals for additional fluxing, opacifying, and bite

- Borax
- Barium (very dangerous and toxic)
- Lime
- Potassium Bichromate
- Soda Ash
- Chrome oxide
- Stannous chloride

Always use Scavo last. It will eat at your punty with each reheat.

Scavo should not be applied to any food-bearing surfaces. Anyone using Scavo does so at their own risk.

I wish to thank Rik Allen for providing the above formula and text. After seeing Rik's beautifully Scavoed surfaces, I knew I had to have his formula for *Glass Notes*.

Mold Separator

There are many different types of mold separators. Everyone seems to have a favorite.

Murphy's Oil Soap

This is one of the oldest separators I know of. I used it when I was a potter many years ago and have used it again recently. It works very well and will impart a very smooth, shiny surface on the plaster, but I only recommend it for plaster to plaster separation. I would not recommend it if you're using it on casting molds. Purchase the Murphy's oil soap in the jar not the one in the spray bottle. It requires 3 coats and you must let it dry between each coat. Buff it after each coat dries.

Vaseline/Kerosene

This is the one I swear by and use most frequently. To mix it, do the following: Melt a container of Vaseline in an old, clean pot. It requires very little heat. After it is melted, take it off the heat, add 2 containers of Kerosene, and stir. Store in a metal coffee can. The mix is rather thin but one coat works really well and can be used on very porous surfaces. The ratio is 1 part Vaseline to 2 parts Kerosene.

Quick and Easy Silicone Rubber Mold

Here is a nifty quick rubber (RTV) mold for small objects. I saw it demonstrated at Pilchuck by Juanita Nye some years ago. She read about it somewhere but varied the process to suit her needs. I was absolutely flabbergasted when I saw the process. It really works.

Materials:

- Silicone Adhesive
- Caulking gun
- Small bucket filled with warm water and some ivory soap.
- Shape to be molded
- Mold separator

Prepare shape to be molded on board and apply separator. Squeeze a thin, continuous stream of silicone into the bucket with the warm soapy water. Soap your hands and pick up silicone blob from bucket. Gently squeeze the water from the silicone ball and gently pat over shape trying not to create any air bubbles. In about ½ hour, gently pat and firm silicone onto shape. Shape can be removed in 3 to 12 hours. Silicone molds can withstand a great deal of heat and are ideal for making wax models. For large molds, it is possible to layer the silicone as it will stick to itself if you keep it clean and free of mold separator.

Crucible Formula for Pot Furnace (for slip casting)

Back in the 70's, some of us made our own crucibles. I did not remember who developed the formula since it was written on a scrap of paper with no names but I suspected that it came from Dudley Giberson originally as he was the one that first published that type of information for the studios and universities in his "Joppa Catalog of Fact and Knowledge." I sent an e-mail to Dudley asking him about the formula and here is his reply.

"The formula you have below is a variant of the one I published in my "Joppa Catalog of Fact and Knowledge," June '77. It came from Mark Peiser and goes like this:"

Mark Peiser Formula (in pounds)
8 quarts water
2 oz. sodium silicate (defloculant)
18 ------- Tenn. Ball
21 ------- Mullite 325 mesh
21 ------- Mullite 200 mesh

Halem variant of the Giberson formula which is a variant of the Peiser formula
7 --------- Tennessee Ball Clay #9 (28 - 30%)
9 --------- 325 Mesh Mullite (36%)
9 --------- 200 Mesh Mullite (36%)
9 --------- Water (38%)

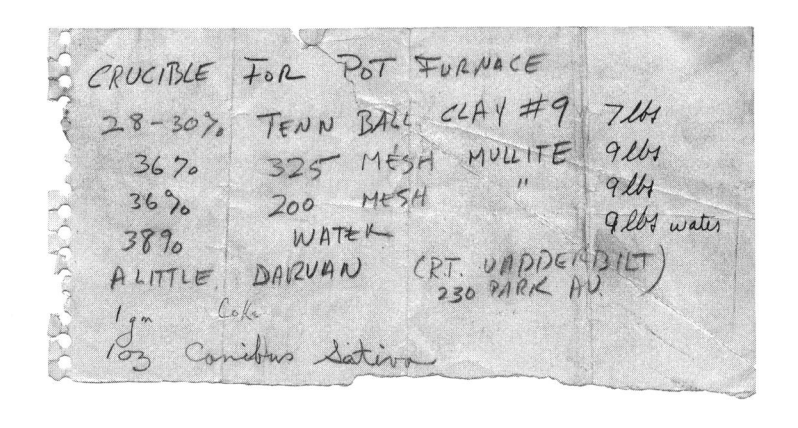

Defloculate with Darvan #7. (Darvan is a deflocculant and used to disperse ceramic suspensions to minimize their water content.)

I have no idea who the smart ass was that wrote the margin notes on the scanned image of the formula.

How to Print a Photograph Inside a Bottle

The original source for this information is unknown.
Some additions have been made by the author.
I include this as a curiosity.

Take the whites of two eggs and add twenty-nine grains of ammonium chloride dissolved in one dram of spirits of wine (a good Beaujolais, no doubt) or wood alcohol and ½ oz. of water. Beat this mixture into a thick froth and then allow it to stand and settle. Filter through a tuft of cotton wool (cheesecloth) and pour into your clear clean bottle. By twisting the bottle around, an even layer of the solution will deposit itself on the sides. Pour off the remaining solution, allow the film in the bottle to dry, and repeat the operation.

The next operation is to sensitize the film with a solution of silver nitrate (use with rubber gloves), forty grains (2.592 grams) to one ounce of water.* The solution should be made in dim light and any extra solution should be stored in a light–tight container. The solution has a minimal shelf life. Pour this in and turn the bottle around for a few minutes; then pour off the superfluous solution and dry again (in a dark room or closet). Hold the neck of the bottle for a few seconds over another bottle containing ammonia so as to allow the fumes to enter it. Hold your breath when doing this.

Printing is the next operation: this is accomplished by tying a film negative around the bottle and covering up all the other parts from the light. Print very deeply by daylight, keeping the bottle turning around all the time to expose your negative evenly. Be careful not to move the negative while you turn it. If you do, your print will be fuzzy. Toning, fixing, and washing can be done in the ordinary way by filling the bottle up with the different solutions. Use a standard photo fix to desensitize and "fix" the silver nitrate coating. Be careful to wash the photo fix from the bottle when finished (about 3 to 5 minutes). This can be accomplished by pouring clean room temperature tap water into the bottle; pour the water out and repeat 4 or 5 times.

The photo effect is very curious and can be improved by coating the inside of the bottle with white enamel paint.

Conversion:	U.S. Avoirdupois
1 dram = .0625 oz.
1 grain = .002286 oz.

Metric
1 dram = 1.772 gms.
1 grain = .0648 gms.

*For converting from one system to another go to www.convert-me.com/en/

Iridizing (Fuming)

The fuming or iridizing of glass was very popular in the earlier days of studio glass and is still used by many studio glass artists. The popularity of enhancing the surface of studio glass with this lustrous metallic overlay came into prominence when the Art Nouveau glass of Louis Comfort Tiffany was being imitated by many of the studio glass artists. This imitation Tiffany glass could be found everywhere and was in great demand by collectors. I do not know who or what studio was the first to iridize their blown vessels, but I do know that Erwin Eisch demonstrated the process to us at the University of Wisconsin in the late 60's. Imitation iridized Art Nouveau glass was so ubiquitous at one time that there were many anti-Tiffany blowers who would declare at GAS meetings, "Let Tiffany Die!" I have to admit that I like many others, briefly went through a Tiffany phase and fumed the hell out of everything I blew. Sales were hot, and that's what the market demanded (what little market there was), or so we thought. Even today, in 2006, one can still find Tiffany look-a-likes in ads from magazines like *Niche* or *American Style*. For many, Tiffany still lives.

The first method we used was actually fuming. It should be noted that fuming and iridizing are different processes but attempt to do the same thing. We would take a metal coffee can lid and place some stannous chloride crystals onto the lid; then, when the piece was on the punty and almost ready to put away, we would take a hot bit and place it on the stannous. The dense, white fumes that were emitted would envelop our slowly turning hot glass piece that was suspended in the fumes. The tin from the fumes would put a beautiful metallic sheen on the surface of the glass similar to the effect found when you mix oil in water. Initially, the surface was very glossy, but reheating the piece in the glory hole matted the surface and sometimes produced a crackled, iridized surface. Eventually we discovered a simpler method which became known as iridizing. In that process we sprayed a fine mist of the stannous onto the surface of the glass rather than our holding the piece in the fumes. More about that later.

I would be remiss if I didn't warn any of you that wish to use this process that it is dangerous and should only be undertaken when you have the right equipment and exhaust system. Tin is a heavy metal, and there are other caustic materials suspended in the liquid spray.

There is an interesting history to the introduction of iridized glass and I have extracted a few paragraphs below from The Robert Koch book, *Louis C Tiffany: Rebel in Glass*, Crown Publishers, New York, 1964.

"Brochures supplied by Tiffany provided scant information on the exact process used in Tiffany glass, declaring only that Tiffany "obtained his iridescent and lustre effects… by a careful study of the natural decay of glass… and by reversing the action in such a way as to arrive at the effects without disintegration." In comparing glass which had developed a natural iridescence after centuries of lying buried in the earth and the antique pitted type of Tiffany's iridescent ware, known as Cypriote, it is apparent that the later pieces have a remarkable verisimilitude. The lustrous patina fitted the lavish taste of the nineties (1890's), with all its fondness for luster, irregularity and richness of detail. Such an effect was described by Tiffany in his patent application of 1880, "The effect is a highly iridescent one and of pleasing metallic luster, changeable from one to the other, depending upon the direction of the visual ray and the brilliancy or dullness of the light falling upon or passing through the glass.""

"Tiffany did not state that he had invented the means for producing iridescent glass, but did describe the method he used in the patent claim filed in 1880. "The metallic luster is produced by forming a film of a metal or its oxide, or a compound of a metal, on or in the glass, either by exposing it to vapors or gases or by direct application. It may also be produced by corroding the surface of the glass, such processes being well known to glass-manufacturers." Gold chloride was used both in suspension in the glass and sprayed on the surface before cooling. The gold in the glass was brought to the surface by a reducing flame. The effect could be intensified by the use of a spray which etched the surface, creating a satin like texture. Twenty-dollar gold pieces were placed in a solution of nitric and hydrochloric acid, which was heated and thinned for use in a spray."

"Sir David Brewster (1781-1868), a Scotch physicist, was the first to experiment with the iridescent patina produced by the decomposition of ancient glass. He patented his colorful kaleidoscope in 1817. In the latter decades of the nineteenth century wide interest was generated in the ancient glass objects, naturally iridescent, which were being evacuated by archaeologists working at many sites in the Middle East. Modern iridescent glass was first made in Bohemia and in Venice before 1880. According to Anne Huether's *Glass and Man*,

Ludwig Lobmeyr exhibited the first iridescent glass to be produced commercially at an exposition in Vienna in 1873; European craftsmen were among the first to see and be influenced by Tiffany's work in this field, since samples were sent abroad even before they were introduced to the New York market."

Iridizing, a how to

The information for this section has been provided by Art Allison, Peet Robison, and myself.

Tiffany first patented an iridescent glassware called *Fabrile* (from the old English, hand-wrought) in the late 1880's. and later changed to the more elegant *Favrile*. This glass was meant to be an artificially aged product, one that closely duplicated the nacreous, rainbow- hued surface of ancient Egyptian and Roman glass. "Egyptian" was all the rage, and Tiffany's glass became all the rage too. Very quickly, all the glass world seemed to be making iridescent ware. Quezal, Loetz, Tiffany, Steuben, and several others made this expensive art glass.

Within a few years, several U.S. companies, most notably Fenton, Millersburg, and Imperial, had begun producing their own cheaper, albeit somewhat gaudy imitations of this art glass. Today we know this type of ware as "Carnival Glass." It too was very popular and is sought after by collectors. This "Carnival Glass" was press molded, then iridized, but the iridizing process for this glass was very different than for the aforementioned Art Glass. I should mention that I have seen some beautiful iridized Art Noveau-style glass made by Fenton Glass in Williamstown, WV. The factory has an excellent museum of the work they produced.

To iridize a piece of glass, all that really needs to be done is to create an object with either a silver bearing glass or a lead glass. The stannous solution that is sprayed onto the surface of the glass does not take well to soda/lime glass although some artists have had a degree of success with those types of glasses. The piece, while hot and on the punty rod is first reduced to its metallic state in the glory hole and then introduced into an atomized mist of stannous chloride in an aqueous suspension. Voila! A rainbow of colors appears on the surface of your glass. The iridescent colors come from light being reflecting off the silvery surface, then refracted by the very thin layers of metallic tin. The effect is not unlike the rainbow created when oil mixes with water. Add a little sunlight and you get a rainbow of color.

To create the iridescence consistently, and to make the best possible colors, 3 variables must be considered and understood:

- **The base glass**
- **Glory Hole atmospheres**
- **The Iridizing spray**

Base Glass

Success or failure when iridizing is dependent on your base glass. As stated above, iridizing does not work very well on soda/lime glass. It will work to some degree, but the full effect is realized when done over metallic-based glasses such as 7% silver-based glass as well as lead-based glasses. The more opaque the glass is, the nicer the iridescent colors will be. I would note though that Frederic Carder did beautiful iridizing over clear glass which he designated as Verre de Soie--sounds so romantic. Remember, you are working with reflected light, so you want to eliminate all the transmitted light. If you're using a soda/lime glass an overlay of color from a lead or silver bearing color bar or frit works well, especially if the base color is dark. Dark cobalt also works well. Interesting effects can further be achieved by using bits or wraps from metallic based color rods on the surface of your piece. When you iridize the surface of your piece, only the areas where you have placed the metal-based wraps or bits will be iridized dramatically.

Glory Hole Atmospheres.

- The glory hole atmosphere has to be set correctly, or your work is for naught.
- Work the piece continually under a strongly oxidizing flame. Continue working the piece under this atmosphere until it's completely finished on the punty and ready to put away.
- Turn down the air until you get a heavy reduction flame (be careful not to overdo it--do not make a smoky or sooty atmosphere. Work the piece in the reducing atmosphere. Watch carefully; the silver or lead will start to reduce to the surface. Do not heat the piece to the point that it is overly soft. This will have an adverse affect on the color. It takes experience, but eventually you will understand how to regulate the atmosphere of your glory hole.

- Heat and cool the piece until the surface takes on a metallic hue. Try to note as you work the piece what kind of metal the surface looks like (silvery gold or coppery). This is a subtle nuance, but with a deft use of the flame, you can change the look of the finished piece. You're now ready to iridize the surface of your piece.

Try different levels of reducing flame in your glory hole. The level of reduction will affect the iridized surface. The difference will be whether you obtain warm or cool colors in the iridized surface. You may need to reheat the piece a couple of times while you are applying the iridizing spray, but leave the reduction atmosphere set as it is, and do not heat the piece to its high softening point.
--Art Allison

Here is how Peet Robison describes his process of iridizing:
"For different effects I use powders that have silver in it and my own black/silver luster glass made from SP87. The big thing with fuming is temperature of the piece and the reduction/oxidation atmosphere. I have found that getting the piece hot enough to move after spraying causes a nice texture on the surface. I did a 'verre de soie series that was just soda lime clear'.

Iridizing Spray

- 32 oz. (.94 liters) tap or distilled water
- 300 gms. stannous chloride (the DiHydrate form is recommended)
- 2 tbl. *muriatic acid (dilute hydrochloric acid). Keeps stannous in solution.

*Muriatic acid can be obtained in a hardware store. It is used to clean concrete.

Lesser volumes of iridizing spray can be mixed in proportional amounts. If the solution gets old, the stannous may precipitate out.

The finished piece of glass, reduced as described above, is sprayed with this solution, and WoWy wow wow wow, colors appear. It really is just that simple. You can vary the colors with some degree of control by adding more or less spray. You might also try small additions of different metallic chlorides to the base solution such as iron chloride, but again, some of these additions are dangerous.

The Sprayer

Since metals are adversely affected by the corrosiveness of the stannous chloride mixture, it precludes the use of any commercially available sprayers. I have built my own from a block of acrylic. Plastics are not affected by the iridizing solution but will clog if not cleaned regularly. The principal for my sprayer is based on an atomizer, like those simple metal spray tubes available in art supply stores. The principle is simple; air is blown across the top of a tube that is immersed in your solution. As the air blows across the top of the tube, a partial vacuum is formed which then pulls the liquid up through the tube where it enters the air stream and exits the orifice as a liquid mist. The illustration on page 302 should help you to understand how to build this device as well as understand the principle if you're building your own. The jar that you keep the solution in must be glass or plastic and the lid must be plastic as well. Remember, no metal.

The Iridizing Chamber

There are two types of exhaust systems that I have either used or seen and illustrated on page 301.

The iridizing chamber is a large plastic trash barrel available from any number of plastic parts suppliers. I use U.S. Plastic Corp. (www.usplastic.com). The barrel is placed on a sturdy support at a comfortable height. An exhaust vent hole is cut into the back or side of the barrel. A large diameter plastic tube (6")--PVC works well-- is attached to the vent hole. You may wish to attach a flange to the PVC exhaust tube so that you can bolt it to the exhaust hole (use plastic connectors) of the plastic barrel. The exhaust system is attached to the PVC exhaust tube as indicated in the two illustrations below. The U.S. Plastic Corp. carries a large selection of plastic tube, pipe, flanges and other types of adaptors that will serve your system.

Fig. 1 depicts a straight-out-the-back system and uses a 6" in line duct booster fan obtainable from Grainger as well as other sources. This system is the least expensive of the two to build. Because the in-line duct booster is not made from plastic it should be checked at regular intervals for corrosion since the iridizing exhaust is corrosive.

The second exhaust system (Fig. 2) employs a flange-mounted, plastic blower also available from Grainger and U.S. Plastics. This system is very efficient. The exhaust tube from the plastic barrel is attached to the intake of the blower. You will probably have to build a stand for the blower in order to position it at the correct height. Remember, both these systems are electrically operated so you should put the on/off switch in a convenient location.

It is important to include a good filter in the barrel as you do not want to vent heavy, metal fumes into the atmosphere. A good foam filter works well and will filter out most of the over spray. Remember, you must suck the fumes away from you and out of the studio. The fumes as well as the spray are dangerous to your health.

It is also wise to keep a pair of long-handled metal tongs on hand in case the hot piece that you're iridizing falls off the punty and hits the bottom of your plastic barrel. Grab it before it burns a hole. Better yet, put a piece of fiber insulation in the bottom of the barrel so that if the piece falls off it will be insulated from the plastic, thus giving you time to remove it.

Words to live by: A little bit of iridescence is nice, a lot and you're making tchotchkies.

Warning

Iridizing glass is hazardous to your health. It involves caustic liquids and heavy metals.

It is important to wear the correct clothing when mixing the iridizing solution: Full face shield when mixing any acids, rubber gloves, appropriate respirator, protective apron, etc. You must observe good lab practices. You must read and understand all the MSDS available on any chemical you work with.

Nearly all of the iridized "Art Glass" surfaces can be recreated using stannous chloride as an iridizing spray. This is fortunate, because stannous chloride is the least dangerous of all the substances that can be used. If you find yourself in possession of old recipes that call for using iron chloride or barium chloride, make sure you use them with caution as these chemicals can cause severe damage to your kidneys.

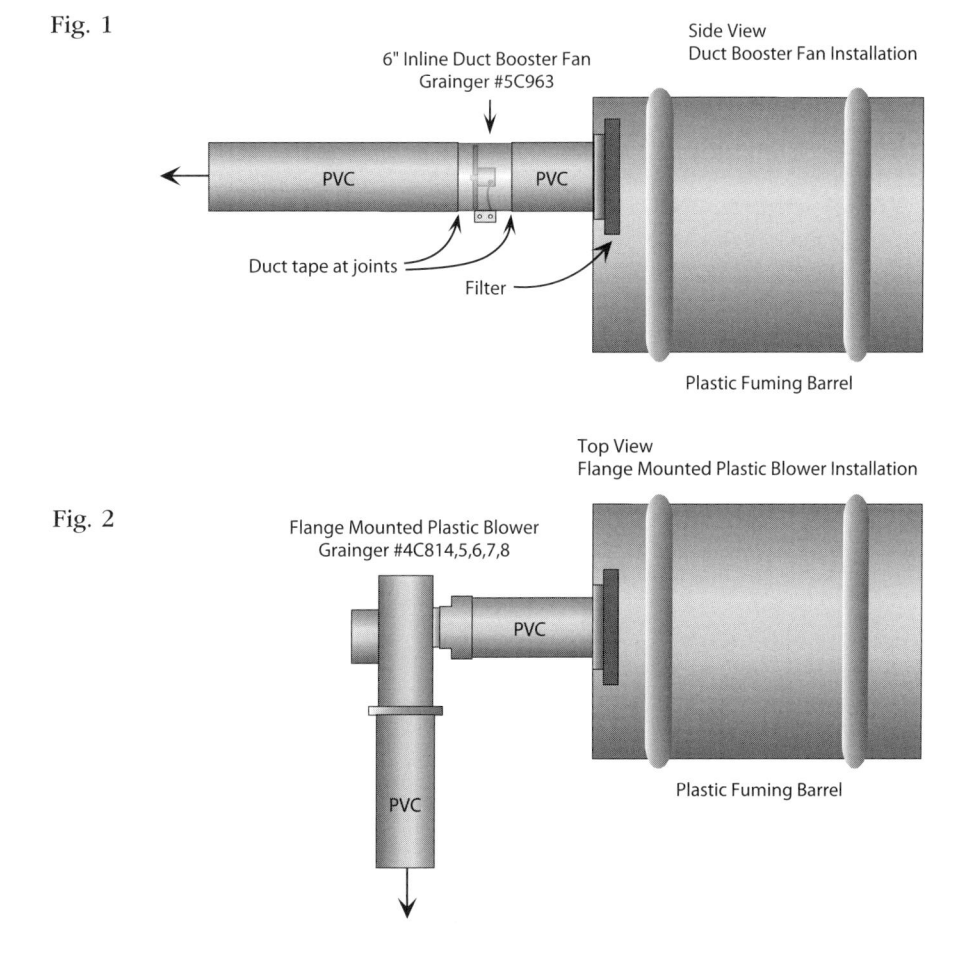

Fig. 1

Side View
Duct Booster Fan Installation

6" Inline Duct Booster Fan
Grainger #5C963

PVC — PVC

Duct tape at joints
Filter

Plastic Fuming Barrel

Fig. 2

Top View
Flange Mounted Plastic Blower Installation

Flange Mounted Plastic Blower
Grainger #4C814,5,6,7,8

PVC

PVC

Plastic Fuming Barrel

Iridizing Sprayer

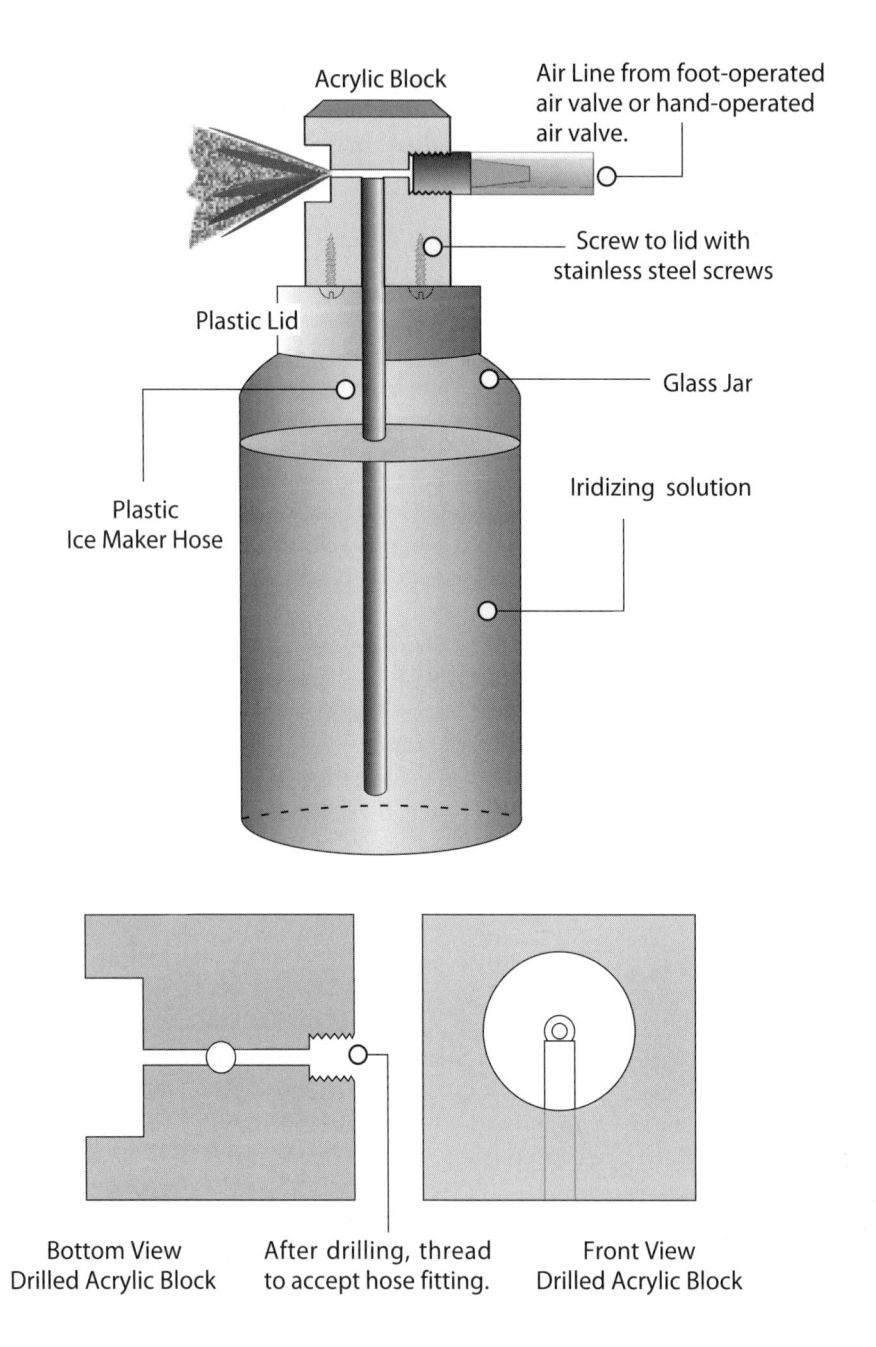

Acrylic Block

Air Line from foot-operated air valve or hand-operated air valve.

Screw to lid with stainless steel screws

Plastic Lid

Glass Jar

Plastic Ice Maker Hose

Iridizing solution

Bottom View
Drilled Acrylic Block

After drilling, thread to accept hose fitting.

Front View
Drilled Acrylic Block

The design for this sprayer was shown to me by Erwin Eisch in about 1972.

Lusters and Bright Metals

Lusters and bright metals applied and fired on glass or glazed ceramics produce unique and appealing decorations of delicate metallic tints. It is important to observe the following suggestions.
- The ware should be perfectly clean and dry. Dust and dirt should be avoided as much as possible to avoid imperfections in the fired film. To prevent dust or lint from settling on the freshly-applied luster, it is good policy to shelter or cover the decorated pieces in some way. The luster will have to set up safely within 30 minutes; thereafter, dust particles will no longer penetrate the film.
- For best results, the luster should be applied evenly with a flat camel's hair brush and in medium strength; too heavy a deposit will cause blistering or flaking in the firing;* uneven coatings will tend to cause color variations. Exceptions in this respect are pearl lusters; they should be applied crisscross and subsequently stippled to bring out the mottled effects characteristic of pearls.

Because of their basic ingredients, lusters differ in viscosity and workability. Those that appear thick and tacky can be conditioned with a few drops of luster essence. Luster essence can be obtained at any quality ceramic supply shop. Lusters can also be sprayed, and while some can be used as supplied, others will stand cutting from 20 to 50%. The proper air pressure for spraying is from 10 to 15 psi. The objects should be held at a distance from 6–12" (15–30 cm), depending on their size. The compressed air should be dried to prevent water from getting into the luster, which will cause the fired film to show white spots.

Unique color combinations result by applying lusters over fired coatings of bright gold, platinum, palladium, and copper.

The firing procedure and temperature are the same for bright gold, platinum, palladium, and copper. The kiln door should be "cracked" until the ware has "smoked off" about 700°–720° F (371°–382° C); it is then closed and fired to maturity. The actual temperature depends on the ware itself and ranges between 1060° and 1250° F (571°–676° C) on glass, depending on the thickness and shape of the object. The recommended temperatures listed below are not absolute. They are offered only as a guide. The principle is to fire as high as the glass will stand; if under-fired, the decoration will wipe off. Another pointer is to avoid crowding the ware in the kiln and give it sufficient air space to permit complete burning out of the combustible matter in the lusters. It is important when firing lusters and bright metals to maintain an equal heat distribution in the firing chamber.

*I cannot stress enough the need to apply lusters and bright metals very thinly. These materials set up very quickly, and you should not go back over what you have laid down. Again, keep the door "cracked" until reaching 700° F (371° C).

Recommended Firing Temperatures

Flint and lime glass ---------------------- 1060°-1120° F (570°-605° C)
Pyrex and quartz glass ----------------- 1200°-1250° F (650°-675° C)
Soft glaze earthenware ----------------- 1150°-1250° F (620°-675° C)
Standard glaze pottery ----------------- 1300°-1360° F (705°-737° C)
Hard glaze china or porcelain -------- 1400°-1500° F (760°-815° C)

Converting Silver Nitrate to Silver Salts

A word of caution before using silver nitrate: Silver Nitrate can cause burns when it comes in contact with skin. It is also believed to be somewhat carcinogenic. Do not breath the fumes. The silver will also transfer to your gloves if you pick up a piece that has the silver nitrate on it; it will subsequently transfer to any other pieces that are touched with those gloves. Do not put silver nitrate on the marver; it will transfer to the metal and is difficult to remove. Use silver nitrate with caution. Always practice safe glass.

　　　　　Silver Nitrate ---------------------- 112.0 gms
　　　　　Sodium Chloride ------------------ 38.8 gms

　　　　　Silver Nitrate ---------------------- 112.0 gms
　　　　　Sodium Bromide ------------------- 77.8 gms

　　　　　Silver Nitrate ---------------------- 112.0 gms
　　　　　Sodium Iodide -------------------- 90.0 gms

1. Mix silver nitrate in one (1) pint of distilled water.
2. Stir until thoroughly dissolved.
3. Mix salt in one (1) pint of distilled water. All the salts must be reagent pure. Stir until dissolved.
4. Pour the nitrate and salt solution together in large beaker and stir. You now have a silver salt precipitate.
5. Pour the solution through a filter paper and funnel. After all the liquid has passed, unwrap the precipitate from the filter paper, place it in hand towels, and squeeze until a hard ball is formed. When the ball is unwrapped, some pieces of precipitate may break off. Save these pieces as they are usable.
6. Dry the precipitate in a warm location, but DO NOT get the drying temperature above 400° F (204° C) as it will melt.

Repeat 1, 2, 3, 4, and 5 to create each of the silver salt precipitates listed above.

The above salts (silver chloride, silver bromide, silver iodide) create different effects when applied to hot glass. The effects vary from very fluid to concise surface marks. Silver salts are used by holding a piece in a tweezer and "drawing" on the surface of the hot vessel. Remember, do NOT breath the fumes. They are dangerous. Use an adequate exhaust hood.

Author's Note: Amounts of silver nitrate and salt can be reduced as long as it is done proportionally. Accuracy of all weights and measures is very important.

A bit of history

Silver nitrate and, to a lesser degree, the related silver salts were used quite extensively by the American Studio and University glass blowers during the latter 60's and into the 70's. I'm not sure anyone really knows who introduced the use of silver nitrate, although it is my belief that Fritz Dreisbach and Joel Myers started using it in the 60's. I know we used it extensively at the University of Wisconsin in the latter 60's. There was a time when I think every blown piece had a silver salt of some sort or other on its surface. We used it because there was nothing else that we knew of to decorate our glass with. Color was rare and Kügler had not come into common usage. Silver nitrate was relatively cheap and easy to use. Although there are a few blowers using silver today, the technique as it was used at that time has all but disappeared. I think its use peaked in about 1972.

Everyone who used silver had a favorite trick. One of our favorites was to create a reducing atmosphere in the glory hole for the last reheat; the silver would sometimes "strike" a beautiful bright silver. Another decorative trick was to gather over a surface that had silver nitrate applied to it; the silver would create a silvery, opaque, bluish veil. As stated on the previous page, silver nitrate is used differently than the silver salts. Silver nitrate takes the form of a very coarse salt, and the hot glass is usually marvered in a few grains of it. The chloride, bromide, and iodide are somewhat solid and must be applied using a tweezer. Many of us learned how to make the silver salts from Dick Huss when he demonstrated the technique at GAS 2.

Niijima Element Configuration

While in Japan, I had the opportunity to work at the glass studio on the beautiful island of Niijima off the coast of Tokyo. The studio is managed and maintained by Osamu Noda, his wife Yumico, and many assistants. The hot glass studio was modern and well equipped. I noticed one of the annealers had a novel solution for hanging the heating elements. Instead of using the standard coiled elements, they simply strung and pinned the straight element wire as indicated in the following diagram. The walls of the annealer were comprised of three or four inches of 1600° F fiber block insulation with the inner face being 1" of fiber board. The elements were pinned to the board every few inches to prevent the drooping of the element. This method also allowed one simply to pin the element to the crown without having to resort to any fancy system of hanging elements. The two side walls, back wall, and crown were wired in parallel. Establishing the length of wire required is a simple procedure as indicated on page 281. For those skeptics who think this system cannot work, I can assure you I have seen it in action and it works quite well. It seems to give excellent and even heat distribution. Remember to "pigtail" the element at each end. A "pigtail" is two thicknesses of element twisted together. This double-thick twist keeps the elements from getting hot at the electrical connection.

Author's note: Pin the elements as indicated in the illustration below for the reasons stated.

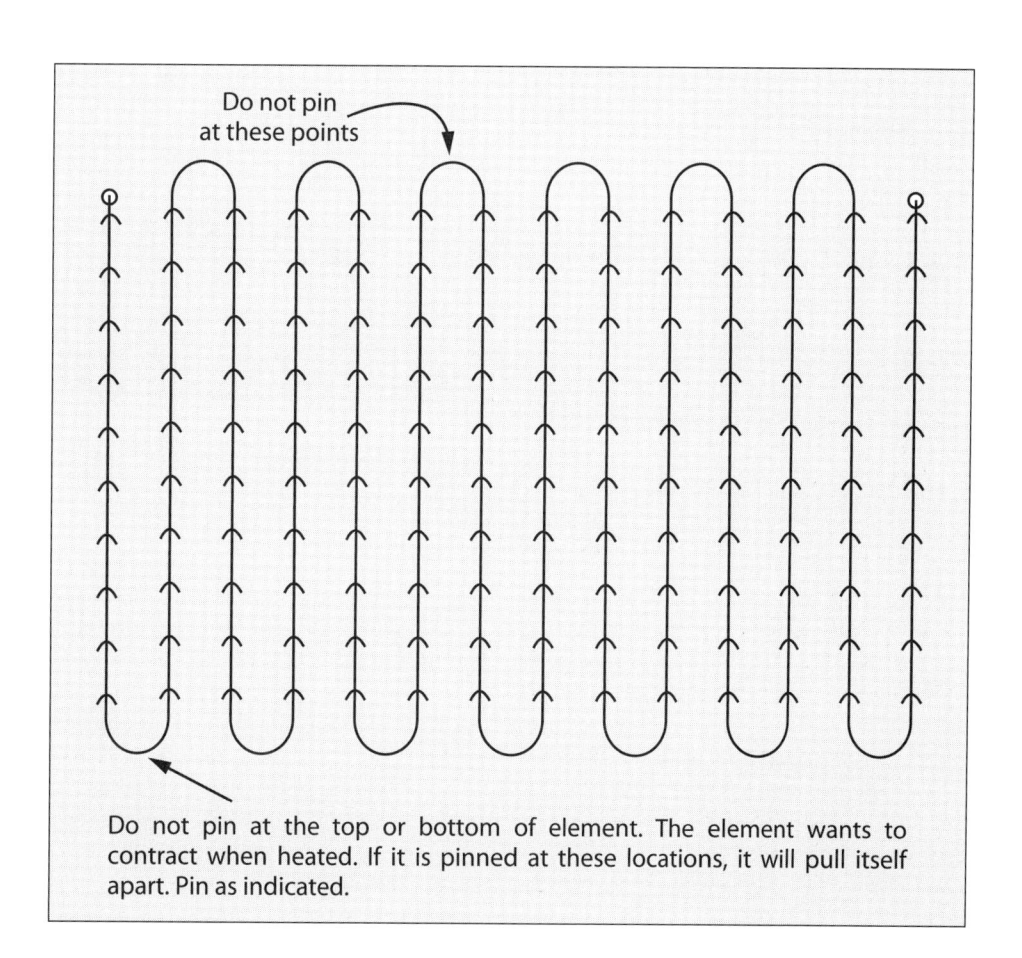

Do not pin at these points

Do not pin at the top or bottom of element. The element wants to contract when heated. If it is pinned at these locations, it will pull itself apart. Pin as indicated.

Precious Leaf Pick-up Table

Take a 12" x 24" by ⅛" piece of aluminum and drill holes ³⁄₃₂" every ½". The holes should be drilled in a grid pattern as shown below. Construct a box as shown and mount a small fan in the the bottom. Too large a fan will suck the leaf through the holes. Make sure you mount the fan so it blows toward the floor. When the fan is on, a slight, negative pressure will be exerted which will hold the gold or silver leaf flat and ready to be picked up on your hot gather.

This little tidbit of information was submitted by Art Allison.

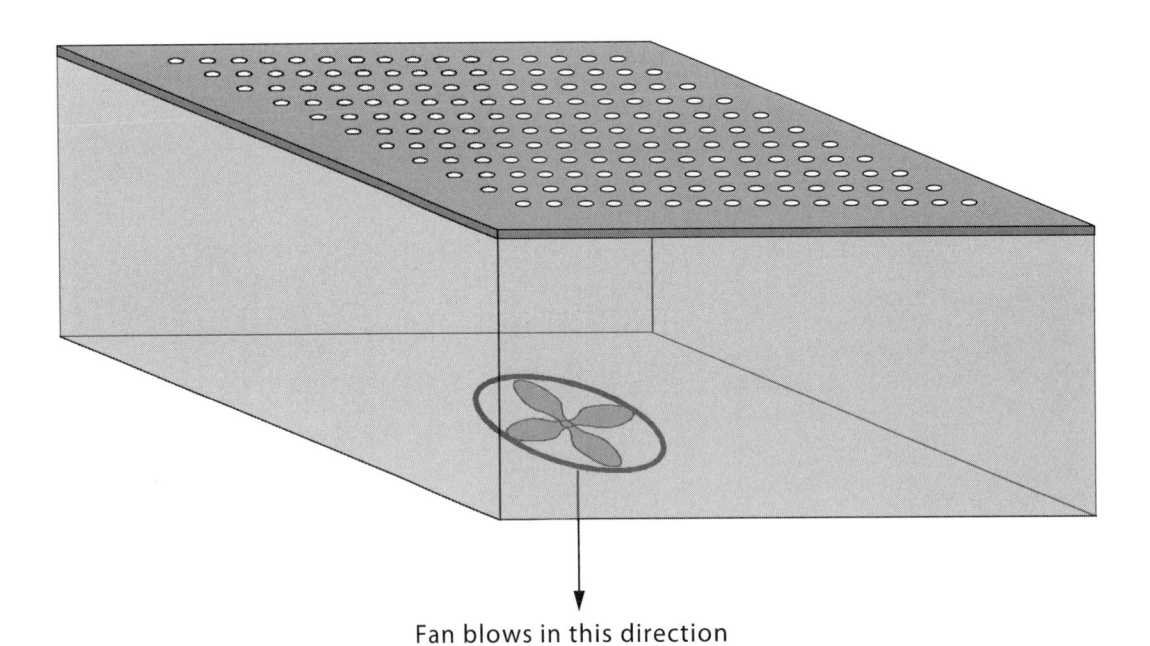

Fan blows in this direction

Color Bar Breaker

I've seen a lot of different types and styles of color bar cutters, some complex and some quite simple. The simplest is a sharp, cold chisel and a hammer, but that's no fun and, more often than not, the color bar breaks into many pieces. The one depicted below I've seen in action and can vouch for the fact that it works. All bar cutters are based on the guillotine. For that invention I think we can thank the French.

The Penland Color Bar Breaker

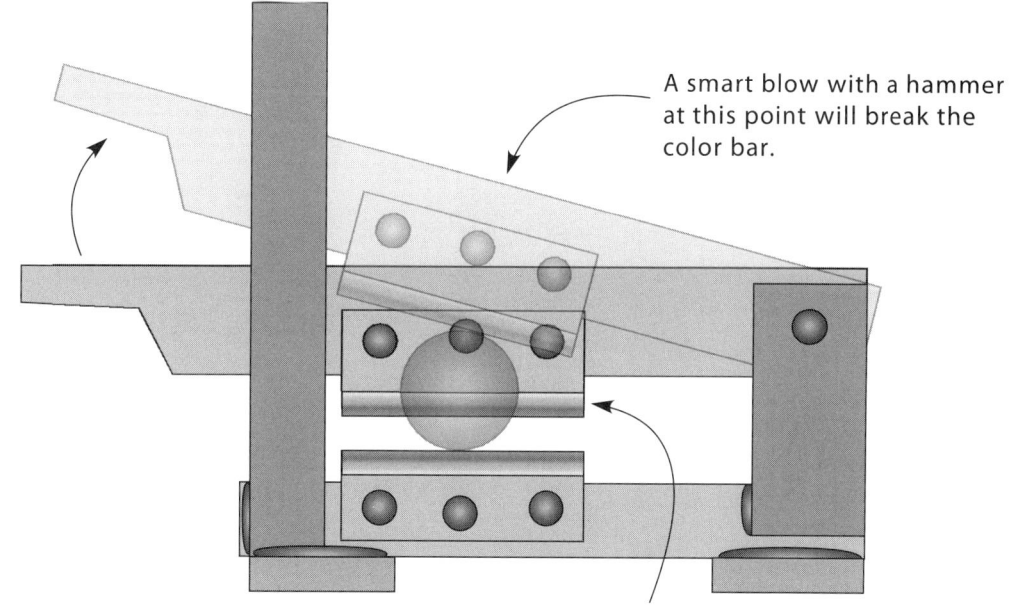

A smart blow with a hammer at this point will break the color bar.

Cutter fabricated from a flat file. The edge of the file is ground sharp.

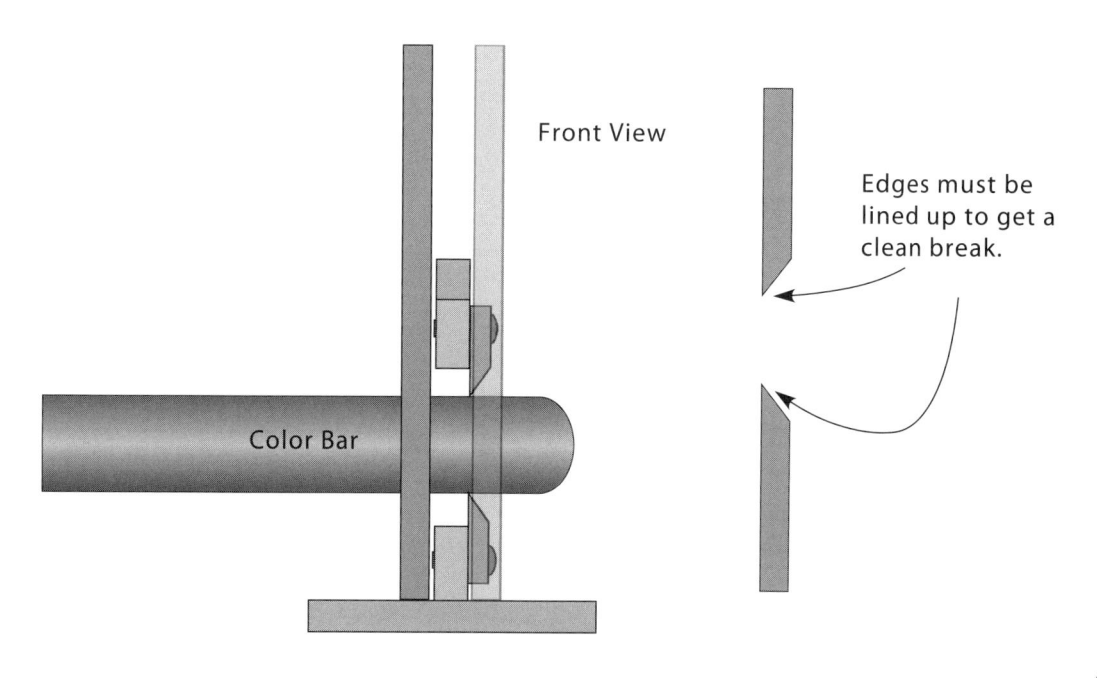

Front View

Color Bar

Edges must be lined up to get a clean break.

Glass Notes 307

More Color Bar Breakers

The color bar breakers shown below are simple to build and they work well. My preference, however, is #2 because it has a sharp edge file under the color bar. It is important to keep the cold chisels sharp in order to facilitate a clean break. When hitting the cold chisel with a hammer, it is important to hit it smartly and not wimp out when striking. If you do wimp out the color bar will sense your apprehension and shatter into many small unusable pieces.

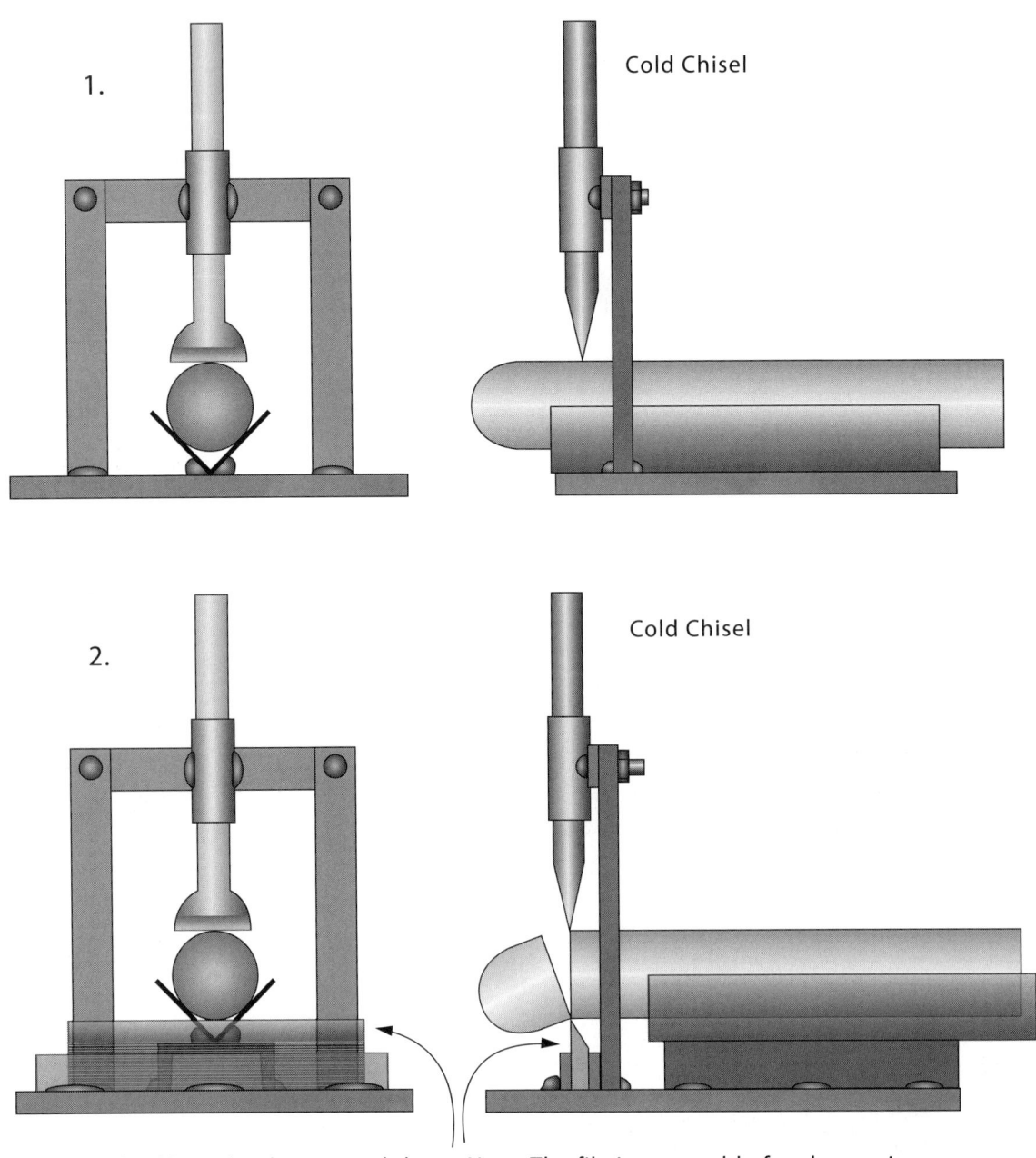

1.

Cold Chisel

2.

Cold Chisel

Flat file with edge ground sharp. Note: The file is removable for sharpening. You will destroy the temper of the file if you overheat it when grinding sharp.

Pipe Cooler, Battery Powered

There are many designs for pipe coolers. It seems as if every studio I visit has their own design. The one illustrated here is a design that has many variations. What I particularly like about this design is that it is fairly simple to build from pieces and parts found in any hardware store. It also can be wheeled to any part of the studio because it is battery operated. The battery charge usually lasts at least one month, but that of course depends on how much use it gets. It's always a good idea to have a spare battery on hand. The photographs will also give you a good idea of how it is constructed.

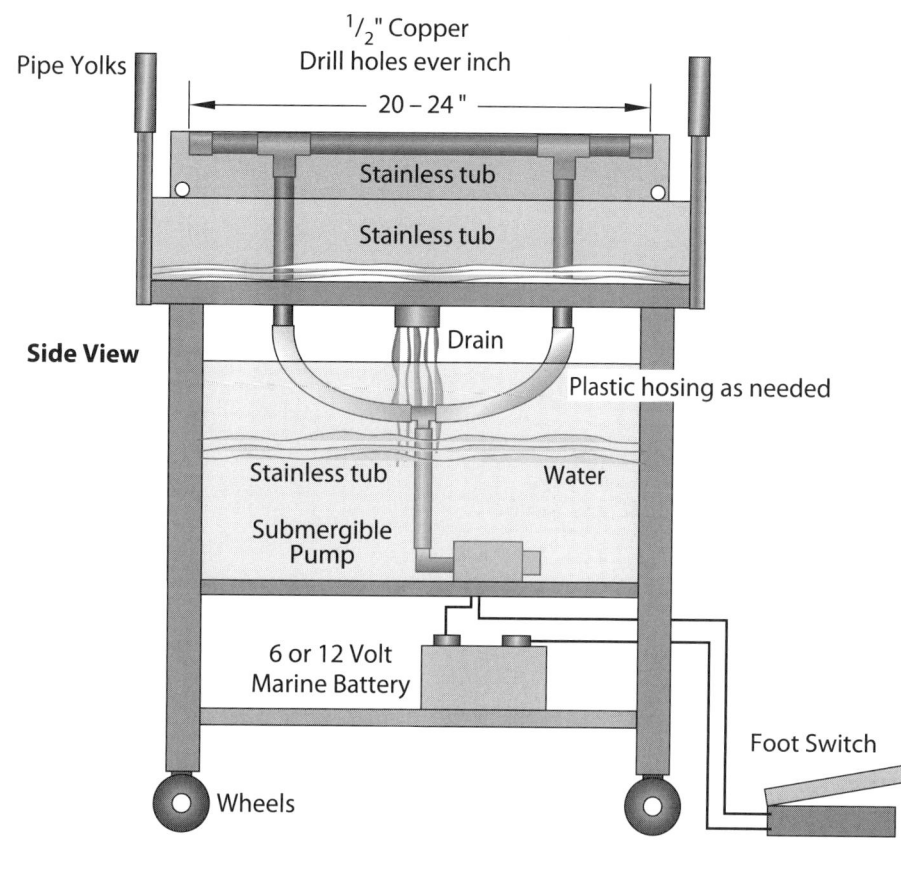

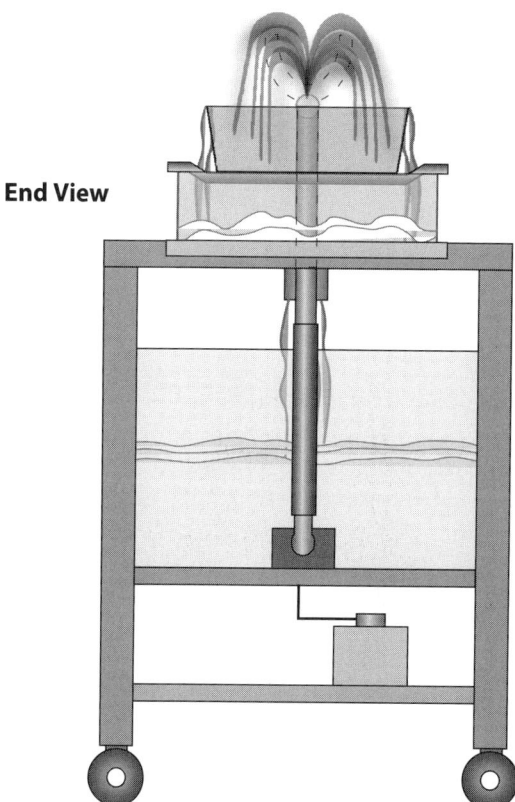

Side View

Pipe Yolks
1/2" Copper
Drill holes ever inch
20 – 24"
Stainless tub
Stainless tub
Drain
Plastic hosing as needed
Stainless tub
Water
Submergible Pump
6 or 12 Volt Marine Battery
Foot Switch
Wheels

End View

Glass Notes 309

Fritz's Original Bench

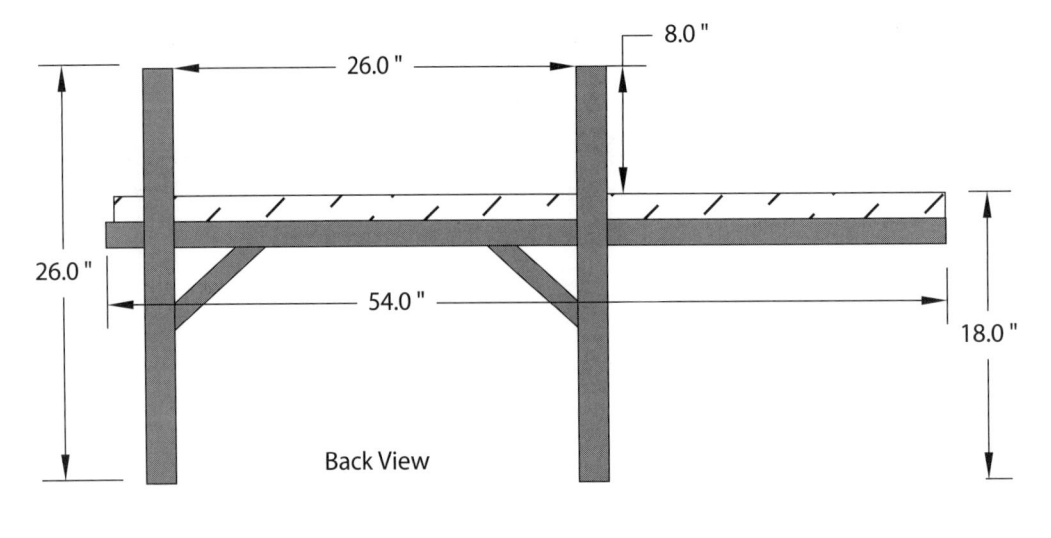

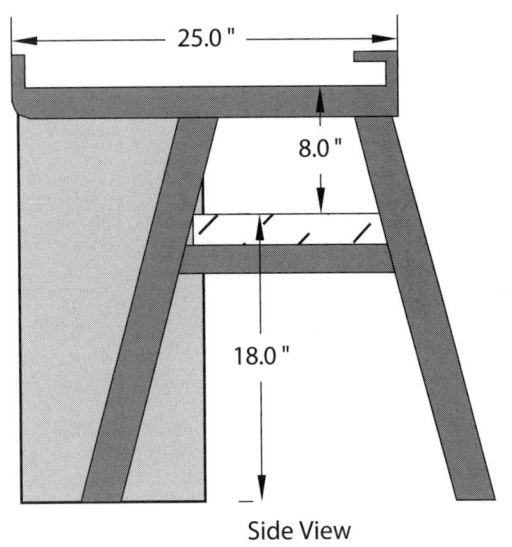

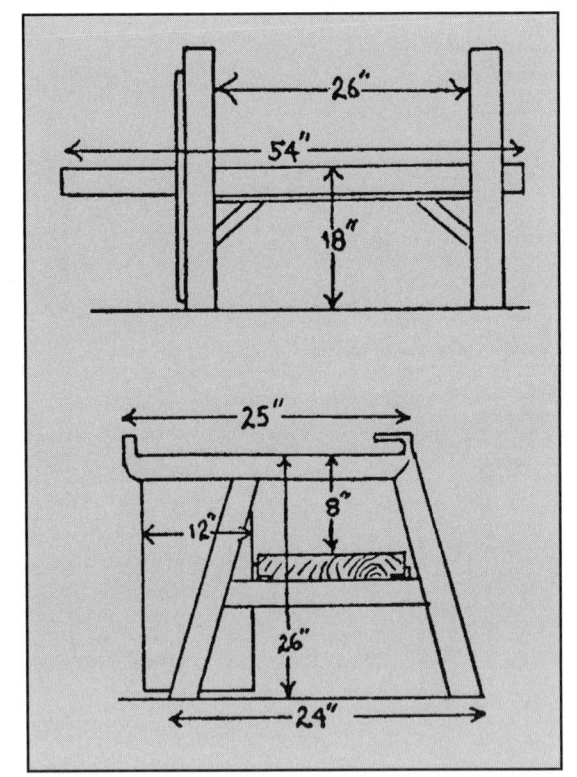

Back View

Side View

When Fritz was building his benches in Toledo, we were building our studio at Kent State University. I found it a great help to have his equipment designs to emulate. This is a very quick bench to build if you are an experienced welder, as the frame is constructed from angle iron and the seat is a piece of 2" x 12". During the early years, this bench design served us well, but in today's world the bench is an anachronism and, to be honest, a bit flimsy. The Italian Gaffers bench on the next page is an up–to–date rendition of what is needed for today's glass blowers. The proportions should be tailored to meet your needs. Some blowers like to sit slightly above standard chair height (18") and some like to sit high, almost in a standing position. Experiment with what is most comfortable for you. Some gaffers like to make the tool shelf autonomous from the bench itself. If the tool shelf is part of the bench, make sure you put a leg on it. If you do not, it might tip over when you lean into the piece. If you blow in the left-handed position, just read all these drawings in a mirror. :-)

These are Fritz Dreisbach's original drawings for a blowing bench. We built our benches based on these proportions and they seem to work just fine.

Blowing Bench

This bench was designed by Lino Tagliapietra and Tom Farbanish. The frame for this bench is made from 1 ¼ x 1 ¼" x ⅛" square steel tube. Do not make the seat from plywood. Use a nice piece of hardwood. Cover the tool area with a nice piece of 16 to 18 gauge copper. The heat shield has thin steel plate on one side and ½" plywood on the other. The bench can be constructed from wood as well as steel. However you wish to construct it, make sure it is strong and has some weight. It's no fun blowing on a flimsy bench. Over the years blowers have added some amenities like a cup holder and a wax tray as shown in the illustration. The placement of the cup holder and the wax tray is up to you.

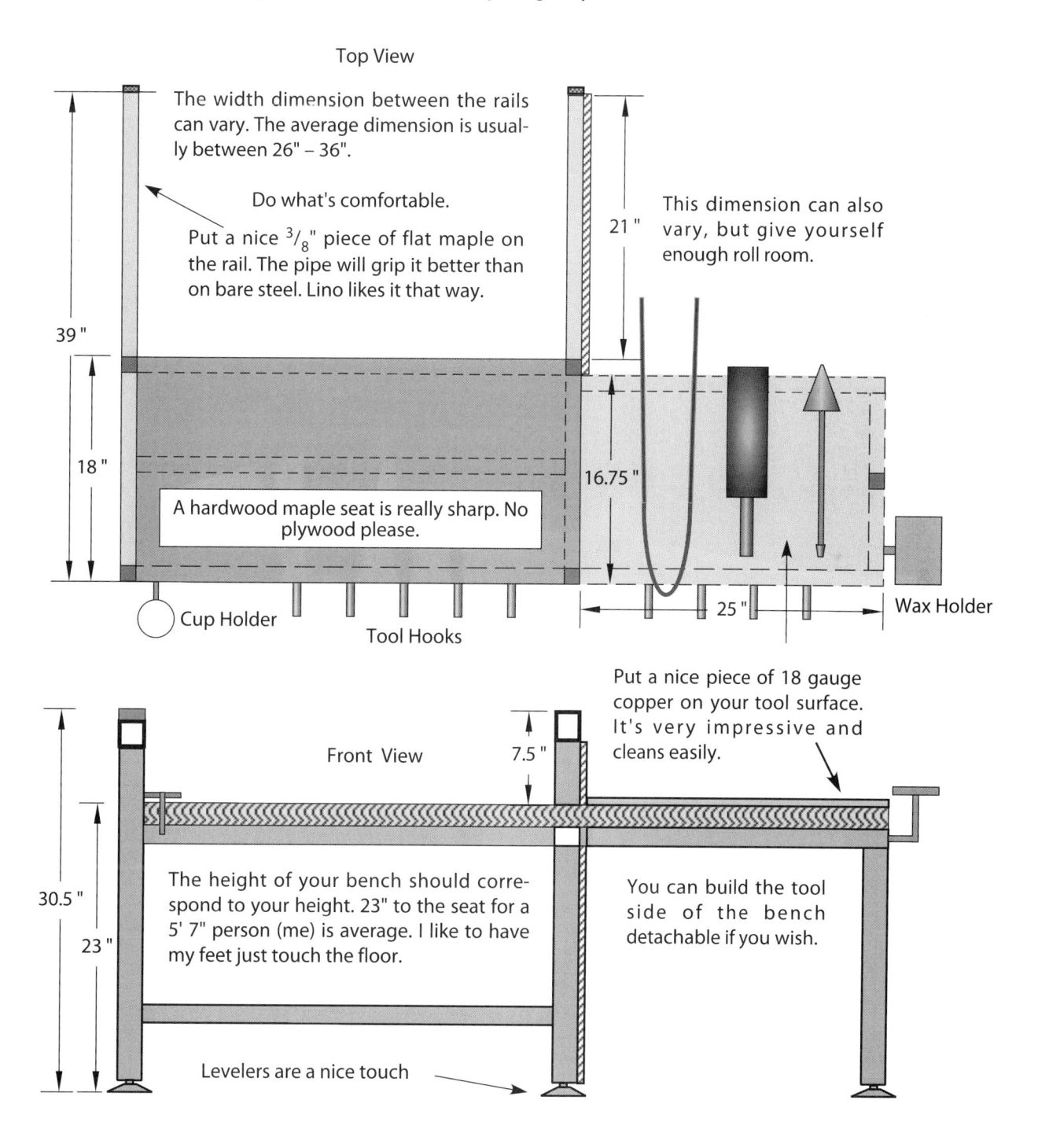

Top View

The width dimension between the rails can vary. The average dimension is usually between 26" – 36".

Do what's comfortable.

Put a nice ⅜" piece of flat maple on the rail. The pipe will grip it better than on bare steel. Lino likes it that way.

This dimension can also vary, but give yourself enough roll room.

21"

39"

18"

16.75"

A hardwood maple seat is really sharp. No plywood please.

Cup Holder

Tool Hooks

25"

Wax Holder

Front View

Put a nice piece of 18 gauge copper on your tool surface. It's very impressive and cleans easily.

7.5"

30.5"

23"

The height of your bench should correspond to your height. 23" to the seat for a 5' 7" person (me) is average. I like to have my feet just touch the floor.

You can build the tool side of the bench detachable if you wish.

Levelers are a nice touch

Bench, Side View

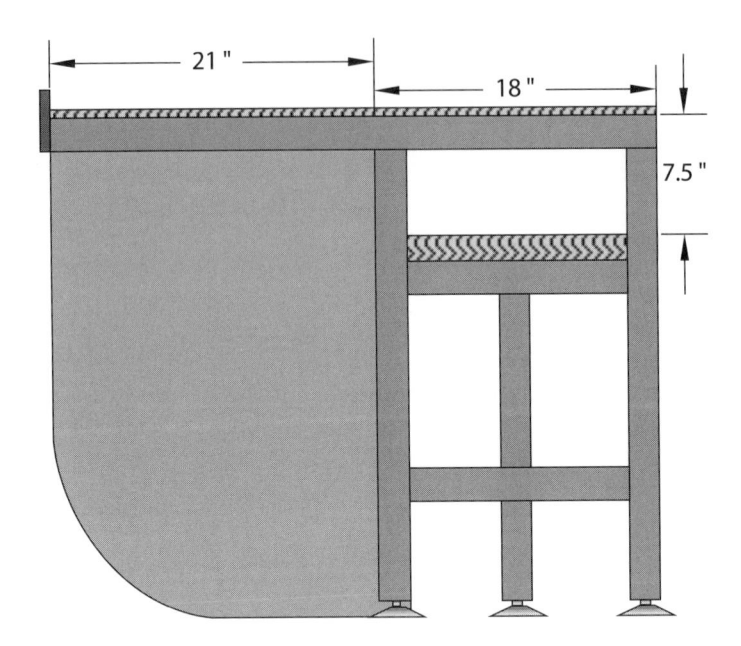

Bench

The bench shown here is based on the Lino/Farbanish bench. It is sturdy and will take years of abuse. It is important to have strong welds. As you can see in the photo, this bench has tool hooks in the front and not in back as I've depicted in the illustration. The choice of where things go is up to you.

312   Glass Notes

Make-Up Air

Why and What is Make-up Air?

Make-up air is outside air introduced into a building to replace the air being exhausted from within the building. Generally, an air make-up system is sized to deliver up to 10% more air than is being removed by the exhaust system. The slight, positive pressure prevents infiltration of contaminated or cold air.

Make-up air heaters are designed to supply this air to the building, heated to room temperature.

If you're in an area that has winter, you will need the air heated if you wish to maintain a comfortable studio. Conversely, if you're in a warm climate you probably do not need an air heater but only what is referred to in the trade as a control panel fan box. As an aside, I remember that when we built the studio at school, we were in a building that was notoriously cold in winter; to add to the problem, the thermostat for the studio was near the furnace which as you can guess kept the heaters from turning on. The result was that your front was warm, your back was cold, and the block buckets were usually frozen when we came into the studio in the morning. Through it all, we still made some really snazzy glass.

Make-up air heaters do not replace the building heating system but rather supplement the space heating equipment by heating the air required for ventilation.

Direct fired make-up air heaters burn natural gas or LP gas directly in the air stream. The resulting products of combustion are diluted with outside air, released into a studio building, and exhausted through the ventilation system. This is in direct contrast to space heating which maintains comfortable temperatures. Ideally, the make-up air system and ventilation system should be independent of the studio heating system.

Direct firing of natural gas or LP gas in a make-up air heater is both safe and economical. Properly designed burners achieve nearly perfect combustion and produce harmless products of combustion. A high degree of dilution occurs when the products of combustion are mixed with the large volume of air being heated, which makes the process completely safe.

The Need for Make-up Air

It is generally accepted that a glass studio with gas-fired equipment should have approximately 18 air changes per hour in order to maintain a healthy environment. If you do not provide a sufficient quantity of make-up air, you will be creating negative pressure within your studio. If this is the case, then you are creating problems that can impact your health. These problems include:
- Dust vapors, fumes, and contaminates are not adequately removed from the building and possibly cause nausea, and headaches.
- Drafty conditions from infiltration.
- Back drafts in stack and ventilators that can lead to combustion problems and spread toxic gases.
- All gas-fired furnaces, glory holes, etc., will run more efficiently in a neutral or slightly positive atmosphere, resulting in less gas consumption.

A properly sized make-up air system takes the load off the heating system and provides cleaner air and a healthier work environment.

Sizing Your Exhaust System (CFM)

Some of the following as well as the information on the preceding page was provided by Steve Abell. Steve's company, Abell Combustion, Inc., provides burner, safety, and air management systems for the glass studio (www.abellcombustion.com; Tel. 610/827-9137).

The following formula will help you calculate the cubic feet per minute (CFM) needed to achieve the number of air changes per hour. There has been much discussion on what is a good number of air changes in order to achieve a healthy work environment. The consensus seems to favor 18 air changes per hr. Although this may seem like a high number, it really is quite easy to achieve given the types of exhaust fans available.

It should be noted that it is not always necessary to maintain 18 air changes per hr. as some studios have very limited equipment that doesn't demand this level of air movement; even the larger studios are not always running all their gas-fired equipment all the time.

In order to have a system that is flexible one can mount 2 exhaust fans with each fan having 2 speeds. This combination gives you the potential to have 13 different CFM's (I think; you do the math).

The ideal situation is to mount the fans in the back wall behind the equipment. The make-up air system should be mounted on the wall opposite the equipment being exhausted.

Calculating CFM

Wanted: 18 air changes per hr. for a studio that is 40 x 20 x 15 feet

- Establish the cu. ft. of the studio, 12,000 cu. ft.
- How many minutes to get 1 air change?
- Divide 60 minutes by 18
- 60/18 = 3.3
- 3.3 = 1 air change every 3.3 minutes
- To convert air changes to CFM:
- Divide the cu. ft. by 3.3
- 12,000/3.3 = 3,636 CFM

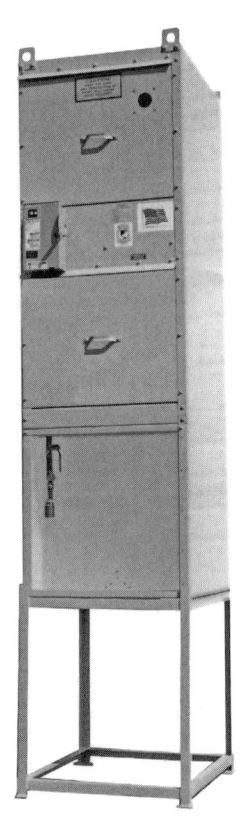

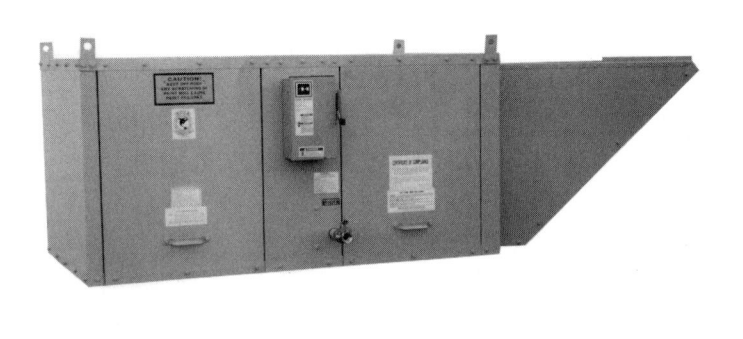

Make-up air units can be mounted either vertically or horizontally indoors, outdoors, or on the roof.

An Inexpensive Make-Up Air System

The drawing below depicts a studio set-up for make-up air using an inexpensive louver system. This system is adequate insofar as it will provide make-up air for the air exhausted by the fans placed behind the furnaces. The louvers need to be of adequate size in order to allow an amount of air equal to what is being exhausted. The louvers do not have to be down low in order to provide sufficient make-up air but can be at ceiling level. Louvers come fabricated from stainless, aluminum, and plastic, and some have bird screens built into them. The system depicted is not a system that I would recommend in climates that have cold seasons since the outside air entering the studio will not be heated; however if you don't mind cold drafts and/or frozen block buckets, then this is the system for you. Notice that the louver is on the wall opposite the exhaust fan. W.W. Grainger and McMaster Carr sell a full range of louver products (www.mcmaster.com, www.grainger.com).

Louvers provide make-up air; dog provides friendship.

Sam Scholes Fudge

In 1932, Dr. Sam Scholes came to Alfred University in Alfred, NY, and founded the glass technology department. In 1935 he wrote *Modern Glass Practice,* which would later become the glass primer for the studio artist who wished to learn the technical aspects of glass. Dr. Scholes used his now famous "fudge" as a way of demonstrating to his students what viscosity was all about. My feeling is that if it was good enough for Dr. Scholes' students, it's good enough for *Glass Notes*. What you find below is Dr. Scholes in his own words.

Having had some success in producing the homely confection known as Fudge, the writer is disposed to impart instructions for the process, in order that others may make this delectable stuff with confidence in the outcome of each effort. Properly made, fudge is a soft solid, consisting of sugar in a microcrystalline condition, bonded by a matrix of highly viscous syrup. It usually carries chocolate as the important flavoring substance, with vanilla as a secondary flavor, and small amounts of milk, fat and proteins.

Recognition of the fact that the production of fondant, fudge, or any similar candy resembles the de-vitrification of a glass leads to the need for writing this brief treatise in a Morey* -or less scientific style.
*(*Dr. Schole's pun, and a pretty good one at that.*)

Raw Materials

PROCEDURE: Measure sugar, chocolate, and milk into a suitable stew pan and place it over a moderate fire. Mix with a large wooden spoon, and and stir frequently as the mixture heats and boils. Stirring at the cooling stage promotes homogeneity and prevents sticking to the pan. The objects of the boiling process are to carry the sugar into complete solution, to concentrate the solution of evaporating

Sucrose (sugar)	680 gm. (3 cups)
Chocolate	85 gm. (3 oz.)
Lac Bovis (whole milk)	220 ml. (1 cup)
Glyceryl Butyrate (butter)	15 ml. (½ oz.)
Vanilla extract	5 ml. (1 tsp.)

water, and to convert a small portion of the sucros to levuclos [fructose]. A secondary object is to create an odor that sharpens the appetite of the household for the product.

As boiling continues, the viscosity of the liquid increases. Cooking is complete when the viscosity is approximately 10^5 poises at 20° C. In the absence of a suitable viscometer, an approximate test can be made by dropping some of the liquid into cold water, testing the "soft ball" with the fingers. Another test for completion is the boiling point of the liquid. Care must be taken to allow for altitude (barometric pressure). Reliance can be placed upon the so-called candy thermometer by correlating the reading, by experience, with the viscosity or soft-ball test.

The pan is removed from the fire. The prescribed quantity of butter is melted around the inside surface of the pan and over the liquid. This procedure covers any stray sugar crystals that might "seed" the melt and induce premature crystallization. The pan is set in a larger pan of cold water (or outdoors, if the weather is cold and predators are absent).

While the product is cooling, a large plate or cake-tin is buttered ready for later use. Quiet cooling continues to about 40° C (100° F). The vanilla is added and vigorous stirring begins. If the mixture has become too cold, it may be warmed until the pan is warm to the touch. Stirring is continued until crystallization is so far advanced that the mass can only with difficulty be removed from the pan and spread on the buttered plate. It will form a layer about one inch deep, covering a nine-inch circle. Before the fudge has completely set, it is well to cut it into squares with a thin knife.

THEORY OF THE PROCESS: The boiled solution, a viscous syrup, becomes a supersaturated solution as it cools, analogous to a glass undercooled below its liquidus. If this solution is stirred while it is hot enough to have relatively little viscosity but is already supersaturated, crystallization will commence and proceed so readily that large crystals will grow. The final product will be coarse-grained. The same result follows over-cooking, because the degree of super saturation is so great, and not enough saturated syrup will be left to keep the mass agreeably soft.

Undercooling to a temperature barely warm brings about a condition of high viscosity along with super saturation. The effect of stirring is then the formation of a crystal nuclei. At the high viscosity of the liquid, the multitude of tiny crystals cannot grow rapidly enough to be large; and the multitude of tiny crystals bonded by the remaining concentrated syrup produces the desired "smooth" texture.

Viscous

Viscosity: a term usually applied to liquids, and means in a qualitative sense, the resistance that a liquid offers to flow; molasses has a high viscosity. Viscosities are expressed in a unit called the poise. The viscosity of water at room temperature is .010 pose: of SAE 30 motor oil is about 1.0 poise. The viscosity of most glasses at room temperature is about 10^{19}-10^{22} poises, which is about as high a viscosity as can be measured. Viscosity is related to temperature.

S. R. Scholes, Ph.d, State University of New York College of Ceramics at Alfred, January 1953. *Morey, G. W., "Properties of Glass"

Materials authored by: Education Department The Corning Museum of Glass One Museum Way Corning, NY 14830-2253

"The Boy's", 1971
Those are some hats!
l to r: Fritz Dreisbach, Jim Tanner, Jack Schmidt

Diamond Drilling in Glass

Lunzer Industrial Diamonds, Inc.

Because of its brittle and abrasive nature, glass can pose serious machining problems. This is especially true when it comes to drilling straight, clean holes through glass components. Unless great care is taken, chipping cracking, as well as drill burn-out or excessive tool wear can occur.

Many people first approach glass drilling with the view that it is essentially similar to drilling metals or wood. A steel twist drill, of course, can be used routinely on these materials. It won't work on glass. And although carbide drills and copper or brass tubes dipped in an abrasive have been successful, the method is slow and laborious. Without question, the ideal tool is a diamond-edged coring drill.

The Drill

Basically, the drill is a metal cylinder to which diamonds have been affixed. This can be achieved in three distinct ways.
1. The impregnated diamond drill. Here, the diamond section consists of a quantity of natural or synthetic diamond grit, correctly sieved to an exact size, mixed with a holding matrix and bonded to the steel core shank.
2. The plated diamond drill. Here, a single layer of diamond particles are plated to the end of the core. The diamond material adheres to the surface of the shank and has far greater concentration than the impregnated type. The principal drawback of the surface-plated drill is that when the diamond surface wears off, the drill must be discarded.
3. The electro-deposited drill. Here, the diamond section is built up in layers by an electroplating process. This type of construction has all the advantages of the impregnated drill, but has a much thinner wall.

Diamond Core Drill

The Diamond

The choice between natural and synthetic diamond is not a simple one, since each type may be superior according to certain conditions. The important point is that there is a diamond abrasive to suit exactly the requirements of any given application. Hence, the glass maker must consult his or her tool supplier in order to determine which type should be used for a specific application.

Diamond Size

Diamond grit for drills comes in sizes generally ranging from 40 to 240 mesh. Choice of mesh size is largely determined by the size of the drill and the material being drilled. It is highly important that the correct size be use. A 40 mesh diamond drill will not give the same production performance as, say 140 mesh unit.

Drill Equipment

The basic requisite in successful glass drilling is a sturdy, vibration-free and well-made drill press. Since the ultimate goal is to achieve chip-free holes, every component involved in the drilling process is important.

Drill Speed

The exact speed of the drill will depend also on the type of drill used, how the coolant is applied, the material being drilled, whether one is starting or finishing a hole, and the experience of the operator.

Coolant

Ideally, drills should be mounted in a collet and attached to a water swivel so that coolant is constantly supplied under pressure through the center of the drill. It is of prime importance to see that the drill is cooled with coolant applied under pressure, thereby freeing the core and preventing core hang-up in the drill.

Coolant can also be supplied externally through a pipe to the drill or hole, or the piece being drilled can be submerged in coolant. Remember that the cooling of the drill is only one of the necessary functions of a coolant. When fluid is applied through the center of the drill, it lubricates the drill and keeps the core from sticking.

Methods and Techniques

Diamond core drilling is an entirely different process than conventional drilling. The diamond drill is actually a grinder that abrades away glass particles. A novice must develop a feel for diamond drills.

Never Force a Diamond Drill!

This will chip the material and clog the drill. It is essential that the drill always be clear and free. As soon as any resistance is felt, clear the drill.

Before using a new drill, run it against a grinding

wheel (120 grit). And whenever the drill feels as if it is going dull or losing its speed, dress it, especially the cutting face, which must be quite square on the corners for optimum cutting performance, with a grinding wheel. A dull drill can cause core hang-up.

Whenever drilling glass, always mount the workpiece to a base plate of glass. This helps eliminate chipping at the end of the hole. For perfect holes, drill half way through the workpiece by setting the drill depth gauge for that distance. Then reverse the workpiece and drill from the other side. Avoid steel or any other metal as base plates. Slate or marble is good.

If a diamond core drill develops dark burn marks at the diamond section, the drill speed is probably too high or the amount of pressure is too great. Reduce

Quick Guide to Recommended Drill Speeds

	Glass, Ceramic, & Porcelain China					
Drill Diameter	¼	½"	1"	2"	3"	4"
Drill Speed	2,000	950	700	525	450	400

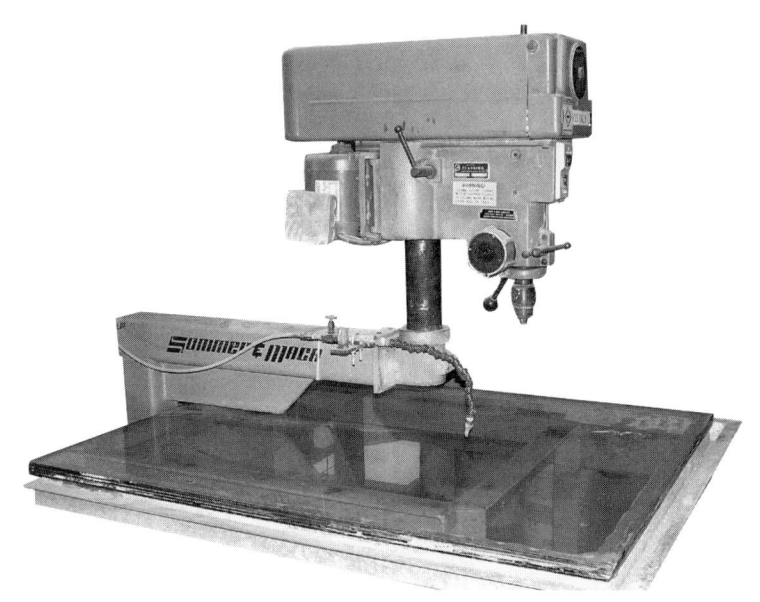

Somaca diamond drill press. No longer in production

Glass Notes 319

NOTES

Suppliers of Products for the Glass Studio

Where to Buy Stuff

Abrasives and Diamond Products --------------------325
    Harbor Freight Tools
    Electro Abrasives
    Washington Mills Electro Minerals Company
    Abrasive Technology, Inc.
    Glastar
    Unbornsky Diamond Tool Co., Ltd.
    Starlite Industries, Inc.
    Braxton-Bragg Corp.
    Daniel Lopacki
    UKAM Industrial Superhard Tools
    UK Abrasives, Inc.
    Diamond Drill & Tool Division
    Salem Distributing Co., Inc.
    diFrenzi Diamond
    HIS Glassworks, Inc.

Adhesives, Silicones, Epoxy, UV and UV Lights --329
    Sommer & Maca
    Dow Corning Corporation
    The General Electric Company
    HIS Glassworks, Inc.
    Dymax Corporation
    Dewey Assoc., Inc.
    Loctite UV Adhesive
    Talas
    W.W. Grainger
    Applied Industrial Technologies (formally Bearings Inc.)

Assorted Everything -------------------------------------324
    McMaster - Carr
    W.W. Grainger

Assorted Products --------------------------------------339
    United State Plastic Corp. (All things plastic)
    Whitehouse Books.com (Hard to find glass books)
    Buffalo Felt Products (Felt and Horsehair wheels)
    Bell Inc. (Decals and decal supplies)
    MIFCO (Muller mixer)

Batch and Cullet --337
    Spruce Pine Batch Co.
    Gaffer Glass, USA Ltd.
    East Bay Batch and Color
    Spectrum Glass Company, Inc.
    Gabbert Cullet Co.

Burners ---337
    Joppa Glassworks, Inc.
    Wilton Technologies
    The Hub Consolidated, Inc.
    Wet Dog Glass
    Pine Ridge Enterprises
    Abell Combustion, Inc.
    North American Manufacturing Co.
    Eclipse Combustion
    Maxon Corp.
    Charles A. Hones, Inc.
    Hauck Mfg. Co.

Casting Supplies, Rubber, Investments, Silica, Fiberglass, Wax ----------------------------------330
    Smooth-On
    Polytek Development Corp.
    Cementex Latex Corp.
    Oglebay Norton Co.
    U. S. Silica Co.
    U.S. Gypsum
    Ransom & Randolph
    ZIRCAR Refractory Composites, Inc
    Mr. Fiberglass
    The Kindt-Collins Company LLC

Chemicals, Colorants for Batching --------------------336
    Unimin Corp.
    Ceramic Color and Chemical Mfg. Co.
    Mason Corporation
    Molycorp, Inc.
    Standard Ceramics
    Seattle Pottery Supply

Coating for Fiber Insulation ---------------------------333
    Alpha Associates, Inc.
    Mon-Eco Industries, Inc.
    Great Lakes Textiles, Inc.

Cold Working Tools for the Glass Studio -----------326
    Steinert Industries, Inc.
    Denver Glass Machinery
    Sommer & Maca
    Kurt Merker Kelheim
    Covington Engineering Corporation
    DNS Engineering, Inc.
    Felker
    Sowers Diamet
    GranQuartz
    third-hand
    MK Diamond Saw

Colloidal Silica & Colloidal Alumina ----------------331
    WesBond Corporation
    ETS Schaefer Corporation

Color Bars ---324
    Olympic Color Rods
    East Bay Batch & Color
    C&R Loo
    Spruce Pine Batch Co.
    Hot Glass Color and Supply
    Colour Fusion (Canadian)

Controllers --339
    Digitry Company, Inc.
    Watlow
    Partlow
    Fuji
    Love Controllers
    Skutt

Crucibles --333
    Engineered Ceramics (EC Crucibles)
    Emhart Glass Inc. (Laclede Christy Crucibles)

Dichroic Glass ---335
    Coatings By Sandberg
    Savoy Dichroic
    Dichroic Alchemy

322   Glass Notes

Elements and Thermocouples ------------------------ **338**
    Duralite Inc.
    I Squared R Element Co.
    Sentro Tech Corp.
    MXI
    Songshan Enterprise Group
    Kanthal Corp.
    OMEGA Engineering, INC.
    Vulcan Electric Company
    Thermo Sensors Corporation
    Trutemp Sensors, Inc.
    Cleveland Electric Laboratories

Enamels, Glass ------------------------------------- **336**
    Reusche & Co.
    Thompson Enamel

Furnaces, and Studio Equipment -------------------- **327**
    Hub Consolidated Inc.
    Wet Dog Glass
    Falorni Gianfranco srl
    Ohm Equipment, LLC
    Stadleman Glass
    Denver Glass Machinery Inc.
    Electroglass Furnaces

Fusing, Slumping and Casting Glass ---------------- **335**
    Bullseye Glass Co., Resource Center
    Uroboros Glass
    Spectrum Glass Company,
    Glass Brokers, Inc. (Schott Crystal)
    Gaffer Coloured Glass Ltd.
    East Bay Batch and Color

General Suppliers ---------------------------------- **324**
    Olympic Color Rods
    C&R Loo, Inc.
    His Glassworks, Inc.

Gold Leaf and Leafing Supplies --------------------- **332**
    M. Swift & Sons, Inc.
    The Gold Leaf Co.
    Gold-Orient Eastman Industrial Company Ltd.

Hand Tools, Blow Pipes, Wood Blocks -------------- **334**
    Cutting Edge Products
    Jim Moore Glass Tools
    Steinert Industries, Inc.
    Spiral Arts, Inc.
    C&R Loo, Inc. (Essemce Hand Tools)
    C.R. Machine
    Star Glass Works
    Putsch (Meniconi Hand Tools)
    Marco Tool, USA

Mirroring Solution --------------------------------- **336**
    Peacock Laboratories, Inc.

Refractories --------------------------------------- **332**
    Unifrax Corporation
    Thermal Ceramics
    ETS Schaefer Corp.
    Cotronics, Corp.
    New Castle Refractories Co.
    ANH Refractories
    Vesuvius/Monofrax
    BNZ Materials
    Resco Products, Inc.
    Skamol Americas, Inc.
    Pryor Giggey Co.
    Missouri Refractories Co., Inc. (Morco Refractories)
    Able Supply Company
    Utah Refractories Corp.
    Danser, Inc.

Relays, SCR's & SSR's ------------------------------ **339**
    Continental Industries International
    Payne Engineering Company

Sandblasters, Resist and Media -------------------- **328**
    McMaster Carr
    Cyclone Blasting Systems
    Clemco Industries Corp.
    Blast-It-All
    TP Tools & Equipment
    Truman's, Inc.
    Ruemelin Mfg. Co., Inc.
    Econoline Manufacturing, Inc.
    PhotoBrasive Systems
    Rayzist Photomask, Inc.
    Armour Products
    B & B Etching Products, Inc.

Wheels --- **331**
    McMaster-Carr Supply Co.
    W.W. Grainger

Wood Blocks -- **334**
    Walter Evans, Cherrywood Mold Shop
    Fantasilaboratoriet
    Hot Block Tools
    Blockhead Tools

Gas 1, Penland, NC - 1970

Glass Notes   **323**

Suppliers

There are original equipment manufacturers of products (OEM) for the glass studio, e.g. Steinert Industries, Felker, etc. and there are companies that are re-sellers of products for the glass studio. Some of those re-sellers have a vast selection of products that service all the glass forming techniques, e.g. Olympic Color Rods and C&R Loo, to name two. There are also manufacturers that re-sell the products they manufacture as well as products from other OEM's that complement the products they manufacturer, e.g, Bullseye Glass Co.

Obviously, it is impossible to list every manufacturer of products and/or re-seller of products that are applicable to the glass studio. I have listed those companies and organizations that I am or was familiar with, or were recommended by others, or seemed worthy enough after perusing their Web site.

I do not accept advertising, nor do I endorse any manufacturer or re-seller of products. Usually you will find distributors on the manufacturers Web site. One of the best starting points is one of the oldest but still one of the best: the Yellow Pages for your region. If you're computer savvy, I would also recommend The Thomas Register, www.thomasnet.com or, www.motionnet.com, recommended by Mark Wilson.

Please note: In some instances, area codes and telephone numbers might change. I have tried to be as accurate as possible when transcribing telephone numbers, Web sites, and E-mail addresses. My apologies if there are any errors. Please send me an E-mail If you find an error in any of my listings.

General Suppliers

Olympic Color Rods
P.O. Box 9240
Seattle, WA 98109
Tel: 206/343-7336
Toll Free: 800/445-7742
Fax: 206/343-2292
E-mail: must use an online contact form
Web: www.glasscolor.com/

C&R Loo, Inc.
1085 Essex Ave.
Richmond, CA 94801
Tel: 510/232-0276
Toll Free: 800/227-1780
Fax: 510/232-7810
E-mail: sales@crloo.com
Web: www.crloo.com

HIS Glassworks, Inc.
91 Webb Cove Road
Asheville, NC 28804 USA
Tel: 828/254-2559
toll free 800/914-7463
Fax: 828/254-2581
E-mail: support@hisglassworks.com
Web: www.hisglassworks.com

Color Bars

Olympic Color Rods (www.glasscolor.com)

East Bay Batch & Color (www.eastbaycolor.com)

C&R Loo (www.crloo.com)

Spruce Pine Batch Co. (www.sprucepinebatch.com)

Hot Glass Color and Supply (www.hotglasscolor.com)

Colour Fusion (Canadian) www.colourfusion.com

Assorted Everything

McMaster - Carr (www.mcmaster.com)
W.W. Grainger (www.grainger.com)

If you do not know about these two companies, you should. They sell everything but the kitchen sink (actually they sell that too.) Their catalogs are very thick. How thick are they? They're so thick my niece uses the Grainger catalog as a high chair for her kid and the McMaster - Carr for a door stop. (rim shot)

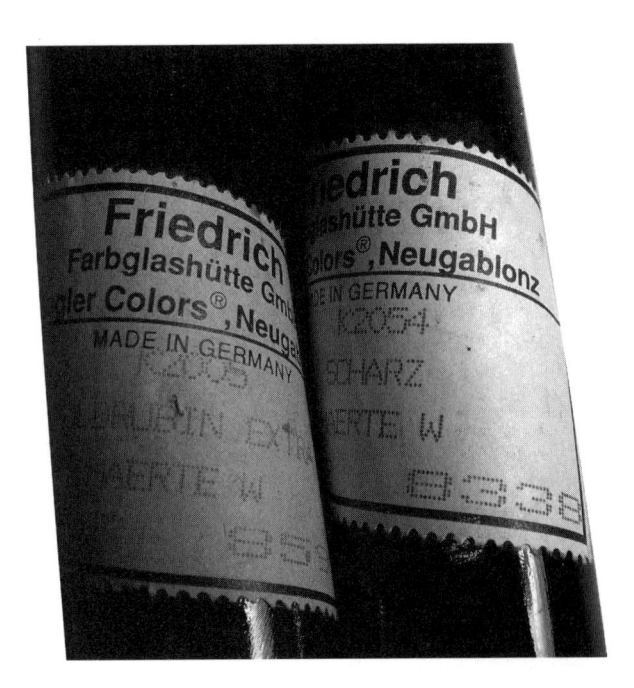

Abrasives and Diamond Products

Domestic abrasive manufacturers use sieves or screens to size abrasive grain. Both the sieve and the grain size must conform to the American National Standards Institute B74.12. Typical abrasive grain designations such as #8, #16, #36, #60, #80, #120, #180, #220, #240, #400, #600 would conform to the same size standard regardless from which domestic manufacturer it was purchased. The sizes are referred to as "macrogrits" or simply "grits". The smaller the number, the courser the grain. Most studios use nothing courser than #80. The number refers to the screen size per sq. inch.

Harbor Freight Tools
Online or by telephone
Tel: 800/423-2567
Fax: 800/905-5220
Web: www.harborfreight.com

Diamond Products from China, cheap but adequate. A 50-piece set of diamonds for your Dremel sells regularly for $24.99, but they put this item on sale for $14.95. The order number is 36252-4ATA.

Electro Abrasives
701 Willet Rd.
Buffalo, NY 14218
Tel: 800/284-4748
Fax: 716/822-2858
E-mail: info@electroabrasives.com
Web: www.electroabrasives.com

Manufacturer of Silicon Carbide abrasive. 50 lbs. is a minimum order.

Washington Mills Electro Minerals Company
P.O. Box 423
1801 Buffalo Avenue
Niagara Falls, NY 14302-0423
Tel: 716/278-6600 or 800/828-1666
Fax: 716/278-6650
E-mail: info@washingtonmills.com
Web: www.washingtonmills.com

The largest producer of abrasives and electro minerals in the world. Washington Mills will only sell abrasive grain in large quantities, but they have distributors across the U.S. The Silicon Carbide they sell for glass grinding is called Silcaride RA. Call for information.

K. C. Abrasive Company, Inc.
3140 Dodge Road
Kansas City, KS 66115-0127
Tel: 913/342-2900
Fax: 913/342-0127
E-mail: info@kcabrasive.com
Web: www.kcabrasive.com

K.C. Abrasives is an excellent source for silicon carbide grinding media. There is a $25 minimum for orders under 25 lbs. They also sell Aluminum Oxide and glass bead.

Abrasive Technology, Inc.
8400 Green Meadows Dr.
P.O. Box 545.
Lewis Center, OH 43035 USA
Tel: 740 548/4100 For Orders 800/964-8324
Fax: 740/548-7617
Web: www.abrasive-tech.com
Abrasive Technology distributes the diamond products manufactured by the Crystalite Corp. Abrasive Technology sells diamond hand pads, files, and configurations for diamonds too numerous to mention. They also carry diamond belts for your large Somaca wet-belt sander.

A highly recommended company. They have an excellent Web site packed with information and a secure order page.

Glastar
20721 Marilla St.
Chatsworth, CA 91311
Tel: 800/423-5635
Local. 818/341-0301
Fax: 818/998-2078
E-mail: askus@glastar.com
Web: www.glastar.com

Glastar manufactures and sells grinding equipment and diamond pads as well as sandblasting equipment.

Unbornsky Diamond Tool Co., Ltd.
502 Room 2
Unit #10
ShiruiYuan Zhangdian Zibo 255000
Shandong CHINA.
Contact Person : Meng Tao
Tel: 86-533-3118780
Fax: 86-533-3118
E-mail: yuxuan@163169.net
Web: www.unbornsky.ebigchina.com

This company's as well as Eternal Star's Web site uses photos and text lifted directly from the companies that are the OEM or distributors of the product they're ripping off. The reason I included this company in the book is to show how some Chinese companies choose to do business. It is indeed a sad commentary on business ethics. Suffice it to say the Chinese do not have a lock on questionable business ethics.

Starlite Industries, Inc.
1111 Lancaster Ave.
P.O. Box 990
Rosemont, PA 190-0911
Tel: 610/ 527-1300
Toll Free: 800/727-1022
E-mail: info@starliteindustries.com
Web: www.starliteindustries.com

Starlite sells diamond files and core drills as well as core drill accessories. They are also a source of diamond band saw blades.

Braxton-Bragg Corp.
P.O. Box 5407
Knoxville, TN 37928
Tel: 800/575-4401
Fax: 800/915-5501
Web: www.braxton-bragg.com

This company is a major re-seller of diamond tools and products.

Daniel Lopacki
P.O. Box 144
Cliff, NM 88028
Tel: 888/593-9462
International Tel: 505/535-2524
E-mail: orders@lopacki.com, catalogrequest@lopacki.com
Web: www.lopacki.com

Lopacki sells a complete line of diamond products from China.

UKAM Industrial Superhard Tools
28231 Crocker Avenue
Unit 80
Valencia, CA 91355
Tel: 661/257-2288
Fax: 661/257-3833
E-mail: lel@ukam.com
Web: www.ukam.com

Ukam sells just about everything needed in diamonds. Very cluttered Web site but filled with all kinds of information about diamonds. They have a zillion .pdf files filled with diamond usage information.

UK Abrasives, Inc.
3045 Mac Arthur Blvd.,
Northbrook, IL 60062
Tel: 847/291-3566
Fax: 847/291-7670
E-mail: info@ukabrasives.com
Web: www.ukabrasives.com

Diamond Drill & Tool Division
AmeriGlas Stained Glass
P.O. Box 27668
Omaha, NE 68127-0668
E-mail: sales@diamonddrillandtool.com
Web: www.diamonddrillandtool.com

Salem Distributing Co., Inc.
5901 Gun Club Rd.
Winston-Salem, NC 27103
Raymond Acosta, Sales
Se habla español
Tel: 336/766-1104
Toll Free: 800/234-1982
Fax: 336/766-1119
Web: www.salemdist.com

At present their Web site gives no information on what products they sell but claims an online catalogue will soon be available. Salem sells many varieties of abrasives including aluminum oxide, silicon carbide, and cerium, belts, and core drills. Call for print catalog; it's a good one.

diFrenzi Diamond
954 Kentucky Street
Louisville, KY 40204
Tel: 502/299-6533
Web: www.difrenzidiamond.com

diFrenzi imports and sells diamond pads and blades from China.

HIS Glassworks, Inc. (see pg. 324)

A note about diamond abrasives: There are any number of companies in Asia manufacturing diamond products and available at cut rate prices. Their Web sites display pictures of their products, but in some instances, the pictures and descriptions are appropriated from other Web sites. The problem is that many of the domestic companies selling diamond abrasive products are reselling what they purchase from Asian manufacturers. The quality of the Asian products in many instances is good, but it is hard to know if that is the case when purchasing their products.

If you're grinding to polish, I do not recommend diamond but rather a good quality SiC. Yes, SiC is messy but it cuts like butta and does not leave odd scratches like diamond pads. When it comes to grinding and polishing, "cleanliness is next to godliness."

Cold Working Tools for the Glass Studio

Steinert Industries, Inc.
1507 Franklin Ave.
Kent, OH 44240
Tel: 800/727-7473
Tel: 330/678-0028
Fax: 330/678-8238
E-mail: glasstools@steinertindustries.com
Web: www.steinertindustries.com

Steinert manufactures heavy–duty glass machinery, optic molds, hand tools, blow pipes, and paperweight making equipment. Send for a free catalog to get an idea of their complete line. Their machines are state-of-the-art.

Denver Glass Machinery, (see bottom of pg. 327)

Sommer & Maca
Offices and warehouses located regionally
E-mail: somacausa@aol.com
Web: www.somaca.com

Excellent Web site with great search engine. They have regional warehouses. Go to to their Web site to locate your regional distributor. Somaca sells the 106" belt sander used by most glass studios and hundreds of other products for the glass industry.

Kurt Merker Kelheim
Elsterstrasse 6
D-93309 Kelheim
Germany
Tel: 49 9441 3355
Fax: 49 9441 12815
E-mail: k-merker@t-online.de
Web: www.merker-kmk.com

Merker is the company that sells the famous Merker engraving lathe used throughout the glass world. This lathe comes in two sizes: small for fine engraving and large for heavy-duty grinding and engraving. Call Isabel for information. They speak your language. Their Web site has nice pictures.

Covington Engineering Corporation
715 West Colton Avenue
P.O. Box 35
Redlands CA 92373
Tel: toll free 877/793-6636
Outside U.S. 909/793-6636
Fax: 909/793-7641
E-mail: sales@covington-engineering.com
Web: www.covington-engineering.com

Covington make a moderately-priced, self feed diamond slab saw. The saw comes in three sizes. These saws are in many college and university glass programs. They also re-sell the Rose Rociprolap.

DNS Engineering, Inc.
640 So. Texas Ave
Redlands, CA 92374
Tel: 909/793-5000
Toll free: 888/890-0419
E-mail: info@rociprolap.com
Web:www.rociprolap.com

This company manufactures and sells the Rose Rociprolap as well as all the pieces and parts for same.

Felker
Corporate Office
17400 West 119th Street
Olathe, Kansas 66061
Tel: 800/365-4003 or 800/825-0028
E-mail: customerservice@felkersaws.com
Web: www.felkersaws.com

Felker diamond cut-off saws are found in many glass studios. The most common saws from Felker are the Mason Mite II and the Mason Mate II. They sell many other diamond saw configurations as well from small 6" tile saws up to the Mason 20".

Sowers Diamet
P.O. Box 1140
Elyria, OH 44036
Tel: 440/458-6790 or 800/653-1978
Fax: 440/458-8836
E-mail: info@sowersdiamet.com
Sales: sales@sowersdiamet.com
Customer Support: support@sowersdiamet.com
Web: www.sowersdiamet.com

This company bought the old Felker cast iron cut-off saw line and is now producing it. If you need a diamond saw that cuts accurately, this is the saw for you.

GranQuartz
P.O. Box 2206
Decatur, GA 30085-2206
Tel: 800/458-6222
E-mail: info@granquartz.com
Web: www.granquartz.com
Web Canada: www.granquartzcanada.cjb.net

GranQuartz sells hand–operated power tools, both air driven and electric with water feeds, for polishing and grinding. They also sell all the diamond pads that attach to these tools.

third-hand
9000 45th Avenue SW
Seattle, WA 98136
Tel/Fax: 206/763-5940
Cell: 206/778-3721
E-mail: third-hand@earthlink.net
Web: none at present

Third-hand imports and sells glass cutting and polishing tools from the Czech Republic. The BMK lathe is a state-of-the-art machine. They also have a nice line of sintered diamond wheels.

MK Diamond Saw
Web: www.mkdiamond.com/index.html

The MK line of diamond saws is very popular for general studio diamond cutting. The MK 101Pro, 10" seems to be the popular model. I own one and find it to be built well. Their Web site has a list of all internet distributors for this saw. Check carefully as prices vary.

Furnaces, Annealing Ovens and Other Studio Equipment

Hub Consolidated Inc.
690 Rt. 73
Orwell, VT 05760
Tel: 802/948-2209
Fax: 802/948-22154
E-mail: info@hubglass.com
Web: www.hubglass.com

Hub builds furnaces, annealers, and all the other equipment that a studio would need.

Wet Dog Glass
3924 Conti St.
New Orleans, LA 70119
Tel: 504/483-1195
Fax: 504/483-3059
E-mail: hotstuff@wetdogglass.com
Web: www.wetdogglass.com

Wet Dog builds furnaces, annealers, and all the other equipment that a studio would need.

Falorni Gianfranco srl
Viale IV Novembre,15
50053 Empoli (FI) ITALY
Tel: +39 0571922333
Fax +39 0571 920816
E-mail: info@falorniglass.com
Web: www.falorniglass.com

Falorni glass is an Italian company that sells what some have dubbed the flying saucer furnace. They also build glory holes and annealers.

Ohm Equipment, LLC
P.O. Box 538
Millville, NJ 08332
Tel: 856/765-0808
E-mail: info@ohmequipment.com
Web: www.ohmequipment.com

Ohm builds furnaces, annealing ovens, and other equipment for the hot shop.

Stadleman Glass
P.O. Box. 453
Forest Grove OR 97116
Tel: 503/709-9922
E-mail: stadelmanglass@earthlink.net

Stadleman Glass builds Moly electric melt furnaces from 100-600 lb. capacities in both single and 3 phase. They also will build to suit your needs.

Denver Glass Machinery Inc.
2800 S. Shoshone St.
Englewood, CO. 80110
Tel: 303/781-0980
Fax: 303/781-9067
Web: www.denverglass.com

Denver builds a wire electric glass melting furnace and other equipment for the hot shop.

Electroglass Furnaces
P.O. Box 908
Portage, MI 49081
Tel: 269/668-2855
Web: www.electroglass.com

Electroglass manufactures an electric furnace fired with SiC elements

Sandblasting, Resist and Media

Every shop should have a good abrasive blast unit. There are two basic types: Pressure pot blasters and siphon blasters. Each is quite different from the other insofar as how they entrain the blasting media as well as the amount of energy they exert on the abrasive material. The pressure blaster holds the abrasive blast material in a tank that is pressurized from a compressor. The pressure in the tank pushes the abrasive material through the nozzle at a very high speed which in turn causes it to cut quickly and deeply into the material being blasted. The pressure blaster is fast and very efficient. For some type of blasting, it's overkill. The pressure blaster requires at least a 5 hp 2 stage compressor. The siphon blaster is the type found in most studios. It works by creating a partial vacuum in the inlet hose which then causes the abrasive media to rise into the gun where it is picked up by a pressurized stream of air coming from the compressor. A siphon blaster does not require a heavy-duty compressor but its efficiency is increased if you have one. It should be noted that the larger (hp) your compressor the less it will cycle. If your compressor is too small, it will not be able to maintain a sufficient quantity of air in its holding tank; subsequently your blasting ability will be severely diminished and your compressor will eventually self destruct. When you purchase a blasting unit, the company selling you the equipment will advise you on what size compressor is necessary. Regardless of the type of unit you use, it is very important to have a good reclamation tank attached to your cabinet. A good reclamation tank will separate the fine dust particles from the usable blast media and recycle it through the blaster. A good reclamation device should also filter the air going through it. The exhaust air should not have any silica particles in it. It is always a good idea to wear a good filter mask when abrasive blasting.

> If you wish to sandblast mold investment from the surface of your casting without sandblasting the glass surface use ground corncobs or walnut shells. These materials are available from many sandblast material suppliers.

Sandblasters

Cyclone Blasting Systems
P.O. Box 815
Dowagiac, MI 49047
Tel: 877/331-5931
Fax: 616/782-9623
E-mail: cyclone@blasters.com
Web: www.blasters.com

Sandblasting cabinets and blasting media for the hobbyist.

Clemco Industries Corp.
One Cable Car Drive
Washington, MO 63090
Tel: 636/239-0300
Fax: 800/726-7559
E-mail: directly from their Web site
Web: www.clemcoindustries.com

Clemco is one of the largest manufacturers of sandblasting equipment in the world. Call or visit their Web site to find a distributor near you. The Clemco line includes pressure pots and the Zero line syphon blasters.

Blast-It-All
P.O. Box 1615
Salisbury, NC 28145-1615
Tel: 704/637-3300 or 800/535-2612
E-mail: sales@blast-it-all.com
Web: www.blast-it-all.com

Blast-It-All makes an excellent syphon blaster and reclamation system for the glass studio. Penland installed one of these and it is excellent. A nice little unit is the Little-Blaster. Call for a catalog.

TP Tools & Equipment
Division of Tip Plus Corp.
7075 Route 446
P.O. Box 649
Canfield, OH 44406
Order On-Line, or call toll free 800/321-9260,
Web: www.tptools.com

TP sells all kinds of blasters and cabinets as well as all the different types of media to go with it. Their pricing is for you if you're on a tight budget. They even have a build your own sandblaster. Get their catalog to see everything they sell.

Truman's, Inc.
7079 State Rt. 446
P.O. Box 678
Canfield, OH 44406
Tel: 888/533-2693 or 330-533-6103
Fax: 330/533-4409
Web: www.san-blast.com

Ruemelin Mfg. Co., Inc.
3860 N. Palmer St.
Milwaukee, WI. 53212
Tel: 414/962-6500
Fax: 414/962-5780
E-mail: sales@ruemelin.com
Web: www.ruemelin.com

Ruemelin is one of the top-of-the-line companies selling state-of-the-art pressure pot blasters. Their pressure pot blaster is heavy duty.

Econoline Manufacturing, Inc.
401 N. Griffin Street
Grand Haven MI 49417
Tel: 616/846-4150
Fax: 616/846-6341
E-mail: info@sandblasting.com
Web: www.sandblasting.com

General purpose syphon sand blasting units at reasonable pricing. W.W.Grainger and McMaster-Carr sell the Econoline units. Go to the Econoline Web site to find a re-seller near you.

Resist for Sandblasting

PhotoBrasive Systems
4832 Grand Avenue
Duluth MN 55807
Tel: 218/628-2002 or 800/643-1037
Fax: 218/628-2064
E-mail: sandcarver@photobrasivesystems.com
Web: www.photobrasive.com

An excellent supplier of photo resist material and a lot of other handy products for sandblasting and sand carving. If you're looking for crystal blanks for trophies and awards, PhotoBrasive has a very complete line.

Rayzist Photomask, Inc.
955 Park Center Drive
Vista CA 92083-8312
Tel: Toll Free: 800/729-9478
Fax: 760/727-2986
E-mail: info@rayzist.com
Web site: www.rayzist.com

They sell blast cabinets as well as a complete line of resist products.

Armour Products
P.O. Box 128
Wyckoff, NJ 07481
Tel: 201/847-0404
Fax: 201/847-0231
E-mail: sales@armourproducts.com
Web: www.armourproducts.com

Armour Products is not a retail company. They only sell wholesale to the craft & hobby industry. You must qualify to purchase product from them. They sell a lot of products for sandblasting as well as Armour Etching Cream. Go to their Web site to find a retail re-seller of their products.

B & B Etching Products, Inc.
19721 N. 98th Avenue
Peoria, Arizona 85382
Tel: 888/382-4255
Fax: 803/584-7316
E-mail: etchall@etchall.com
Web: www.etchall.com

Etchall dip 'n etch and etchall etching creme. Re-usable liquid and creme that produces a matte, opaque, permanent, etched finish on glass.

Author's Note: The ultimate blast resist is a product manufactured by 3M called Buttercut. It is about 1/16" thick, rubbery, with an adhesive backing. It is used by those who blast tombstone monuments. It allows the the user to blast deeply into the surface without fear of the resist deteriorating. It can be obtained by looking in your Yellow Pages under Monuments or doing a Google search for Buttercut. Be advised though that some re-sellers markup their price astronomically.

Sandblasting Media

For every type of media available for sandblasting and blast cleaning, go to:

McMaster Carr (see pg. 324)

Adhesives, Silicones, Epoxy, UV and UV Lights

There are many distributors of adhesives, and there are many different types of adhesives (see pg. 284). The three most common adhesives used by studio glass artists are UV adhesives, silicones, and epoxy. The UV type is fairly easy to use and is quite strong. Because it needs a UV (ultra violet) light source to harden, it can for the most part only be used with glasses that will permit a UV light to pass through it unfiltered. It also requires the parts being glued to have intimate contact. That is, UV adhesive does not jump gaps. The parts must be in total contact with each other. UV adhesives also work very well for glass to metal adhesion. When used correctly, UV adhesives have excellent life expectancies.

Silicones are quite strong and, if used correctly will last forever. Most general purpose silicones are available in hardware stores. There are no optically clear silicones. Although they say clear, they arc cloudy. If you wish to purchase silicone in bulk, Sommer & Maca, W.W. Grainger, and McMaster-Carr are good suppliers. Hardware store style epoxies can be used for general glass work but are not recommended for laminating. The epoxy adhesive HXTAL used by most studio artists is for laminating and not prone to failure if used correctly. It is very expensive and requires some facility in its use. HXTAL has very high optical qualities.

Sommer & Maca
Offices and warehouses located regionally and listed on their Web site.
E-mail: somacausa@aol.com
Web: www.somaca.com

Their house brand of silicone is designated (88R). They also carry the GE silicones. The great thing about the Somaca brand silicone cartridges is that they can be resealed.

Dow Corning Corporation
Midland, MI 48686-0994
Tel: 517/496-6000 customer service
Web: www.dowcorning.com

There are Dow general silicones available at many hardware stores. You may purchase general usage silicone in bulk from SOMACA (see Somaca for address). There is a denser, stronger, and harder silicone (actually RTV) available. It's called Dow Corning 732 RTV. The 733 is for glass to metal. Go to their Web site for information.

The General Electric Company
260 Hudson River Rd.
Waterford, NY 12188
Tel: 800/332-3390 (customer service)
Web: www.gesilicones.com

GE Silicones, two-part RTV potting compounds, and a host of assorted adhesives are available from Grainger and other distributors. The higher strength silicones are usually labeled "Construction Grade." Their Web site is not easy to navigate.

HIS Glassworks, Inc.
91 Webb Cove Rd.
Asheville, NC 28804
Tel: 800/914-7463
Fax: 704/254-2581
E-mail: diamond@hisglassworks.com
Web: www.hisglassworks.com/

HIS is a re-seller of adhesives including HXTAL.

Dymax Corporation
   51 Greenwoods Road
   Torrington, CT 06790
   Tel: 860/482-1010
   Fax: 860/496-0608
   E-mail: info@dymax.com
   Web www.dymax.com

This company makes state-of-the-art UV adhesives. You can purchase their product directly from the Web site, or you can call Dewey for sales and advise (my recommendation).

Dewey Assoc., Inc.
   459 Main St.
   Suite 102
   New Rochelle, NY 10801
   Tel: 800/448-2306
   Fax: 914/633-4175

Re-seller of Dymax UV adhesives. This company sells many different types of Dymax UV adhesives. Call for information on which Dymax UV adhesive is right for your application. This company carries the UV adhesive for glass to glass adhesion. They have one that "forms sparkling, crystal–clear bonds with lead crystal" (GB225UV or JB225UV). Many of their adhesives can be cured with an activator when the cure area is UV blocked. It takes somewhat longer to effect a cure when using an activator but seems to work quite well and is very strong (JGR210/535A). This is just the stuff for those of you using opaque glasses. They also sell a very diverse line of UV lights. Send for a free catalog. Great phone help.

Loctite UV Adhesive
   Sold through Distributors
   Assistance in the U.S,: 800/LOCTITE (562-8483)
   Assistance in Canada: 800/263-5043
   E-mail: info@loctite.com
   Web: www.loctite.com

Loctite UV Adhesive #349931 is a super strong, optically–clear adhesive used by many glass folk for general-purpose adhesion of clear glass. They sell many other types of UV adhesives. Loctite sells their products through local distributors. Call them for the nearest distributor.

Talas
   568 Broadway
   New York, NY 10012
   Tel: 212/219-0770
   Fax:/212/219-0735
   E-mail: info@talasonline.com
   Web: www.talasonline.com

Talas is a reseller of HXTAL.

Author's Note: You can spend a good sum of money for a UV light. If your not doing a great deal of UV adhesive work it's possible to work with an inexpensive black light. If your doing some serious UV adhesive work, it does pay to spend a few bucks and get yourself a UV light built specifically for this type of work.

W.W. Grainger
   Web: www.grainger.com

Applied Industrial Technologies (formally Bearings Inc.)
   Web: www.applied.com

Re-seller of Loctite UV adhesives. Go to their Web site and click on Location Service Centers to find a reseller near you.

Casting Supplies, Rubber, Molding, Silica, Fiberglass, Wax

Smooth-On
   2000 Saint John Street
   Easton, PA 18042
   Tel: 800/762-0744
   Fax: 610/252-6200
   Technical Help Line: 610/252-5800
   E-mail: smoothon@smooth-on.com
   Web: www.smoothon.com

Smooth-On is one of the mainline suppliers of casting rubber products. They have excellent phone help. I have used their products for many projects. I've used their ReoFlex line of rubbers with great results. Visit their Web site to get an idea of how extensive their line of products is. They have distributors all across the U.S. and in Europe.

Polytek Development Corp.
   Address: 55 Hilton St.
   Easton, PA 18042
   Tel: 610/559-8620
   Toll Free: 800/858-5990
   Fax: 610/559-8626
   E-mail: sales@polytek.com
   Web: www.polytek.com

Polytek is one of the mainline supplier of casting rubber products. They have an extensive line of casting rubbers and an excellent Web site. The Poly 74 series of casting rubber seems to be one commonly used.

Cementex Latex Corp.
   121 Varick St.
   New York, NY 10013
   Tel: 800/782-9056
   In NY: 212/741-1770
   Fax: 212/627-2770
   E-mail: info@cementex.com
   Web: www.cementex.com

Cementex Latex Corp. provides a variety of materials for making rubber molds. They compound natural latex, urethanes, polysulfides, and silicones.

Silica

Oglebay Norton Co.
   1001 Lakeside Ave.
   Cleveland, OH 44114
   Tel: 216/861-3300
   Fax: 216/861-2863
   E-mail: info@onco.com
   Web: www.oglebaynorton.com

U. S. Silica Co.
   P. O. Box 187
   Berkeley Springs, WV 25411
   Tel: 800/243-7500
   Fax: 304/258-8295
   E-mail: sales@ussilica.com
   Web: www.u-s-silica.com/index.htm

Oglebay Norton and U.S. Silica are two of the mainline Companies. If you're going to be using a lot of silica, I recommend buying in bulk. The product you want for casting is 200-300 mesh silica. Go to their Web site to find a distributor near you. If you only need a small quantity of silica for your casting molds, then I recommend buying from a ceramic supplier like Standard Ceramic Supply. There are many ceramic chemical suppliers throughout the U.S.

Plaster

U.S. Gypsum
Local building suppliers
Web: www.gypsumsolutions.com

Plaster of Paris, Pottery Plaster, and Moulding plaster are all one and the same except that the pottery plaster as a bit of hydrocal in it. Web site for distributors and nifty consistency calculator.

Other Mold Materials

Ransom & Randolph
Tel: 419/794-1290
Fax: 419/865-9997
E-mail: dnixon@ransom-randolph.com
Web: www.glass-cast.com

R&R offers three products for the caster: R&R 910, R&R 400, and R&R 101. Their Web site has all the information pertaining to these products.

ZIRCAR Refractory Composites, Inc
P.O. Box 489
Florida, NY 10921
Tel: 845/651-2200
Fax: 845/651-1515
www.zrci.com/

"ZIRCAR Luminar is Mold Mix 6 and is a refractory-molding compound designed to allow replication of three-dimensional objects in glass. It comes as a paste, which is applied to a suitably prepared pattern and hardens on drying." Mold mix 6 is resold by other companies, but I believe your best deal is to purchase directly. Go to their Web site for up to date pricing.

Fiberglass

Fiberglass cloth and loose fiber is used to strengthen molds especially when constructing pâte de verre molds. To obtain this material, I suggest you look in the Yellow Pages under Marine Supplies or Plastics. Fiberglass is a common product used by boat builders.

Mr. Fiberglass
204 Arabian Circle
Yorktown, Virginia 23693
Tel: 757/865-6281
E-mail: dave@mrfiberglass.com
Web: www.mrfiberglass.com

This company sells all types of fiberglass including chopped fiber.

Wax

The Kindt-Collins Company LLC
12651 Elmwood Avenue
Cleveland, Ohio 44111
US Toll Free: 800/321-3170
Local Tel: 216/252-4122
Fax: 216/252-5639
E-mail: info@kindt-collins.com
Web: www.kindt-collins.com

The Kindt-Collins Co. has the most complete line of waxes for the artist. Their Micro-Crystalline waxes come in different degrees of hardness. Excellent Web site.

Colloidal Silica & Colloidal Alumina

WesBond Corporation
1135 East 7th Street
Wilmington, DE 19801
Tel: 302/655-7917
Fax: 302/656-7885
Web: www.wesbond.com

ETS Schaefer Corporation
See pg. 332 for contact information.

Wheels

McMaster-Carr Supply Co. (pg. 324)

W.W. Grainger (pg. 324)

"V" Groove wheels; If your looking for those hard to find wheels McMaster - Carr and Grainger is the place

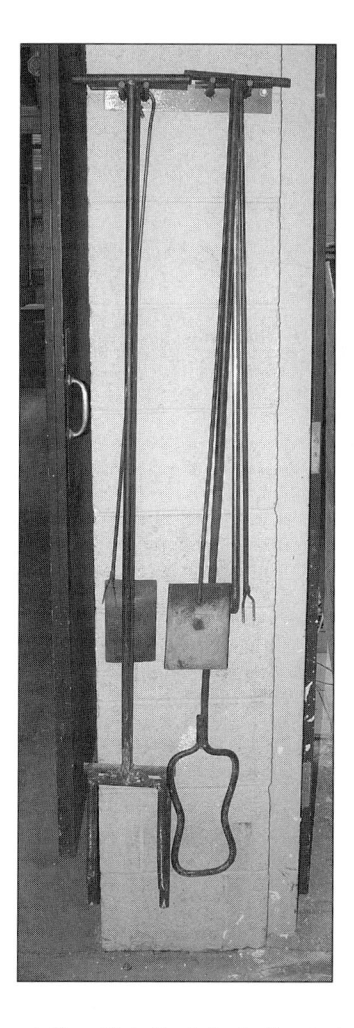

Garage and Glory Hole Tools for Italian Style Work

Gold Leaf and Leafing Supplies

Many sign companies sell gold leaf as well as other types of leaf. They may have a limited supply of other materials for leafing. You will probably pay a premium price when buying from a sign company or hobby store. There are many companies that sell gold leaf as well as all the other materials that go along with leafing. I suggest you Google "Gold Leaf" and find a re-seller on the internet.

M. Swift & Sons, Inc.
10 Love Lane
Hartford, CT 06112
Tel: 860/522-1181 or 800/628-0380
Fax: 860/249-5934
Web: www.mswift&sons.com

Manufacturer of gold leaf. Competitive pricing.

The Gold Leaf Co.
27 Fort Place
Staten Island, NY, 10301
Tel: 718/815-8802 - Steve Martinez
Fax: 718/720-7027
E-mail: info@goldleafcompany.com
Web: www.goldleafcompany.com

Gold-Orient Eastman Industrial Company Ltd.
Unit 505 No.50 Changbin Road
Huli, Xiamen,
China
Tel: 0086-592-7663676
Fax: 0086-592-5607887
E-mail: export@metal-leaf.com
Web: www.metal-leaf.com

I'm not sure how one can do business with this company, but they have some varigated leaf designs that I have never seen anywhere. They advertise low prices.

Refractories

Many companies sell refractory products. I have only listed the mainline companies. To find a local distributor of these products, go to the Yellow Pages of your phone directory and look under Refractories. I would also suggest that you go online and peruse the Thomas Register for refractory companies.

Unifrax Corporation
2351 Whirlpool Street
Niagara Falls, N.Y. 14305-2413
Tel: 716/278-3800
Fax: 716/278-3900
Web: www.unifrax.com

Fiberfrax is the one product used in every glass studio in the world. Fiberfrax comes in many forms, paper, felt, board, rope and many others. To find a distributor of this product call them directly at the number above. Unifrax has manufacturing plants throughout the world.

Thermal Ceramics
Go to their Web site:
www.thermalceramics.com/home.html

Thermal Ceramics is a mainline company that manufactures fiber insulation, fiber boards, IFB, and a host of other refractory products. A visit to their site will give you an idea of what they manufacture. They have some excellent high density high temperature boards. Go to their link to data sheets to see all the products they sell.

ETS Schaefer Corp.
8050 Highland Pointe Pkwy.
Macedonia, OH 44056
Tel: 800/863-5400 or local: 330/468-6600 ext. 211
Fax: 330/468-6610
E-mail: sales@etsschaefer.com
Web: www.etsschaefer.com

ETS manufactures a soft inexpensive fiber board, fiber blanket, bulk–shredded fiber, fiber paper, colloidal silica. Their prices are lower than the mainline companies. The fiber board is a soft rigid board. Because of its softness I would only recommend it for back up insulation on annealers unless you rigidize it with colloidal silica. The board comes in 1" and 2 " thicknesses with a standard width of 2' and standard lengths of 36", and 48". It has a binder in it that must be burned off before using. They sell 8 lb. density fiber blanket in the standard 2300° F temperature range and high temperature blanket (2600° F).

Cotronics Corp.
3379 Shore Parkway
Brooklyn, NY 11235
Tel: 718/646-7996
Fax: 718/646-3028
E-mail: sales@cotronics.com
Web: www.cotronics.com

Beside having a range of fiber and board products, Cotronics sells fiber papers starting at a thickness of $\frac{3}{32}$" and ultra high temperature castable refractory ceramics.

New Castle Refractories Co.
915 Industrial St.
New Castle, PA 16102
Tel: 724/654-7711
Fax: 724/654-6322
E-mail: ncr@dixonusa.com
Web: www.newcastlerefractories.com

They manufacture silicon carbide kiln shelves and IFB brick.
If you have a casting oven with elements in the floor, this is the shelf of choice for your raised floor. It is very strong but has little to no insulating value (which is a plus). They manufacture to your order and take about 12 weeks for delivery. Their product is fairly expensive but well worth the cost.

ANH Refractories
Go to their Web site
Web: www.hwr.com

ANH is the big gorilla on the block as they are the holding company for North American Refractories (NARCO), A.P. Green, and Harbison/Walker. Most of the products that are manufactured by these three companies are distributed from warehouses all across the U.S. as listed on their site. They have an excellent Web site listing all the products they carry with a .pdf data sheet.

Vesuvius/Monofrax
1870 New York Avenue
Falconer, NY 14733-1797
Tel: 716/483-7238
Fax: 716/483-7273
E-mail: info@monofrax.com
Sales and engineering: bud.davis@us.vesuvius.com
Web: www.monofrax.com

This is the last company in the U.S. to manufacture AZS block. An AZS liner is very pricey, but for many glass melting applications is well worth the investment. Cavaet: I only recommend you use this type of liner if you know how to use it. AZS has characteristics that must be understood by the end user. The main problem with this type of liner is that it heat shocks very, and I mean very easily. If you live in an area that is prone to power failures I would not recommend this product.

BNZ Materials
191 Front St.,
Zelienople, PA 16063
Tel: 412/452-8650 or 800/999-0890
E-mail: info@bnzmaterials.com
Web: www.bnzmaterials.com/zelienople.html

BNZ is a major manufacturer of IFB. They also manufacture high temperature board products, specifically, Marinite and Transite. Both of these products are now non-asbestos and very applicable to encasing annealers. Call them for a distributor or order direct.

Resco Products, Inc.
2 Penn Center West
Suite 430
Pittsburgh, PA 15276
Tel: 412/494-4491
Toll Free: 888/283-5505
Fax: 412/494-4571

They manufacture castables and plastic refractories

Skamol Americas, Inc.
11151 S.E. Cedar Way
Happy Valley, OR 97236
Tel: 503/698-3998
Cell: 503/780-7157 (Kevin Keeler)
Fax: 503/698-5369
E-mail: krk@skamol.com
Web: www.skamol.com

See pg. 140 for technical information on Skamol boards.

Pryor Giggey Co.
Go to their Web site for a distributor near you.
Web: www.priorgiggey.com

Pryor Giggey manufactures a complete and excellent line of castables for the glass studio.

Missouri Refractories Co., Inc. (Morco Refractories)
1198 Mason Circle Dr.
Pevely, MO 63070
Tel: 636/479-7770
Fax: 636/479-7773
E-mail: dennish@morco-inc.com

Morco manufactures and sells a very complete line of castables. Their Morcocast 95 & Morcolite 95 are good products.

Able Supply Company
5220 Texas Ave
Houston, Texas 77011
Tel: 713/926-9623
Fax: 713/926-6541
E-mail: internetsales@ablerefractory.com
Web: www.ablerefractory.com

Utah Refractories Corp.
P.O. Box 12536
Pittsburgh, PA 15241
Sales: Tom Mulholland
Tel: 412/851-2430
Fax: 412/851-2425
E-mail: tlmpgh@aol.com
Web: www.utah-refractories-corp.com

Utah Refractories serves the glass industry worldwide with Type "A" Gen-Sil® silica brick, Gen-Sil Lite® insulating silica brick and Gen-Sil® Bond silica mortar.

Danser, Inc.
P.O. Box 4098
Murphytown Rd.
Parkersburg, WV 26104
Tel: 304/679-3666
Fax: 304/679-3354
E-mail: sales@danserinc.com
Web: www.danserinc.com

Danser casts fiber panels to your specifications and requested density. They also fabricate hi-temperature fiber cylinders that can be used as a glory hole.

Coating for Fiber Insulation

Alpha Associates, Inc.
Two Amboy Ave.
Woodbridge, NJ 07095
Tel: 732/634-5700 or 800/631-5399
E-mail: Web E-mail
Web: www.alphainc.com

Alpha Temp-Mat safety coating for fiber insulation.

Mon-Eco Industries, Inc.
5 Joanna Court
East Brunswick, NJ 08816
Tel: 732/257-7942
Toll Free: 800/899-6326
Fax: 908/257-6525
Web: www.mon-ecoindustries.com

Manufactures Coating liquid for uncoated glass fiber lagging. Product designation, 11-30 Eco-Lag Adhesive. Call them to find a distributor of this product.

Great Lakes Textiles, Inc.
7200 Northfield Rd.
Walton Hills, OH 44146
Tel: 800/551-9759
Local Tel: 440/439-7236
Web: www.gltproducts.com
Regional distributors:
Greensboro, NC, Tel: 800/551-9760
Stockton, CA, 800/833-4500

Re-wettable fiberglass cloth good to 1000° F. They sell other hi-temp products for encapsulating fiber blanket.

Crucibles

Engineered Ceramics (EC Crucibles)
Resold by Pete VanderLaan of Guadalupe Glassworks and also sold by Olympic Color Rods
Tel: 603/323-7900
E-mail: glassgu@earthlink.com
Web: www.guadalupeglass.com

Order directly from Pete.

Emhart Glass Inc. (Laclede Christy Crucibles)
  405 East Peach Street
  P.O. Box 580
  Owensville, MO 65066
  Tel: 573/437-2132
  Fax: 573/437-3146
  Web: www.emhartglass.com

Fomlac is the crucible formulation for melting most all soda/lime glasses. They have a .pdf catalog of their glasshouse crucibles.

Hand Tools, Blow Pipes, Wood Blocks

These are the mainline companies that sell hand tools for hot glass.

Cutting Edge Products
  P.O. Box 3809
  Chico, CA 9592795927
  Tel: 530/342-1970
  Fax: 530/342-0771
  E-mail: info@cuttingedgeprdx.com
  Web: www.cuttingedgeprdx.com

Jim Moore Glass Tools
  P.O. Box 1151
  Port Townsend, WA 98368
  Tel: 360/379-2936
  E-mail: Has online E-mail
  Web: www.toolsforglass.com

Steinert Industries, Inc.
  1507 Franklin Avenue
  Kent, OH 44240
  Tel: 330/678-0028
  Out of State: 800/727-7473
  Fax: 330/678-8238
  E-mail: glasstools@steinertindustries.com
  Web: www.steinertindustries.com

Spiral Arts, Inc.
  2940 Westlake Avenue North
  Suite #100
  Seattle, Washington 98109
  Tel: 206/768-9765
  Fax: 206/768-9766
  E-mail: fmetz@spiralarts.com
  Web: www.spiralarts.com

C&R Loo, Inc. (Essemce Hand Tools)
  1085 Essex Ave.
  Richmond, CA 94801
  Tel: 510/232-0276
  Toll Free: 800/227-1780
  Fax: 510/232-7810
  E-mail: sales@crloo.com
  Web: www.crloo.com

C.R. Machine
  Nickelite Tools
  30 Danforth Road
  Rindge, NH 03461
  Tel: 603?899-9871
  Fax: 603/899-6591
  E-mail: crm@monad.net
  Web: www.crmachine.net

Star Glass Works
  Palmer Tools
  10506 Crestridge Dr.
  Minnetonka, MN 55305
  Tel: 612/546-60215

Putsch (Meniconi Hand Tools)
  P.O. Box 5128
  Asheville, NC 28813
  Toll Free: 800/847-8427
  Tel: 828/684-0761
  Fax: 828/684-4894
  E-mail: info@putschusa.com
  Web: www.putschusa.com

Marco Tool, USA
  27232 59th Ave. NE
  Arlington, WA 98223
  E-mail: marco-tools@hotmail.com
  Web: www.mfi.or.jp/marco45c/

Wood Blocks

Walter Evans, Cherrywood Mold Shop
  2725 Mill Branch Rd
  Kenova, WV 25530
  Tel: 304/453-2279

Call Walter directly to order blocks. Contrary to rumor Walter has no intention of retiring. He says he'll probably make blocks till he drops. Actually his wife told me that.

Fantasilaboratoriet
  Sodra Orsjo
  210 SE 38297
  Orsjo Sweden
  Tel/Fax +46 (0) 481 200 40
  Cell. 0705559040
  E-mail: contact@fantlab.com
  Web: www.fantlab.com

Hot Block Tools
  3710 Liberty Ave
  Pittsburgh PA 15201
  Tel: 412/683-1700
  E-mail: hotblocktools@earthlink.net
  Web: www.hotblocktools.com

Blockhead Tools
  Wood tools sold through Olympic Color Rods
  Web: www.glasscolor.com

Fusing, Slumping and Casting Glass

Fusers please take note of the following: There are many re-sellers of products for the fuser. The companies listed below are the manufacturers. I recommend you visit their sites to find a distributor in your region.

Bullseye Glass Co., Resource Center
Order line: 888/220-3002 (toll-free)
Fax: 503/227-3130
E-mail: resourcecenter@bullseyeglass.com
Web: www.bullseyeglass.com

The Bullseye Glass Co. was the first company to manufacture fusable compatible glass. To complement their sheet glass, they also manufacture complementary products, frit, stringers, etc. Bullseye also manufactures billets of casting glass in a full range of colors. They have a very complete catalog of other products as well. Excellent Web site.

Uroboros Glass
2139 N. Kerby Ave.
Portland, OR 97227 USA
Tel 503/284-4900
Fax 503/284-7584
Web: www.uroboros.com

Uroboros manufactures a line of fusing-compatible glass and casting glass in billet form and, like Bullseye, has complementary products. They manufacture sheet glass in two ranges of expansion, 90 and 96. Some of their product line is manufactured by the Spectrum Glass Co.

Spectrum Glass Company,
P.O. Box 646,
Woodinville WA 98072.
Tel: 425/483-6699.
Fax: 425/483-9007.
E-mail: hotglass@System96.com
Web: www.spectrumglass.com

Glass Brokers, Inc. (sells direct)
4 Mill Street
Pittston, PA 18640-1922
Tel: 570/602-8833
Fax: 570/602-8844
E-mail: glassbrokers@adelphia.net
Web: www.glass-brokers.com

This company resells Schott lead casting glasses. The lead glasses are LF-5, 35% Pb and F2, 45% Pb. These glasses have a very high index of refraction and casts like butta. They also sell N-BK7, a boro optical casting glass, and S8 used for casing by paperweight makers.

Gaffer Glass, USA Ltd.
Unit #4
19622 70th Ave. South
Kent, WA 98032
Toll Free: 877/395-7600
Local: 253/395-3361(2)
Fax: 253/395-3363
E-mail: info@gafferglassusa.com
Web: www.gafferglassusa.com

Gaffer Glass can be purchased directly. Gaffer glass manufactures a line of casting glasses in stunning colors. Their casting glass contains lead, but for those of you fearful of glass products that contain lead, it behooves you to visit this site and read about the testing done within a glass studio environment.

East Bay Batch and Color
169 South First St
Richmond, Ca 94804
Tel: 800/322-6567
Local: 510/233-0708
Fax: 888/442-3337
E-mail: ebbatch@aol.com
Web: www.eastbaycolor.com

EB is a re-seller of, Ornela, and Uroboros casting glasses. The Ornella casting glass is 45% lead. It comes in billets and chunks. Call for ordering instructions and pricing.

Dichroic Glass

Coatings By Sandberg
856 N. Commerce Street
Orange, CA 92867
Tel: 714/538-0888
Fax: 714/538-2767
E-mail: info@cbs-dichroic.com

Sandberg manufactures dichroic glass and is compatible with the mainline fusing manufacturers glasses.

Savoy Dichroic
Web: www.savoystudios.com

Savoy manufactures dichroic glass and is compatible with the mainline fusing manufacturers glasses. Savoy glass is only sold through distributors. Go to the Web site listed above.

Dichroic Alchemy
Eugene, OR
Toll Free: 866/434-2476
Local: 541/726-7339
E-mail: order@dichroicalchemy.com
Web: www.dichroicalchemy.com

Manufactures Boro dichroic glass coatings.

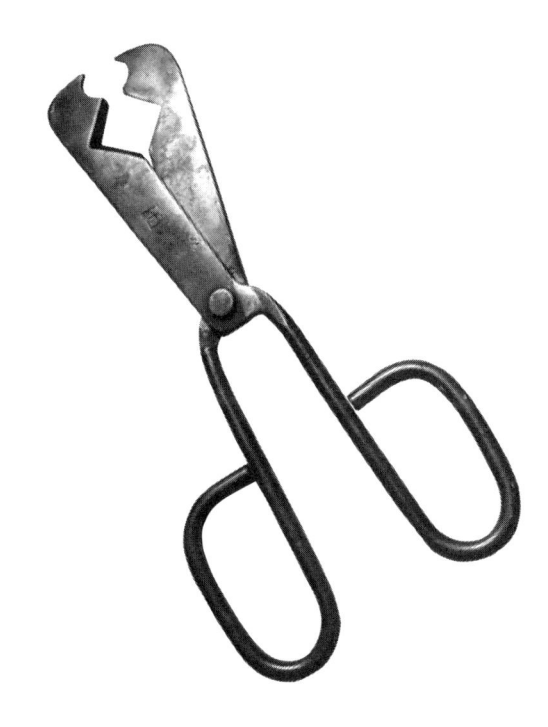

Glass Enamels

Reusche & Co.
1299 H St.
Greeley, CO 80631
Tel: 970/346-8577
Fax: 970/346-8575
E-mail: sales@reuscheco.com,
Web: www.reuscheco.com

Reusche makes and sells very high end glass enamels. They have a complete line of enamels for high and low fire. They also sell the Hanovia line of liquid bright metals and lustres. Reusche also has a few distributors. Go to their Web site for the list.

Thompson Enamel
P.O. Box 310
Newport, KY 41072
Tel: 859/291-3800
Fax 859/291-1849
E-mail: nfo@thompsonenamel.com
Web: www.thompsonenamel.com

Thompson enamels are a course ground enamel (80 mesh) and not appropriate for painting. They do advertise that they will special order 325 mesh ground enamels.

Chemicals, Colorants for Batching

Unimin Corp.
258 Elm St.
New Canaan, CT 06840
Tel: 203/966-8880
Fax: 203/966-3453
Web URL: www.unimin.com

Produce and market silica sands, ground and microcrystalline silica, feldspar, and nepheline syenite.

Ceramic Color and Chemical Mfg. Co.
P.O. Box 297
13th St. & 11th Ave.
New Brighton, PA 15066
Tel: 724/846-4000
Fax: 724/846-4123
E-mail: cccmfg@ccia.com

Manufactures and distributes colorants and other chemicals for batching. Check for minimum quantities.

Mason Corporation
1049 US RT 41
Schererville IN 46375
Tel: 219/865-8040
Fax: 219/322-3611
E-mail: E-mail@masoncorp.org
Web: www.tinchemical.com/

Mason sells tin products in less than 100 lb. quantities.

Molycorp, Inc.
67750 Bailey Road
Mountain Pass, CA 92366
Tel: 888/577-7790
Fax: 760/856-2344
E-mail: johnb@molycorp.com
Web: www.molycorp.com

Distributor of rare earths

Standard Ceramics
P.O. Box 4435, Pittsburgh, PA 15205
Tel: 412/276-6333
Fax: 412/276-7124
E-mail:: info@standardceramic.com
Orders: orders@standardceramic.com
Web: www.standardceramic.com

Standard sells small or large quantities of chemicals for batching. Send for a catalog of all the products they handle. They also have distributors all over the U.S.

Seattle Pottery Supply
35 S. Hanford St.
Seattle, WA 98134
Toll Free: 800/522-1975
Local & Canada: 206/587-0570:
Local Fax: 206/587-0373
Nationwide free Fax: 888/587-0373
E-mail: info@seattlepotterysupply.com
Web: www.seattlepottery.com

Seattle Pottery Supply is similar to Standard insofar as they sell many of the chemicals needed for batching. Their Web site has a listing of all the materials they sell.

Mirroring Solution

Peacock Laboratories, Inc.
54th & Paschall Ave.
Philadelphia, PA 19143
Tel: 215/729-4400
Fax: 215/729-1380
E-mail: sales@peacocklabs.com
Web: www.peacocklabs.com

Peacock offers chemicals, solutions, coatings, equipment, and supplies for the manufacturing of mirrors.

Roman Bowl
Fused and Slumped

Glass Batch and Cullet

Spruce Pine Batch Co.
P.O. Box 159
2490 Burnsville Highway (19E)
Spruce Pine, N.C. 28777
Tel: 828/765-9876
Fax: 828-765-9888
Web: www.sprucepinebatch.com

The ubiquitous Spruce Pine Batch Co. The formula was originally developed by Nick Labino.

East Bay Batch and Color
169 South First St
Richmond, Ca 94804
Tel: 800/322 6567
Local: 510/233 0708
Fax: 510/233 3438
E-mail: ebbatch@aol.com
Web: www.eastbaycolor.com

East Bay Color distributes Phillips pellets and Electroglas pellets. They will also mix your private batch formula.

Gaffer Glass, USA Ltd.
Unit #4
19622 70th Ave. South
Kent, WA 98032
Tel: 877/395-7600 Local: 253/395-3361(2)
Fax:253/395-3363
E-mail: info@gafferglassusa.com
Web: www.gafferglassusa.com

Gaffer now sells direct. Excellent casting glass and color rods.

Spectrum Glass Company, Inc.
P.O. Box 646
Woodinville, WA 98072
Tel: 425/483-6699
Fax: 425/483-9007
E-mail: hotglass@System96.com
Web: www.spectrumglass.com

Spectrum sells a system 96 "Studio Nugget" cullet.

Gabbert Cullet Co.
P.O. Box 63
Williamstown, WV 26187
Tel: 304/375-6434
Web: www.gabbertcullet.com

Gabbert was the first company to supply the universities and studios with cullet, and they're still at it.

Burners

Joppa Glassworks, Inc.
P.O. Box 202
Warner, NH 03278
Tel: 603/456-3569
Fax: 603/456-2138
E-mail: joppaglass@conknet.com
Web: www.joppaglass.com

Joppa Glassworks is Dudley Giberson. It manufactures and sells the Giberson tip (U. S. Patent #3697000) as well as ribbon burners and lots of hard-to-find stuff for the studio.

Wilton Technologies
2932 Via Loma Vista
Escondido, CA 92029
Toll free: 800/928-7637
Local: 760/745-5956
Fax: 760/745-1944
E-mail: paul@paulwilton.com
Web: www.paulwilton.com

Manufactures and sells a flame retention tip and glass booth display materials.

The Hub Consolidated, Inc.
690 Route 73
Orwell, VT 05760
Tel: 802/948-2209
Fax: 802/948-2215
E-mail: info@hubglass.com
Web: www.hubglass.com

Hub sells complete combustion systems

Wet Dog Glass
3924 Conti St.
New Orleans, LA 70119
Tel: 504/483-1195
Fax: 504/483-3059
E-mail: hotstuff@wetdogglass.com
Web: www.wetdogglass.com

Wet Dog sells the Spiral Arts burner tips and complete combustion systems.

Pine Ridge Enterprises
P.O. Box 121
Paradise, CA 95967
Tel: 530/877-9793
E-mail: pineridge@earthlink.com

Tom Ash introduced the ribbon burner to the U.S. The burner is quiet and hot. E-mail Tom for information on ordering.

Abell Combustion, Inc.
P.O. Box 198
Kimberton, PA 19442-0198
Tel: 610/ 827-9137
Fax: 610/ 827-7156
E-mail: sabell@abellcombustion.com
Web: www.abellcombustion.com

Steve designs and sells complete combustion systems.

The mainline manufacturers for burners are:

North American Manufacturing Co. - Cleveland, OH
www.northamericanmfg.com/
Eclipse Combustion - Rockford, IL
www.eclipsecombustion.com
Maxon Corp. - Muncie, IN
www.maxoncorp.com
Charles A. Hones, Inc. - North Amityville, NY
Venturi High Pressure Nozzle Burner
www.charlesahones.com
Hauck Mfg. Co. - Lebanon, PA
www.haukburner.com

There are many other manufacturers of burners and other burner related equipment for the glass studio. I recommend you surf over to The Thomas Register, www.thomasnet.com. The online Thomas Register is one of the best resources available for finding the manufacturer of any product you seek.

Elements and Thermocouples

Duralite Inc.
15 School St.
Riverton, CT 06065
Toll free: 888/432-8797 (Toll Free)
Local: 860/379-3113
Fax: 860/379-5879
E-mail: sales@duralite.com
E-mail to engineer your oven: engineering@duralite.com

Duralite is probably the main provider of metallic elements for the glass studio in the country.

I Squared R Element Co.
12600 Clarence Center Road
P.O. Box 390
Akron, New York 14001-0390
Tel: 716/542-5511
Fax: 716-542-2100
E-mail: info@isquaredrelement.com
Web: www.isquaredrelement.com

Manufactures and sells Moly and SiC elements.

Sentro Tech Corp.
804 W. Bagley Rd.
Cleveland, OH 44017
Tel: 440/260-0364
Fax: 440/260-0413
E-mail: info@sentrotech.com
Web: www.sentrotech.com

Manufactures and sells Moly and SiC elements.

MXI
613 Redna Terrace
Cincinnati, OH 45215
Tel: 513/772-0404
Fax: 513/672-3333
E-mail: sales@mhi-inc.com
Web: www.mhi-inc.com

Manufactures and sells Moly and SiC elements.

Songshan Enterprise Group
Sanlizhuang High & New Tech. Zone,
Dengfeng Zhengzhou Henan 452483
China
Tel: 86 - 371 - 62768046
Fax: 86 - 371 - 62768249
E-mail: online E-mail
Web: www.songshan.en.ec21.com/

Songshan manufactures Moly and SiC elements at very reduced pricing. If you know what you want or wish to make and inquiry, they have a Web mail connection.

Kanthal Corp.
119 Wooster St.
P.O. Box 281
Bethel, CT 06801
Tel: 203/744-1440
Web: www.kanthal.com

The Kanthal Corp. is a Swedish Co. with offices all over the world. They manufacturer Kanthal Super Moly elements. Kanthal also manufactures SiC as well as wire for metallic elements. Who hasn't used Kanthal A-1 elements in their ovens?

Thermocouples, Type K, R, and S

OMEGA Engineering, Inc.
One Omega Drive
P.O. Box 4047
Stamford, Connecticut 06907-0047
Tel: 800/848-4286 or 203/359-1660
E-mail: custom@omega.com
Web: www.omega.com

Vulcan Electric Company
28 Endfield Street
Porter, Maine 04068
Tel: 800/922-3027 In State: 207/625-3231
E-mail: sensorsales@vulcanelectric.com
Web: www.vulcanelectric

This company also reclaims precious metals from used thermocouples.

Thermo Sensors Corporation
P.O. Box 461947
Garland, TX 75046
Tel: 800/889-5478
Fax: 972/272-2112
E-mail: andy@thermosensors.com
Web: www.thermosensors.com

Trutemp Sensors, Inc.
465 Pike Road Bldg. #110
Huntingdon Valley, PA 19006
Tel: 888/878-8367 or 215/396-1550
Fax: 215396-1551
E-mail: sales@trutempsensors.com
Web: www.trutempsensors.com

Cleveland Electric Laboratories
1776 Enterprise Pky.
Twinsburg, OH 44087
Tel: 330/425-9021
Fax: 330/425-7209
E-mail: celabs@raex.com
Web: www.clevelandelectriclabs.com

CEL carries a full line of thermocouple products.

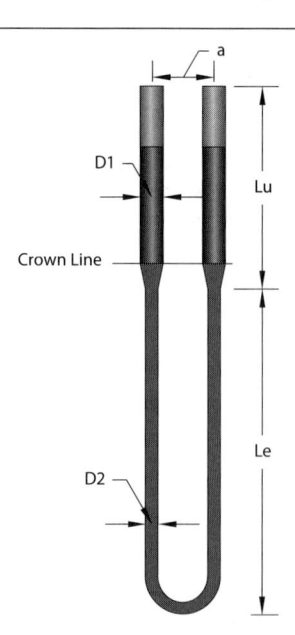

Typical Moly Element

Controllers

A few mainline companies manufacture and distribute controllers throughout the U.S. (and the world, for that matter). I have listed the main manufacturers of controllers that service the glass studio. All the companies listed manufacture reliable controllers at reasonable prices. Most have distributors in all 50 states and probably a distributor near where you live. Digitry sells direct. Over the years these mainline companies have tried to simplify their programming sequence and in some cases have succeeded. One aspect of interest are those controllers that are tunable, that is, after being calibrated, they are capable of anticipating overshoot and can give you an accuracy within one degree. Call a representative from one of these companies and have the rep pay you a visit so that he or she can see your operation and recommend a model that fits your needs. In all my years of looking at controllers, though, I have never found one as simple to operate as the GB line by Digitry.

Digitry Company, Inc.
188 State Street, Suite 21
Portland, ME 04101
Tel: 207/774-0300
Fax: 617/484-5220
E-mail: info@digitry.com
Web: www.digitry.com

Digitry was the first to develop a simple controller for the university glass programs as well as the studios. The GB line of controllers has proven to be reliable and simple to operate. The GB-5 can be obtained with communication capability for a PC interface. Go to their Web site to find out what that means.

Watlow
Web: www.watlow.com
The 998/999 was supposed to replace the 981/982 series but they left out restart on power failure and ramping. I recommend sticking with the 981/982 or the high end series F4 line of controllers. The SD line of controllers is their economy class.

Partlow
Web: www.partlow.com
The MIC series of controllers

Fuji
Web: www.fujielectric.com

The PXG, PXR and PYX series. The PYX uses fuzzy logic to anticipate your process.

Love Controllers
A subsidiary of Dwyer Instruments Inc.
E-mail: info@dwyer-inst.com
Web: www.love-controls.com

Skutt
E-mail: skutt@skutt.com
Web: www.glasskilns.com

Their GlassMaster controller is reasonably priced and has some excellent features.

Relays, SCR's & SSR's

Continental Industries International
741 - F Miller Drive
Leesburg, VA 20175
Tel: 571/258-2105
Fax: 703/669-1302
E-mail: support@ciicontrols.com
Web: www.ciicontrols.com/contact

This company has a very large selection of relays. Their Web site lists distributors.

Payne Engineering Company
P.O. Box 70
Scott Depot, West Virginia 25560
Tel: 304/757-7353
Fax: 304/757-7305
E-mail: info@payneng.com
Web: www.payneng.com

Go to their Web site to find a rep near you.

Author's Note: You can also purchase relays from W.W. Grainger and McMaster-Carr. Look in the yellow pages under electronics and you may find what you need.

Assorted Products

Plastics

United State Plastic Corp.
1390 Neubrecht Rd.
Lima, Ohio 45801-3196
Tel: 800/809-4217
Fax: 800/854-5498
E-mail: usp@usplastic.com
Web: www.usplastic.com

This company has everything plastic including balls for your rociprolap, order #91507.

Books

Whitehouse Books.com
P.O. Box 16
Corning, NY 14830
Tel: 607/936-8536
Fax: 607/936-2465
E-mail: julia@whitehouse-books.com
Web: www.whitehouse-books.com

Whitehouse books is a major resource for books on and about glass.

Felt Wheels

Buffalo Felt Products
14 Ransier Drive
West Seneca, NY 14224
Tel: 716/674-7990 Ext. 205
Fax: 716/674-3631
E-mail: salesdesk@buffalofelt.com
Web: www.buffalofelt.com

Decals

Bell Inc.
6905 NW 25th
Miami, Florida 33122
Tel: 305/593-0911
Fax: 305/593-1011
E-mail: sales@beldecal.com
Web: www.beldecal.com

The company will make fire on 4 color decals from your artwork. They have a minimum order.

Muller Mixers

MIFCO
700 Griggs Street
P.O. Box 31
Danville, Illinois 61834
Tel: 217/446-0941 extension 112
Fax: 217/446-0943
E-mail: online form for e-mail
Web: www.mifco.com

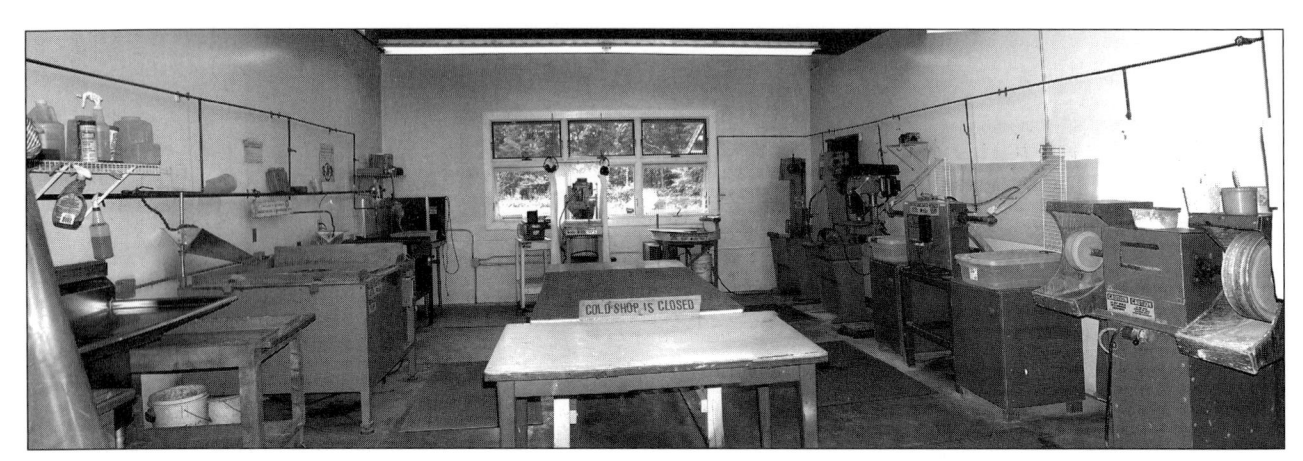

Cold Shop, Penland School of Crafts

MK 10" Diamond Cut-off Saw

Merker Lathe

Steinert Polishing Machine

Felker Cut-off Saw

340 Glass Notes

Conversions, Letters to Dr. Glass, & The Index

Chapter Contents

Temperature Conversion Chart	342
Comparison of Metric and U.S. Systems of Weights and Measures	343
Length	343
Volume	343
Area	343
Energy, Heat, and Work	344
Power and Heat Flow	344
Electric Heating	344
Temperature Conversions	344
To Convert Degree Increments	344
To Calculate the Length of a Pulley	344
To Calculate RPM's	344
Conversion References	344
Your Weight in Stones	344
Letters to Dr. Glass	345
Index	348

Temperature Conversion Chart

To convert from Fahrenheit to Centigrade or vice versa, simply find the temperature you wish to convert from in the center column and read the temperature directly to the left or right. The center column represents either Centigrade or Fahrenheit. The equivalent temperature is found in either the right or left hand columns.

**Reading
°F or °C
to be converted.**

°C.		°F.	°C.		°F.
-18	0	32	383	720	1328
-7	20	68	393	740	1364
+4	40	104	404	760	1400
16	60	140	416	780	1436
27	80	176	427	800	1472
38	100	212	438	820	1508
49	120	248	449	840	1544
60	140	284	460	860	1580
71	160	320	471	880	1616
82	180	356	482	900	1652
93	200	392	493	920	1688
104	220	428	504	940	1724
116	240	464	516	960	1760
127	260	500	527	980	1796
138	280	536	538	1000	1832
149	300	572	549	1020	1868
160	320	608	560	1040	1904
171	340	644	571	1060	1940
182	360	680	582	1080	1976
193	380	716	593	1100	2012
204	400	752	604	1120	2048
216	420	788	616	1140	2084
227	440	824	627	1160	2120
238	460	860	638	1180	2156
249	480	896	649	1200	2192
260	500	932	660	1220	2228
271	520	968	671	1240	2264
282	540	1004	682	1260	2300
293	560	1040	693	1280	2336
304	580	1076	704	1300	2372
316	600	1112	716	1320	2408
327	620	1148	727	1340	2444
338	640	1184	738	1360	2480
349	660	1220	749	1380	2516
360	680	1256	760	1400	2552
371	700	1292	771	1420	2588

°C.		°F.
782	1440	2624
793	1460	2660
804	1480	2696
816	1500	2732
827	1520	2768
838	1540	2804
849	1560	2840
860	1580	2876
871	1600	2912
882	1620	2948
893	1640	2984
904	1660	3020
916	1680	3056
927	1700	3092
938	1720	3128
949	1740	3164
960	1760	3200
971	1780	3236
982	1800	3272
993	1820	3308
1005	1840	3344
1016	1860	3380
1027	1880	3416
1038	1900	3452
1049	1920	3488
1060	1940	3524
1071	1960	3560
1082	1980	3596
1093	2000	3632
1104	2020	3668
1116	2040	3704
1127	2060	3740
1138	2080	3776
1149	2100	3812
1160	2120	3848
1171	2160	3884
1182	2160	3920
1193	2180	3956

Comparison of Metric and U.S. Systems of Weights and Measures

To convert from metric to U.S. equivalent or vice versa multiply your weight or measurement (column A) by its equivalent (column B).

For example: 345 grams= 345 X .035274= 12.1 oz.

A	B
1 gram	.035274 ounce
1 kilogram	2.2046 pounds
1 ounce	28.3495 grams
1 pound	453.5924 grams
1 millimeter	0.03937 in.
1 centimeter	0.3937 in.
1 meter	39.37 in.
1 in.	2.54 centimeters
1 foot	30.48 centimeters

Length

1 ft	=	12 in.
1 yd	=	3 ft.
1 mi.	=	5280 ft.
1 in.	=	25.40 mm.
1 in.	=	2.54 cm.
1 meter	=	3.281 ft.
1 mile	=	1.609 km.

Volume

1 cu. ft	=	1728 cu. in.
1 cu. yd.	=	27 cu. ft.
1 cu. in.	=	16.39 cc.
1 liter	=	61.02 cu. in.
1 U. S. gal.	=	231 cu. in.
1 cu. ft.	=	7.481 U. S. gal.

Area

1 sq. ft.	=	144 sq. in.
1 sq. yd.	=	9 sq. ft.
1 sq. in.	=	6.452 sq. cm.
1 sq. mi.	=	2.590 sq. km.
1 sq. mi.	=	640 acres

Glass Notes

Energy, Heat, and Work

1 B.t.u.	=	252.0 cal.
1 B.t.u.	=	0.2520 kg.-cal.
1 therm.	=	100,000 B.t.u.
1 B.t.u	=	778.2 ft.-lb.
1 B.t.u.	=	1055 Joules
1 cal.	=	4.187 Joules
1 h.p.-hr.	=	2544 B.t.u.
1 kwh.	=	3412 B.t.u.
1 h.p.-hr.	=	1,980,000 ft.-lb.
1 kg.-m.	=	7.233 ft.-lb.

Power and Heat Flow

1 kw.	=	1.341 h.p.
1 hp.	=	550 ft.-lb./sec.
1 h.p.	=	42.41 B.t.u./min.
1 B.t.u./sec.	=	1.055 kw.
1 kw.	=	3412 B.t.u./hr.
1 h.p.	=	2544 B.t.u./hr.

Electric Heating

Volts x Amps	=	Watts
Watts x 3.41	=	B.t.u./hr.
1 Amp. at 110V.	=	375 B.t..u./hr.
Amp.	=	$V \div R$ (ohms).
Watt = V. x Amp.	=	$V_2 \div R$.

Temperature Conversions

To change Centigrade to Fahrenheit, multiply by ⁹⁄₅, and add 32.

To change Fahrenheit to Centigrade, subtract 32 and multiply remainder by ⅝.

That is:

F = (C x 1.8) + 32

C = F -32 ÷ 1.8

The Centigrade degree is a longer temperature interval than the Fahrenheit degree in the ratio of 9:5

To convert degree increments

F degree ÷ 9 x 5 = degree C

To Calculate the Length of a Pulley

$$L = 2C + 1.57(D+d) + (D-d)^2 \div 4C$$

L = Pitch Length of Belt
C = Center Distance from Both Pulleys
D = Pitch Diameter of Large Pulley
d = Pitch Diameter of Small Pulley

To Calculate RPM's

Motor speed in RPM's x diameter of motor pulley (drive pulley) ÷ diameter of shaft pulley (driven pulley) = speed of equipment.

Conversion References

The ultimate reference guide for conversions is the *Pocket Ref* published by Sequoia Pub. Inc. (www.sequoiapublishing.com.) The internet reference for conversions can be found at, www.convert-me.com/en/

Your Weight in Stones

Stones is an odd British weight calculation

Pounds ÷ 14 = weight in stones

I weigh 147 lbs. but in Great Britain I would weigh 10.5 stones
And you think pounds is an odd measurement?

The United States is the only major country in the world that has not adopted the metric system.

Letters to Dr. Glass

Over the years I have received many letters asking for advice on or about glass. As you will see, the letters come from all manner of people with urgent needs and a desire to have their problem solved by Dr. Glass, that's me. I have reprinted some of those letters exactly as they were written, misspellings and all. The names have been changed to protect the innocent.

Hi there

I am very interested in starting a business in glassblowing. I need to know however if there is anything i need to be able to run business. For example Specialist qualifications. I will obviously learn how to blow glass but this is my long term goal.

I have been fascinated by glass blowing ever since i was a child and i would love to take this fascination and turn it into an actual business. I have thousands of ideas and luckily i am good at art and design.

So if you could give me any advice what so ever i would be very grateful.

Thank you very much

pardon me and with all respect

I'm not only a hot glass manipulator and devoted searcher of the mystery of glass but I would fancy myself an antique dealer/historian also and therefore. If this is a contradiction I would not be the slightest surprised. I find myself on this side of the mirror often.

Anyway I became aware of the right path concerning glass and its properties suspected and predicted, after having read Mr. Brills article many years ago. It would seem there are many more urban myths buried in the phenomenon we describe as glass. If you would have any need of elucidation I would be pleased and honored to clarify.

Respectfully

hellow Dr

my name is Svi and i live in Israel.

I hope you can help me. I am building now a kiln from mud based on burning wood in a rounded shape in order to melt glass. my hobby is constructing mosaic floor and i am planning to melt glass in to thick plates then brake them into small tessarae. please can you give me a direction.

thank you

I have a lot of questions since i am writing a report on glass blowing. what machinery is used? After you blow how long does it need to dry? what is the glass made of? How do you make it? How do you put in the different colors? How do you make shapes with the glass?

Who buys the glass? How much money does a glass blower make? Where is it displayed? Do you have to go to college to be a good glass blower? what are the dangers? what are the rewards? what kind of things do glass blowers do?

hello,

I'm a belgian student and i make a studies about the burning of glass to eliminate some defaults on the glass. I'll ask you to submit some documents about this subject please!

I thank you very much;

i awnt to amke red colour through single boiling of broken white (recycling) glass. i wiil be grateful if you guide me .

Hello IM an electronics genius working in VT. during my three years here I have built a mountain of dead computer monitor tubes. My idea is to melt them down and cast them into 26" high rectangular 5 gallon bottles that will hold a special type of lead acid storage battery. My observations are that the glass will contain allot of lead due to the conductive coating used on them and that if thick enough really takes the punishment. So in conclusion will glassnotes tell me how, and do you think the bottles will last 60+ years. Thanks

Okay, this may sound a little strange, but I'm sure you've heard stranger: Let's say you get a gun, about

.22 caliber (really darn small) with a copper bullet. Now Let's say you've got a punty or blowpipe with a really fat gob of glass on it--Maybe four sizable gathers. Still with me? We'll say the temperature of the glass on that pipe is uniform the whole way through. If the glass is warm enough to be malliable, but not so hot that it's dripping, and the gun is fired at the glass, will the shock of the bullet make the glass break? will the bullet make it through the glass, or will it be slowed down so much that it is preserved inside, similar to an insect preserved in amber? Keep in mind that in addition to moving forward at an extremely high rate of speed, the bullet is also spinning around on a path set by the rifling in the barrel of the gun. Is there a table showing the viscosity of glass at various temperatures? This has seriously been a burning question for about a year. I'm very tempted to try it out, but I blow glass at college, and I don't know how kindly they'd take to me discharging a firearm on the campus.

Thank you for your time and thoughts.

Hi.My name is John Smith I'm doing a colonial village project for my fourth grade class. We got to pick a trade and I picked glassblowing. I was interested in learning as much as I can about glassblowing in colonial times. I wanted to see if you could answer the questions following:
1. What did glassblowers do in colonial times?
2. What tools did glassblowers use in colonial times?
3. Were there certain clothes that glassblowers wore?
4. What kinds of designs did glassblowers make in colonial times?
Thank you for your help.

hello dr glass
i want to ask you abuot problem with color bottle, when i prodect bottle for beer or wine and i check the durability in pressing then the bottle blowing up, so if you can tall me pleas what is the reason of the blowing up,

hi doc. hennry names John and just thanking you, your book for helping me build my studio.
glass rules dont it?

Hello,
I was wondering if there is any technical or colloquial name for the neck, inclusive or not of the mouth, spout or lips, of a bottle?
I understand there is one for the shoulders as well?
Thank you for your time

Dear Dr. Glass,
 Will you please send me everything you know about Pâtè De Verre, and some internet addresses about this technique. I don't know where to find it on the net. Thank you for your trouble, I will really appreciate it.

Dr. Glass,
What do you give the Fire Marshall when he asks for the UHL approvals on your equipment? I have a 100 lb.free standing pot furnace and a small glory hole complete with safety system. All the gas lines and hook-ups were installed by a mechanical contractor. Any insight into this matter would be appreciated. Let me know if you need more info.

What I like to know is when was glass invented in what year. Thank you

I'm just writing to thank you for the site, and to ask you if your book covers everything I'll need to know about start-up costs, typical monthly gas bills, and other commitments that are likely/commonly overlooked.
Otherwise, I would greatly appreciate any general reality checks and advice you have to offer.
One very specific question I have is regarding "day furnaces." I'm not familiar with them. Would a day furnace present an opportunity to keep a day job and fire up the furnace at night, as opposed to 24-hour heating? Or am I more likely looking at a desire that inherently requires more of a total commitment?

Well there you have it. These letters sort of sum up the need for Glass Notes.

The Index

l to r, Yvon Streetman, Bill Brown, Unknown, GAS 1, 1970

Chihuly, Libensky, Halem, 1991

Henry Halem, 1968

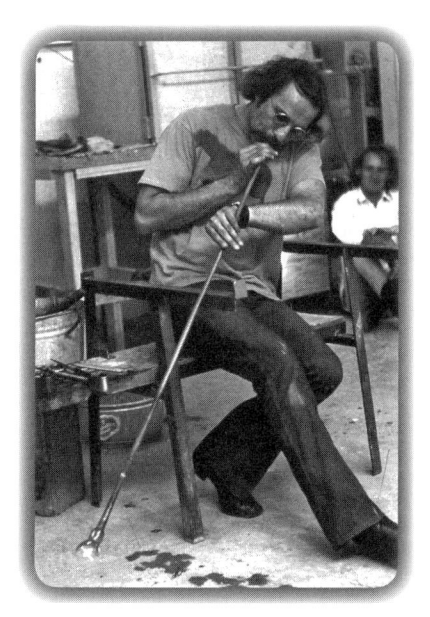

Fritz Dreisbach, 1970

Marvin Lipofsky, 1971

Harvey Littleton, 1984

Glass Notes 347

Index

A

Adhesives 284
  Dymax 288
  guidelines for using 288
  HXTAL-NYL-1 285–286
  Loctite 288
  Silicone 289
  UV adhesive 287
Air, Make-up 313–315
Alumina Block *See* **Refractories**
Annealing 39
  a few words about 75
  annealing temperature, determining 48
  castings, annealing of 50
  charts 49
    castings and thick pieces 51
  charts, about 46
  Dr. Woolley explains 42
  effect of shape on 43
    illustrations of shapes 44
  explanation of 40
  Libensky method 52
    Libensky chart 53
  problems and solutions 41
  testing, annealing and strain point 54
  testing for stress and compatibility 55
    illustrations 58
  thermal gradation 47
Annealing Ovens 241
  Convection Oven 277
  IFB annealing oven 242
    an overview 242–245
    annealer dimensions 245
    counter weight, hinges 249
    digital controllers and relays 246
    element placement 246
    insulation 247
    the lids 248
    power to the annealer 244
    some electrical talk 245
    starting to build 247
    the annealer 244
    materials for 260
    photos and illustrations 250–252
    the hinge 259
    the lid 258
  Roll-Out Oven 266
    flat crown construction 275–276
    illustrations of 270–274
    overview and details 266–269
  Skamol annealer
    how to build 261–265
AZS Block *See* **Refractories**

B

Batch 15
  batch your own glass 25
    introduction 26
  composition of raw materials 18
    reciprocals 18
  developing a batch 17
  assorted notes 31
    fining agents 31
    opals 31
  opacifying agents 19
  properties of chemicals 15
  reasons for raw materials 16
  some real batches 32
    two reds, a phosphate and an opal white 32
Blowing Benches 310–312
Turbo Blower 229
Break-Away Box, Bob Carlson 110
  Illustrations 111, 112, 113
Burners 223
  Alfred Style 234
  aspirator 229
  aspirator premix system 233
  burner systems 228
  what is combustion 225
  combustion of Fuel 226
  determining btu's 228
  function 228
  Giberson burner 235
  illustrations of parts 232
  inspirator 228
  Labino burner 226
    illustration 227
  mechanical 229
  nozzle mix 229
  ribbon burner 236

C

Castables *See* **Refractories**
Cast and Blow 108
Casting Techniques 67, 80
  billet casting 81
  calculating glass quantity 73, 82, 87
  investments 87
  Libensky/Brychtova 67
    Pilchuck hand-out 72
    studio photos 71
  molten casting 81
  what type of casting oven? 80
  which glass to use? 80
CFM *See* **Exhaust System**
The Chardiet Method of Casting 108
Color Bar Cutter 307–308

Colored Glasses 21
  adding colorants to batch 21
  adding colorants to cullet 22
  colorants for batch 23
  colorants for cullet 24
  effect of atmosphere 22
  interaction
    color and fining agents 21
  nature of coloration 21
  solution colorants 21
Compatibility 34
  composition and its effects on 36
  factors for calculating LEC 37
  thermal expansion 35
  why glasses are incompatible 34
Controllers and Relays 49
Convection Oven 277
Conversions, Metric to U.S. 341
Crucible, Make Your Own 296
Crucibles 166
  where to buy 169

D

Day Tank *See* **Furnaces**
Diamond Drilling 318
  drill speeds 319
Durability Testing 60

E

Electrical Stuff 241
Electric Elements 253
  amperage conversion 280
  designing of 278, 281
  Japanese configuration 305
  quartz tubes for 279
  slots in IFB brick 253–256
    illustration of electrical connection 257
Enameling on Glass 290
Exhaust System 314

F

Fiber Insulation *See* **Refractories**
Firebrick *See* **Refractories**
Flame Safety 237
  NFPA approved system 238
  pressure switches 240
  shut off valves 239
  UV scanner 240
  what is flame safety 239
Flame Turbulence 231
Sam Scholes Fudge 316
Fuming (Iridizing) *See* **Iridizing**

348 Glass Notes

Furnaces 144
   building a day tank 145
      alumina block liner 150
      AZS liner 148–149
      casting the crown 156–157
      determining flue size 145
      illustrations 151–155
      list of materials 146
   freestanding crucible furnace 166
      burner and gathering port 173
      description of 171
      door illustration 174
      illustration of 170
   invested crucible furnace 158
      casting the beehive crown 162
      crown illustrations 163–165
      illustrations of 159–161
   read before building 147
Fusing *See* **Kiln Casting**

G

The Garage 222
Gas Cock, Supervising 231
Gas Pressure 230
Glass Properties 10
   formers
   fluxes
   stabilizers 10
Glory Holes 189
   fiber 190
      cost of materials 197
      general information 190–193
      illustration 193–196
   HUB IFB Glory Hole 198
      calculations 200
      construction of 201
      explanation 199
      illustrations 202–218
   Tom Ash square glory hole 219
      illustrations 219–221

H

Heat Transfer
   btu's 227
History, brief 12
   JM 475 marbles 12
   Labino, Nick 12
   Littleton, Harvey 12
HXTAL *See* **Adhesives**

I

Insulating Firebrick (IFB) *See* **Refractories**
Insulation, Understanding 142
Insulation Value Charts 143

Investments *See* **Mold Making & Casting Techniques**
Iridizing (Fuming) 298–301
   illustration of sprayer 302

J

Jack Wax (Milton Mud) 294

K

Kiln-Forming 121
   temperature ranges, 121
   fusing & slumping chart, 122
   Jeremy Lepisto, Kiln Forming 123
Kiln Casting 84
   flower pot casting 84
      Illustrations 85
      more illustrations 86
Klaus Moje Technique 115–120

L

Labino, Nick viii, 12, 60, 226, 227
Letters to Dr. Glass 345–346
Libensky, Stanislav 52, 67, 72, *see* **Casting Techniques**
Littleton, Harvey viii
Lusters & Bright Metals 303

M

Mineral Block Board *See* **Refractories**
Mold Making & Casting Techniques 61
   basic mold making 62
   different calculations 81
   mold additives 62
   mold coatings 63
   mold making illustration 66
   mold materials 62
      Ann Robinson's investments 88
      Luminar, mold mix 6 89
      R&R 910 and other products 89
   more mold making illustrations 76
   plaster/silica ratios 83
   steaming out wax 65
Mold Problems & Solutions 64
Molds, Plaster Blow 97
Mold Seperator 295

O

Ohm's Law *See* **Electric Elements, design of**
Orifice, Limiting Adjustable 231

P

Paradise Paint Pick-up 293
Pâte de Verre, Alicia Lomné 124
   firing 130
      with core 131
   inlay 128
   mixing glass 127
   packing a mold 126, 127
   working with powders 129
   process of construction 125
Photo Inside a Bottle 297
Pick-up Table, precious leaf 306
Pipe Cooler, battery power 309
Plaster Blow Molds *See* **Molds, Plaster Blow**
Making a plaster positive 79
Plastic Ram & Patches *See* **Refractories**
Pot Furnace, Freestanding *See* **Furnaces**
Pot Furnace, Invested *See* **Furnaces**

R

Recuperation 175
   energy savings for propane 183
   illustrations 179–182
   operation and maintenance 184
   overview 177
HUB Recuperator
   illustration 186–187
Refractories 135
   AZS 137
   pressed AZS block 138
   castables 138
   definition of 136
   fiber Insulation 139
   firebrick 136
   high alumina 137
   insulating brick, IFB 136
   mineral block board 140
   plastic ram & patches 139
   vermiculite board & calcium silicate board 140
Robinson, Ann *see* **Casting Techniques, investments**

S

Sandblast Resist 294
Sand Casting 90
   Bentonite sand 99
      how to cast process 102, 105

    how to ladle 103
  Chem Bond 4905, resin bond 96
  ladles 101
  sodium silicate, CO_s 90, 92
    making the mold 93
    illustrations of process 95

Scavo 295
Separator, Mold *see* **Mold Separator**
Silicone *See* **Adhesives**
Silver Nitrate to Silver Salts 304
Skamol *See* **Refractories (vermiculite board)**
Skamol Annealer 261 *See* **Annealing Ovens**
Suppliers Index 321–340

T

Thermal Expansion *See* **Compatibility**

U

UV adhesive *See* **Adhesives**

V

VanderLaan, Pete 25
Vermiculite Board & Calcium Silicate Board *See* **Refractories**

W

Wax, Jack *See* **Jack Wax**
Wax Positive, Making a 77
Woolley, Dr. Frank E. 20, 34, 42, 55

Attention Educational Institutions

Order *Glass Notes* for your class and receive a 25% discount off the cover price.

Franklin Mills Press will reprint any section or sections of *Glass Notes* for your class. Inquire about discounts and pricing.

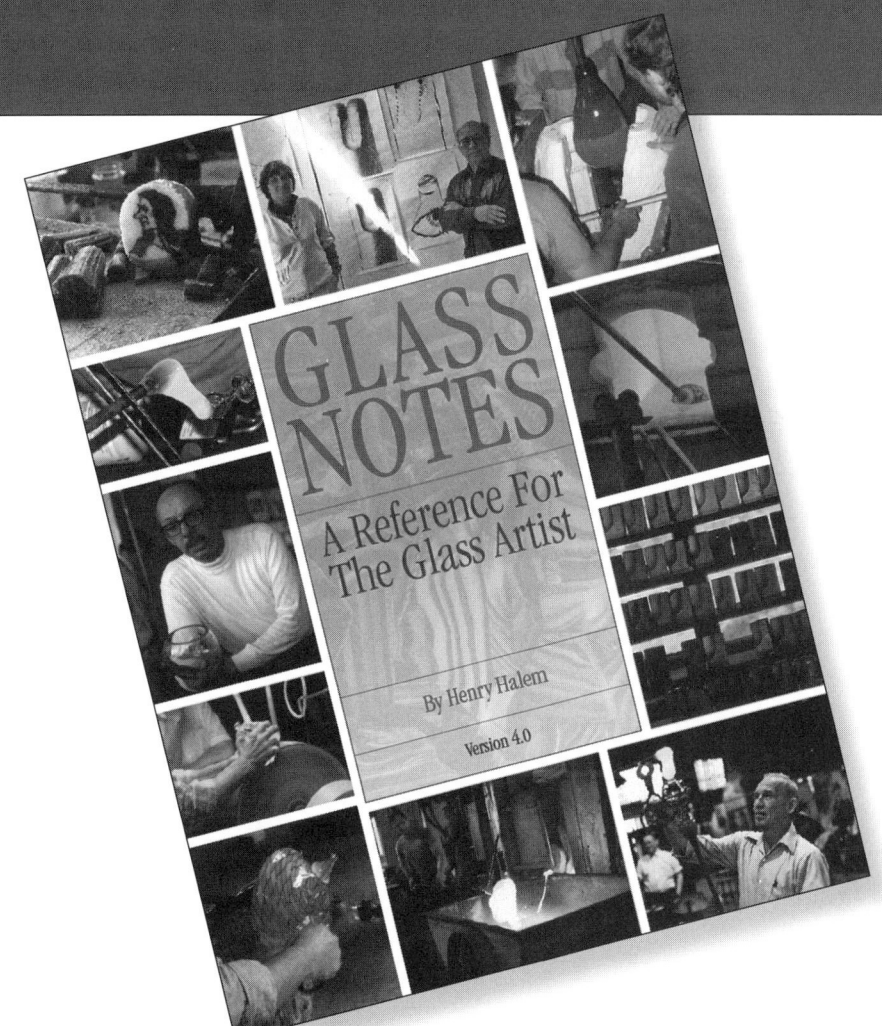

Franklin Mills Press
P.O. Box 906
Kent, OH 44240
Tel: 330/673-8632
Fax: 330/677-2488
E-mail: hhalem@glassnotes.com